RESEARCH AND PRACTICE

IN

PROFESSIONAL DISCOURSE

T0307311

RESEARCH AND PRACTICE
IN
PROFESSIONAL DISCOURSE

Edited by
Christopher N CANDLIN

City University of Hong Kong Press

First published 2002
Printed in Hong Kong

ISBN 962-937-071-9
Published by
City University of Hong Kong Press
Tat Chee Avenue, Kowloon, Hong Kong

Website: www.cityu.edu.hk/upress
E-mail: upress@cityu.edu.hk

Contents at a Glance

Section II: Discourses and Practices

Discourses of Health and Social Care

Discourses of the Academy

Discourses of Literature and Creativity

Media Discourses

Discourses of Business Communication

Detailed Chapter Contents

Acknowledgements

This volume derives from an International Conference which was held at the City University of Hong Kong under the auspices of the Centre for English Language Education and Communication Research and the Department of English and Communication. In addition to the presence of major scholars in the field, whose invited papers are represented in the volume, the Conference was a truly international affair with researchers and teachers from over 30 countries represented. A selection of the papers refereed for publication are included here.

I would like, as Editor of this volume, to thank them for their support, but also in particular my academic colleagues: Professor Vijay K. Bhatia, Dr. Ken Hyland, Dr. Tim Boswood and Professor John Flowerdew of the Department of English and Communication, for their assistance in devising the programme and selecting the conference papers.

Particular thanks are due to Ms Vivienne Shuet, the Executive Officer of the Centre for English Language Education and Communication Research, for her imaginative and very dedicate organizational support for the conference and for this publication, and to those research associates and graduate students who worked hard to make the Conference, on which this volume is based, such a notable success.

Finally, thanks are due to the staff of the City University of Hong Kong Press, particularly Ms Farrah Ching and Mr. Edmund Chan, for their very effective editing and publishing skills.

I hope that the chapters in this volume will serve not only to emphasize the academic richness and variety increasingly displayed in the field of the analysis of professional discourse and its application — entirely and characteristically in keeping with the stated mission of the City University of Hong Kong — but something of its international range, inter-cultural inclusiveness, and methodological diversity.

Christopher N. Candlin

List of Illustrations

Tables

Figures

Research and Practice
in
Professional Discourse

1

Introduction

Christopher N. Candlin

Organization and Scope

The body of chapters in this volume is organized into two Sections. The first Section contains seven chapters (Bhatia, Swales, Bazerman, Sarangi, Gu, Martin and Wodak) which form an invited set of papers whose purpose — apart from their own inherent contributions in terms of topics, data and analysis — is to provide a range of distinctive but relatable perspectives on the overall focus of the volume. These chapters — *Themes and Issues* — are designed to provide the reader with a sense of diversity in terms of intellectual origins, epistemologies and research methodologies in the field of research and practice in professional discourse, but at the same time to display particular coherence seen against a number of pervasive themes. One of these, as I shall try to show below, is that of reconciling the differing perspectives of analysts and participants, and, arising from that the need for a model of research which does not subordinate the macro to the micro or vice-versa, and which honours a range of research methodologies.

The second and more numerous Section — *Discourses and Practices* — consists of some seventeen chapters drawn from selected and refereed papers constructed around a number of Discourses, each relating broadly to one of a set of related organizational and institutional contexts. In keeping with the title of the volume, the authors of chapters within these Discourses themselves exhibit an appropriate occupational and professional diversity: discourse analysis in the academy, nursing and healthcare practice, social work, engineering, literary and creative arts, languages for specific purposes, law and legal practice, media studies, information technology, and business studies. The authors of these chapters, as with those of the first Section, are drawn from a wide range of countries and institutions, thus providing an international conspectus to the volume, its themes and topics. In terms of research methodologies, authors are equally diverse, drawing on interactional sociolinguistics, (critical) discourse analysis, genre analysis, ethnography, linguistic and textual description using systemic functional linguistics, accommodation theory and social psychology, pragmatics, conversational analysis, mediated action theory, corpus linguistics; and, in some cases, illustrating a multiple methodological approach combining quantitative and qualitative methods.

Finally, the two sets of chapters in the two Sections of the volume are mediated by an invited chapter from Tom Huckin which draws on the invited chapters in identifying some key issues and themes, and which at the same time provides a lens through which the issues and data of the main body of chapters can be viewed.

Section I: Themes and Issues

Given that Tom Huckin's mediating chapter focuses, as I note above, on the themes and issues that arise from his perspective in the various invited chapters in the first Section of the book, but also with a view to their implications for the theme-based chapters that follow in Section II, I would like here not to reiterate his arguments, with which I very much agree, but to introduce this first Section by focusing on issues of perspectives on research and on research practices as I see them arise in the invited chapters.

In a recent publication (Sarangi and Candlin, 2001)[1], Srikant Sarangi and I sought to effect an alignment between researchers and the professional partners with whom they worked as co-participants, on the basis of a mutual recognition of their respective perspectives on the study of discourse in social life. Such a recognition is itself a

---

1.   Sarangi, S. and C. N. Candlin. 2001. Motivational elevancies: Some methodological reflections on social theoretical and sociolinguistic practice. In *Sociolinguistics and social theory*, edited by N. Coupland, S. Sarangi and C. N. Candlin. London: Pearson, 350–388.

challenge, as we indicated, and turning the recognition of diversity into co-operative and collaborative action engages both parties in a problematic methodological choice:

> "......*we revisit the main methodological problematic that pervades both social theoretical and sociolinguistic studies of social life. This has to do with striking a relationship between participants' and analysts' perspectives on social data. Two positions can be discerned. First we could say that participants and analysts bring different perspectives to data, very much in the objectivist, scientific mode of inquiry. Such an assumption of difference leads to the analyst imposing or transforming the "observed" into a form of order. A second position would maintain that participants and analysts view the world in the same way, through the same lens, using the same coding devices — very much in the hermeneutic, ethnomethodological mode of inquiry. Here the assumption is one of similarity demanding that both perspectives need to be aligned in any study of social events.*" (p. 379)

Addressing the issues of this methodological choice lies explicitly or implicitly before all the invited chapters in this first Section of the book. Bhatia's scene–setting chapter makes this plain in its adumbration of the goals of what he explicitly refers to as "shared practice": the requirement of the presenting and accounting for the realities of the professional world, the understanding of private intentions, the investigating of language as action, the exploring of relationships between professional discourses and social structures, identities and practices, the negotiating through discourse of professional boundaries, and, above all, the integrating of discourse analytical procedures and professional practices. The challenges he identifies resonate closely with the problematic of the Sarangi and Candlin quotation above: how *shared* can the practices be of investigating professional expertise, how *shared* the research methodologies?

Swales' discussion about the nature of models as metaphors for testable hypotheses about genres and discourses is not only directed at the researcher's models — more or less linguistic, more or less discursive — but is implicitly directed at the issue of the possibility of sharedness of models between analysts and practitioners, and, in that, the challenge posed to the testability of the predictive adequacy of theoretical models not just by the need to meet theory-internal conditions but, externally, those of socio-institutional practices.

Bazerman's elevation of the personal, reflexive narrative is not just an underwriting of the hermeneutic — Sarangi and Candlin's second position above — but is *both* a guide to ways of achieving the analyst-participant partnership, *and* a reinforcement of the importance of the data of experience as input to theory-building. Reflexivity, for Bazerman, is a way of monitoring, guiding and regulating action; it keeps both theory and practice, as it were, on track. More than that, it extends theory by requiring it to be more encompassing, more tolerant of variation and diversity, more integrated with human purposes and human action. It is perhaps the most powerful means by which analyst and practitioner can share perspectives.

For Sarangi, this reflection on the practices of researchers — what he calls "making discourse research consequential" — lies at the heart of the problematic. For assigning the research perspective to the analyst alone grossly misrepresents the situation. Practitioners are themselves researchers into the discourses of their own professional practices. They, too, are discourse workers. The shared role is what Sarangi genially calls that of the *discourse practitioner* — only with the caveat that this is not only the role of the analyst but of both analyst and practitioner. As with Bazerman, the articulation of personal experience is legitimized here as a research practice, and the professional site is one where what constitutes professional knowledge and expertise can be negotiated in the context of interdisciplinary collaboration. This negotiation is however not just about the aligning of professional identities or a search for reciprocity, it characterizes the ecology of the research process itself and directly impacts on the thickness of the description, the likelihood of its plausibility, and, perhaps, its acceptance as a basis for action.

At first glance, Gu Yueguo's descriptively extensive and rich sociolinguistic chapter might seem innocent of these issues of perspective more straightforwardly foregrounded in previous chapters, but only apparently so. His asking of the question: "what is a workplace?" serves, in fact, to problematize the status of the data upon which any response would rely, and to raise, though more indirectly, the same issues. Whose data, and whose workplace? That of the analyst or that of the participant? As Gu unerringly identifies, the textualized discourses of workplace discourse analysis are not authentic, but can serve only as abstractions from the workplaces of the real world. In part this is so because they lack the link to action, but more because they exist outside time and space, and, as Sarangi also warns, they inevitably underestimate the forces of human agency. As Gu points out, "workplace discourse is thus the actualization of some potential talks/doings by a population who make use of the available discourse resources within social and spatial-temporal constraints". For the participants, then, workplace discourse is a process; for the analyst it is inevitably a product, and so achieving a reciprocity of perspectives is not only a matter of mutualising view and stance, it is also a matter of (re)vitalizing what is necessarily an ecology. Furthermore, the dead bodies of texts are not time-bound, as Bakhtin and Layder in different ways acknowledge, they are historical. In Gu's terms they represent *time-space networks of activity* and what he terms *trajectories of life-paths*. The issue of perspective now becomes one of the ultimate impossibility of the analyst capturing the processes of human ecological and socio–cultural existence.

Perspectives imply orientation, not to say tendency, and where analysts select texts as a conscious and socially-motivated act of solidarity with a cause — as most obviously with writers in the Critical Discourse Analysis tradition — the issue of alignment between analyst and participants becomes not only an issue of mutuality in terms of access to models and methods, but also to ideology. This matter of orientation is avowedly in play in Jim Martin's chapter, where he aims his analysis, at least in part, at effective intervention in those social sites which motivate him as here, towards seeking reconciliation — what he terms Positive Discourse Analysis. The critical question of which discourses, and which interpretations participants draw on to attempt the co-operative reconciliation of differences imbues his chapter. The issue here in relation to perspectives is both one of aligning social and political orientations and also one of evidence. Implicit in his analysis — or any analysis for that matter — is the status of evidence, what counts as evidence, and what claims can be made on the basis of such evidence. The Truth and Reconciliation Commission in South Africa had that as its impelling question, and so does Martin's chapter. Determining that status lies at the bottom of any process towards the alignment of perspectives between analyst and participants, as Sarangi and Candlin (*op cit.*, 2001) make plain.

The workings of an institutionality such as that silent but present participant in Martin's chapter, the Truth and Reconciliation Commission, provides just that nexus of discourse, politics, organization and identity that is at the heart of Ruth Wodak's final invited chapter in this Section. What does her focus on the discursive construction of identity add to this discussion of distinctive perspectives and motivational relevancies among analysts and participants? Principally, I believe, it emphasizes the importance of history. Texts do not just fall off the back of trucks, they also don't just crack out of eggs. Unravelling the recontextualized chaining of incorporated texts is not just a matter of managing some intertextual and interdiscursive methodology in discourse analysis; it is also a matter of the writing of history. And as in all histories, the issue is one of power, as Wodak says, of inclusion and exclusion as constituents of political communication, and — as Gu also noted — the central significance of time and space. Alignment of perspectives here is again not just a matter of mutual agreement on the interpretation of semiotic analysis, it has to do with the political mutuality among the participants, among the analysts, and among them both. Wodak's contribution, more than most, is to add that political element to the perspectives debate, but also, as with Sarangi, in emphasizing the fluidity of organizational and professional boundaries, thus emphasizing the dynamism of the reconciling and mutualizing process. Acknowledging and reflecting the ecology, in fact.

The discussion so far has concentrated on what may appear to be an essentially theoretical issue of the warranting of data and claims, and the need to be aware of the dangers of some inequitable transformation of such data by the analyst, in the search for harmonization with some pre-established analytical order. As the chapters above make plain, the issue could not be more alive, but in addressing it, two further matters need to be considered. Firstly, that of the connection to be made between "motivational relevancies" and what Sarangi and Roberts (1999)[2] refer to as "practical relevance" [3]. As Sarangi and Candlin suggest (2001:370), following Sarangi and Roberts (1999), such a connection is not only itself an issue for negotiation, its inception and characterization must principally be a participant's not an analyst's prerogative. The second, and related matter, is that of the dependencies between the macro dimensions of discourse and micro instantiations in social practice, and how these dimensions may be connected within an inclusive methodology.

Taking first that of the connection between relevancies, the implications from the discussion of these invited chapters so far is that a reflexive acknowledgement of tacit assumptions about research — much in the manner perhaps of Bazerman, but not only in that way — is a basic premiss for any analyst-participant alignment. Accounting for practices is, of course the issue, especially the terms in which the accounting is to be done and the ways in which the accounts are to be presented. Now, to have any measure of likely achievement, alignment of perspectives through such accounting cannot be restricted to the theoretical, to the explanation of a model. This is a point made especially by Swales, but also by Sarangi. It will, for the practitioner-participant, have to connect with their lived experience — what Bhatia refers to as the problematic complexities of the real world. I take it that this, following Sarangi and Roberts (*op cit.*, 1999), now becomes

---

2. Sarangi, S. and C. Roberts, eds. 1999. *Talk, work and institutional order: Discourse in medical, mediation and management settings.* Berlin: Mouton de Gruyter.

3. I am grateful to my Ph.D. student at Macquarie University, Sydney, Jonathan Crichton, for underlining this link in his thesis, and for numerous discussions on this point.

a matter not just of explaining technicalities of accounts, but one of acknowledging potentially distinctive perspectives in terms of value. In short, it becomes a matter less of theory and more one of acknowledging and addressing the ethics of professional behaviour. Several of the chapters in this first Section acknowledge this, in particular those of Martin and Sarangi. Roberts and Sarangi (1999: 473[4]) see this as depending on analyst-participant dialogue, but more than just that, on what they call a process of "joint problematization" between analysts and participants. This may be less easy to achieve. Not only because of the difficulties surrounding achieving of mutuality of analysis and explanation, but rather one of the assignment of prerogatives. Who determines the problematic issues and in what terms are they formulated? As Wodak illustrates in her chapter in relation to the bureaucracies of the European Union, there would be, and is, much reluctance to a shift of such power to the analyst, and this may be much more generally the case in sponsored research. Nonetheless, it is hard to see how the alignment of perspectives, which is theoretically valuable, will have much practical relevance if such a process of joint problematization is not initiated. As Jonathan Crichton indicates (personal communication), there is a reflexive relationship between motivational relevance and practical relevance: the analyst's decisions on how to balance the analyst's and participants perspectives both shape and are shaped by the analyst's mode of engagement with the problems of participants. A related but distinctive point is made by Coupland, when he writes: "... there is a permeable membrane between academic and theoretical sociolinguistics and social action itself" (Coupland, 2001:20[5]). Indeed there is, but I don't think that anyone can guarantee the reflexivity of the transmission.

---

4.   Roberts, C. and S. Sarangi. 1999. Hybridity in gatekeeping discourse: Issues of practical relevance for the researcher. In *Talk, work and institutional order: Discourse in medical, mediation and management settings*, edited by S. Sarangi and C. Roberts. Berlin: Mouton de Gruyter.

5.   Coupland, N. 2001. Introduction: Sociolinguistic theory and social theory. In *Sociolinguistics and social theory*, edited by N. Coupland, S. Sarangi and C. N. Candlin. London: Pearson, 1–26.

The second matter, that of macro-micro dependencies and inclusivity, raises a number of issues which can only be adumbrated briefly here: firstly, how to situate discursive practices, texts and accounts within a model which is inclusive of all relevant features of discourse; secondly, how to accommodate the distinctive perspectives and relevancies outlined above, both "motivational" and "practical"; thirdly, how to make a connection between the macro-sociological focus on the testing of theory, underpinned by large-scale quantitative analysis, and micro interactional analysis, emphasizing qualitative and grounded, participant-centered accounts; finally, how to incorporate these descriptive methodologies into a useful, workable, and accountable system. In their different ways, the chapters in this Section address these issues but what is perhaps needed is a framework in which they can be incorporated. One such framework has been made available by the sociologist and social theorist Derek Layder in a number of recent publications (Layder, 1993[6]; 1998[7]) under the general title of a resource map for research (*op cit.*, 1993:72) the essentials of which I sketch in what follows. It may be that this map, or developments of it, could serve to situate the issues I raise, and to harmonize the methodologies of the chapters in this first Section[8].

In this cartography, Layder sets out four research elements, each of which is interconnected with the others, and each of which has a particular, and equally connectable, *research focus*. Layder argues that none of the elements is prime, and research may begin with any, providing that all are severally and differentially addressed. From the interplay of the data arising from each element, theory "emerges". I take it this is the basis of his construct of "adaptive theory" (Layder, 1998:132ff).

---

6. Layder, D. 1993. *New strategies in social research*. Cambridge: Polity Press.
7. Layder, D. 1998. *Sociological practice: Linking theory and social research*. London: Sage Publications.
8. I have found this Resource Map, and developments from it, especially valuable in university teaching in the field of professional and workplace communication, and in collaborative work with professional communities, for example lawyers and healthcare workers (CNC).

Figure 1.1
A Resource Map for Research

	Research Element	Research Focus
HISTORY	CONTEXT	*Macro social organization* Values, traditions, forms of social and economic organization and power relations. For example, legally sanctioned forms of ownership, control and distribution; interlocking directorships, state intervention. As they are implicated in the sector below.
	SETTING	*Intermediate social organization* Work: Industrial, military and state bureaucracies; labour markets; hospitals; social work agencies, domestic labour; penal and mental institutions. Non-work: Social organization of leisure activites, sports and social clubs; religious and spiritual organizations.
	SITUATED ACTIVITY	*Social activity* Face–to–face activity involving symbolic communication by skilled, intentional participants implicated in the above contexts and settings. Focus on emergent meanings, understandings and definitions of the situation as these affect and are affected by contexts and settings (above) and subjective dispositions of individuals (below).
	SELF	*Self-identity and individuals's social experience* As these are influenced by the above sectors and as they interact with the unique psychobiography of the individual. Focus on the life–career.

The case for a research cartography (Layder, 1993:72)

It is significant also that the four research elements: *context, setting, situated activity, self* are all set within a frame of *history,* although we need to note that in Layder's conception, all elements, as social processes, have their own time-space frames. Interactions among persons for example, operate within a different time-space perspective than do changes in social institutions, although both may influence the conduct and practices of the other, and these differences are significant. We have seen in the chapters by Gu and Wodak how significant this focus on time-space dimensions is for any analysis.

How are these research elements and this research resource relevant to the issues I identify above and to the chapters in this first Section of this volume?

Beginning with the relevance to the invited chapters, Layder first (though not necessarily as prime) identifies *context* as that element which implicates the macro social organization, the values, traditions, forms of social and economic organization and power relations within the social formation, and illustrates these in terms of "legally sanctioned forms of ownership, control and distribution: interlocking directorships, state intervention". The chapters by Martin, Wodak, Gu, Sarangi all speak to this, Wodak and Martin especially directly.

Layder's second element, that of *setting*, focuses on the intermediate social organization, categorized as *work-related* and *non-work related*. Important to setting is what Layder calls — "its already established character", that is the social and institutional structure and practices within which a particular situated activity occurs. Of the invited chapters, those of Gu and Sarangi perhaps most obviously characterize this focus on *setting*, but from distinct perspectives. Gu most concerned to chart the time-space of quotidian activities and their effect on discourse performance but also with identifying what his settings imply beyond their obvious physicality; Sarangi, *inter alia*, describing the issues of access to crucial settings and sites. Sarangi introducing a double interpretation of setting, drawing on Goffman to emphasize the frontstage and the backstage of setting and performance, expanding and deepening Layder's element.

If settings are in Layder's terms *established* — though we should be cautious here not to equate establishment with stability, as such stability will be highly relative across and within social formations, and certainly relative to sectors of the population — then Layder's third element of *situated activity* involves a focus on that face-to-face, or mediated social activity involving what he calls "symbolic communication by skilled, intentional participants implicated in the contexts and settings". Note here how Layder explicitly draws on the discursive turn in sociological research referring to "emergent meanings, understandings and definitions of the situation as these affect and are affected by contexts and settings, and the subjective dispositions of individuals." The message is plain, and it is one that imbues these chapters, most programmatically in that of Bhatia. The message is that the appraisal of discourse in action requires a clearly defined program of sociolinguistic and discourse analytical study of a range of differentiated encounters, and one which goes beyond what may otherwise be a dangerously reductionist reliance on uttered text, as Sarangi warns. But *description* is not enough. Description needs to be accompanied by interpretive, ethnomethodological accounts of the meaning-making of individuals in interaction in particular situated activities, emphasizing the members' resources that can be brought to bear, or are prevented from being brought to bear, on the communicative challenges of the moment. However, even such a focus on interpretation will not adequately include and bring to bear in and of itself Layder's elements of *context* and *setting*, and certainly not the overarching construct of *history*. As Wodak's chapter illustrates par excellence, their significance only emerges from the talk and writings of the participants, from their narratives when set against socio-historical accounts and studies of organizational change, shifts in national policies, analyses of decision-making over time. Including this dimension, as Layder argues one must, moves the research agenda from description and interpretation to what one can call critical explanation.

Finally, in Layder's resource map, what is the significance for the researcher of his fourth element, the *self*? If we see self, with Layder, as invoking identity within the context of social experience, what he refers to as the "unique psychobiography of the individual" located within the time-space of a life career, then the struggle between the individuality and the collectivity of the self as at once body, mind and person is revealed. As Bazerman's self-related narrative reveals, *history, context, setting and situated activity* all impinge strongly on this self in its various identities. No-one who reads the selves involved in, say, Martin's or Gu's accounts could possibly characterize them as merely personal and idiosyncratic, innocent of history, unaffected by situated actions in particularly contextualized settings.

Those accounts, and others in this Section, point up the relationship between the macro and the micro inherent in Layder's map. As he writes:

> *"Although I have presented the resource map as a set of separable elements with their own properties, I have also continually stressed their interconnected nature in relation to the analysis of specific research problems. In this regard, macro phenomena make no sense unless they are related to the social activities of individuals who reproduce them over time. Conversely, micro phenomena cannot be fully understood by exclusive reference to their internal dynamics so to speak; they have to be seen to be conditioned by circumstances inherited from the past. In other words, micro phenomena have to be understood in relation to the influence of the institutions that provide their wider social context. In this respect, macro and micro phenomena are inextricably bound together through the medium of social activity and thus to assert the priority of the one over the other amounts to a "phoney war"* (Giddens, 1984[9]) (1993:102–103)

More than this, however, and in making this micro-macro connection, these chapters offer, taken together, a way towards establishing a research methodological apparatus which will work towards achieving that inclusivity of discursive features I refer to earlier. The challenge for research into professional discourse is just that; to find ways in which, say, the methodologies of text analysis, of social interaction, of narrative ethnography, and of social-institutionally–focused structural and historical analysis can be effectively combined in an integrated research agenda. But even if we were to achieve that — and I believe the signs are increasingly looking good — there is still the issue of *alignment*. Alignment between the model and the social action (as Swales reminds us here); alignment between the body-mind of the self and the time and space-bound person (as Gu evidences); alignment between the motivations of the analyst and those of the sources of his data (as Martin's paper seeks); alignment between the analysis of individual discursive actions and that of the chronicled archive of a

9. Giddens, A. 1984. *The constitution of society*. Cambridge: Polity Press.

polity (as in Wodak's critical discursive history); alignment between the analyst and the practitioner in the project of a negotiated re-invention of each other's perspectives in the identification of what is problematic and the terms in which this may be addressed (as in Sarangi's co-constructionist enterprise); and alignment between the analyst and his personal researcher history (as in Bazerman's reflexively interpreted biography). Nevertheless, alignment can still imply the maintenance of two albeit harmonized identities. The real challenge for research and practice in professional discourse lies in some reinvention of professional boundaries, as Bhatia's chapter implies, where the distinctive perspectives of analyst and professional practitioner are maintained but understood and linked in a common enterprise. The project of seeking practical relevance provides the stimulus to the harmonizing, not the merging, of motivational relevancies.

Section II: Discourses and Practices

Discourses of Health and Social Care

This theme comprises four chapters (Askehave, S. Candlin, Firkins and Smith, Zhang and Shang) which address topics of the reception and usability of pharmaceutical documents (Askehave), relationships between discourse analysts and practitioners in nursing care (S. Candlin), judgement and decision-making in child protection in social work (Firkins and Smith), doctor-patient interaction seen contrastively (as between Chinese and Western practices) (Zhang and Shang).

Their data draws on the comparative study of specialized professional documents conveying pharmaceutical information, spoken narratives from contexts of professional-patient interaction in aged care, bureaucratic and institutional documents directed at the management of judgements in child protection, interactional data from doctor-patient communication in clinical consultations.

In terms of topics, what we identify in the chapters is a concern for interdiscursivity and intertextuality (see Fairclough, 1992[10],

Candlin and Maley, 1997[11]), itself linked to an increasing breaking down of boundaries between discourse communities; the multiple identities inhabited by participants in professional–client relationships and, linked to that the issue of analyst-participant relationships (see Sarangi and Candlin, 2001)[12] and their distinctive — "motivational relevancies"; the recontextualization of messages across a range of modes (see Linell, 1998)[13]; the distinctiveness of reflective professional (as opposed to more generally social) interactions; the discourses of the processes of decision-making; the nature of "professional vision" (see Goodwin, 1994)[14] and the importance of identifying key communication strategies linked to the identification of participant goals. More generally, all chapters in this theme set close analysis of texts, whether spoken or written, in the context of the social practices of which they are a part, emphasizing how the study of professional interaction, direct or indirect, serves as a mediator between close analysis of texts and the study of tendencies within the broader social formation, in part elucidated through reference to a range of social theoretical positions. (see Sarangi, 2001)[15]

10. Fairclough, N. L. 1992. *Discourse and social change*. Oxford: Polity Press.

11. Candlin, C. N. and Y. Maley. 1997. Intertextuality and interdiscursivity in the discourse of alterative dispute resolution. In *The construction of professional discourse*, edited by B.-L. Gunnarsson, P. Linell and B. Nordberg. London: Longman, 201–222.

12. Sarangi, S. and C. N. Candlin. 2001. Motivational elevancies: Some methodological reflections on social theoretical and sociolinguistic practice. In *Sociolinguistics and social theory*, edited by N. Coupland, S. Sarangi and C. N. Candlin. London: Pearson, 350–388.

13. Linell, P. 1998. Discourse across boundaries: On recontextualizations and the blending of voices in professional discourse. *TEXT* 18 (2): 143–158.

14. Goodwin, C. 1994. Professional vision. *American Anthropologist* 96 (3): 606–633.

15. Sarangi, S. 2001. A comparative perspective on social theoretical accounts of the language-action interrelationship. In *Sociolinguistics and social theory*, edited by N. Coupland, S. Sarangi and C. N. Candlin, 29–60.

Inge Askehave

Drawing on her and her colleagues' work in Denmark on the structure and interpretability of pharmaceutical texts, Askehave explores the relationships between the complexity of contemporary discourse communities to discursive variation within informational texts, but also to their receptivity and usability. Her focus on Internet-mediated informational texts introduces a dimension of variability by modality, and her close analysis of the texts themselves is linked to her account of the rhetorical strategies adopted by their author(s)/designer(s) in relation to expert and non-expert audiences.

Sally Candlin

Central to Candlin's chapter are two topics of intense contemporary relevance in professional discourse studies: the relationships between discourse analysts and professional practitioners and their patients/clients; and the need to take account of multiple identities adopted among both professionals and their patients/clients, and the consequent hybridity of their discourses. The explanatory value of a recourse to social theory — in particular to the work of Bourdieu — is evidenced in the distinction drawn between nursing interactions and social interactions, and the suggestion that close analysis of text needs to be informed by what may be, as here, differences in purposes, values and underlying professional ideologies among participants.

Arthur Firkins and Sue Smith

Of all the chapters in this first theme, Firkins and Smith argue the case for the analysis of texts to be embedded in the analysis of the social structures and institutional practices which give rise to them and which they also construct and maintain. Child protection as a distinctive field of practice within social work has judgement and decision-making as key practices, both of which are carefully discoursed in terms of legitimated and sanctioned coded forms of talk and writing. The focus of the chapter on the assessment of risk is linked to the appraizal of professional judgement, and this, in turn, is connected to issues of the evaluation of professional expertise. (See Candlin and Candlin, 2002)[16].

Zhang, Zuocheng and Shang, Wei

Beginning with an emphasis on the genre-based analysis of doctor–patient interaction in terms of move structures, Zhang and Shang expand to discuss such interaction in terms of communication strategies, deriving their analysis from work in Communication Accommodation Theory (see Giles, Coupland, and Coupland, 1991)[17]. They argue for a convergence of these two modes of analysis — one more (socio) linguistic the other more social psychological — and see this construct of *strategy* as one such means. A contrastive analysis of Western and Chinese medical encounters provides an opportunity for inter–cultural comparison within a single institutional context, and, as with other chapters in this theme, there is emphasis on the data set as evidence, and the sites of engagement as arenas, for a discussion of social and institutional struggle and change.

Discourses of the Academy

This theme comprises six chapters (Barron, Cheung, Gotti, Hewings, Jensen and Woodward–Kron) which address topics of the nascence of an academic discipline, its practices and discourses (Barron), the value of a multiple methodological approach to the study of a particular academic genre (Cheung), the arguments in favour of a broad linguistic approach (incorporating discourse analysis, text analysis and pragmatics) to the analysis of specialist genres (Gotti), issues concerning the influence of disciplinary norms on the writing of professionals and students (Hewings), accounting for the written rhetorical strategies of students of law in answering problem-questions (Jensen), and the issue of "apprenticeship" of teacher educators into their professional discipline (Woodward-Kron).

---

16. Candlin, C. N. and S. Candlin, eds. 2002. Discourse, expertise and the management of risk in health care settings. Introduction to the special issue of the *Research on Language and Social Interaction Journal* 13 (2): 115–137.

17. Giles, H., J. Coupland and N. Coupland. 1991. *Contexts of accommodation: Developments in applied sociolinguistics.* Cambridge: Cambridge University Press.

As befits the general site of engagement of the theme, chapters draw on texts taken from disciplines within the academy. These range across student–produced analytical reports in engineering, scholarly writing in economic theory, student essays and academic journal articles in geography, students' written answers to problem-questions in law, and textbooks, essays and interview data from the discipline of teacher education and its participants.

In terms of topics, chapters here are deeply concerned with the ways in which disciplines are constructed through their Discourses (Gee, 1992, 1996[18]), how disciplines themselves come into being, and, in turn, how members of such disciplines are apprenticed into their practices (Lave and Wenger, 1991[19]), and via what discursive means. The loosening of boundaries between disciplines and a consequent increase in discursive hybridity (Bhatia, 1999[20] and this volume), raises issues of disciplinary identification, and this in turn poses challenges to description. The contribution of linguistics (writ broadly) to this endeavour is emphasized, drawing on a range of methodologies, textual, statistical and computational, and corpus-based. The value of combining analysis of text with qualitative accounts drawn from interview-based interpretations by experts is characteristic of several chapters (see Hyland, 2000[21]), and a key theme of some is the relationship to be made between the broadly linguistic and discursive analysis of students' written performance and the systems and values employed by disciplinary specialists in assessment of such writing (see

18. Gee, J. P. 1992. *The social mind: Language ideology and social practice.* New York: Bergin & Garvey.
   Gee, J. P. 1996. *Social linguistics and literacies: Ideology in discourses.* London: Falmer.
19. Lave, J. and E. Wenger. 1991. *Situated learning: Legitimate peripheral participation.* Cambridge: Cambridge University Press.
20. Bhatia, V. K. 1999. Integrating products, processes, purposes and participants in professional writing. In *Writing: Texts, processes and practices,* edited by C. N. Candlin and K. Hyland. London: Pearson, 21–39.
21. Hyland, K. 2000. *Disciplinary discourses: Social interactions in academic writing.* London: Pearson.

Candlin and Plum, 1999[22]). The focus on complex texts with multiple sources brings into focus here the concern for intertextuality we have noted in the chapters in Section I, and the tensions in play among distinctive disciplinary Discourses in the contemporary academy, between learning, teaching and evaluating, and between the world(s) of the academy and those of professional work, raise parallel discussions about interdiscursivity.

Colin Barron

Drawing on detailed study of the discipline of mechanical engineering, Barron explores how it is that a discipline becomes established, how it differentiates itself from either parent(s) or sibling(s), and, in particular, the role played by its Discourse(s) and its texts in such a process. The historical attempts to resolve tensions between theory and practice that he discerns in mechanical engineering are not unfamiliar; applied linguistics would be another case in point, especially in the debate whether a discipline like engineering is "applying" a theory (in this case physics, and in that, linguistics), although some may feel that engineering has achieved a greater harmony of the scientific and the empirical than has (applied) linguistics. The interrelationship he delineates between "rules" and "laws", and the double understanding of rules to mean those governing scientific method and those governing human activity, resonates equally in applied linguistics, especially in current discussion about participant perspectives (Sarangi and Candlin, 2001, *op cit.*).

Paul Cheung

Multi-modality is a current subject of considerable interest (see Kress *et al.*, 2001[23]) in the study of complex texts, and is matched by a growing investment in multi-modality in research methodology. Cheung's chapter argues for directing a range of methodological

---

22. Candlin, C. N. and G. Plum 1999. Engaging with the challenges of interdiscursivity in academic writing: Researchers, students and tutors. In *Writing: Texts, processes and practices*, edited by C. N. Candlin and K. Hyland. London: Longman, 193–217.

techniques (what he terms "textual-analytical-statistical" and "psychometric-statistical") on the analysis of engineering reports, and displays how these different methodologies can be combined to give an account of the integrity and diversity of engineering analytical reports. A second major focus of the chapter is to provide comparative data from NS and NNS student writers and between student writers and their "professional" counterparts. In making these comparisons, Cheung combines the twin foci of research into second language writing on the one hand, in particular, the relationship to the first language writer; and, on the other, research in writing in the academy more generally, in particular the relationship between that and writing by professionals in non-academic contexts.

Maurizio Gotti

A key issue in the study of academic discourse is the relationship between the disciplinary specialist and the linguist/discourse analyst professionally concerned with the study of academic discourse. Such a relationship, as Gotti argues in this chapter, is complicated not only by the degree of their shared knowledge of the disciplinary subject matter, but also because of the claim to descriptive linguistic expertise that *both* parties exercise as a consequence of the central role that language plays in the expression of that disciplinary expertise. Drawing on examples from Maynard Keynes' *General Theory*[24], Gotti argues for the linguist, and for analysis on linguist's terms. This is not a matter of exercising some professional *egemonia*, rather that the professional focus of the linguist (and the term is used broadly) on the central relation between form and meaning, and on the writer-reader relationship, is more likely to offer explanatory evidence for textual complexity or infelicity than an approach, which while focused on language, is essentially literary and text-bound. Nonetheless, as Gotti emphasizes,

23. Kress, G., C. Jewitt, J. Ogborn and C. Tsatsarelis. 2001. *Multimodal teaching and Learning: The rhetorics of the science classroom*. London: Continuum International.
24. Keynes, J. M. 1937. The general theory of employment. *The Quarterly Journal of Economics* (February).

the disciplinary specialist-linguist partnership is crucial; the issue is one of territory, orientation and expertise.

Anne Hewings

Writing in the academy is always more than merely a matter of genre analysis. From the pioneering work of Berkenkotter and Huckin (1995)[25], the situatedness, and the ideologically invested situatedness, of writing in the academy has become a central theme in applied linguistic research. Characteristic is not only the pervasiveness of disciplinary norms exercised and enforced through a range of practices and documents of authority, but also the associated sanctions in terms of the criteria drawn upon for the assessment of success and failure among student writers. That such criteria are often unclear and obtuse has been widely recognized (see the papers on academic discourse in the collection by Candlin and Hyland, 1999[26]), and in part because of uncertainties concerning the epistemological placement of many disciplines, especially in the hybridizing conditions of the late modern academy. Hewings identifies Geography as one such uncertainly poised discipline, and drawing on a corpus of student writing and of academic papers in the discipline, links this uncertainty with variations in the expected disciplinary norms of writing prescribed for students as they move between more phenomenological (humanities-based) towards more epistemic (science-based) views of the discipline.

Christian Jensen

We have noted in relation to Gotti's chapter above the potential for tension between the discipline specialist's views of language and language structure in relation to their specialized texts, and the approach taken by discourse analysts and applied linguists. The genre of legal problem questions provides a further example. Jensen's chapter

25. Berkenkotter, C. and T. N. Huckin. 1995. *Genre knowledge in disciplinary communication: Cognition/culture/power.* Hove: Lawrence Erlbaum.
26. Candlin, C. N. and K. Hyland, eds. 1999. *Writing: Texts, processes and practices.* London: Longman.

explores the rhetorical strategies used by students of law in a second language (English) as they seek to adjust to the commonly used genre schema employed by legal academics (viz. Issue, Rule, Application, Conclusion (IRAC)). The chapter in part addresses the question of whether a more discourse analytically derived technique (Rhetorical Structure Theory (RST)) (Mann and Thompson, 1986[27]) would be more valuable as an analytical tool which could be taught to students as a heuristic device for improving their own written responses. In the event, Jensen opts for IRAC as being well embedded in the armoury of the legal academic, but introduces a greater precision in his association of the "moves" in IRAC with particular lexico-grammatical choices, thus incidentally evidencing ways in which inter-professional cooperation can augment and refine a well-established professional technique. This greater precision of evidence allows him to make important links between the quality of student responses and the grades they receive, with not entirely harmonious results.

Robyn Woodward-Kron

Drawing on the important work of Basil Bernstein into the relationships between changes in disciplinary knowledge and students' educational progress (Bernstein, 1975, 1990, and see also Bernstein, 1996[28]) — a topic which resonates with that of Hewings' chapter earlier — Woodward-Kron draws on data from textbooks, statements of disciplinary subject aims and objectives, student essays and interviews, to explore contrasts between Bernstein's "disciplinary knowledge" and the perceptions by student-learners of that knowledge. A critical

---

27. Mann, W. C. and S. A. Thompson. 1986. *Rhetorical structure theory: Descriptions and construction of text structures*. ISI Reprint Series, ISI/RS–86–174 October, 1986, USC/Information Sciences Institute. Marina del Rey, California.

28. Bernstein, B. 1975. *Towards a theory of educational transmissions: Class, codes and control*. Vol. 3. London: Routledge & Kegan Paul.
    Bernstein, B. 1990. *The structuring of pedagogic discourse: Class, codes and control*. London: Routledge.
    Bernstein, B. 1996. *Pedagogy, symbolic control and identity: Theory, research, critique*. London: Taylor & Francis.

exploration of the problematic construct of "apprenticeship" (see Lave and Wenger, 1991, *op cit.*) into the academic community, and in particular the so-called "novice–expert" relationship, is exemplified by detailed studies of three Discourses Woodward-Kron discerns as being in play — the Discourse of pedagogy, the Discourse of learning, and the Discourse of the discipline, especially as they differentially construct the nature of knowledge and its representation. A close study of the disciplinary subject of *Child Growth and Development* in respect of these issues, identifies (once again) the intertextual and interdiscursive demands on student writing, and also how meeting the normative challenges of assessment occasions greater pressure on conformity than the exercise of liberated intellectual enquiry would appear to advocate.

Discourses of Literature and Creativity

This theme comprises two chapters, the first of which (Burton and Mahoney) focuses on the tensions induced into classroom practice in the field of the teaching and learning of creative expression by contradictory interpellations of the Discourses and practices of "creativity" associated with the discourse of current educational reform policies in Hong Kong; the second chapter (Hermes) addresses the practices of group-based development of learner autonomy in the study of creative texts in a tertiary education context.

In the introductory comments to the first Section of invited chapters in this book, I make explicit reference to the work of Layder (Layder, 1993) as an important stimulus for the design of a socially-situated and historically-grounded research methodology, and in particular as a source for warranting the combination of a range of distinctive research strategies. As with those invited chapters, I mention this work not only because it has proved insightful for the study of professional-client communication and sites of teaching and learning (Candlin, 2000[291]), but also chiefly because it explicitly identifies what is key to the understanding of the Burton and Mahoney, and the Hermes chapters in this theme. In particular, in relation to the former chapter, how a construct such as "creativity" becomes critical when subjected to contradictory interpretations in the framework, as here, of educational reform, and in the second chapter how the historically well-established practices of university teaching, in particular the traditionally didactic role of the teacher, can be challenged by a innovative pedagogy itself deriving from an association between one concept of learning and practice (here autonomy) and another associated with a specific discipline (here the study of literary creativity). In both cases, Layder's call for a historical and social structured grounding for the analysis of context, setting, and situated activity is made explicit and well-motivated, and the focus on creativity marries perfectly with Layder's most micro focus, on the self, on individuality, and on socio-biographical accounts of personality.

Pauline Burton and Dino Mahoney

Drawing on a close analysis of classroom interaction and retrospective accounts from involved teachers set against a reading of official publications from government sources, both administrative and those intended for popular consumption, sharp contrasts emerge through this chapter between official framings of "creativity" and those espoused by the teachers in the context of secondary education in Hong Kong. Fairclough's model of text, social practice and discourse practice (Fairclough, 1992, 1995[30]) and his subsequently available discussions of contemporary discourses of welfare reform (Fairclough, 2000[31]), provide a theoretical framework for their comparative analysis. Pedagogically, Burton and Mahoney's chapter demonstrates clearly that classroom actions are never unconnected to external factors in the social, which always impinge on the school as institution and community and the practices of its members (see Lin, 1999[32]), however

---

29. Norton, B. 2000. General editor's preface to *Identity and language learning: Gender, ethnicity and educational change,* by C. N. Candlin. London: Longman.

30. Fairclough, N. L. 1992. *Discourse and social change.* Cambridge: Polity Press.
    Fairclough, N. L. 1995. *Critical discourse analysis: The critical study of language.* London: Longman.

31. Fairclough, N. L. 2000. Discourse, social theory and social research: The discourse of welfare reform. *Journal of Sociolinguistics* 4 (2): 163–195.

attenuated and indirect these influences may appear. The authors' explanatory methodology provides a clear illustration of how such external factors do so impinge, as seen by teachers' reactions to official formulations and through their and their students' own classroom activity. The classroom is thus an environment for what is always a conditioned creativity.

Liesel Hermes

As the author points out, "autonomy" is now a buzzword, not only in Germany — the site for her chapter — but much more generally, at least in the Western-influenced educational world (for extensive critical and research-informed accounts, see Benson and Voller (1997[33]) and Benson, 2000[34]). Constructed within the world of literary studies in the academy, autonomy is seen, in Germany at least, to have an intellectual antecedent in reception theory (Warning, 1975[35]) with a focus on the creative engagement of the reader in the construction of meanings in negotiation with the source text. Such an engagement serves, in Hermes' view, to develop the students' own discursive abilities and, concurrently, to stimulate their own autonomy as learners. Crucial to this process is the conducive design and construction of the classroom as a site of engagement. It is here that Hermes' chapter demonstrates how the encouragement of individuality within classroom group-work not only establishes the conditions for this negotiation of meaning, but also presents a clear alternative to the traditional university classroom seen as didactic institution.

---

32. Lin, A. M. Y. 1999. Doing-English-lessons in the reproduction or transformation of social worlds. *TESOL Quarterly* 33 (3). [Reproduced in C. N. Candlin and N. Mercer, eds. 2001. *English language teaching in its social context*. London: Routledge, 271–286.

33. Benson, P. and P. Voller, eds. 1997. *Autonomy and independence in language learning*. London: Longman.

34. Benson, P. 2000. *Teaching and researching autonomy*. London: Pearson.

35. Warning, R., ed. 1975. *Rezeptionsaesthetik*. Munich: Fink.

Media Discourses

This theme comprises three chapters (Burger and Fillietaz, Lu, and McKenna) which sample something at least of the increasing range and variety of genres, modalities and interactional sites within the media. In locating media interviews as site of engagement (Scollon, 1998, 2001[36]) in which multiple social practices intersect, the chapter by Burger and Fillietaz re-emphasizes an earlier topic of what van Dijk calls "social discourse analysis" (van Dijk, 1997[37]) essentially iterating the argument of Burger and Luckman (Burger and Luckman, 1967 [38]), and also that of Boden and Zimmerman, (1991[39]) that social "reality" is negotiated through the production and reproduction of social practices, and is in part discursively mediated. It is important, however, not to see such mediation as entirely or even essentially textualized. As Hak points out in a significant paper in relation to health communication (Hak, 1999[40]), there is a considerable "talk bias" in the analysis in many studies in that field. We might say that there is equally a text bias in discourse analysis of the media, a point brought out strongly by Burger and Fillietaz, in respect of two key themes; the need to link what and how something is textualized with the study of how participants' socio-cognitive processes of making matters salient affect the textualization and its reception, and, secondly, how media interviews (in their case here) are exemplars of *mediated*

---

36. Scollon, R. 1998. *Mediated discourse as social interaction: A study of news discourse.* London: Longman.
    Scollon, R. 2001. Action and text: Towards an integrated understanding of the place of text in social (inter)action. In *Methods in critical discourse analysis*, edited by R. Wodak and M. Meyer. London: Sage, 139–183.

37. Van Dijk, T. A. 1997. Discourse as interaction in society. In *Discourse as social interaction*, edited by T. A. van Dijk. London: Sage, 1–37.

38. Burger, P. and T. Luckman. 1967. *The social construction of reality: A treatise in the sociology of knowledge.* Harmondsworth: Penguin.

39. Boden, D., and D. Zimmerman, eds. 1991. *Talk and social structure.* Cambridge: Polity Press.

40. Hak, T. 1999. "Text" and "con–text": Talk bias in studies of health care work. In *Talk, work and institutional order: Discourse in medical, mediation and management settings*, edited by S. Sarangi and C. Roberts. Berlin: Mouton de Gruyter, 427–452.

action (Wertsch, 1991[41]) in which the texts become interpretable only in conjunction with an interpretive analysis of the actions — say of interviewing, or of multimodal illustrative exemplification — in which the texts are embedded, or at least associated. There is a further complexification, in that media discourse is by no means a simple social site, but multiple in respect of its texts and actions, and the roles and assumed or ascribed identities of its participants. The linkage to the social is more than the locally institutional; as Lu, Xiaofei makes plain in respect of his chapter on Internet mediated news discourse in Taiwan and the PRC, broader and more pervasive ideological issues are always in play, connected, of course, with the power of that medium and that modality to technologize (Fairclough, 1996, 1998[42]) particular positions and subjectifications. Finally, as a topic in this theme, McKenna's chapter focuses on mediated communication in the use of hypertext in the setting of the academy, making a critical and a critiqued link between what he refers to as the "hype" of hypertext and issues of economic efficiencies and effectiveness of learning.

The data for these chapters, and their modes of analysis, once again evidence the diversity and hybridity of methodology we have noted earlier; live video interview data (Burger and Fillietaz) interpreted using techniques from mediated discourse analysis (see Scollon, 1998, 2001[43]), and frame analysis (see Goffman, 1974[44]); data from Internet news discourse (Lu), analyzed drawing on critical discourse analysis

41. Wertsch, P. 1991. *Voices of the mind: A sociocultural approach to mediated action.* Cambridge, MA: Harvard University Press.

42. Fairclough, N. L. 1996. The technologization of discourse. In *Texts and practices: Readings in critical discourse analysis*, edited by C. R. Caldas-Coulthard and M. Coulthard. London: Routledge, 71–83.
Fairclough, N. L. 1998. Political discourse in media: An analytical framework. In *Approaches to media discourse*, edited by A. Bell and P. Garrett. Oxford: Blackwell, 142–162.

43. Scollon, R. 1998. *Mediated discourse as social interaction: A study of news discourse.* London: Longman.

Scollon, R. 2001. Action and text: Toward an integrated understanding of the place of text in social (inter)action. In *Methods in critical discourse analysis*, edited by R. Wodak and M. Meyer. London: Sage.

(see Wodak and Meyer, 2001, *op cit.*) but incorporating corpus concordancing techniques as a main mode (see Garside *et al.,* 1997 [45]) and displaying some alignment to mass communications theory; review and analysis of data from specialist commentaries and also of data from primary educational administration and bureaucracy sources (McKenna), again drawing broadly on critical discourse analysis but incorporating reviews of relevant educational, pedagogical, and educational psychological literature.

Marcel Burger and Laurent Fillietaz

In keeping with their reference to mediated discourse analysis, the authors' key concern is to address the question of how participants carry out complex social practices — in this case the television interview — and to tease out what they see as three overlapping and at times contested Discourses within that practice: the Discourses of media information, of private meetings, and of media interviews per se. Such Discourses construct, and are constructed by particular understandings of participant goals, social and discursive; by discursively mediated constraints on particular actions; and by the processual evidencing of particular identities at different moments in the interaction. Valuable in the chapter is its introduction to a methodology: Burger and Fillietaz go to some pains to demonstrate how connections can be made between social-institutional analysis, socio-cognitive interpretation of participant discursive choices, and the realization of such choices in the lexico-grammar. Questions are raised as to the most appropriate way of representing those multiply-oriented and multiply-voiced Discourses within the social practice the authors are studying; one generally relevant question that arises from their discussion is whether an analytical framework premised on constructs such as sequencing or embedding is not too derivative of the linguistic, and whether a more Venn-like dynamic metaphor would not be more suitable. If so, how

44. Goffman, E. 1974. *Frame analysis: An essay on the organization of experience.* New York: Harper and Row.
45. Garside, R., G. N. Leech and T. McEnery, eds. 1997. *Corpus annotation: Linguistic information from computer text corpora.* London: Longman.

this is to be effectively mapped remains a challenge, although recent work by Hasan (Hasan, 2000[46]) exploring the interplay between Action, Relation and Contact offers a possible way forward, as did, much earlier, Levinson's work on the linguistic realization of Goffman's construct of footing (Levinson, 1988[47]). Certainly, Burger and Fillietaz's careful enunciation of the ways in which social practices are realized in social actions and how participants negotiate these practices as acts of identity provides the reader with an effective example of what Scollon refers to as *mediated discourse analysis*. (Scollon, 2001, *op cit.*).

Lu, Xiaofei

With Fairclough's framework for critical discourse analysis as a theoretical point of departure, (see Fairclough, 1993, 1998[48], Wodak and Meyer, 2001[49]), in particular his proposal that discourse events are to be seen as concurrently realized as text, discursive practice and as social practice, the author subjects a corpus of data drawn from US and mainland Chinese news media to computer-aided quantitative and qualitative analysis. Constructs and techniques of systemic functional grammar provide the descriptive tools for close analysis of transitivity, allowing statements to be made about agency and semantic processes, while concordancing routines focused on identifying key lexicalizations and collocations provide quantitative support for ideational analysis of preferred themes and topics in the compared corpora. Methodologically, therefore, Lu's paper provides an excellent example

46. Hasan, R. 2000. The uses of talk. In *Discourse and social life*, edited by S. Sarangi and M. Coulthard. London: Pearson, 28–47.

47. Levinson, S. 1988. Putting linguistics on a proper footing: Explorations in Goffman's concepts of participation. In *Erving Goffman: Exploring the interaction order*, edited by P. Drew and A. Wootton. Cambridge: Cambridge University Press, 161–227.

48. Fairclough, N. L. 1993. Critical discourse analysis and the marketization of public discourse: The universities. *Discourse and Society* 4 (2): 133–168.
Fairclough, N. L. 1998. Political discourse in media: An analytical framework. In *Approaches to media discourse*, edited by A. Bell and P. Garrett. Oxford: Blackwell.

49. Wodak, R. and M. Meyer, eds. 2001. *Methods in critical discourse analysis*. London: Sage.

of the deployment of an ensemble of quantitative and qualitative tools to address variation in the choice of discursive strategies in the two sets of texts, and the ideological significance of alternative positions on the "Taiwan question" suggested by these choices — namely controversy surrounding issues of statehood. Finally, much in the manner of Layder's research map we refer to earlier (see Layder, 1993, *op cit.*), Lu provides the necessary historical and political grounding for the positions adopted by the chosen texts.

Bernard McKenna

As I indicate above, the study of media discourse has proved a fruitful site of engagement for both mediated discourse analysis and critical discourse analysis. Typically, such studies have been directed at documenting the multimodality of media discourse, displaying linkages to the social practices of (subsets) of the media-making and media-using communities, and, in some, have sought to set their analysis within a broader social theoretical framework, seeing media discourse as an ideologically invested site characteristically involving the exercise of power and hegemony. One such media-making and media-using community, though perhaps not the most obvious, is the contemporary academy. Both in terms of its access to public media and, more characteristically, in its production and use of narrowcast online educational media, the academy deserves to receive the critical attention otherwise directed at the practices and outputs of more broadcast-oriented media organizations. With some reflection, and assisted by McKenna's carefully documented critical analysis, it becomes clear that the introduction of mediated learning in the academy raises a wide gamut of contested issues concerning the purposes, economies, properties, practices and participation of the academy as an institution. As he indicates, mediarization and technologization are always accompanied by claims, though only tenuously, it appears, with warrants. Hyping hypertext is a metaphor not only for Fairclough's marketization of the academy (Fairclough, 1993, *op cit.*), but also as a redefining of learning and teaching. It is not only the institution that has become a commodity, but also its central practices, and the modality of those practices has become a crucial and contested site. For, if technologized and mediated practices cannot warrant their claims, as McKenna argues, then not only do the products *per se* which sustain the claims of the commodified institution come under critical challenge, but the institution itself, like the emperor, loses its clothes. You cannot market failure, and if you market hyperbole you soon lose credibility, as the reinvented virtual academy is discovering to its considerable cost.

Discourses of Business Communication

This final theme comprises two chapters (Nickerson and Zhu) which provide two examples of characteristic research into Business communication; the first, Nickerson, focusing on a comparative study of email messages within a single corporation in English and Dutch, the second, Zhu, exploring genre changes in sales invitations in China in the context of major social and ideological shifts over the time period of the so-called "pre-reform" and "post-reform" eras in the PRC. It may be useful to locate these two papers in the context of what Louhiala–Salminen refers to as "the surprisingly small amount of research done in business languages" (Louhiala-Salminen, 1995:12). While the numbers of such research might not agree with her analysis, certainly the range of topics addressed might justify her comment, with their principal focus (overwhelmingly) on examples of business writing, terminology and Fachsprache, text types, and, more recently, on new modalities introduced alongside new technologies. Much less common are those studies which either integrate spoken and written communication; or those which take an avowedly inter-cultural communication stance, although this is changing as researchers focus on languages other than English, or English in relation to other languages. As Louhiala-Salminen points out, more work is undertaken in management studies and international business departments than in departments of languages; or those which link discursive practices and styles with external social pressures and forces; or those which view the study of business communication as closely linked to organizational practices and structures within the firm or the corporation. Paradoxically, it appears that business communication has been much more focused on communication (and particularly on the study of written genres) than it has been on business, and almost exclusively on documenting existing communication practices as diagnostic accounts rather than adopting a more prognostic stance concerned with changes in organizational practices and their corresponding organizational discourses. Louhiala-Salminen (*op cit.*, p. 12) quotes Nigel Holden (1989:43)[50] in making a related point:

> "...*we know surprisingly little about language usage and performance in business contexts and in relation to companies' competitive quest for resources and strategic advantage... There is a need all in all for empirical investigations, which attempt to study language in the business world for what it is. These studies are .... necessary in order to enhance our understanding of language as a facet of corporate communication.*"

Holden was, of course, writing in 1989, and there have been changes, for example the two chapters included in this Section, and items in their bibliographies, the extensive collection of papers in Bargiela-Chiappini and Nickerson (1999)[51], and recent publications in the *Journal of Business Communication*. There also exist commissioned studies undertaken for particular corporations and companies which very clearly connect business practices with business communication and are oriented towards system change. However, many if not most of these are commercial-in-confidence and as such not publicly available, although Boswood and Pearson-Smith (in press)[52] is an accessible counter-example. Interestingly, although perhaps not surprisingly, such contextualized studies are often reported

50. Holden, N. 1989. The Gulf between language studies and management studies: Introducing communication competence as an interfacing concept. In *Language learning in business education, Proceedings from the 1st ENCoDe Conference*, Barcelona, edited by P. Silcock, 33–46.

51. Bargiela-Chiappini, F. and C. Nickerson, eds. 1999. *Writing business: Genres, media and discourses*. London: Longman.

in the management literature, rather than in the business communication journals *per se*. Examples here would be Orlikowski and Yates (1994)[53], Rogers and Hildebrandt (1993)[54]. As studies of business communication become more of a partnership enterprise with business and organizational studies specialists, as they increasingly are sponsored by commercial companies and entities, it is inevitable that such studies will not only gain in authenticity, but will require to be underpinned by theories of social and organizational structure and change. Not only, therefore, will practitioners and writers in business communication need in-depth awareness and knowledge of organizational practices, but they will also need a social theoretical base. This general point is argued in the papers in Coupland, Sarangi and Candlin (2001, *op cit.*) and in Sarangi and Roberts (1999, *op cit.)* As one example, any study of workplace communication in the environment of rapid changes in the workplace environment (reorganization or industrial and commercial tasks, workplace restructuring involving increased team work, greater accountability within the organization in terms of quality management, and, publicly, outside the organization, to warrant the organization) needs to take account of such changes in its analysis of communicative modes and modalities (see Coleman, 1989[55]; Gee, Hull and Lankshear, 1996[56]; Iedema, Degeling and White, 1999[57]; Levett and Lankshear, 1994[58]; Scheeres and Solomon, 2000[59]). There are continuing and growing demands on the communication skills levels of all employees, requiring

---

52. Boswood, T. and A. Pearson-Smith. An ESP program for management in the horse-racing business. In *English for specific purposes: Case studies in TESOL practice*, edited by T. Orr. Fairfax, VA: TESOL. In press.

53. Orlikowski, W. J. and J. Yates. 1994. Genre repertoire: The structuring of communicative practices in organizations. *Administrative Sciences Quarterly* 39: 541–574.

54. Rogers, P. S. and H. W. Hildebrandt. 1993. Competing values instruments for analyzing written and spoken management messages. *Human Resource Management* 32 (1): 121–142.

55. Coleman, H. 1989. The present and the future of work. In *Working with language: A multidiciplinary consideration of language use in work contexts*, edited by H. Coleman. Berlin: Mouton de Gruyter, 109–128.

not only a capacity to understand and to convey information to fellow-specialists, but also, increasingly, to other specialists in different fields, to upper management, or to the public at large, both directly and in a range of mediated forms. At very least, we can no longer happily equate research into business communication with the analysis of de-contextualized examples of typical genres, useful although they may be for establishing terminological databases or style-sheets for pedagogic practice. As Louhiala-Salminen writes:

> *"...However, the emphasis (in workplace communication [CNC]) is not on the "pure" linguistic aspects, but the umbrella covers the whole workplace, and communication is seen as a dynamic real-life process between the participants, which is influenced by various individual, organizational, social, and societal factors."*
> (1995:31)

This argument from business communication resonates strongly with that advanced in this book as a whole, and in the preambles to earlier disciplinary sub-sections, that one cannot study discourse and discursive practices in isolation from the study of social, cultural, disciplinary or organizational practices if one wishes to make some impact on understanding how such institutions and organizations function, and how their practitioners and members operate.

---

56. Gee, J., G. Hull and C. Lankshear. 1996. *The new work order: Behind the language of the new capitalism*. Sydney: Allen & Unwin.

57. Iedema, R., P. Degeling and L. White. 1999. Professionalism and organizational communication. In *Challenges in a changing world: Issues in critical discourse analysis*, edited by R. Wodak and C. Ludwig. Vienna: Passagen Verlag, 127–155.

58. Levett, A., and C. Lankshear. 1994. Literacies, workplaces and the demands of new times. In *Literacies and workplaces: A collection of essays*, edited by M. Brown. *Geelong*: Deakin University, 25–54.

59. Scheeres, H. and N. Solomon. 2000. Research partnerships at work: New identities for new times. In *Research and knowledge at work*, edited by J. Garrick and C. Rhodes. London: Routledge, 178–199.

Catherine Nickerson

The data for Nickerson's study comes from e-mail communication in two languages (English and Dutch) from a range of English and Dutch employees (writers) within a multinational organization. Informed by Bhatia's now classic characterization (Bhatia, 1993)[60], she provides a detailed genre analysis of the collected texts, focusing on the textualization of the messages, an appraisal of their purposes within the organization, and an interpretation of the strategies employed by the writers for effecting interpersonal stance. In keeping with the thrust of the comments in the preamble to the sub-section above, this multi-perspectived analysis allows Nickerson to address not only corporate events and tasks, but also to offer evidence of how members perceive the corporate structure and the corporate environment within which they work, its affordances and constraints. Inter-culturally, Dutch and English employees were seen to textualize their messages in a number of distinct ways, but what was of greater interest was the extent to which ethno-linguistic differences were revealed as less significant than were institutional commonalities. Thus the study of intra-cultural similarities and differences within the organizational culture of such a multinational company takes on more importance than does the traditional focus of studies on ethno-linguistically intercultural differences. This double interpretation of 'culture', and the importance of not conflating the two, has been the subject of other studies, notably by Sarangi, (1996)[61].

Zhu, Yunxia

That inter-cultural does not necessarily imply ethnolinguistic difference either, is well exemplified in Zhu's study of generic variation in the textualizations and underpinning values of a single genre at two stages of a nation's social and political development. Taking two historical

---

60. Bhatia, V. K. 1993. *Analyzing genre: Language use in professional settings*. London: Longman.
61. Sarangi, S. 1996. Conflation of institutional and cultural stereotyping in Asian migrants' discourse. *Discourse and Society* 7 (3): 359–387.

points in the social history of contemporary China — the pre-reform period (1949–1978) and the post-reform period (1978–to date) — the author documents generic differences in the form of sales invitations. As with Nickerson above, Zhu aligns the description of the internal generic structure of these sales invitations with the interpersonal stance revealed by a study of politeness and face. Changes in the economic system in China in the two periods are evoked as partial explanations of the distinctive formulations studied, in particular in relation to changes in salesperson/organizational-to-customer/client stance. What the chapter invites is a greater attention in business communication to the effects on such communication and its genres of wider social change, outside the organization itself. Seen this way, the chapter provides a valuable illustration of the theme of Fairclough's book on discourse and social change (Fairclough, 1992, *op cit.*) and also, in this present volume, of the study of workplace and personal discourses of contemporary *putonghua* evidenced in the invited chapter by Gu, Yueguo.

Section I
Themes and Issues

2

Professional Discourse: Towards a Multi-dimensional Approach and Shared Practice

Vijay K. Bhatia

Introduction

Research and practice in professional discourse has been one of the most inspiring developments in multi-disciplinary applied linguistics (which includes socio-psycho-linguistics) in the last 30 years or so. It has engaged the attention of a variety of scholars and practitioners, not only from linguistics (both applied and computational), discourse analysis, document design, communication studies and rhetoric, but also from sociology, discourse psychology and other cognitive sciences, translation studies, practising disciplines such as business studies, marketing and management (advertising, and accounting, in particular), law (plain English campaigns), to name only a few. Long-term investment in and affiliation to different linguistic and socio-linguistic frameworks and to some extent geographical and disciplinary boundaries have encouraged people to define and pursue research in professional discourse and practice to somewhat differing frameworks leading to a range of conclusions. Oftentimes, such a variation in approaches has also been prompted by different motivations for such analyses: a specific application of findings, a more socio-critical look at what people do with language, a particular theoretical issue, or a specific focus. It has often been assumed, with some justification I think, that many of these areas of study have their own preferred research methodologies and frameworks, depending upon the nature of their research questions, the perspectives they prefer to develop in their practices, and the applications they have in mind. However, in recent years the research in professional discourse is becoming increasingly multidisciplinary and multidimensional. In this chapter, I would like to give some indication of the way and the extent to which research and practice in professional discourse has developed and changed our perception of and perspectives on the nature of and engagement with the study of language, which has traditionally been claimed as a somewhat less important aspect of linguistics.

However, before embarking upon such a course, I would like to give a brief account of the historical development of the field of professional discourse. The emergence of discourse analysis in the form of structural analyses in the sixties, more communicative ones in the seventies, via somewhat more functional frameworks within linguistics, indicates a consistent development of the art, or maybe, craft of discourse analysis. This development, in a way, can be characterized in terms of an increasing quest for what Geertz (1973) refers to as "thick" descriptions of language use, incorporating and often going beyond the immediate context of situation. This quest for thicker descriptions of language use has led researchers from a variety of disciplinary backgrounds to increasingly innovative and often multi-disciplinary frameworks, some of which have become popular as text-linguistics (de Beaugrande and Dressler, 1981; van Dijk, 1980) discourse analysis (Sinclair and Coulthard, 1975; Brown and Yule, 1983), genre analysis (Swales, 1990; Bhatia, 1993; Berkenkotter and Huckin, 1995) critical discourse analysis (Fairclough, 1989, 1992; Gee, 1999), and several others, where the intentions have always been to offer an increasingly grounded description of language use in institutional, academic, professional or other workplace settings. It is a significant development and over the years, the discipline has gradually moved away from formal linguistics more towards socio-cultural orientations. Let me give some substance to this claim by looking more closely at two of the more typical and interesting explications of discourse analysis separated by a span of about 15 years, one in Brown and Yule (1983) and the other very recent one in Gee (1999).

Brown and Yule (1983) claimed that the term "discourse analysis" covered "a wide range of activities ... at the intersection of disciplines as diverse as sociolinguistics, psycholinguistics, philosophical linguistics and computational linguistics." (p. viii) A little later they add, "It must be obvious that, at this relatively early stage in the evolution of discourse analysis, there is often rather little in common between the various approaches except the discipline which they all, to varying degrees, call upon: linguistics" (ix). They further point out, "We call on insights from all of the inter-disciplinary areas ... but our primary concern is the traditional concern of the descriptive linguist, to give an account of how forms of language are used in communication" (ix). This relationship between discourse analysis and formal linguistics is further emphasized in the following quote:

> *"We try to show that, within discourse analysis, there are contributions to be made by those who are primarily linguists, who bring to bear a methodology derived from descriptive linguistics. We have assumed a fairly basic, introductory knowledge of linguistics and, where possible, tried to avoid details of formal argumentation, preferring to outline the questions addressed by formalisms in generally accessible terms."*
>
> (Brown and Yule, 1983: ix)

Fifteen years later, James Gee (1999), in his book entitled *An Introduction to Discourse Analysis: Theory and Method* at the very outset declares:

> *"Many people, including many linguists, think that the primary purpose of human language is to "communicate information". In fact, I believe this is simply a prejudice on the part of academics who believe, often falsely, that what they themselves primarily do to and with each other is "exchange information". Language, in fact, serves a great many functions and, "giving and getting information", yes, even in our new "information age" is but one, and, by no means, the only one.... If I had to*

*single out a primary function of human language, it would
be not one, but the following two: to scaffold the
performance of social activities (whether play or work
or both) and to scaffold human affiliation within cultures
and social groups and institutions.*

*These two functions are connected. Cultures, social
groups, and institutions shape social activities ... At the
same time though, cultures, social groups, and institutions
get produced, reproduced, and transformed through
human activities."*

(Gee, 1999:1)

Comparing Gee's very recent view of discourse with what was
prevalent in the early eighties, one can see very clearly the movement
in time from a more linguistic and perhaps textual view of discourse
to a more social view of discourse, which can be visually captured in
the following diagram.

Figure 2.1
Research and Practice in Professional Discourse

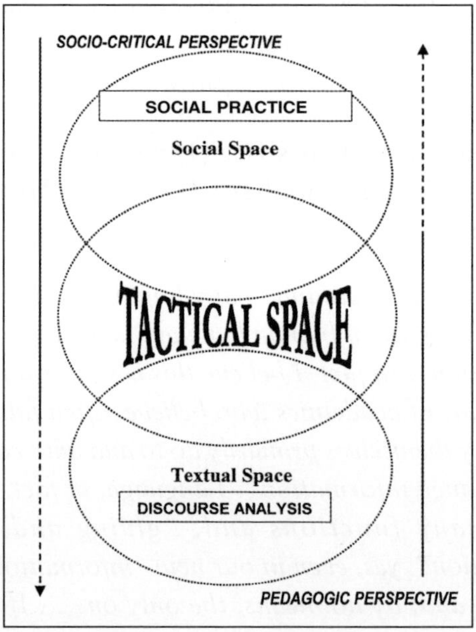

SOCIO-CRITICAL PERSPECTIVE

SOCIAL PRACTICE

Social Space

TACTICAL SPACE

Textual Space

DISCOURSE ANALYSIS

PEDAGOGIC PERSPECTIVE

As one can see, this gradual development of the field of professional discourse analysis has operated sometimes exclusively, but often selectively within or across, three rather overlapping concepts of space, starting off with a predominantly linguistic view of discourse primarily confined to what may be called "textual space" in the late seventies and early eighties, of which Brown and Yule (1983) is a typical example, and then, moving on to a more socio-pragmatic view of discourse exploring what may be called "tactical space", and more recently, to a more socio-cultural and critical view of discourse, operating more centrally within a "social space". One of the most typical questions addressed within a "textual perspective" on discourse is, "What forms of language are realized in communication? On the other hand, the most typical question addressed within a "socio-pragmatic or tactical perspective" on discourse is, "Why do members of professional discourse communities use the language the way they do in the conduct of their daily activities?" In a predominantly "socio-critical perspective", however, the focus shifts from discourse to socio-cultural and institutional aspects of discourse, and the kinds of typical questions raised within "social space" are: "How do social actions (which include language use) express social changes, social structures, identities, and institutions, and in turn, how are they themselves determined by such social institutions and processes?"

It is necessary to mention at this stage that for language teaching purposes, PDA (professional discourse analysis) could be seen as operating within several concepts of space, and as we move away from the issues of language teaching and learning, we seem to be drifting toward social space, where as we can see, context and therefore, complication becomes crucial to an understanding of professional discourse. However, just as focusing on text, which represents lexico-grammatical and discoursal structures, is likely to deprive the language teacher and the learner of the most useful contextual information, in the absence of which it is likely to make very little sense, similarly an exclusive focus on the social space is likely to lead the language teacher and the learner away from linguistic concerns. It may create a less serious problem in first language contexts, where linguistic systems are assumed to have already been acquired, but in the second language learning contexts, it is likely to lead both, the teacher and the learner, to somewhat uneven and unfamiliar territory.

The three perspectives seem to show somewhat distinct boundaries and in some respects, there may be some advantage in taking such a view; in actual practice however, they show a kind of progression that is somewhat typical of the development of such a discipline. They also have an essentially multidisciplinary focus in its concerns, methodology, and even applications. The process of gradual development is also visible even within each perspective. Within the textual space, for example, we have seen gradual, though distinct, developments in the mid-sixties to mid-eighties, which is shown visually in Figure 2.2 on page 45.

We also see several rather distinct stages of the development in the field of professional discourse studies within a predominantly "textual perspective". The first significant stage of development we find in the movement from the characterization of *statistically significant features of lexico-grammar* to the *study of textualization* in discourse, i.e., a characterization of values these features of form realize in discourse. The second stage of development extended the study of textualization to the *study of macro-structures* in texts, thereby bringing into focus the notion of discourse structure. The third stage of development marked a more significant shift of focus from the object of analysis itself, i.e., *text*, to the *context* in which it is constructed, used, interpreted and perhaps manipulated. It is at this stage that the focus shifted *from text* to *what makes* a *text possible*, from surface structure to deep structure of discourse, from discourse to genre, and finally from "what?" to "why?" and "to what effect?" in language use. The next stage was to widen the horizon, as it were, which concerns more centrally the study of social structures, social and organizational identities, discourse systems and hybridization and marketization of discourse practices.

We also see how linguistic analyses have become much more than mere descriptions, often attempting to offer explanation for a specific use of language in institutionalized, social, educational, academic and professional settings. These efforts to offer more explanatory linguistic descriptions often attempt to answer the question "why a particular use of language takes the shape it does".

Figure 2.2
Levels of Linguistic Description

Surface— Deep	Type of Analysis	Type of Finding	Typical Examples
Level A	Identification of statistically significant lexico-grammatical features of discourse	Predominant use of passives in scientific discourse; overwhelming use of complex prepositions in legislative discourse; etc	Barber (1962); Gopnik (1972); Bhatia and Swales (1982);
Level B	Study of form-function correlation, or textualization in discourse, i.e., relating lexico-grammar to text-types, rhetorical principles and grammatical choices	-en participles in chemistry texts; tense usage in reporting past literature in research writing; nominals in academic writing	Swales (1978); Oster (1981); Dubois (1982); Selinker et al. (1973)
Level C	Analysis of information, or rhetorical structuring, and discourse organization; schematic patterns, predictive elements, rhetorical shifts in discourse	Analysis of classroom discourse, problem-solution structures, doctor-patient communication, schematic patterns in service encounters, and predictive structures in economics	Sinclair & Coulthard (1975); Winter (1977); Hoey (1983); Candlin et al. (1974); Tadros (1985); Ventola (1983); Trimble (1985); Selinker et al. (1978);
Level D	Enquiries into institutionalized aspects of discourse; cognitive structuring in discourse; rationale for discourse construction	Move structures in abstracts, article introductions, sales promotional letters, qualificational patterns in legislative discourse	Swales (1981); Bhatia and Tay (1987); Swales (1990); Bhatia (1993)
Level E	Socio-critical investigations of institutionalized discourses	Discourse, identities, and social structures; power and politics of institutionalized discourses; generic hybridization (mixing, embedding and appropriation); recontextualization in discourse	Fairclough (1993, 1995); Bhatia (1995, 1997, 1998); Berkenkotter & Huckin (1995); Sarangi and Roberts (1999)

Adapted and developed from Swales, "unpublished notes".

In spite of such a consistent development of the theory and practice of professional discourse analysis in the last 40 years, there are a number of myths still prevalent about our current understanding of professional discourse, some of which include the following:

- Professional discourse analysis is only a passing fad, or fashion, and not really an area of serious intellectual engagement.

- Professional discourse research, like much of sociolinguistic research, is a theory-deficit field, in the sense that it has no serious theoretical framework(s).

- Qualitative investigation procedures, including those used in socio-linguistics, are non-empirical/non-scientific, hence less reliable, and therefore less interesting.

Without going into any elaborate argument over these issues, I would like to emphasize that these impressions may have had some historical value two decades ago but in the context of today, when we have a number of international conferences every year, some of them almost regularly in areas centrally related to professional discourse research and practice, several international journals, a number of prestigious book series from almost all major international publishers, and a discourse community of several thousands of members, these impressions are nothing more than mere myths. Another very strong indication of the establishment of research field is evident from a comparison of references to and indications of affiliations with formal linguistics in professional discourse studies in the sixties and in the nineties. In the sixties, almost every article published in applied linguistic journals had some reference to the formal linguistics literature (either generative linguistics or some other), but today we rarely if ever find any serious reference to any formal linguistics framework, except references to systemic functional linguistics which have survived because of the functional nature of this linguistic framework. While analysis of professional discourse has moved away from formal to functional linguistics, at the same time, it has been increasingly influenced by a more socio-cultural as well as socio-pragmatic orientations.

Although this brief and rather subjective interpretation of developments of the last four decades indicates that professional discourse analysis whether it is formal, functional, generic, institutional, or social has moved away from its original leanings on formal linguistics towards a more socio-cultural practice, it is misleading to think that linguistic perspectives have been completely abandoned or undervalued. On the contrary, links with functional linguistics have become increasingly central to some forms of discourse analysis, as is evidenced in much of discourse and genre analysis from the systemic-functional perspective (Martin, 1985, 1993).

Research and Practice in Professional Discourse Today

Like any other area of multidisciplinary activity, professional discourse analysis (PDA) has also been sliced off as a rather independent territory by individual disciplines, with somewhat differential spotlights, specific perspectives, varied applications, and more importantly, distinct methodological procedures. Consequently, we have seen a diverse range of multidisciplinary engagements with the discursive practices of disciplinary and professional cultures. Although there is an acknowledged diversity of interests for undertaking analyses of professional discourses, there has been, at the same time, a growing realization that we can understand the critical moments of engagement better if we are in a position to see the whole of the elephant, as it were, rather than only a part of it. As a result, there is a rather selective interest towards an appropriation of research methodologies across disciplinary boundaries. Secondly, since interest in the analyses of professional discourses has been motivated by a variety of applications within and across disciplinary boundaries, many of which tend to benefit from a multidimensional view of analysis, there has been calls for integration of research methodologies and frameworks for analyzing professional discourses and practices.

Another recent development in the field seems to be an attempt to redefine and extend the conventional disciplinary boundaries in applied linguistics. This is motivated by strong applications of PDA to a range of disciplinary concerns, which have prompted researchers and practitioners to look well beyond the narrow boundaries drawn by earlier concerns with the teaching and learning of languages. Although much of the work on professional discourse continues to be primarily motivated by applied linguistic concerns, attempts to extend the scope of research in professional discourse (and hence professional practice) have been on the increase. Whatever the focus of research, it is difficult to undermine the complex and dynamic realities of professional practice. It is often more convenient to focus on a narrow application, in particular, on the search for analytical models and outputs suitable for language training or writing, where it can be used either as exemplary texts or as a resource. As a model, linguistic description is often used as a representative, typical, or ideal example of a generic construct as input for learners to analyse, understand and to exploit in their writing to innovate and respond to novel situations. However, there is also a strong emphasis on using discourse description as a resource, in which case the focus shifts from the textual description as a model to the knowledge of procedures, practices, and conventions that make the text possible and relevant to a particular socio-rhetorical context. This knowledge might be seen in terms of a "generic potential" to extend Halliday's (1975) use of the term "meaning potential", which enables one to make appropriate decisions as to the choice of lexico-grammatical as well as generic resources to respond to familiar and not so familiar rhetorical situations. However legitimate and strong the need for a narrow focus on applications to language learning and teaching, it is always important to have a broader vision to capture the realities of social, institutional and professional practices. The main goals of research and practice in professional discourse therefore are manifold, some of which include the following.

To Represent and Account for the Realities of the Professional World

Much of work on professional discourse analysis has focused on standardized and conventionalized generic forms, which has served the cause of language teaching and learning extremely well. There has been a negative impact of this practice, in the sense that it has kept focus on idealized and somewhat pure generic forms to the neglect of the realities of the professional world. In more recent years however, PDA has started exploring the complexities, dynamism, and versatility of professional practices in academic, institutional, professional, and other workplace contexts, which has led to the identification and investigation of issues related to generic hybridization (which include mixing, embedding, bending or other forms of exploitation of genres), colonization of genres (marketization, and various others forms of appropriation of generic resources), and to disciplinary and institutional conflicts within and across generic boundaries. In spite of the prevailing complexities of the world of professional discourse, especially in terms of its generic patterns, one may often come across typical exponents of pure, and other closely related genres, which seem to form a colony, with varying degrees of shared generic features; one may even find colony members sharing features across colonies. It is this interestingly complex patterning of genres within and across disciplinary boundaries, which makes the PDA enterprise worth the excitement and the trouble it may cause.

To Understand and Account for the "Private Intentions" in Professional Genres

With the invasion of new media and modes of communication in public life, on the one hand, and the more recent increase in the interdisciplinary nature of academic and professional discourse, on the other, appropriation of lexicogrammatical resources and discoursal strategies across discourse communities and genres is becoming increasingly common. Fairclough (1993, 1995) and Bhatia (1993, 1995, and 1997a) give extensive coverage to this aspect of discourse manipulation by expert members of professional communities. The phenomenon of generic hybridization is a complex one incorporating various forms of "generic appropriation" giving rise to mixed and embedded forms, sometimes even creating conflicts in this process of hybridization, as often in the case of memoranda of understanding, joint declarations (Bhatia, 2000), and potentially in some forms of fund-raising discourse (Bhatia, 1998a). Some of the prominent examples discussed in published literature are the following.

- Academic job and course advertisements (Fairclough, 1993)
- Academic course descriptions (Fairclough, 1995)
- Book introductions and book blurbs (Bhatia, 1997a)
- Fund-raising discourse (Bhatia, 1998a)
- Memoranda of understanding, joint declarations (Bhatia, 2000)

These can be represented as follows:

Figure 2.3
Colonization of Academic, Professional and Institutionalized Genres

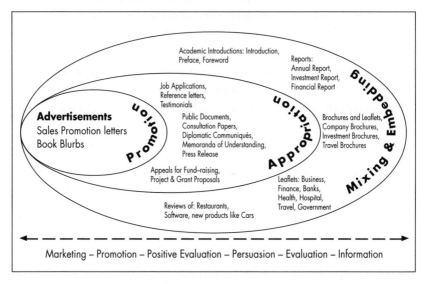

In addition to such hybrid forms, expert writers of professional discourse often exploit generic conventions to implicitly express their private intentions within the context of socially recognized communicative purposes, which is often seen as bending of generic forms. Some of the most discussed forms of such generic appropriation in professional contexts are questions in conferences and seminars, "stance" or "angle" in news reporting, summarizing others' contribution in meetings (Fairclough, 1995), and often exploitations in the form of much of organizational variation in professional discourse, whether it is in the context of newspapers, business corporations, or any industrial unit.

To Investigate Language as Action in Socio-critical Environment

Professional genres are invariably used to do things; to give voice to social actions (Miller, 1984; Martin, 1985, 1993; Martin *et al.* 1987). It is often claimed that since language is only an instrument to achieve social ends, we do not need to pay so much of attention to the analysis of language, and will do well to focus more or rather exclusively on "action" (Gee, 1999). This emphasis on social action in recent literature is on the increase, especially from scholars from a predominantly socio-cognitive background. However, people from other backgrounds, applied linguistics and language education, in particular, would like to see a balance between language and social action. The tendency to focus on what was earlier identified as "social" or "textual" space is more likely to discourage analysts from making informed judgements about the use of professional discourse.

To Investigate the Relationship between Professional Discourse and Social Structures, Social and Professional Identities and Professional Practices

Although it is important to study how professional and organizational discourses are constrained by professional practices, identities and organizational hierarchies, it is equally important to study how discursive practices in professional organizations determine and redefine professional and organizational identities and practices (Boswood, 2000). PDA has focused on how expert members of the community not only create and express their own identities but also question and undermine social identities of the outsiders to the community (Candlin, *et al.*, 1999). Although it is relatively easy to see the relationship between professional discourse and social structures, it is not easy to investigate the tensions between social and professional identities, on the one hand, and preferred professional or organizational practices, on the other. There are several identities that professionals may be required to give expression to simultaneously in the same piece of discourse: professional identities as members of a particular disciplinary community, organizational identities as members of specific organizations or institutions, social identities, as valued members of social groups, and of course individual identities as indications of self-expression. It is interesting for PDA to investigate how established professionals negotiate these different, and often conflicting identities in their discourses.

To Understand how Professional Boundaries are Negotiated through Discourse Practices

Recontextualization of discourse in professional and institutional contexts is yet another interesting area of language use because it raises very significant issues about variation in disciplinary and institutional practices and their use of contrasting methodologies. As Sarangi and Candlin (2001:383) rightly point out:

> *"In the context of communication in public and professional life, discourse analysts are bound to remain outsiders while seeking to make sense of the practices of the professional group, in a very similar way to the workings of Lave and Wenger's (1991) concept of "legitimate peripheral participation". Considerable time and effort, and considerable negotiation, is needed in order to immerse oneself in the research site so as to enable access to necessary tacit knowledge. Equally, a lack of methodological fit, as for example entering a site of professional and public communication without any motivational relevancies, as is the case with so-called open-ended discourse analytic studies, has to be viewed with considerable suspicion (Clark, 2000). Against this backdrop, reflexivity and collaborative interdisciplinary research become a necessity. Nor is this merely a matter of "professional" sites. The issue of shared perspectives of analyst and participant is, quite clearly and routinely, an issue of access to mutuality."*

In addition, it also underpins the issues of *power* and *dominance*, *authority* and *relevance* in institutionalized discourses (Candlin, Bhatia and Jensen, 2000; Sarangi, 1999; Wodak, 1999).

To Investigate Integration of Discourse Analytical Procedures and Professional Practices

The tension between discursive practices and professional or organizational practices is probably one of the most difficult areas to handle. There seems to be little understanding of the two processes across disciplinary boundaries. Often it has been found that two disciplinary cultures do not even share the same language. The *identity* and *membership* of different discourse communities are more likely to create tensions rather than bridge the gap between their varying epistemological orientations, even in a context in which it is advantageous for both to co-operate and collaborate (Sarangi, 2000).

To Offer Effective Solutions to Pedagogical and Other Applied Linguistic Problems

Although a significant effort in PDA research has been devoted to the teaching and learning of languages under English for Specific Purposes, or more popularly known as ESP (Swales, 1990, Bhatia, 1993), there has been very little understanding or collaboration between the two communities, either in the form of jointly undertaken research projects or team taught ESP courses. There is little shared interest in each other's practices. There is still very little understanding of what counts as specialist expertise in a particular professional community. For instance, it is important for ESP practitioners to understand the nature and acquisition of professional expertise in specialist disciplines in order to design and teach ESP programmes to uninitiated members of various professions, but our understanding of the nature, function and acquisition of specialist expertise is still very rudimentary (Bhatia, 2000). We still have no reliable answers to questions like the following:

1. What constitutes expert behaviour in a specific professional field? In other words, how do we characterize an expert accountant or lawyer?
2. What role does discursive competence play in professional practice?
3. Is it possible to specify professional expertise in terms of key competencies?

4. How does one acquire and use these professional competencies?

5. Are these competencies teachable/learnable?

6. How does one appraise/measure expertise in a specialist area?

This area is rather blurred and under-developed and there is a need to bridge the gaps across disciplinary boundaries to lead to a better understanding of PDA and professional practice.

In the preceding sections I have made an attempt to focus on some of the main concerns of professional discourse analysis. Let me now conclude by identifying some of the major challenges facing us in the coming years.

Investigations of Professional Expertise

If discursive practice is an important part of professional practice, and there is no reason to think that it is not, then it seems reasonable to think that expertise in a professional context is invariably acquired in different ways and at different stages of one's career development. Some of the key contributors to this process of acquisition are:

- Education
- Professional Training
- Apprenticeship
- On the Job Learning (Legitimate Peripheral Participation)
- ESP (English for Specific Purposes)
- Communication Skills Training

Considering the diverse range of likely contributors to the development of professional expertise, it is inevitable that research in professional discourse must be more sensitive to and informed by all aspects of professional practice. This kind of research must account for or explain professional practice, on the one hand, and influence the outcome of professional practice, on the other. Although we know that discursive competence and disciplinary knowledge both contribute significantly to professional practice, all three of them help in the development of what we know of as professional expertise. This can be represented as follows:

Figure 2.4
Development of Professional Expertise

Professional Practice

Bridging the Gap between Discourse Analysis and Professional Practice

It follows from the first challenge above that it is important to develop a common language between PDA (Professional Discourse Analyst) and PDP (Professional Discourse Practising) communities through inter-professional understanding and greater appreciation and integration. As Sarangi (2000) rightly points out, it may not be an easy task, as every discipline has its own concerns and priorities, and ways of doing things. It may therefore be necessary to develop an understanding of each other's methods and procedures, epistemological and ideological orientations, their typical issues of concerns, membership practices, and varying discursive practices.

Working towards a Multi-dimensional Research Methodology

Following from the first and second challenges above, it is necessary to work towards enrichment of analytical procedures by integrating interdisciplinary variation or tensions in research methodologies and analytical frameworks. This kind of integration will bring in a much greater level of delicacy and intricacy in the recontextualization and hybridization of discourses, including mixing, embedding, appropriating and bending of professional genres in a much more interesting and exciting manner, which at the moment is partly reflected in some aspects of promotional genres.

Creativity and Conformity in Professional Discourse

A.   *The Social vs. Individual Constructions of Discourse*

This tension between *socially constructed discourse forms* and *individual expressions or identities* has been one of the major issues in the past few years. A further complication is added when we consider the case of those who have the social sanction, institutional power, and authority to bend or exploit conventions to achieve individual identities, or undermine the identities of other participants (Bargiela-Chiappini *et al.*, 1999). This also reflects the tension between *generic integrity* and *generic innovation* (Bhatia, 1993, 1998b, 1999b, 2001).

B.   *The Complexities of the Real World vs. The Contrivances of the Pedagogic World*

The tension between real and the pedagogic worlds, which, to a large extent raises the question:

"To what extent should *pedagogical practices* reflect or account for the *realities of the world* of discourse?"

And, finally, assuming (a) and (b),

"To what extent should the *analytical procedures* account for the *full realities of the world* of discourse?"

Or in other words,

"To what extent, it is necessary or even desirable to see *the whole of the elephant*?"

References

1.   Barber, C. L. 1962. Some measurable characteristics of scientific prose. In *Contributions to English syntax and phonology*. Stokholm: Almquist & Wiksell, 1–23.

2.   Bargiela-Chiappini, F. and C. Nickerson, eds. 1999. *Writing business: genres, media and discourse*. London: Longman.

3. Berkenkotter, C. and T. N. Huckin. 1995. *Genre knowledge in disciplinary communication: Cognition/culture/power*. New Jersey: Lawrence Earlbaum Associates.

4. Bhatia, V. K. and M. Tay, eds. 1987. *Teaching of English in meeting the needs of business and technology*. Vol. 1 and 2. Singapore: Department of English Language and Literature, National University of Singapore.

5. Bhatia, V. K. 1993. *Analyzing genre — language use in professional settings*. London: Longman.

6. _____ . 1994. Generic integrity in professional discourse. In *Text and talk in professional contexts*, edited by B.-L. Gunarsson, P. Linnell and B. Nordberg. ASLA: Skriftserie nr 6, 61–76.

7. _____ . 1995. Genre-mixing in professional communication: The case of "private intentions" v. "socially recognized purposes". In *Explorations in English for professional communication*, edited by P. Bruthiaux, T. Boswood and B. Bertha. Hong Kong: City University of Hong Kong, 1–19.

8. _____ . 1997a. Genre-mixing in academic introductions. *English for specific purposes* 16 (3): 181–196. Forthcoming.

9. _____ . 1997b. Power and politics of genre. *World Englishes* 16 (3): 359–372.

10. _____ . 1998a. Discourse of philanthropic fund-raising. *Working Papers*, IU Center for Philanthropy, University of Indiana, Indianapolis.

11. _____ . 1998b. Generic conflicts in academic discourse. In *Genre studies in English for academic purposes*, edited by F. Inmaculado, J. C. Plamer, S. Posteguillo and J. F. Coll. Bancaixa: fundacio Caixa Castello, 15–28.

12. _____ . 1999a. Disciplinary variation in business English. In *Business English: Research into practice*, edited by M. Hewings and C. Nickerson. Prentice Hall, 129–143.

13. _____ . 1999b. Integrating products, processes, purposes and participants in professional writing. In *Writing: Texts, processes and practices*, edited by C. N. Candlin and K. Hyland. London: Longman, 21–39.

14. _____ . 1999c. Analyzing genre: An applied linguistic perspective. Keynote address given at the 12th World Congress of Applied Linguistics, Tokyo, Japan, 1–6 August 1999.

15. _____ . 2000a. Genres in conflict. In *Analyzing Professional Genres*, edited by A. Trosborg. Amsterdam/Philadelphia: John Benjamins Publishing Company, 147–162.

16. _____ . 2000b. Acquisition of generic competence. Paper presented at the International Conference on Language and Cognition, Kuala Lumpur, Malaysia, 14–16 July 2000.

17. Bhatia, V. K. 2001. Genres in the world of reality. Paper presented at the American Association of Applied Linguistics (AAAL) Conference, St. Louis, USA, 24–27 February 2001.

18. de Beaugrande, R. and W. U. Dressler. 1981. *Introduction to text linguistics*. London: Longman.

19. Brown, G. and G. Yule. 1983. *Discourse analysis*. Cambridge: Cambridge University Press.

20. Candlin, C. N., C. J. Bruton and J. H. Leather. 1974. *Doctor-patient communication skills: Working papers 1–4*. University of Lancaster, Lancaster, UK.

21. _____ and G. A. Plum. 1999. Engaging with challenges of interdiscursivity in academic writing: Researchers, students and tutors. In *Writing: Texts, processes and practices*, edited by C. N. Candlin and K. Hyland. London: Longman, 193–217.

22. _____, V. K. Bhatia and C. Jensen. 2000. Must the worlds collide? Professional and academic discourses in the study and practice of law. In *Domain-specific English: Textual practices across communities and classrooms*, edited by G. Cortese and P. Riley. Bern: Peter Lang.

23. Clark, A. 2000. On being a subject of discourse research. Paper presented at the International Conference on Text and Talk at Work, Ghent, 16–19 August 2000.

24. Coupland, N., S. Sarangi and C. N. Candlin, eds. 2001. *Sociolinguistics and social theory*. Harlow: Pearson Education Limited.

25. van Dijk, T. A. 1980. *Text and context: Explorations in the semantics and pragmatics of discourse*. London: Longman.

26. Dubois, B. L. 1982. The construction of noun phrases in biomedical journal articles. In J. Hoedt, *et al.*, eds. *Pragmatics and LSP*. Copenhagen: Copenhagen School of Economics, 49–67.

27. Fairclough, N. 1989. *Language and power*. London: Longman.

28. _____ . 1992. Discourse and text: Linguistic and intertextual analysis within discourse analysis. *Discourse and Society* 3 (2): 193–217.

29. _____ . 1993. Critical discourse analysis and the marketization of public discourse: The universities. *Discourse and Society* 4 (2): 133–168.

30. _____ . 1995. *Critical discourse analysis: The critical study of language*. London: Longman.

31. Freedman, A. and P. Medway, eds. 1994. *Genre and the new rhetoric*. London: Taylor and Francis.

32. Gee, J. 1999. *An introduction to discourse analysis: Theory and method*. London: Routledge.

33. Geertz, C. 1973. *The interpretation of cultures.* New York: Basic Books.

34. Gopnik, M. 1972. *Linguistic structures in scientific texts.* The Hague: Mouton.

35. Halliday, M. A. K. 1975. *Learning how to mean: Explorations in the development of language.* London: Edward Arnold.

36. Hoey, M. 1983. *On the surface of discourse.* London: George Allen & Unwin.

37. Kress, G. 1987. *Genre in a social theory of language: A reply to John Dixon.* In *The place of genre in learning: Current debates,* edited by I. Reid. Geelong: Deakin University Press.

38. Kress, G. R. and T. van Leeuwen. 1996. *Reading images: A grammar of visual design.* London: Routledge.

39. Lave, J. and E. Wenger. 1991. *Situated learning: Legitimate peripheral participation.* Cambridge: Cambridge University Press.

40. Martin, J. 1985. *Factual writing: Exploring and challenging the experiential world.* Geelong: Deakin University Press.

41. Martin, J. R. 1993. A contextual theory of language. In *The powers of literacy— A genre approach to teaching writing.* Pittsburgh: University of Pittsburgh Press, 116–136.

42. _____, F. Christie and J. Rothery. 1987. Social processes in education: A reply to Sawyer and Watson (and others). In *The place of genre in learning: Current debates,* edited by I. Reid. Geelong: Deakin University Press.

43. Miller, C. R. 1984. Genre as social action. *Quarterly Journal of Speech* 70:157–178.

44. Myers, G. 1992. The textbooks and the sociology of scientific knowledge. *English for Specific Purposes* 11:13–18.

45. _____. 1995. *Disciplines, departments and differences.* In *Writing in academic contexts,* edited by B.-L. Gunnarsson and I. Backlund. Uppsala University, 3–11.

46. Oster, S. 1981. *The use of tenses in reporting past literature.* In *English for academic and technical purposes: Studies in honor of Louis Trimble,* edited by L. Selinker, E. Tarone and I. Hanzeli. Rowley, Mass: Newburg House, 76–90.

47. Sarangi, S. 2000. Discourse practitioners as a community of interprofessional practice: Some insights from health communication research. This volume.

48. _____. and C. Roberts, eds. 1999. *Talk, work and institutional order: Discourse in medical, mediation and management settings.* Berlin: De Gruyter.

49. _____. and C. N. Candlin. 2001. Motivational relevancies: Some methodological reflections on social theoretical and sociolinguistic practice. In *Sociolinguistics and social theory,* edited by N. Coupland, S. Sarangi and C. N. Candlin. Harlow: Pearson Education Limited, 350–388.

50. Scollon, R. 1998. *Mediated discourse as social interaction — A study of news discourse*. London: Longman.

51. Selinker, L., J. Lackstrom and L. Trimble. 1973. Technical rhetorical principles and grammatical choice. *TESOL Quarterly* 7 (2) (June 1972): 127–136.

52. _____, M. T. Trimble and L. Trimble. 1978. Rhetorical function shift in EST discourse. *TESOL Quarterly* (September): 311–320.

53. Sinclair, J. M. and M. Coulthard. 1975. *Towards an analysis of discourse: The English used by teachers and pupils*. London: Oxford University Press.

54. Swales, J. M. 1974. Notes on the function of attributive en-participles in scientific discourse. Papers for Special University Purposes No. 1, ELSU, University of Khartoum.

55. _____ . 1981. Aspects of article introductions. *Aston ESP Research Report No. 1*, Language Studies Unit, University of Aston in Birmingham, UK.

56. _____ . 1990. *Genre analysis: English in academic and research settings*. Cambridge: Cambridge University Press.

57. _____ . 1998. Other floors, other voices: A textography of a small university building. *Rhetoric, Knowledge and Society Series*. Marwah, NJ: Lawrence Erlbaum Associates.

58. _____ and V. K. Bhatia. 1982. An approach to the linguistic study of legal documents. *Fachsprache* 5 (3): 98–108.

59. Tadros, A. 1985. *Prediction in text*. Birmingham: English Language Research, The University of Birmingham.

60. Trimble, L. 1985. *English for science and technology*. Cambridge: Cambridge University Press.

61. Ventola, E. 1983. Contrasting schematic structures in service encounters. *Applied Linguistics* 5:275–86.

62. Winter, E. O. 1977. A clause relational approach to English texts: A study of some predictive lexical items in written discourse. *Instructional Science* 6 (Special Issue).

63. Wodak, R. 2000. Multinational organizations: Europe in the search of new identities. This volume.

3

On Models in Applied Discourse Analysis

John M. Swales

One day a man comes up to Mozart in the street in Vienna and asks "Excuse me, Herr Mozart, could you tell me how to write a symphony?" "Sure", says, Mozart, "this is what you do" and the man gets out his notebook to write it all down.

"First, you write a piece for solo piano, then a duet, then a quartet, and then a concerto for a small orchestra, and then finally you are ready to write a symphony". The man in the Viennese street writes it all down but then looks up and exclaims "But that's not how you did it, Herr Mozart". "Ahh," replies Mozart, "you see there's a big difference between you and me; I didn't have to ask the question."

Mozart was, of course, an exceptional human being; he was both a musical genius and he had received some remarkable and remarkably intensive early training in the musical arts from his illustrious father. Doubtless there are few other "naturals"; a few other successful auto-didacts who do not need to ask the question of how to create a major work; a few others like Conrad and Nabokov who can write brilliantly in languages not originally their own. However, the vast majority of us need some kind of scaffolding, some kind of progressive and nested structure that education, curriculum, syllabus, and graded tasks and individual mentoring at their various levels and in their various ways typically provide. From the important but partial rhetorical perspective we can see this education as a series of generic ladders — although of course there are, in British parlance, some snakes or, in American parlance, some chutes as well. In terms of written academic discourse, the top rungs of these generic ladders might consist of an 8-page researched paper at the end of a high school, an honours thesis for a BA, a major group research project for an MA, a dissertation for a Ph.D., and a substantial article in a top journal for an assistant professor.

In our new textbook for NNS doctoral students and junior researchers around the world (Swales and Feak, 2000), Chris Feak and I try to parallel this kind of progression in most of our eight units. The titles of these eight units are as follows:

1. The positioning of the research writer
2. Stepping onto a wider stage — the conference abstract
3. Research on display — the conference poster
4. The literature review
5. More complex literature reviews
6. Further steps and stops on the dissertation road
7. Academic communications in support of the research process
8. Academic communications in support of a research career

After an orientation opening unit, the next five units deal with official genres or part-genres, starting with the conference abstract, since this is typically the first piece of writing that a graduate student does that is aimed outside his or her own institutional setting and, not coincidentally, is one that is short enough to be suitable for peer-review. The last two units deal with what I have elsewhere called "occluded genres" (Swales, 1996); these are requests, applications, reminders, recommendations and so on that support a burgeoning academic career, but are not themselves part of the formal record. Most of both types of these genres and part-genres are susceptible to structural modeling (i.e., there are propensities for what is likely to happen in their opening, continuing and closing moves). However, according to our research, one exception is the literature review which appears to be much less susceptible to such an approach (Swales and Lindemann, 2001), but that is another story.

Reflections on Structural Models

In this chapter, I would like to reflect at some length on the status and deployment of this kind of structural model in applied discourse analysis and, by extension, in academic and professional writing and, by further extension, to academic and professional speaking. The kind of model I have in mind is one that purports to account for discourse structure, such as Michael Hoey's situation-problem-solution-evaluation structure (Hoey, 1983) for many types of technical and expository texts; and it can be noted in passing that the first definition of "model" in my Oxford dictionary is "a representation of structure". In discourse analysis, these structural models are typically either in schematic form, often accompanied by arrows, or in the form of numbered lists, sometimes with various kinds of sub-categorization.

But before I attempt to develop my main argument, it may first be helpful to place this aspect of applied linguistic research in a wider context lest I am thought to be even more obsessive-compulsive about the importance of genre analysis than is actually the case. For this, I will use Anne Beaufort's excellent but insufficiently known 1998 volume entitled *Writing in the Real World*. She produces a model (that word again) for "five context-specific knowledge domains for writing expertise". The following four overlap and coalesce to shape an expert text:

- Subject matter knowledge
- Rhetorical knowledge
- Writing process knowledge
- Genre knowledge

All these four are further encapsulated within, or bounded by, what she calls "discourse community knowledge" (p. 64), or what Ken Hyland (2000) calls "disciplinary cultures", or what others have called "communities of practice" (Lave and Wenger, 1991), or perhaps what Bourdieu calls "habitus" (Bourdieu, 1991). Whatever the terminology, the point I want to stress at this early juncture is that my focus omits only one part — in Beaufort's model only a fifth part — of what we might conceive of as writing expertise; the other parts are important but cannot be encompassed in this small a space.

Despite their potential importance as demonstrations of what discourse analysis can produce and elucidate at a level above that of the sentence or utterance, serious meta-analytic reflection on the uses and roles of structural models would seem to be rare in the applied linguistic/ESL literature. Rather the models tend to be glossed in two lesser ways. On the one hand, they are often accompanied by various disclaimers that the model is "provisional" or a "simplification". On the other, they are often presented as landmarks of achievement as when authors announce that their lengthy discussions can now be summarized in their upcoming models or that their models demonstrate what schematized analyses can achieve from both a heuristic and a pedagogical viewpoint. Beyond this kind of hedge-boost verbal commentary, we seem to have little.

This reticence may of course be connected to the fact that models are not universally approved of in writing circles, partly because of their widespread but research-uninformed use in textbooks in business and technical communication, and their L2 alternates. Models have also tended to sit uneasily with those who adopt a process approach to writing, with those who privilege individual expression and creativity, and for those who believe that models are inherently conservative and constraining and therefore diminish opportunities for learners and teachers to deconstruct the hierarchical systems of which they are part (Pennycook, 1997).

Despite these concerns, the models themselves have a venerable place in the short history of discourse analysis. In written textual analysis, the first was probably Vladimir Propp's 1928 account of the European/Slavic folktale (Propp, 1968) , with his analysis of the 31 elements that characterized such a genre and his finding that however many of these elements were realized in any particular tale they always followed a set order (and one that is miraculously reflected in the Harry Potter books).

One of the earliest attempts in spoken discourse was Mitchell's (1957) neo-Firthian account of market transactions in North Africa (based on data collected in 1949), entitled "Buying and selling in Cyrenaica; a situational statement". This was a study clearly ahead of its time; apparently rejected by British linguistics journals as "not being linguistics" (and later dismissed by Langendeon as "ethnography", (Ventola, 1998)), it was eventually published in a Moroccan journal devoted largely to archeology entitled *Hesperis*, and has had an obscure existence ever since. All the same, the paper remains an important precursor, not least for its close interweaving of context and linguistic expression. Here is one of Mitchell's models:

Market (non-auction) and Shop Transactions

These categories share a common pattern of stages as follows:

1. salutation
2. enquiry as to object of sale
3. investigation of the object of sale
4. bargaining
5. conclusion

(Mitchell, 1957:45)

Note: in addition to the numbered list, the use of the phrase "a common pattern of stages", which Mitchell then proceeds to gloss, qualify and illustrate. Here is how he opens his account of Stage 1:

> "Shop and market situations differ in that for the latter it is possible that in the instance no greetings are exchanged. This is **on the whole** more likely to be so when the buyer is a townsman. **As a rule**, however, both because of the importance attached in the society to the greeting of one's fellows and, more particularly, **because of the possible attendant benefits in the transaction**, proceedings are opened by the buyer with an appropriate salutation."

(p. 45; my emphases)

Although this is a project initiated 50 years ago, the first two elements in bold type point to what would become a long-standing concern to allow for exceptions to the model, and the third to providing some explanatory account for the preferred choice. These features, plus others such as its superb linguistic documentation, would not make its appearance in a contemporary journal either untoward or unexpected.

Certain other models have, of course, established a certain popularity, or perhaps even notoriety. Here are four, all of which are more than ten years old:

Labov (1972) Oral Narratives
   Abstract
   Orientation
   Complicating action
   Evaluation
   Resolution
   Coda

Hoey (1983) Problem-solution Texts
   Situation
   Problem
   Solution
   Evaluation

Ventola (1987) Service Encounters
   Offer of service
   Request for service
   Transaction
   Salutation

Swales (1990) Article Introductions
   Establishing a territory
   Establishing a niche
   Occupying a niche

So, next I would like to raise three closely-related questions about such models in applied discourse analysis, concentrating on the last of the four cases in part because I know that model quite well and know something of the literature it has engendered, but mostly because it was designed specifically for ESL academic and professional writing. These questions are:

1. What makes "a good" model?

2. What are the preferred relationships between models and their associated discourses?

3. What can we learn from the above about the role of models in (applied) discourse analysis?

One seemingly predisposing feature for the acceptance of structural models is a certain simplicity. Although all of the four models I have selected are rather more complex than my own representations (Labov deals with missing elements, Hoey with alternate sequences, Ventola with recursive elements and Swales with "steps" within his three "moves"), none is complicated in basic outline. In contrast, elaborate models, for all their sophistication and for all the time and effort put into their evolution, somehow typically fail to attract the attention of the relevant applied discourse communities in a sustained way, however much they may appeal to coteries of like-minded scholars. It looks as though being simple engenders being memorable, and this in turn engenders being usable, quotable, and perhaps teachable (in some sense to be discussed).

A second obvious common characteristic of the four models is that their elements are depicted in terms of pragmatic or rhetorical categories, rather than linguistic or formal ones. A third important feature is that, with the possible exception of Hoey, the elements chosen have been labelled according to the exigencies of specific discourse-types or genres. A fourth would seem to be that all are well grounded in various corpora of real-world data, since none has emerged from introspection or speculation and none has been directly inherited from Aristotle or some other rhetorical luminary.

For a fifth winning characteristic it may be helpful to recall Murray S. Davis' famous 1971 article on what makes a theory — in sociology, primarily — interesting. His answer, in a nutshell, is that interesting theories or propositions — or in our case structural discourse models — deny certain assumptions of their audiences. His first category for what he calls an "Index of the Interesting" is the one most relevant to the present discussion.

Organization

a.   What seems to be a disorganized (unstructured) phenomenon is in reality an organized (structured) phenomenon.

He interestingly goes on to comment that the former is the typical ambition of a "younger ripening discipline", which seems to fit the field of discourse studies pretty well. In our case then "good" models of discourse structure would seem to be those which offer order where order might not be expected, or might not yet have been reported. In effect, "good" models must bring to their readership, or at least to a sufficient part of that readership, some small sense of revelation; they need to invoke, at least initially, some feeling of "Oh okay I see what's going on here in a way I didn't quite see before; before there were just trees, but now I can see the wood". In this way, our original rather jumbled and inchoate perceptions of a spoken story, of a short technical report, of a sales encounter, or of an article introduction become replaced by a schema that model inflicts upon us. There is, in other words, some exegetical power apparently at work here. It is not surprising then that models that have all the five characteristics I have mentioned are rare. Indeed, despite some trying, I have not so far been able to repeat my earlier success. Perhaps in the same way that composers only seem able to write one violin concerto, discourse analysts can produce only one successful model.

Murray Davis can also help us think about the other two questions, particularly whether a model is "good" if it accounts well for the data to which it might (more or less) appropriately be applied. At first sight, the answer would seem to be a straightforward, obvious and unmitigated "Naturally, there should be a good fit between data and model". Indeed, science would seem to argue along these lines; here is a brief quote from Stephen Hawking, who is of course talking about the theoretical physical sciences: "A theory is a good theory if it is an elegant model, if it describes a wide class of observations, and if predicts the results of new observations" (Hawking, 1993:6). However, I would like to propose that, at least in our applied field, there is nothing transparently obvious or self-evidently correct about such a position, and this despite the large numbers of "test-the-model" studies that have been undertaken for MA and Ph.D. theses.

A Test Case

It might be helpful at this juncture to consider a simple hypothetical situation. Imagine we want to construct a model to account for what happens linguistically after somebody asks a question. Here is one such based on the well-known turn-taking model of Sacks, Schegloff and Jefferson (1974):

1. Question
    2a) Response, or
    2b) Question, or
    2c) Silence ➜ 3a) Repetition of question
                          3b) Other response

Let us assume for the sake of my argument that this model covers all possible contingencies for question-following verbal behaviour. It might therefore seem that this model is a "good" one; however, it is not in Murray Davis' sense a very interesting one. Even if it might appeal to philosophers and the like, it tells us nothing very specific about the propensities of human verbal behaviour, and how these propensities are affected by various kinds of context, in exactly the same way that Grice's maxims (Grice, 1975) need to be recalibrated for each context of situation for them to have any practical value. For example the Maxim of Quantity ("Say as much as you need but no more") is an empty truism until we can interpret it within the conventions of what is allowable and expected within a particular genre.

So let's offer this simple alternative:

1. Question
2. Answer

Now this is more "interesting" (in the sense that I have been using the adjective) because the model captures the Conversation-analytic "preference" system whereby answer is the preferred response; it can also capture the well-attested phenomenon that experts in institutional dyads (in legal, medical and educational contexts) have rights to posit questions that require answers from non-expert interactants, while the latter have reduced rights in terms of questions they can ask. Equally importantly, the model is now falsifiable in Popperian terms. We could show that in, say, Perez-Gonzalez' study of 911 calls that requests for various kinds of response by callers are typically followed by dispatcher's questions asking for more information (Perez-Gonzalez, 1998), and that this typically happens in service encounters and in "asking the way" sequences (Scotton and Bernsten, 1983):

Q: Could you tell me the way to the Post Office?
Q: How well do you know the town?

At this juncture, a third and alternative model emerges and would look like this:

1. Question

2. [When interlocutor 1 underspecifies relevant information] Question

This less expected model now has "news value" in Berkenkotter and Huckin's (1995) terms; it is more "interesting" than the other two in Davis's conceptualization; it has some interesting explanatory potential; and it would be likely to attract further empirical investigation in areas in which it might apply. It now looks as though goodness-of-fit-with-the-overall-data might not be after all a defining, nor a necessary nor a sufficient, criterion for pedagogically or practically useful structural models in our field.

Article Introductions Revisited

The 1990 Create-a-Research-Space model has been comparatively successful, in both descriptive and pedagogical terms (or so I fondly believe) because it is relatively simple, functional, corpus-based, *sui-generis* for the part genre to which it applies, and at least at the outset offered a schema that had not hitherto been widely available. A probable sixth predisposing element for its success may have been its strong metaphorical colouring — that of ecological competition for research space in a tightly-contested territory. However, the deployment of a controlling metaphor of this particular type has had the consequence of producing two conflicting effects. On the one hand, it has contributed to the model's "interestingness"; on the other, it has contributed to its apparent fallibility. These effects derive from the fact that the Create-a-Research-Space metaphor privileges an environment in which academic promotionalism and boosterism are strong (Lindeberg, 1998; Hyland, 2000); it primarily reflects research in a big world, in big fields, in big languages, with big journals and big libraries.

Elsewhere on the academic scene, matters may be very different, as Mauranen (1993) has shown for Finnish economists, Ahmad for Malay scientists (Ahmad, 1997), Duszak (1997) and Golebiowski (1999) for Polish scholars, and Fredrickson and Swales (1994) for Swedish linguists, to name but a few of such studies. We could now, I suppose, construct an alternate model to account for these new kinds of data, one which might be called the OARO, or Open a Research Option, Model. It might look like this:

Figure 3.1
The OARO (Open a Research Option) Model

0	*[Attracting the Readership]* Optional Opening (Fredrickson and Swales)
1	Establishing Credibility a) Sharing background knowledge (Golebiowski) b) Justifying need for research *per se* (Ahmad) c) Presenting interesting thoughts (Clyne) d) Introducing general goal (Golebiowski)
2	Offering a Line of Inquiry a) Discussing current problems b) Expressing interest in an emerging topic
3	Introducing the topic

This alternative thus captures a kinder, gentler research world where there is little competition for research space, but where there may be competition for readership (as in the case of Fredrickson and Swales' Swedish linguists writing in Swedish), where justifying doing any research at all may have higher priority than establishing some small gap in an extensive previous literature (as with Ahmad's Malay scientists), and where a beginning researcher, such as a junior graduate student, might find a wider comfort zone. We could schematize this polarity in the following way:

Figure 3.2
Comparing Two Models

OARO (Open A Research Option)

- Non-antagonistic
- Mostly softer fields
- Small discourse communities
- Non-anglophone cultures
- Unsectioned/unconventional

CARS (Create a Research Space)

- Antagonistic
- Mostly harder fields
- Large discourse communities
- Anglophone cultures
- Conventional (IMRD)

At this stage, some might think that the above contrast represents some small kind of *tour de force* and that its author should be congratulated on his contribution to our understanding of academic discourse and to its potential utilization in teaching academic and research writing. However, rather than being seduced by such a superficially attractive polarity, we in fact need to be aware that such expansions are only the beginning of a story, rather than the end of one. This is because we next need a model that would, as it were, be able to characterize — and perhaps later guide — introductions that would occupy some mid-position in the above polarity. We might call this a Present-a-Research-Topic, or PART model. However, once we have opened Pandora's Box, we now need a model to account for those elaborated introductions in English wherein authors oppose conventional beliefs or attempt to instigate a Kuhnian paradigm shift. Paul and Charney (1999) have valuably compared early and late articles in Chaos Theory and showed that the ground-breaking early articles contained "Exemplar Moves". As they say, "Examples remain common ground that can be shared both by researchers pursuing normal science and those attempting to launch a revolution or paradigm shift" (1999: 406). We might call this The-Take-On-The-Establishment or TOTE model. In terms of increasing rhetorical effort or strain, we now have four models:

OARO (Open a Research Option)

∨

PART (Present a Research Topic)

∨

CARS (Create a Research Space)

∨

TOTE (Take on the Establishment)

In this way models for article introductions proliferate and thus begin to raise the question as to whether such proliferation leads to a sharper specification or, on the other hand, to a valuable loss of generality. And we can note that, even within the research article, we have come nowhere close yet to accounting for all the variables. Hyland (2000) in his analysis of disciplinary discourses, shows considerable linguistic and rhetorical variation in the eight fields that he studies. In addition, there have often been suggestions that the options available for established researchers can be very different to those available for beginning ones; in consequence, in addition to a "Young Turk" (for which a CARS-type schema might suffice), we also need one to capture the rhetorical movement of "Old Fart" introductions.

At this juncture I would suggest that the better policy is to pick up Occam's Razor ("do not multiply entities unnecessarily") and engage in some model-culling for both descriptive analyses and pedagogical materials. On the former, Golebiowski (1999) has recently compared introductions in English and Polish and concluded "variation between Anglo-American and Polish styles of scholarly writing is too significant to justify the implementation of the same investigative tool [the CARS model] in both cases" (p. 239). Now this is an interesting statement indeed. On the one hand, given the discrepancies she found, it is undoubtedly true that the CARS model could not and should not be used in any applications directed toward the teaching of Polish scholarly writing. On the other, it is very unclear whether Golebiowski would have been able to point up the differences so starkly without using some relatively simple, metaphorically-rich and rhetorically-pointed schema such as the CARS model provides. It also directly raises an equally important issue: not whether such disparities exist, but why they do so. Are they determined by inherited cultural tradition, socio-political ethos, academic training, size of the discourse community, or maturity of the national field, and in what proportions and combinations?

Concluding Remarks

In this chapter I have presented some arguments for seeing rhetorical or structural models as potentially revealing metaphors for discoursal arrangements that function as testable and rejectable hypotheses for communicative planning by writers, readers, listeners and speakers. One obvious reason for doing so is an apprehension about so-called "boiler-plate" and a concern about how descriptive analysis can become normative control, as when my linguistics undergraduates tell me that they write their resumés "out of a book".

In terms of actual teaching practice, I have little to offer of startling novelty, but rather align myself with contemporary practice. As Anthony recently observed in *TESOL Matters* as follows: *"The proposed methods for teaching genres have also changed from explicit approaches to those in which features of genres are 'negotiated' through classroom discussion or 'reinvented' through elaborate writing tasks"* (Anthony, 2000:18) In this "negotiated" approach, particularly as it becomes both personalized and particularized for the individual rhetorical situation of the individual NNS writer, and wherein schemata become recontextualized, simple, fallible but "interesting" structural models lose their authority and rightly so, especially in an era when professional genres are in dynamic movement and in rapid evolution.

We also live in an era in which international graduate students are flooding into universities across the English-speaking world; an era in which English is regrettably establishing a stranglehold on the world's international academic communications; an era in which there is (again regrettably) increasing pressure across the world to publish in international and now overwhelmingly English-medium journals; an era in which there are growing expectations that doctoral students, especially in the U.S., will also contribute to those burgeoning literatures; an era in which an increasing stream of publications aims at delineating the features of academic English; and an era in which cross-cultural studies are on the rise and are at the same time increasingly problematized, as in Kubota (1997).

In response to such trends, as an EAP practitioner I now mostly teach academic writing to third, fourth and fifth year Ph.D. students who all volunteer for these classes. The level at which Chris Feak and I operate can perhaps be seen as a sign of the growing maturity of our field; it at least shows that we have something useful to teach at these levels. It shows a recognition that senior graduate students may need some support as they ascend the higher rungs of the generic ladders in their chosen disciplines. In the multidisciplinary "laboratories" of our classes — and our participants can come from any of the university's 19 schools and colleges — non-normative depiction and discussion of generic structures provides a locus for enhanced metalinguistic awareness on the part of the participants and for further adjustment and enlightenment on the part of the instructors. If, as Wollman-Bonilla (2000) argues for first graders in Boston, and Jim Martin and his colleagues in Sydney have long argued for Australian primary schools, native-speaker children are capable of recontextualizing genre information, and are capable of seeing genres as "resources for meaning" rather than "systems of rules" (Halliday and Martin, 1993: 22), then that is surely equally true of our NNS elite, who often have superb analytic skills in their own areas of speciality. If, as part of raising rhetorical consciousness and metalinguistic awareness, our class participants are all discourse analysts now, then such part-timers do better critiquing and modifying simple models rather than learning and applying complicated ones.

References

1. Ahmad, U. K. 1997. Research article introductions in Malay: Rhetoric in an emerging research community. In *Cultural and styles of academic discourse*, edited by A. Duszak. Berlin: Mouton de Gruyter, 273–303.

2. Anthony, L. 2000. Implementing genre analysis in a foreign language classroom. *TESOL Matters* 10 (3): 18.

3. Beaufort, A. 1999. *Writing in the real world: Making the transition from school to work*. New York: Teachers College Press.

4. Berkenkotter, C. and T. N. Huckin. 1995. *Genre knowledge in disciplinary communication*. Hillsdale, NJ: Lawrence Erlbaum.

5. Bourdieu, P. 1991. *Language and symbolic power*. Oxford: Polity Press.

6. Davis, M. S. 1971. That's interesting! Towards a phenomenology of sociology and a sociology of phenomenology. *Social Science* 1:309–344.

7. Duszak, A. 1997. Analyzing digressiveness in polish academic texts. In *Culture and styles of academic discourse*, edited by A. Duszak. Berlin: Mouton de Gruyter, 323–341.

8. Fredrickson, K. M. and J. M. Swales. 1994. Competition and discourse community: Introductions from "Nysenska Studier". In *Text and talk in professional contexts*, edited by B.-L. Gunnarsson, P. Linell B. Nordberg. Uppsala: ASLA, 9–22.

9. Golebiowski, Z. 1999. Application of Swales' model in the analysis of research papers by Polish authors. *International Review of Applied Linguistics* 37:231–247.

10. Grice, H. 1975. Logic and conversation. In *Syntax and semantics, 3: Speech acts*, edited by P. Cole and J. Morgan. New York: Academic Press, 41–58.

11. Halliday, M. A. K and J. R. Martin. 1993. *Writing science: Literacy and discursive power*. Pittsburgh: University of Pittsburgh Press.

12. Hawking, S. 1993. *Black holes and baby universes and other essays*. New York: Bantam.

13. Hoey, M. 1983. *On the surface of text*. London: Allen & Unwin.

14. Hyland, K. 2000. *Disciplinary discourses: Social interactions in academic writing*. Harlow, UK: Pearson Education.

15. Labov, W. 1972. *Language in the inner city: Studies in black English vernacular*. Philadelphia: University of Pennsylvania Press.

16. Lave, J. and E. Wenger. 1991. *Situated learning: Legitimate peripheral participation*. Cambridge: Cambridge University Press.

17. Lindeberg, A.-C. 1998. Promotional rhetorical steps and linguistic signalling in research articles in three disciplines In *LSP: Identity and interface research*, edited by L. Lundqvist *et al.* Copenhagen: Copenhagen Business School, 698–699.

18. Mauranen, A. 1993. *Cultural differences in academic rhetoric.* Frankfurt: Peter Lang.

19. Mitchell, T. F. 1957. The language of buying and selling in Cyrenaica: A situational statement. *Hesperis* 44:31–72.

20. Paul, D. and D. Charney. 1995. Introducing chaos (theory) into science and engineering: Effects of rhetorical strategies in scientific readers. *Written Communication* 12: 396–438.

21. Pennycook, A. 1997. Vulgar pragmatism, critical pragmatism and EAP. *English for Specific Purposes* 16: 253–269.

22. Perez-Gonzalez, A. 1998. The conversational dynamics of interactional dispute in conflictive calls for emergency assistance: A single case study. *Current Issues in Linguistic Theory* 158: 265–290.

23. Propp, V. 1968. *Morphology of the folk tale.* Austin, TX: University of Texas Press. (First published in Russian in 1928.)

24. Sacks, H., E. A. Schegloff and G. Jefferson. 1974. A simplest systematics for the organization of turn-taking in conversation. *Language* 50:696–735.

25. Scotton, C. M. and J. Bernsten. 1988. Natural conversations as a model for textbook dialogue. *Applied Linguistics* 9:372–84.

26. Swales, J. M. 1990. *Genre analysis: English in academic and research settings.* Cambridge: Cambridge University Press.

27. _____ . 1996. Occluded genres in the academy: The case of the submission letter. In *Academic writing: Intercultural and textual issues*, edited by E. Ventola and A. Mauranen. Amsterdam: John Benjamins, 45–58.

28. _____ and C. B. Feak. 2000. *English in today's research world: A writing guide.* Ann Arbor, MI: The University of Michigan Press.

29. _____ and S. Lindemann. Teaching the literature review to international graduate students. In *Genres and the classroom: Theory, research and practice*, edited by A. M. Johns. Mahwah, NJ: Lawrence Erlbaum. Forthcoming.

30. Ventola, E. 1987. *Structure of social interaction: The semiotics of service encounters.* London: F. Pinter.

31. Wollman-Bonilla, J. E. 2000. Teaching science writing in first graders: Genre learning and recontextualization. *Research in the Teaching of English* 35:35–66.

4

Rhetorical Research for Reflective Practice: A Multi-layered Narrative

Charles Bazerman

Sometimes it may seem that research into the rhetoric of disciplines and professions is an arcane endeavour, concerning philosophic issues, epistemological critique, or the structure of language. However, for some — myself included — such research is motivated by practical concerns, with results immediately applied to our classrooms and writing. Rhetorical knowledge provides means for practical reflection and reflective practice. This intimate and dynamic link between knowledge and practice has nourished my experiences as a writer, a teacher, a researcher, and a theorist.

I am about to engage in reflexive autobiography as a form of academic argument. Some see this genre as a postmodern American abomination. But if it is an abomination, its history is much deeper and its sources more international. Many of the postmodern advocates are European (vide Giddens; Ashmore; Woolgar). And not all recent advocates are postmodern theorists. The highly practical Donald Schon wrote about the reflective practitioner and founded a highly influential movement that has invaded such unpostmodern places as business, medicine, the law, and engineering. In the middle of the twentieth century Robert Merton argued that sociological concepts ought to be tested, extended, and used for personal wisdom through self-exemplification — seeing how general theories apply to yourself and your kindred. At the beginning of that twentieth century, the Soviet psychologist Lev Vygotsky argued that language provided us the means of reflexive action and reflexive learning — which suggested that accounts of ourselves were the beginnings and ends of knowledge. Joseph Priestley in the eighteenth century argued that science ought to be presented as discovery accounts of how we addressed and overcame our intellectual quandaries. And his contemporary Adam Smith struggled throughout his career with what it meant for him to be a practical philosopher.

As writers we are all reflective practitioners; as speakers we are often reflective when we are not just running off at the mouth. We think about what we write and speak; we think about our situations, goals, audiences, and available means of expression. Such thought is the foundation of rhetoric, which provides tools for examining communicative situations, for making choices about what we speak and write for making deeper sense of what others speak and write. The more we learn about what our words do to whom under what conditions, the more thoughtful and considered we become about our expression and the more understanding we become of the force of others' statements.

Writing is particularly open to reflection because it affords so much time to think, to compose, to revise, to examine. Studies of writers in professional workplaces consistently reveal that experienced writers spend far more time planning prior to beginning the first draft than they spend in the actual drafting. Further in writing we have the opportunity to read over what we have written, both before we send it off to our intended audience and after. Writing's externalization gives us much to reflect on and gives us more than the usual opportunity to see ourselves as others see us. Looking back on what we wrote yesterday we can wonder, what could we have been thinking? Time makes us strangers to our texts, but the texts hang around to haunt us with our former presences.

Similarly in our teaching we reflect as we plan day by day, revise curricula, develop materials, review the results of each term. And then we are haunted by the writing of our students. What could they have been thinking? What is it they didn't understand? What is it that we said that they so misconstrued or perhaps understood only too well? What should we be changing in our teaching to increase students' success and save us from seeing the shortcomings in student productions that haunt us?

We study language to provide us better tools to write more

effectively, to discover what choices skilled users make, to reveal what would help our students find their way in this wondrously teeming and endlessly creative world of language. Such knowledge is especially needed for the languages, registers, and practices that we and our students are not born and deeply socialized into. But writing is a second language to us all. Especially in our university years and after, as we confront more specialized forms of writing, we are caught in worlds where pre-reflexive habits of language are not enough. Who, after all, is born to write grammars or analytic philosophy or legal briefs?

I must admit I was late and resistant to more reflective attitudes toward writing. I was, as many who wind up teaching writing, a successful and fluent writer in school, trying many styles, thinking about what I wanted to say, sometimes worrying about it, but doing that thinking behind my own back. I wrote papers in a single draft at the last minute. I took my skills as a sign of genius rather than the result of fortunate early experience that led to increasingly frequent, successful, and confident experiences. So when asked in my own first–year university writing class to consider what my strengths and weaknesses as a writer were, I wrote a defensively resistant parable arguing that it was a waste of time to reflect — just let the genius grow and flower, keep doing what is in front of you.

Despite the defensiveness, I did keep thinking about what I was doing, and even regularly looked back on my papers from previous years, mostly to remember the glory of thinking those thoughts. Yet I rarely had the courage to face the writing as something that could be consciously worked and reworked; for many years I found revision an extremely painful process. However, when teaching college writing in the early seventies, I found myself passionately preaching the latest doctrines of the process movement — including revision. I also started to use my own experience as a writer, as current doctrine urged, to form a writing community with the students and help them face their own writing processes. My conscience eventually got to me and I decided that I needed either to practise what I preached or change my preaching to reflect my practice.

I tried to use drafts more deeply, to inspect not only sentence style, but the underlying logic and presentational strategies. I was pleasantly surprised to learn that this helped me understand what I was doing and do it better. This experience of becoming more reflective about our own writing is, I believe, a common experience of writing teachers and researchers. The Bay Area and the National Writing Projects, born about this time, encouraged teachers to think of themselves as writers and to reflect on their processes, so as to be able to lead students to think of themselves as writers. I was soon set on a conscious trajectory of investigating what can be done through writing, what competences and skills and practices are part of making writing do these things, and then how to use that knowledge to refine my own practice.

Throughout my career, every study in some way has extended my understanding of my positioning or practice as a writer, or the available forms of writing, or the systems within which writing flowed. I expanded my repertoire and strategic thinking as a writer by recognizing and managing the process; by understanding traditional tools of rhetorical analysis such as, situation, *kairos* and *enthymeme*; by drawing on recent work in linguistic pragmatics and anthropology, such as *deixis* and footing; by considering writing as interaction and as a means of self-development in interaction through the lenses of interpersonal psychiatry, sociocultural psychology, phenomenological micro-sociology, and structural sociology. Out of these and others I have developed an ever more integrated synthesis of the act and consequence of writing, which I am currently trying to bring together in a multi-volumed theoretical work.

One core trajectory as a writer, scholar, and teacher that has given me tools to engage in multidimensional synthesis involves what has become known as intertextuality. However, the issues now clustered under the widely circulated term intertextuality have sources and implications broader than those that arise in the literary discussion that shaped the term's familiar meanings. A reflection on my history of grappling with these issues may suggest broader sources and implications of the term within writing studies, as well as the significance of using the concept in writing and teaching practice. My developing understanding of intertextuality suggests the way in which writing, as many other human activities, is a reflective boot-strap operation, allowing us to go further and do more, the more we do and understand what we do. We make it up as we go along, in the very best sense of that phrase.

The term intertextuality was first coined in literary theory by Julia Kristeva in *Desire in Language*, published in 1980. She drew on Bakhtin and Vološinov to suggest that any text is a mosaic of quotations. She argues against the radical originality of any text and locates common experience in the sharing of text rather than any more fundamental shared intersubjective state. Orientation to common utterances, she argues, creates the ongoing culture and evokes common objects of desire. Intertextuality, for Kristeva, is a mechanism whereby we write ourselves into the social text, and thereby the social text writes us.

The origins of the concept in Bakhtin and Vološinov — and I would distinguish between the two — have different motives and forces than used by Kristeva. In Vološinov's *Marxism and the Philosophy of Language* the relation among texts is used to argue against Saussure's langue/parole dichotomy and to suggest an utterance-based approach to language, always located in immediate moments and relation. Further, the relations among utterances are used to argue against Saussure's diachronic/synchronic dichotomy by pointing out that every utterance draws on the history of language use and carries forward that history. In the interplay with past utterances, each new utterance takes on a stance toward previous utterances. Vološinov, furthermore, begins a technical analysis of how texts position themselves to each other through linguistic systems of direct and indirect quotations. Vološinov's work raises fundamental issues about the nature of all language and does not prejudge which set of relations are more valuable. He points out that the relations exist and different linguistic forms and practices facilitate different sets of relations. Bakhtin, on the other hand, uses the relations of utterances to pursue narrower questions of literary value in the way that novels represent the utterances of the characters and narrators. In *Problems of Doestoevsky's Poetics*

(1984) and *The Dialogic Imagination* (1981) he praises the form of novel (which he associates with a form of consciousness) that recognizes the variety of utterances incorporated and thus adopts a stance of multivocality, dialogism, or heteroglossia rather than authoritative univocality, monologism, or monoglossia, which obscures the complexity of human language, consciousness and relation. In these and other works, such as *Rabelais and his World* (1984), Bakhtin is also interested in the stance or attitude or evaluation one utterance makes toward others, such as through double-voicing or carnivalesque.

Later literary critics such as Kristeva, Barthes and Riffaterre narrow the literary and ideological questions even further to issues of the status of the author and originality. Among the literary critics only most recently has Genette begun to start mapping out in an orderly the possible sets of relations among texts, what he calls transtextuality: intertextuality (explicit quotation or allusion), paratextuality (the relation to directly surrounding texts, such as prefaces, interviews, publicity, reviews); metatextuality (a commentary relation); hypertextuality (the play of one text off of familiarity with another); and architextuality (the generic expectations in relation to other similar texts). (1992, 1997a, 1997b.)

My work in academic writing, begun in the early 1970s before much of this literature was available in the US, raised the issues of what I called then writing about reading and took me down a different pathway, showing different things. The problem first appeared to me in the form of the ill-defined assignment of the research or term paper, endemic to American composition courses of the time, and in its variants still endemic to many courses in many disciplines. In such assignments students are expected to investigate and discuss some issue relevant to the course subject matter. Nobody quite knew what this assignment entailed, and the only teaching materials available were little more than lists of references and resources along with footnote-style prescriptions. Teachers regularly complained, long before word processing and Internet research, of cut-and-paste jobs that simply strung together quotations, paraphrases, or verbatim plagiarism.

As a successful student, however, I knew that there was a lot more to writing good research papers than locating some sources and following correct bibliographic form. There was a journey of learning, of problem formation and reformulation, of careful and thoughtful reading, of being able to interpret and restate what sources had to say, of evaluation and comment, of synthesis, of fresh argument. I had begun to learn this myself through the assignments in middle and high school, and then amplified through undergraduate assignments in literary studies where I did much experimenting on positioning my commentary with respect to the text discussed and the prior commentaries on texts, and in papers in other disciplines where I was forced to take an evaluative, argumentative, synthetic, or analytical stance towards the materials. These were not lessons necessarily learned by all my classmates — so these skills were what marked me as one of the better students. Why I was first able to get on this train when many of my classmates weren't, I am not quite sure — perhaps it had something to do with my early development of language and ability to speak with adults and then a series of fortunate experiences that flowed from that. I do know that by high school I was writing far more ambitious research assignments than my classmates. My university experience of switching majors every six months, from physics to political science, to literary studies, taught me that intellectual inquiry and use of prior disciplinary utterances was not a uniform generalized skill but involved understanding different disciplinary styles of investigation, thought, projects, values, data. When I started teaching, I did not articulate these things very well, but little was well articulated about these issues then. Some textbooks of previous decades and centuries taught summary or precis writing, some used annotating texts, some provided advice on how to read a book or a page. Mina Shaughnessy in her 1977 book *Errors and Expectations* had a few lines on the importance of reading in writing (p. 223), mostly in relation to literary texts.

I took encouragement from those words of my colleague at the City University of New York, but I had already for several years been redesigning the research paper course around how to write about non-literary, knowledge-focused reading. I eventually rebuilt the entire 15–week course around a sequence of assignments that took apart and practised separately different clusters of skills and activities that went into successful library research projects — including response realized in journals and informal essays, close restatement of details and gist of source texts through paraphrase and summary, understanding the rhetorical characters of text in their aims and techniques, linking a text's meanings and implications to one's own experiences and observations, evaluation of texts through book reviews and critical essays, comparison and synthesis of texts, framing research problems and plans in proposals and moving through sequences of discovery and reconceptualizations, culminating in a final paper. As I started to analyse these skills, I developed more focused smaller assignments and teaching sequences, so that the research paper ultimately became an optional component of the course. The course became about how you write about things you read. Although there had been for a while a tradition of books about how to write about literature, there existed no book that took up such issues for non-literary texts. *The Informed Writer*, which I worked on throughout the mid-seventies, appeared at the end of 1980. I also co-authored an integrated reading and writing skills handbook at this time, first appearing in 1977.

The Writing Across the Curriculum movement was being born at this time, and my work on academic reading and writing suggested to me that we needed a much better understanding of what was entailed in academic course work and writing in disciplines than the then dominant expressivist and writing-to-learn theories. I did some surveys of the relation between reading and writing in the assignments students were doing in other courses throughout the university. This led me then to begin investigating differences in disciplinary discourses, and I soon moved to a sociological understanding of how texts were situated within fields. As I already had a rhetorical view of the way texts mediated social interaction, I began to look at how texts served various functions within different fields, engaged in different kinds of arguments, and developed appropriate forms. I also began to see how texts structured role relationships. I had the good fortune to be introduced to the sociology of science and the eminent sociologist Robert Merton.

My introduction to sociology resulted in a review of the literature of science studies applying to scientific writing — "Scientific Writing as a Social Act" (1983) and the essay "What Written Knowledge Does" (1981). In this latter article, in comparing texts from literary studies, sociology, and biology, I foregrounded the use of prior texts of the field, the character of the prior texts, and the position of the new text with respect to those prior texts. My analytic heuristic expanded the traditional Aristotelean communication triangle of author-audience-subject matter by adding a fourth vertex — the literature — to create a communication pyramid. Thus intertextuality became built into my fundamental model of communication. I went on to examine the historical emergence of features of scientific writing as writers constantly built on and exceeded prior texts. This was coincident with my settling on genre as a key concept. Although I had not read Bakhtin, Kristeva, or any of the others at this time, I was influenced by Vygotsky's account of the social origins of language and the way the interpersonal became the grounds for the intrapersonal. I was also influenced by similar notions from the psychiatrist Harry Stack Sullivan about how the self is formed through histories of social relations. I found in these much more fundamental accounts of utterance relations than I was later to gain from Bakhtin and even Vološinov.

How did these research and theory interests affect my own practice as a writer and a teacher? The changes in my teaching practice can be traced through the various editions of *The Informed Writer*, through which I reflectively developed my teaching not only for the second-term course but other courses before and after in our sequence. In the second edition (1985), I added an introductory chapter on writing as situated problem-solving, purposeful within rhetorical contexts. I also added a new section of five chapters on writing in the disciplines, considering how the organization of investigative work leads to different forms of writing, argument, and knowledge. The most important addition of the third edition (1989), by which time I had read Bakhtin, was a chapter on analyzing the many voices within the text. I remember distinctly thinking that this chapter brought out the underlying logic of the book, making explicit the core concepts upon which the book was already built. The writing in the disciplines section also put more emphasis on how to read materials in the disciplines — for you had to read before you wrote knowledgeably. Since students were more in a position to make sense of and use disciplinary texts for their own purposes than to create novel contributions to knowledge, I started to put more emphasis in the following editions of students as consumers of disciplinary texts rather than producers. My pedagogy took distinct shape as I understood the intertextual landscape of professions and the ways individuals took up positions in those landscapes as producers, learners, neophytes, citizen consumers. I saw my students as part of the same complex world as I was investigating.

Similarly, as my understanding of intertextual disciplinary knowledge worlds deepened through teaching as well as research, I better understood what I was doing as a writer. My commitment to practising what I preached and preaching what I practised was reinforced by Vygotsky's account of reflectivity as a way of monitoring, guiding, and regulating action. Spilling the beans about how to do academic writing started as a kind of introspective consideration of what I did that allowed me to succeed, but as I articulated this more to my students and then saw related patterns emerge in my research, I sharpened and refined my own practice. I became more adept at encapsulating the meaning of new texts, synthesizing literatures, developing my own evaluative position and stance, and using the literature in my own arguments. Thus my own writing kept gaining intertextual richness, drawing very close to a number of literatures while sharpening my distinctive uses and differences. I used reviews of literatures to master fields and reorganize them for my own purposes, as when I wrote "Scientific Writing as a Social Act."

This interdisciplinarity became a self-conscious ability to move across disciplines as well as to analyse the shape of different disciplinary discourses in my research. I was able to draw on numerous fields in my work from history to sociology by sorting through what they had to offer, what stances they took on what theoretical underpinnings, and how they fit together or contradicted in more than superficial ways. Yet I still was able to maintain a sense of my own project of the study of writing for practical purposes. Because I had become so self-conscious about the techniques of handling literatures in various fields, I could quickly identify what the fields had to say on issues of interest to me, to figure out where in their literatures to go to, and to recognize given the dynamics of discussion in the fields what kinds of findings were and were not likely to be available. I also learned to assess quickly the kinds of theories, perspectives, and assumptions underlying the research and the ways those theories might or might intersect with my own theoretical assumptions and concerns. I became practised and self-consciously planful of how to synthesize diverse empirical and theoretical materials in relation to my own projects, which carried their own baggage. Paradoxically, the more I found points of contact with other forms of inquiry the more unusual the positions and methods and forms of argument are that I took. The oddity of my work is not the result of individual characteristics or personal virtue — though I might have believed that in my earlier days — but precisely because I have become broadly conversant with the standard writing tools and the historical particulars of work within a range of academic disciplines. As I developed a pedagogy and textbooks, I became the student in my own classes on academic writing — allowing me to push my research and theoretical essays farther, in turn providing deeper insights to be applied to my own writing and teaching.

Specifically, with respect to intertextuality, my own sense of the agency of the individual to move through complex literatures and create new positions and practices through developing new forms of argument went hand in hand with specific scholarly projects. My interest in the historical emergence of modern explicit citation practices, for example, led to my study of Joseph Priestley, who was one of the key figures in that development. I took up the consequences of modern citation practice for the way the publication game is played now by examining a modern virtuosic *tour de force* of citation, Gould and Lewontin's "Spanderels of San Marcos." During this period several other people were working on parallel studies to understand the workings of reviews of literature to position new contributions (Swales) and to advance research agendas (Myers), the way graduate students learn to navigate the literatures of their field to establish professional identities (Berkenkotter, Huckin and Ackerman), the way intertextuality structures the work of a profession (Devitt), and the way particular charter documents organized all the discourse of a field (McCarthy).

These various studies helped me see my own writing and the writing of my students as strategic, purposeful action within emergent structures of texts that conditioned the situation for future actions. Each text we write is a speech act, and the success of that text is in the consequences for what follows after, how the text creates a landmark of something done that needs to be taken into account in future utterances. One may even start taking a felicity condition approach to writing — what conditions must be met for each text to have the desired effect. This moves the evaluation of texts — and thus the trajectory of conscious production — away from formal standards or general rhetorical or aesthetic principles, or even presupposed persuasive or expressive ends, to a detailed analysis of situations and how they evolve with various textual interventions and accomplishments. My framing of these ideas was influenced by contact with linguistic anthropology, pragmatics, and conversational analysis. These concerns in turn helped evolve the pedagogic practice revealed in my recent textbook *Involved* (1997). Much of this pedagogy is to enable the student to size up the situation and the stakes, and then to identify what the writing must accomplish to meet the student's need. Only through commitment to action and continuing successful action is to be found strong motivation to write, a sense of self-fulfilling reward, and increasingly meaningful feedback. These in turn lead one to solve ever more difficult problems of writing, to continuing hard work, and to focused attention through which one grows as a writer. This perspective has increasingly informed my mentoring practice with a wide range of writers, from underprepared first year students through graduate students and mature professionals. Even my professional service as editor, creator of professional forums, and departmental administrator are informed by these perspectives.

The theme of agency through creating presence in intertextual landscapes directed my major scholarly project of the 90's, a book on the *Languages of Edison's Light*. The book examines how Edison took up positions in major discourses of his time — patent law, finance, corporations, technology and science, politics, journalism, consumer culture — as part of making incandescent light and power a reality. He had to complete many speech acts and create many social facts in multiple discursive worlds to give his emergent technologies presence, meaning, and value.

Where this concern for agency within intertextual worlds leaves me now is wondering about what it means to live in an information age, and what intellectual and rhetorical skills students will need to negotiate the informational world. I see this as urgent not only because information technologies are now reshaping all educational, social, and economic institutions but additionally because the ideology and representation of information misleadingly represents information as disembodied from human purposes and meaning-shaping contexts. I have several recent and current projects looking at the emergence of our modern understandings of information, how agency is being reshaped in Internet environments, and how students can learn to use large data sets in meaningful ways for their own purposes and for purposes of social improvement.

The odd public performances of a seventeenth century West Prussian engineer, the different drafts of Newton's work on optics, the social ideology behind early reviews of literature, or the political strategies of a citizen's information movement in 1950s St. Louis give glimpses into the rhetorical world we have made and how people manage to act in the world through words. I have tried to apply the lessons of these cases to provide students the tools they need to make their own lives and the lives of us all a little better.

I warned you at the beginning that this reflective narrative might be seen as purely a creature of American ambition and self-aggrandisement. If that is the case, there is even more reason to consider the reflective dynamics of other forms of communicative research, theory, pedagogy and practice — for we each make our communicative worlds out of what we know, believe, and desire. The diversity of language pedagogy and practice reflects the diversity of the worlds we believe we live in or desire to live in. Further, language pedagogy creates the meanings and uses of language within which our students will make their lives. And that is something worth reflecting on.

References

1. Ashmore, M. 1989. *The reflexive thesis*. Chicago: University of Chicago Press.

2. Bakhtin, M. 1981. *The dialogic imagination*. Austin: University of Texas Press.

3. _____ . 1984. *Problems of Doestoevsky's poetics*. Minneapolis: University of Minnesota Press.

4. _____ . 1984. *Rabelais and his world*. Bloomington: Indiana University Press.

5. Barthes, R. 1974. *S/Z*. New York: Hill and Wang.

6. Bazerman, C. 1991. How natural philosophers can cooperate. In *Textual dynamics of the professions*, edited by C. Bazerman and J. Paradis. Madison: University of Wisconsin Press, 13–44.

7. _____ . 1981; 1985; 1989; 1992; 1995. *The informed writer*. Boston: Houghton Mifflin.

8. _____ . 1993. Intertextual self-fashioning: Gould and Lewontin's representations of the literature. In *Understanding scientific prose*, edited by J. Selzer. Madison: University of Wisconsin Press.

9. _____ . 1997. *Involved*. Boston: Houghton Mifflin.

10. _____ . 1999. *Languages of Edison's light*. Cambridge, MA: MIT Press.

11. _____ . 1983. Scientific writing as a social act. In *New essays in technical writing and communication*, edited by P. Anderson, J. Brockman and C. Miller. Farmingdale, NY: Baywood, 156–184.

12. _____ . 1981. What written knowledge does: Three examples of academic discourse. *Philosophy of the Social Sciences* 11 (3): 361–388.

13. Berkenkotter, C., T. Huckin and J. Ackerman. 1991. Social context and socially constructed texts: The initiation of a graduate student into a writing research community. In *Textual dynamics of the professions*, edited by C. Bazerman and J. Paradis. Madison: University of Wisconsin Press, 191–215.

14. Devitt, A. 1991. Intertextuality in tax accounting: Generic, referential, and functional. In *Textual dynamics of the professions*, edited by C. Bazerman and J. Paradis. Madison: University of Wisconsin Press, 336–380.

15. Genette, G. 1992. *The architext*. Berkeley: University of California Press.

16. _____ . 1997a. *Palimpsests*. Lincoln: University of Nebraska Press.

17. _____ . 1997b. *Paratexts*. Cambridge: Cambridge University Press.

18. Giddens, A. 1984. *The constitution of society*. Berkeley: University of California Press.

19. Kristeva, J. 1980. *Desire in language: A semiotic approach to literature and art*. New York: Columbia University Press.

20. McCarthy, L. P. 1991. A psychiatrist using DSM-III: The influence of a charter document in psychiatry. In *Textual dynamics of the professions*, edited by C. Bazerman and J. Paradis. Madison: University of Wisconsin Press, 358–378

21. Merton, R. K. 1968. *Social theory and social structure*. New York: Free Press.

22. Priestley, J. 1767. *The history and present state of electricity*. London.

23. Riffaterre, M. 1984. Intertextual representation. *Critical Inquiry* 11 (1): 141–162.

24. Schon, D. 1983. *The reflective practitioner*. New York: Basic Books.

25. Shaughnessy, M. 1977. *Errors and expectations*. New York: Oxford University Press.

26. Smith, A. 1980. *Essays on philosophical subjects*, edited by W. P. D. Wightman. Oxford: Clarendon Press.

27. Swales, J. 1990. *Genre analysis*. Cambridge: Cambridge University Press.

28. Vološinov, V. N. 1973. *Marxism and the philosophy of language*. London: Seminar Press.

29. _____ . 1986. *Marxism and the philosophy of language*. Cambridge, MA: Harvard University Press.

30. Vygotsky, L. 1986. *Thought and language*, translated by A. Kozulin. Cambridge: MIT Press.

31. Wiener, H. and C. Bazerman. 1977. *English skills handbook: Reading and writing*. Boston: Houghton Mifflin.

32. Woolgar, S., ed. 1988. *Knowledge and reflexivity*. London: Sage.

5

Discourse Practitioners as a Community of Interprofessional Practice: Some Insights from Health Communication Research

Srikant Sarangi

Introduction

In this chapter my main concern is to show how discourse and communication based studies in the context of health and social care do provide a basis for reflecting on our practices as discourse researchers. For current purposes, I take all discourse analysts as belonging to a shared professional community of practice — despite their differences in the use of analytic tools, and their engagement with different types and sites of data. Indeed, such differences within a professional community are rather commonplace and do not warrant concern. In the health care setting — which will be the focal site of my discussion here — patients and professionals are used to the idea of contested treatment regimes and differential patterns of healthcare delivery, which sometimes culminate in seeking "second expert opinions". It is quite likely that another health professional will either interpret the same symptoms and evidence differently, or might divert his/her gaze elsewhere, seeking new evidence and/or tests as a sound basis for offering a more informed assessment. Apparently, in discourse research we are all too familiar with scenarios of different interpretations of the same data leading to different claims. Such differences come to no harm most of the time, as our variable and situated interpretations may not have any consequence for the people whose text/talk-data we may be analyzing.

There is another dimension to our professional practice. The participants who we make our subject of study (doctors, nurses, therapists) are themselves discourse workers. They are using language to elicit and narrate symptoms, offer diagnosis, arrive at treatment decisions, etc. This then begs the question of what it is that is distinctive about our way of looking at the practices of other professionals. To what extent will our observational account help them to understand their discourse work and perhaps trigger any change in practice? It is worth mentioning that both the reporting of discourse-based findings and their actual uptake by professional communities remain largely unexplored (Sarangi and Roberts; 1999, 2000). This is not to say that discourse research cannot be made consequential, but such an injunction will depend on a whole set of other things: how we go about negotiating our researcher identity and expertise; how we seek endorsement of the research topic and design; where we look for data and how we interpret such data; how we package our research findings and manage the situations beyond the reporting stage. Here I will limit my discussion to the extent to which working on the interface of professional communities (e.g., medical, legal, educational) makes it possible to reflect on what we do as discourse researchers and what constitutes our practice. In the spirit of constructionism, we may end up researching the research process — how we construct other professions, and our own, through our own discourses. To extend this position, from a discourse/communication perspective, any professional discourse site is interprofessional by definition. There remains the difficulty of having acquaintance with another professional genre, and the willingness to socialize into these communities of practice (Lave and Wenger, 1991). I will use the healthcare site to illustrate my argument, but my discussion would extend to other sites — especially language education — where there is a long tradition of collaborative action research, but not without the tensions I allude to on page 116.

I will use the term "discourse practitioner" as a convenient identity label, keeping in mind the out-group with which we need to interact for carrying out collaborative work. Unwittingly, I started using this label to describe myself in the company of healthcare professionals before I realized its usefulness. Whenever I used the unmarked term "discourse analyst", I was called upon to elaborate further what this entailed in terms of tasks and knowledge. The accounts that I gave were more like glosses of language-as-discourse — a kind of explanation of our object of study rather than what it meant to be have a professional identity as a discourse researcher. Also, I realized that the term "analyst" pointed to the fact that discourse researchers were outsiders to the event that they were studying. Inevitably, it had the connotations of an investigative — and at times, moral — stance, as if we were breathing down our subjects' necks in insisting on our co-presence while recording their interactions. This is partly reflected in the ethnographic field study involving General Practitioners (GPs — equivalent to family doctors, see page 106 on professional socialization) when GP-examiners, at the end of the oral interviews, turn around and ask the observer-researcher: "do you think I asked the right questions?", "could I have done this better?". It is through such direct questioning that they nearly challenge your "neutral" participant-observer status and push you towards your consultancy role. For some reason, by labelling myself as a discourse practitioner I was not only able to draw a parallel to my subject cohort — the general practitioners — it also somehow helped to minimize the outsiderness, and to project the professional status of discourse researchers. Our identity is cast as one of professional practitioners who do discourse research.[1]

The Overlay of Professional Knowledge and Professional Practice

Freidson (1970) offers a blue-print of what constitutes a profession: following Cogan's (1953) classic study, he identifies, among other things, the legal basis, licensing and freedom of action as relevant benchmarks (see Hughes, 1958; also Candlin, 1997). As far as the

---

1. In a recent multi-disciplinary meeting of the National Assembly for Wales, I found myself in the midst of experts from health policy, health economics, biochemists, sociologists, environment studies — who had difficulty in understanding what discourse analysis is all about. The meeting was about Health Impact Assessment (HIA), so apart from labelling myself a discourse practitioner, I also started using the acronym CDP (to stand for Communication and Discourse Perspective) on health care issues.

medical profession is concerned, Freidson suggests that it is the clinical mentality as opposed to the scientific mentality which defines the practitioner's professional status. Doctors are mainly action-oriented, as they apply scientific knowledge rather than contribute to the growth of knowledge. The application of scientific knowledge, however, has to be mediated through one's clinical experience. In casting the professional as a practitioner, Freidson legitimizes the role of personal experience in professional practice.[2] As he (1970:169) summarizes it: "In his commitment to action, his faith, his pragmatism, his subjectivism, and his emphasis on indeterminacy, then, the practitioner is quite different from the scientist". Ravetz (1971) draws a similar distinction between scientific problems and practical problems. Historically, this distinction can be traced to Ryle's (1949:32) proposed separation between *knowing that* and *knowing how*:

> *What distinguishes sensible from silly operations is not their parentage but their procedure, and this holds no less for intellectual than for practical performances. "Intelligent" cannot be defined in terms of "intellectual" or "knowing how" in terms of "knowing that"...*

The "procedure" that practitioners follow, in Schon's (1983:50) terms, constitutes "knowing-in-action" and it goes beyond the simple application of technical/rational knowledge to practice. Professional practice becomes a form of "knowing how" in an accumulative sense.

The gap alluded to above between scientific knowledge and professional practice applies to the profession being studied as much as to the discourse practitioners who are doing the looking. As discourse researchers, we may be preoccupied with what Schon (1983:viii) characterizes as "inquiry into the epistemology of practice":

> *"What is the kind of knowing in which competent practitioners engage? How is professional knowing like*

---

2. For Freidson, "practitioner" is a relatively neutral term, unlike "professional" which connotes status, specialized work knowledge, etc.

*and unlike the kinds of knowledge presented in academic
textbooks, scientific papers and learned journals?"*

In situations where we study other professions, do we see ourselves
as knowledge workers (in the sense of "know that") or practitioners
(in the sense of "know how")? More realistically, where in the
continuum between scientism and practice do we position ourselves?

This already poses a tension. As discourse researchers, one of our
interests must be to contribute knowledge to discourse theory. But
with regard to our commitment to a professional group, a discourse
practitioner identity will need to foreground concrete action — "a
rather thoroughgoing particularism, a kind of ontological and
epistemological individualism" (Freidson, 1970:170), in the sense that
our observations and findings can lead to some kind of a resolution of
professional dilemma. It is not enough simply to ask questions and
delve into problematization *per se*. What is needed is "meaningful
problematization" (Luhmann, 1990), so that discourse research fulfils
the criterion of accountability.

Accessing, Problematizing and Interpreting Professional Discourse

There is a long tradition of sociolinguistic and discourse analytic studies
in different areas of professional practice, e.g., legal, medical,
therapeutic, educational settings. Studies of professional-client
encounters focus on themes such as power asymmetry, expert-lay
knowledge systems, role-relationships, face management, co-operation.
Many discourse researchers are primarily interested in how language
mediates professional activities, and not all of them may engage
explicitly in what constitutes professional knowledge and practice
beyond language performance. Exceptions here are the
ethnomethodological and ethnographic studies into professional work
(see, e.g., Atkinson, 1995; Goodwin, 1994) which go deeper than the
linguistic and interactional surface in their attempt to understand
professional practice and knowledge representations from the insiders'
perspective.

My aim here is not to summarize the wide range of topics and findings from discourse-based studies of different professions, but to raise the following three issues as a way of anticipating the tensions I will address on page 116. The three issues are : (1) accessibility; (2) salience/problem identification; (3) coding/interpretability/ articulation. Let me in turn elaborate each of these very briefly.

Firstly, access to professional data sites has remained a longstanding problem for discourse researchers. With special reference to the legal domain, O'Barr (1983) problematizes the issue of gaining access. Generally speaking, in addition to blunt denials and failed attempts, negotiations for routine access to different professional sites can be time-consuming and frustrating. At the far extreme, there is an element of suspicion, and perhaps mistrust, especially when the practitioners under study do not have any (or, limited) access to the discourse research process and outcome.[3] In many cases, discourse researchers are seen as outsiders, only driven by their own motives to access real-life data, and armed with their own expertise to analyse talk and text and use such analyses to verify linguistic/pragmatic theories of interaction, meaning construction, etc. Such an agenda is the counterpoint to being a discourse practitioner in the sense I am using the term here.

The issue of access is linked to a sense of mutual usefulness. With regard to negotiating access, Humphreys (cited in Agar, 1980), in his study of "Tearoom trade", talks about the researcher taking on the identity of a "watch queen" — how the researcher is allowed to observe homosexual acts, but in return is required to watch out for the police or straight males. In professional discourse studies, one also needs to be mindful of the competitive research ethos. In the health care setting, for instance, discourse researchers have to vie for space and credibility. There is keen interest from other stakeholders representing different disciplinary backgrounds: medical sociology, medical anthropology,

---

3. Even when participants give informed consent for being recorded, they have very little idea about how the data would be analysed in the future. It is often not clear what rights and obligations they have over the interpretation of "their data", nor do we know much about the liabilities that a discourse researcher may have to live with.

medical law/ethics, medical education; health psychology, health economics, health technology. The competition, however, becomes diffused when we learn that other researchers may have different agenda (topics of study) and methodologies. Sociolinguistics- and discourse-based researchers have to show how they can make a distinctive contribution to a given field of professional practice, while underscoring the fact that language is one of the major social variables that can account for differences at the level of performance. We find here a client-practitioner relationship, where subject-clients will seek out different professions and practitioners for solving their practical problems.

This leads me to my second point, i.e., the extent to which the issue of problem identification is central to carrying out professional discourse studies. Assuming that we are successful in obtaining access, we are then faced with the problem of identifying what we choose to make the focus of our study. In many instances, however, our prior formulation of research problems does mediate the negotiation of access. Does our motivation for a given topic or problem align with what the professional group see as worth investigating? What kinds of data do we need to collect in order to be able to address our research questions? In approaching our research questions and data in this way, we are already introducing an analytic bias. Moreover, we start to emphasize that linguistic and interactional data are necessary and sufficient conditions for our study of professional practice. As Schon (1983:viii) rightly points out,

> "*Competent practitioners usually know more than they can say. They exhibit a kind of knowing-in-practice, most of which is tacit. Nevertheless, starting with protocols of actual performance, it is possible to construct and test models of knowing. Indeed, practitioners themselves often reveal a capacity for reflection on their intuitive knowing in the midst of action and sometimes use this capacity to cope with the unique, uncertain, and conflicted situations of practice.*"

If we follow this line of argument, talk and text does not always constitute the whole of professional practice. Hak (1999), among others, draws our attention to the talk-bias in most conversation-analytic and discourse-analytic studies with their preoccupation on analyses of talk-in-interaction. Not only does this scientific/analytic mentality reveal a misconception that "talk is work" but it also suggests a reductionist approach in the sense of the researcher-analyst not engaging fully with professional practice. As I have already suggested, it is hard enough to access talk and text data in a professional setting. When we succeed, all we get access to is what constitutes the frontstage activities. The backstage activities which constitute the core of professional practice are very well guarded and may not be made accessible to researchers perceived as outsiders.[4] This is very much the case in professions such as medicine, where other-initiated gaze and criticism may be a dispreferred activity.

Thirdly, coding and interpreting talk/text data of another profession requires on our part adequate insider knowledge of the professional practice we are investigating. It is very likely that we will identify a problem based on the access we are given to in professional sites, and based on our analytic tool boxes. As Ravetz (1971:354) puts it, "The solution of a practical problem ... is determined by the categories in which it is conceived." Coding therefore assumes priority. The identification and naming of a problem is often constituted in the act of seeing. Cicourel (1968), among others, argues in favour of adopting an insider perspective in order to understand professional practice. As he points out, talk and text which is produced in a professional context, such as police case notes, are other-directed. The "other" here refers to one who already belongs to this community of practice, i.e., medical case notes, police case records as being targeted at other co-professionals and specialist readers (Goffman, 1961; Garfinkel, 1967). Even typical professional-client encounters serve other-directed institutional purposes, so there will be gaps in our understanding of how a specific interaction develops. The discourse

---

4. See Goffman (1959) on the notions of "frontstage" and "backstage", and Sarangi and Roberts (1999) on their relevance in professional discourse studies.

researcher in this setting occupies an "other other" position — one who does not belong to this community of practitioners, and so may lack the necessary perspective to interpret what is going on. It is one thing to say, along the ideological lines of conversation analysis (CA), that we do not need to bring any contextual baggage to the data we are looking at. But it is not far from admitting that we might end up with misinterpretations, although such misinterpretations do not have any consequences for either professionals or clients. This brings me back to my earlier point that if our work were to be practically relevant, we need to align our interpretation with professional practitioners' "knowing in action", which is not always linguistically manifest. Hence, what we may regard as real-life linguistic or interactional data can in itself pose a limitation as to what we can say about professional practice, especially when we take on board Schon's (1983:viii) observation that "competent practitioners usually know more than they say".

In light of our inadequate knowledge of "other" professional practice, Cicourel (1992) advocates the idea of collaborative interpretation as a necessary condition, and so emphasizes the need for seeking support in the form of feedback data and triangulation as a way of ensuring ecological validity. Collaborative interpretation is at par with Garfinkel's (1967) notion of "documentary method of interpretation". If types and tokens are intricately linked, then when we observe a token of professional practice, we need to have an understanding of the type against which the token is to made sense of. Many CA researchers orient themselves to a participant perspective, but they hesitate in embedding "the participant" whole-heartedly into their analysis. The talk data in its transcribed form becomes a constraint and the ensuing interpretation becomes a scientific rather than practice-driven enterprise.

Conducting collaborative research is fraught with difficulties if we do not engage our professional practitioners in the act of interpretation of data. An early example of (lack of) collaborative interdisciplinarity is the study of therapeutic interaction by Labov and Fanshel (1977). As we know, the final outcome of this study is a corpus of generic rules of discourse coherence. In this sense, it is an example of "knowledge that" in Ryles' sense above, as it stands out as a theoretical contribution to discourse comprehension, rather than providing us any insights into the "know how" of therapeutic practice. Indeed this looking for general principles in a scientific vein is counter-productive in terms of a practitioner identity (see our discussion of Freidson above). Collaborative modes of inquiry, which include collaborative interpretive practices, are still very rare in professional discourse studies. This is particularly striking when we note the overall interpretive turn in the study of professions.

The Interpretive Turn in Professional Discourse Studies

Within sociology, there has been a shift from normative to interpretive work as a continuation of the hermeneutic tradition (Wilson, 1971). The focus, to varying degrees, has been on aligning participants' and analysts' perspectives rather than imposing categories external to the object of study. This trend is most prominent in the studies labelled "sociology of deviance" or "social problem construction" (e.g., Becker, 1963; Stoddart, 1974; Wieder, 1974; Whyte, 1955; Best, 1989) — both in terms of topic and method. Rather than address bigger social issues such as suicide, kinship, marriage in the Durkheimian tradition, researchers in this interpretive paradigm identify almost any everyday activity as their topic of inquiry — the street corner society, drug addict communities, the half-way house, etc. Ethnography and ethnomethodology have offered the methodological tools necessary to study such everyday sites. Even this hasn't been very easy — in terms of access to sites and interpretation of data. A few researchers have gone for disguise — i.e., they pass as one of the group/community being studied in order to access data and to become socialized into another interpretive community of practice — but this is perhaps more difficult in professional and institutional settings.

Stoddart (1974), for instance, sought to pass as a group member in order to study the lives of heroin users. He talks about the power of argot, i.e., specialized register, and how it can impede the interpretive process. Not just learned professions, but every community of practice is constitutive of their specialized genre. How do we as outsiders understand others' language use, especially when words are used to signal some non-conventional meaning and when it is counterproductive to ask explicitly what something meant? Stoddart gives the example of "pinched" as it was used in this community of heroin users to denote the unconventional meaning of "someone has been arrested for junk". In my work with the genetic counsellors, I had difficulty in making sense of what they meant by DNA. They were using the term in a non-technical way to refer to patients who "Did Not Attend".[5] I waited for a considerable amount of time before I could ask for clarification about this unconventional use. I had to pretend to have understood it until then (see Cicourel, 1992 and Becker, 1993 for similar accounts).

MacKay (1974) talks about children's "interpretive competence" in the context of child socialization studies. In a similar vein here we are concerned with the researcher's interpretive competence in discourse socialization studies. We need to seek membership into the professional community under study, while acknowledging the limits of our interpretive practice (see page 120 on analyst paradox). If meaning is embedded in context (Duranti and Goodwin, 1992), then discourse researchers need the help of professionals to understand what is going on in a given situation in order for their interpretation to be ecologically valid. One needs to go beyond what Heritage (1984) refers to as "double contextualization" — every action shapes and is shaped by context. In the professional discourse studies, we need to make an attempt to integrate the broader context (in the sense of institutionalized framing of activities, hence the need for ethnographic fieldwork) with the narrow context (in the sense of locally organized and negotiated interaction). The assumption here is that participants (professionals and clients) draw upon both levels of context, and so this leaves the discourse researchers with no choice but to engage with the context at all levels in order to be able to put into practice Garfinkel's "documentary method of interpretation" (see page 127 on contextual

---

5. According to my consultant colleague, they now use FTA (failed to attend) instead of DNA to refer to absent patients. This new acronym will need explaining to other non-medical researchers.

constructionism). In this sense, Giddens' (1976) idea of "brought about" and "brought along" contexts apply to both participants and researchers. We have evidence of this ecological interpretive practices in the medical domain in studies such as Becker *et al.* (1961), Cicourel (1992) which attempt to combine ethnographic and micro-analytic methods of observation and interpretation.

In what follows I first briefly introduce the three health care sites where my current work can be located and then identify some key areas of tension in conducting inter-professional research in terms of knowledge, identity and genre, as well as the linkage between discourse research and its potential uptake.

An Overview of Discourse/Communication-based Studies in Three Health Care Sites

From the discussion above, it is apparent that decisions about where to look for data are bound up with what insights we are likely to get about professional knowledge and practice. Also, it is important to bear in mind the extent to which we may feel competent and comfortable in analyzing such data given our own level of knowledge about professional practice. Here I draw on three data sites from my ongoing health communication research — all of which pose challenges of "expert" interpretation and intervention.

Professional Socialization: The RCGP Study

The mainstream studies in healthcare are doctor-patient encounters (especially in general practice settings), with the analytic focus on what doctors do.[6] The clinic is still the site of study when one orients to the patients' perspective (with the exception of narrative studies of patients'

---

6. Mainstream discourse analytic studies seem to have identified prototypical sites of investigation. As with the focus on the clinic in medical discourse, there is more focus on courtroom interaction than between lawyer-client interaction outside the courtroom (or lawyer-lawyer talk for that matter); more focus on teacher-pupil interaction inside the classroom rather than what happens outside the classroom (or teacher-teacher talk, for that matter).

accounts of illness). Earlier I have drawn attention to frontstage and backstage activities of a professional community and the problems associated with gaining access to backstage activities. In some cases, the backstage activities may be regarded as constituting "the core" of a profession's knowledge and identity. For instance, talk between doctors in gatekeeping settings such as the oral examination brings to the fore how professional knowledge and practice are constructed, maintained and contested at any given time.

Here let me briefly outline one such research project which Celia Roberts and I carried out as part of consultancy research. During 1995–1996, we were approached by the Royal College of General Practitioners (RCGP) to record and analyse the oral exam interviews (for details see Roberts and Sarangi, 1999; Roberts *et al.* 2000; Sarangi and Roberts, in press). Our brief was to see if the oral examination was in any way discriminatory as far as GP candidates from different linguistic and cultural backgrounds were concerned. The consultancy paradigm however allowed us to redefine our/their research interest. Rather than jumping into conclusions about racial discrimination, we chose to concentrate on the oral examination in its entirety as a discourse event. This led us to look closely at what the examiners were looking for in terms of successful candidates, and not just focus on how candidates from ethnic and linguistic minorities fared. Were the examiners, for instance, looking for good doctors (competent in professional practice in Ryle's sense of "know how") or good interview performers (competent in displaying abstract scientific knowledge in Ryle's sense of "know that")? To what extent did the examiners' questions and interactional moves index one or the other outcome? This connects with my earlier point about keeping knowledge and practice analytically separate.

In this study we identified three modes of talk — institutional, professional, personal experience — which seemed to be present in different degrees in all of the oral interviews. Here we are not talking about different and oppositional voices — voice of medicine vs. voice of the lifeworld in Mishler's (1984) sense — but about different layers of hybrid modes within the voice of medicine. Further analysis revealed that the examiners were not particularly privileging one or the other mode of talk, although overall it seemed that the institutional mode (in Ryle's sense of "know that") took priority over the professional and personal experience modes (in Ryle's sense of "know how"). Indeed smooth transitions between these modes seemed to be the right kind of recipe for success. The maintenance of hybridity became a key issue for both examiners and candidates.

One thing that soon became apparent was the difficulty in identifying and labelling, in a rigorous way, these different modes of talk in the discourse data. A related difficulty was to note all the transition points and then to locate which ones were particularly awkward and might have been consequential in terms of interactional outcomes. The consultancy format provided an excellent opportunity to access further insider knowledge from the examining doctors. So, we produced a checklist of possible awkward moments for a group of selected examiners to respond to as part of their video training sessions. (See Appendix 1 on page 134 for a sample filled-in form, with the numbers in italic referring to the time frame of a specific video.) This then became a kind of collaborative coding — like collaborative interpretation — which led us to look specifically for those interactional moments which had been identified by the examiners as being awkward.

For me, this amounts to integrating participant and analyst perspectives at the time of identifying and coding data — a kind of discoursal construction of problems. Also, in identifying awkward moments, the examiners can be said to be reflecting on their practice — or "knowing in action" (Schon, 1983).[7] In this instance, it then made sense to map the three modes of talk on to the awkward moments as a way of finding out what contributed to success and failure of individual candidates. Through such systematic analysis of data, aided by professional insights at the stage of coding and also later, we were able to develop a comparative perspective which was crucial to making our work practically relevant. As one of the by-products of this

---

7. Following from this activity, the examiners (as part of their annual convention meeting) sent us more instances of awkward moments — almost voluntarily.

collaboration, we were in fact able to formalize better what we meant by the different modes of talk. Interestingly, these same modes of talk became salient in our negotiation of expertise with our medical colleagues (Sarangi and Roberts, 2000). In other words, the institutional and professional modes of talk that we had identified in the oral interview data also defined the research process: how we went about demarcating our (in)expertise, how we mixed institutional, professional and personal experience modes and, more importantly, how we mapped discoursal evidence onto aspects of cultural difference and potential discrimination.

Communication Skills in Medical Education

My second site concerns oral exam interviews involving final year medical students in the UK. This study was also designed as consultative, with Celia Roberts and myself working closely with medical educators and practitioners. This is a fertile area for discourse research to have an impact — especially when medical curricula are taking the issue of communication skills training seriously (see Cameron, 2000, more generally). Our work, unlike a psychological package of skills training, had an applied angle as we tried to show how a micro-analysis of interaction can reveal what kind of socialization is expected of student doctors before they get rites of passage to the community of medical practice. It broadly falls within the strand of studies in medical socialization (Merton *et al.*, 1957; Becker *et al.*, 1961).

The site here — like the RCGP one — is also a gate-keeping occasion, except that we are looking at how novices move from the periphery to the centre of what constitutes medical knowledge, practice and identity. One of our primary concerns was to see if ethnicity of candidates was linked to rate of failure. Like in RCGP, however, we chose to look at the entire event and across the candidates from all backgrounds in order to be able to determine whether or not culture and ethnicity are the proper predictors of success/failure (the same can be said about gender). A general point here is that consultancy research in intercultural settings should not fall into the trap of pure academic research on cross-cultural differences. A lot can be gained (and prevented) if we looked at cases of intercultural encounters alongside others, not just the ones involving ethnic participants as that might restrict our sphere of interpretation and our assessment of the exact effect of ethnicity on interactional process and outcome.

These oral interviews consisted of professional role players acting as patients. The student-doctors moved from one patient case to another taking histories, giving or not giving treatments, but above all, performing their physician identities through various interactional routines. This oral talk, like the RCGP one, consisted of a mixture of institutional, professional and personal experience modes. Unlike our analysis of RCGP data which focused on awkward moments, here we decided to have full mappings of the orals in order to capture the interactional flow and the thematic staging (Roberts and Sarangi, 2001). This was easily accomplished because these were fairly standard encounters, with fixed topics, involving the same actor-patient and each session lasting about six minutes. Through the full mappings we identified two major involvement styles — which we termed empathetic and retractive — each one with a further set of sub-categories. It seems candidates can be assessed overall as being empathetic or retractive, with their preferred styles underpinning different ideologies. Hybridity of the kind we found in the case of RCGP data is also a characteristic feature of this data. It is perhaps too early to predict what relevance our findings will have for purposes of training examiners, student-doctors and/or actor-patients.

Communicative Frames in Genetic Counselling

The third and final site of this overview is my ongoing work in genetic counselling. Genetics as a new area of expertise poses specific challenges to discourse researchers. Unlike mainstream doctor-patient encounters, here the boundaries between lay and expert knowledge systems are hard to demarcate. The complexity is also manifest in a dispersed notion of patienthood, the range of topics that can be discussed in any one counselling session, including aspects of non-treatability and non-diagnosable nature of certain genetic conditions. As an activity, it wavers between being consultation, counselling and therapy with regard to information, explanation and advice giving sequences (Sarangi, 2000).

As I began to sit in the clinics to collect data, I became increasingly aware of the nuances associated with different genetic conditions. Compared to the two other healthcare sites mentioned above, I was no longer dealing with a structured activity. I soon realized how genetic counsellors had to constantly grapple with issues of uncertainty and non-directiveness — two key aspects of genetic counselling — in condition-specific ways. For instance, it may be possible to become directive when one has the relevant scientific evidence and clinical knowledge about the genetic condition in question. Or, based on results from a predictive test concerning, say, Huntington's Disease, one can be very certain about inheritance, but not about the exact onset.

A discourse researcher coming from outside the profession needs to have a certain amount of knowledge about genetics and genetic counselling in order to be able to assess the status of any information as advice or as explanation. This is not even taking into account the fact that any information offered by a counsellor could be taken up as potential advice by clients — putting them on course to make specific decisions as if that was what the counsellor intended. Equally, dealing with matters of uncertainty, a discourse researcher will be unable to keep at pace with the ever-expanding genetic knowledge base. New genes and new gene functions are being discovered on a regular basis, as are new technologies and tests. Such developments are bound to have an impact on how uncertainty is managed in the clinical setting.

As I started to look for interactional patterns in the data, I was constantly asking myself questions of a different nature: Why didn't the counsellor elicit more details about the family history? Why was the counsellor reluctant to give a diagnostic label when the clients desperately wanted one? Why was the counsellor repeating himself/herself when the clients seemed to know what was being talked about? To some extent, I felt that I needed to know more about the genetic conditions themselves and about specific family histories before my analysis of the clinical interaction could have any credibility. Let us consider here an example of a post-clinic discussion between the researcher (R) and the consultant geneticist (G), related to a condition called Rett Syndrome.[8]

Genetic Counselling: Post-clinic Discussion

1. R: I was saying looking at it from the last clinics I went to [(.)] where a <u>lot</u> was =

2. G: [mm]

3. R: = going back to (.) you know much more .hh (.) family tree and [(.)] all the =

4. G: [yes]

5. R: = question about the risk and so on and so forth (.) and that was very much tied up with (.) future planning and [(.)] so on (.) er the the two cases we =

6. G: [yeah]

7. R: = looked at today were nothing to do with (.) family trees I mean [that didn't come up at all] and therefore it was much more (.) naming =

8. G: [no that's one of the things (.) yeah]

9. R: = and labelling and (.) the other things rather than [(.)] you know the risk =

10. G: [yes]

11. R: = and so on even th- the whole issue of another child wasn't even raised here

12. G: *mm (.) yeah* (.) no it's a very different context (.) from (.) from that ((name of town)) clinic

13. R: mm

14. G: *yeah and* (.)

---

8. I will use the following transcription conventions: dots or numerical between round brackets denote pause; texts within double round brackets are glosses; square brackets signal overlaps; equal sign (=) means latching; extended colons stand for lengthened sound and untranscribable segments are signalled by [^^^^^]. Asterisks on both sides of an utterance denote words spoken in relatively lower voice.

15. R: and how do these things get framed so differently [(.)] is it because of the =

16. G: [mm]

17. R: = nature of (.) I mean w- what I was thinking of is um (.) these are the test cases you don't have a label (.) you can't trace it back to the (.) the the mainstream family tree kind of [(.)] er er logic and therefore (.) the case =

18. G: [mm]

19. R: = comes with the (.) with the child [(.)] so you can't name it until (.) it is =

20. G: [mm]

21. R: = there if you like (.) and for it to be there (.) you need to wait and see (.) with tests and developments and so on [(.)] so so the whole question of <u>naming</u> =

22. G: [mm]

23. R: = something now [(.)] is is not an option because you have to wait for it to =

24. G: [mm]

25. R: = happen or occur

26. G: yes (.) s- sometimes (.) I mean people will (.) differ in their skill I mean some people will be able to (.) be quite sure (.) about (.) er (.) a diagnosis (.) and a child's (.) growing into a diagnosis sooner than others so I mean

27. R: people meaning (.) medics yes

28. G: geneticists

29. R: right

30. G: so some will (.) will spot something quicker and (.) er (.) than than others will and you know I'm not dysmorphology (.) is is something that I <u>do</u> in terms of (.) trying to recognize syndromes [(.)] but I'm not a natural at it I'm not =

31. R: [mm]

32. G: = brilliant at it (.) so that's why I rely on taking pictures and discussing with colleagues an' (.) sometimes asking er ((name of G)) in ((town)) or someone else elsewhere even (.) to look at one of my children's (files) and (.) send a family to see (.) someone else [(.)] if I think there is a label there to be =

33. R: [mm]

34. G: = named but I can't make it (.) um but but this last child (.) I really don't think there is a label to be made um

35. R: but you would take it back to (.) your colleagues [and] does it (.) I mean is it =

36. G: [well I]

37. R: = one of those ones

38. G: well there's not much point I mean because she's not dysmorphic I mean physically just looking at her ((discusses medical symptoms)) [...]

39. G: and so one's really left with (.) very little (.) to go on and the one (.) if her if ((CF's)) (.) hand use had been different had been affected much more than it is then I'd have (.) been saying yes she's got Rett Syndrome (.) 'cause everything else would fit with it [(.)] so I mean I want I'm <u>like</u>ly to end up =

40. R: [mm]

41. G: = saying when I see them next time (.) I'll see what the EG shows but probably what I'll say is (.) that she's got a (.) sort of (^^^^) or <u>vari</u>ant of Rett Syndrome and that's going to be an unsatisfactory label but the best one there is and if they're not well I mean they can always=

42. R: =that's something you probably already hinted at (.) [even] without the test =

43. G: [yes]

44. R: = that it has a bit of both [(.)] or these features <u>do</u> match up
with something =

45. G: [yes]

46. R: = that goes with that but not entirely so

47. G: but she hasn't got it in a classical form=

48. R: =right right

49. G: and (.) they'll probably probably end up asking another
paediatric neurologist to see her (.) because they probably
won't be happy with just me seeing her I think they'll want
somebody else to confirm it (.) I think (.) I'll probably send
her to (.) well there's no one else in ((name of city)) they'll
probably send her to ((name of hospital)) or somewhere (.)
er (.) you know to see if there's somebody else who sort of
(.) go along the same story that I'm (.) telling them

Such post-clinic discussions, for me, constitute collaborative
interpretation. This episode is triggered by the researcher who notices
a striking difference between counselling sessions: how on one occasion
the clinician may choose to dwell upon the family tree in order to
attempt diagnosis, whereas on another occasion s/he may decide not
to follow a similar route. The latter scenario captures the clinic being
talked about here. R obviously needs the insights of G so as to make
sense of the linkage between genetic explanation based on family trees
on the one hand, and how such information is to be utilized for purposes
of diagnosis and labelling on the other hand. This tension characterizes
what happens in the clinic, although there are reasons behind what
gets explicitly said or not said. The follow-up discussion therefore
provides a means for explicating some of the "unseen but noticed" —
giving a twist to Garfinkel's (1967) idea of "seen but unnoticed" —
aspects of the counselling session. In turns 26–32, G draws R's attention
to the existence of differential practice as far as degree of certainty
about diagnosis is concerned — "some people will be able to be quite
sure about a diagnosis". G also points to his zone of expertise, including
his inclination to seek a second opinion (see also turn 49). We also

have evidence here (see in particular turns 26, 30 and 32) of how clinical expertise is acquired through exposure to individual cases in practice. The idea of "taking pictures and discussing with colleagues" constitutes an important route to enhancing one's professional "knowing-in-action". Backstage considerations such as these are bound to affect the quality of the interaction in the frontstage clinical setting. It seems to me that insider perspectives on tacit knowledge are a necessary condition for analyzing what surfaces at the level of talk and interaction. Each interaction that a discourse researcher is looking at, especially in the clinical genetic context, will always come with a biographical history of its own. So, the discourse researcher will remain an outsider unless some attempt at collaborative interpretation is made.

Tensions in Negotiating Inter-professional Boundaries

On the basis of my discussion so far (see in particular page 97 on overlay of professional knowledge and professional discourse), let me single out four types of overlapping tensions which characterize the study of professional discourse.

Deconstructing the Researcher Identity

For a long time communication scholars have urged us to deconstruct the research process (see, for example, Cameron *et al.*, 1992). However, the role of the researcher has largely remained a monolithic concept. This is particularly striking in view of the fact that many of us adopt the Goffmanian participation structure framework to talk about different producer and receiver roles in social interaction, but we are somewhat less forthcoming when it involves the characterization of the multi-faceted researcher role-identities in inter-professional discourse settings. As discourse researchers, when we decide to gain access to professional research sites, it is very likely that we will need to negotiate our own identities on a contingent basis. It will bear on the notion of presentation of self as "professional strangers" and how our subjects "will draw on their own repertoire of social categories to find one that fits you" (Agar, 1980:54). In other words, how the researcher is perceived by the subjects is as crucial as how the researcher manages his/her presentation of self. We can think here of multiple possibilities, e.g., researcher as insider, as outsider, as agent of change, as animator, as overhearer etc (Sarangi and Hall, 1997). These different identities index different levels of participation and involvement (including trust and accountability) with research subjects. A good example here is Gubrium (1975) who constantly shifted between doing menial work (toileting) and being a gerontologist at staff meetings, as part of his ethnographic study of a nursing home.

The issue of socialization of the discourse researcher into another professional practice needs to be taken seriously. It is bound to be an incremental process, similar to how novices get socialized into their professions — moving from the periphery to the centre (in the sense of Lave and Wenger, 1991, see page 104 on socialization and ecological validity in terms of interpretive practices). In the ethnographic tradition, when researchers carry out their fieldwork in "other" surroundings, they make an attempt to socialize into their subjects' ways of doing things. Becker's (1963) highly influential paper "Becoming a marihuana user" can serve here as a metaphor. According to Becker, the technique of marihuana use needs to be first separated from smoking tobacco: unlike tobacco smokers, marihuana users take in a lot of air, get it deep down their system and keep it there for as long as they can. This results in getting sufficient dosage for intoxication. Becker breaks this inhaling process down into three components: (1) learning the technique; (2) learning to perceive the effects and (3) learning to enjoy the effects. In terms of interprofessional research sites, this means that discourse researchers need the practice to get enough of professional air into their system in order to understand what they are observing and enjoy the collaborative research experience.

If discourse is a form of marihuana, then professionals also need to inhale discourse slowly and steadily in order to become competent practitioners of discourse. In other words, what we have here is a relation of complementarity: not only do discourse researchers become socialized into professional practice, but professionals also learn to become socialized as discourse practitioners. This will then amount to redefining the role-relationship between the researcher and the professional practitioner as we are no longer positioning ourselves as experts, making explicit recommendations for change of professional practice. In any case, as Freidson (1970) alerts us, practitioners do not always seem to be keen on changing their practice based on scientific findings (see also Bloor, 1997). Professional practitioners work with different kinds of knowledge, including their own cumulative practical knowledge, so any new findings — such as the ones arising from discourse-based studies — need to be seen against other competing knowledge resources available to practitioners. Self-appraisal is more likely to result in change of practice than other-initiated-advice. This is not very different from the preference of self-initiated repairs in the conversation analytic sense. In very modest terms, discourse practitioners can make it their goal to turn their subjects into discourse practitioners which would lead to self-appraisal. It is then a matter of developing a way of seeing (gaze) and use of (meta)language or specialized register. Does this then pose a threat to our livelihood as discourse researchers? Not any more than discourse researchers in large part being ignored by professional communities of practice.

Aligning Differential Knowledge Bases

The role of discourse analysts when dealing with professional sites needs further scrutiny. Goodwin (1994) exemplifies how each profession is constituted in different ways of seeing, leading to differential practices of coding, highlighting and articulating material representations. In his discussion of the Rodney King trial, he shows how the police have a distinct way of coding evidence from that of the lawyers. He also draws our attention to how even within the legal profession, the defendant's lawyer and the prosecution lawyer will adopt different ways of presenting evidence. These differences are likely to be heightened further when we cross inter-professional boundaries.

Goodwin's characterization above concerns the act of interpretation. When extended to our interprofessional sites, it may not be so easy to attain a reciprocity of participants' and analysts' perspectives. As Cicourel (1968:15) remarks:

"I assume the critical task of the researcher is to show the reader how the research materials are always understood by reference to unstated and seen (but unnoticed) background expectancies both members and observers employ to recognize and to understand their activities."

There seem to be two extreme choices: alignment with participants' perspectives or transformation of what is observed (Sarangi and Candlin, 2001). Alignment may be seen as a form of contextualization in search for "ecological validity" — which is different from the process of transformation since it impinges on analysts' imposition of external categories and labels. Transformation is thus a form of recontextualization (for an overview, see Linell and Sarangi, 1998). Alignment is also a matter of feasibility as well as desirability (see page 127 on strict and contextual constructionism). It is quite possible that different participants, say, lawyers and defendants, will pursue different goals in a given encounter. When we find ourselves torn between different participant perspectives, on whose side do we lean (Becker, 1967)?

Let us return to the genetic counselling context and ask: what happens when there are differences between researcher and participant perspectives; or what happens when we have a counsellor's perspective which may differ from that of the patient/client? As I have suggested already, the method of getting participant feedback is one of gaining access to what participants think is going on and to align their views with the analyst's perspective. But from a social constructionist position, we need to be aware that seeking feedback constitutes another speech event and does not provide reliable data to assess *what actually happened*. But a participant perspective must recognize that the participant is a discourse practitioner who is entitled to reflect on his/her practice, as the geneticist does in the post-clinic session discussed earlier. Also, when interacting, participants no doubt analyse each other's conversational exchanges on a contingent basis. Once we bestow upon our participant the analyst status, then their post-hoc accounts are as authentic and credible as any outsider discourse analyst's commentary. But what may make a discourse analyst's task different is his/her motivated lookings for patterns and rules.[9] It is worth noting that not all practitioner-participants will bring with them a similar degree of discourse analytic insights (in the same way that not all discourse analysts will approach a professional data site in the same way). It will depend partly on how much discourse they were prepared to inhale during the collaborative research process. There also remains the issue of knowledge differences within a given a profession (practitioners vs. practitioner researcher vs. policy makers). In the case of our RCGP consultancy study, medics who were only practitioners, as opposed to those who were researchers, responded to our discourse analytic work rather differently.

The Interplay of Observer's Paradox, Participant's Paradox and Analyst's Paradox

In sociolinguistic research, the notion of observer's paradox (coined by Labov, 1972) has been discussed at length, and has probably been overstated at the expense of other paradoxes — participant's and analyst's — which characterize discourse studies in the professional settings (see Appendix 2). Labov (1972) claims that we can only get authentic data when we are not observing the interaction — that is, our observation (which also includes the use of audio and video recording equipment) contaminates the data. Whatever we observe becomes a product from an observer's viewpoint. In Labov's formulation, the researcher as observer is conceptualized as having a unified identity. But as we have discussed in deconstructing researcher identity on page 116, researchers may be accessing professional sites in various capacities. We can therefore extend the notion of observer's paradox to think about the activity of participants observing the observer — which is what I would call the "participant's paradox". For instance, some participants may be completely oblivious of the

---

9. Here we can refer to the problem inherent in practitioners becoming full-fledged researchers, i.e., the difficulty of negotiating researcher identity with people with whom they previously have had professionally sanctioned role-relationships.

presence of the researcher-observer and/or the recording equipment during various stages of the interaction. Indeed, many participants admit this to be the case after a recording session. Other participants may remain conscious of the researcher's presence and even wish that the researcher were a legitimate participant, albeit with restricted interactional rights and obligations. It is the latter group who may find the "uninvolved" stance of the researcher-observer as unnatural and distracting (Clarke, 2000). Following Goffman's participation categories, we can think of a cline of involvement — at one end the researcher remains a "participant as observer" and at the other end, s/he becomes a "participant as interactant". This distinction between the sphere of observation and the sphere of interaction is likely to be a matter of practical concern for many researchers in the field. Participant observation without becoming involved in the ongoing activity may not be so problematic if one is observing, say, classroom lessons or hospital ward rounds. But it is different in the clinical setting. Doctors and patients are very much used to the presence of various participants in a clinic and are aware of the fact that different participants may have activity-specific rights and obligations. So, in such a setting, if the researcher-observer remains fully uninvolved, then it may not go unnoticed. As far as participants are concerned, observer neutrality cannot be taken for granted, so it may be useful for the researcher-observer to participate, however minimally, in the interaction without influencing the course of events.[10]

Let us now consider yet another paradox: the analyst's paradox. This connects with our earlier discussion about collaborative interpretation and ecological validity. I have already made the point that we need not only data of professional practice, but also professional practitioners' insights to inform our data analysis. The notion of collaborative interpretation, in my view, accommodates the participant perspective as it is upheld in CA studies, but it is not reduced to it. Collaborative interpretation does not privilege participant perspectives

---

10. It is perhaps worth mentioning here that in our RCGP research site, it has been difficult to keep separate the roles of "researcher as observer" and "researcher as participant/consultant".

unduly: instead it tries to align participant's perspective with analyst's perspective. This, of course, includes participants taking on the role of analysts in their own right (see aligning differential knowledge bases on page 118). Research interviews as an activity is in fact based on the assumption that participants know best what they do and why — i.e., they have the knowledge which discourse researchers are seeking to uncover. This does not mean that research interviews should not be interpreted as situated events, which make specific demands on participants to maintain a given role-relationship. The accounts of professional practice that we access in an interview are not necessarily the same as what constitutes professional practice in action. As discourse researchers, we remain, for most part, peripheral but legitimate participants, eager to rely on our subjects' insights so that we align (rather than transform) analyst and participant perspectives.

Discourse Ecology and Discourse Ethics

The ecology of context argument, as we have discussed earlier, bears upon the significance of aligning analyst and participant perspectives. This form of interpretive alignment is not only different from conversation analytic preference for "members' method", it is also distinctly different from how critical discourse analysts draw upon the external, socio-political context in a ritualized manner to account for talk and text data. Indeed this latter kind of context-embeddedness — or, "brought along" context by the researcher (in Giddens' sense) — runs the risk of overriding the participant perspective, i.e., the "brought along" and "brought about" contexts from the participants' perspective. So, we have to see ecology not just in the sense of context-embeddedness but also in the sense of interpretive alignment.

In a recent interview, Candlin (2000) teases out the various meanings associated with the ecology metaphor to include (1) an interactional view of language which coincides with how everyday people perceive language use; (2) a notion of dynamic (and systematic) change as in the case of language acquisition/socialization or colonization/globalization; and (3) uptake in interprofessional settings. The latter has to do with how discourse researchers relate to practitioners such as lawyers, doctors, social workers who use language professionally and for whom language is the essence of what they do.

The above ecological considerations will have to be supplemented with ethical issues. In the field of discourse and communication research, the issue of ethics has been mainly confined to matters of data collection and data presentation (see Cameron *et al.*, 1992). I feel that when we work in professional discourse sites such as healthcare, ethical issues go beyond data collection and researcher-researched field relations. This is where my earlier discussion of collaborative interpretation again comes to the forefront. In addition, we need to be open about what might happen to the data in the future in terms of re-interpretations.[11] This is particularly relevant when professional practitioners — individually or collectively — and professional organizations are showing a keen interest in the value of communication and discourse analytic studies.[12]

Let me formulate the ethical issues in the form of some key questions.

Where do we look?

My answer to this is "almost everywhere". In addition to the difficulties in accessing various frontstage and backstage activities of a professional community, we are also constrained by our own expertise. For instance, our interest may be only in talk and text rather than professional practice as such. We may then tend to select those moments of professional practice that are constituted in talk and text. In fact discourse scholars working with text do not even consider examples of professional talk. The reverse is also true. For instance, researchers interested in medical discourse seem to take for granted that medical

---

11. This point came home to me when a genetic counsellor whose clinics we have been taping for quite some time showed signs of concern about what kinds of analyses we were doing. Although we have had consent for the clinics to be taped, it is legitimate to be apprehensive about what happens to the data and who gets to read the analyses (despite assurances of anonymity). There is a parallel here to the current debates about genetic tissue banking and how such tissues are utilised for research or other commercial purposes.

work is constituted in talk in the clinic, and so ignore the practising of medicine as it happens elsewhere, including in the text format. What Hak (1999) refers to as the talk bias can also be extended to discuss text-bias. Basically our naming of a topic of inquiry can be reductonist. Both strictly motivated lookings (like Labov and Fanshel, 1977) and open-ended lookings can be unhelpful for professionals.

Do we identify a set of problems that might be of interest to our participants?

My preferred response here would be "Yes, as far as practicable". If the problem identification is jointly negotiated, the research findings are more likely to be interpreted favourably. But this needs to be seen against Peräkylä's (1995) warning that the primary motivation of interaction research is not to solve problems faced by professionals. This is a cautious and honest assessment and it partly coincides with my point that we may be lacking adequate knowledge to solve another profession's dilemmas. However, this kind of an opposition between discourse research and professional practice can be bridged through collaborative interpretive work. Also, solving problems, raising awareness and reporting of findings are different activities, although in a consultancy model these two may become inseparable. More generally, discourse-based studies must try to orient their work for professional uptake — whether or not this leads to change of practice and solution of specific problems. On the contrary, adopting an indifferent stance or approaching professional discourse sites with an

---

12. Recently I met an oncologist to discuss possible collaborative research on cancer communication. Routinely, he taped all his clinics and handed the tapes to the patients so that they could listen to the clinic discussions again. Following the usual consent procedure, the oncologist invited me to listen to a few tapes as a way of identifying topics of mutual interest. When I was asked, what I might say in relation to problems of communication, I saw it as similar to a kind of referral practice which blended research design and consultancy. As discourse practitioners, then, we need to come up with a concrete set of points and make clear our intentions and speciality (or lack of it) in dealing with such sensitive data. In approaching us, professionals are both worried about our sense of ethics and confidentiality, but at the same time they are indicating that we can do something that would help improve their day-to-day practice.

"open mind" can be viewed with suspicion by professional colleagues.

To what extent do we involve participants in the interpretive process?

The notion of collaborative interpretation, as I have discussed so far, needs to be reassessed on a case-by-case basis. As we have seen in the RCGP study, it can be at the stage of identifying key moments for analysis, or it can be, as in the genetic counselling site, to back up or clarify preliminary analysis of data. Much will depend on the level of involvement and understanding that the discourse researcher brings to the research site. In a sense, it is similar to anthropologists' use of the native informant on the top of participant observation in order to make sense of "other" cultural practices. Levi-Strauss (1978:26) calls this the "anthropological doubt" which he glosses as "knowing that one knows nothing, but of resolutely exposing what one thought one knew — and one's very ignorance". In a similar vein, here we are talking about "discoursal doubt" which is bound to be a feature of interprofessional research.

Do we tell our participants everything we find?

The answer to this question has to be a cautious "No". This is partly because we have only done a motivated looking, but also because our interpretations may not be sophisticated at all levels. The final decision as to what to offer as feedback will depend on what problems have been jointly defined for scrutiny. As Becker *et al.* (1961) point out in their study of medical education:

> *"But our purpose is not criticism, but observation and analysis. When we report what we have learned, it is important that we do so faithfully. We have a double duty — to our own profession of social observation and analysis and to those who have allowed us to observe their conduct. We do not report everything we observe, for to do so would violate confidences and otherwise do harm. On the other hand, we must take care not to bias our analyses and conclusions. Finding a proper balance*

> *between our obligations to our informants and the*
> *organization, on the one hand, and our scientific duty,*
> *on the other, is not easy."*

Cameron *et al.* (1992:14) make a similar point when they say that "the interests of the researched are a negative force limiting what researchers can do". This perhaps relates to the general issue about studying social problems. Our involvement as discourse researchers needs to be assessed in light of contributions from neighbouring fields — especially from sociologists, anthropologists and psychologists. It is not just a matter of problem construction but also how we construct our findings for the uptake of the professionals involved, as Becker *et al.* so clearly attest. Discourse researchers need to verify their interpretations not so much against theories of language use but against the participants' theories of practice. That will have a double benefit of participants becoming reflexive about their practice, as well as discourse researchers challenging their own theories that are not always data-driven and in doing so, reflect upon their own discourse and interpretive practices.

When it comes to determining the audience of discourse research, we need not fall into the ethnographic trap where research accounts have to be produced to conform to established genre and in the process amount to decontextualisng the native's practices and the very act of participant observation/involvement (Marcus and Fischer, 1986). An additional tension concerns what Bloor (1997) refers to as the provision of feedback based on contrastive performance. In presenting our audience with instances of good and bad practice (say, examples of empathetic and retractive encounters, see page 109) can be regarded as part of good pedagogy for raising awareness among practitioners. But this may raise ethical dilemmas. Apart from threatening the individual face of some practitioner, it can amount to non-cooperation for future research.

It seems that our usefulness as discourse practitioners can be enhanced in a model of "professional consultancy" research. But can we imagine ourselves as discourse clinicians listening to other professionals' troubles-telling and being able to offer concrete advice, not theorize? It need not be therapeutic, but a kind of on-line gloss on what's going on, as is the case with medical education and training. Collaborative interdisciplinarity, which is part and parcel of the professional consultancy model as I see it, has the promise of successful uptake. This is partly because practitioners invariably analyse their practice, so they may naturally see the value of discourse-based insights. The professional collaborator may change his/her practice based on findings and this then may have the ripple effect — change happening over time in ever increasing circles. This is very different from a model of mass preaching or backstage engineering.

Conclusion: Professional Discourse Research as a Co-constructionist Enterprise

In this chapter I started with the promise discourse research has for the study of professional sites — especially in the healthcare domain — in light of the interpretive turn in social sciences generally. Discourse research can offer a range of linguistic and rhetorical categories to capture the "know how" of a professional group, while also being able to distance oneself from passing judgement about individual practice. This raises the question as to whether discourse analysis is a science or an art or a form of practice. Clearly, as we have seen, one needs more than linguistic skills and knowledge in order to engage with professional practice. The strength of discourse research lies in our ability to identify suitable data for analysis, while underscoring the fact that no single interpretation is valid in itself and that alternative interpretations are always inevitable. Our discourses have to be flexible to accommodate different ways of seeing and doing across professional boundaries. For this to be the case, we need to have an understanding of the professional practice before we can analyse any discourse data (S. Candlin, 2000).

It is therefore important to recognize the limits of discourse research. The irony is that much of our work may lack the kind of rigorous scientificity for the claims we make to be credible. And for professional practice to change, our discourse-based claims need to be robust. Starting from collecting data to interpreting data to reporting findings, we are bound to be selective. Our analytic findings, in Durkheimian sense, may simply be aimed at illustration rather than demonstration. But illustration in this context can be a useful exercise, especially when what we are illustrating coincides with what professionals might intuitively think to be the case (Sarangi and Roberts, 2000). The outcome of discourse research may simply be that our subjects will know more about their own discourses — with a new metalanguage offering a window on their discourse practices — as we also come to realize our own individual disciplinary preferences.

Throughout the chapter I have highlighted the need for collaborative interdisciplinarity where the collaborators are also professional practitioners. This is different from discourse scholars joining with sociologists or psychologists in order to achieve a fuller understanding of a given professional practice. Working with professional practitioners, I have argued, will guarantee interpretive ecology, while also facilitating the potential uptake of findings. Wherever possible, such collaborative work needs to be carried out over a longer period of time, rather than being designed as one-off relationships which begin and end with access to data sites. There is the need for discourse practitioners and professional experts to align their ways of seeing and accounting as they attempt to understand the phenomenon under study and try to bring about changes in everyday practice through reflexivity. This is not a reductionist position, since the discourse researchers have at their disposal other kinds of contextual information which they can draw upon to evaluate various participants' contributions. Joel Best (1989) makes a useful distinction between strict and contextual constructionist positions. The first one — characteristic of the purist form of conversation analytic research — constrains the analyst by not allowing him/her to evaluate what members say. The analyst is seen as just one other member and as not having a privileged status. In the case of the latter, the analyst is obliged to contextualize what members say with other kinds of available data. In their preface to the Best volume, Kitsuse and Schneider (1989) summarize this as follows:

> *"Best's distinction between a contextual and strict constructionist analysis, then, is one that differentiates research on social problems where the researcher participates, with members, in the practical projects of documenting and explaining a state of affairs that they find objectionable or important and that they may want to change, and research where an analyst pursues a distinct, theoretical project organized around the description and understanding of the form, substance, and development of the members' practical project."*

Indeed collaborative interpretation — which will constantly seek insights from professional practitioners — must become a guiding principle for discourse research, much in line with multidisciplinary, team-based work in professions such as medicine, social work, law, education etc. The onus is on discourse practitioners to present themselves as a "community of interprofessional practice" in order to make their research both credible and socially relevant across professional boundaries.

References

1. Agar, M. 1980. *Professional stranger: An informal introduction to ethnography.* New York: Academic Press.

2. Atkinson, P. 1995. *Medical talk and medical work: The liturgy of the clinic.* London: Sage.

3. Becker, H. S. 1963. *Outsiders: Studies in the sociology of deviance.* New York: Free Press.

4. _____. 1967. Whose side are we on? *Social Problems* 14:239–248.

5. _____. 1993. How I learned what a crock was. *Journal of Contemporary Ethnography* 22 (1): 28–35.

6. _____, B. Geer, E. C. Hughes and A. L. Strauss. 1961. *Boys in white: Student culture in medical school.* Chicago: Chicago University Press.

7. Best, J., ed. 1989. *Images of issues: Typifying contemporary social problems.* Hawthorne, NY: Aldine de Gruyter.

8. Bloor, M. 1997. Addressing social problems through qualitative research. In *Qualitative research: Theory, method and practice*, edited by D. Silverman . London: Sage, 221–238.

9. Cameron, D. 2000. *Good to talk?* London: Routledge.

10. _____, E. Fraser, P. Harvey, B. Rampton and K. Richardson. 1992. *Researching language: Issues of power and method.* London: Routledge.

11. Candlin, C. N. 1997. Editorial preface to *The construction of professional discourse*, by B–L. Gunnarsson, P. Linell, and B. Nordberg. London: Longman, viii–xiv.

12. _____ . 2000. An interview with Christopher Candlin by Claire Kramsch. *Berkeley Language Centre Newsletter* 16 (1): 1–4.

13. Candlin, S. 2000. Nurses, patients and discourse analysts: Identifying problems, meeting challenges and facing the future. Paper presented at the International Conference on Text and Talk at Work, University of Gent, 16–19 August.

14. Cicourel, A. V. 1968. *The social organization of juvenile justice.* New York: Wiley.

15. _____ . 1992. The interpenetration of communicative contexts: Examples from medical encounters. In *Rethinking context: Language as an interactive phenomenon*, edited by A. Duranti and C. Goodwin. Cambridge: Cambridge University Press, 291–310.

16. Clarke, A. 2000. On being a subject of discourse research. Paper presented at the International Conference on Text and Talk at Work, University of Gent, 16–19 August.

17. Cogan, M. L. 1953. Toward a definition of profession. *Harvard Educational Review* 23:33–50.

18. Duranti, A. and C. Goodwin, eds. 1992. *Rethinking context: Language as an interactive phenomenon.* Cambridge: Cambridge University Press.

19. Freidson, E. 1970. *The profession of medicine: A study of the sociology of applied knowledge.* New York: Dodd, Mead and Company.

20. Garfinkel, H. 1967. *Studies in ethnomethodology.* Englewood Cliffs, NJ: Prentice Hall.

21. Giddens, A. 1976. *New rules of sociological method.* London: Hutchinson.

22. Goffman, E. 1959. *The presentation of self in everyday life.* New York: Doubleday Anchor.

23. _____ . 1961. *Asylums: Essays on the social situation of mental patients and other inmates.* New York: Doubleday Anchor.

24. Goodwin, C. 1994. Professional vision. *American Anthropologist* 96 (3): 606–633.

25. Gubrium, J. F. 1975. *Living and dying at Murray Manor.* New York: St Martin's Press.

26. Hak, T. 1999. "Text" and "con-text": Talk bias in studies of health care work. In *Talk, work and institutional order: Discourse in medical, mediation and management settings,* edited by S. Sarangi and C. Roberts. Berlin: Mouton de Gruyter, 427–451.

27. Heritage, J. 1984. *Garfinkel and ethnomethodology.* Cambridge: Polity Press.

28. Hughes, E. C. 1958. *Men and their work.* Westport, Connecticut: Greenwood Press.

29. Kitsuse, J. I. and Schneider. 1989. Preface to *Images of issues: Typifying contemporary social problems,* edited by J. Best. Hawthorne. NY: Aldine de Gruyter.

30. Labov, W. 1972. Some principles of linguistic methodology. *Language in Society* 1:97–120.

31. _____ . and D. Fanshel. 1977. *Therapeutic discourse: Psychotherapy as conversation.* New York: Academic Press.

32. Lave, J. and E. Wenger. 1991. *Situated learning: Legitimate peripheral participation.* Cambridge: Cambridge University Press.

33. Levi-Strauss, C. 1978. *Structural anthropology II,* translated by M. Layton. London: Penguin.

34. Linell, P. and S. Sarangi. 1998. *Discourse across professional boundaries.* Special Issue of *Text* 18 (2): 143–318.

35. Luhmann, N. 1990. *Essays on self-reference.* New York: Columbia University Press.

36. Mackay, R. W. 1974. Conceptions of children and models of socialization. In *Ethnomethodology,* edited by R. Turner. Harmondsworth: Penguin, 180–193.

37. Marcus, G. E. and M. M. J. Fischer. 1986. *Anthropology as cultural critique.* Chicago: The University of Chicago Press.

38. Merton, R., G. G. Reader and P. L. Kendall. 1957. *Student-physician: Introductory studies in the sociology of medical education.* Cambridge, MA: Harvard University Press.

39. Mishler, E. G. 1984. *The discourse of medicine: Dialectics of medical interviews.* Norwood, NJ: Ablex.

40. O'Barr, W. M. 1983. Addressing social issues through linguistic evidence. *Journal of Language and Social Psychology* 2:241–251.

41.   Perakyla, A. 1995. *AIDS counselling: Institutional interaction and clinical practice*. Cambridge: Cambridge University Press.

42.   Ravetz, J. R. 1973. *Scientific knowledge and its social problems*. Harmondsworth: Penguin Books.

43.   Roberts, C. and S. Sarangi. 1999. Hybridity in gatekeeping discourse: Issues of practical relevance for the researcher. In *Talk, work and institutional order: Discourse in medical, mediation and management settings*, edited by S. Sarangi and C. Roberts. Berlin: Mouton de Gruyter, 473–503.

44.   Roberts, C., S. Sarangi, L. Southgate, R. Wakeford and V. Wass. 2000. Oral examination — equal opportunities, ethnicity, and fairness in the MRCGP. *British Medical Journal* 320:370–375.

45.   Ryle, G. 1949. *The concept of mind*. London: Hutcheson.

46.   Sarangi, S. 2000. Activity types, discourse types and interactional hybridity: The case of genetic counselling. In *Discourse and social life*, edited by S. Sarangi and M. Coulthard. London: Pearson, 1–27.

47.   _____ and C. N. Candlin. 2001. "Motivational relevancies": Some methodological reflections on sociolinguistic and social theoretical practice. In *Sociolinguistics and social theory*, edited by N. Coupland, S. Sarangi and C. N. Candlin. London: Pearson, 350–388.

48.   _____ and C. Hall. 1997. Bringing off "applied" research in inter-professional discourse studies. Paper presented at the BAAL/CUP Seminar on Urban Culture, Discourse and Ethnography. Thames Valley University, 24–25 March.

49.   _____ and C. Roberts, eds. 1999. *Talk, work and institutional order: Discourse in medical, mediation and management settings*. Berlin: Mouton de Gruyter.

50.   Sarangi, S. and C. Roberts. 2000. Uptake of discourse research in inter-professional settings: Reporting from medical consultancy. Paper presented at the International Conference on Text and Talk at Work, University of Gent, 16–19 August.

51.   _____ . Discoursal (mis)alignments in professional gatekeeping encounters. In *Language socialization and language acquisition: Ecological perspectives*, edited by C. Kramsch. London: Continuum. Forthcoming.

52.   Schon, D. A. 1983. *The reflective practitioner: How professionals think in action*. New York: Basic Books.

53.   Stoddart, K. 1974. Pinched: Notes on the ethnographer's location of Argot. In *Ethnomethodology*, edited by R. Turner. Harmondsworth: Penguin, 173–179.

54.   Turner, R., ed. 1974. *Ethnomethodology*. Harmondsworth: Penguin.

55.   Whyte, W. 1955. *Street corner society: The structure of an Italian slum*. Chicago: Chicago University Press.

56. Wieder, D. L. 1974. Language and social reality: *The case of telling the convict code.* The Hague: Mouton.

57. Wilson, T. 1971. Normative and interpretative paradigms in sociology. In *Understanding everyday life: Toward the reconstruction of sociological knowledge,* edited by J. Douglas. London: Routledge and Kegan Paul, 57–79.

THE ROYAL COLLEGE OF GENERAL PRACTITIONERS
ORAL EXAMINATION
<u>AWKWARD MOMENTS</u>

Thank you for agreeing to help us with our study of the RCGP Oral Examination.

There is a considerable amount of research which suggests that ethnic/ cultural/linguistic differences lead to communicative difficulties, and these show up as awkward moments in talk. However, such awkward moments can occur in the oral examination situation, irrespective of the candidate's ethnic/linguistic background. Please use the following checklist and any other criteria to pick up any examples where things are not going so well in the oral. You might wish to look out for the following:

<u>Checklist</u>

1.   Long pauses, often filled by further questions from the examiner.
     9.25 / 9.26 / 9.43 / 12.36
2.   Interruptions.
3.   Too many questions in succession, without allowing adequate time for candidates to respond.
     10.59 / 11.58
4.   Asking simple, factual questions, while the exam requires higher level questioning.
     12.20
5.   Problems of understanding, which require examiners to rephrase or give more context.
     9.26 / 11.18-11.20
6.   Any other difficult moments, such as culturally different styles of communicating, as perceived by you.

Please note that this is only a guide; there may be other aspects of awkwardness and discomfort in the video data you're looking at.
Thank you once again for your cooperation.

Celia Roberts/Srikant Sarangi
Consultant Researchers, RCGP

25 July 1996

Interplay of Observer's, Participant's and Analyst's Paradoxes

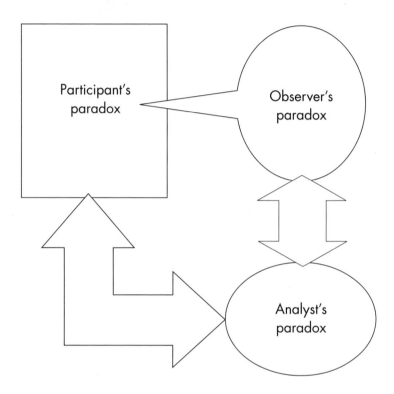

6

Towards an Understanding of Workplace Discourse: A Pilot Study for Compiling a Spoken Chinese Corpus of Situated Discourse

Yueguo Gu

Preamble [1]

A six man team was set up in 1999 to compile a 500-hour spoken Chinese corpus of situated discourse in Beijing area (the project known as SCCSD BJ-500 in short) under the auspices of the Chinese Academy of Social Sciences. It is hoped that enough experience will be accumulated at the end of this project for the launching of a nation-wide programme of compiling a similar corpus bearing the name *Spoken Chinese*. The project reported in this paper was initially intended as a pilot study for the SCCSD BJ-500, a way to test the water, so to speak. By the time this chapter was submitted to the editor of this collection, 309 hours of situated discourse in Beijing area have already been collected. So although the observations made about workplace discourse in this chapter were largely based on the initial pilot study samples, other samples from the corpus will also be occasionally made use of for demonstrative purposes.

In his study of negotiation in the workplace, David Bell (1995: 42) makes a brief historical survey of what place counts as workplace. Historically in the early industrial period, the workplace was typically

---

1. The author wishes to express his gratitude to Professor Ron Scollon for several informal discussions about the project over meals together. He is equally grateful to Professor Christopher Candlin for unfailing support and encouragement. Thanks also go to the participants in the conference and the seminars whose questions and comments have made the author think harder and become less vulnerable to errors.

associated with the factory or the shop. Nowadays, non-workplace seems to be difficult to find. One man's leisure is another man's work. "So perhaps," Bell concludes, "the workplace *is* everywhere" (italics original). In this paper, however, we distinguish regular workplaces from temporary ones. For example, Professor Xu had a tutorial at home or under a tree. It is true that the professor was working, but "at home" and "under a tree" are temporary make-do "workplaces", not proper ones. So a regular workplace is a socially recognized setting where people are employed to work for pay or without pay.

Workplace is a relative concept. Beijing is a workplace in the context of China. In Beijing itself there are many workplaces in the context of one against another. For the sake of clarity, the term workplace is reserved to refer to the grass roots level in the hierarchy. Take a university, for example. The workplaces are prototypically classrooms where teachers teach. Administrative offices are also workplaces. Departments, faculties, unions, etc. will not be counted as workplaces, although they are often used to answer the question of "Where are you working?" They will be referred to as "work units".[2]

Workplace discourse can simply be taken as discourse generated in workplaces (see a more technical definition on page 147). It is in contrast, if you like, with family discourse, i.e., discourse generated in a familial setting among family members or relatives. The last few decades have witnessed booming studies of workplace discourse. Doctor-patient discourse (e.g., Pendleton, 1983; Mishler, 1984; West, 1984; Steward and Roter, 1989; Gu, 1996; Kim, Smith and Gu, 1999), legal discourse (e.g., Penman, 1990; Gibbons, 1994), scientific discourse (Gunnarsson, 1997), classroom discourse (e.g., Coulthard, 1977), institutional discourse (e.g., Drew and Heritage, 1992; Anward, 1997), organizational discourse (e.g., Boden, 1994), discourse of negotiation in the workplace (Firth, 1995), media discourse (e.g., van Dijk, 1988; Bell, 1991; Scollon, 1998), can all be said to be workplace discourse analyses. Since the analysts conduct their studies from their own perspectives, and with varied academic backgrounds, the similarities

2.   Work unit is equivalent to 單位 in Chinese. It is one level higher than workplace in the hierarchy.

among them seem to be as great as their diversities. A detailed review of the literature is obviously impossible here for lack of space. However, three reservations need to be voiced, at the risk of overgeneralization, for they are the factors that bear direct relevance on this research project.

First, all those types of discourse mentioned above are not workplace discourses in their original forms. Rather they are abstractions of what the researchers are interested in from the real world workplace discourses, with the unwieldy elements that do not fit the perceived categories being weeded out. This can be methodologically defensible, but is liable to present a misleading account of what is actually happening in the real world. Second, time and space as both constraining and enabling factors of discourse production, consumption and reproduction are generally overlooked. Third, human agency as discourse-maker making discourse is not made the primary object of discourse analysis. Discourse and discourse structure have been examined without giving primary recognition to the fact that they are both constituted by human agency and yet at the same time are the very medium of this constitution.

This paper takes a step further down the abstraction ladder, so to speak, by examining workplace discourse as it is, without first putting it through the lens of categorization. We do not start with an intuitive preconception of a type of interaction/discourse, or a particular discourse phenomenon, which is followed by looking for data. Rather, it is paramount that we preserve the naturalness of workplace discourse. The research strategy we take is as follows. A Beijing professional was "cajoled" to audio-tape his workplace talks for a week, wherever he went doing his work. Another Beijing community social worker was also "cajoled" to audio-tape the talks taking place in her office for a week (she actually overdid it for two weeks). The chapter argues that it is more profitable to start from the very basics before we move onto a higher and more abstract level.

In what follows we first say a few words about the data collection and processing. We then discuss the sociological theories that underpin the research strategy we have adopted. The bulk of the chapter will be devoted to the analysis of the data. As the data are extremely rich and complex, this chapter will only focus on the former case, leaving the latter for another study.

Data Collection and Processing

The Beijing professional mentioned above, to be referred to as Mr. X hereafter, was kind enough to audio-tape his week long talks in his workplaces. Permissions to record were also kindly given by the authorities of the workplaces concerned. However, the other participants in the activities were not informed beforehand. The recording started with Mr. X's arrival in the office, and switched off when he left it. Although the recording device was a quality digital MD with a highly sensitive digital microphone, not all the actual recordings turned out to be usable due to background noise, or too great a distance between the microphone and the actual speakers. The usable MD disks last 18 hours and 2 minutes. They were converted and segmented into wave files, each of which lasts about 5 minutes long. For the present purpose they were transcribed in Chinese characters. Situational and biographical details concerning the workplaces and the participants were noted down by Mr. X who carefully filled in the recording information sheets as requested. Table 6.1 shows some general logistics.

Table 6.1
The Usable Recordings

Date	Duration of Usable Recording	Physical Setting	Active/Passive Participants
Monday	2 hours 51 minutes	office	6/0
Tuesday	2 hours	office	15/30
Wednesday		Absent from workplace	
Thursday	5 hours 43 minutes	Office, meeting room	18/21
Friday	1 hour 53 minutes	office	6/0
Saturday	3 hours 17 minutes	Conference hall	4/480
Sunday	2 hours 20 minutes	hotel suite	11/0
Total	*18 hours 2 minutes*		*60/531*

Time, Space, and Trajectories of Workplace Discourse

Hägerstrand's Socio-environmental Web Model of Society and Habitat

Work is a fundamental necessity in human life. Society depends on work for the production of food, machines, computers, newsprint, etc. As individuals, people work to satisfy their material needs as well as their social and psychological needs, i.e., to meet certain obligations, to be seen as significant and feel significant to themselves. All these take place in workplaces. Workplace discourse is therefore, too, a fundamental necessity in human life. It is from this vantage point that this chapter looks at workplace discourse.

One of the fundamental organizing principles of workplace discourse is by time and space. Time and space traditionally enter into linguistic theorization in historical linguistics and dialectology respectively. In de Saussure's influential distinction between diachrony and synchrony, time is virtually frozen and plays an immaterial role in the synchronic study of langue. It is examined in connection with tense in grammar, and with temporal deixis in pragmatics. Space, outside dialectology, has only recently drawn considerable attention from linguists who are not primarily interested in regional variations of language use (e.g., Fauconnier, 1985; Langacker, 1987; Levinson, 1997; Bickel, 1997). These studies focus on the relation between time and space on the one hand, and language internal structure on the other. The effects of real/social time and space on discourse production via social practice and routinization of daily life are generally overlooked.

One of the everlasting contributions made by ordinary language philosophers in the last century (e.g., Austin, 1962, 1979; Searle, 1969, 1979) and CA oriented sociologists, is the treatment of language use as action. Assessing CA oriented works, Drew and Heritage (1992: 17) remark that:

> *"[t]he decisive feature that distinguishes the CA treatment of interaction and language use from others that are current in the field is what may be termed its* **activity focus.** *... CA begins from a consideration of the* **interactional accomplishment of particular social**

*activities. These activities are embodied in specific social
actions and sequences of social actions." (emphasis
original)*

Attention has been, however, focused on such local mechanisms
(e.g., turn-taking, adjacency pair, self-repair) with the result that more
general and hence more fundamental social processes with actions as
constitutive elements have been generally not touched upon. Social
processes here do not refer to such macro phenomena as ideology,
super structure of society, social stratification, etc., but to "human
socio-cultural ecology" (Carlstein, 1982), "life paths in time-space",
and "time geography" (Hägerstrand, 1975). "Most social analysts,"
Giddens (1984:110) observes, "treat time and space as mere
environments of action and accept unthinkingly the conception of time,
as measurable clock time, characteristic of modern Western culture. ...
social scientists have failed to construct their thinking around the modes
in which social systems are constituted across time-space". This remark
is equally applicable to pragmaticians, discourse analysts and CA
analysts alike. As the writings of Hägerstrand and of his associates
such as Carlstrein "remain unknown to the majority of those working
in the rest of the social sciences, although they contain ideas of very
general application" (Giddens, 1984:111), they are sadly just as obscure
in DA and CA.

Elucidating Hägerstrand's time-geographic model of society and
habitat, Carlstein writes (1982:39) that in ecology, food-energy
relations are conventionally modeled as food chains between different
species. The total system of chains in an ecosystem is referred to as a
food-web. In fact in any population system, one can find another web
which is composed of the paths of the individuals describing their
movements in space over time. Hägerstrand calls his model "a socio-
environmental web model". The essence of the model is that "the
human population is looked upon as a *web of paths* which flow through
a set of time-space locations" (Carlstein, 1982:40; italics original).
"In a time-space region, each individual can be visualized as a
continuous path starting in a point of birth and ending in a point of
death. Depending on the observation period, individual-paths can be

referred to as day-paths, year-paths or life-paths."

In general terms, time and space both constrain and enable human activities. According to Hägerstrand (1975), human activity is basically constrained by:

1. the indivisibility of the human body, and of other living and inorganic entities in the milieux of human existence;
2. the finitude of the life span of the human agent as a "being towards death";
3. the limited capability of human beings to participate in more than one task or activity at once, coupled with the fact that every task has a duration;
4. the fact the movement in space is also movement in time;
5. the limited packing capacity of time-space;
6. the fact that every situation is inevitably rooted in past situations.

The paths of individuals do not, of course, occur as isolated instances. They come into contact with one another and "are coupled into bundles" (Carlstein, 1982:42). Moreover, humans form bundles with materials, equipment, domestic and non-domestic organisms, vehicles, and so on.

> *"The physical environment in which individuals act may be said to consist of **channels of transport and communication and stations**, such as dwellings, work places, establishments for education and welfare, shops, and arrangements for recreation. Individuals reside in these stations, move about or send messages between them in order to collaborate economically and socially, make use of services, or otherwise having their needs and wishes met. These stations appear in the country /or region/ in different numbers and form geographic patterns with varying relative distances, from the high degree of packing and differentiation in city areas to the low degree of packing and lesser differentiation in the sparsely settled regions." (Carlstein's translation of Hägerstrand, 1966; emphasis original)*

As Carlstein points out, "what this approach essentially signifies is an attempt to commence with the more general parameters of human ecological and socio-cultural existence first and then move on towards more specified forms of analysis." (Carlstein, 1982:51). It is exactly the analysis of this human ecological and socio-cultural existence that DA and CA are lacking. This chapter hopes to be an attempt to fill in the gap.

The time-space "stations", e.g., workplaces, in which individuals qua discourse-makers act and talk constrain and enable the way discourse is produced and reproduced. "A rhythmic pattern of behaviour is established, and is transmitted culturally in the form of a known 'timetable' of activities." (Shapcott and Steadman, 1978:49–50). In Mr. X's case, on Mondays and Thursdays, he must report to his post at the General Office before 8:45. His arrival later than this cut-off time will be counted as being late for work and will be penalized. The time/space left for him after the registration, on the other hand, is relatively freer at his own disposal: he can choose to do a range of things inside the building, even things having little to do with his job descriptions. However, should he get outside the building, he is expected to "let someone know" before he departs, otherwise his move is considered undesirable and even unacceptable at times.

Such constraints provide the overall "boundaries" limiting behaviour across time-space. They condition the webs of interaction formed by the trajectories of the daily, weekly, monthly and overall life paths of individuals in their interactions with one another. The trajectories of agents "have to accommodate themselves under the pressures and the opportunities which follow from their common existence in terrestrial space and time". In other words, as Shapcott and Steadman (1978:54, italics original) put it, "the *arrangement* of constraints serves to define the ranges of available opportunity" for human activities.

Mr. X's Trajectories of Weekly Workplace Discourse Paths

The trajectories of Mr. X's audio-taped weekly life paths go like this: He gets up in the morning and talks with his family before going to work. On Monday he goes to Workplace A in Building A. On Tuesday he goes to Workplace B in Building B. He was absent from his work on Wednesday. On Thursday he goes to Workplace A in Building A again. On Friday he goes to Workplace B in Building B again. In the afternoon he goes to the annual review conference of the Firm he works for as his moonlighting job in Building C, and remains working there until Sunday afternoon before returning home in the evening. In the workplaces he does his work and talks with his colleagues. Back home, he goes shopping and talks with shopkeepers. And of course he does other things and talks a lot before going to bed. His daily life is to a large extent routinized, and recycled on daily and weekly bases. Mr. X's trajectories of the weekly workplace discourse activities can be plotted on a time/location plane as in Figure 6.1.

Figure 6.1
Mr. X's Trajectories of Weekly Activities

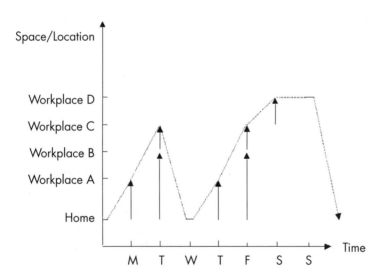

Similar weekly path trajectories can be drawn for Mr. X's colleagues, as for all language users.

Life path trajectories of a population are sometimes converging, sometimes dispersing, and sometimes interwoven. This is so because interactions of individuals moving in time-space compose "bundles" (encounters or social occasions in Goffman's terminology) meeting at "stations" or definite time-space locations within bounded regions (e.g., homes, streets, cities, states, the outer limit of terrestrial space being the earth as a whole). Take Mr. X's Monday morning for example. It is a bundle of 2 hours and 51 minutes' interactions among 6 interactants. The details of the bundle are given in Appendix 1 on page 182. (Mr. X is coded as Zhao in the corpus.) Adopting the graphic representation used by Hägerstrand and Carlstein, the bundle can be described in Figure 6.2:

Figure 6.2
Trajectories of Monday Morning Workplace Discourse in Building A

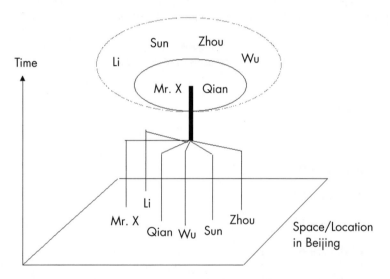

Note: The rectangle represents the space/location of Beijing area. Mr. X, and his colleagues Qian, Wu, Sun, Zhou and Li converge from their homes to the office in Building A to work there. The central solid bar represents the bounded spatial-temporal setting; the dotted line oval captures the bundle of the interactions; the inner solid line oval represents a sub-bundle of interactions with a higher intensity.

Similar graphic representations of the trajectories of workplace discourses can be drawn for the remaining days of the week. As there are many more interactants who are involved, the graphics can be simplified by showing bundles of interaction rather than individuals. Take Saturday for example. Mr. X went to a conference, the annual review meeting of the Firm. It lasted 3 hours and 17 minutes. Three senior managers spoke on the platform to an audience of 480 employees. The conference site was the conference hall of a summer resort in Beijing suburb. Eight buses were used to drive them from the Firm's headquarters to the site.

Figure 6.3
Trajectories of Saturday Workplace Discourse in Building B

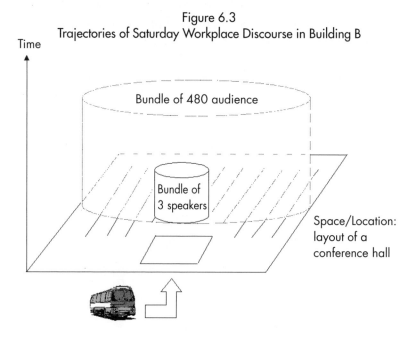

Note: The space/location plane shows the layout of the conference hall. The solid line cylinder represents the bundle of speakers speaking on the physical platform. The dotted line cylinder represents the bundle of the audience of passive participants. The two cylinders represent the social/psychological time-space configuration of workplace discourse.

Workplace Discourse Geography

Time and Space as the Fundamental Organizing Principle of Workplace Discourse

Objections can be foreseen to our stance towards time and space, and towards weekly or yearly or life trajectories. They may seem a bit far removed from the core issues of workplace discourse. As pointed out in the previous section on page 141, we think that they are fundamental. Work is basically organized in time and space, so is workplace discourse. According to the *Beijing Yellow Book 1999*, there are 67,783 work units[3], so are there at least that many workplaces. These units/workplaces are spread in the plane of space/location. Work and workplace discourse start with the working population of several millions pouring and converging in workplaces at scheduled times, and end with the population dispersing home in separate places and at scheduled times. Adopting Shapcott and Steadman's (1978:51) three-dimensional representation scheme, workplace talks/doings can be imagined to be configured in time, space and place, as shown in Figure 6.4.

Figure 6.4
A Potential Spatial-temporal Configuration of Talks/Doings by a Population

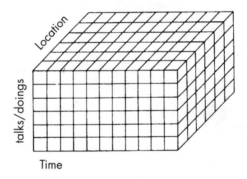

A cell stands for time, location and talks/doings. The cube can be imagined to represent all the potential talks/doings by Beijing working population. The total population in cells in each talk/doing/location plane must obey the population constraint, as shown in Figure 6.5.

---

3. This figure cannot be taken as an accurate one, for the Yellow Book is not exhaustive on account of the fact that military and security units are not listed.

Figure 6.5
Talks/Doings/Location Plane

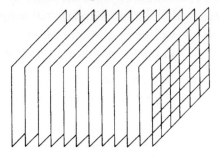

The total population in cells in each location/time plane must obey the time budget constraint for that talk/doing, as shown in Figure 6.6.

Figure 6.6
Location/Time Plane

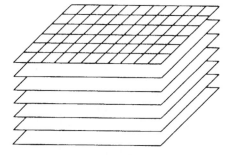

"The daily activity patterns of the population in question," Shapcott and Steadman (1978:50) observe, "may then be imagined as a distribution of that population to the cells of this three-dimensional array, each entry in any cell signifying a number of people engaged in an activity at a particular place and at a specific time of day." In the case of the present study, the talks/doings by Mr. X and his colleagues, having been audio-taped, can be seen as actualizations of some cells, in the meantime the social and spatial-temporal constraints prevent Mr. X and his colleagues from doing otherwise potentially available activities.

Workplace discourse is thus the actualization of some potential talks/doings by a population who make use of the available workplace discourse resources within the social and spatial-temporal constraints. The actualization takes place in a web of bundles that evolve along workplace practices, and the life path trajectories of the population.

Figure 6.7 illustrates some workplace discourses over a time span of 7 a.m. to 24 p.m. The home discourse is included for contrast.

Figure 6.7
Workplace Discourse Geography

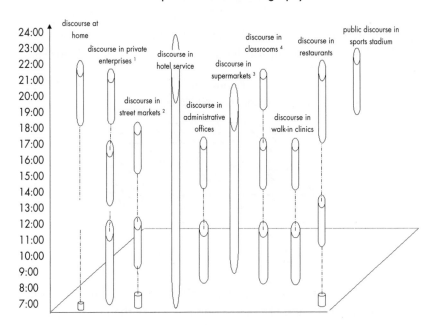

Notes: 1. People in private enterprises work much longer hours than those in state owned ones.
   2. It is only in recent years that street markets in Beijing offer early morning service. This is in sharp contrast with street markets in southern parts of China which have a long tradition of early morning service.
   3. It is also quite a recent phenomenon that supermarkets in Beijing have long non-stop opening hours from 8.00 a.m. to 8.30 p.m. or even 10 p.m.
   4. Evening classes are now taught at primary, secondary and tertiary levels. The practice used to be rare, but is now widespread. All these changes mean, with regard to workplace discourse, that Beijing citizens spend more time/space on workplace discourse than they used to do. In other words, they would spend less time/space on home discourse than they would do previously.

Time, Space and Their Relative Values in Workplace Discourse Production/Consumption

Time and space are physical properties, of course. They enter into the discourse domain when they constrain and enable discourse production and consumption. We need to distinguish, for example, time and space as measurable physical units (abbreviated as T/S-ph hereafter) from time and space as social and psychological dimensions of discourse (abbreviated as T/S-dis hereafter). Compare Mr. X talking to the staff meeting on Tuesday morning with him talking to his family. The amount of time he spent may be the same. Think of time as a constraining and enabling factor on discourse production, and we shall see that the same T-ph does not have the same value of T-dis. Time is less "precious" at home than that at a crowded meeting.

In the Monday morning office, the allocation of physical space to the office personnel is almost equal: for example, the head of the department and the staff share the same amount of space in the same room — each assigned with a desk and a PC computer. The coupling effects created by the close co-presence in the public space, on the other hand, are quite considerable. For example, when two are talking while the others are working, or two talking to their own separate partners, the pressure of the co-presence is felt and calls for mitigating measures to be taken, e.g., lowering voices.

On Saturday, in contrast, the social allocation of the participants to T/S-ph is not equal. The senior directors of the Firm are given some space on the platform, with the managing director sitting at the centre. All the other participants sit in rows separated by aisles. Only three senior directors are given time to speak with the managing director speaking most of the time. The coupling effects created by this unequal allocation of T/S-ph are just as great as in the office situation, but are quite different. The speakers, due to their given prominence under the spotlight of public glare, have to put on their best show, worried about making mistakes and about wasting everyone's time by saying things not interesting to them. The participants sitting in the row, on the other hand, are so close to one another that quite a good number of them conduct a whispered conversation, from time to time sharing comments about the speakers or gossiping about things of their own interest. For the speakers T/S-dis is compact and intense, whereas it can be relaxing or boring to some participants in the rows.

Approaching Workplace Discourse: As a Process and as a Product

The workplace discourse that is audio-taped is an audio snapshot of the flowing stream of events. The snapshot is thus both a process and a product. It is a process in the sense that it was originally an integral part of a larger social process. It is a product in the sense that it was taken out of the larger social process and was frozen for inspection and analysis. Confronting the process/product snapshot, discourse analysts have two, albeit closely related, tasks: (1) work out an analytic framework to anatomise it, and (2) define a set of metalanguage that is adequate for descriptive purposes. The tasks are of such magnitude that it takes years of research to complete. What is attempted here is programmatic at best.

Situatedness

The face-to-face talks actually audio-taped in the workplaces are always some particular individuals' discourses taking place at a particular historical spatial-temporal setting. That is, they are situated, specifically in the sense that they are:

1. situated to the spatial and temporal setting of the work unit;
2. situated to the existing functions and goals of the work unit;
3. situated to the on-going activities of the work unit;
4. situated to the more or less routinized practice of the work unit;
5. situated to actual particular staff members who implement their roles in individualized fashion;
6. situated to an inter-subjective world of discourse;
7. situated to the performance contingencies of speakers who are engaged in spontaneous talking with little pre-planning;
8. situated to the immediate and remote history of the situation.

Time, space, workplace facilities, functions and goals of the workplace, routinized workplace practices, are the main non-personal constraining/enabling factors on the staff members' performance of workplace discourse. There are, on the other hand, personal constraining/enabling factors: members vary, e.g., in their ideological orientation towards work, towards workplace practice, and in their ability in making use of the discourse resources, and in their sociability and communicative ability. Thanks to these diversified constraining/enabling factors, the actual talks recorded from the actual workplaces have a mosaic quality, resisting the classification into hard and fast ready-made categories of discourse. Consider this dialogue:

Thursday 28.wav

B : 某某回來啦 (the so-and-so is back)

A : 嗯 (pardon)

B : 某某哇 (the so-and-so)

A : 啊回來了 (ah back)

B : 回來啦 (back)

A : 某某很年輕的 (the so-and-so's very young)

B : 對 (yeah)

A : 可能比你小吧 (younger than you perhaps)

B : 什麼樣子 (what does she look like)

A : 好像以前是他的學生 (seems to be his former student)
   <10 sds>

B : 好可惜呀 (what a pity)
   應該要早點過來念書 (should have come to study here earlier)
   <start giggling>
   這樣就有機會 (that will give an opportunity)
   嘿嘿… (giggling)

A : 誰呀 (whose opportunity)

B : 誰是誰不管啦 (never mind whose opportunity)
   反正是早點過來念書 (should have come to study here earlier)

誰有機會當他的 (she'll have an opportunity to be his)

A ： 太太 (wife)

B ： 嘿嘿 (giggling)

A ： 我還不幹呢 (I don't want to be)

B ： 你要嗎 (you don't want)

A ： 當然不要 (certainly not)

B ： 哎喲 (oh—)

      我覺得不錯呀 (I think he's not bad)

A ： 你要嗎 (do you want)

B ： 我 — 考慮一下 (I — think about it)

      我已經誇他了一次呀 (I already paid him a compliment)

A ： 誇他什麼啦 (praise him for what)

B ： 偉大的丈夫 (great husband)

A ： 哈哈哈…… (laugh)

From what is being talked about, we can tell that the two speakers are students, and moreover, female unmarried students. The spatial-temporal setting is likely to be their dormitory. As it is, we may very well classify it as dormitory talk. The actual setting is however in Mr. X and his colleagues' office in Building A. The time was on Thursday morning. The office was deserted for the time being except for the presence of the two students. The recorder was left operating, hence the recording of the dialogue (it gave the two a good laugh when the tape was played back).

In another instance, in a walk-in clinic, the doctor practising Chinese medicine was examining his patient. His mobile phone rang. He then did two things at the same time: while he was giving instructions over the phone to his assistant in another city on the business of setting up a new clinic, he intermittently dictated to his assistant the names of the herbs to be used for the patient he was examining.

Official Legitimacy and Prototypicality

How do exchanges of talk like these found in the workplaces fit into workplace discourse or professional discourse? As we suggested at the beginning of the paper, professional discourse is to some degree idealized, with the unwieldy elements like the two instances being weeded out. Workplace discourse is in fact primary at the lower ground level. In order to accommodate the complexity and richness found at this level, we need to make the following distinctions. The activities done by the workplace staff can be described by using five scalar categories:

1. *from the officially prototypical to the officially non-prototypical*, that is from the activities primarily performed to fulfil the social or institutional functions of the work unit, to those performed to maintain the normal operation of the unit.

2. *from the officially acceptable to the officially prohibited*, that is from the activities that are strictly speaking out of place in terms of the function of the unit, but tolerated, to those that are not allowed by the unit.

3. *from the focused to the unfocused*, that is from the activities which have an agreed (written or unwritten) agenda with clearly defined goals, to those without agreed agenda or clearly defined goals.

4. *from talking-oriented to doing-oriented*, that is from the fact that the items and goals being pursued are achieved through talking, to the fact that the items and goals being pursued are achieved through doing.

5. *from the boundary clear to the boundary fuzzy*, that is from the T/S-ph clearly marked with the beginning and ending, to the T/S-ph without any landmarks.

The five are compatible with one another except the first two which are mutually exclusive, i.e., if an activity fits the scale of *from the officially prototypical to the officially non-prototypical*, it cannot at the same time be described as one of *from the officially acceptable to the officially prohibited*. Table 6.2 shows the first two scalar distinctions with reference to the hospital workplace.

Table 6.2
The First Two Scalar Distinctions

Continuum of Activities	Continuum of Doing and Talking
Officially prototypical activities	Doing, e.g., treating the patient's illness according to the standard practice
	Talking, e.g., talking about the symptoms, counselling
Officially non-prototypical activities	Doing, e.g., cleaning, catering
	Talking, e.g., political meeting
Officially tolerated activities	Doing, e.g., lying down or sleeping in the corridor
	Talking, e.g., gossiping, talking over the mobile phone
Officially unacceptable activities	Doing, e.g., smoking, spitting
	Talking, e.g., talking about death

Note: Hospitals in Beijing, and probably all over China, put up notice–boards in the hospital lounge informing patients what the standard practices are that can be expected from doctors. Boards are also found telling the hospital staff and patients a list of "do's" and "don'ts".

Talking/Doing Structure

The fourth scalar distinction between talking and doing drawn above deserves more detailed analysis here, as it is rather complicated in the real life world of workplace discourse. In our corpus data, talking and doing are found to be interwoven in the following ways:

1. *Talking is doing*, e.g., seminar on Thursday afternoon, between 1.30–3.30; annual review meeting on Saturday morning between 8.45–12.00.

2. *Talking is the main constitutive part of the task*, e.g., some classroom discourse, doctor-patient discourse.

3. *Talking is a constitutive part of the task*, which is mostly doing-oriented. Doing is dominant, and talking tends to be fragmented, if taken out of the action sequence, e.g., Mr. X giving instructions from time to time to Qian on how to operate the scanner (see also Appendix 1 on page 182).

4. *Talking and doing run in a conflicting parallel*, the achievement of the latter serves as a means to the goal of the former, e.g., business dinner (i.e., business table talk — eating and talking are conflictive, but they are intended to achieve the same business goal).

5. *Talking is an embedded social part of the task*, e.g., Mr. X talking over the meal with his wife. Note that in comparison with the previous business table talk, this instance of talking serves the social purpose of keeping the husband-wife relation warm.

6. *Talking is a decorative part of the task*, e.g., talking accompanying tea-making.[4]

7. *Talking is a hindrance to the task*, e.g., talking during a written exam.

8. *Talking and doing are independent of each other* (see below).

Talking and doing among the interactants, on the other hand, are interwoven on another dimension: they can be conflictive, parallel, independent, relevant, etc. Let us take a closer look at the first five minute activities carried out early in the Monday morning bundle in Building A.

---

4. Tea-serving restaurants are getting popular again in China. In some expensive ones, tea-making is a very complicated process. To drink Wulong tea, for instance, it will take 18 steps. The tea waitress will chant each step while preparing the tea, e.g., the first step being fendian tanxiang (焚點檀香, meaning "light the fragrant incense"). The purpose of this step is to refresh the air with fragrant smell. All the 18 step names are four-character long, and sound poetic and imaginative. From the names, e.g., wulong ru gong (烏龍入宮) one can hardly figure out what it really refers to without watching the real action. Wulong ru gong literally means "black dragon enters the palace". What it really means is that the waitress puts the black tea into the tea pot! The decorative function of such talk is quite apparent.

Table 6.3
Performance Analysis of Five Minute Activities

Spatial-temporal	Doing		Talking	
	Relations between doing-acts	Doing	Relations between doing and talking	Talking
00:00 – 1:15	Parallel and independent	X helps himself to instant noodles	Conflictive	X and Qian talk about an author's paper
		Qian sorts out the things on the table	Parallel and independent	
1:27 – 2:6	Parallel and independent	X puts away the bowl and the chopsticks	Parallel and independent	X and Qian talk about the journal editing
		Qian switches on the computer		
2:11 – 3:06	Parallel and independent	X sorts out the things on the table	Parallel and independent	Qian gossips about a politician
		Qian sorts out the journal files		
3:19 – 4:25	Parallel and independent	X starts to reinstall his computer	Parallel and relevant	X talks to Qian about the journal layout
		Qian continues sorting out the journal files		
4:34 – 4:40	Parallel and independent	X continues reinstalling	Parallel and relevant	X continues talking to Qian about the journal editing
		Qian continues sorting out the journal file		

It is worth noting that this was the beginning of doing-oriented talking/doing discourse. The sense of the achievement for the day is measured against the amount of doing, i.e., "work", having been carried out. Talking is a constitutive part, not the main part, of the process. However, not all the talks (i.e., instances of talking about specific matters) are constitutive. The staff may occasionally gossip, as Qian does, or take telephone calls, or entertain visitors, etc. Furthermore, changes in their doing may prompt them to talk about something which would have otherwise never have been talked about. Here is the excerpt from a Monday morning discourse. Mr. X was setting a new password for Qian's computer.

Monday 7.wav

		Comments

<11 sds,計算機轉動聲><computer operating sounds for 11 seconds>

Computer was re-booting.

Mr. X : 那個我們剛才想的數字是 456 (that the figure we thought just now was 456)

Qian : 啊 456 (yeah 456)

Mr. X : 456 <輸入聲音>(456) <keyboarding sounds> <7sds>

Qian : 那個原來咱們那個機子 TIEN21 (that our former tien21 in our that computer)
然後呢小馮就不知道 (after that Xiao Feng didn't know)
她就問我好幾次 (she asked me about it several times)
問我好幾次呢 (asking me about it several times yeah)
然後我也不告訴她 (but I didn't tell her)
後來在那兒苦思苦想 (then thought very hard)
最後她自己破譯了 (eventually she cracked it herself)

The setting of the password prompts Qian to talk about her former colleague's anecdote with the password.

Mr. X : 啊 (ah)

Qian : 嗯 (yeah)
<6 sds>

Mr. X : <咯咯笑> <giggling>

Qian : 啊 (yeah)
噢今天是不是你兒子生日呀 (ohh today is your son's birthday isn't it)

The former password tien 21 makes Qian suddenly recall the birthday of Mr. X's son, which triggers off a new topic.

Mr. X ： 對(right)

Qian ： 我想起來了您不是說情人節
嗎? (I remember you said it's
Valentine Day)

Mr. X ： 對(right)

Qian ： 哎，你兒子生日這個日子挺好
(aih, your son's birthday is a
very good day)

The sudden switch from one topic to another, visitors' intruding discourse (see page 168), inter-bundling discourse sharing (see page 173) are generally true of non-talking-oriented unfocused workplace discourse. When the talks of this kind are separated from their hosting sequence of events, they may sound incoherent or abrupt and sometimes even incomprehensible to outsiders.

Capturing Workplace Dynamics

The time/space of workplace offers natural anchoring landmarks for assessing the process/product snapshot, e.g., beginning, closing, stages of the process, etc. For Mr. X and his colleagues, the official time to begin work in office is 8:45 am, and the lunch time is between 12:00–13:30. The afternoon work begins at 13:30 and ends at 16:45. Talking/doing that falls within the office time/space is office time/space talking/doing. Talking/doing that spills over the margins is ultra (pre/post) office time/space activities. In the current work practice in China, doing things that have nothing to do with one's job within office/time space invites sanctions and criticisms, and doing one's job in ultra office time/space deserves discovery[5] and rewards (e.g., praise from the authority, a free meal, bonus, etc.).

The office time/space, talking/doing distinction, and the five scales discussed on page 155 offer the initial grid in which workplace discourse can be anatomized. For demonstrative purposes, this initial grid is applied to Mr. X's Monday morning discourse and Thursday afternoon's discourse respectively.[6] Details concerning the two discourses are spelt out in Appendices 1 and 2.

The Monday morning discourse is unfocused, with the T/S-ph boundary fuzzy. The officially non-prototypical talking takes more time/space than the officially prototypical talking. The officially prototypical doing is obviously a dominant activity. Most of the doing by the interactants is carried out separately, and independent from talking. The officially accepted doing (2 instances), intruding discourse (4 instances), and inter-bundle discourse sharing (3 instances) are found. Pre-office time/space talking/doing is present. This shows that the staff arrived in the office earlier. However, they left earlier than the official time for lunch. Table 6.4, based on Appendix 1, tabularizes the configuration of talking/doing.

In comparison with the Monday morning discourse, Thursday afternoon discourse poses a sharp contrast. It is a focused seminar on American functionalism, and the T/S-ph boundary is clear. The room serves as an exclusive space/location for the purpose. All the talking/doing is officially prototypical, with doing related and subordinate to talking. There are pre-office time/space talks/doings, but these were carried out in separate offices. As on Monday morning, the staff left earlier than the official time for home. Table 6.5, based on Appendix 2, tabularizes the configuration of talking/doing.

The tabular representation of the two discourses treats discourse as a product. It fails to show the dynamic process that generates the product. However, it can be amended with the graphic representation scheme used by time geographers, as shown in Figures 6.8 and 6.9 respectively.

5. The word *discovery* is used here because the doer is not supposed to advertise his/her extra work in order to attract attention. It should be left for others to discover and let the authorities know.

6. The two are selected on the ground that one is the unfocused doing-oriented, and the other focused talking-oriented.

Table 6.4
The Initial Grid for Describing Monday Morning Talking/Doing

Time/space anchoring	T/S indicator		Talking/doing ▸ Prototypical T	Prototypical D	Non-proto-Typical T	Non-proto-Typical D	Officially accepted T	Officially accepted D	Officially prohibited T	Officially prohibited D	Intruding T	Intruding D	Inter-bundle sharing T	Inter-bundle sharing D
Pre-office time/space	8:35		+		+	+		+						
Office time/space	8:45				+	+					+			
	9:00		+		+	+								
	9:15		+		+	+								
	9:30		+		+	+								
	9:45		+		+	+					+			
	10:00	boundary fuzzy / unfocused			+						+			
	10:15				+						+			
	10:30				+	+							+	
	10:45				+	+		+					+	
	11:00				+	+							+	
	11:15				+	+								
	11:45													
	12:00													
	lunch													

Table 6.5
The Initial Grid for Describing Thursday Afternoon Talking/Doing

Time/space anchoring	T/S indicator	Talking/doing											
		Prototypical		Non-proto-Typical		Officially accepted		Officially prohibited		Intruding		Inter-bundle sharing	
		T	D	T	D	T	D	T	D	T	D	T	D
Pre-office time/space	12:54-13:30	+		+	+					+		+	
Office time/space	13:30	+	+										
	13:45	+	+										
	14:00	+	+										
	14:15	+	+										
	14:30	+	+										
	14:45	+	+										
	15:00	+	+										
	15:15	+	+										
	15:30												
	15:45												
	16:00												
	16:15												
	16:30												
	16:45												
Post office time/space													
Home													

(T/S indicator column for Office time/space reads vertically: "boundary clear to focused")

Figure 6.8
The Talking/Doing Configuration of Monday Morning Discourse

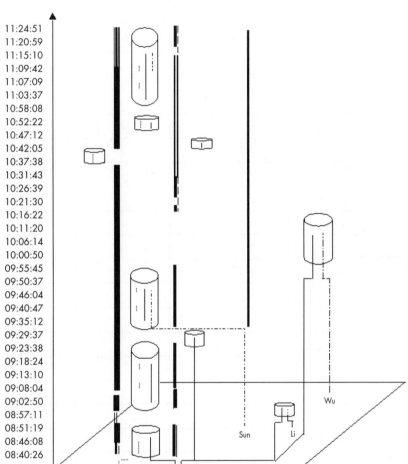

Note: Different shapes of black bars = various doings by Mr. X, Qian and Sun; different sizes
         of cylinders = various talks among Mr. X, Qian, Sun, Li and Wu.

Figure 6.9
The Talking/Doing Configuration of Thursday Afternoon

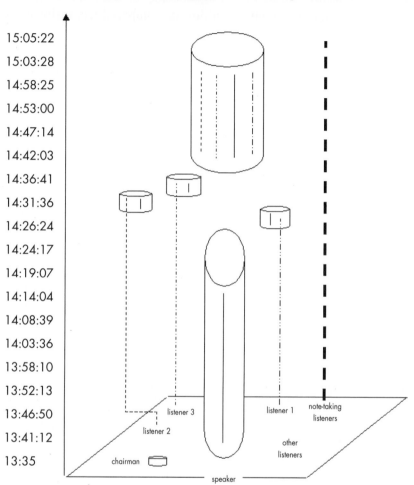

Note: Different sizes of cylinders = various talks among the speaker, listeners 1, 2, 3, and others; the broken bar = note-taking by some listeners.

The advantage of graphic representation lies in the fact that the dynamic configurations of talking/doing over time are iconically captured. Types of discourse can thus be compared iconically at an immediate glance.

Tripartite Approach to Workplace Discourse to be Amended

In a way, the analytic grid demonstrated in previous section can be used to differentiate, in descriptive terms, one type of workplace discourse from another. It is however not fine-tuned enough to capture the way workplace discourse evolves on a turn-by-turn basis. For this purpose, the present author has elsewhere (Gu, 1996, 1997, 1999a) outlined a scheme of tripartite analyses. Given a situated workplace discourse, the task of a discourse analyst is to construct a know-that account of how the know-how participants conduct their joint discourse in pursuit of their communicative and extra-communicative goals. The account can be constructed on a three-line analysis: goal development analysis, talk exchange development analysis, and interpersonal management analysis. The analytic scheme is shown graphically in Figure 6.10 (see Gu, 1997, 1999a for details).

Workplace/situated discourse is a goal-directed and dynamic social process. The issues of how goals are developed, how talk exchanges are developed, and how interpersonal management is carried out, of course, vary from person to person, hence from one discourse to another. Goal development primarily refers to the process of pursuing extra-communicative goals. It captures the interface between linguistic communication (in Habermas's sense, (Habermas, 1984)) and social interaction at large. Talk exchange development captures the actual talking among participants. Interpersonal management refers to interpersonal tie work on the basis of the participants' recognition of each other as responsible subject, and of their relative social positions and roles in that particular transaction.

With fresh workplace data and hindsight, the main weakness of the tripartite approach lies in it being unable to handle the doing-oriented discourse or talking/doing mixed discourse. It needs to be

Figure 6.10
A Tripartite Analysis of Workplace/Situated Discourse
Workplace/Situated Discourse as a Joint Purposeful Social Process

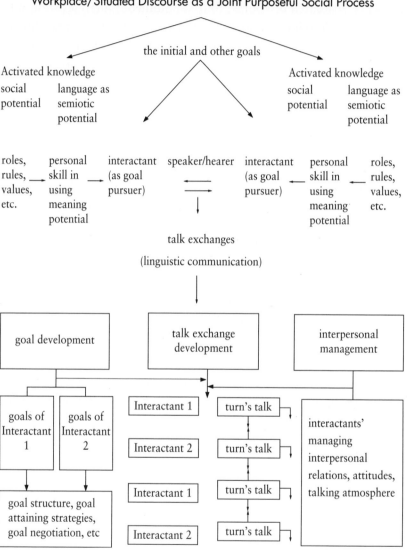

supplemented with one more dimension of analysis, viz. talking/doing development analysis. So, given a piece of naturally occurring workplace/situated discourse, four simultaneous analyses should be made, doing/talking development analysis (some way on the line of analysis given on page 156), goal development analysis, talk exchange development analysis and interpersonal management analysis. More research is required before it can become a viable frame of analysis.

Workplace Identity and Intruding Discourse

In a workplace where two or more people work separately, or occasionally jointly, the enclosure and division of space creates together-ness, belonging-ness, i.e., a sense of workplace identity, which emerges strongly when the flow of the work is interrupted by visitors or telephone calls. For example, the workplace members can gossip among themselves and enjoy it. When visitors come and gossip, on the other hand, this can cause resentment among the uninvolved members. Resentment also arises when visitors come for serious business but talk too loudly. This even holds true of the cases in which the visitors/intruders and hosts belong to the same organization or institution. Instances are found in the Monday and Thursday bundles of workplace discourse in Building A.

Mr. X was asking Qian about the location of the journals when Li stepped in. Both know the visitor very well, since they all work for the same institution.

X Monday 4.wav

Comments

......

X : (對錢)......喂我們那些雜誌放在哪一層啊 (To Qian)...... hi which floor are our journals put
我要查的一些書啊 (I'd like to check for some books)

Qian is checking files. X's question slips her attention.

(李走進來) (Li comes in)

    喂你好 (hi how're you) ......

    怎麼樣(How're things getting on)

    新年怎麼樣的 (How was the New Year OK)

> Li's entering draws Qian's attention away from X's question put to her.
> X knows Li very well. But Li comes to talk to Qian, not to him.

Li : 還行 (So so)

X : 阿 (I see)

Li : 過年了 (the New Year)

    歇着 (have a rest)

    玩兒 (have fun)

X : 歇着玩的 (aha rest, have fun)

    (笑聲)(laugh)

......

> X raises the question of locating journals again. Qian and Li help him with it.

Li : mm

> Li signals to Qian that he wants to talk to her alone.

(3:29-5:30 小聲跟我説話，聽不清楚) *(Li talks with Qian in low voice. Not clear.)*

> The two talk in such a low voice that the recording is illegible.

Li : 哎謝謝你啊 (yeah thank you very much)

Qian：不送 (don't see you off)

The italics shows the intruding discourse. Since the talkers share space with the rest of the office members, they have to lower their voice (1) to reduce interference, and (2) to create a sphere of privacy for themselves. Considering the flow of workplace discourse, Li's visit interrupts X's original topic and the talk exchanges between him and Qian. Mr. X has to suspend his talk with Qian and initiates small talk with the visitor, before leaving them to talk between themselves.

Here is another instance of intruding discourse. Mr. X was preparing the office scanner to do some scanning for Qian, and at the same time to teach Qian how to operate it by herself. Their work was interrupted by Wu's visit. As in the previous example, Wu also works for the same institution. Wu is a senior and respected staff member.

X Monday 15.wav	**Comments**
X ： 我來給你把這個掃描 (Let me do this scanning for you)	
再給你弄好 (and do that for you ......)	Accompanying the action
Qian： 好來 (good)	
X ： 給你 (here you are)	Accompanying the action
再一個就是 (another thing is)	Accompanying the action
那個白的打開 (open that white thing)	Accompanying the action
做掃描 (do the scanning)	Accompanying the action
掃描儀 (the scanner)	Accompanying the action
(Wu 走進來)(Wu comes in)	
Qian： 吳老師 (Teacher Wu)	
Wu ： 你好 (how're you)	
Qian： 你好 (how're you)	
過年好 (Happy New Year)	
X ： 嘿 (hi)	
Wu ： 拜個晚年吧 (give you a late-coming greeting)	
......	
Qian： 應該説你那個房子 *(it should be said that your flat)* ...	Qian sits on the house allocation committee. Wu wants to know the committee's recommendation about his flat.
Wu ： 怎麼樣 *(how're things going)*	

Qian and Wu had a long conversation while Mr. X was doing the scanning. Unlike the first instance, neither of the two lowered their voice (which is largely due to Wu's seniority). The recording was quite intelligible. As Wu was conscious of the inconvenience his visit caused, he was quite apologetic from time to time. For example:

X Monday 18. wav

......

Qian：為什麼為什麼這次這次決定呢 (that's why why this time the decision this time)

Wu　：X老師，我吵你一下啊 (Teacher X I disturb you with my loud talk for once)

X　　：沒問題 (no problem)

Incoming telephone calls can also be counted as intruding discourse. On Thursday afternoon, Wang and Qian are talking separately to their partners when the telephone rings.

X thurs aftnn 7.wav

......

Wang：這個問題呢 (about this question)

<有女人低聲說話的聲音> <a female voice is heard talking in a low voice>

　　　我們明年才能行 (we'll do it next year)

Qian：那個呆會兒 (that just a minute)

　　　給我那個把你那個分的住的那個房子...... (give me that your that allocated flat ......)

<電話鈴響> <telephone rings>

　　　對 (right)

<接電話> <pick up the phone>

　　　喂 (hello)

　　　是我 (speaking)

　　　你不用着急 (don't worry)

　　　你等會兒打電話就是了(you can call it later)

他可能吃飯還沒回來 (it's likely he is out for lunch)

......

好 (OK)

就這樣啊 (that's it)

<掛電話> <hang up>

Qian : 這還是辦公室呢 (this is an office)

要是在家更找不着這幫人......(one can never find these folks at home)

Intruding discourse often produces follow-up backlash or echo effects. The three instances above all have the follow-up echo effects. In the first instance, immediately after Li left, Qian says to Mr. X:

X Monday 5.wav

......

Qian : (對 X) 他讓我看他的請調報告 (he lets me see his resigning letter)

<不清楚，Qian, X 笑> <not clear, Qian and X are heard laughing>

X　　: 啊 (yeah)

Qian : 不過 (but)

他確實是 (really he's)

有句話 (to say)

我説句實在話(to speak my mind)

鑒於他自己年齡(considering his age)

......

Qian and Mr. X go on gossiping over the matter for a further while before resuming their normal work.

Note that not all visitors to workplaces bring in intruding discourse. Whether it is intruding or not depends on the function/goal of the workplace concerned, and on any prior appointment required. Take a walk-in clinic, or a department store. Visitors are always welcome provided that the goal of the visit fits the function of the clinic or the department store. The distinction of intruding discourse is necessary and useful when the way workplace discourse develops is examined (see also page 156 on talking/doing/structure).

Inter-bundle Discourse Sharing

Intruding discourse imposes its immediate presence on its host discourse. There is another way of merging one discourse into another, viz. *inter-bundle discourse sharing.* When people converge in workplaces, they bring some of the products generated in other interactive bundles to share with the workmates. Here are some examples.

Qian and Wu had a talk about his flat allocation a few days ago. When she and Mr. X came to work on Monday, she told him this story:

Qian (to Mr. X):

現在呢我愛人單位説了 (Now the work unit where my wife works said this)
原來交的那兩套平房 (the two flats previously handed in)
現在原封退給你們 (were now going to be returned to *you* in the original form)
然後我們一算某某單位就虧了 (then *we* did some calculation only to find the so-and-so work unit is going to lose)

Comments

Qian uses direct speech to report Wu's words as if she were Wu talking to Mr. X.

"*Nimen*" (i.e., you) refers to the work unit where Wu works.

"*Women*" (i.e., we) refers to the flat allocation committee. Qian here is reporting the committee's discourse to Mr. X.

Qian then goes on to retell her talk at the flat allocation meeting to Mr. X by using indirect speech:

Qian (to Mr. X):

> 我說如果你們領導拍板同意 (*I said* if you the authorities decided to give him)
>
> 我們分房委員吧不反對 (we the flat allocation committee would not object to it)
>
> 最後反正責任所裏兜着 (Eventually if anything happens, the work unit will shoulder the responsibility)

Inter-bundling discourse sharing is also found in a more formal speech. Mr. Feng is making an annual work review speech on Saturday morning.

Mr. Feng (to an audience of employees)

> 我們是當英語教師
> (*We* are teachers of English)
> 20年30年沒有聽過的
> (have never listened to it for last 20 or 30 years)

"*Women*"(i.e., we) refers to the teachers who talked to Mr. Feng during his visit to their university). Mr. Feng is using direct speech to report his talk with them.

> 有的教師甚至說聽某某《單位名》這樣的高層次的教授的報告 (*some* even said that listening to so senior professor's talk)
> 今生今世也就這麼一次 (will be only once in a life-time)

Mr. Feng switches to indirect speech.

It must be pointed out that, unlike the direct and indirect speech used to portray characters in literary works, they are part of discourse/language reproduction process in workplaces, and serve among other functions as in our data, as gossiping materials or are used to prove a point or forward an instruction.

Some Theoretical Issues and Implications

So far we have looked at workplace discourse in the light of human life and existence over time and space. Now it is time to look at it from the point of view of language production, consumption, reproduction, and spoken corpus compilation in particular. As pointed out above, work is a fundamental necessity in human existence, so is workplace discourse. It can also be said that it plays a fundamental role in language production, consumption and reproduction. There is a general tendency emerging, at least in Beijing, that time/space spent on home discourse is dwindling. Workplace discourse sucks in most of the waking time/space of the working population. Routinized workplace practice leads to routinized workplace discourse, which is in turn embodied in routinized patterns of discourse production, consumption and reproduction.

In the long history of linguistics, the postulates of dualism, viz. langue vs. parole, abstract system vs. actual use, collective mind vs. individual user, have been taken for granted. Human agency has been given a marginized role in studies of language. We are so used to saying that language does this or that, almost forgetting the fact that it is human language users who do things in and by language. Once human agency is given its due prominence, we face the problem of whose language it is. Take Beijing with a population of over ten million. It is no exaggeration to say that you can find people with all kinds of background there. Is the discourse they produce in the workplace an instantiation of an abstract language system, as assumed by the Saussurean and Hallidayan tradition (for a critical review of the issue see Gu 1999a, 1999b)? When we look at workplace discourse in its original, situated, un-idealized form, we cannot help doubting the validity of the old wisdom. When people come to workplaces to work, what they bring in to operate with is their internalized "languages" which are on-going temporary products of the trajectories of the life paths taken up to the spatial-temporal point of speaking. The extent to which they can successfully communicate with one another depends largely on the shared intersection of the trajectories of their life paths. In our data, it is found that within a family, Father may talk with a strong Jiangsu accent, Mother with a North China accent, and children with local accents. Father speaks with such a strong accent that he is quite often misunderstood by his colleagues and even by his children from time to time. He is however seldom misunderstood by his wife thanks to the shared intersection of their life path trajectories.

Figure 6.11
Shared Intersection of the Trajectories of Life Paths

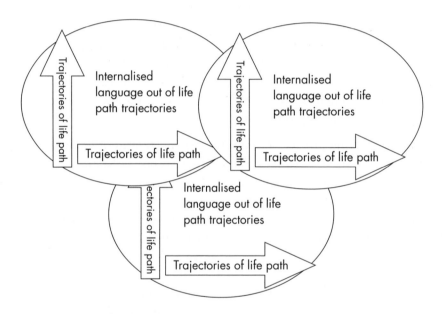

Given three people, we can draw Figure 6.11 to illustrate the point made above.

The overall picture of language use emerges like this. The standard language, viz. Putonghua, is a construct made by grammarians/linguists for political, educational and communicative purposes. It is prototypically the discourse of the workplaces such as national radio and TV stations. Since it is made available through radio and TV, it is imposed on people who have access to the media. In our analysis, the interaction between radio/TV discourse and the discourses of other workplaces is an inter-discourse sharing phenomenon. To what extent the latter is affected by the imposed former remains to be investigated.

Viewed from the perspective of individual language users, it is the intersections of their life path trajectories that make their communication possible and meaningful. We have no reason to believe that there exists an abstract language system that lies in store for them to make use of when they produce discourse. They activate the internalized "languages" in response to the situated needs. The internalized languages, as pointed out above, are the on-going, constantly updating processes/products along their life path trajectories.

This view of language use challenges the standard variety approach to corpus compilation. Chafe, Dubois and Thompson (1991:69), compilers of the Corpus of Spoken American English, introduce their design thus:

> "*Spoken SAE encompasses formal and informal styles, preaching, cursing, bureaucratese, slang, Southern accents, New York accents, and a host of regional, class, gender and ethnic accents. What unifies it is a shared set of grammatical rules and structures, which among spoken varieties of American English come closer than any other to the written variety as used in journalism, government publications, textbooks, and so on, while of course still differing from the written variety in the many ways that speaking may differ from writing. Because SAE encompasses a variety of accents, registers and styles, it is not the sole property of any particular group in American society. For every ethnic group of any size in the United States, there are members who speak SAE and members who do not.*"

This standard variety approach, though advantageous in its own way, is subject to serious criticisms relating to the reservation of the naturalness of language use. The standard variety, e.g., SAE, is given its identity before the corpus is compiled. The corpus cannot be used to represent its naturalness, nor be used to establish or demonstrate its identity. One cannot point to the corpus and say: Look, this is what

SAE looks like. One can only say: This is what the compilers believe
SAE looks like. Subjective judgment is also involved in sampling SAE
speakers by filtering non-standard speakers out. When they are being
audio-taped, the assumed SAE speakers may be interacting with non-
standard speakers. Unless they are "commissioned" to talk among
themselves, the activities the standard and non-standard interactants
are engaged in have to be properly filtered as well.

Sinclair (1991:13) writes:

> *"The specification of a corpus — the types and
> proportions of material in it — is hardly a job for linguists
> at all, but more appropriate to the sociology of culture.
> The stance of the linguist should be a readiness to describe
> and analyze any instances of language placed before him
> or her. In the infancy of the discipline of corpus linguistics,
> the linguists have to do the text selection as well; when
> the impact of the work is felt more widely, it may be
> possible to hand over this responsibility to language-
> oriented social scientists."*

The job is probably more profitably done jointly by linguists and
language-oriented scientists. But anyway for the time being, corpus-
compiling linguists have to make serious and difficult decisions. The
sampling strategy we have adopted is alluded to workplace discourse
geography on page 147 above. The 67,783 work units listed in the
Beijing Yellow Book 1999 and the workplace discourse distributions
of space/location over time (illustrated in Figure 6.7) are adopted as
guides for sampling. The details concerning the sampling and other
issues in compiling a spoken corpus of situated discourse cannot of
course be spelt out here and have to be dealt with elsewhere.

References

1. Anward, J. 1997. Parameters of institutional discourse. In *The construction of professional discourse*, edited by B.-L. Gunnarsson, P. Linell and B. Nordberg, London, NY: Longman, 127–150.

2. Atkinson, J. M. and J. Heritage, eds. 1984. *Structures of social action.* Cambridge: Cambridge University Press.

3. Austin, J. L. [1962] 1980. *How to do things with words*. Oxford: Oxford University Press.

4. Bell, A. 1991. *The language of news media*. Oxford: Blackwell.

5. Bell, D. V. J. 1995. Negotiation in the workplace: The view from a political linguist. In *The discourse of negotiation: Studies of language in the workplace*, edited by A. Firth. Oxford: Pergamon, 41–58.

6. Bickel, B. 1997. Spatial operations in deixis, cognition, and culture: Where to orient oneself in Belhare. In *Language and Conceptualization*, edited by J. Nuyts and E. Pederson. Cambridge: Cambridge University Press, 46–84.

7. Boden, D. 1994. *The business of talk: Organizations in action*. Cambridge: Polity Press.

8. _____ and D. H. Zimmerman, eds. 1991. *Talk and social structure: Studies in ethnomethodology and conversation analysis*. Cambridge: Polity Press.

9. Bryant, C. G. A. and D. Jary, eds. 1991. *Giddens' theory of structuration: A critical appreciation*. Routledge.

10. Carlstein, T. 1982. *Time resources, society and ecology*. London: George Allen & Unwin.

11. _____, D. Parkes and N. Thrift, eds. 1978a. *Human activity and time geography*. London: Arnold.

12. _____ , D. Parkes and N. Thrift, eds. 1978b. *Making sense of time*. London: Arnold.

13. Chafe, W. L., J. W. du Bois and S. A. Thompson. 1991. Towards a new corpus of spoken American English. In *English corpus linguistics: Studies in honour of Jan Svartvik*, edited by K. Aijmer and B. Altenberg. London: Longman, 64–82.

14. Coulthard, M. 1977. *An introduction to discourse analysis*. London: Longman.

15. Drew, P. and J. Heritage, eds. 1992. *Talk at work*. Cambridge: Cambridge University Press.

16. Fairclough, N. 1989. *Language and power*. London: Longman.

17. Fauconnier, G. 1985. *Mental spaces: Aspects of meaning construction in natural Language*. Cambridge, Mass: MIT Press.

18. Firth, A., ed. 1995. *Discourse of negotiation: Studies of language in the workplace*. London: Pergamon.

19. Fisher, S. and A. D. Todd, 1983., eds. *The social organization of doctor-patient communication*. Washington DC: Centre for Applied Linguistics.

20. _____ . 1986., eds. *Discourse and institutional authority*. New Jersey: Ablex Publishing Corporation.

21. Freidson, E. 1970. *Profession of medicine: A study of the sociology of applied knowledge*. New York: Harper & Row.

22. Gibbons, J., ed. 1994. *Language and the law*. London: Longman.

23.   Gibbons, J. 1984. *The constitution of society*. Cambridge: Polity Press.

24.   _____ . 1991. *Modernity and self-identity*. Cambridge: Polity Press.

25.   Goffman, E. 1967. *Interaction ritual: Essays on face to face behaviour*. New York: Anchor Books.

26.   _____ . 1974. *Frame analysis*. New York: Harper and Row.

27.   _____ . 1981. *Forms of talk*. Philadelphia: University of Pennsylvania Press.

28.   Graham, B. and J. R. E. Lee, eds. 1987. *Talk and social organization*. Clevedon: Multilingual Matters Ltd.

29.   Gu, Y. 1996. Doctor-patient interaction as goal-directed discourse. *Journal of Asian Pacific Communication* 7 (3) & (4): 156–176.

30.   _____ . 1997. Five ways of handling a bedpan. *Text* 17 (4): 457–475.

31.   _____ . 1999a. Towards a model of situated discourse. In *The semantics/ pragmatics interface from different points of view*, edited by K. Turner. Oxford: Elsevier, 150–178.

32.   _____ . 1999b. Users'– discourse: Its status in linguistic theorization. *Contemporary Linguistics* 3:3–14.

33.   Gumperz, J. J. 1982. *Discourse strategies*. Cambridge: Cambridge University Press.

34.   Gunnarsson, B-L. 1997. On the sociohistorical construction of scientific discourse. In *The construction of professional discourse*, edited by B.-L. Gunnarsson, P. Linell and B. Nordberg, 99–126.

35.   _____ , P. Linell and B. Nordberg, eds. 1997. *The construction of professional discourse*. London: Longman.

36.   Habermas, J. 1984. *The theory of communicative action, vol. 1: Reason and the rationalization of society*, translated by T. McCarthy. London: Heinemann.

37.   Hägerstrand, T. 1975. Space, time and human conditions. In *Dynamic allocation urban space*. Farnborough: Saxon House.

38.   Halliday, M. A. K. 1973. *Explorations in the functions of language*. London: Edward Arnold.

39.   _____ and R. Hasan. 1989. *Language, context and text*. 2nd ed. Oxford: Oxford University Press.

40.   Heritage, J. 1984. *Garfinkel and ethnomethodology*. Cambridge: Polity Press.

41.   Kim, M. S., D. H. Smith and Y. Gu 1999. Medical decision making and Chinese patients' self-construals. *Health Communication* 11 (3): 249–260.

42.   Hodge, R. and G. Kress. 1992. *Language as Ideology*. 2nd ed. London: Routledge.

43.   Langacker, R. W. 1987. *Foundations of cognitive grammar*. Stanford: Stanford University Press.

44.   Levinson, S. 1997. From outer to inner space: Linguistic categories and non-

linguistic thinking. In *Language and conceptualization,* edited by J. Nuyts and E. Pederson. Cambridge, NY: Cambridge University Press, 13–45.

45. Mishler, E. G. 1984. *The discourse of medicine*: Dialectics of medical interviews. Norwood: Ablex Publishing Corporation.

46. Nuyts, J. and E. Pederson, eds. 1997. *Language and conceptualization.* Cambridge: Cambridge University Press.

47. Parret, H., ed. 1993. *Pretending to communicate.* Berlin: Walter de Gruyter.

48. Pendleton, D. and J. Hasler, eds. 1983. *Doctor-patient communication.* London: Academic Press, Inc.

49. Penman, R. 1990. Facework and politeness: Multiple goals in courtroom discourse. In Tracy and Coupland, eds., 15–38.

50. Pietro, R. J. D., ed. 1982. *Linguistics and professions.* New Jersey: Ablex Publishing Corporation.

51. Scollon, R. 1998. *Mediated discourse as social interaction.* London: Longman.

52. Searle, J. R. 1969. *Speech acts.* Cambridge: Cambridge University Press.

53. _____ . 1979. *Expression and meaning: Studies in the theory of speech acts.* Cambridge: Cambridge University Press.

54. Shapcott, M. and P. Steadman. 1978. Rhythms of urban activity. In Carlstein, Parkes and Thrift, eds. pp. 49–74

55. Sinclair, J. 1991. *Corpus, concordance, collocation.* Oxford: Oxford University Press.

56. Stewart, M. and D. Roter, eds. 1989. *Communicating with medical patients.* London: Sage Publications.

57. van Dijk, T. A. 1993. *Elite discourse and racism.* Newbury Park, Calif: Sage Publications.

58. _____ , ed. 1985. *Handbook of discourse analysis,* 4 vols. London: Academic Press Limited.

59. _____ . 1988. *News as discourse.* Hillsdale, NJ: Lawrence Erlbaum Associates.

60. _____ , ed. 1997. *Discourse as social interaction.* London: Sage Publications.

61. _____ , ed. 1997. *Discourse as structure and process.* London: Sage Publications.

62. West, C. 1984. *Routine complications: Troubles with talk between doctors and patients.* Bloomington: Indiana University Press.

63. Weston, W. W. and J. B. Brown 1989. The importance of patients' beliefs. In *Communicating with medical patients,* edited by M. Stewart and D. Roter. London: Sage Publications, 77–85.

64. Wodak, R., ed. 1989. *Language, power and ideology.* Amsterdam: John Benjamins Publishing Company.

Appendix 1: Monday Morning Talking/Doing Record

Clock time	No. of files	Doing	Talking (30 60 90 120 150 180 210 240 270 300 330)
8:40:26	326	X helps himself to noodles, Qian sorts out things on the table	X talks about journal editing (T1, 00–1:15); X talks about editing on computer (T2, 1:27–2:6); Qian gossips about a politician (T3, 2:11–3:06); X talks about journal business (T4,); X inquires about their colleague (T5, 4:34–4:40)
8:46:08	342	X reinstalls computer; Qian continues to sort out things on the table	Qian talks about house allocation (T6, :09–2:15); Qian answers the phone (T7, 2:16–2:32); Qian talks about house allocation (T6, 2:33–5:38)
8:51:19	311	X and Qian continue what they are doing	Qian talks about house allocation (T6, :03–1:24); Qian gossips about a colleague's intention to quit the job (T8, 1:26–5:11)
8:57:11	352	X sorts out things on his table, Qian stops and talks with the visitor	Qian gossips about the colleague's intention to quit the job (T8, :00–00:17); X inquires about the library service/X & Qian greeting Li (T9, T10, 1:49–2:14); X inquires about the library service (T9, 2:24–3:17); Qian and Li talked in low voice (T11, 3:29–5:30, not clear); Qian told X what they talked about (T12, 5:38–5:42)
9:02:50	339	X intermittently checks the reinstalling process; Qian checks her files	Qian gossips about the colleague's quitting the job (T8, :00–00:47); X talks about the proof-reading problem (T13, 2:25–3:54); X talks about the royalties (T14, 4:06–4:14); Qian told X the thing she forgot to tell him earlier (T15,)
9:08:04	314	X out and back, Qian continues	Qian told X the thing she forgot to tell him earlier (T15, :00–00:26); X talks about proof reading (T13, 00:41–2:29); X talks about a password for computer (T16, 3:04–4:28); Qian talks about keyboarding papers (T17,)

Clock time	No. of files	Doing	Talking
9:13:10	306	X continues reinstalling; Qian does proof-reading	Qian talks about keyboarding papers (T17,) and corpus data collection (T18, :02–1:48); X talks about password for computer (T16, 2:08–2:41); Qian talks about password to X's son's birthday (T16, T19, 2:53–3:03); X talks about how to reset the password (T16,)
9:18:24	314	As above	Qian talks about house allocation (T :18–3:00)
9:23:38	314	As above	Qian talks about the shortage of research papers (T20, :21–1:02); Qian talks about the rejected paper and made a phone call (T21, T22, 2:38–5:11)
9:29:37	359	X continues reinstalling; Qian makes a phone call	Qian talks on the phone (T22, :00–00:35); Qian tells X about the phone call (T23, 00:39–00:57); Qian asked for password (T24, 2:57–; Qian and X greet Sun, then talk about computer and proof-reading (T25, 4:01–5:59)
9:35:12	335	X continues reinstalling; Qian does proof-reading	Qian, X and Sun talk about proof reading (T25, :00–2:00)
9:40:47	335	X and Qian as above; Sun comes in	X and Sun gossip (T26, 3:50–5:8)
9:46:04	317	X and Qian as above; Sun reads	X, Qian and Sun gossip about flu, and about journal CD-Rom (T27, T28, :00–4:)
9:50:37	273	As above	X and Sun talk about computer virus (T29, 1:45–2:10)
9:55:45	308	As above	X receives a phone call (T30, 2:19–2:36); X and Qian greet Wu (T31,); Wu and Qian talk about house allocation (T32, 2:30–5:08)
10:00:50	304	X and Sun as above; Qian talks with a visitor	Qian and Wu talk about house allocation (T32, :00–5:04)
10:06:14	324	As above	Qian and Wu talk about house allocation (T32, :00–5:24)

Talking timeline scale: 30, 60, 90, 120, 150, 180, 210, 240, 270, 300, 330

Clock time	No. of files	Doing	Talking
10:11:20	306	As above	Qian and Wu talk about house allocation (T32, :00–5:06)
10:16:22	302	As above; Wu left; X and Qian operate scanner	Qian and Wu talk about house allocation (T32, :00–4:15); X and Qian talk over scanning (T33, 4:16–5:02)
10:21:30	308	As above	X commenting on scanning, intermingled with Qian talking about house allocation (T33, T32, :00–5:08); X and Qian talk about how to scan papers (T33, 3:40–5:08)
10:26:39	309	X and Sun as above; Qian does layout	X showing Qian how to operate the scanner (T34, :00–4:06)
10:31:43	304	As above	X receives a phone call (T35, 4:38–5:54)
10:37:38	355	As above	X receives a phone call (T35, :00–2:21); X talks with a passing-by colleague (T36, 2:31–3:10)
10:42:05	327	As above	Qian phones her father (T37, 4:08–4:40); Qian gossips about her sister's job (T38,
10:47:12	307	As above	(silence)
10:52:22	310	As above	X talks about scanning papers (T33, :00–4:15)
10:58:08	346	As above	(silence)
11:03:37	329	As above	X talks about scanning papers (T33, :00–4:37)
11:07:09	212	As above	Qian talks about her sister's job (T38, :00–1:49); Qian and Sun gossip about their colleague (T39, 2:00–2:30)
11:09:42	163	As above	X talks about a colleague's phone call (T40, 1:42–2:08)
11:15:10	328	X and Qian operate the scanner;	X and Qian talk about problem-solving (T41, :00–2:51); X talks about picture-editing (T42, 3:28–5:28)
11:20:59	349	As above	X talks about picture-editing (T42, :00–5:48)
11:24:51	232	As above	X talks about picture-editing (T42, :00–1:36); X invites Sun to lunch (T43, 2:11–3:50)

The Talking column is divided into time intervals: 30, 60, 90, 120, 150, 180, 210, 240, 270, 300, 330.

Note: This is taken from the corpus database. The location remains unchanged throughout. All the actual names are replaced by the surnames in the order listed in the Book of Hundred Surnames.

Appendix 2: Thursday Afternoon Talking/Doing Record

Clock time	No. of files	Doing	Talking										
			30	60	90	120	150	180	210	240	270	300	330
13:35– 13:41:12	372	Some audience take notes		Speaker talks about US functionalism									
13:46:50	338	Some audience take notes		Speaker talks about US functionalism									
13:52:13	323	Some audience take notes		Speaker talks about US functionalism									
13:58:10	357	Some audience take notes		Speaker talks about US functionalism									
14:03:36	326	Some audience take notes		Speaker talks about US functionalism									
14:08:39	303	Some audience take notes		Speaker talks about US functionalism									
14:14:04	325	Some audience take notes		Speaker talks about US functionalism									
14:19:07	303	Some audience take notes		Speaker talks about US functionalism									
14:24:17	310	Some audience take notes		Speaker talks about US functionalism									
14:26:24	127	Some audience take notes		Speaker talks about US functionalism									
14:31:36	312	Some audience take notes		Speaker talks about US functionalism (–00:45)									
							Question/answer 1 (00:46–3:18)						
14:36:41	305	Some audience take notes		Question/answer 2 (:00–3:01)							Question/answer 2 (3:30–5:11)			
14:42:03	322	Some audience take notes	discussion									Question/answer 3 (3:03–5:04)		
14:47:14	311	Some audience take notes	discussion											
14:53:00	346	Some audience take notes	discussion											
14:58:25	325	Some audience take notes	discussion											
15:03:28	303	Some audience take notes	discussion											
15:05:22	116	Some audience take notes	discussion											

7

Blessed are the Peacemakers: Reconciliation and Evaluation

J. R. Martin

Reconciliation [1]

In this paper I want to open up, in a very programmatic sort of way, the question of the role of evaluation in discourses of reconciliation. I see this as an important site for what I call positive discourse analysis (PDA), a style of analysis that engages with processes of change that we sense make the world a better place (Martin, in press). I sometimes get the feeling that modernity has mesmerized critique, to the point where an obsession with hegemony rules virtually all critical inquiry; as a result all we end up doing is exposing power and showing why the world is a terrible place. This is not only depressing, but frustrating, since it doesn't tell us what we need to know about change for the better. There is more to challenging power than critiquing it; in addition we need to know how people commune in ways that rework its circulation (Gore, 1993) — personally, locally, nationally and globally. I think it is time to get off the high moral ground and take a look at people we admire and how they get on with what they do. We can learn some things from them that we need to know if we are going to intervene effectively as discourse analysts in the sites that motivate us. Such as reconciliation, for example, in our post-colonial world — I will focus on discourses from Australia and South Africa here, in relation to the legacy of European invasion and the way European and Indigenous peoples are learning to live together in their "new" worlds.

---

1. I am much indebted to David Rose for his work analysing the texts from Tutu 1999 and to Joan Rothery and Chris Jordens for their help with the suggestions about attitude and reconciliation developed here.

Making Peace: Language in Education

I will begin by coming at the question of reconciliation in one local site, where a kind of peace had to be made in relation to the politics of language in education. The moment was the discussion culminating in what came to be known in Australia as the "Christie Report", the result of a project of national significance on the preservice preparation of teachers for teaching English literacy directed by Professor Frances Christie (Christie *et al.*, 1991). By way of preparing this report Christie assembled a team which projected at least three major voices — education, functional linguistics and critical theory. This was a wise choice at the time, since these groups had been working together for a few years and coming up with some innovative programming that would be widely acclaimed in the ensuing years. But we certainly did not agree about everything, even most things... and the line between complementarity and difference can be a thin one, and we did not always toe the line.

What made difference difficult was the pressure from both curriculum and pedagogy to linearize — whether you are talking about scope and sequence in curriculum, or teaching strategies that enable zones of proximal development in pedagogy, you have to decide what comes first. And coming first necessarily privileges one perspective over another as an orienting point of departure. In debate this would come round to a question of what was really important — what mattered most. And educators, linguists and critical theorists have different views, as we would expect.

As part of the peace-making solution to these differences, one of the team's linguists suggested setting up three macro-regions underlying curriculum — which came to be called (i) Communities of learners, (ii) Informing theories and (iii) Curriculum. Each of these macro-regions included several components reflecting our group's major concerns, as outlined in Figure 7.1. The idea was that each unit of work would have to draw on each of the three macro-regions in its formulation, but that within macro-regions curriculum designers could choose which communities of learners, which informing theories and which of pedagogy, curriculum and evaluation they wished to focus on. This seemed to us to make room for differences across training institutions as far as the interests of staff was concerned, at the same time as avoiding privileging in our own recommendations one voice over another. All in all, this made the formulation of the final report possible; and in discussions, peace more or less broke out.

Figure 7.1
Three Macro-regions Underlying Curriculum

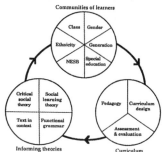

Differences were further resolved by agreeing on the notion of a spiral curriculum, which would allow pre-service programs to return to ideas as often as necessary, in increasing depth, as training unfolds. Our perspective on this is outlined in Figure 7.2.

Figure 7.2
A Spiral Curriculum

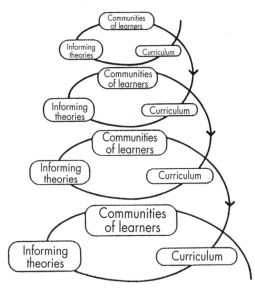

The way in which the macro-regions and spiral curriculum notions might influence programs of study is exemplified below for the training of secondary English teachers.

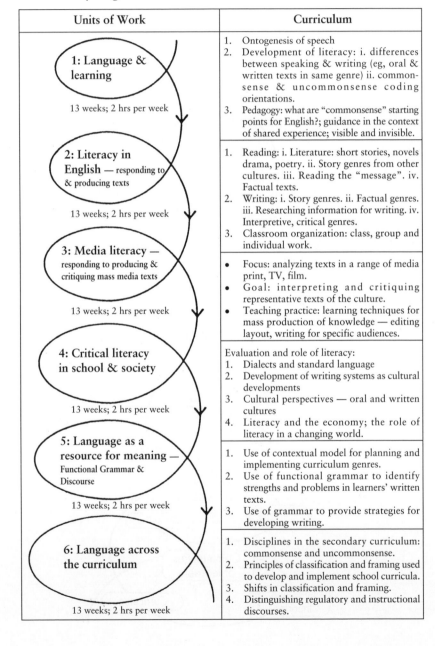

Units of Work	Curriculum
1: Language & learning 13 weeks; 2 hrs per week	1. Ontogenesis of speech 2. Development of literacy: i. differences between speaking & writing (eg, oral & written texts in same genre) ii. common-sense & uncommonsense coding orientations. 3. Pedagogy: what are "commonsense" starting points for English?; guidance in the context of shared experience; visible and invisible.
2: Literacy in English — responding to & producing texts 13 weeks; 2 hrs per week	1. Reading: i. Literature: short stories, novels drama, poetry. ii. Story genres from other cultures. iii. Reading the "message". iv. Factual texts. 2. Writing: i. Story genres. ii. Factual genres. iii. Researching information for writing. iv. Interpretive, critical genres. 3. Classroom organization: class, group and individual work.
3: Media literacy — responding to producing & critiquing mass media texts 13 weeks; 2 hrs per week	• Focus: analyzing texts in a range of media print, TV, film. • Goal: interpreting and critiquing representative texts of the culture. • Teaching practice: learning techniques for mass production of knowledge — editing layout, writing for specific audiences.
4: Critical literacy in school & society 13 weeks; 2 hrs per week	Evaluation and role of literacy: 1. Dialects and standard language 2. Development of writing systems as cultural developments 3. Cultural perspectives — oral and written cultures 4. Literacy and the economy; the role of literacy in a changing world.
5: Language as a resource for meaning — Functional Grammar & Discourse 13 weeks; 2 hrs per week	1. Use of contextual model for planning and implementing curriculum genres. 2. Use of functional grammar to identify strengths and problems in learners' written texts. 3. Use of grammar to provide strategies for developing writing.
6: Language across the curriculum 13 weeks; 2 hrs per week	1. Disciplines in the secondary curriculum: commonsense and uncommonsense. 2. Principles of classification and framing used to develop and implement school curricula. 3. Shifts in classification and framing. 4. Distinguishing regulatory and instructional discourses.

Informing Theories	Communities of Learners
• Learning theory: zone of proximal development; the spiral curriculum; models of literacy development in English. • Linguistic theory; from proto-language to the adult system. • Sociological theory; development of coding orientations • Functional grammar: analysis of language development from the grammar	• All learners: different experiences of language learning depending on ethnicity, class and gender. • Focus on experience of learners from NESB and "disadvantaged" backgrounds and mismatches with school learning.
• Text and context; genre/register theory. • Critical theory; (fictional and non–fictional) genres as sociocultural constructs (narrative theory, discourse, intertextuality, textual polysemy); the reading subject (compliant, resistant and tactical readings); institutional constraints on readers; discourse analysis; feminist and post-colonialist critiques; social subjects negotiating texts; subjective positioning of the writer (authoritativeness in/and writing, gendered texts).	• Different genres produced by different socio-cultural groupings: dominant, dominated, "marginalized". • Problems of NESB and Aboriginal students in accessing cultural knowledge assumed to be shared by readers. • Culturally specific linguistic resources.
• Critical theory: theories of realism; theories of subjectivity; fragmented and interactive audiences, audience targetting. • Discourse analysis: nature and function of news, whose news?, gender positioning. • Media technologies and histories. • Text in context: genres in different media.	• All learners to develop critical knowledge of mass media production. • Incorporating different perspectives and knowledge of NESB and Aboriginal learners as resources for deconstruction of contemporary media texts.
• Text and context: development of written genres and registers. • Functional grammar: history of development of language system. • Critical theory: social significance of literacy. • Role of literacy in (i) specialized knowledge, (ii) management and public administration.	• All groups of learners: high levels of literacy are essential for all students for choicies in educational, occupational and community participation. • Focus on needs of NESB and disadvantaged learners.
Functional grammar: • participating in dialogue (mood & modality), • distributing information (theme), • analysing experience (transitivity), • chaining clauses (expansion and projection, parataxis and hypotaxis), • assessing events and settings in time (verbal group), • modifying events (adverbial phrases).	• All groups of learners: different orientations to grammatical resources depending on ethnicity, class and gender. • Focus on problems for NESB learners: differences between L1 and L2 — interference from grammar of L1 in English learning.
• Text in context; genres and registers of subjects in focus; techniques for analyzing text structure. • Functional grammar: subject specific language — technicality, abstraction, personality. • Critical theory: problematising knowledge; critiquing educational knowledge.	• All groups of learners bridging from commonsense to uncommonsense. • Needs of NESB, Aboriginal, disadvantaged learners moving from culturally specific commonsense to uncommonsense language. • Reinforcing cultural knowledge through problematizing educational knowledge.

The linguist's solution is an interesting one in retrospect, with respect to the ways it draws on linguistic theory. One dimension of this is stratification — the idea of setting up "higher order" resources which can be instantiated in various ways "below". Another is the notion of choice — of establishing sets of options as resources from which designers can select. Yet another is the trinocular vision motif — the idea that the same thing can be looked at in different ways and implementations are about phasing perspectives together in engaging ways. An example of how linguists might go about making peace for others by drawing on their metalanguage (the very last thing of course that they ever do with one another).

This example is a local kind of peace, I know. And I could never have blessed myself this way within Australia; for that kind of thing Aussies have to speak abroad. But there was an engaging local politics at play, and differences did hurt; but we were in the long run committed to making a statement together, and so we had to get our act together — find a way to get along. In the post-colonial worlds we live in differences both large and small are everywhere and we are all negotiating a space for our ever-changing voices in every sphere of our lives — home, work, play, nation, biosphere and so on. The dimension of this I want to concentrate on here is feelings.

Appraisal: Communities of Feeling

For this we will need a framework, and one which moves beyond the well-known work on functional grammar by Halliday (1994) and Matthiessen (1995). The view of interpersonal meaning in that work focuses on interaction — the function of the clause to negotiate propositions (statements, questions and responses to these) as exemplified in Irene and Ivy's remarks below:

> *"I never thought you'd remember me," said Irene, 37, as the two women threw their arms around each other on the stoep (veranda), crying and laughing at the same time. Ivy, 59, replied: "But after I was assaulted it was you who was there to help me, who entered my cell at night. Can you ever forget someone like that?"*
>
> [Tutu 183]

Related resources negotiate proposals (offers, commands and replies to these) as exemplified in Irene's remarks below:

negotiating proposals [imperative realm]

> *She said, "It is fine, do not worry yourself. I will help you."*

> [Tutu 183]

Related to this, via polarity, is modality — resources for expressing probability and usuality in propositions, and obligation, inclination and ability in proposals, as exemplified in the modal verbs and adverbs below:

usuality	*He and his friends **would** visit **regularly**.*
probability	*there **must** have been someone out there who is still alive...*
obligation	*If **I had to** watch how white people became dissatisfied with the best...*
inclination	*I **would** have done the same had I been denied everything*
ability	*who **can** give a face to "the orders from above" for all the operations*

For work on feelings we need to move beyond these closed system resources and gaze lexically on lexicogrammar. The key system here is attitude and comprises gradable resources for construing evaluation (Martin, 2000a, b). Over the years we have developed a framework which deals with three types of feeling — affect, judgement and appreciation (our take on emotion, ethics and aesthetics if you will). Affect is concerned with construing emotional reactions:

> ***Humorous, grumpy**, everything in its time and place. Then he says: He and three of our friends have been promoted. "We're moving to a special unit. Now, now my darling. We are real policemen now." We were ecstatic. We even **celebrated**.*

Judgement is concerned with construing norms of esteem and behaviour:

> A *bubbly, vivacious* man who beamed out **wild energy.**
> **Sharply intelligent.** Even if he was an Englishman, he was
> popular with all the "Boere" Afrikaners.

Appreciation focuses on the worth of things, including semiotic objects such as songs, poems, paintings, sculptures and buildings and natural phenomena of various kinds — including semiotic objects such as questions and issues in the example below:

> So is amnesty being given at the cost of justice being done?
> This is not a **frivolous** question, but a very serious issue,
> one which challenges the integrity of the entire Truth
> and Reconciliation process.

In systemic theory (e.g., Halliday and Matthiessen, 1999) interpersonal meaning is associated with prosodic patterns of realization, and this is certainly true of attitude. Lexical choices resonate with one another to establish the mood of a phase of discourse, generally with one or another of affect, judgement or appreciation setting the tone. Here are some longer examples of emotional, ethical and aesthetic stance:

AFFECT ("emotions"; reacting to behaviour, text/process, phenomena)

He became <u>very quiet</u>. **Withdrawn.** Sometimes he would just **press his face into his hands** and **shake uncontrollably.** I realized he was <u>drinking too much</u>. Instead of resting at night, he would <u>wander from window to window</u>. He tried to hide his **wild consuming fear,** but I saw **it.** In the early hours of the morning between two and half-past-two, I jolt awake from his **rushed breathing.** <u>Rolls this way, that side of the bed</u>. He's <u>pale</u>. <u>Ice cold in a sweltering night</u> — <u>sopping wet with sweat</u>. Eyes **bewildered,** but dull like the dead. And **the shakes.** The **terrible convulsions** and **blood-curdling shrieks of fear and pain** from the bottom of his soul. Sometimes he <u>sits motionless</u>, just <u>staring in front of him</u>.

JUDGEMENT ("ethics"; evaluating behaviour)

> I envy and respect the people of the struggle — at least their leaders have the guts to stand by their vultures, to recognize their sacrifices. What do we have? Our leaders are too holy and innocent. And faceless. I can understand if Mr (F.W.) de Klerk says he didn't know, but... there must have been someone out there ... who can give a face to 'the orders from above'.... Dammit! What else can this abnormal life be than a cruel human rights violation? Spiritual murder is more inhumane than a messy, physical murder. At least a murder victim rests. I wish I had the power to make those poor wasted people whole again.

APPRECIATION ("aesthetics"; evaluating text/process, phenomena)

> This legendary 1983 debut by the fallen torchbearer of the 80s–90s blues revival sounds even more dramatic in its remixed and expanded edition. Stevie Ray Vaughan's guitar and vocals are a bit brighter and more present on this 14-track CD. And the newly included bonus numbers (an incendiary studio version of the slow blues "Tin Pan Alley" that was left off the original release, and live takes of "Testify," "Mary Had a Little Lamb," and the instrumental "Wham!" from a 1983 Hollywood concert) illuminate the raw soul and passion that propelled his artistry even when he was under the spell of drug addiction. Texas Flood captures Vaughan as rockin' blues purist, paying tribute in his inspired six-string diction to his influences Larry Davis (who wrote the title track), Buddy Guy, Albert King, and Jimi Hendrix. His own contemplative "Lenny," a tribute to his wife at the time, also suggests a jazz-fueled complexity that would infuse his later work. — Ted Drozdowski, Amazon.

At heart, each of these three kinds of stance involves feeling. But with judgement and appreciation the affectual dispositions we are all born with (and which parents have to tame) get institutionalized so that we can enter into communities with one another. Judgement

recontextualizes feeling in the realm of proposals about how to behave —
our ethics and morality, which may in fact be codified by church and
state. Appreciation recontextualizes feeling in the realm of propositions
about what things are worth — our sense of beauty and value, which
may in turn be codified as medals, prizes, marks or monetary rewards.
This orientation to feeling is outlined in Figure 7.3 below.

Figure 7.3
Judgement/Appreciation as Recontextualized Affect

ethics/morality (rules and regulations)
feeling institutionalized as proposals

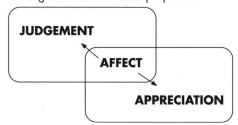

feeling institutionalized as propositions
aesthetics/value (criteria and assessment)

It is important to recognize that attitude is an interpersonal
resource which we draw heavily on in relation to solidarity. Feelings
are meanings we commune with, since we do not say what we feel
unless we expect the person we are talking with to sympathize or
empathize with us. We express feelings in order to share them... to
build relationships; where we misjudge the situation and get rebuffed,
then a sense of alienation sets in. The deployment of this resource for
building relationships in casual conversation is insightfully treated in
Eggins and Slade (1997).

Rhetoric of Reconciliation: Australia

Here I am asking questions about the use of feelings in discourses of
reconciliation. We will begin with a speech by the then Prime Minister
Paul Keating, at the Australian Launch of the International Year of
the World's Indigenous People in November 1992. Keating spoke at
Redfern Park, and is generally known in Australia as "The Redfern
Park Speech" (e.g., Gratton, 2000); Redfern is a well-known Aboriginal

settlement in Sydney. It is a very moving speech, which I think ranks as Australia's Gettysburg address... like many Australians I find it a source of inspiration, and at the same time a source of frustration when I consider how far we have slipped backwards in the absence of comparable moral leadership during the governance of Australia's current churl of a Prime Minister, John Howard. I will deal with just part of the speech here, using the layout from Keating's website, which I suspect reflects more closely the phrasing of his delivery (when compared with the written presentation edited by Gratton 2000:60–64).

Paul Keating at Redfern Park

> *...It begins, I think, with that act of recognition.*
>
> *Recognition that it was we who did the dispossessing.*
>
> *We took the traditional lands and smashed the traditional way of life.*
>
> *We brought the diseases. The alcohol.*
>
> *We committed the murders.*
>
> *We took the children from their mothers.*
>
> *We practised discrimination and exclusion.*
>
> ***It was our ignorance and our prejudice.***
>
> ***And our failure to imagine these things being done to us.***
>
> ***With some noble exceptions, we failed to make the most basic human response and enter into their hearts and minds.***
>
> ***We failed to ask — how would I feel if this were done to me?***
>
> *As a consequence, we failed to see that what we were doing degraded all of us.*
>
> *If we needed a reminder of this, we received it this year.*
>
> *The Report of the Royal Commission into Aboriginal Deaths in Custody showed with devastating clarity that*

the past lives on in inequality, racism and injustice.

In the prejudice and ignorance of non-Aboriginal Australians, and in the demoralization and desperation, the fractured identity, of so many Aborigines and Torres Strait Islanders.

For all this, I do not believe that the Report should fill us with guilt.

Down the years, there has been no shortage of guilt, but it has not produced the responses we need.

Guilt is not a very constructive emotion.

I think what we need to do is open our hearts a bit.

All of us.

Perhaps when we recognize what we have in common we will see the things which must be done — the practical things.

There is something of this in the creation of the Council for Aboriginal Reconciliation.

The Council's mission is to forge a new partnership built on justice and equity and an appreciation of the heritage of Australia's indigenous people.

In the abstract those terms are meaningless.

We have to give meaning to "justice" and "equity" — and... we will only give them meaning when we commit ourselves to achieving concrete results

I am not trained in rhetoric, but it seems to me there is some significant repositioning going on here as far as feelings are concerned. As part of the drift Keating begins with affect — *how would I feel if this were done to me?* He then moves on to judgement — *we failed to see that what we were doing degraded all of us.* The he tries to move beyond guilt and recrimination to the vision of the then newly created Council for Aboriginal Reconciliation — *The Council's mission is to forge a new partnership built on equity and justice and an appreciation of the heritage of Australia's indigenous people.* As the text unfolds, emotion is in a sense reworked as ethics, which is in turn reworked as what I will develop below as politicized aesthetics:

> "Emotion" recontextualized by "ethics", re/recontextualized by "aesthetics"

FROM [affect — **feel empathy**] ... We failed to ask - how would I <u>feel</u> if this were done to me?

THROUGH [judgement — **respect humanity**] ...we failed to see that what we were doing <u>degraded</u> all of us.

TO [appreciation — **reconcile difference**] The council's mission is to forge a new <u>partnership</u> built on equity and justice and an <u>appreciation of the heritage</u> of Australia's indigenous people.

This movement is outlined as an image in Figure 7.4, drawing on Lemke's (e.g., 1995) notion of metaredundancy (the idea of patterns of patterns of meaning). The drift of the recontextualization process in the speech can be usefully compared with the phylogenetic drift suggested for the institutionalization of feeling in Figure 7.3.

Figure 7.4
Recontextualizing Feeling in Keating's Speech

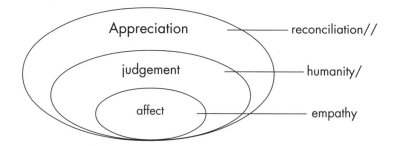

The main extension to the current model of attitude I am proposing here involves expanding appreciation beyond a concern with the beauty and value of things towards a concern with the composition of community — as reflected in Keating's choice of the evaluative terms *partnership* and *appreciation*:

> *The council's mission is to forge a new <u>partnership</u>*
> *built on <u>equity and justice</u> and an <u>appreciation of the</u>*
> *<u>heritage</u> of Australia's indigenous people.*

This politicized aesthetics is further developed later in his
presentation, as outlined below:

> *... Mabo is a historic decision. We can make it an*
> *historic turning point, **the basis of a new relationship***
> ***between indigenous and non-Aboriginal Australians...***
> *And if we have a sense of justice, as well as common*
> *sense, we will **forge a new partnership...** ... And I say it*
> *because in so many areas we have proved our capacity*
> *over the years **to go on extending the realms of***
> ***participating, opportunity and care...** Just as Australians*
> *living in the relatively narrow and insular Australia of*
> *the 1960s imagined a **culturally diverse, worldly and***
> ***open Australia**, and in a generation **turned the idea into***
> ***reality**, so we can **turn the goals of reconciliation into***
> ***reality**. There are very good signs that **the process has***
> ***begun**. The **creation of the Reconciliation Council** is*
> *evidence itself. The **establishment of the ATSIC — the***
> ***Aboriginal and Torres Strait Islander Commission —** is*
> *also evidence....*

So what I am suggesting here is that we bring political values into
the picture, and look at the ways in which discourses of reconciliation
construe a better world — what kind of better world is it? What
matters there?

Truth and Reconciliation: South Africa

Let us pursue this now in the context of reconciliation in South Africa,
beginning with the opposite of reconciliation — living hell. The story
I am dealing with here comes from Desmond Tutu's book *No Future
without Forgiveness*, and tells the story of a white South African woman
and her partners' involvement in human rights violations. We will
look at Helena and her second partner here:

My story begins in my late teenage years ... I met a young man in his twenties... It was the beginning of a beautiful relationship... .

After my unsuccessful marriage, I met another policeman. Not quite my first love, but an exceptional person. Very special. Once again a bubbly, charming personality. Humorous, grumpy, everything in its time and place. Then he says: He and three of our friends have been promoted. "We're moving to a special unit. Now, now my darling. We are real policemen now." We were ecstatic. We even celebrated. He and his friends would visit regularly. They even stayed over for long periods. Suddenly, at strange times, they would become restless. Abruptly mutter the feared word "trip" and drive off. I ... as a loved one...knew no other life than that of worry, sleeplessness, anxiety about his safety and where they could be. We simply had to be satisfied with: "What you don't know, can't hurt you." And all that we as loved ones knew ... was what we saw with our own eyes. After about three years with the special forces, our hell began. He became very quiet. Withdrawn. Sometimes he would just press his face into his hands and shake uncontrollably. I realized he was drinking too much. Instead of resting at night, he would wander from window to window. He tried to hide his wild consuming fear, but I saw it. In the early hours of the morning between two and half-past-two, I jolt awake from his rushed breathing. Rolls this way, that side of the bed. He's pale. Ice cold in a sweltering night — sopping wet with sweat. Eyes bewildered, but dull like the dead. And the shakes. The terrible convulsions and blood-curdling shrieks of fear and pain from the bottom of his soul. Sometimes he sits motionless, just staring in front of him. I never understood. I never knew. Never realized what was being shoved down his throat during the "trips". I just went through hell. Praying, pleading: "God, what's happening? What's wrong with him? Could he have changed so much? Is he going mad? I can't handle the man anymore! But, I can't get out. He's going to haunt me for the rest of my life if I leave him. Why, God?"

Today I know the answer to all my questions and heartache.... . I finally understand what the struggle was really about. I would have done the same had I been denied everything. If my life, that of my children and my parents was strangled with legislation. If I had to watch how white people became dissatisfied with the best and still wanted better and got it. I envy and respect the people of the struggle — at least their leaders have the guts to stand by their vultures, to recognize their sacrifices. What do we have? Our leaders are too holy and innocent. And faceless. I can understand if Mr (F.W.) de Klerk says he didn't know, but dammit, there must be a clique, there must have been someone out there who is still alive and who can give a face to "the orders from above" for all the operations. Dammit! What else can this abnormal life be than a cruel human rights violation? Spiritual murder is more inhumane than a messy, physical murder. At least a murder victim rests. I wish I had the power to make those poor wasted people whole again. I wish I could wipe the old South Africa out of everyone's past. I end with a few lines that my wasted vulture said to me one night: "They can give me amnesty a thousand times. Even if God and everyone else forgives me a thousand times — I have to live with this hell. The problem is in my head, my conscience. There is only one way to be free of it. Blow my brains out. Because that's where my hell is."

[Tutu 1999:49–51]

As we would expect from a narrative, there is lots of affect — basically a pulse of happiness followed by a sustained prosody of anguish. It is hard not to feel some sympathy for Helena and her vulture, although the more we know about what the special forces were up to the less likely we are to empathize; reading position is absolutely crucial as far as aligning with attitude is concerned. Below I have highlighted the lexis which explicitly construes emotion; for a richer reading we could extend this to include behaviour which indexes emotion (for example, becoming very quiet, drinking too much, wandering from window to window and so on):

> *After my unsuccessful marriage, I met another policeman. Not quite my first love, but an exceptional person. Very special. Once again a bubbly, charming personality.* **Humorous, grumpy,** *everything in its time and place. Then he says: He and three of our friends have been promoted. "We're moving to a special unit. Now, now my darling. We are real policemen now." We were ecstatic. We even* **celebrated.** *He and his friends would visit regularly. They even stayed over for long periods. Suddenly, at strange times, they would become* **restless.** *Abruptly mutter the* **feared** *word "trip" and drive off. I ... as a* **loved** *one ... knew no other life than that of* **worry,** *sleeplessness,* **anxiety** *about his safety and where they could be. We simply had to be* **satisfied** *with: "What you don't know, can't hurt you." And all that we as loved ones knew ... was what we saw with our own eyes. After about three years with the special forces, our hell began. He became very quiet.* **Withdrawn.** *Sometimes he would just* **press his face into his hands and shake uncontrollably.** *I realized he was drinking too much. Instead of resting at night, he would wander from window to window. He tried to hide his* **wild consuming fear,** *but I saw it. In the early hours of the morning between two and half-past-two, I jolt awake from his* **rushed breathing.** *Rolls this way, that side of the bed. He's pale. Ice cold in a sweltering night — sopping wet with sweat. Eyes* **bewildered,** *but dull like the dead. And* **the shakes.** *The terrible* **convulsions** *and* **blood-curdling shrieks of fear and pain** *from the bottom of his soul. Sometimes he sits motionless, just staring in front of him ...*

> *Today I know the answer to all my questions and*
> *heartache ... . If I had to watch how white people became*
> *dissatisfied with the best and still **wanted** better and got*
> *it. I **envy** and **respect** the people of the struggle — at*
> *least their leaders have the guts to stand by their vultures,*
> *to recognize their sacrifices ... **I wish** I had the power to*
> *make those poor wasted people whole again. **I wish** I*
> *could wipe the old South Africa out of everyone's past ...*

In the part of the story that recounts her husband's disintegration
there is more affect than judgement, although her husband's character
is dealt with briefly. But once Helena starts interpreting the significance
of his activities a burst of judgmental evaluation sets in around the
themes of propriety and inhumanity:

> *After my unsuccessful marriage, I met another*
> *policeman. Not quite my first love, but an **exceptional***
> *person. **Very special.** Once again a **bubbly, charming***
> *personality... Praying, pleading: "God, what's*
> *happening? What's **wrong** with him? Could he have*
> *changed so much? Is he going **mad**? I can't handle the*
> *man anymore! But, I can't get out. He's going to haunt*
> *me for the rest of my life if I leave him. Why, God?"*

> *Today I know the answer to all my questions and*
> *heartache... . I finally understand what the struggle was*
> *really about. I would have done the same had I been*
> *denied everything. If my life, that of my children and my*
> *parents was strangled with legislation. If I had to watch*
> *how white people became dissatisfied with the best and*
> *still wanted better and got it. I envy and respect the people*
> *of the struggle — at least their leaders **have the guts** to*
> *stand by their vultures, to recognize their **sacrifices**. What*
> *do we have? Our leaders are **too holy** and **innocent**.*
> *And **faceless**. I can understand if Mr (F.W.) de Klerk*
> *says he didn't know, but dammit, there must be a clique,*
> *there must have been someone out there who is still alive*
> *and who can give a face to "the orders from above" for*

*all the operations. Dammit! What else can this abnormal life be than a **cruel human rights violation**? Spiritual **murder** is more **inhumane** than a messy, physical **murder**. At least a **murder victim** rests. I wish I had the power to make those poor **wasted** people **whole** again. I wish I could wipe the old South Africa out of everyone's past. I end with a few lines that my **wasted** vulture said to me one night: "They can give me amnesty a thousand times. Even if God and everyone else **forgives** me a thousand times — I have to live with this hell. The problem is in my head, my **conscience**. There is only one way to be free of it. Blow my brains out. Because that's where my hell is."*

Appreciation in the story is relatively sparse. Early on it is used to value relationships (and arguably personality); later on the main theme is that of life as living hell:

*My story begins in my late teenage years ... I met a young man in his twenties ... It was the beginning of a **beautiful** relationship ... .*

*After my **unsuccessful** marriage, I met another policeman. Not quite my first love, but an exceptional person. Very special. Once again a **bubbly, charming** personality. Humorous, grumpy, everything in its time and place. Then he says: He and three of our friends have been promoted. "We're moving to a **special** unit. Now, now my darling. We are real policemen now... Suddenly, at **strange** times, they would become restless. Abruptly mutter the feared word "trip" and drive off... After about three years with the special forces, our **hell** began... I just went through **hell**...*

*Dammit! What else can this **abnormal** life be than a cruel human rights violation? Spiritual murder is more inhumane than a **messy**, physical murder... I end with a few lines that my wasted vulture said to me one night: 'They can give me amnesty a thousand times. Even if*

God and everyone else forgives me a thousand times — I
*have to live with this **hell**. The problem is in my head,*
my conscience. There is only one way to be free of it.
*Blow my brains out. Because that's where my **hell** is."*

As we can see, as far emotional equilibrium is concerned the
characters in the story have reached a kind of impasse. Because of
ethics (*The problem is in my head, my conscience*), Helena's husband
cannot find peace (*There is only one way to be free of it. Blow my*
brains out); and while Helena can now sympathize with the people of
the struggle, admire their leaders and condemn her own, she cannot
find a way to make her husband whole again. The pain in the story
does not resolve. For this couple amnesty is not a solution; they end
up trapped in a debilitating dialectic of affect and judgement without,
apparently, resources to transcend.

The next text we will consider on the other hand is transcendent.
It comes again from Tutu's book (the story we just looked at is in fact
used to exemplify its first argument). This text is an exposition, which
presents an issue and then gives three arguments as to why amnesty is
not being given at the cost of justice being done. I have highlighted the
conjunctions which scaffold the key stages of this structure:

So is amnesty being given at the cost of justice being done?
This is not a frivolous question, but a very serious issue,
one which challenges the integrity of the entire Truth
and Reconciliation process.

The Act required that where the offence is a gross
violation of human rights — defined as an abduction,
killing torture or severe ill-treatment — the application
should be dealt with in a public hearing unless such a
hearing was likely to lead to a miscarriage of justice (for
instance, where witnesses were too intimidated to testify
in open session). In fact, virtually all the important
applications to the Commission have been considered in
public in the full glare of television lights. Thus there is
the penalty of public exposure and humiliation for the

perpetrator. Many of those in the security forces who have come forward had previously been regarded as respectable members of their communities. It was often the very first time that their communities and even sometimes their families heard that these people were, for instance, actually members of death squads of regular torturers of detainees in their custody. For some it has been so traumatic that marriages have broken up. That is quite a price to pay. ...

It is <u>also</u> not true that the granting of amnesty encourages impunity in the sense that perpetrators can escape completely the consequences of their actions, because amnesty is only given to those who plead guilty, who accept responsibility for what they have done. Amnesty is not given to innocent people or to those who claim to be innocent. It was on precisely this point that amnesty was refused to the police officers who applied for it for their part in the death of Steve Biko. They denied that they had committed a crime, claiming that they had assaulted him only in retaliation for his inexplicable conduct in attacking them.

<u>Thus</u> the process in fact encourages accountability rather than the opposite. It supports the new culture of respect for human rights and acknowledgement of responsibility and accountability by which the new democracy wishes to be characterized. It is important to note too that the amnesty provision is an ad hoc arrangement meant for this specific purpose. This is not how justice is to be administered in South Africa for ever. It is for a limited and definite period and purpose.

<u>Further</u>, retributive justice — in which an impersonal state hands down punishment with little consideration for victims and hardly any for the perpetrator — is not the only form of justice. I contend that there is another kind of justice, restorative justice, which is characteristic of

traditional African jurisprudence. Here the central concern is not retribution or punishment but, in the spirit of ubuntu, the healing of breaches, the redressing of imbalances, the restoration of broken relationships. This kind of justice seeks to rehabilitate both the victim and the perpetrator, who should be given the opportunity to be reintegrated into the community he or she has injured by his or her offence. This is a far more personal approach, which sees the offence as something that has happened to people and whose consequence is a rupture in relationships. Thus we would claim that justice, restorative justice, is being served when efforts are being made to work for healing, for forgiveness and for reconciliation.

[Tutu 1999: 48–52]

In contrast to the narrative, there is very little affect in Tutu's exposition — and a couple of instances arguably fuse affect with judgement in any case (humiliation, respect):

... (for instance, where witnesses were too intimidated to testify in open session). In fact, virtually all the important applications to the Commission have been considered in public in the full glare of television lights. Thus there is the penalty of public exposure and humiliation for the perpetrator... For some it has been so traumatic that marriages have broken up. That is quite a price to pay ...

Thus the process in fact encourages accountability rather than the opposite. It supports the new culture of respect for human rights and acknowledgement of responsibility and accountability by which the new democracy wishes to be characterized ...

But from the perspective of judgement, the text is full of feeling — not surprisingly since it deals with a moral dilemma:

So is amnesty being given at the cost of justice being done? This is not a frivolous question, but a very serious *issue, one which challenges the **integrity** of the entire Truth and Reconciliation process.*

*The Act required that where the offence is a gross violation of human rights — defined as an abduction, killing, torture or severe ill-treatment — the application should be dealt with in a public hearing unless such a hearing was likely to lead to a miscarriage of justice (for instance, where witnesses were too intimidated to testify in open session). In fact, virtually all the important applications to the Commission have been considered in public in the full glare of television lights. Thus there is the penalty of public exposure and **humiliation** for the **perpetrator**. Many of those in the security forces who have come forward had previously been regarded as **respectable** members of their communities. It was often the very first time that their communities and even sometimes their families heard that these people were, for instance, actually members of **death squads** or regular **torturers** of detainees in their custody. For some it has been so traumatic that marriages have broken up. That is quite a price to pay. ...*

*It is also not **true** that the granting of **amnesty** encourages **impunity** in the sense that perpetrators can escape completely the consequences of their actions, because **amnesty** is only given to those who plead **guilty**, who accept responsibility for what they have done. **Amnesty** is not given to innocent people or to those who claim to be **innocent**. It was on precisely this point that **amnesty** was refused to the police officers who applied for it for their part in the death of Steve Biko. They denied that they had committed a crime, claiming that they had assaulted him only in **retaliation** for his inexplicable conduct in attacking them.*

*Thus the process in fact encourages **accountability** rather than the opposite. It supports the new culture of*

> *respect for **human rights** and acknowledgement of **responsibility** and **accountability** by which the new democracy wishes to be characterized. It is important to note too that the **amnesty** provision is an ad hoc arrangement meant for this specific purpose. This is not how justice is to be administered in South Africa for ever. It is for a limited and definite period and purpose.*
>
> *Further, retributive **justice** — in which an **impersonal** state hands down punishment with little consideration for victims and hardly any for the perpetrator — is not the only form of **justice**. I contend that there is another kind of **justice**, restorative **justice**, which is characteristic of traditional African jurisprudence. Here the central concern is not **retribution** or **punishment** but, in the spirit of ubuntu, the healing of breaches, the redressing of imbalances, the restoration of broken relationships. This kind of **justice** seeks to rehabilitate both the victim and the **perpetrator**, who should be given the opportunity to be reintegrated into the community he or she has injured by his or her **offence**. This is a far more **personal** approach, which sees the **offence** as something that has happened to people and whose consequence is a rupture in relationships. Thus we would claim that **justice**, restorative **justice**, is being served when efforts are being made to work for healing, for **forgiveness** and for reconciliation.*

Some of his judgements are like Helena's — everyday evaluations of character involving respectability, responsibility, accountability and veracity:

respectable members of their communities

who accept **responsibility**

encourages **accountability**

It is also not **true**

But many more of his judgements are judicial — they work as a kind of technicalized morality that we associate with legal institutions. Note for example that he offers a definition of a gross violation of human rights, taken from the Promotion of National Unity and Reconciliation Act. Definitions are a sure sign that we are moving from common sense into uncommon sense knowledge:

a **gross violation of human rights** — defined as an abduction, killing, torture or severe ill-treatment

Here are some more examples of Tutu's judgmental legalese:

had committed a **crime,**
sees the **offence**

the **perpetrator**
regular **torturers** of detainees
the **victim**

who plead **guilty**
innocent people
those who claim to be **innocent**

of **reprisals**
in **retaliation**
not **retribution** or **punishment**
encourages **impunity**
the granting of **amnesty**

a **miscarriage of justice**

For certain analytical purposes we might argue that these technical judgements should be left out of an appraisal analysis, since each in a sense refers to a precisely situated ideational meaning within legal institutions. But I do not think their technicality totally robs them of their evaluative role — most seem to carry with them some of their everyday attitudinal power, certainly for lay readers. When Robert Manne wrote for example that Australia's policy of removing

Aboriginal children from their families by force was "technically an act of genocide", I doubt that for most Australians its technicalization completely softened the moral blow:

> *A national inquiry last year found that the government policy of forced removal was a gross violation of human rights and **technically an act of genocide** because it has the intention of destroying Australia's indigenous culture by forced assimilation.*
>
> [Manne 1998: 63]

Appreciation is sparse until the third argument in the exposition where Tutu develops his notion of restorative justice:

> *So is amnesty being given at the cost of justice being done? This is not a **frivolous** question, but a very **serious** issue, one which challenges the integrity of the entire Truth and Reconciliation process.*
>
> *... In fact, virtually all the **important** applications to the Commission have been considered in public in the full glare of television lights...*
>
> *... They denied that they had committed a crime, claiming that they had assaulted him only in retaliation for his **inexplicable** conduct in attacking them.*
>
> *... It is **important** to note too that the amnesty provision is an **ad hoc** arrangement meant for this specific purpose. This is not how justice is to be administered in South Africa for ever. It is for a limited and definite period and purpose.*
>
> *Further, retributive justice — in which an impersonal state hands down punishment with little consideration for victims and hardly any for the perpetrator — is not the only form of justice. I contend that there is another kind of justice, restorative justice,*

*which is characteristic of traditional African jurisprudence. Here the central concern is not retribution or punishment but, in the spirit of **ubuntu**, the **healing of breaches**, the **redressing of imbalances**, the **restoration of broken relationships**. This kind of justice seeks to **rehabilitate** both the victim and the perpetrator, who should be given the opportunity to be **reintegrated** into the community he or she has **injured** by his or her offence. This is a far more personal approach, which sees the offence as something that has happened to people and whose consequence is a **rupture in relationships**. Thus we would claim that justice, restorative justice, is being served when efforts are being made to work for **healing**, for **forgiveness** and for **reconciliation**.*

Tutu's use of the term justice in the context of *ubuntu* seems at first blush to indicate that he is judging behaviour here. But in fact he is more concerned with restoring the fabric of social relations than with western notions of retribution and punishment contested in an adversarial legal system. Setting up *ubuntu* as a superordinate concept is not unlike the stratification strategy outlined in the first section on page 180. Here is Tutu's characterization of the concept during a visit to Sydney in 2000:

*But we have another kind of justice, restorative justice, based on something that we find difficult to put into English. **Ubuntu** is the essence of being human. It speaks of compassion and generosity, of gentleness and hospitality and sharing, because it says: "My humanity is caught up in your humanity. I am because you are." A person is a person through another person.*

*An offence breaks a relationship, ruptures an interconnectedness, a harmony so essential for a full human existence. **Ubuntu** does not give up on the perpetrator and sees him with a capacity to change for the better and so **ubuntu** seeks to heal a bridge, to restore relationships,*

> *to forgive and to have reconciliation. [Tutu: taking the*
> *costly path to peace. The University of Sydney Gazette.*
> *1. April 2000. 12–13.]*

Instantiating *ubuntu*, on the positive evaluation side, we have terms concerned with communal healing:

the **healing of breaches**
the **redressing of imbalances**
the **restoration** of broken relationships
rehabilitate both the victim and the perpetrator
the opportunity to be **reintegrated into the community**
restorative justice
healing
reconciliation.

On the negative side we have terms concerned with damage done:

broken relationships
the community he or she has **injured** by his or her offence
a **rupture** in relationships

The key term for Tutu, judging from the title of his book, is **forgiveness** — which seems in this context to comprise aspects of both judgement and appreciation. Judgement in the sense that someone is generous enough to stop feeling angry and wanting to punish someone who has done something wrong to them; appreciation in the sense that peace is restored. It also seems that for Tutu, forgiveness involves a spiritual dimension, underpinned by his Christianity; the concept transcends ethical considerations towards a plane of peace and spiritual harmony. **In appraisal terms what this means is** *that a politicized aesthetics of appreciation has recontextualized the moral passion plays of judgement.*

If we take communal healing as one emerging dimension of value analysis as far as the discourse of reconciliation is concerned, then the act which formed Tutu's T & C Commission can also be seen to be concerned with repairing social relations.

OFFICE OF THE PRESIDENT
No. 1111.
26 July 1995
NO. 34 OF 1995: PROMOTION OF
NATIONAL UNITY AND RECONCILIATION
ACT, 1995.

It is hereby notified that the President has assented to the following Act which is hereby published for general information:-

ACT...

*SINCE the Constitution of the Republic of South Africa, 1993 (Act No. 200 of 1993), provides a historic bridge between the past of a **deeply divided society** characterized by **strife, conflict,** untold suffering and injustice, and a future founded on the recognition of human rights, **democracy** and **peaceful** co-existence for all South Africans, irrespective of colour, race, class, belief or sex;*

AND SINCE it is deemed necessary to establish the truth in relation to past events as well as the motives for and circumstances in which gross violations of human rights have occurred, and to make the findings known in order to prevent a repetition of such acts in future;

*AND SINCE the Constitution states that the pursuit of **national unity**, the well-being of all South African citizens and **peace** require **reconciliation** between the people of South Africa and the **reconstruction of society**;*

AND SINCE the Constitution states that there is a need for understanding but not for vengeance, a need for reparation but not for retaliation, a need for ubuntu but not for victimization;

*AND SINCE the Constitution states that in order to advance such **reconciliation** and **reconstruction** amnesty shall be granted in respect of acts, omissions and offences associated with political objectives committed in the course of the **conflicts** of the past;*

AND SINCE the Constitution provides that Parliament shall under the Constitution adopt a law which determines a firm cut-off date, which shall be a date after 8 October 1990 and before the cut-off date envisaged in the Constitution, and providing for the mechanisms, criteria and procedures, including tribunals, if any, through which such amnesty shall be dealt with;

(English text signed by the President.)
(Assented to 19 July 1995.)

For this analysis I have concentrated on items that do not directly involve judgement. But the following paragraph gives us pause:

*AND SINCE the Constitution states that there is a need for **understanding** but not for vengeance, a need for **reparation** but not for retaliation, a need for **ubuntu** but not for victimization;*

Here the act systematically opposes what I treated as appreciation above to terms which more explicitly involve ethical considerations:

appreciation (healing)	**judgement** (impropriety)
understanding	vengeance
reparation	retaliation
ubuntu	victimization

Afro-Christian values are constructed as transcending western justice. Perhaps a better reading of the drift of feeling in the act would be one that follows Tutu's comments in his cost of justice exposition on the meaning of ubuntu:

the spirit of ubuntu, the healing of breaches, the redressing of imbalances, the restoration of broken relationships

Here order subsumes disorder; peace is restored. These are the values the act wants people to align with in the new rainbow republic. Accordingly it might be wise to group judgement and appreciation together here, under the headings of order and disorder — by way of displaying the attitude to reconciliation the act is designed to enact.

order

bridge, democracy, peaceful co-existence, national unity, peace, reconciliation, reconstruction of society, understanding, reparation, ubuntu, reconciliation, reconstruction;
recognition of human rights, truth, well-being, amnesty, amnesty

disorder

deeply divided society, strife, conflict, conflicts; injustice, violations of human rights, vengeance, retaliation, victimization, omissions, offences

It might be even wiser to pause for a moment and consider the extent to which the affect, judgement and appreciation framework represents a western modernist construction of feeling. Tutu's Afro-Christian heritage might not factor attitude along these lines. I am not wise enough to gaze beyond my categories here. But I am confident that other cultures should take pause, and look at what I have done through different eyes.

Emergent Discourse: Cultures of Peace

At this point it might be useful to step back a little and reconsider textual instances from the perspective of system, since I am suggesting that the drift of local weather is changing the climate of our culture in significant ways. Systemically, attitude is part of a more general system called appraisal, in the interpersonal discourse semantics of English. Alongside attitude this system includes resources for incorporating a number of voices in text (engagement) and resources for grading categories (graduation) — as outlined in Figure 7.5.

Figure 7.5
Appraisal Systems (ATTITUDE, ENGAGEMENT, GRADUATION)

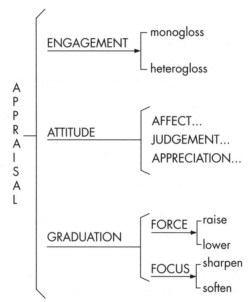

The main options for engagement are monogloss and heterogloss. In monoglossic discourse, evaluation is presented as sourced unproblematically to a single authority — as when Helena introduces herself at the beginning of her story:

> *monogloss (elide dialogism) — As an eighteen-year-old, I met a young man in his twenties. He was working in a top security structure. It was the beginning of a beautiful relationship.*

Later of course she uses a variety of resources to dialogize her text, including various types of "projection" as highlighted below:

> *heterogloss (reference dialogism)* — *I can understand if Mr (F.W.) de Klerk says he didn't know,* but dammit, there must be a clique, there must have been someone out there who is still alive and who can give a face to *"the orders from above"* for all the operations.

Engagement has been designed by Gillian Fuller, Henrike Körner and Peter White, among others (e.g., Fuller, 1998) as a resource for construing heteroglossia in texts. It's capacity for introducing and aligning voices makes it critical to developing the programmatic discussion of evaluation and reconciliation undertaken here.

Another resource which needs to be brought into the picture is graduation. This involves resources for adjusting the intensity of gradable items (turning the volume up and down as it were):

> *force (raising intensity)* — For some it has been *so traumatic* that marriages have broken up. That is *quite a price* to pay.

Related to these are resources for making categorical distinctions gradable:

> *focus (sharpening focus)* — We are real policemen now.

We have already seen the significance of these resources with respect to Robert Manne's use of the term *genocide* above (*technically an act of genocide*). By moving the issue from the ethical to the legal realm he makes it arguable on the basis of United Nations legislation — in a discourse that foregrounds reason over feeling, however morally charged remains the charge.

Appreciation as an emerging discourse of peace is outlined in Table 7.1, taking into account the texts reviewed here and a few closely

Table 7.1
Appreciation as an Emerging Discourse of Peace

Reconciliation	Positive	Negative
reaction: impact [notability]	important, significant	
reaction: empathy [caring]	understanding, appreciation, valuing, care;	demoralization, hurt, desperation dispossessed
	tolerance, acceptance, respect, trust	
composition: order	ubuntu;	
	reconciliation;	
	peaceful coexistence, peace;	strife, conflict;
	united Australia, national unity, partnership, relationship, relations, cooperation, sharing, cross-party commitment;	deeply divided society, fractured identity;
	redressing of imbalances, restoration of broken relationships, reintegrated into the community, reconstruction of society, reparation, building bridges;	broken relationships, a rupture in relationships, smashed the traditional way of life;
	healing of breaches, rehabilitate, healing	injured
composition: diversity	culturally diverse, worldy, open	
valuation [social justice]	democracy, participating, opportunity, equity;	racism, discrimination, inequality, exclusion injustice
	restorative justice, justice, addressing disadvantage	

related examples I had to hand (for a comparison with work on appreciation developed initially for the visual arts see Martin, 2000a, and Appendix 1 on page 226. As we can see, the largest group of terms falls under the heading of composition and has to do with recomposing social order in a fractured post-colonial world. This is just a glimpse of what is going on and we need lexically focussed corpus studies to follow up this lead. Over to you Birmingham, to carry on.

What we might ask are the implications of this perspective for Human Rights initiatives around the world? If true reconciliation involves transcending ethics, then what role does morality (however defined, by whom) play in making peace? The many tensions over Human Rights issues in relation to "Asian Values" can perhaps be re-evaluated in light of this discussion. Imposing ethical regimes is a modernist solution to difference; this is not a solution that is likely to succeed in a multi-voiced post-colonial world.

We also need to ask in what sense transcending ethics involves recontextualizing ethics. A number of the terms in Table 7.1 can arguably be read as involving judgement, although I do not think this does justice to their impact in the texts I considered above, as I argued there. A recent conference at Curtin University in Perth for example advertised itself as "Human rights: a fair go for all". Is this just an ethical title? Or, does the meaning of "fair go" in Australian English in a sense transcend morality? Does it mean making room for difference, in the spirit perhaps of the inspiring communality of the Olympic Games in Sydney in September 2000? As Joan Rothery has suggested to me in relation to her work with Maree Stenglin, there is probably more than morality involved in the "deep grammar" of resonant Australian ideals such as the "fair go" and "mateship"; there is a sense of peace and social order there as well, of community and support — a set of resources for reconciliation which indigenous and non-indigenous Australians need to draw on in this time of desperate need.

Political Aesthetics: Reconciling Values

What I have tried to do here is open up one site for positive discourse analysis, reconciliation, and suggest an emerging resource at play — political aesthetics, which I have flagged here as evaluative resources for re/composing communities. My suggestions can be checked against related processes in other sites, such as diplomacy, mediation, collective bargaining, meetings, counselling and so on — sites where people set aside competitive adversarial posturing, whether codified as judicial proceedings or not, and try to reconcile differences co-operatively. I am asking what kinds of discourse they use to do so.

> **sites** (reconciliation and beyond):
> diplomacy, mediation, collective bargaining, meetings, counselling...

I am sure appraisal is not the only resource we need to consider. What is the role of stratification, for example? Do we need higher order concepts like *ubuntu*? I recall that during his presentation at a literacy conference at Bachelor College in 1987 that Mandawuy Yunupingu introduced the concept of two-way education in relation to his indigenous language's name for a fish that darted one way, then another, as it swam in streams near his home (cf. Walton and Eggington, 1990). What then is the role of metaphor? Or of symbols, such as the version of the Australian flag with the Aboriginal flag in the upper left hand quadrant instead of the British ensign? What is the role of humour? What is the role of abstract images like the macro-regions introduced in section 1? What is the role of ritual and ceremony? What is the function of display and design as far as the spaces we try to co-operate in are concerned? And the many more resources I cannot yet bring to mind.

> **resources** (appraisal and beyond):
> appraisal, stratification, humour, metaphor, symbols, diagrams, ceremony, design...

As a systemic functional semiotician, I am interested in all of these. But let me end with a poignant linguistic example, which comes from a draft of the Declaration for Reconciliation which has been developed by the Council for Aboriginal Reconciliation. At stake here is John Howard's refusal to support an official national apology for the injustices suffered by indigenous peoples in Australia. Here is his "official" as opposed to his "personal" position (for discussion see Martin, in press):

> *The Prime Minister acknowledges and thanks you*
> *for your support for his personal apology to indigenous*
> *people affected by past practices of separating indigenous*

children from their families. However, the government does not support an official national apology. Such an apology could imply that present generations are in some way responsible and accountable for the actions of earlier generations, actions that were sanctioned by the laws of the time, and that were believed to be in the best interests of the children concerned. [Senator Herron writing on behalf of the Prime Minister, John Howard, to Father Brennan in late 1997]

In an attempt to finesse their way around this sticking point the Council drafted as follows:

...And so we take this step: as one part of the nation expresses its sorrow and profoundly regrets the injustices of the past, so the other part accepts the apology and forgives. ... [Draft version, Council for Aboriginal Reconciliation 2000]

As a linguist I was struck by the clever use of participant identification, bridging to be precise (Martin, 1992). Howard's profession of sorrow and regret (affect) is reconstrued through nominalization as an apology (judgement) — his voice is recontextualized by another in a perfectly balanced clause complex linked by *as* and *so* (appreciation) — what Howard is willing to say becomes what other Australians want to hear. It is a nice compromise, enacting and symbolizing reconciliation through the identification, nominalization and clause linking strategies deployed. Something for a linguist's aesthetic perhaps, but a nice piece of rhetoric as well, in anyone's terms.

one part of the nation
expresses its sorrow and
profoundly regrets the injustices of the past

=

the apology

Of course, John Howard was too concerned about the 51% of Australians who are opposed to an official apology to accept this wording. Accordingly the Council replaced *expresses its sorrow and profoundly regrets* with *apologises* in later drafts. The finesse failed; an opportunity for peace was lost. And Australia is diminished for it. But there are many more resources to try. In such processes, can linguists play a part?

References

1. Christie, F. and J. R. Martin. 1997. *Genre and institutions*: *Social processes in the workplace and school*, Open Linguistics Series. London: Cassell.

2. Coffin, C. 1997. Constructing and giving value to the past: An investigation into secondary school history. In *Genre and institutions*: *Social processes in the workplace and school,* edited by F. Christie and J. R. Martin. London: Cassell, 196–230.

3. Eggins, S. and D. Slade. 1997. *Analyzing casual conversation*. London: Cassell.

4. Fuller, G. 1998. Cultivating science: Negotiating discourse in the popular texts of Stephen Jay Gould, edited by Martin and Veel, 35–62.

5. Gore, J. 1993. *The struggle for pedagogies: Critical and feminist discourses as regimes of truth*. London: Routledge.

6. Gratton, M., ed. 2000. *Reconciliation: Essays on Australian reconciliation*. Melbourne: Black Inc.

7. Halliday, M. A. K. 1994. *An introduction to functional grammar*. London: Edward Arnold.

8. _____ and C. M. I. M. Matthiessen. 1999. *Construing experience through meaning: A language-based approach to cognition*. London: Cassell.

9. Hunston, S. and G. Thompson, eds. 2000. *Evaluation in text: Authorial stance and the construction of discourse*. Oxford: Oxford University Press.

10. Lemke, J. L. 1995. *Textual politics: Discourse and social dynamics*. London: Taylor & Francis. (Critical Perspectives on Literacy and Education).

11. _____ . 1998. Resources for attitudinal meaning: Evaluative orientations in text semantics. *Functions of Language* 5 (1): 33–56.

12. Manne, R. 1998. The stolen generations. *Quadrant* 343 (XLII) (1–2): 53–63.

13. Martin, J. R. 1992. *English text: System and structure*. Amsterdam: Benjamins.

14. _____ . 1995b. Interpersonal meaning, persuasion and public discourse: Packing semiotic punch. *Australian Journal of Linguistics* 15 (1): 33–67.

15. Martin, J. R. 1999. Grace: The logogenesis of freedom. *Discourse Studies* 1 (1): 31–58.

16. _____ . 2000a. *Beyond exchange: Appraisal systems in English*. Hunston & Thompson, 142–175.

17. _____ . 2000b. Factoring out exchange: Types of structure. In *Working with Dialogue,* edited by M. Coulthard. Tubingen: Niemeyer, 19–40.

18. _____ . Positive discourse analysis: Power, solidarity and change. *Social Semiotics*: (Special Issue — "Critical Semiotics", edited by C. Caldas-Coulthard). Forthcoming.

19. Matthiessen, C. M. I. M. 1995. *Lexicogrammatical cartography: English systems.* Tokyo: International Language Sciences Publishers.

20. Tucker, G. 1999. *The lexicogrammar of adjectives: A systemic functional approach to lexis.* London: Cassell.

21. Tutu, D. 1999. *No future without forgiveness.* London: Rider.

22. _____ . 2000. Tutu: Taking the costly path to peace. *The University of Sydney Gazette* 1:12–13.

23. Unsworth, L., ed. 2000. *Researching language in schools and communities: Functional linguistic perspectives.* London: Cassell.

24. Walton, C. and W. Eggington, eds. 1990. *Language: Maintenance, power and education in Australian aboriginal contexts.* Darwin, NT: Northern Territory University Press.

25. White, P. 1997. Death, disruption and the moral order: The narrative impulse in mass "hard news" reporting. In *Genre and institutions: Social processes in the workplace and school,* edited by F. Christie and J. R. Martin. London: Cassell, 101–133.

Appendix 1: Appreciation in the Visual Arts

The framework for APPRECIATION is outlined below. APPRECIATION can be thought of as the institutionalization of feeling, in the context of propositions (norms about how products and performances are valued). Like AFFECT and JUDGEMENT it has a positive and negative dimension — corresponding to positive and negative evaluations of texts and processes (and natural phenomena). The system is organized around three variables — *reaction, composition* and *valuation. Reaction* has to do with the degree to which the text/ process in question captures our attention (reaction: impact) and the emotional impact it has on us (reaction: quality). *Composition* has to do with our perceptions of proportionality (composition: balance) and detail (composition: complexity) in a text/process. *Valuation* has to do with our assessment of the social significance of the text/process.

	POSITIVE	NEGATIVE
reaction: impact "did it grab me?"	arresting, captivating, involving, engaging, absorbing, imposing, stunning, striking, compelling, interesting... fascinating, exciting, moving... remarkable, notable, sensational... lively, dramatic, intense...	dull, boring, tedious, staid... dry, ascetic, uninviting... unremarkable, pedestrian, ... flat, predictable, monotonous...
reaction: quality "did I like it?"	lovely, beautiful, splendid... appealing, enchanting, pleasing, delightful, attractive, welcome...	plain, ugly... repulsive, off-putting, revolting, irritating, weird...
composition: balance "did it hang together?"	balanced, harmonious, unified, symmetrical, proportional...	unbalanced, discordant, unfinished, incomplete...
composition: complexity "was it hard to follow?"	simple, elegant... intricate, rich, detailed, precise...	ornamental, over-complicated, extravagant, puzzling... monolithic, simplistic...
valuation "was it worthwhile?"	challenging, significant, deep, profound, provocative, daring... experimental, innovative, original, unique, fruitful, illuminating... enduring, lasting...	shallow, insignificant, unsatisfying, sentimental... conservative, reactionary, generic... unmemorable, forgettable...

These variables are relatable to the kind of mental processing (Halliday, 1994) involved in the appreciation, in following proportions:

	reaction	is to	*affection*
as	*composition*	is to	*perception*
as	*valuation*	is to	*cognition*

8

Multinational Organizations: Europe in the Search of New Identities

Ruth Wodak

Introductory Considerations on the Relationships between "Discourse, Politics, Organizations and Identity"

Vaclav Havel, Czech President, famous poet and hero of May 1968 in Prague, gave a very important and widely acknowledged speech in Germany, on 24 April 1997, in the Deutscher Bundestag, the German National Assembly. This marks a new phase in the European integration, and Havel started his speech after some introductory greetings in the following way:

> "After some initial agonizing I decided not to think about what is expected of me, to set aside all lists of politically appropriate remarks, and not to experience this responsibility as a trauma but to make the most of this opportunity to concentrate on a single theme, one which to my mind is exceptionally significant and topical. This theme is nothing more nor less than our perception of one's homeland. I have made this choice for two reasons: the first is that the Czech Republic and the Federal Republic of Germany have one important thing in common. In their present form they are very young states that in many ways are still looking for their identity and are consequently redefining what makes them the homeland of their citizens. And yet, paradoxically enough, both our countries have a long tradition of

investigating the nature of their national identity and of cultivating or criticizing different forms of their patriotism. The second reason is the ongoing, unprecedented process of European integration, which compels not only you and us but all Europeans to reflect again on what, in this new age, their homeland means or will mean to them, how their patriotism will coexist with the phenomenon of a united Europe and, principally, with the phenomenon of Europeanism. To what extent is it still true that our native land means simply the nation-state in the classic sense of the term and patriotism merely love for our nation?"

In this speech and already in this short quote, Havel alludes to the past, present and future of the two countries and also of Europe[1]. The tensions between the traditional nation state and new supranational entities, like the EU are mentioned as relevant for the discursive construction of identities. At the same time, Havel also mentions the most important strategy and component of identity construction: The question of being same or equal or being different then others (see Ricoeur, 1992). Thirdly, the past is talked about, a most difficult past for the joint history of these two countries and the respective past of both states, implicating the Nazi past, the communist past and the attempt of both states to face and confront these memories. Fourthly, Havel talks about the tension between "homeland" and "global entities" which we find expressed nowadays in "Globalization rhetoric" on the one hand, in "homeland rhetoric" on the other hand (Muntigl,

---

1. Discourses about the past, present and future are characteristic for the construction of national identities. The analysis, for example, of presidential speeches (see Wodak *et al.*1999; Kovacs and Wodak 2001) illustrates that most speeches integrate passages about the past of the nation state (a founding myth), the present and some visions of the future.

2. Due to space restrictions, it is not possible to elaborate the discourse theory and all the linguistic strategies and categories for the analysis of "discourses of sameness and difference", prevalent in the construction of national identities. I have to refer readers to Wodak *et al.* (1999) and to Reisigl and Wodak (2001) for details.

Weiss and Wodak, 2000; Weiss and Wodak, 2000). All these *topoi* which Havel refers to are important in the attempt to construct a new "European identity", along the frontiers of a New Europe which — of course — means Western Europe plus maybe some of the former Eastern Bloc countries. In the attempt to construct this New Europe, new borders have been drawn, mainly on an economic level, to other European countries, and we hear the slogan of the "fortress Europe" again and again.[2]

These thoughts of Havel are to be found with other politicians and scholars throughout the countries and disciplines. Thus, starting off with Benedict Andersen's idea of the "imagined community" (see Anderson, 1983; Wodak *et al.*, 1999) to Stuart Hall's "narratives of identity" (see Hall, 1996a,b), the reflection and study of this "New Europe" on many dimensions (cultural, economic, values, etc.) has become mainstream for many and politically relevant for others. Remi Brague (1992, 1993) distinguishes between several dichotomies, which characterize Europe, a Europe, which, as he writes, carries a "face full of scars". There are dichotomies, which are geographical (East–West, North–South) and dichotomies, which are religious (catholicism and reformism), finally dichotomies which belong to the past (the role of the Third Reich) etc. As Brague summarizes, "to retain the memory of such ruptures can avoid confusion" (page 16).

In this chapter, I reflect — on the basis of the research from recent years, particularly in our research unit in the Austrian Academy of Science (www.oeaw.ac.at/wittgenstein) — upon the extent, to which globalization trends and the associated coming together of nation-states have exposed new discourses of inclusion and exclusion; and the extent to which today, on the basis of these changes, traditional values and institutions/organizations also change. Thus, identity research today must be especially concerned with the tensions that arise between supra-national and national identities, which may all be captured discursively, which produce and reproduce the tensions, and which may therefore be grasped by means of an analysis of the discourse.

Specifically, I would like to branch out from a large

interdisciplinary study (Muntigl, Weiss and Wodak, 2000): "EU Discourses on Un/Employment". I will consider new developments in the European Union organizations and in European nation states, like Austria, which we have found striking in our ethnographic fieldwork and empirical research on European Union organizations and discourses on Un/employment in very different public spaces therein. We studied the recontextualization of certain arguments about employment policies in interviews, committee meetings, in the European parliament and also in written genres, like policy papers, resolutions and presidential conclusions of the EU. In this study, among many other significant results, we found the above mentioned tensions very relevant and dominant. Also, secondly, we could follow the process of development in Europe from an economic interest group to a value oriented identity. The tension between globalization rhetoric and homeland rhetoric is a third major finding, which will be shortly presented in the course of this chapter. The following two claims serve to organize all these findings in relationship to identity construction:

The first thesis is that discourses of inclusion and exclusion have remained a constitutive element of political communication, of a politics of identity and difference. At the same time significantly new dynamic borders have been and are being created, in both time and space. These new developments have been described by Anthony Giddens, in apposite terms, as "time and space distanciation" (Giddens, 1984). David Harvey has also demonstrated these tensions empirically in a number of areas of politics and culture (Harvey, 1996). The sense of unsettlement, that is resulting from different types of globalization, yearns for simple answers, and these in turn lead to ever more fragmentations, contradictions, insecurities and dichotomies, as already well described by Stuart Hall some years ago and taken up by Zygmunt Baumann in his most recent book *In Search of Politics* (1999). Baumann distinguishes between three forms of insecurity: uncertainty, insecurity and unsafety. Thus, concepts such as time, space, border, "we" and "others" need to be thoroughly reviewed in the light of new public spaces and the loss of traditional political values. The "New European identity" is torn between "globalization rhetoric and homeland rhetoric". Moreover, the development of the EU from an economic unit to a "*Wertegemeinschaft*", to a supranational entity concerned with values of justice, democracy, diversity and equality are visible.

Over the past thirty years Western Europe has been one region in which pan-national integration appeared to have some positive prospects. At least, this is the region that has attracted the most empirical and theoretical attention. Of course, predictions about integration in Western Europe ran the gamut from forecasts of a United States of Europe, through various federal and loose decentralized functional cooperative unions, to predictions that the system of sovereign states would hardly change at all. Some of the cooperative and integrative efforts Western Europe states did make were often attributed to the influence of the United States and its desire to contain the Soviet Union. With the end of the Cold War, predictions again ran the gamut with some forecasting continued and even deeper integration, partly because of the predicted continuing influence of the West European institutions that had been established, and others forecasting the breakdown of these Cold War era institutions and a return to nationalist contests and conflicts reminiscent of the 1930s.

Over the past four decades a complex set of institutions has evolved at the European level. These often were designed to manage growing interdependencies and to coordinate cross-national policy-making. Political sovereignty may have remained ultimately with states but in important areas, policy-making is also the responsibility of European institutions. How the proliferation and deepening of European institutions have affected the political identities of people living in Europe is not clear. Certainly, the history of some nations begins with the state and its cultivation of national feelings. Are European institutions having this effect on political conceptions in Europe? Are they producing a perception of common fate and unified political identity in Europe? The process of institutionalizing Europe, might also heighten state and national fears and produce backlash efforts to defend state sovereignty and cultural autonomy. Moreover, the debate about a constitution and new organization of the EU is dominant nowadays (Henningsen, 1998; Weiler, 1999). Thus, it is important to study the role of the sub organizational systems, the development of new public spaces, networks, and the debate about the aims and goals of the EU, which started out as an economic entity (and of course still is) and is now discussing values and ideals (Moisi, 1999; Höffe, 1999).

The second thesis is that experts, using knowledge management and networking strategies, replace more and more previously used decision-making structures in organizations, governments and nation states. This is an immediate consequence of globalization: supranational dynamic and flexible commissions and committees are replacing cumbersome national institutions to an ever greater extent. In this way, in many areas of life, rapid decisions and judgements, that took too long and that were beset with too many obstacles in static bureaucratic systems, have become both vital and possible. Time has become faster, and now transcends borders. Problems have become more complex, and so knowledge and expertise are more relevant than ever before, old-style bureaucrats are no longer able to maintain an overview of this complexity (Wilke, 1999). We therefore speak of new elites, of elites of knowledge.

Organizational Discourses and Identity Construction

These thoughts have to be tied to research on organizations. The study of organizational discourses and practices has always centred around the parameters of time and space. In this work, organizational meanings have been considered as both diachronic or logo-genetic, and synchronic or intertextual (Wunderlich, 1972; Ehlich and Rehbein, 1986; Fairclough, 1992; Clegg, 1990; Lemke, 1995). More recently, as mentioned above, the notions "time-space distantiation" (Giddens, 1984) and "time-space compression" (Harvey, 1989) have been used to describe both organizations in general and organizational interactions specifically (see Iedema, 1997a; Harvey, 1996). Time-space distantiation enables social, organizational and spatial relations to be extended over time, mainly through the storage of both meanings and resources (in, for example, data banks, expert practices and procedures, but also interior spaces and buildings). Time-space compression is mainly that which results from the newly emerging communications technologies, and concerns the consequences which these technologies have on situated interaction (Iedema, 1999).

This perspective acknowledges historical and technological dimensions and how they impact on the temporal and spatial aspects of interaction as crucial for understanding organizational discourses and interactions. Inherent in this perspective is that the structuration of organizations is achieved through recontextualization. Recontextualization is the process through which different practices and discourses are inter-linked, and become translated into one another (Bernstein, 1990; Linell, 1998; Wodak, 1999; Iedema, 1997a, 1999).

Lastly, and this is where I would like to tie my two claims together, the impact of globalization and internationalization on organizational research has to be acknowledged. The boundaries between professions are becoming increasingly uncertain and challenged; organizations are becoming increasingly fluid and less hierarchical, and bureaucratic; political as well as expert-professional allegiances are changing (see Clegg, 1996; Muntigl, Weiss and Wodak, 2000; Fairclough, 1999; Wilke, 1999, Bach, 1998; Wodak and Vetter, 1999). Clegg (1990) defines the organization as a domain where differences in skills, tasks and expertise are managed, thus relying on the Weberian model. He sees organizational structure as a framework which enables both the differentiation and the interlinking of professional and occupational work practices. Historically, organizations enabled the transference of skills from craftspeople and guilds to commercial corporations and administrative bureaucracies, relegating knowledge to organizational charts and related storage devices and reconstituting craftsmanship into simple, repetitive and mechanized tasks. "Divisions of products and divisions of tasks no longer coincided nor were they related by any normative community. Instead relations within organizations were increasingly mediated though mechanisms of market exchange and state regulations rather than through moral sentiment" (Clegg, 1990: 11; also Reed, 1996, Wodak and Iedema, 2001).

While modern organizations are characterized by increased professional and occupational differentiation, post-modern organizations, Clegg claims, experience "a blurring of the boundaries" (Clegg, 1990: 11; also Clegg and Hardy, 1996). It is because of such blurring among professional orientations and specializations that it is becoming difficult to privilege any one kind of account, approach or analysis as explanatory meta-narrative. It is also becoming increasingly difficult to take either an entirely structural or agentive perspective on organizational phenomena, and not in some way account for the complex dialectics that characterizes the interplay between embodied and objectified organizational phenomena. Thus, instead of subscribing *a priori* to either a structural or agentive account, the focus is on "what is actually involved in managing and accomplishing organization" (Clegg, 1990:13).

After these first theoretical observations on the coming together of supranational organizations and the discursive construction of identities in the EU, the first example presents interviews with members of the EU commission and of the EP, asked about their own feelings about being "European" and about "European employment policies". The second example looks more specifically at the search for a New European Identity in a typical EU network, the CAG, and considers the functions of new knowledge elites and networks using the models and analysis which Peter Muntigl, Gilbert Weiss and myself developed as an ethnographic approach in CDA.

In my conclusions, the Austrian example, as one of the 15 member states, serves as example for the tensions between "homeland rhetoric" and "globalization rhetoric". The conflict management implemented by the 14 other member states after the instalment of the new government in Austria, on the 4th of February 2000, — the so-called sanctions and the committee of the "Three wise men", the first official intervention into governmental politics of a nation state by the EU, will be discussed. This latter example illustrates very strongly both the search for certain democratic values by the EU and the role of expert committees.

The Politics of Identity and Difference

Let us now turn to our main subject, the discursive construction of identities in the EU organizations. The politics of identity and difference has become decisive in our globalized world: "Globalization rhetoric" and "homeland rhetoric" are in a state of dialectic opposition that is manifest in the fragmentations and contradictions between supranational identities (such as the EU) and national (nationalist) and populist movements. Sheyla Benhabib (1996:56ff) had the following to say on this matter:

> *"Since every search for identity includes differentiating oneself from what one is not, identity politics is always and necessarily a politics of the creation of difference. One is a Bosnian Serb to the degree to which one is not a Bosnian Moslem or a Croat...What is shocking about these developments, is not the inevitable dialectic of identity/difference that they display but rather the atavistic belief that identities can be maintained and secured only by eliminating difference and otherness. The negotiation of identity/difference is the political problem facing democracies on a global scale."*

The dichotomization of this complex world into such simple categories is — in my opinion — truly the constitutive feature of political linguistic usage, persuasive communication and political action, but in particular of populist rhetoric, even when we look at it from an historical point of view (Wodak, 2001a,b).

At this point it is necessary to say a few words, as a short digression, on the term "Globalization" (Weiss and Wodak, 2000). This term has achieved an incredible prominence, and in the Social Sciences there are many different approaches to globalization. Many people see it as a myth that dispenses with any foundation in economic and political reality. Others believe that globalization is truly a reality and that it should be criticized radically, because it is leading to a dominance of international capital, of the financial markets and of *global players*. (Pierre Bourdieu in particular sees it in this way, see Bourdieu, 1993). Others are very enthusiastic because they smell the opportunity finally to realize the idea of "world citizen" and a new form of cosmopolitan democracy. (Ulrich Beck is an example here, see Beck, 1998). Still others adopt an ambivalent position and see both the political opportunities and the economic risks (Habermas, 1998). Others again describe in relatively sober terms the tensions that arise between globalization on the one hand and fragmentation and regionalization on the other (Luhmann, 1997).

The battle between these different positions cannot be settled here. And what makes a precise definition of the term additionally difficult is that it is applied to a variety of processes: economics, politics, the media, and so on. In this chapter, we are dealing with several important discursive rhetorical figures. I would just like to mention one: the decline of the nation state and the impact of globalizing economies.

One of the uses of the division between "us" and "them", between globalization rhetoric and homeland rhetoric, is to present one's own actions positively and, conversely, the actions of others negatively. This is a phenomenon that may be given a clear social-psychological explanation, and which researchers like Gordon Allport or Henri Tajfel spoke of many years ago (see Allport, 1993; Tajfel, 1981). This fundamental pattern has several functions, and in particular that of constituting identity but thereby also that of delimiting and excluding. From this point on, therefore, I would like to devote my attention almost exclusively to these kinds of "we-and-the other-discourses", as the most important example of the discursive construction of identities. What linguistic and discursive functions, therefore, can we distinguish and what are the consequences?

> Complex phenomena are explained in simple terms, and thereby distorted.

> Complex questions are given simple answers.

Complex arguments are replaced by simple assertions.

Complex problems rapidly find simple solutions: the scapegoat strategy is available as an example of this. "The others are to blame!"

Friends and foes are always being redefined, and those in power determine who shall be included and excluded.

This basic structure permits generalizations to be made about the out-group, which is a pre-condition of prejudiced linguistic usage.

Winning and being included into the positive in-group is constitutive of persuasive communication, for instance in an election campaign. In this way identities are perpetually being reconstructed discursively.

The we-discourse, therefore, serves ultimately to create and define identities, to bring about continuous re-ordering of identity, similarity and difference (*idem* and *ipse* in Ricoeur's sense) and to manipulate exclusion and delimitation.

Multiple Identities

In the first example from our study of EU organizational systems, I would like to summarize some results from our interviews with commission employees and MEPs, focusing on the "Us" and "Them" discourses.

The data for this analysis consist of 28 interviews with 14 Members of the European Parliament, all members of the Committee on Employment and Social Affairs; 10 Commission officials, and the Commissioner in charge of employment and social issues; and four Austrian delegates to the Council of Ministers (see Straehle, 1998).

The question in focus here (one of the many questions asked) is "Do you consider yourself to be European and, if so, what are the characteristics of being European?" which requests rather direct labelling of self-identity. Since the question involves two components,

Table 8.1
MEPs' Self-definitions

	European	Region in Europe, e.g., Scandina-via	Country/ National -ity	Region in Country, e.g., Bavaria	City, Town	World Citizen; not just EU	Not in terms of citizen-ship	Definition variable in relation to others
MEP1	X		X		X			
MEP2	X	X	X					
MEP3	(X)[1]				X			
MEP4	X					X		
MEP5	X			X				
MEP6	X							
MEP7	X	X	X			X		
MEP8	N/A							
MEP9	X		X					
MEP10	X	X	X		X	X		
MEP11	N/A							
MEP12	N/A							
MEP13				X			X	
MEP14	(X)[2]		(X)		(X)	X		X
	9/13 (10)/13	3/13	5/13	2/13	3/13 (4)/13	4/13	1/13	1/13

Notes:

1   MEP states that she is and is not European, depending on how one looks at it.

2   Characteristics for this MEP hold only in contrast to other countries, e.g., feeling European when in the USA, etc.

N/A   these respondents gave characteristics of what European means, but did not explicitly state that they felt European the self-labelling and the listing of specific qualities, the presentation here is also handled in two parts. And because response patterns appear to correspond with the interviewees' respective EU organizational affiliation, my discussion looks at MEPs, Commission officials, and Council representatives, respectively.

Members of Parliament

In Table 8.1, we see that most MEPs of those who were asked, responded to the first part of the question, "Do you consider yourself to be European?", explicitly with "I am European" (one MEP simply stated "yes") and five of these further added their self-identification with the country they represent in the Parliament, e.g., "I am European and I am Dutch". At the same time, other characteristics are relevant, for example coming from a particular region, supranational or national, such as Scandinavia or Hessen, or labelling oneself as from a particular city, such as Berlin. Four MEPs mentioned explicitly that 'being European" involved more than simply the EU, but entailed being a "world citizen" or "cosmopolitan" as well. Interestingly, all four MEPs who added this to their self-definition are affiliated with the Green Party. One MEP defines herself in several "layers" of these characteristics:

> *First I feel like I come from Västerbotten in the North of Sweden. I feel like a Västerbotten. I don't live there, but I feel like that. I feel like a Swede. I feel like a Scandinavian. I feel like a European and I feel like a world citizen. MEP10*

Commission Officials

The responses of Commission officials, suggest somewhat more homogeneity than the MEPs:

Table 8.2
Commission Officials' Self-Definition

	European	Region in Europe	Country/National-ity	Region in Country,	City or Town	World Citizen; not just EU	Not in terms of citizen-ship	Definition variable in relation to others
EC1	X							
EC2	X							
EC3	(X)[*]		(X)					
EC4	X		X					
EC5	X		X					
EC6	X		X		X			
EC7	X		X					X
EC8	X							X
EC9	X							X
EC10	X							
	9/10 (10)/10		4/10		1/10			9/10

Note: * This respondent noted that he felt no more European than before coming to the Commission and that he never felt particularly bound to his home country.

Specifically, all except one Commission official made an explicit statement to the effect of "Yes I feel European" or responded with an unequivocal "Sure! or "Yes." Here, too, about half of the interviewees added that they also identified themselves in terms of their home country/nationality, in other words, a standard response was to the effect of "Yes, I am European, but I am also French."

> *I think the Commission officials tend to be European, who have a vision of trying to get the best of each component of the EU. At the same time, I'm always a*

> *Finn. My philosophy is that you cannot really be a*
> *European if you don't have your roots anywhere.*
>
> EC5

Some also indicated feeling European when they are abroad, that is, in contrast to some other nation:

> *You feel European when you're in the middle of New*
> *York. That's when I feel European.*
>
> EC8

No other characteristics appear particularly salient. Unlike the Parliamentarians, none of the Commission respondents made the point of explicitly describing themselves as reaching beyond Europe, as "world citizens", and generally they did not speak in terms of regional or more local affiliations.

According to these data, then, it seems that the EC officials we interviewed are slightly more oriented to the idea of a European identity, one that is clearly compatible with maintaining one's national roots. The MEPs here expressed "Europeanness" as well, but tended to emphasize more regional and local identities as well as specifically national ones. One might speculate that these tendencies reflect on the one hand another of the roles commonly associated with the Commission, and on the other hand, the nature of the EP electoral system. The Commission is obviously sometimes viewed as "the conscience of the Community", which among other things, emphasizes the role of the Commission as "multinational organization, which does not seek to represent any one particular governmental position within the Union" (Cini, 1996:16), but aims to look for what is good for the Union as a whole, as a supranational entity. In the words of one EC official:

> *I'm a Swede and I'm a European because I'm working*
> *on the European level and that means that I'm not here*
> *to represent Sweden. I'm here to see to all-the interest of*
> *ALL countries...*
>
> (EC4)

In other words, much of what the Commission does is somehow connected with promoting what is European rather than the interests of (a) particular Member State(s).

In contrast, the broader palette of identities mentioned by MEPs in this context could reflect the nature of the Parliamentary electoral system, which is not yet unitary across the EU. While some countries abide by a system of constituency representation (e.g., UK), others have more proportional systems where the entire country serves as the representative's electoral area (see Corbett *et al.*, 1995:13–29). As such, MEPs may in their self-definitions tend to orient to the factors that are relevant to their particular electoral situation, thereby variably emphasizing national, regional, or other such identities.

Council of Ministers Representatives

As was the case in assessing the responses of Council delegates above, here, too, we have difficulty making any clear generalizations because of the limited data. One of the four, like many of the MEPs and Commission officials above mentions feeling both European and Austrian. Another identifies herself as Austrian, and fourth merely signals "yes" in response to the question "Are you European", but does not elaborate further. Finally, two of them emphasize their scepticism with regard to the present existence of a united "Europe(an) Union)", citing the relative strength of *Nationalstaat*:

> *Ich glaube, es ist etwas was sich wandelt...es wird immer mehr, irgendwann werden, werden wir wahrscheinlich alle mal Europäer sein und werden...aber für mich ist Europa keine geschlossene Veranstaltung. Und je langer ich im Coreper und im Rat sitzt, unsomehr denke ich "Jessus, nein, das kann nie was werden!"...in Brüssel werden mit einer Brutalität nationale Interessen vertreten, das mit Europa, oder einem europäischen Gefühl nix zu tun hat.*
>
> CM2

I think it is something that is changing...it is increasing steadily, someday we will probably all be and become Europeans...but for me, Europe isn't something that's finished. And the longer I'm in Coreper and the Council, the more I think "Jesus, no, this can never amount to anything!" ...in Brussels national interests are represented with a brutality that has nothing to do with Europe or with a European feeling. (my translation)

This particular description also supports the perception expressed by Commission officials and MEPs that it is the Council, or rather the Member States that compose it, that sometimes impedes developments in the direction of a more united Europe, namely, brutally representing national, as opposed to supranational, interests.

Characteristics of European

We can compare the features of what constitutes "European" by examining Table 8.3. The characteristics here represent those most frequently mentioned by all interviewees, grouped according to their EU organizational affiliation:

Table 8.3
Characteristics of "European"

	Way of thinking; Exchanging ideas; Being concerned with own and others' problems	Different but shared cultures, traditions, history, languages	Way of dealing with social, environmental problems; Social model; not USA, Japan	Part of geographic map, more than E.U.	Globally competitive, especially against USA and Japan	Whole is bigger than its parts: being under one roof; Added value of EU; Strength in diversity	Vision, way, direction for the future	Model for peace
MEPs	4/13	5/13	4/13	4/13	2/13	3/13	4/13	1/13
EC	1/10	3/10	4/10	2/10	3/10	6/10	1/10	1/10
CM	0/4	2/4	1/4	0/4	0/4	1/4	2/4	1/4
	5/27	9/27	9/27	6/27	5/27	10/27	7/27	3/27

While no definitive comparison among groups can be made, it appears that MEPs and EC officials, while overlapping in their mentioning of several characteristics, may stress certain features differently. Note, for example, that 6 out of 10, more than half of the Commission officials stress the "added value" of the Member States being united in the European Union. In the words of one official (EC8), it is necessary to "capture Europe's diversity in an economic way", that "Europe's strength is its diversity." In other words, this economic characteristic underscores the legitimacy of the EU. Working together under "one roof", Member States can prosper more than if they were to act independently.

Among MEPs no one cluster of characteristics is particularly prominent — instead, several attributes receive similar mention — except, perhaps, for emphasizing Member States share a certain cultural, historical and linguistic richness that binds them together, despite differences in specifics.

When we combine the responses of all three groups, however, we see that certain characteristics of "European" are somewhat more prominent than others: (1) Differences notwithstanding, generally shared cultural, historical, linguistic traditions; (2) the "added value" of a united Europe; (3) the European social model, one that is emphatically *not* the same as in the US or in many Asian countries; and (4) Europe as a way for the future. If we look at these attributes more closely, we could argue that they resemble the "matrix of contents" that Wodak *et al.* (1999:57–60) see as capturing the themes relevant to the discursive construction of a nation in their study: the linguistic construction of the *homo Austriacus*, a common culture, a common political present and future, a national body and the "narration and confabulation of a common political past". Among the characteristics of "European" highlighted by the interviewees, we see repeated reference to a common culture and past (i.e., shared cultural, historical, linguistic traditions; similar social models) and a common present and future (i.e., European social model; "added value" of being united; a way for the future). Moreover, if identity is to some extent "based on the formation of sameness and difference", we see this in the frequent referral to Europe, especially in terms of its social model(s), as not the U.S. or Asia (most prominently, Japan). Thus, all our examples point to discourses of sameness and difference. Moreover, all the interviews illustrate that the different sub organizations of the EU require different forms of identification with Europe due to their manifest and latent functions. In the EP, specifically, the multiple identities of regional, national and supra national belongings conflict with each other.

Identity and Difference: The CAG

The CAG, i.e., the body under investigation, was set up by Jacques Santer, former President of the European Commission, in order to prepare specific drafts and proposals directly for the Council of Ministers. The group consists of 12 members, two women and ten men, who represent industry, politics and the trade unions; the European Commission itself is also represented by one member. These representatives discuss highly sensitive issues and draw up a report every six months. The CAG is chaired by Jean Claude Paye, former Secretary-General of the OECD, whom I interviewed in Paris in September 1998. Meetings are audio-taped, there are hand written minutes as well as resolution papers. In autumn 1997, the CAG was asked to draw up an employment policy paper for the Council of Ministers in November 1997. The CAG is an example of an "epistemic community" or "transnational knowledge community" which "proposes problem definitions, argumentations and policies" (Beck, 1998:39) The policy paper finally manifests clearly the conflicts between employers and trade unions on many levels. It is an attempt to lay out a European employment policy, a policy, which changes the social welfare states but nevertheless retains European values.

First, I would like to illustrate the ideological debates on the New European Identity from inside this small group of prominent experts:

M3
Dans les points forts, President, d'abord l'effort d'ajustement structurelle de beaucoup d'entreprises, avec la recherche d'économie d'échelle et les fusions, les regroupements, le redressement de la rentabilité de beaucoup de sociétés, un climat social finalement les

derniéres années quand même relativement stable, un peu de, de grandes gréves et des conflits sociaux, l'évolution favorable de la balance extérieur de l'Union Européenne, les effets favorables de l'ouverture du marchés des capitaux, et l'approximité de marché émergeant, je pense à l'Europe Central et l'Europe de l'Est, tout ça est positif. Et mon dernier point c'était, mais vous l'avez déjà mentionné, le niveau élevé de l'éducation et de la formation professionel dans la plupart des pays Europeens. Ca sont des atouts.

Paye
Merci, M9
M9
I think, another strong point ehm, which we're just beginning to see, is, in the context of a global market place. Ehm, Europe's historical positioning around the world. And the fact that uniquely in terms of the main blocks of economic activity, the United States, Europe and Japan, ehm, we in Europe are best positioned to cover the world with cultural and commercial links. And if I can turn to my left, you take Spain, I mean, Spain has rediscovered an Hispanic market which extends not just throughout most of Latin America but also of course in the United States. Ehm, and we're beginning to find in other parts of the world that we have links, which are old links, which have been dormant and which can come forth, and in terms of, you know Europe in a global market place, that inheritance is very very strong. But we've got to capitalize it, and use it.

Paye
Just, a, a sentence adding to that point. European is more international than, than other ones, and ....

M9
Exact, and it's very much easier as a European to develop commercial partnerships outside your domestic country than it is for Americans, or Japanese. And that's partly because of our inheritance and history.
M4
....maybe, our diversity...

M9

...that too...

M3

Diversity is a richness, not a weakness, to a large extent.

M9

There are two layers to it: I mean, the, the, there is the diversity and that in one sense or another we cover the globe, eh, but there is also the, the history and the way in which we have operated, we, we do have a more global view of the world than the Americans, far more so.

M3

Exact, it is the long-term favour of fall-out of our colonial past. Yeah, after 30 years of independence of all our former colonies we can say that now, today. Without being accused of neo-, neo-colonialism. Yeah.

F1

In a more friendly way, in our entrepreneurship. Our ancestors went out, sailing, to do business.

M6

Well, American multinationals have done well but, I mean you, I mean the, the, the, many sectors, I'm not saying your sector, but I mean, one cannot forget that......

M9

I, I, I'm not xxx the Americans, in that sense, and eh, all I'm saying is that ehm, they do have a blind spot. And their blind spot is often their ability to make partnerships outside their domestic base. Ehm, and they have significant blind spots within Europe, in, Europe is Europe is Europe, except there is an English speaking bit in the UK, and the, they ha, they have difficulty in sensing the differences between countries, and it, it's much tougher for them. Whereas we have something which we haven't used for a long time, but is, is, is coming forward here, and, I, I, I do take the Hispanic point is very strong as you know and me too well, in eh, in all sorts of businesses, telecommunications, financial services, you name it, it's eh, they've found a new market.

Paye

Alright, that, you, do, do you see any other eh, strong eh, points, or should we move to the next session?

This sequence is one of the few where spontaneous discussion occurs. It is like a brainstorming session where everybody contributes to the characteristics of a new European identity, one, which stands in contrast to the USA and Japan. One might have the impression that the members of the committee try to convince each other that specific European aspects are actually to be viewed as positive and not negative. This sequence also functions to emphasize group solidarity. Without analyzing this sequence in a detailed way, we would just like to point out two main linguistic strategies employed here: legitimation and difference (Van Leeuwen and Wodak, 1999). All the characteristics mentioned in this short dialogue point to Europe's traditions in justice and welfare, education and professional expertise. Specifically, Europe's internationalism is mentioned, its tradition in contacting other parts of the world (colonialism!), in contrast to the USA, which does not have such a tradition. Some other characteristics are added on during this brainstorming session: diversity and knowledge. Specifically, the debate about "diversity" (Essed, 1998) is of interest here. Diversity is defined in a positive way, as richness of cultures and traditions and languages, not as something negative which often happens in racist discourse on immigration (Wodak and Sedlak, 1999). All the positive characteristics reassure the members of the committee that Europe has a chance in the world market even though taxes are higher and labor laws stricter. The specific Europeanness is co-constructed interactively. The other strategy consists of distinguishing oneself from others, the USA and Japan, of constructing uniqueness. This is typical for discourses on identity (see Wodak *et al.*, 1999, de Cillia, Reisigl, and Wodak, 1999). The whole passage is very significant in the meeting. It has the function of creating optimism and showing solutions to the European economic problems. A positive self-assessment makes everybody feel stronger. Thus, this passage also constructs the identities of the committee members. Note that a national identity is used as an example, pars pro toto, namely Spain. The "Hispanic example" provides an illustration of what Europe could achieve. Summarizing: Europe is in search of new employment policies because of big structural changes in the world but this new policy should be different from the USA and Japan. The politics of identity and difference — to take up our *topos* from the beginning and throughout the chapter — becomes very visible as well as the impact of regional, national and supranational identities. Secondly, it must also be emphasized that even in a committee dealing with pure economics, with un/employment as an economic and not social problem, such a debate could occur.

In the interview with the chairperson Paye, I asked about the decision-making process and his impressions about it as well as about the impact of such a document: who reads the report, what is the impact of this policy paper? There must be important functions of the CAG, because otherwise such busy and influential people would not take the trouble to meet and spend their time together. As already mentioned in the introduction, networking is one of the main characteristics of such transnational bodies. The second important function is most certainly legitimation. The policy paper serves as legitimation device for the politicians if they need it. The chairperson himself is well aware of these functions. "I think that his self-assessment is of interest:

I: WHAT HAPPENS with these reports. who who READS them

P: THIS is this is äh: this is a problem I ähm spoke aBOUT with öh: with the (xxx) Président Santer, because — my impression is that öh öh the agenda of öh of öh the (European) Council — according to what I read in — in the [*laughs*] (press communiqué)

I: ja,

P: is so: — HEAVy. so heteROGENEOUS so diVERSE, that they CANnot — devote öh öh much TIME to to every SUBject. — I don't know how it is going NOW, ähm — let me take the example of this äh report in November, [*coughs*] — there were — two reports to the European Council, coming from a wide vaRIETy of öh of institutions and I've been TOLD that the European PARLiament made report, the (Hungarian social council) made a rePORT, öh: the — there were — two or three other reports in addition to OURS. — of COURSE — the

the heads of (State and government) haven't been able to to read all all that STUFF, and not even their AIDES.

I: ja.

P: %have been able [*softly*]% - THEREfore I don't know. — I don't know what the the the real IMpact öh öh IS, — which öh of course is a bit öh: — well discouraging

Paye himself thus is very pessimistic about the influence of a group such as the CAG. Nevertheless, he believes in his work and that the debates are important. The papers are circulated widely and maybe — as Paye argues — might have an impact somewhere at sometime.

So, we are left with the question what the functions of such a group are and why so much work is invested into a policy paper, which is maybe not read by the audience it addresses. I believe — as mentioned above — that the main function lies in the establishing of solidarity and networks, of having discussion fora where European citizens meet. Only in such a way, at very many different places and times, is the construction of a new European identity possible. And at the same time, only through extended debates between the social partners are new economic policies to be developed. The CAG provides a stage for such ideological debates, a public space where different ideologies and opinions can meet and negotiations take place. This, in my view, is the most important function of such advisory groups.

Discourse and Politics: Us and Them

In the last example, I would like to turn to the homeland rhetoric, to illustrate the tensions between the EU and its member states. I would like to discuss briefly the very interesting first attempt of the EU to "punish" member states if they do not act according to values of the "dispositif idéel": "The Three Wise Men" judging the behaviour of the new coalition government in Austria since 4 February 2000.

With the instalment of the new government, the 14 other member states implemented "measures against the new government", which were recontexualized as "sanctions against Austria" in official discourses. Most people had the feeling (and were deeply hurt) that the EU did not "like" them and they felt punished, again victims of conspiracies, as Austrians have felt throughout history time and again. As soon as the EU member states realized that these measures had the reverse effect (they strengthened the government and did not weaken it), they searched for an exit strategy. And the "Three Wise Men" were called upon: the former Finnish president, the Spanish chancellor and a prominent German political scientist. These three men visited Austria twice, spoke to many delegates, officials and NGOs and came out with an extensive report on 8 September 2000. The report also judged the populist discourse of the FPOe, from which I would just like to quote the following:

c) Der fortwährende Gebrauch zweideutiger Formulierungen durch fuehrende Mitglieder der FPÖ

88. Es scheint tatsächlich zu einem typischen Kennzeichen in der Österreichischen Politik geworden zu sein, dass Vertreter der FPÖ äußerst mißverständliche Formulierungen verwenden. Hohe Parteifunktionäre der FPÖ haben über eine lange Zeit hinweg Stellungnahmen abgegeben, die als fremdenfeindlich oder sogar als rassistisch verstanden werden können. Viele Beobachter erkennen in den verwendeten Formulierungen nationalistische Untertöne, manchmal sogar Untertöne, die typisch nationalsozialistischen Ausdrücken nahe kommen, oder sie sehen in ihnen eine Verharmlosung der Geschichte dieser Zeit".

[c) The continual use of ambiguous formulations by leading members of the FPÖ.

88. It seems indeed to have become a typical feature of Austrian politics, that representatives of the FPÖ use extremely misleading formulations. Senior party members of the FPÖ have, over a long period of time, adopted attitudes that could be understood as xenophobic or even as racist. Many observers have recognized, in the formulations used, nationalistic undertones, and sometimes even undertones that come

close to typical national-socialist expressions, or they sense in them a trivialization of the history of that period.]

The report then becomes more specific and less vague:

89 Offenbar hat die FPÖ keine Masznahmen gegen Mitglieder ergriffen, die öffentlich fremdenfeindliche Stellungnahmen abgegeben haben; sie hat diese Stellungnahmen weder verurteilt noch unterbunden und sich auch nicht eindeutig fur sie entschuldigt. Wenn diese Äußerungen ihren Urhebern vorgehalten werden, bestreiten sie jegliche national-sozialistische Absicht oder einen entsprechenden Charakter der Äußerung".

[89. Clearly the FPÖ has taken no measures against members who have publicly projected xenophobic attitudes; it has neither condemned nor curtailed these attitudes and has made no clear apology for them. Whenever the perpetrators are confronted with these utterances, they deny any national-socialist intention or any corresponding character of the utterance.]

These two paragraphs — and they are followed by several more in similar vein —, which discuss very critically the actions of FPÖ functionaries, and document the fact that even a prominent commission of two "elder statesmen" and a highly respected political scientist attribute an inherent role to political communication, to the language of politics, and also to language in politics and to the prejudiced discourse of the FPÖ. The reactions to this report were manifold: The government posted that everything was now okay, that the EU had judged Austria democratic and acting according to the European values. The quoted paragraphs were almost not talked about at all. If some government officials reacted to the judgement of the FPÖ, they tried to change the judgement and — for example — changed the negative connotation of "radical" to a positive one. I dealt with these aspects elsewhere extensively (Wodak 2001, a,b). On the surface, the conflict has thus been "managed" and solved; and the EU sanctions were taken from the agenda in the media, which they had dominated for months. This makes it possible now to confront other problems in Austria again.

Which Functions can One Detect while Analyzing the Status and Impact and Working of Such an Expert Committee?

First, there is the important question concerning the status of "Experts" and "Knowledge Management". Nowadays, commissions frequently have a transnational brief. I recall the Waldheim Commission and the Historians' Report, or the moratorium on the Wehrmacht Exhibition (Wodak *et al.*, 1994). The Three Wise Men do not fit into this schema, because "elder statesmen" under considerable pressure of time had to exercise diplomatic and political conflict management and legitimize the "exit strategy" on which one had already informally agreed upon. As Romani Prodi, the president of the EU commission, said in June 2000 when the Three Wise Men were put to work, they should be "quick, quick, quick" in their judgement. Diplomacy is reflected in the language they used: a language that is not scientific, but which is characterized — at least in part — by vagueness. The vagueness relates particularly to those statements in the report that are based on documents and evidence from NGOs, thus on reported speech.

The takeover of political action by such political entrepreneurs, as Paul Krugman has described them, is a characteristic of the globalized society (Krugman, 1994). Both Paul Krugman and Ulrich Beck even talk of a "committee regime", referring to Van Schendelen (1996). Static national organizations are to a great extent being replaced by such transnational networks. This could be demonstrated already with reference to our study of decision-making mechanisms in the EU and the CAG (cf. Muntigl, Weiss and Wodak, 2000). The intervention of such international committees of experts shows, however, that traditional national borders are no longer valid, that is to say that "abroad" and "home" are becoming blurred, that foreign policy is becoming internal policy, and that the language of experts is being given a dominant role. Professional roles and definitions are changing: in our EU research it was quite evident that we are approaching a politicization of the bureaucracy and a depoliticization of politics.

An entire register of competences is expected and used, bureaucrats have to be able to negotiate like diplomats, they are often experts in a particular subject and prepare decisions. Politicians administer these decisions and attempt to "sell them". And it as this point that political rhetoric takes over. We are dealing here with an example — even in the case of the Three Wise Men — of those epistemic communities or transnational communities of knowledge and expertise who, as Ulrich Beck says, "develop, own and provide common definitions of problems, causal assumptions and political recommendations". International organizations depend increasingly on this kind of transnational rationale of experts, which, conversely, is entering ever more areas of social practice. What is characteristic of such communities is that the border between reflective-distanced expertise on the one hand and political action on the other (or policy-making as we call it today) is disappearing. In fact it is no longer possible to determine clearly who is a politician and who is an expert.

Secondly, this conflict management also has huge impact on the search for new European values and identities. It was the first time that "measures" were taken against a nation state and member which seemed to have behaved "badly", or not according to values of democracy, justice and equality. The action taken by the 14 other member states clearly that the EU organizations have developed from purely economic interest groups to something else, to a system of values, in their search for a European identity. This is what makes this Austrian example so interesting for the whole European development which Tony Judt calls "an idea" not "a region" (1996). Of course, many questions remain unanswered: what happens to other member states with populist parties in their governments, to larger and more powerful member states, for example? Is national sovereignty still respected?

The political models presented for Austria are not, of course, restricted only to Austria or to the present day. "Globalization and Homeland Rhetoric", and also right-wing populism, are on the increase throughout Western Europe, as a number of election campaigns, such as the recent one in Belgium by the Vlaams Blok, have demonstrated powerfully. It is for precisely this reason that the measures against the new Austrian government must also be seen against this background: and the specifically Austrian stimulus — the "sloppy handling of its National Socialist past" — became the decisive reason for action. We will have to continue to observe these European experiences for new cases of value judgements, as attempts to construct the New European Identity.

Conclusions

If one comes to Brussels or Strasbourg, one is struck by the semiotics of the buildings: they are like fortresses or churches, big stable organizations where the entrance is controlled by many passwords, bodyguards and x-rays. Everybody runs around very busily, through endless corridors, 11 languages are to be heard, and many intercultural gestures and misunderstandings can be perceived. In this most complex organization, where gender, age, ideologies, political parties, lobbies, national, regional and European interests clash, consensus is nevertheless achieved, as in the CAG or also by the Three Wise Men. These very slow and bureaucratic organizations have created means, which enable quick decisions and consensus without having to pass all possible hindrances. But exactly these small and dynamic networks are non-transparent, not accessible by the European citizens. These are heard and interviewed and reported sometimes, like in our latter example; or very prominent elites decide without even listening to them, like in the CAG. We are dealing with symbols of identity formation, on the one hand, like the buildings and the explicit power formation; on the other hand, one is confronted with decisions by experts "behind closed doors". The knowledge society has substituted these transnational networks of experts for all our well established forms of institutional actions and knowledge. They meet anywhere, quickly, and are dynamic and flexible. Their discourses are ideological and serve as legitimation for political actions, whereas the traditional organizations like the European Parliament, for example, discuss the details and organizational aspects. These differences are visible even in their use of verb processes or agents as we have documented elsewhere (Weiss and Wodak, 2000b).

These considerations point to the beginning of this paper, to Vaclav Havel and his claims of the functioning of the new globalizing processes and the search for patriotism and supra national identities: our whole perceptions of national identities and of political organizations have changed.

In his book *A Grand Illusion. An Essay on Europe*, Tony Judt (1996) summarizes the European "problem" as follows referring, of course, to Benedict Anderson's concept of "imagined communities":

> *"If we look to European Union as a solution for everything, chanting 'Europe' like a mantra, waving the banner of 'Europe' in the face of recalcitrant 'nationalist' herectics and screaming 'Abjure, abjure', we shall wake up one day to find that far from solving the problems of our continent, the myth of 'Europe' has become an impediment to our recognizing them. We shall discover that it has become little more than the politically correct way to paper over local difficulties, as though the mere invocation of the promise of Europe could substitute for solving problems and crises that really affect the place. Few would wish to deny the ontological existence of Europe, so to speak. And there IS a certain self-fulfilling advantage in speaking of it as though it existed in some strong collective sense…. 'Europe' is more than a geographical notion but less than an answer." (140/41).*

References

1. Allport, G. W. 1993. Vorwort. In *Antisemitismus*, edited by E. Simmel. Frankfurt am Main: Fischer, 9–11.

2. Andersen, B. 1988. *Die Erfindung der Nation. Zur Karriere eines erfolgreichen.* Konzepts: Frankfurt a. Main/New York.

3. Bach, M. 1999. *Die Bürokratisierung Europas. Verwaltungseliten, Experten und politische Legitimation in Europa.* Frankfurt a. M./New York: Campus.

4. Baumann, Z. 1999. *In search of politics.* London: Polity Press.

5. Beck, U. 1998. *Politik der Globalisierung.* Frankfurt am Main.

6. Benhabib, S. 1996. The democratic movement and the problem of difference. In *Democracy and difference: Contesting the boundaries of the political,* edited by S. Benhabib. Princeton, NJ: Princeton University Press, 3–18.

7. Bernstein, B. 1990. *The structure of pedagogic discourse: Class, codes and control.* Vol VI. London.

8. Bourdieu, P. 1993. *Soziologische Fragen.* Frankfurt/Main.

9. Brague, R. 1992. *Europe, la voie romaine.* Paris: Criterion.

10. _____. 1993. *Europa. Eine exzentrische Identitaet.* Frankfurt: Campus.

11. Clegg, S. 1990. *Modern organizations: Organization studies in the postmodern world.* London.

12. _____ and C. Hardy. 1996. Organizations, organization and organizing. In *Handbook of organizations studies,* edited by S. Clegg, C. Hardy, and W. North. London, 1–28.

13. Corbett, R. *et al.* 1995. *The European parliament.* 3rd ed. London: Cartermill.

14. De Cillia, R., M. Reisigl and R. Wodak. 1999. The discursive construction of national identities. *Discourse & Society* 10 (1): 149–173.

15. Ehlich, K. and J. Rehbein. 1986. *Muster und Institution. Untersuchungen zur schulischen Kommunikation.* Tübingen: Niemeyer.

16. Essed, P. 1998. *Diversity: Gender, colour and culture.* UMP. Amherst.

17. Fairclough, N. 1992. *Discourse and social change.* Cambridge: Polity Press.

18. _____. 1999. Democracy and the public sphere in critical research on discourse. In *Challenges in a changing world,* edited by R. Wodak and C. Ludwig. Vienna, 63–85.

19. Giddens, A. 1994. *The constitution of society.* Cambridge: Polity Press.

20. Habermas, J. 1988. *Die postnationale Konstellation. Politische Essays.* Frankfurt am Main.

21. Harvey, D. 1996. *Justice, nature and the geography of difference.* London.

22. Henningsen, M. 1998. Die politische Verfassung Europas. Merkur: *Deutsche Zeitschrift für europäisches Denken* 5 (5): 454–461.

23. Höffe, O. 1999. *Demokratie im Zeitalter der Globalisierung.* München: Beck.

24. Iedema, R. 1997a. Organizational dynamics and social change. Ph.D Diss., University of New South Wales, Australia.

25. _____. 1999. The formalization of meaning. In *Special issue of discourse and society on organizational research.* Volume 10.1, edited by R. Wodak and R. Iedema, 49–66.

26. Judt, T. 1996. *A grand illusion. An essay on Europe.* London: MacMillan.

27. Kovacs, A. and R. Wodak, eds. 2001. *NATO, neutrality and national identity: The case of Austria and Hungary.* Vienna: Boehlau. In Press.

28. Krugman, P. 1994; *Peddling prosperity. Economic sense and nonsense in the age of diminished expectations.* New York: Norton.

29. Lemke, J. 1995. *Textual politics: Discourse and social dynamics.* London: Falmer Press.

30. Linell, P. 1998. Discourse across boundaries: On recontextualizations and the blending of voices in professional discourse. *Text* 18 (2): 143–157.

31. Luhmann, N. 1997. *Die Theorie der Gesellschaft.* 2 Volumes. Frankfurt: Suhrkamp.

32. Moisi, D. 1999. Dreaming of Europe. *Foreign Policy* 115:44–61.

33. Muntigl, P., G. Weiss and R. Wodak. 2000. *European Union discourses on un/employment. An interdisciplinary approach to employment policy-making and organizational change.* Amsterdam: Benjamins.

34. Reed, M. 1996. Organizational theorising: A historically contested terain. In *Handbook of organization studies,* edited by S. Clegg, C. Hardy and W. Nord. Newbury Park, 31–35.

35. Reisigl, M. and R. Wodak. 2000. *Discourse and discrimination. Rhetorics of racism and antisemitism.* London: Routledge.

36. _____ . 2001. *The semiotics of racism. Approaches in critical discourse analysis.* Vienna: Passagen.

37. Ricoeur, P. 1992. *Oneself as another.* Chicago.

38. Straehle, C. 1998. *We are not Americans and not Japanese, we are Europeans. Looking inside the European Union.* Vienna: Manuscript.

39. Tajfel, H. 1981. *Human groups and social categories. Studies in social psychology.* Cambridge: Cambridge University Press.

40. Van Leeuwen, T. and R. Wodak. 1999. Legitimizing immigration control. A discourse-historical analysis. *Discourse Studies* 1 (1): 83–118.

41. Van Schendelen, M. P. C. M. 1996. EC Committees: Influence counts more than legal powers. In *Shaping European law and policy. The role of committees and commitology processes in the political process,* edited by R. Pedeler and G. F. Schaefer. Maastricht, 25–38.

42. Weiler, J. 1999. *The constitution of Europe.* Cambridge: Cambridge University Press.

43. Weiss, G. and R. Wodak. 1999. Organization and communication. On the relevance of Niklas Luhman's systems theory for a discourse-hermeneutic approach to organizations. Working Papers, Kopenhagen .

44. _____ . 2000a. European Union discourses on employment. Strategies of depoliticizing unemployment and ideologizing employment policies. In *International Journal of Action Research and Organizational Renewal* 5 (1): 2000.

45. _____ . 2000b. *Debating Europe. Globalization rhetorics in European Union committees.* Amsterdam: John Benjamins.

46. Wilke, H. 1999. Inevitable unemployment: On the impact of the knowledge society on the labour market. University of Bielefeld.

47. Wodak, R., F. Menz, R. Mitten and F. Stern. 1994. *Sprachen der Vergangenheiten. Öffentliches Gedenken in österreichischen und deutschen Medien.* Frankfurt: Suhrkamp.

48. _____. *et al.* 1999. *The discursive construction of national identity.* Edinburgh: University Press.

49. _____. 1999. Critical discourse analysis at the end of the 20th Century. *Research on Language and Social Interaction* 32 (1&2): 185–193.

50. _____. 2001a. Multiple identities: The role of female parliamentarians in the EU parliament. In *Handbook of language and gender*, edited by J. Holmes and M. Meyerhoff. Forthcoming.

51. _____. 2001b. *Diskurs, Politik, Identität, Tagungsband Wissenschaftstag, Österreichische Forschungsgemeinschaft.* Forthcoming.

52. _____ and M. Sedlak. 1999. We demand that foreigners adapt to our life-style: Political discourse on immigration laws in Austria and the United Kingdom. In *Combating racial discrimination. Affirmative action as a model for Europe*, edited by E. Appelt and M. Jarosch. Oxford, NY: Berg, 217–237.

53. _____ and E. Vetter. 1999. Competing professions in times of change: The discursive construction of professional identities in TV talk-shows. In *Challenges in a changing world*, edited by R.Wodak and Chr. Ludwig. Wien: Passagen Verlag, 209–237.

54. Wunderlich, D. 1972. *Linguistische Pragmatik*, Frankfurt am Main.

9

Retrospect and Prospect

Tom Huckin

In what follows, I would like to identify what I think are the *four main themes* of the plenary papers from the *Research and Practice in Professional Discourse Conference* which are presented as chapters in the first major section of this book from pages 39 to 261. In all cases, the authors of the plenary papers address, touch on, or emphasize these themes.

The first theme, which I will call the *dynamism of disciplinary boundaries and genres,* has clearly taken hold in the field of discourse analysis and genre theory. Discourses and genres are not static structures and forms but flexible, dynamic and malleable constructs that can be manipulated for rhetorical purposes. Disciplines are not carved out in a hard and fast fashion but are constantly inter-penetrated by neighbouring disciplines. It is this dynamism which makes the field exciting as an area for study.

The second theme, which I will call *the use of rhetorical analysis,* fits well with the dynamism I have just mentioned because rhetorical analysis allows you to discern how speakers or writers try to produce discourse for specific purposes for specific audiences, tailoring their communication to particular situations. In this sense, therefore, one might expect the dynamism of disciplines and genres to go hand in hand with the use of rhetorical analysis. Not all of the plenary papers engaged in rhetorical analysis but most of them did to a certain extent.

As a third theme, I would identify what I will call *analyst reflexivity* — how willing analysts are to engage in reflection and second thoughts about their methodology and what it is that they are performing as analysts. This kind of reflectiveness is, I think, inherent in good discourse analysis and in some cases it is particularly important and salient. Most of the plenary papers engaged in this kind of reflexivity, the only exceptions being those where the research was still in midstream.

Finally, and as a fourth theme, I identify what I will call *interactivity between discourse analysts and professionals in the workplace,* where discourse analysis and workplace applications are seen to be mutually beneficial. I find this kind of direct engagement in the workplace an exciting development in discourse analysis, providing a kind of ethnomethodological thrust, one which was taken up as a theme in many, though not all, of the plenary papers.

Dynamism

Turning first to the theme of dynamism, John Swales's chapter is devoted mostly to a historical survey of structural non-dynamic models. While giving general support for their value, it is interesting to note, however, that in the end he aligns himself with what he calls *contemporary teaching practice* which he describes as follows: "In a negotiated approach to teaching genres particularly as it becomes both personalized and particularized for the individual rhetorical situation of the individual NNS writer, and wherein schemata become recontextualized, simple, fallible but interesting structural models lose their authority, and rightly so especially in an era when professional genres are in dynamic movement and in rapid evolution". So we may conclude that he recognizes and accepts the dynamic theme I have identified.

Vijay Bhatia draws our attention consistently to the issue of hybridization and the mixing of genres and professional discourses. This has been a theme of his scholarly writings for some time, and so his support for this initial theme might be expected. What his current research has taken us to, however, is towards a dynamism of dynamism if you like, whereby dynamic discursive practices dynamically colonize other discourses and genres across disciplinary and professional boundaries.

As Charles Bazerman indicates in his chapter, his research throughout most of his career has focused on discursive and rhetorical differences between disciplines, but perhaps more from the perspective of differences that are embedded *within* disciplines than of differences that emerge from *cross*-disciplinary analysis. As might be expected, however, of someone so prolific in his output, his approach has continued to evolve towards one which seems now to be more locally-rhetorically situated. Towards the end of his chapter he writes about the need to have *"a detailed analysis of situations and how they evolve with their various textual interventions and accomplishments"*. Writing for him is now *"strategic, purposeful action within unfolding inter-texts"*. If we were to compare that statement with some of his earlier writings from, say, ten years ago, I think we would recognize a shift in the direction of more dynamic and interdisciplinary analysis and study.

Gu Yueguo's chapter displays an extremely interesting and what one might call a natural "grassroots" methodology that seeks to record language in use — here spoken Putonghua in Beijing — and to privilege its naturally occurring non-standardized forms rather than seeing language as the instantiation of a language system. Accordingly, we may note that he takes a very strong position in embracing the dynamism of natural language in use. As he writes, *"workplace discourse can be seen as evolving along with the life-path trajectories of discourse-making agents"*.

Ruth Wodak, working on a more macro-level, emphasizes in her chapter how much of the work being done to create a united Europe is not being accomplished through traditional, large institutions but through the interactions of smaller, more dynamic committees and networks. As she writes: "As a consequence of globalization, super-national dynamic and flexible commissions and committees are replacing cumbersome national institutions. Discourses of inclusion and exclusion are constitutive elements of political communication of as politics of identity and difference. Significantly new dynamic borders have been and are being created in both time and space". So here is a form of dynamism at the very macro level as opposed to a kind of individual, rhetorical event between individual actors. Her work, therefore, while illustrating my first theme, is quite unique among the different chapters that are presented here.

Jim Martin, it seems to me, is less concerned with documenting changing disciplinary boundaries than with advocating the setting-up of teams from different disciplines in such a way as to encourage peaceful co-existence between them so that they might learn from each other. This supported his larger goal of moving beyond modernist discourses of conflict resolution towards embracing newer, post-colonial ways of finding real reconciliation, or *ubuntu* in the case of South Africa. In his words, "Peace-makers can overcome the volatility of strong emotion and conflicting moralities to construct an aesthetically-balanced community in which feelings and differences are valued as resources for future generations". This is in a sense also an acknowledgement of what one might call a negotiated and harmonious dynamism.

Finally, Srikant Sarangi's model of inter-professional collaborative research in the health professions is primarily and fundamentally constituted in discursive hybridity and recontextualization practices across discourse boundaries. It is, then, essentially a dynamics of discourse. His chapter offers a range of examples from the medical and healthcare context, identifying different kinds of hybridity, the appropriation of genres by professional experts, and how discourses are inevitably recontextualized by the researcher in the process of analysis and account.

Rhetorical Analysis

With the exception of the chapter by Gu Yueguo, where his study was at this point focussed on corpus building and has not reached the point where he can pay attention to individual, situated communicative events, all the other plenary papers acknowledge in various ways the value of rhetorical analysis, though to different degrees.

In John Swales's case, rhetorical analysis provides perhaps the key element in his argument for the use of simple models in applied discourse analysis. Instead of aiming for highly accurate, full-blown descriptions of genres, he recommends, as an alternative, simple models which need to be critiqued, recontextualized and modified according to their particular rhetorical situations and contexts of use. In this sense, rhetorical analysis plays a fundamental role in his advocacy of simple models.

In the writings of Vijay Bhatia, rhetorical factors play an implicit role in all of his work on mixed genres, hybrid genres, and what he terms "genre-bending" by expert members of professional communities. For example, in his paper he defines genre-bending as "implicitly expressing private intentions within the context of socially-recognized communicative purposes". More generally, he points to a tension between language seen as form and language seen as action, a tension which constitutes a formula for rhetorical action.

Charles Bazerman's writings have always been suffused with a rhetorical sensibility and his chapter in this volume is no less so. As he announces, "As writers we are all reflective practitioners. Similarly we are often reflective speakers when we are not just running off at the mouth. We think about what we write and speak. We think about situations, goals, audiences and available means of expression. Such thought is the foundation of rhetoric which provides tools with which to think about communicative situations to make choices about what we speak and write to make deeper sense and judgements of what others speak and write. The more we learn about what written language can do, what our words do to whom under what conditions, we become more thoughtful and considered about our expression and more understanding of the force of other statements". I would be hard put, and it would be otiose, to restate his position. He declares it clearly. There could be no stronger endorsement of rhetoric and the centrality of rhetorical analysis.

Ruth Wodak's study includes the term *rhetoric* in its broad popular sense when she writes of the "rhetoric" of Austria's Freedom Party or of European unity more widely. But she also dug deeper in her ethnographic interviews. For example, consider the question she puts to the European Community's CAG [Competitive Advisory Group] chairman. *"Who reads these reports?"* A great question which unerringly addressed the real purposes behind the reports. Further, consider the analysis in her chapter of the three wise men's deliberate use of ambiguity in their criticism of the Freedom Party; in particular when they talked about the Freedom Party being a populist party with radical elements and how she neatly and persistently uncovers the built-in ambiguity in the term "radical". This is rhetorical analysis in action.

I would not consider Jim Martin's chapter as explicitly rhetorical, except in his treatment of the example case of the Paul Keating speech. However, in that Martin's trans-disciplinary approach is nonetheless explicitly about *negotiating futures*, this presumably must involve the analysis of purposes, identities, roles and other rhetorical elements involved in persuasive action. However, I am not sure that he would want to characterize Bishop Tutu's verbal art as deliberately persuasive or even rhetorical *per se* given the agonistic tradition of classical rhetoric. In any case, as a linguist, his chapter is strongly text-based with virtually no mention of audience, so in my understanding at least, one might say that rhetorical analysis was not present in the matrix of the paper though it appeared in one or more of the examples.

Srikant Sarangi does not write either about rhetoric *per se*. However, in his approach, he highlights the need for discourse practitioners and professional experts to align their ways of seeing and accounting as they attempt to understand the phenomena under study and try to bring about changes in their everyday practice through reflexivity. Although this is something that is not inherently rhetorical in the strict sense of the term, one could easily extend his research methodology to allow for some attention to be paid to the broader audience by addressing the issue of the effect of his research on actual patients. To do that would allow for more discussion of audience and audience reception, and through that one might incorporate something more of the understanding of rhetoric and rhetorical analysis I have identified.

Analyst Reflexivity

From the plenary papers we may discern different takes on the value, the possibility, and perhaps the desirability of analyst reflexivity. For some, such reflexivity is inherent and integral to their research and their methodology. For others, it may be wished-for, desirable, but essentially tangential to their research project; for others, again, it may be a stage to be achieved after essential descriptive and analyst-focused research has been undertaken. It may indeed be eschewed altogether in that such participant reflexivity is seen to detract from the objectivity of the analyst's descriptive account. Perhaps we see these latter two positions most clearly in the chapters by Ruth Wodak and Gu Yueguo.

In the case of John Swales' chapter, he interrogated his own history, his own take on the CARS model and why it has been so successfully adopted in a wide range of parallel studies of academic writing. I see this as constituting at least a small measure of analyst reflexivity although there is a sense in which he — and others — could take this much further. To be fair, one has to acknowledge that he has taken this step in other writings, for example, in *Other Floors, Other Voices* and in *"Discourse and the projection of corporate culture"* (with Priscilla Rogers).

Vijay Bhatia cites Sarangi and Candlin[1] on the need for reflexivity: "Entering a site of professional and public communication without any motivational relevancies as is the case with so-called open-ended discourse analytic studies, has to be viewed with considerable suspicion. Against this backdrop, reflexivity and collaborative interdisciplinary research becomes a necessity". But while acknowledging its relevance, his chapter does not go beyond this injunction in practice.

Reflexivity does not have to engage the Other, necessarily. Charles Bazerman, for example, in his chapter, begins by labelling it as a "reflexive autobiography"; and in tracking his own intellectual growth from his student years he provides a *self-oriented* interpretation of reflexivity which is as much part of its definition as that achieving reciprocity of perspectives among researcher and researched which Cicourel and others have sought to achieve in their analyses.

1. Sarangi S. and C. N. Candlin. 2001. Motivational relevancies: Some methodological reflections on social theoretical and sociolinguistic practice. In *Sociolinguistics and social theory*, edited by N. Coupland, S. Sarangi and C. N. Candlin. London: Pearson, 350–388.

At first glance, it would seem to me that the very systematicity of systemic functional grammar would work to militate against analyst reflexivity. But in his chapter, on page 217, Jim Martin writes "It might be even wiser to pause for a moment and consider the extent to which the affect, judgement and appreciation framework represents a western modernist construction of feeling. Tutu's Afro-Christian heritage might not factor attitudes along these lines. I'm not wise enough to gaze beyond my categories here. But I am confident that other cultures should take pause and look at what I have done through different eyes". So, in such a gracious and self-reflective remark, we can acknowledge, with Jim Martin, the potential value in the Other perspective, characteristic of analysts' reflexivity.

Srikant Sarangi's chapter clearly emphasizes at length the importance of reflexivity. The type of discourse analytic practice he describes implies the exercise of reflexivity by both discourse analyst and professional expert working together. Indeed, at one point he comments that such mutual and reciprocal activity is parallel to reflexive ethnography.

Interactivity

Finally, I turn to the theme of interactivity between discourse analysts and professionals in the workplace. This is something that Vijay Bhatia advocates very strongly and he does so in his chapter. In particular, he calls for discourse analysts to do field research in the professional workplace. He even coins a new acronym for it — PDA (professional discourse analysis). He urges that analysts as PDAs should investigate the complex realities of PP (professional practice). What we should do is to avoid falling back on idealizations, and rather get our hands dirty in the professional workplace. We need to know more about the nature of professional expertise and how professional discursive practices affect the use of genres, and how these genres relate to the construction of individual and personal identities. In the end Vijay raises these interesting questions: "To what extent should pedagogical practices reflect or account for the realities of the world of professional practice"and: "To what extent should the analytical procedures that we use account for the full realities of the world of discourse?" The latter question could lead to an interesting debate perhaps between himself and Martin, who does, I believe, look for full accounting of the world of discourse.

Jim Martin, in his chapter, seems to advocate a similar kind of interactivity between discourse analysts and professional experts that Bhatia does. One of his projects for example, involves educators learning about linguistics and linguists learning about education. "The more fluent the teacher-linguists we produce, the more productive our interventions". He calls for a type of "trinocular" vision that he feels is needed for a peace-making solution to long-standing problems. So, in this, he seems also to be committed to this kind of interactivity, even given the strong-text nature of his approach.

Charles Bazerman does not talk about workplace interaction in the normal sense. Nonetheless, his work does fit here if we think of the university itself as a workplace. And I think that is perfectly legitimate — after all, people at universities do spend most of their time working. "As I developed a pedagogy and textbooks, I became a student in my own classes in academic writing allowing me to push my research and theoretical research further, in turn providing deeper insights into my own writing and teaching". So, it seems almost like a self-ethnography or like Srikant Sarangi's collaborative arrangement where one part of Charles Bazerman is collaborating and interacting with the other part.

There is always a danger in reading from a single chapter an author's stance generally about issues such as those contained within the themes I have identified here. Such is the case with John Swales's chapter. Although his chapter in this volume does not talk about interactivity, one has only to consult his most recent book, *Other Floors, Other Voices*[2], to see that interactivity is at the heart of his textographic research methodology, engaging observer and observed in a way somewhat akin to ethnography. In that work, John's interactions with the professionals on each level of the building (especially the botanists

---

2.   Lawrence Erlbaum Associates (Mahwah, NJ), 1998.

and the applied linguists) were key to his insightful analyses of their discourse.

There is a need to distinguish *interactivity* (as between the participants in the research enterprise) and the description of interaction in the workplace. In one sense Gu Yueguo's chapter in this collection exemplifies this distinction. There is no doubt whatsoever that his research is strongly committed to investigating the complexities of *interaction* in workplace discourse. The compiling of a week's worth of spoken data from a worker in Beijing as he went about his daily life is bound to pay off not only for the study of modern spoken Putonghua, but also for the rich insights into workplace practices and interactions that it provides. However, the discourse analysts gathering this data remain to an extent, and perhaps necessarily, distant, so far as I can tell, from the workplace itself. Perhaps this is a matter of the analyst's preferences in presenting his or her data. For this theme of interactivity, however, it would be the mutualities (and the differences) of interpretation and approach among the participants that would be criterial.

Ruth Wodak's conducting of 28 interviews with European Union officials grounds her analysis centrally in actual workplace data. I think that is very much an exciting part of her research. Even her brief semiotic description of the European Union buildings in Brussels and Strasbourg contributes to the empiricism of her study. But like Gu Yueguo, she and her team are hardly mentioned in her chapter. Considering the special access that Ruth and her team enjoyed in this project, and the importance of the work, I think that we all would like to know her thoughts of the possibility of discourse analysts working together with the political experts in these massive buildings.

Finally, to Srikant Sarangi. His chapter has more to say about interactivity and collaboration than any of the other plenaries. Indeed, it was the principal theme of his talk. Using the term collaborative interdisciplinarity, he argued that the notion of a researcher is not monolithic and that it needs deconstructing. The researcher plays multiple roles including that of outsider, insider, expert, agent of change, befriender, assessor, animator, and resource. His chapter speaks about professional discourse as a co-constructionist enterprise, and in doing so invokes a number of paradoxes, drawing a parallel between the Participant-Observer's Paradox (where the researcher is simultaneously a participant and an observer, including an observer of his own participation) and what might be called the Analyst-Observer's Paradox. He talks about textual constructionism and gives very heavy emphasis to the important theme of discourse analysts and professionals in the healthcare workplace working hand-in-hand together in a direct engagement in the workplace.

Section II
Discourses and Practices

Discourses of
Health and Social Care

10

Drug Information for Laymen: Good or Bad Medicine?

Inger Askehave

Introduction

Recent years have seen a considerable increase in differentiated product information within the pharmaceutical industry, where companies produce product information aimed at two different target groups, namely doctors and consumers. Linguistically differentiated product information poses great challenges. The text for the consumer and the text for the doctor share the same special discourse domain (both texts are about a pharmaceutical product). However, the change in target group, where we move from communication between equals (pharmacist to doctor) to asymmetrical communication between experts and non-experts (pharmacist to consumer) calls for the recognition of a special discourse domain realized at different levels of abstraction. The aim of this chapter is to address the situational and linguistic aspects of differentiated product information. Drawing on the concept of "discourse communities", the chapter discusses the characteristics of symmetrical and asymmetrical communication and comments on the challenges and pitfalls of the so-called "pure" and "mixed" discourse communities. Furthermore, the chapter presents an analysis of two texts from the website of the pharmaceutical company Eli Lilly to throw light on the linguistic aspects of differentiated product information. The analysis also serves to illustrate how differentiated product information often comes into existence; namely by "translating" the text aimed at experts, adapting its form and content to a non-expert target group.

Background

In 1999 a colleague and I worked on a research project funded by the Danish Medicines Agency and a number of Danish pharmaceutical companies (Askehave and Zethsen, 2000a). The aim of the research project was to improve the readability of Danish patient package inserts (PPI) — the small instructions included in a package of medicine. Package inserts are a fairly recent phenomenon in a Danish context. As a result of EU legislation, it became a legal requirement in Denmark in 1993 to include a sheet of product information in all packages containing medical products aimed directly at the consumer. The PPI has been made a legal requirement in order to inform and protect the consumer and the law is quite specific:

> *"The package leaflet [PPI] must be written in clear and understandable terms for the patient and be clearly legible in the official language or languages of the Member State where the medicinal product is placed on the market."*

(Council Directive 92/27/EEC of 31 March 1992 — article 8)

The problem, however, is that many Danish PPIs are *not clearly* legible and that the PPIs often confuse and even frighten consumers instead of informing and protecting them.

EU legislation requires a close relation between the package insert and a more scientific document called the product summary (PS). Both documents deal with a particular drug, i.e., they describe how it works, its side effects, dosage, etc. However, the PS is intended for experts — i.e., the approving authorities issuing a marketing approval and doctors who look for additional information about a drug. Whereas the package insert is intended for non-experts — consumers who simply want to know how to use the drug. In most cases the legal requirement of a relation between the two documents is met to such an extent that not only content but also form is directly transferred form the PS to the PPI. This means that the pharmaceutical companies transfer special language features directly from the PS to the PPI instead of differentiating their product information and explaining medical concepts at a lower level of complexity.

Characteristics of Differentiated Product Information

The Danish product summaries and package inserts are examples of two texts where differentiated product information is required but unfortunately has not been successfully achieved. In order for differentiated product information to become successful, the authors of such texts need to be aware of the following:

- The special discourse domains are by and large the same.
- The addressees are different (some are experts others non-experts).
- The functions of the texts are different.
- This requires an adaptation of language use.

As it appears from the presentation of Danish package inserts and Danish product summaries, both texts belong to the special discourse domain of medicine, more specifically that of medical products. However, it also appears that the product summary is intended for experts within the medical field, whereas the package insert provides information about the product to laymen who have no pre-knowledge of the field as such. This change in extra-linguistic features (such as target group and function of the text), where we move from communication between equals to asymmetrical communication between experts and non-experts, calls for less complex language use at a lower level of abstraction. In practice this means that texts, which originate from an expert discourse community but serve as the basis for a consumer-oriented version, need to be "translated" to become meaningful to non-expert readers. It follows that one of the reasons why package inserts are difficult to understand for the ordinary Dane is the inability of the pharmaceutical companies to downgrade and simplify their expert language and medical jargon to accommodate a non-expert target group (Askehave and Zethsen, 2000b).

In order to explain why a simplification of medical texts poses great challenges to the pharmaceutical companies, it would be relevant to address the concept of "discourse community".

According to Swales (1990:24–26) a discourse community is characterized by:

- a broadly agreed set of common public goals
- mechanisms of intercommunication among its members
- participatory mechanisms primarily used to provide information and feedback
- one or more genres
- specific lexis
- a threshold level of members with a suitable degree of relevant content and discoursal expertise.

Considering the linguistic aspects of discourse communities, it appears that as people acquire knowledge of a special field (e.g., medicine), and become full members of a discourse community, they learn to communicate with peers using the linguistic tools (genres, lexis, etc.) appropriate in a special context.

The product summary, for example, is used within a discourse community which is "pure" in the sense that the community is composed of equals or near-equals in knowledge and professional role. However, with the advent of differentiated product information, the walls of the pure discourse community are demolished and the concept of a "mixed" discourse community (where the addresser is an expert and the addressee is the general public) is required. This broader view of discourse communities differs from Swales' (1990), who sees discourse communities as consisting of equals where all participants take part in the discourse by reading and writing (see Frandsen, 2000).

Needless to say, communication within a mixed discourse community is somewhat more problematic because the parties communicating are often unequal in knowledge. Killingsworth and Gilbertson (1992:180) provide an example of a mixed discourse community, the so-called "human services discourse community", where the target group is the general public and the author may be a company, institution, etc. providing some service to a group of people. Thus a company and its customers for example form a mixed discourse community and communicate through manuals, sales brochures, advertisements, etc.

It goes without saying that human services discourse communities force members of an expert community to communicate with outsiders. However, from the research into the Danish package inserts (Askehave and Zethsen, 2000a) it appears that many medical experts lack the ability to downgrade their special language to accommodate a non-expert target group. The reason for this inability is obviously that the authors are experts within *medicine* — not language experts. And their knowledge of medicine is intertwined with a particular language use (the very idea of discourse communities). Therefore, instead of explaining the medical concepts at a lower level of complexity, the authors tend to use "expert language" in all their documents in spite of the fact that it hampers the readability and usability of the more consumer-oriented ones. In other words, the authors seem to neglect the fact that they sometimes move outside their pure discourse community and need to comply with the discoursal conventions of a discourse community consisting of experts and non-experts. And even though the authors of such texts are aware of the shift in discourse community and target group, they may not have the linguistic tools for implementing this shift (Askehave and Zethsen, 2000b). What is more, following the work of the German philosopher, H. G. Gadamer (1996), the very notion of "experts" may also constitute a barrier to successful communication in mixed discourse communities. Experts are often accepted as "experts" because of the way they act — not least linguistically. If they start communicating differently, their expertise and authority within a particular field may decrease in their own eyes, and in the eyes of the public.

An Example of Successful Differentiated Drug Information

As we began to improve the readability of Danish inserts, I started wondering whether differentiated drug information in general faced a target group problem, or whether the problems were restricted to the genre of patient package inserts. Recent years have seen a significant increase in drug and healthcare information on the Internet. Thus apart from providing information about themselves (company history, organizational structure, career possibilities, etc.) most pharmaceutical companies use the Internet to promote their medical products. The Internet texts are particularly relevant for the study of medical information at different levels of abstraction because the texts concerned with drug information are specifically aimed at different target groups. This appears when entering the pharmaceutical company Eli Lilly's site concerned with the drug Prozac. At the Prozac Home page (http://www.prozac.com/prozac/Main/Index.jsp) the reader is provided with two possibilities — either entering the site as a patient or entering the site as a healthcare professional. Thus here the researcher has an outstanding possibility of investigating how the company customises its product information and addresses two different target groups.

The Prozac Texts

I have analysed two texts from the Prozac site; one primarily targeted at experts (doctors) and one at non-experts (consumers). The two texts are ideal for comparison because they are concerned with the same thing — namely a description and explanation of how Prozac works. Text 1 is a product summary, called Product Label, which provides detailed prescribing information about the drug (referring to clinical trials and tests carried out in the research lab). In the actual analysis I focus on one particular section of the Product Label called Pharmacodynamics which explains how the drug works. The author of Text 1 is an expert (a pharmacist/scientist) and the primary addressee is another expert namely doctors who would like to get complete prescribing information. Text 2, called About Prozac, forms part of the site intended for consumers and provides the reader with the most important information related to the use of Prozac — again how Prozac works. The author of Text 2 is also an expert/technical writer but the primary addressee is consumers i.e., non-experts within the field of medicine. The term primary addressee is used here to make room for the fact that other people, apart from the intended target group, may access the site. In fact the hypertext nature of websites makes it possible for consumers to access the Product Label and for doctors to access the site intended for consumers via links. Table 10.1 below presents the two texts in a schematized form.

Table 10.1
Texts 1 and 2 Compared

Discourse Component	TEXT 1: Product Label/ Pharmacodynamics	TEXT 2: Prozac/About Prozac/How Prozac works
1. What causes depression		Depression is not fully understood, but a growing amount of evidence supports the view that people with depression have an imbalance of the brain's neurotransmitters, the chemicals that allow nerve cells in the brain to communicate with each other. Many scientists believe that an imbalance in serotonin, one of these neurotransmitters, may be an important factor in the development and severity of depression.
2. How Prozac works	The antidepressant, antiobsessive-compulsive and antibulimic actions of fluoxetine are presumed to be linked to its inhibition of CNS neuronal uptake of serotonin. Studies at clinically relevant doses in man have demonstrated that fluoxetine blocks the uptake of serotonin into human platelets. Studies in animals also suggest that fluoxetine is a much more potent uptake inhibitor of serotonin than of norepinephrine.	Prozac may help to correct this imbalance by increasing the brain's own supply of serotonin.
3. Prozac compared	Antagonism of muscarinic, histaminergic, and a1–adrenergic receptors has been hypothesized to be associated with various anticholingergic, sedative, and cardiovascular effects of classical tricyclic antidepressant drugs. Fluoxetine binds to these and other membrane receptors from brain tissue much less potently in vitro than do the tricyclic drugs.	Some other antidepressant medicines appear to affect several neurotransmitters in addition to serotonin. Because Prozac selectively affects only serotonin, it may cause fewer side effects than other medications.
4. What Prozac is used for		While Prozac cannot be said to "cure" depression, it does help to control the symptoms of depression, allowing many people with depression to feel better and function more normally.

Comparison of Content and Structure

Differentiated product information involves adaptations at two levels, namely in terms of the text organization (more specifically the discourse components of the text) and the rhetorical strategies used to realize these components. Let us begin by considering the discourse components of the two Prozac texts. Texts 1 and 2 use the following discourse components to explain the *pharmaco-dynamics* of Prozac — or to put in it plain English how Prozac works:

Table 10.2
Discourse Components of Texts 1 and 2

Discourse Component	Text 1	Text 2
What causes depression	-	+
How Prozac works	+	+
Prozac compared to other antidepressants	+	+
What Prozac is used for	-	+

Both texts include a description of how Prozac works, what Prozac is used for, and finally provide a comparison of Prozac to other drugs. The main difference is the presence of a discourse component called "what causes depression" and "what Prozac is used for" in Text 2. The general introduction to depression in Text 2 is most likely motivated by the fact that readers of Text 2 are non-experts who may not know what depression is or what causes depression, whereas one can safely assume such information to be known to the readers of text 1 who are experts in medicine. In other words, this section serves as a brief introduction to the medical field and helps non-expert readers make sense of the information about Prozac which follows. The addition of discourse component 4, "What Prozac is used for" is probably motivated by the fact that consumers may want to know the effect of the drug outside the brain — that is how the restoration of neurotransmitters improve their life in general.

When considering the discourse components present in both texts, it appears that one obvious sign of differentiated product information lies in the amount of information and the level of detail provided in Texts 1 and 2. Here is an example: When comparing Prozac to other antidepressants in discourse component 3, Texts 2 simply states that other antidepressant medicines appear to affect several neurotransmitters but Prozac only affects one neurotransmitter and therefore cause fewer side effects. Text 1, however, provides a very detailed description of *how specific types* of antidepressants affect *specific* neurotransmitters and comments on the kinds of side effect which they usually cause. Furthermore, Text 1 refers to studies in humans and animals to provide an explanation as to *why* fluoxetine (Prozac) only affects serotonin. Text 2 contains no reference to clinical trials but focuses on the final outcome of these trials, i.e., the fact that Prozac selectively affects only serotonin.

So in terms of the overall structure and contents of the two texts, Eli Lilly succeeds in including information which is relevant to the two target groups. The choice of information in the two texts clearly reflects the pre-knowledge of the different readers and meet their different information needs.

Comparison of Rhetorical Strategies

I shall now move on to a more detailed examination of the different rhetorical strategies used in the texts to inform doctors and the patients respectively about Prozac. More specifically I shall focus on the linguistic means used to adapt Text 2 to its non-expert target group. The analysis will be concerned with the following adaptations:

A. *Rhetorical strategies concerned with lexis:*

- Medical terms are replaced with ordinary, common words
- Medical terms are replaced with more general, less detailed terms
- Medical terms are kept but made accessible to the reader by a paraphrase

B. *Rhetorical strategies concerned with syntax:*

- The "noun style" is replaced with the "verb style"

As the two texts differ in terms of discourse components, and consequently content, it is not always possible to illustrate the "replacement" by providing examples from both texts. Thus when using examples from discourse components 1 and 4 (which are only present in Text 2) only Text 2 will be listed.

Rhetorical Strategies Concerned with Lexis

When two experts talk to each other, they will use the terms and expression characteristic of their expert discourse community. However, when they step outside their usual community and talk to laymen, they have to adjust their language accordingly. Generally it appears that Text 2 contains very little medical jargon compared to Text 1. An obvious reason is that Text 2 is less detailed compared to Text 1. Another reason is that Text 2 quite successfully replaces the medical jargon with common, more general terms. And in the few examples where a medical term is kept, a paraphrase of the term is provided. Here are a few examples:

Medical terms replaced with common, ordinary words:

Text 2: Prozac cannot be said to "cure" depression (instead of the medical term 'treat')

Text 2: people with depression (instead of the medical expression "patients with depression")

Text 2: the chemicals that allow the brain cells to communicate with each other (instead of the medical expression "that transmit nerve impulses across a synapse")

Medical terms replaced with general, less detailed terms:

Text 1: Fluoxetine (active ingredient)
        is replaced with
Text 2: Prozac (product name)

Text 1: classical tricyclic antidepressant drugs
        is replaced with
Text 2: some other antidepressant medicines

Text 1: muscarinic, histaminergic and a1-adrenergic receptors
        is replaced with
Text 2: several neurotransmitters

Text 1: anticholingergic, sedative, and cardiovascular effects
   is replaced with
Text 2: side effects

Text 1: tricyclic drugs
   is replaced with
Text 2: other medications

Paraphrase of medical terms:

Text 2: neurotransmitters, the chemicals that allow nerve cells in the brain to communicate with each other

Text 2: serotonin, one of these neurotransmitters

Rhetorical Strategies Concerned with Syntax

It is a well-known fact that specialist discourse communities favour a passive, impersonal, and condensed style which *inter alia* focuses on things rather than actions. Syntactically, this style may be achieved through the use of heavy noun phrases where actions are realized by nouns which again are modified by a range of pre and postmodifiers. This allows experts to provide condensed information for other experts who are trained to perceive and consequently to talk about the physical world in terms of concepts. Text 1 is characterized by this so-called *thingish* style (noun style) (see Killingsworth and Gilbertson, 1992: 131) whereas Text 2 for the most part uses an active style (verb style). The use of the thingish style results in a text concerned with *things* such as "antidepressant actions", "inhibition of CNS neuronal uptake", "antagonism of muscarinic", "histaminergic, and a1–adrenergic receptors", "anticholingergic, sedative and cardiovascular effects" and how these things are interrelated. Text 2 "unpacks" the complex noun phrases and realizes the content of the noun phrase in a sentence; i.e., actions are represented by verbs, and subjects realize the persons or things performing the action. Below I have tried to compare excerpts from Texts 1 and 2 to illustrate the syntactic differences. However, it should be noted that the examples compared cannot be said to contain exactly the same information, the point is simply to find related examples.

"Noun style" replaced with "verb style":

Text 1: The antidepressant, antiobsessive-compulsive and antibulimic actions of fluoxetine

Text 2: Prozac may help to correct this imbalance

or

Text 2: It [Prozac] does help to control the symptoms of depression

Text 1: inhibition of CNS neuronal uptake

Text 2: by increasing the brain's own supply of serotonin.

Text 1: antagonism of muscarinic, histaminergic, and a1–adrenergic receptors

Text 2: some other antidepressant medicines appear to affect several neurotransmitters in addition to serotonin

Text 1: various anticholingergic, sedative, and cardiovascular effects of classical tricyclic antidepressant drugs

Text 2: it (Prozac) may cause fewer side effects

The examples above demonstrate that the thingish style promotes lengthy, information-packed noun phrases where strings of modifiers allow the specialist to cram considerable information into just one sentence. However, this style tends to hamper the readability of consumer-directed documents as it presents a picture which is fundamentally detached from what we experience in the real world where participants perform actions e.g., inhibit something, act in a particular way, etc. (Halliday and Martin, 1993; Killingsworth and Gilbertson, 1992; Killingsworth and Steffens, 1989, *Plain English Handbook* 1997).

This small analysis of the two Prozac texts provides a rather limited but nonetheless realistic view of what successful differentiated product information may look like. It appears that important changes take place in terms of content (discourse components and level of detail) and form (lexis and syntax). However, it should be noted that only some of the means suitable for making drug information accessible to patients have been described here (see, for example, Kitching, 1990 for other ways to improve the readability of medical texts).

Conclusion

The aim of this chapter was to address the situational and linguistic aspects of differentiated product information within the pharmaceutical industry. The chapter threw light on the nature of differentiated production information focusing on the symmetrical and asymmetrical communication involved. The discussion of pure and mixed discourse communities provided insights into the challenges and pitfalls of differentiated product information. It appeared that the production of differentiated product information required an awareness of the different linguistic conventions associated with the different types of discourse community. The chapter also presented a "real" example of differentiated product information and threw light on some of the linguistic means available to produce differentiated product information. The text from the Eli Lilly website showed that several adjustments in content and form had been made in order to transform the expert text on *pharmacodynamics* to the non-expert text on *how Prozac* works.

No doubt the demand for and supply of differentiated product information is on the increase. The advent of the Internet, with its possibilities of providing easily accessible drug information to consumers and doctors, is bound to increase the number of product information texts aimed at different target groups within the pharmaceutical industry. The negative and positive aspects (including moral issues) of such information, especially in connection with direct-to-consumer (DTC) advertising, have not been addressed in this chapter (see for example Cohen 1990, Davis 1999, Kopp and Sheffet 1997). Instead the chapter suggests that if pharmaceutical companies want to produce differentiated production information, they have to consider the situational and linguistic aspects of such information and address the premises of readability and user-friendliness — not least in consumer-oriented texts.

References

1. Askehave, I. and K. K. Zethsen. 2000a. *The patient package insert of the future.* Aarhus: Aarhus School of Business.

2. _____ . 2000b. Medical texts made simple — dream or reality? *Hermes* 25: 63–74.

3. Cohen, E. P. 1990. Are pharmaceutical ads good medicine? *Business and Society Review* 2:8–10.

4. Council Directive 92/27/EEC of 31 March 1992 on the Labelling of Medicinal Products for Human Use and on Package Leaflets.

5. Davis, J. J. 1999. Imprecise frequency descriptors and the miscomprehension of prescription drug advertising: Public policy and regulatory implications. *Journal of Technical Writing and Communication* 29 (2): 133–152.

6. Frandsen, F. 2000. What do members of discourse communities have in common? *Hermes.* Forthcoming.

7. Gadamer, H.-G. 1996. The *enigma of health: The art of healing in a scientific age.* Stanford: Stanford University Press.

8. Halliday, M. A. K and J. R. Martin. 1993. *Writing science: Literacy and discursive power.* Pittsburgh: University of Pittsburgh Press.

9. Killingsworth, J. M. and M. K. Gilbertson. 1992. Signs, *genres and communities in technical communication.* New York: Baywood Publishing Company.

10. _____ and D. Steffens. 1989. Effectiveness in the environmental impact statement. A study in public rhetoric. *Written Communication* 6 (2): 155–189.

11. Kitching, J. B. 1990. Patient information leaflets — the state of the art. *Journal of the Royal Society of Medicine* 83 (May): 298–300.

12. Kopp, S. W. and M. J. Sheffet. 1997. The effect of direct-to-consumer advertising of prescription drugs on retail gross margins: Empirical evidence and public policy implications. *Journal of Public Policy and Marketing* 16 (2): 270–276.

13. Swales, J. M. 1990. *Genre analysis — English in academic and research settings.* Cambridge: Cambridge University Press.

14. The Office of Investor Education and Assistance. 1997. How to create clear SEC disclosure documents. In *Plain English Handbook.* Washington D.C. Available from http:/www.sec.gov/consumer/plaine.htm.

11

A Triple Jeopardy:
What can Discourse Analysts
Offer Health Professionals?

Sally Candlin

Introduction

This chapter begins with the "So what?" question. The data discussed are grounded in a practice discipline but it is to the discourse analyst that the practitioner must turn for an answer to the questions: "The practitioner has this data, so what?" "What can the discourse analyst tell the practitioner about what's going on?" How can discourse analysis inform practice? "What is going on backstage, and how does this relate to, and affect the performance on the front stage?" (cf. Goffman, 1981); "What can the practitioner do about the situation?" "How then can the discourse analyst advise the practitioner about how to use the data, to take appropriate actions which will improve a situation?" If the practitioner does not ask the questions, and if the discourse analyst does not provide answers, then the data collection is nothing more than an esoteric exercise which makes use of clients for the researcher's own ends and gives nothing in return. Together, practitioners and analysts can explore, explain and discover, and provide a basis for professional action.

Because older women outnumber their male counterparts, but also have higher morbidity rates, it is suggested that an analysis of the discourse of interactions of older women and nurses will have utility in the provision of appropriate health and nursing care. The conclusions drawn from this analysis draw parallel results with those drawn by Watson and Mears (2000) in their book *Women, Work and Care of the Elderly*. The evidence which supported what many had believed intuitively, often as a result of personal experience, was that in spite of the so-called freedom which was won by women for women, particularly in the field of employment, the situation of many women seems not to have been improved. In fact for some, the strides made in the equal opportunities enjoyed by women in the workforce is not translated into benefits for women who need to work (for whatever reason) *and* at the same time take on the role of caring for sick family members.

And so the next questions to be raised are: How do women see themselves? How are they identified? And what in their experience contributes to their perceptions — or indeed — to these identities? What does the discourse tell us about the multiplicity of identities enacted and displayed by the individual? The presentation of multiple identities appears to be very evident in the discourse of many women, but with these identities there are certain roles which are undertaken, each of these necessitating different functions. The data which will be examined here illustrate that women seemingly take on the identity of wives/mothers but they also take on the identity of members of the workforce (albeit sometimes self-employed and partnered by their husbands) (Norton, 2000). One women is identified as a housewife and proprietor of a cafe; and another as a housewife, mother, farmer, carer. These roles might require the accomplishing of a number of functions. Do the women, as a result, speak with distinct voices, or has their discourse become hybridized (cf. Fairclough, 1992)? And if this is so, what does it say about their roles in society?

One cannot talk about the identity of women without raising the issue of gender differences. This is not, however, the purpose of this chapter and the reader is referred to the work of, for example, Connell (1987), Tannen (1987), and Coates and Cameron (1988), for differing perspectives on the issues. Cameron's view is that the discourse of women is not so much related to their gender but to their powerless position, one shared by all powerless people regardless of gender. On this view one would expect to see differences in the discourses of women who are empowered and those who see themselves as victims of circumstance. To a certain degree this chapter will illustrate such comparisons. What really should be addressed, however, not totally unrelated to the discussions of others, concerns the expectations of women themselves, and how much these expectations are grounded in their history and in the society in which they live. To do this their voices must be "listened" to, acknowledged, and heard.

Methodology

The data were gathered by audio-recording nurses and older patients talking during the process of giving and receiving nursing care. The places of care were in hospitals, extended care facilities and the community. The following extracts were recorded in the patients' own homes. The talk was not idle chatter. This was not the social communication which occurs between friends. The discourse might appear to be friendly in tone, but it nevertheless illustrates the nurse engaging in therapeutic communication, a mode of talk which is not, and never can be, considered to equate to the social conversation which takes place between friends (cf. Hunt, 1991). The nurse in each situation was gathering information, during the course of which the patients were encouraged to reminisce. The nurse, in the process, was able to make an assessment of health needs. Such an assessment allowed the nurse to determine nursing goals and plan appropriate interventions which must be based on the patient's history, cultural background, values, beliefs and understanding of his/her physical, social, mental and emotional health status. The nursing goals and interventions should be mutually identified and agreed. This is accomplished by means of the nurse actively listening, and by so doing, developing a trusting relationship which will encourage more self-disclosures — often painful — on the part of the patient (see Coupland, Coupland, and Giles, 1991 for further discussion on the handling of painful self-disclosures (PSDs).

Data Collection and Analysis

Transcription symbols used in the text.

• (.) seconds of silence

- (*) seconds of indecipherable talk

Here is a part of Mrs C's story:

1. Nurse: You were saying the other day that you retired up here and took over a little business when you retired.
2. Mrs C: Yes.
3. Nurse: That kept you fairly busy — the coffee shop.
4. Mrs C: Yes kept me busy all right — half the night sometimes.
5. Nurse: You didn't have that for too long though did you?
6. Mrs C: Five years just under five years.
7. Nurse: What sort of work did you and your husband do before that?
8. Mrs C: Clerical.
9. Nurse: Both of you?
10. Mrs C: Yeah.
11. Nurse: Is that where you met?
12. Mrs C: No no actually when I first met him he had a garage he was a (***) a motor man. Of course he was always into motor cars but I was just a clerk

In this extract there is the first indication of Mrs. C's identity. Following some probing questions it can be seen that Mrs. C revealed that she had been a working woman, even after retirement. This might be regarded as an unusual phenomenon in her generation, but what is even more telling is her self-deprecating expansion in utterance 12.

"...But I was *just* a clerk" (my emphasis). This is even stranger when one listens to her previous replies. Both Mr. and Mrs. C had engaged in clerical work, but Mrs. C gives the nurse a hidden message. Somehow her husband, in her eyes, was elevated by being "into motor cars". The self-deprecating "just a clerk" appears to indicate that her perception was that she was in a position of subservience. Utterance 4 is also interesting: "Yes kept me busy all right — half the night sometimes." It is not known if this is an inclusive first person of course, but it just might be that she was the one who "did the washing up" — used as she was, to accepting a lower position. More support for this suggestion is found in the next extract.

Later in the conversation

13. Nurse: So what are you hoping to do — when you feel a little bit better? What are you hoping to get back into — your normal — what normally — just tell us what em (...) what's life like normally?

14. Mrs C: Well I love to get in with a broom that's my (..) I'm that's my long (**).

15. Nurse: Yeah that might be a good while yet.

16. Mrs C: I wouldn't dare go downstairs and look around because I'd be ashamed you know I know the rubbish that is out the front there.

Here is her identity surfacing as a housewife. She takes pride in her cleaning. What is interesting is that the nurse, in utterance 15, confirms this token of her identity. The conversation then revolves around health and Mrs. C's ability to cook and maintain a healthy diet.

For further discussion one must also listen to Mrs Y's story

Mrs Y had been talking to the nurse about the events which led up to her needing the community nurse help her with her showering.

1. Nurse: Why how long ago is this since your husband died?

2. Mrs Y: Oh fifteen years last er September.

3. Nurse: Oh right and did he help you have your shower before he died? Is that why it was a problem?

4. Mrs Y: Oh no he was — I nursed him.

5. Nurse: Did you?

6. Mrs Y: For nearly seven years he was paralyzed.

7. Nurse: Oh was he? What? Was he in a wheelchair?

8. Mrs Y: Paralyzed oh yes ... paralyzed all down one side.

He couldn't walk and I taught him to talk and I tried to teach him different things but I found it was hopeless.

9. Nurse: It must have been pretty hard for you.

10. Mrs Y: Well yes it meant getting out of bed at night because he was paralyzed down one side so you know he'd fall over one side and I'd always have to put him straight again so I'd be getting in and out of bed all night.

11. Nurse: And that was for how many years?

12. Mrs Y: Nearly seven years.

13. Nurse: Gee that's a long time.

14. Mrs Y: It's a long time well my nurses told me that they never knew anyone to nurse a person that long isn't it?

15. Nurse: Did he have a stroke is that what happened?

This, on the surface, identifies Mrs Y as a loving and concerned wife: taking on the identity of a carer. In itself this involved attempting to take on the functions of a nurse, physiotherapist, and speech therapist. An examination of the choice of the lexico-grammatical structures of Mrs Y's discourse evidences her perceptions of her strength. In utterance 4 for example, she corrects herself and replaces herself in thematic position. In utterance 8, she thematizes her husband but with negative polarity. She dwells on his weaknesses which appears to contrast with the adjacent clause where she is then thematized. The modality is positive — although weakly so: "I tried to teach him". However, the tone of this weak positive modality is strengthened and affirmed in utterance 10 to: "I'd always have to..." Again she is thematized throughout. (See Hasan, 1985 for further illumination of the structure of power relations as reflected in the lexico-grammatical features of discourse.) More self-disclosures are encouraged by the nurse's active listening and empathetic responses (particularly utterances 9, 11, 13), demonstrating an alignment, by both, to the goals of the interaction, but also to Mrs. Y's agenda.

The story continues, however, with more details of her husband's illness during which time she herself had an accident. Eventually he went into a nursing home nearby until she insisted on caring for him at home. The next extract gives considerably more information and explains to a certain extent why Mrs. Y behaved as she did. We see the tacit identity of a loving wife — "but he was so broken-hearted..." — and in spite of her own disability, she was going to care for him somehow. The telling statement comes in the last clause: "I'm a very determined person".

Her story then continues:

> 16. Mrs. Y: They were still building it well they took him there but he was so broken hearted with it all that I said to the doctor couldn't he come home and I said that we could get a nurse in and I said we could get a wheelchair and so he said it wouldn't be worth the trouble so he let him come home and he stayed home afterwards but he brought a letter form the matron saying she didn't think I'd be able to cope because I was still on a crutch, yes so anyhow I was quite determined — I'm a very determined person.

Again the lexical choices demonstrate the comparison between her husband's weakness and her strength, exemplified by the repetition in the last line of her determination, confirming her perception of her strength. In this there is a subtle defiance which indicates her control of the situation since she made the choice, against the advice of the powerful institution. This power is something which is confirmed numerous times in her story, as she later talked about her family and her life in the Australian bush, her work on the sheep farm which she and her husband ran, and her work as an official of the Country Women's Association.

Then her story continues as she discusses the upbringing of her sons.

> 17. Nurse: Are you a good cook were you a good cook in those days

18. Mrs. Y: Oh I think my sons are better cooks than I am

19. Nurse: Oh are they? That's wonderful that you taught them

20. Mrs. Y: I tell you what they used to do when they were boys. Whatever I was doing they'd want to do you see. So they can sew they can knit they can do everything

21. Nurse: Great you were ahead of your time weren't you teaching your son things like that that's wonderful.

22. Mrs. Y: Oh when we were on the farm I used to drive the harvester and a tractor and all those things.

Here, and not unexpectedly it is seen that Mrs. Y is identifying herself as a mother. And it is here that the similarities can be seen between Mrs. C and Mrs. Y. Utterances 17 and 19 which demonstrate her identity as a homemaker and mother involves her taking on the functions of a cook and those of a teacher. But what is revealing is utterance 17: "Oh I think my sons are better cooks than I am". This appears to be reminiscent of Mrs. C's self-deprecating remarks about her employment situation in relation to her husband's status.

Her power, however is echoed in utterance 22: "Oh when I was on the farm I used to drive the harvester and a tractor" emphasized in the next clause by "and all those things". Again Mrs. Y is thematized. The differences between the two texts lie not in the discourse of the patients but in the responses of the nurse. While they both engage in active listening, and both confirm the identities of the patient (Mrs. C as a housewife, and Mrs. Y as a wife and mother), the first nurse does nothing to enhance the patient's identity where the second nurse makes an evaluative comment in utterance 20: "Great you were ahead of your time weren't you teaching your son things like that that's wonderful". It is this positive evaluation which seems to encourage Mrs. Y to maintain her position as a woman of strength.

Much later in the conversation the nurse brought the topic of conversation around to Mrs. Y's health.

23. Nurse: So up until when you came to live here I guess you never had time to be sick did you?

24. Mrs. Y: Well he (...) I've had several operations and em I have been sick — as a matter of fact the last two chest X-rays I've had they've said that I've had TB

And a little later

Nurse: Yeah yeah what sorts of illnesses did you have say up to the time that you came here

Mrs Y: Oh I have the gall bladder removed and I've had a big throat operation — the thyroid ... oh and I had ...

The following pages of text describe the illnesses she had experienced until her present health status is discussed. Even at this stage the determination of Mrs. Y is seen to be maintained as she admits to the nurse that there are things which she refuses to tell the doctor because she doesn't want to be "put in a home". The whole text confirms and re-confirms her identity as an Aussie battler, a woman from the bush who is tough and overcomes adversity. The conversation lasted nearly two hours.

Discussion

In these conversations the women are seen to be adopting multiple identities, but what they have in common, apart from age and a certain degree of ill-health — is a history of hardship and a background of work and more work. How does this compare with their younger counterparts? I began by believing that the women of today have achieved very little in real terms. While today's women may enjoy a greater degree of equality in the workforce, the work of Watson and Mears (2000) does not demonstrate a greater degree of freedom and independence. Not all women indicated that they were in control of their situation. Their allotted tasks were assigned to them, for example one woman said: "It was expected of me; It's my duty". The interviews of Watson and Mears with 40 carers, ranging in age from late adolescents to older women, demonstrate a situation where women not only take on a caring role, but maintain their work outside the home (sometimes only made possible by the actions of understanding female employers), maintain their own home and family, and often the home of a frail parent as well. Marriages are threatened and social lives impoverished as was indicated in the words of one carer (not in the study of Watson and Mears) in a conversation with a carer: "I lost ten years of social development caring for her, I lost so many of my social skills, — but I don't resent it". Why do women do what they do? Their reasons range from:

- It's expected of me;
- It's my duty;
- She cared for me, I am only returning what she has done;
- I want to do it;
- She's my mother, I love her.

It is in the last response that we see the similarity with Mrs. Y who cared for her husband "He was heart broken". But there the similarities end — or do they? The younger women all work — but Mrs. Y was a farmer, and Mrs. C also worked. They both maintained their homes. We can only imagine the effects on their health since the negative effects on the health of carers is well documented (e.g., Braithwaite,1990). But this argument gives us little explanatory value for discourse analysis.

Pragmatic Features

An analysis of the pragmatic features of the extracts might cast further light on the situations. What is interesting about the extracts of data which have been discussed are the similarities in the framing of the interactions. It is in the framing of the encounter that the boundaries are established, with both partners establishing an understanding of the "rules of the game".

Framing

Each nurse had framed the interaction as "talk about you"

Nurse and Mrs C : ...we are just going to be talking about you (...) and how you are how you manage at home that sort of thing. We've been coming to you for some months now haven't we?

Nurse and Mrs Y: What we're going to do is just a little bit about what's happened to you since the nurses have been coming to you.

Perhaps because the frames are absolutely explicit, the patients are able to maintain them and align to the goals which the nurses imply: the talk is about the patient, but only as it relates to the nursing situation. It is "talk" and not "interview" and therefore there is the tacit assumption that they are equal partners in the interaction. An interview implies dominance of one party over another. It is a question/ answer situation and only one person knows the questions. That person, who is the partner in the interaction with the institutional power is the one calls the shots. The other person has no institutional power, and has little choice but to conform to the agenda of the more powerful partner — if of course she wished to maintain harmony in the interaction. A conversation, however, is less threatening, and in this particular situation the one partner, the patient, knows more than the other (the nurse). This is significant since it is the nurse, with the authority vested in her by society by virtue of her education, professional knowledge and experience who represents the institution. It is also the presence of the institutional representative which makes this a public, and not a private, event. Notes will be taken and records kept. The gist of the conversation is there for others (albeit professionals) to access.

Turn Taking and Topic Management

"Talk" implies a casual conversation. It would be expected, therefore, to see a sharing in turn-taking and topic management. This, as the extracts demonstrate, is achieved, and in fact throughout the texts — which are not given here — we see that the topics appear to be controlled by the patients, certainly they have the longer turns. Fisher and Groce (1990:240) state of doctor-patient interactions that patients' accounts function strategically to allow the patient the conversational floor, to insert information and establish credibility. Such strategies are evident in both interactions. Neither patients nor nurses are constrained by the bureaucratic institution. But these strategies, far from making this an informal conversation, is a deliberate attempt to get the patient to disclose more and more, and by so doing places the institutional agent in a very powerful position indeed. Foucault describes power as

> "... something which circulates, ... something which only functions in the form of a chain. It is never localized here or there, never in anybody's hands, never appropriated as a commodity or a piece of wealth. Power is employed or exercised through a net-like organization. And not only do individuals circulate between its threads; they are always in the position of simultaneously undergoing and exercising this power. They are not only its inert or consenting target; they are always also the elements of its articulation." (Foucault, 1980, p. 98)

The Practical Application of Discourse Analysis and Personal Reflections on Practice

I, too, was caught up in this rhetoric until I examined my own practice. And I realized that by strategically adjusting my discourse behaviour, I not only was empowered by the patient, but so too was the institution empowered. Self-revelation and painful self-disclosures could not be retracted — they were now on public record. The power was *not* necessarily circulating. And it is here that any argument that equates an informal conversation being similar to any social interaction falls down. Nursing interactions are not, and never can be, social interactions. They are professional interactions and unlike social interactions where the disclosures can be made to a party who may use and/or abuse the information, the power given to the nurse is equalized by her response as the agent of the institution. Her response is guided by interdependent ethical principles, such as those articulated by Thiroux (1980) as the principles of:

- The value of life
- Goodness and rightness

- Justice or fairness
- Truth-telling or honesty
- Individual freedom

Her response *must* therefore be of benefit to the patient and it is in the response that the interaction must be therapeutic, taking it above the realms of a friendly social interaction.

Such a response draws also for its explanation upon the notions of habitus, field and capital proposed by Bourdieu (1990d). He argues:

> "... The source of historical action, that of the artist, the scientist, or the member of government just as much as that of the worker or the petty civil servant, is not an active subject confronting society as if that society were an object constituted externally. The source resides neither in consciousness nor in things but in the relationship between two stages of the social, that is between the history objectified in things, in the form of the institutions, and history incarnated in bodies, in that form of enduring dispositions which I call habitus..."
> (Bourdieu, 1994).

Habitus reflects cultural aspects of the individual and is very powerful in our presentation of self to others and our interpretation of the behaviour of others. As a concept it is particularly significant in the nurse-patient relationship, and in the situation in health care, since a nurse's beliefs and behaviours about health are culturally encoded. Thus we can consider a person's health, "a system of durable transposable dispositions" in terms of habitus. It is particularly significant in the health care situation since the system of lasting transposable dispositions integrates past experiences and functions as a matrix of patients' and nurses' perceptions and actions making possible the achievement of infinitely diversified tasks.

Each person brings into the field of health certain capital — not in any Marxist sense, but as a capital which is in non-material form —

cultural, symbolic and social. Such capital is seen always as a means of exerting power as Bourdieu states:

> "...These fundamental social powers are according to my empirical investigations, firstly economic capital, in its various kinds; secondly cultural capital or better, informational capital, again in its different kinds; and thirdly two forms of capital that are strongly correlated, social capital, which consists of resources based on connections and group membership, and symbolic capital, which is the form different types of capital take once they are perceived and recognized as legitimate... "
> (Bourdieu,1987f cited in Calhoun 1993, p. 70)

Within the nurse-patient situation, we are particularly concerned with firstly, informational capital since competent nursing practice demands a sound nursing knowledge base not usually available to the patient, and secondly, social capital where the nurse might be seen as a professional, thus excluding patients. But symbolic capital cannot be ignored since the capital of the nurse has been legitimized by society because she is a member of two powerful institutions: the professional institution (membership of which is accorded to her by virtue of her information capital), and the health care system (membership of which is accorded to her because of her membership of the nursing institution). The patient is excluded from these institutions because she has no legitimate capital by which she can become a member. She can therefore, in spite of her apparent strengths, never be on a par with the nurse because she has no capital and therefore no legitimate power. The best that can be achieved in the nurse patient situation, is a mutual alignment to goals. In this sense patients might be seen as a group within the bureaucratic institution. But this is not a strong argument since so much depends on the choices and strategic adjustments made by the individual nurse. In such instances, one would expect to see the alignment and affiliation between agents that was manifest in the text analysed here, particularly through the discursive practices of turn-taking and topic exchange.

Conclusion

This work has indeed seen these expected pragmatic features of alignment and affiliation manifest in the topics, topic management and turn taking, but I have argued that their utilization is a reflection of the strategic adjustments of the nurse to obtain information from another, thereby seizing power from the patient. However once in possession of such power, the nurse's behaviours must be guided by ethical principles so that the patient receives the benefits of these strategies. The application of these ethical principles is not solely the prerogative of the nurse, but of other professional groups also. But do they not also guide the behaviours of any who are involved in caring? Perhaps what we are seeing is not so much a similarity between women of different generations in their workloads, but similarities between all those who take upon themselves the care of others, whether professional or family carers. They are all guided by ethical principles: whether they are conscious of this or not. They all operate within the field of caring and they all draw from their capital to inform their caring practices, and their actions are all part of their habitus since habitus always has an expressive dimension. Habitus gives expression to certain meanings that things and people have for us.

I argue, finally, that it is just such an acceptance of the habitus of women as carers that allows society to make utility of the so-called caring female attributes. By accepting the human attributes of caring, a society can determine the ideological stance which is reflected in its policy making decisions. But this is more than overt policy. It is a means of confirming the status of women. Not only do women constitute the greatest number of informal/family carers; they also number in the health care system as the largest group — and not amongst the highest paid. The data analysed here, unfortunately see women themselves confirming the status given them by society. Their lives seem to be forever jeopardized by their habitus: a dialectic between the institutions, and history incarnated in bodies.

References

1. Bourdieu, P. 1987f. In C. Calhoun. 1993. Habitus, field and capital: The question of historic specificity. In *Bourdieu: Critical perspectives,* edited by C. Calhoun, E. LiPuma and M. Postone. Cambridge: Polity Press, 61–88.

2. _____ . 1990d. *In other words: Essays towards a reflexive sociology,* translated by M. Adamson. Cambridge: Polity Press.

3. Braithwaite, V. 1990. *Bound to care.* Sydney: Allen and Unwin.

4. Coates, J. and D. Cameron, eds. [1988] 1991. *Women in their speech communities.* Harlow: Longman.

5. Connell. R. W. 1987. *Gender and power.* Oxford: Polity Press in association with Basil Blackwell.

6. Coupland, N., J. Coupland and H. Giles. 1991. *Language, society and the elderly.* Oxford: Blackwell.

7. Fairclough, N. 1992. *Discourse and social change.* Cambridge: Polity Press.

8. Fisher. S. and S. B. Groce. 1990. Accounting practices in medical interviews. *Language in Society* 19:225–250.

9. Goffman, E. 1981. *Forms of talk.* Oxford: Blackwell.

10. Hasan, R. 1985. *Linguistics and verbal art.* Victoria: Deakin University Press.

11. Tannen, D. 1987. *That's not what I meant.* London: Dent.

12. Thiroux, J. P. 1980. *Ethics, theory and practice.* 2nd ed. Encino, Cal: Glencoe Publishing Co Inc.

13. Watson, E. A. and J. Mears. 2000. *Women, work and care of the elderly.* Aldershot, Hants: Ashgate Publishing Ltd.

12

Judgement as a Resource in Child Protection Practice

Arthur Firkins and Sue Smith

The Context of Child Protection Practice

The field of child protection has developed as both a professional and social practice, arising out of pressure from the community for state intervention to protect children from possible abuse or neglect. Child abuse and neglect is a social problem which has significant consequences for children and their families. Child protection, as a social practice, gains significant attention in the media, particularly when things go wrong. In New South Wales, responsibility for the wellbeing and safety of children is spread across agencies between professions and within the community. One agency, generally a state institution, has lead responsibility for the initial response, when a child is considered to be at risk of harm.

In most countries in the western world, this responsibility and the mandate for action is embedded in a legislative framework. In New South Wales this is the Children and Young Persons (Care and Protection Act 1998). This could be described as a *super-text,* a text to which all other texts, created within the practice, relate inter-textually and which directs the social practice of child protection. In short, child protection is situated in a context characterized by a mixture of crises, response, limited resources and pressure for accountability.

Within this shifting context of practice, child protection agencies have responded by limiting their role to investigation, intervention and referral. The practice is not the domain of any single profession but is increasingly reliant on inter-agency and inter-professional cooperation. In New South Wales, this move has been encouraged through the recommendations of large public enquiries such as the Royal Commission into New South Wales Police Service (1997), which recommended a greater emphasis on inter-agency cooperation, collaboration and partnerships with community organizations.

The mandate to intervene therefore rests within the practitioner's institutional and often statutory role, not necessarily their membership of a specific professional group. Practitioners need to balance the pressures of identifying any issues of abuse and neglect and ensuring that measures are taken to address any harm or potential harm to a child while ensuring that adequate support services are provided to families and children. This requires practitioners to respond to the unique circumstances of each situation of often crises for the individuals concerned, particularly the child. Effective communication between practitioners is central to the practice and underpins the process of decision making. Child protection can be considered as a field of practice with its own discourse community and discourses unique to the practice.

The Discourse of Decision Making

Child protection is embedded in the discursive practices established by the state agencies responsible for the practice. Decision making, is shaped by the interactions of the practitioner with a number of other professionals and informants throughout a decision making process.

Errors in communication can have serious repercussions on the case (Munro, 1999).

In the 45 reports reviewed by Munro, such errors were a significant source of criticism levelled against the practitioners and child protection agencies. Errors cited by Munro are listed in the following:

- Failure to revise risk assessments
- Basing decisions on to little information or evidence
- Relying on evidence gathered in only one context
- Failure to use past history
- Differential levels of scepticism about new evidence

- Reliance on people's testimony rather than written records of information
- Written information overlooked in preference to oral reports of professionals present at case conference or meeting.
- Persistent influence of first impressions
- Information known to others but not collated

The exchange of information between professionals, agencies and key people in a child abuse/neglect case can be problematic, and the major cause of avoidable errors within the practice (Munro, 1996). In a recent inquiry surrounding the death of a child in NSW, the Community Service Commission identified similar problems in practice:

> *"A significant factor contributing to a failure in the interagency approach used was the Department's failure to clearly communicate its decisions about the case to agencies involved with the family. Poor intra-departmental communication also led to a departmental failure to coordinate its own intervention."*

(NSW Community Service Commission Report, 1999)

Munro (1996) uses the metaphor of a *jigsaw* to describe decision making within child protection practice. Information around a child abuse/neglect case is spread between professionals, agencies and other community members. A practitioner may only have a few pieces of the puzzle and cooperation is essential to gain the other pieces. Munro (1999 and 1996) stresses that a decision taken in one context, using particular information may be correct. However, it may led to an adverse outcome because the information base available to the practitioner at the time of decision may be too small. Practitioners are often working with an incomplete picture and must constantly weigh up the time needed to collect further information against the necessity to ensure the immediate safety of the child.

This indicates a significant difference between information available to the practitioner on which he/she can base a timely decision, and information, which is technically in existence, but unavailable to the practitioner. Important information may not be available to the practitioner at a particularly crucial point in the case. Sarangi (1988) in a detailed discussion of the construction of evidence, supports this view. His study focuses on the exchange of evidence and information between professionals. He emphasizes that evidence selection and evidence focus vary among different professional groups. These professional groups may withhold information from each other and this is rationalized on the grounds of confidentiality, codes of ethics and professional conduct. The core problem is a differing notion of the concept of client between the professionals involved in the case. This determines which evidence is available and which evidence is actually used by the child protection practitioner on which to base a judgement.

Munro (1999) accepts that these problems in communication will occur suggesting that errors in communication are probably inevitable. Munro suggests that *"people hear each other incorrectly, make mistakes writing up records and practitioners express themselves in vague terms that leave scope for misinterpretation by others"* (Munro, 1999;753). Work in sociolinguistics suggests that communication, specifically the discourse of professions and institutions, is extremely complex but amenable to research. The errors in communication identified by Munro have their basis in discourse production and interpretation as well as in the discursive practices of the institution and the professional groups involved in the practice.

Waugh (2000) suggests that the context of how the information is presented as well as the social position of the person who presents the information often determines how seriously the child protection practitioner views information (Waugh, 2000). In a study into the workings of a child protection office in New South Wales, Waugh identified factors which impacted on decision making and the judgements practitioners were making as in the following :

- Personal beliefs and attitudes
- Workplace practices
- If the child had been previously notified.
- If a parent rang in a distressed state threatening to harm the child.

- A child ringing in a distressed state.
- If the informants were other professionals.
- The mode of the information ie by fax, telephone.

Waugh also found that the nature of the practitioner's response was also determined by the following factors ;

- The practitioners' ability to listen and empathize
- The practitioners' qualifications, training and experience
- The practitioners' understanding and definitions of abuse and neglect.
- The practitioners' knowledge of work-place practices
- The practitioners' attitudes to the agencies intervention into families

Waugh's study identifies the complexity of the context of practice in which practitioners are making decisions on a day-to-day basis.

Decision making within child protection practice involves more than one person and information gathered at one point is communicated to other points withn a decision making chain. Munro (1999 and 1996) in a study into common errors of reasoning in child protection practice in Britain, cites errors of communication within these information chains as the significant source of inaccuracy in decision making in child protection.

Problems of communication may themselves be avoidable by making explicit to practitioners the discourse processes within the social practice. Munro's research points practitioners in directions that begin to examine how information is used in decision making processes. However, it does not go far enough in unpacking exactly what these communication errors are and how they occur. Hall, Sarangi and Slembrouk (1997a, 1997b) analyse some of the communication problems surrounding a child abuse/neglect case, at the level of discourse. Their work shows how an understanding of the discourse strategies, at both the professional and institutional levels, can begin to unpack the problems in communication, which Munro accepts as inevitable. Hall, Sarangi and Slembrouk (1997 a, b, c) identify key discourse strategies which underpin some of the errors in communication highlighted by Munro:

- Genre: particularly story construction
- Contrast
- Mediation of voices and the silencing of voices in reports and narratives
- Representation of speech in narratives and reports
- Audience, super-Addressee
- Recontextualization
- Narrative Transformation
- Persuasion
- Evaluation
- Intertextuality

Social practices, such as child protection, have various orientations, economic, political, cultural and ideological as well as a considerable number of social actors and points of view. Discourse may be implicated in all of these factors without any of them being reducible to discourse (Fairclough, 1993:80). Complex discourse strategies arise in complex work situations in day to day practice. This makes an understanding of communication in a highly complex and often chaotic social practice, such as child protection, essential. The whole practice is reliant on written and spoken discourse. However, what is missing from discussions of communication problems in the child protection literature are the explanatory connections between the nature of the discourse processes (in this instance discourse in decision making) and the nature of the social practices of which they are a part (Fairclough, 1992:80).

Child protection is an arena where the technologicalization of discourse (Fairclough, 1992) is evident and where the considerable research into professional and institutional discourses can make a difference at the broad level of practice. This is not only through a critical investigation of the discourse of the professions concerned with carrying out the practice, but also by offering methods to critically analyse the information. It would be reasonable to suggest that discourse strategies, attributed to failures in practice, may also be responsible for the success of the vast majority of cases as well as the errors seized upon so readily when things go wrong. For example a practitioner's refusal to change their initial assessment of a case (cited by Munro, 1999 as an error) may in one context result in positive outcome, whereas in another context result in negative outcome. It is problematic to pass evaluation on the strategies of practitioners without a firm understanding of the situational contexts in which the practitioners have to work and arrive at decisions.

Complex social practice requires reflective practitioners (Schon: 1987). This means accounting for the problems of real-world practice, which do not present themselves as well formed structures and often present themselves not as defined problems, but messy, indeterminate situations (Schon, 1987:4). This chapter picks up the challenge to respond to complex social practice and child protection specifically, in a critical and reflective manner A critical and reflective approach will encompass an understanding of the discourse processes which underpin the practice at a micro as well as a macro level and which encompass the multiple relations between linguistic means and social meaning (Hymes, 1977).

Risk Assessment and Decision Making

The key discourse event in child protection practice is decision making surrounding an allegation of abuse or neglect. Central to decision making is the assessment of risk, the outcome of which is to arrive at a *judgement* and to decide on a course of action. Within this debate a dichotomy is established between various models and approaches to decision making. A focus of the literature is on empirical comparisons between different models. We have singled out decision making and within this judgement as the focus of this discussion. Decision making has been examined predominantly as an individual cognitive process, however in child protection practice this is clearly not the case. Information is passed along an information chain. Munro (1999:752) illustrates an example of an information chain

> *"His relatives went to the police to report their concerns that this little boy might be at risk of physical injury from*

his mother's boyfriend and they were unable to find either
the child or his mother. The duty senior social worker,
at the end of a long chain of communication, heard that
that a little girl, living with her mother at a specified
address, was in danger of neglect. He visited and, like
the relatives, found no-one at home, but since the case
did not sound urgent, he took no further action until the
relatives raised the alarm...."

Decision making involves a number of practitioners throughout the process. Adding an inter-agency element to this means that the quantity of involved professionals is significantly increased, from the point of intake to the point of final decision and beyond. Decision making therefore involves at least two people, and could be described as a *decision making chain,* where information is passed between practitioners.

Within a decision making chain, both the socio-cognitive dimensions of text production and interpretation are crucial. This centres upon the interplay between the individual practitioner's resources, which they have internalized and bring with them to the text processing, as well as the text itself, as a set of cues for the interpretation of process (Fairclough, 1992: 80). These resources include attitudes, beliefs, values and experience. A typical decision making chain would be a report to a child protection agency by a professional, such as a doctor, of a possible child abuse/neglect situation. Information would be passed through the chain as outlined below.

Doctor → Intake officer → Supervisor → Practitioner →

Within a decision making chain the cohesion (connection) of the information as well as, the interpersonal and ideational (information) functions of communication production and interpretation are all equally important. As information is passed through the chain it is contextualized and recontextualized. Recontextualization is the procedure by which a set of original and actual events is transformed into the currency of fact (Sarangi, 1998). This is primarily done by way of *stories* (Sarangi, 1998). Hall, Sarangi and Slembrouck (1997 a, b) point towards the narrative genre as being particularly privileged within child protection practice, and highly prone to the process of recontextualization. An example of narratives which are peculiar to child protection practice are a *disclosure*, where a child may confide in an adult or professional regarding a possible abuse or neglect situation, or a *notification* where an incident of alleged neglect or abuse is reported.

It also appears that report and recount genres are also influential in decision making. In child protection practice information available at a particular stage of a case can be transferred or transformed at another stage (Sarangi, 1998). The process of recontextualization underpins decision making, as the practitioner is called upon to synthesize information and material evidence. Information becomes transferable and transportable in the form of spoken and written reports, narratives or recounts. These primary genres have been incorporated within the secondary practice genre of risk assessment.

Judgement as a Resource

In an analysis of decision making, it is important to draw a distinction between decision and judgement. Judgements are inferences and impressions made from information available, whereas a decision is a choice between alternative courses of action (Dalgleish, 1997). *Judgement* is a mental process whereas *decision* could be seen as a behavioural process, being the outcome of judgement, and implying a commitment to an action. There is a fine-grained distinction between these two cognitive processes, nevertheless an important one with implications for practice. Decisions reached lead to material outcomes for children and families. These outcomes could be positive or negative. The two terms are used interchangeably in the literature, however researchers such as Dalgleish (1997) argue that the two processes represent distinct schemata and as such should be kept separate in discussions surrounding decision making. This provides the rationale for focusing on judgement as an important element of decision making in child protection.

Both are cognitive-linguistic processes at the level of the individual practitioner. However, the further both judgement and decision is removed from the locus of the case, the more the process becomes social and reliant on language. In other words the further up the chain the decision is made the more the process becomes linguistic-social and embedded in the discourse strategies of all the professionals involved. Essentially, judgement is reaching a decision using one's experience and knowledge and is based on the information available. As such, in this chapter we are suggesting that judgement itself could be conceptualized as a resource.

Judgement is not a neutral concept. Judgement is shaped by *individual, professional* and *institutional influences* (see Figure 12.1). The concern of child protection agencies is that judgements left entirely to the individual practitioner are subjected to highly individual influences. The child protection research widely supports this view. Munro (1999 and 1996) and Dalgleish (1997) point out that people take mental short cuts, are prone to initial impressions based on attitude and belief, are quick to formulate judgements and have difficulty articulating how a judgement was formed. *Professional judgement,* where a practitioner draws on experience and professional knowledge is also highly individualistic in an area of practice where practitioners may be from diverse professional groups and have differing levels of training.

Figure 12.1
Influences on Judgement

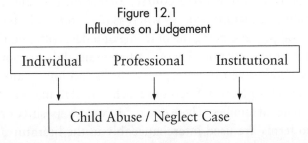

Munro suggests that professional judgements should be regarded as valuable but fallible, needing to be treated as hypotheses requiring further testing (Munro, 1999). Dalgleish (1997) foregrounds the unpredictable and subjective nature of judgement in a comprehensive discussion of decision making in child protection practices. Wald and

Woolverton (1990) also discuss the advantages of risk assessment processes over professional judgement. This research concludes that expert judgement is a necessary component of decision making, which cannot be removed from the process. However such judgement is highly evaluative and subject to factors (pointed out by Dagliesh, 1997 and Munro 1999) which lead to inconsistent decision making. Given the scale of a child protection agency's responsibility, the consequences of decisions and public accountability to the community, it is reasonable that child protection agencies would seek to control, guide or direct judgement.

Child protection agencies influence judgement through decision making or risk assessment models. English and Pecora (1994), Doueck, English, DePanfilis and Moote (1993) and Wald and Woolverton (1990) all offer detailed discussions of the considerable benefits to child protection agencies in using risk assessment models and point to such things as consistency and validity. These models loosely follow two approaches, the more qualitative based structured decision making approaches, which attempt to guide expert judgement and decision making and the quantitative actuarial approaches which attempt to quantify and categorize decision making based on norms in the community. A considerable literature is devoted to arguing the positive and negative aspects of these approaches (Baird, Wagner, Healy and Krister, 1999). The weight of findings suggests the superiority of quantitative decision making models over models that use purely expert judgement. As a result, this chapter will not duplicate this discussion but instead recognize these models as genres of practice and focus on the degree to which risk assessment genres shape the resource of judgement.

Risk Assessment as a Genre of Practice

The framework through which the agency constrains and enables judgement could be described as a genre. Genre here is both a tool in the form of a text and a process in the form of a set of actions. Risk assessment could therefore be described as a *genre* of practice. Agencies across the world differ in how they implicitly or explicitly guide, steer or control judgement. The degree to which practitioners are influenced by individual, professional and institutional factors is an important consideration. The aim is to gain consistency and uniformity in judgement across the whole agency. The theory is that given the same case, the same information and the same context, practitioners should arrive at similar judgements.

Risk assessment models are ways in which the child protection agency can exert institutional influence over judgement. This amount to what Goodwin (1994) describes as socially organized ways of seeing and understanding events that are answerable to the distinctive interests of particular social groups.

Goodwin's discussion centres on how *professional* vision is shaped towards the expertise of a profession. However, in child protection practice risk assessment models are ways in which the institution organizes ways of seeing around a child abuse/neglect case and influences judgement and could be described as ways of shaping *institutional vision* (see Figure 12.2)

Coding transforms phenomena observed in a particular setting into the object of knowledge. *Highlighting* makes specific phenomena in a complex perceptual field salient by marking them in some fashion. *Material and graphic representation* are symbolic representations of the phenomena to be observed. Goodwin's three categories are useful ways of analysing how risk assessment models organize desperate events and information into a common analytical framework. (Goodwin, 1994).

Figure 12.2
Goodwin's Three Categories

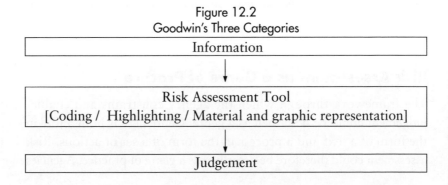

Information

Risk Assessment Tool [Coding / Highlighting / Material and graphic representation]

Judgement

This makes judgement a site of struggle and contested ground within child protection practice. What is at stake is the control of what may be termed *professional judgement* or *clinical judgement*. In Goodwin's terms, this is a struggle for how judgement is focused, individually, professionally or institutionally. The degree to which an agency may attempt to control or guide judgement through coding, highlighting and material representation, may reflect the degree of confidence the agency places in the practitioner's ability to exercise professional judgement over individual judgement. This may be influenced by the agency's perception of the practitioner's professional background, pre-service qualifications, experience and inservice training, but also its own supervision and quality assurance processes surrounding decision making.

No child protection agency in the world would leave judgement totally to the practitioner's individual opinion, and the debate centres on how to use the resource of judgement in the most consistent and effective manner. Dalgliesh (1997) suggests that any model of decision making needs to take expert judgements into account and work with it rather than against it.

Picking up on Dalgliesh's point, the final part of this discussion is an analysis of a risk assessment model using a systemic functional linguistic methodology (Halliday, 1985) focusing on how the resource of judgement is guided through institutional vision using a risk assessment genre. Much of the research around risk assessment models is an attempt to validate one over another. This is not an evaluation of the model's validity or effectiveness in practice, but of how the model accounts for expert judgement and institutionally steers it within the decision making process.

Judgement as a Resource within the Victorian Risk Framework (VRF)

The Victorian Risk Assessment Model (VRF) is explicitly a *Guided Professional Judgement Approach to Risk Assessment in Child Protection*. The VRF is a series of social actions mediated through a number of texts, which represent schematically the practice genre. We have selected this model to examine how judgement as a resource is focused through such an institutionally imposed genre. The VRF model was developed through considerable consultation with Victorian child protection practitioners and accounts for both the experiences of expert practitioners and impirical research.

The VRF has been in development since 1997 with the purpose of developing a standardized approach to risk assessment in the Victorian Framework (Boffa and Armitage, 1999). It therefore explicitly acknowledges judgement as a cognitive resource and the need to focus it institutionally within this complex area of social practice. The model attempts to reconcile the competing demands within the practice.

- Professionals in other fields are trained to be specialists in specific domains, the child protection worker is required to be specialists across many domains (Boffa and Armitage, 1999)
- Although risk assessment sounds like a single focus activity, it is in fact the container for many specialist domains of knowledge (Boffa and Armitage, 1999)
- Different case information may have different significance at different decision making points, however the process of thinking through this information in order to make a professional assessment remains the same (Boffa and Armitage, 1999).

The information on which to base a risk assessment also comes from diverse sources and must satisfy the needs of several audiences. Given such a context of practice, the VRF implicitly acknowledges the complexity of any social practice involving multiple actors in the decision making process. Different risk factors may lead to different decisions.

The VRF defines risk as the relationship between the degree of harm and the probability of harm occurring. (Boffa and Armitage, 1999).

The model argues for the assessment of risk throughout the decision- making process. This relates to both the time frame and context of the judgement and argues that the tension between immediate safety and future risk which recurs continuously through the decision making process needs to be assessed. Risk analysis at any phase of intervention therefore must lead workers to a judgement of risk or safety over the immediate assessment period as well as to a judgement about risk of future harm that requires ongoing work.

Judgement as an individual cognitive resource is refined through a series of institutionally derived filters described in the analysis below. Through the use of the risk framework, judgement is turned from an individual cognitive resource into a social resource, which is spread across the practice. How then is the resource of judgement institutionally constructed with in the Victorian Risk Framework and how is judgement guided institutionally through coding, highlighting and graphic/material representation?

The Textual Framework of Judgement

The text is the institutional vehicle for materially and graphically representing the framework within which judgements are made. This is primarily achieved through the resources of transitivity. Transitivity is the grammatical resource for constructing representation and knowledge in English. This follows an Actor-Process-Goal pattern, where the Actor is the participant who controls action, the Process is type of action and the Goal is where the action is directed. Transitivity also construes the Circumstances of action. Decision as Material Action rather than decision as Cognitive Process is dominant within the VRF.

Within the VRF, grammatical metaphors of action are dominant. For example: *A worker is required to gather, analyse and judge information.* This is a metaphor of obligation, with the Department as Agent requiring an action from the practitioner. Within the VRF it is believed important to provide indicative descriptors of the different judgements Agency and causation of action is realized in the grammar of the VRF, with "The Department" as agent causing the practitioner to engage in the material action of assessing risk. An example of this is outlined in Figure 12.3:

Figure 12.3
The Framework of Judgement

To guide	the key activities [of information gathering analysis and judgement]	
Process/Material:Action	Goal	

To adapt	The risk assessment process	across the different phases [of protective service action and recording/accountability requirements]
Process/ Material : Action	Goal	Circumstance/ Extent

To provide	Access to comprehensive knowledge	
Process/Material : Action	Goal	

To promote	Thorough and informed assessment of risk	
Process/Material : Action	Goal	

To promote	The assessment [of health, welfare and development needs]	where appropriate
Process/ Material Action	Goal Circumstance / Contingency	

Within the VRF, it is the text itself, which is constructed as Actor, construing Material Action, with a strong emphasis on outcome. The action is directed towards the Goals of *activities, process, needs, assessment, and access.* All of these are definable processes, to which the text steers action. Circumstances of Extent (how long?) and Circumstances of Contingency (under what conditions?) set the frame within which judgement can occur. In terms of Agency it is the Department of Human Services who makes the practitioner analyse risk thoroughly through the VRF. The VPF therefore is grammatically constructed as a definable set of Material Actions moving towards the specific outcome of judgement. Grammatical metaphors of action and Material Processes of action are dominant, suggesting that the VRF constructs the assessment of risk as material action.

Coding Judgement

Institutional discourses can be typified as concerned with the realization of constraint on the one hand and the construal of levels of enablement and power on the other (Iedema, 1997). The VRF guides action through the Interpersonal resources of Subject-Finite. In reality the action is an imperative (direction) or a declarative (directive statement). This suggests that the VRF is directed judgement as opposed to guided judgement. Judgement is the practitioner's cognitive resource, however judgement is clearly directed and defined in terms of the agency's outcomes, i.e., a judgement around risk and safety;

- A worker *is required* to gather, analyse, and judge information.
- Judgement of risk *requires* an evaluation of the degree and probability of harm.
- At any point in the protective process, however, the worker's assessment focus *is balanced* between actions to secure safety over the immediate assessment period and actions to reduce any future need for protection.
- Consideration of information relating to these four dimensions *is essential* to achieve the goal of the risk assessment process.
- The VRF *requires* workers to answer a question about the child or young person's safety over the immediate assessment period.

The Department as agency also expresses an opinion through the grammatical resource of modality, clearly indicating to the practitioner its preferred action. For example:

- Within the VRF *it is believed important* to provide indicative descriptors of the different judgement
- Different judgements *may however* arise from information included within the analysis

Judgement is the dominant concept throughout the document. The VRF places an emphasize on the worker's expert judgement at each key decision making point, actively highlighted through a series of statements. There is importance placed on consistency and uniformity and judgement is rested in the collective expert wisdom of the combination of child protection workers who contributed to the research and development of the framework. Judgement is institutionally construed as a resource of the individual workers and the resource of a collective of practitioners. This is realized grammatically through projected relational attributive clauses. For example:

- A worker *is required* to gather, analyse and judge information in relation to what the VRF refers to as the five essential information category.

- Protection *is* action demonstrated as keeping the child and young person from harm.

- The substantiation decision *is* the judgement made by the protective worker following a period of initial investigation which reflects the workers opinion ...

- The substantiation decision *is* the judgement made by the protective worker following a period of initial investigation which reflects the workers opinion

- Risk analysis *must lead* workers to a judgement of risk or safety over the immediate assessment period as well as to a judgement about risk of future harm relating to the child's ongoing need for protection.

Decision as Material Action and Judgement as Material Outcome

The VRF foregrounds decision making as material action. Action is realized through relational attributive clauses. The VRF attributes assessment as being a material outcome, as opposed to a semiotic outcome. Examples of this are provided below.

- The Victorian Risk Framework *provides a guided professional judgement approach to risk assessment.*

- It is the purpose of risk assessment to *determine the need for protection throughout the protective process.*

Focusing Institutional Vision

The VRF institutionally focuses judgement on the key areas of protective practice, harm and safety. This is achieved through a series of focus questions. The goal of the VRF is to steer the practitioner towards a judgement based on a key safety question:

The Safety Question

- Is there any risk of significant harm to the child or young person over the immediate assessment period or is sufficient safety demonstrated?

The VRF further refines the focus of judgement through constraining judgement to consider two risk question:

Risk Analysis Question

- Harm Consequences

What is the actual or believed harm to the child or young person?

- Harm Probability

Judgement is then guided through a series of assessment indicators in the form of questions in order for the practitioner to answer these key risk questions.

Comprehensive Assessment Questions

- Is the alleged perpetrator the primary carer for the child/ren?
- Are there frequent reports of exposure to environmental neglect/substance abuse/violence or other factors?
- Did the abuse result in physical injury to the child/ren?

Judgement is then strategically focused on questions which foreground particular areas within the collected information for particular consideration.

Analysis Questions

- What are the factors that increase or decrease the probability of this harm occurring or recurring?

Text as Process

Practitioners follow three definable processes in decision making around risk. The VRF provides a series of tools to guide the practitioner through each of these processes.

- Gathering information
- Analysis of information
- Judgement of information

In the complex perceptual field of practice the VRF highlights the field of vision through categorization. It highlights five essential information categories on which judgement is based:

- The child or young person
- The parents
- The source of the harm
- The opportunities of harm
- Social networks

Judgement is confined by the risk framework and institutionally filtered through the series of textual tools. The VRF also provides forms on which the practitioner can record the information, as well as a series of textual guides:

- Risk Profile
- Risk Factors Warning List
- Risk Analysis Guide
- Case and Risk Assessment Summaries

These categories are made prominent through the provision of questions and tools to aid the practitioner in gathering the information. Essentially the VRF draws the line in the sand around the accepted definition of risk and further refines the highlighted field through specific specialized tools. The practitioner selects the required tools on the basis of the complexity of the situation, however the selection is limited to four choices:

- Assessments of parenting capacity: substance abuse
- Assessments of parenting capacity: family violence.

- Assessment of adolescent: suicide potential
- Assessment of adolescent: risk

The VRF codes analysis into four areas of risk judgement. All of these are evaluations and the VRF clearly defines how evaluation around these categories should happen through the provision of focus questions for the practitioner to base their evaluation.

- Severity
- Vulnerability
- Likelihood
- Safety

Judgement is further coded towards two schemata, which lock in the parameters of judgement. The decision to act is based on the practitioner's judgements surrounding Future Risk and Immediate Safety:

- Harm consequence
  - extreme
  - serious
  - concerning
- Harm probability
  - high
  - medium
  - low

Conclusion

Decision making is underpinned by the discursive practices of the child protection agency. Judgement is institutionally directed within child protection practice through the use of risk assessment models. These models have significant variation across the world, but all depend on the resource of judgement. Each model uses the resource of judgement in different ways. The Victorian Risk Assessment Model explicitly acknowledges the importance of judgement and provides a framework which is effective in focusing judgement, yet allows semantic space in which the practitioner can exercise judgement, within the decision making process. The model reflects a high degree of confidence in practitioners exercising some form of professional judgement. Expert judgement is a professional resource.

The extent to which judgement as a resource is guided, controlled and directed differs significantly across the social practice. However, when it is institutionally coded, highlighted, directed and guided, it becomes socially distributed across the practice and becomes an institutional resource. As such, risk assessment could be described as a genre of practice, complex patterns of repeated social activity and rhetorical performance arising in response to recurrent situations (Pare and Smart, 1994). The VRF is an example of how an agency can focus institutional vision through the use of a practice genre. The VRF uses the practice genre to guide rather than to control. The effect of this is to harnesses the resource of professional judgement rather than to attempt to suppress it.

Note: The views expressed in this paper are the authors' own and do not represent the views and policies of the NSW Department of Community Services.

References

1. Baird C., D. Wagner, T. Healy and K. Johnson. 1999. Risk assessment in child protective services: Consensus and actuarial model reliability. *Child Welfare League of America* LXXVIII (6 November–December): 723–748.

2. Boffa J. and E. Armitage. 1999. The Victorian risk framework: Developing a professional judgement approach to risk assessment in child protection work. Unpublished manuscript, Child Protection and Juvenile Justice Branch, Department of Human Services Victoria.

3. Children and Young Persons (Care and Protection) Act. 1998. New South Wales Government.

4. Community Services Commission NSW. 1999. *Inquiry into the death of a two-year-old child-final report of an enquiry into the death of a two-year-old child.* Report no. 97/1979.

5. Dalgleish, L. 1997. *Risk assessment and decision making in child protection.* Paper presented lectures at the Normandy Stakis Hotel, Glasgow Scotland, 20 September 1995.

6. Department of Human Services Victoria. 1999. *Victorian risk framework: A guided professional judgement approach to risk assessment in child protection version two.* Practice Leadership Unit Child Protection and Juvenile Justice Branch.

7. Doueck, H. J., D. J. English, D. DePanFilis and G. T. Moote. 1993. Decision-making in child protection services: A comparison of selected risk assessment systems. *Child Welfare League of America* LXXII (5): 441–452.

8. English D. J. and P. J. Pecora. 1994. Risk assessment as a practice method in child protective services. *Child Welfare League of America* LXXIII (5): 451–472.

9. Fairclough. 1992. *Discourse and social change.* Cambridge: Polity Press.

10. Goodwin, C. 1994. Professional vision. *American Anthropologist* 96 (3): 606–633.

11. Hall, C., S. Sarangi and S. Slembrouck. 1997. A moral construction in social work discourse. In *The construction of professional discourse*, edited by P. Linell and B. Nordberry. Nordberg: Longman, 265–291.

12. _____. 1997b. Silent and silenced voices: Interactional construction of audience in social work talk. In *Silence: Interdisciplinary perspectives*, edited by A. Jaworsk. Berlin: Mouton de Gruyter, 181–211.

13. _____. 1997c. Narrative transformation in child abuse reporting. *Child Abuse Review* 6:272–282.

14. Hyme, D. 1977. Studying the interaction of language and social life. In *Foundations in sociolinguistics.* London: Tavistock.

15. Iedema, R. 1997. The language of administration: Organizing human activity in formal institutions. In *Genre and institutions: Social processes in workplace and school.* Open Linguistic series. London: Cassell, 75–100.

16. Munro. 1999. Common errors of reasoning in child protection work; Child abuse and neglect; *Child Abuse and Neglect* 23 (8): 745–758.

17. _____. 1996. Avoidable and unavoidable mistakes in child protection work. *British Journal of Social Work* 26:793–808.

18. Pare, A. and G. Smart. 1994. Observing genres in action: Towards a research methodology. In *Genre and the new rhetoric*, edited by A. Freeman and P. Medway. London: Taylor and Francis, 146–154.

19. Sarangi, S. 1998. Interprofessional case construction in social work: The evidentiality status of information and its reportability. *Text* 18(2): 241–270.

20.   Schon, D. A. 1987. *Educating the reflective practitioner: Towards a new design for teaching and learning in the professions.* California: Jossey-Bass.

21.   Wald, M. S. and M. Woolverton. 1990. Risk assessment: The emperor's new clothes? *Child Welfare League of America* LXIX (6): 483–511.

22.   Waugh, F. 2000. Initial assessment: A key stage in social work intervention. *Journal of Australian Social Work* 53 (1): 57–63.

13

Enquiry into Inquiry: A Study of Chinese Medical Consultation

Zhang Zuocheng and Shang Wei

Introduction

GP practice in the Western surgery has been found to be more than merely medical work. It involves quite complicated interaction between doctor and patient. In the conclusion to their comprehensive study of verbal behaviours of British GPs in medical consultation, Byrne and Long (1976:191) state that "the consultation is a complicated mixture of the discipline we call medicine and the effective utilization of behavioural skills." This interaction is important to both doctors and patients. For doctors, they need to obtain information on patients. This information can help them build up hypotheses concerning the condition and its treatment. In addition to this need, doctors have to persuade patients to accept their diagnosis and comply with their prescription. For patients, they need to voice their concern and give a proper account of their condition so that doctors may have a good grasp of their problems. They also need to take part in the decision making process which leads to the treatment of their condition.

This interaction is necessarily complicated. Doctors and patients alike are not blank sheets, as it were, when they enter into interaction. Both have their own set of knowledge and experience. Patients have knowledge of their body. At least they know what is unusual at the moment, which is why they come to the clinic in the first place. They are also likely to have a lay perspective of illness and causes, which represent "health beliefs derived from folk-models of illness, alternative forms of medical practice, the mass media and "common sense" understandings derived from personal experience or from consultation with friends and family" (Lupton, 1994:100–101). They are also likely to know what medical consultation is like. Doctors, on the other hand, are medical experts by training. They represent the scientific model of disease. Typically, they have acquired their particular consulting styles (Byrne and Long, 1976). To add to this list, other factors such as social class, age, gender, ethnic group, participant personality, nature of the condition, physical setting, time constraint, and bureaucratic practices, etc. can contribute to the complicated nature of medical consultation (Cicourel, 1985; Street, 1991). Due to all these, miscommunication can occur from time to time.

There have been studies of the patterns of interaction between doctors and patients. Researchers have identified the phases of the interaction. For example, Byrne and Long (1976:21) find that medical consultation falls into six consecutive phases:

1. The doctor establishes a relationship with the patient.
2. The doctor either attempts to discover or actually discovers the reason for the patient's attendance.
3. The doctor conducts a verbal or physical examination or both.
4. The doctor, or the doctor and patient, or the patient (in that order of probability) consider the condition.
5. The doctor, and occasionally the patient, detail treatment or further investigation.
6. The consultation is terminated usually by the doctor.

The first three phases are grouped under "diagnostic phases" and the next three under "prescriptive phases" (104).

Researchers are also able to provide details of the phases. The work of ten Have (1991) focuses on the questioning sequence. He demonstrates that doctors typically take the initiative to ask questions while patients often just answer the questions. This is especially true during the diagnostic phases. Additionally, he notes that doctors behave peculiarly in the Third Turn. They typically acknowledge receipt of the information rather than assess it or mark as news what they have just heard.

Heath (1992) studies the prescriptive phases, particularly the fourth and fifth phases. Unlike Byrne and Long, who maintain that the fourth phase is brief or does not exist at all in some cases, Heath argues that this phase usually does exist and "the doctor's opinion of the patient's condition is presented in a distinct utterance or turn at talk which is solely concerned with the delivery of diagnostic information" (239). He identifies a three-stage pattern of interaction: doctor delivering diagnosis or medical assessment; patient making no response, or uttering downward-intoned *er* or *yeh*; doctor making recommended management, treatment, arrangements, and the like (241).

The way doctors and patients interact in the Western GP surgery has been interpreted in terms of institutional asymmetries. An excellent summary can be found in ten Have (1991:140–141). This set of asymmetries is considered to be the driving force behind the pattern of medical talk. But as has been demonstrated convincingly by ten Have (1991) and Heath (1992), the interaction is not automatically restricted or facilitated by the institutional order but is rather an interactional accomplishment.

Another approach is to look at the interaction from the perspective of Communication Accommodation Theory (CAT). CAT derives from social psychology which sets out to explain why people shift their speech styles during social encounters, and to explore the social consequences of such shifts (Giles, Coupland, and Coupland, 1991). Three basic strategies are associated with CAT: convergence, maintenance, and divergence. Convergence means that speakers move toward or approximate each other's communication or communicative needs by manipulating a range of verbal and nonverbal features. Divergence means that they move away from each other or accentuate their differences. Maintenance refers to the way that speakers continue to use their own styles. Street (1991) applies CAT to medical consultations. He argues that medical consultation as a goal-driven social encounter entails two accommodative strategies: convergence and complementarity. By complementarity, he means that both participants make mutual attempts to maintain their social differences in their interaction. By these strategies, patients and doctors can produce positive medical outcomes.

While doctor-patient interaction in Western medicine has been actively researched, or even "over-researched" in the words of Sarangi and Roberts (1999:12), similar work seems to be lacking in Chinese Medicine. Such studies can be potentially interesting. The system of medicare in China differs from that of Western welfare societies. It is also believed that there exist some fundamental differences between Chinese medicine and Western medicine. Xie (1995) identifies some major ones including the conception of human body, cause of disease, diagnostics, and treatment. In Chinese medicine, the human body is regarded "both as a whole organism with the various parts closely related to each other and as an organic unit which adapts to the environment. Health implies harmonious co-ordination among the various parts of the body and adaptation to the physical environment. When normal co-ordination and adaptation break down, illness occurs.... In traditional medical terms, this is called an imbalance of *yin* and *yang*. Medical treatment is thus aimed at restoration of normal equilibrium, bringing *yin-yang* back into balance" (16). Chinese medicine values the differentiation of syndromes, which is "based upon an overall analysis of symptoms and signs, including cause, nature and location of the illness as well as the confrontation between pathogenic factors and the body resistance" (21). Standard methods for obtaining information on the symptoms and signs include the Four Examinations: Inspection, Smelling and Listening, Inquiry, and Palpation. Inquiry, for example, mainly involves practitioners in obtaining information about "the origin and development of the present condition, as well as of pre-existing and previous complaints and reactions to medication" (Wiseman, 1994:89). It is usually oriented to 12 set areas of information: Cold and Heat, Sweating, Heat and Body, Stool and Urine, Diet and Taste in the Mouth, Chest and Abdomen, Hearing and Vision, Sleep, Old Illnesses, Attitude Emotions Lifestyle and Working Environment, Gynecological Matters, and Children (in the case of child patient). Summarizing the tradition of Chinese medicine, Xie concludes that "a doctor practising traditional Chinese medicine treats the patient rather than the disease" (1995:24).

So it will be very interesting to see how doctors and patients interact in a medicine culture that is unique in so many ways. In this study we attempt to investigate discourse practices during Inquiry. We will also look at instances of convergence, complementarity, and divergence. It is our hypothesis that the immediate and larger cultural contexts can have considerable bearing on the goings-on of the interaction.

Data

We tape-recorded a whole morning session of the practice of a Chinese medicine practitioner. The practitioner was aged 70 and had been practising Chinese medicine for over 40 years. The recording was made in his hospital office. The morning session produced altogether six pairs of talk. The patients happened to be all females, six altogether. They were of different ages, ranging from a teenage girl to middle-aged women. The patients all claimed to have tried other doctors before. There was one repeat patient. Except two patients, all the other were accompanied by either a male family member, or a female family member.

We planned to video-tape the talks. But for various reasons, this was made infeasible. So we accepted the much-used option of tape-recording. There are limitations to tape-recording, as we will not be able to refer to the nonverbal communication accompanying verbal communication. But as our purpose is on verbal exchange, we feel the data is acceptable. In addition, bearing in mind that consulting styles of doctors are likely to be idiosyncratic, we decided to limit to one doctor in this pilot study so that we can keep one party constant in studying the consultation.

The talk was transcribed in detail following standard transcription notations. The original extracts are presented in the Appendix on page 359. We went through the transcripts for information with reference to our research questions, namely the overall pattern of consultation, the questioning sequence, the ways in which the doctor and patient converge to, complement, and diverge from each other, and linguistic cues signalling communicative intentions that are used by the patients and the doctor.

Overall Pattern of Consultation

The data reveals lengthy verbal exchanges, lasting from 8 to 19 minutes. It emerges from the transcripts that the doctor and his patients are engaged in a series of activities.

1.   Doctor identifying patient and patient giving factual information. The doctor used almost the same wording across the cases. The sequence can be diagrammed below:

DR:	asking name:	"你叫啥名"
P:	giving name:	
DR:	asking for repeat	"嗯？"
P:	repeating the name	
DR:	repeating the name	
DR:	asking age	"多大歲數？"
P:	giving age	

It is worth describing the appointment system in Chinese hospitals. Patients register at the reception and pay to attend an appropriate department or doctor. If they are not sure which department to go to, they can give their condition to the receptionist who will give some general information as to which department to attend or which doctor to see. Patients are usually issued a blank case record and a patient number at the reception which they take to the department or doctor. Their number together with their case record are usually piled up on the doctor's desk. They have to wait for their turn when there are more patients. When their number is called by either a nurse or the doctor, they go inside to have their consultation or treatment. It is thus necessary for doctors to check that their name and the case record match each other. This is usually done by asking such simple questions like "你叫...？" (Your name is ...?). The doctor enters symptoms and diagnostic information and prescription into the case record, for the patient's record.

In the case where patients do not have a case record, the doctor usually fills in the information into a case sheet, part of his stationery. It appears that in this study case records are not available to the patients and the doctor is filling in information on his case sheet. This may explain why the doctor asks the two main set questions.

2. Doctor inviting patient to talk about her condition and patient describing condition. The doctor usually starts with (“你都怎麼的”(“how are you doing now”)). The patients usually describe their present condition(s).

This pattern seems to be the expected one by the doctor. That is, he expects patients to say something first before he does anything for them. There is one case where the patient says, “你給我看看吧。” (can you give me a check-up.) The doctor replies by inviting her to “你先說說吧。”(You talk about it yourself first.)

3. Doctor asking various questions concerning the condition and other matters and patients giving information. This is what is usually associated with Inquiry.

The doctor’s questions are very much in line with the 12 questions mentioned earlier. But the doctor does not ask all the 12 questions. His questions seem directly related to the complaint the patient has just made.

4. Doctor palpating patient and patient responding with regard to whether there is pain at the location the doctor has just palpated. Palpation takes the form of pulse examination and other physical examination.

Pulse examination is an indispensable activity in Chinese medicine practice. One patient complains about a doctor because he has not examined her pulse. It seems to be the standard practice of this doctor. He usually initiates pulse examination. Sometimes the patients ask for it. During pulse examination, the patient and the doctor are both silent. The patients often ask for information regarding their pulsation and what their pulse pattern indicates. Similar to pulse examination, other physical examination also prompts questions from the patients and thus initiates a new round of Inquiry. Essentially, they return to (3).

5. Doctor giving diagnostic information and patient asking about
    the diagnosis. This is a very extensive process. The patients ask
    about the diagnosis with regard to their condition, its causes.
    Patients frequently poses a new condition and prompt the doctor
    to make further Inquiry or Palpation. The doctor gives individual
    diagnostic information for each condition under question. So there
    can be several rounds of Inquiry and Palpation and Diagnostic
    Informing. See the following Extracts:

Extract 1

0001 DR=doctor P=patient PR=husband accompanying the patient
191   PR: she is (1.0) so thin. she doesn't do any work. just stay
          at home.
192   DR: she has stomach trouble, her assimilation is not good,
          (her) digestion is poor, poor assimilation, how can
          she be plump?
193   (1.0)
194   P: everyone says I=
195   PR: =Can you check if she has other trouble? Has she or
          has she not?
196   DR: no other trouble.
197   PR: no?
198   DR: no. no other trouble.
199   PR: I see.
200   (2.0)
201   P: Can you see if I have other trouble.
202   DR: I haven't found other trouble. just your stomach is
          not good. haven't you had all the necessary
          examinations?
203   P: have you found any trouble through feeling my pulse?
204   DR: sorry?
205   P: you [felt my pulse]
206   PR: [I suspect   ] she has heart disease=
207   DR: =nothing of the kind (.) nothing serious.
208   P: nothing serious.
209   DR: sorry?

210 P: nothing ↓ serious.
211 DR: right.
212 PR: her heart, her family seem to have the gene. her family
       have, not good.
213 DR: sorry?
214 PR: her heart?
215 DR: what's wrong with her heart?
216 P: [he says my family] (.) my parents have the disease.
       his father has the hereditary disease.
217 PR: [( ) parents   ]
218 DR: no. heart (disease) is not hereditary. ((smiling voice))

In this extract, the PR (husband of the patient) initiates a concern
why she is so thin (line 191). He argues that she does not work and
just stays at home, which implies that she should not be thin. The
doctor takes over by explaining that her stomach is not functioning
properly, with poor digestion in line 192. The patient and her husband
are not convinced. The husband takes over from his wife (line 195). (It
is worth noting that this kind of interruption is quite frequent in this
consultation.) He asks if she has something else wrong. It takes the
doctor quite a while to defend his diagnosis until he resorts to
biochemical tests (line 202). This seems to work. But the patient
ambushes in line 203, where she asks the doctor what he has found
about her heart through pulse examination. Her husband joins in line
206 by voicing his suspicion that she has heart disease. The couple
present their reasons in lines 212 and 216. They feel that her parents
have heart disease and she may have inherited the problem. Again, the
doctor has to explain the problem and in the consultation following
this extract, he explains in greater detail why their assumption is invalid.

Extract 2

0004 DR=doctor   P=patient

159 P: it comes out in half an hour. how much does it cost?
160 DR: 21.
161 (1.0)
162 P: 21?

163 DR: right. [yes.]
164 P: [just](.) just my (1.0) waist does the waist need an x ray?
165 DR: x ray (.) waist if the waist is x-rayed you add another 21.
166 P: another 21.
167 DR: that's right.
168 (3.0)
169 P: (what do you say about my liver?
170 DR: liver?
171 (2.0)
172 P: can you please give me a good examination, doctor.
173 DR: take off your shoes take off your shoes.
174 P: okay. ( )
175 (5.0)
176 DR: you need to have an ECG.
177 (1.0)
178 P: I need to have an ECG?
179 DR: your head faces this way. (.) that's right.
180 (3.0)
181 P: have an ECG is it to test if I have heart disease or not?
182 DR: yes. your heart is not working properly.

When this extract starts, the doctor has just palpated the patient's neck and told her to have an x ray of the neck. The patient asks about the cost (line 159). She is concerned whether she needs to have an x ray at the waist (line 164) , as it is one of the two main complaints (the neck and the waist) she has made to the doctor. The doctor does not seem to see any need for the latter. Then the patient asks about her liver in line 169 and implores the doctor to give her a thorough examination in line 172. The doctor obviously complies with the request in line 173 and prepares for the examination by asking the patient to take off her shoes (and lie on the bed). He prescribes an electrocardiogram (line 176). The patient asks why (line 181) and the doctor explains in line 182.

6.   Doctor prescribing treatment and giving instructions and patient asking about the treatment and medication. The discussion of treatment is again quite long. There are clear signs of negotiation between the two parties. Patients may bring in a number of factors, such as economic condition, allergy to certain medication, not complying with the prescription. See the Extracts below:

Extract 3

0006   DR=doctor   P=patient

10   P: can you give me a test request form, test my blood sugar?
11   DR: what about your urine?
12   P: urine I won't have it tested now.
13   DR: why not?=
14   P: =nothing wrong with the urine.
15   DR: your eyelid is swollen, how come it is alright?
16   (3.0)
17   P: after this, after this I will go to another place for the [test.]
18   DR: [all right.]
19   P: test this first.

This patient does not comply with the prescription of biochemical test of her urine (line 12). She explains that she would do it else where (line 17). The doctor accepts this.

The extract below is between the doctor and a middle-aged woman from the countryside. She has claimed at the outset of the consultation that she can hardly afford to see a doctor. When the doctor prescribes an electrocardiogram (line 253), she tries to negotiate with the doctor in line 254:

Extract 4

0004   DR=doctor   P=patient

253   DR: x ray and ECG.

254   P: and ECG? (DR: right.) (.) an ECG have ((in-taken
            breath)) now (.) does it seem necessary? °have an
            ECG°?
255   (2.0)
256   DR: I wouldn't have mentioned it should it not be
            necessary.
257   P: I am cornered. my family condition, if you try your
            best and give me a definite diagnosis, I now (.) spend
            less money.(DR: fine.) have an x ray (2.0) where do I
            go to have the x ray?

This has obviously annoyed the doctor (line 256). The patient quickly justifies herself in the next turn by referring to her economic condition.

7.   Doctor and patient parting with each other. This again can be quite long. Usually the doctor repeats the instruction and reminds patients of a later appointment. The doctor may offer detailed directions for the x ray room. This is also the place where patients relate to the doctor. They ask his name or age, or comment on advantages of Chinese medicine, and express thanks to the doctor. The consultation closes when both have done their part of this work.

It should be noted that the way the activities are presented above does not imply that they constitute a linear process. As is demonstrated in (5) and (6), the process has the potential of being recursive and productive. It is also the case that the activities essentially overlap with the six-phase model of Byrne and Long. The differences lie in the extent of discussions and negotiations that are found in our data.

Questioning Sequence

The questioning sequence discussed in ten Have (1992) is present in our data as well. Inquiry is basically realized in the questioning sequence. The doctor offers a series of queries and patient provides the information. The doctor does not always reveal what is on his mind. The presence of a Third Turn depends on how the patient speaks. Where the patient talks more about her condition, the less the doctor speaks, and the more likely it is for the doctor to have a Third Turn. He usually acknowledges reception of the information and may encourage the patient to go on with their narration or description. Consider at the Extract below:

Extract 5

0004　DR=doctor　P=patient

18	P:	that (2.0) I you say just always have pain in the bone at the back of the neck and waist.
19	DR:	I see.
20	P:	that is in the bone at the back of the neck(.) quite painful.
21	DR:	I see.
22	P:	pain in the waist too.
23	DR:	I see.
24	P:	the heart beats fast.
25	DR:	I see.
26	P:	I feel dazed, always feel the head is pulled by the bone at the back of the neck the head feels very uncomfortable
27	DR:	I see I see.
28	P:	just don't feel energetic [　] don't seem to have the energy.
29	DR:	[er].

This patient is a very fast and outspoken person. She narrates her condition and paraphrases her words (She speaks a dialect different from the doctor's. She repairs herself when she uses her own dialectal expressions) . The doctor acknowledges reception of the informing and encourages her to go on.

In contrast, where a patient speaks little, a two-turn sequence emerges, as is shown in Extract 6:

Extract 6

0005 DR=doctor   P=patient   PR=male accompanying the
      patient

17   DR: what else?
18   P: bloated (.) stiff (.) painful.
19   DR: how long has it been?
20   P: more than 20(.) days.
21   DR: more than 20 days (.) have you not had this condition
      before?
22   P: yes (.) but it used to be minor.

Obviously, the patient simply answers questions and there is no
Third Turn at all.

Another interesting thing in the data is that patients with clear
agendas effectively influence the direction of the talk. There is real
competition for the floor during the consultation and overlappings
and interruptions are quite common.

Extract 7

0004 DR=doctor   P=patient

84   DR: ↑huh. tingle in the shoulders.
85   P: exactly.
86   DR: ↑huh.
87   P: yes. but?
88   DR: sometimes there's a pain in the back.
89   P: pain in the back.
90   DR: yes.
91   P: pain in the back [this is the location] ↓ [this is the
      location] this location =
92   DR: [mainly   ]   [sometimes panting.]
93   P: = the bone at the back of the neck (DR: I see.) (.) so
      painful. (DR: I see.)
      [(   )]
94   DR: [sometimes] panting.

The patient pursues her agenda rather than just following the doctor's report of pulse examination. In line 91, she seizes the floor by stressing the location where she has the acute pain.

Out data lends support to the position that in medical consultation doctors shape the interaction. Although patients may initiate a question (a new condition), they only enter into a new round of Inquiry. The overall process is still regulated by the medical professional.

Accommodation in the Consultation

Street (1991:137–139) summarizes findings in converging and complementing behaviours in medical consultations. He argues that convergence includes behaviours "indicative of communicative involvement (i.e., verbal responsiveness, agreements, gaze, body position, gestures, response latencies) and complementarity includes behaviours "related to control, dominance, and communicative role (i.e., topic initiation, criticism, directives, unilateral touch, extended floor holding durations, interruptions, and pauses within speaking turns)". Doctor and patient are converging when they are reciprocating the exchange of information and developing a topic together. They are complementing each other when they observe their roles in the communicative event.

In this section we will focus on the way the doctor and the patients develop a topic and the way they reciprocate the exchange of information.

The data reveals that convergence does occur. The doctor converges to his patients in four ways.

Firstly, the doctor shifts downward in his lexical choices, that is he avoids medical jargon in favour of everyday language in explaining a condition. In Extract 8, the doctor is explaining the cause of the stomach discomfort to a patient who is not a local person.

Extract 8

0001   DR=doctor   P=patient   PR=husband accompanying the patient

51   PR: her stomach condition what has caused it?
52   (2.0)
54   DR: having meals (1.0) dieting ((prolonged sound.)) yes.
55   PR: eh, dieting =
56   DR: = full this meal and little the next (   ).

In response to the question concerning the cause of the stomach condition (line 51), the doctor starts with "chi fan" (eating), which is everyday language. Then he changes to "yin shi" (dieting, a technical word). When the PR shows some lack of understanding, the doctor reverses to an everyday expression in line 56.

Secondly, the doctor develops the patients' topics. In Extract 9, the doctor takes the patient's topic and makes use of it for his medical purpose.

Extract 9

0006 DR=doctor   P=patient

25   P: I come here it's close to home (.) or else I' d rather go
           to the clinic in my work unit. ↑huh.
26   DR: who do you work for?
27   P: Xin Xing.
28   DR: do you have a clinic?
29   P: yes.
30   (1.0)
31   DR: have you ever had Chinese medicine?

The patient explains why she has chosen this clinic in line 25: the hospital is close to her home. Otherwise, she would have gone to her own work unit. The doctor asks whom she works for in line 26 and then whether there is a clinic there in line 28. In line 31, he relates this patient information to his agenda: whether the patient has had Chinese medicine.

Thirdly, the doctor gives more information during the discussion of treatment and medication.

Extract 10

0003 DR=doctor   P=patient   PR=mother accompanying the patient

96   PR: have an x ray what (.) is it for?
97   DR: I suspect she may have had myocarditis in the past.
98   PR: she had it in the past?
99   DR: That's right. her cardiac muscle was inflamed.(.) in childhood (.) or (what's this). easy to catch cold or have a fever (.) [viral] infection viral myocarditis.
100   PR: [right right.]

The extract begins shortly after the doctor advises the patient to have her heart examined. The PR (mother of the patient) asks what that is for in line 96. The doctor presents the suspicion that the patient may have suffered from myocarditis in line 97. When the mother seems puzzled, the doctor explains his point by giving a set of symptoms associated with the condition. The mother validates them in line 100.

Fourthly, the doctor shows sympathy towards the suffering and difficulties of the patients, and appears willing to discuss options of treatment. Extract 11 shows how the doctor expresses sympathy towards the patient who suffers rheumatism (line 35).

Extract 11

0002 DR=doctor   P=patient

34   DR: You just give it a thorough treatment. (P: okay.) when you are fully cured (.) you stop the medication. (P: I see.) don't stop until you are fully cured. ↓ huh.
35   P: okay.
36   (.)
35   DR: this this disease causes suffering (.) you see (1.0) you can eat and drink, but have to suffer. hhh.

His sympathy to the patients may extend to their economic difficulties. They often bring in their economic difficulties as a prelude to requests for a thorough examination, or to the negotiation of less expensive alternatives of treatment. The doctor generally acknowledges this and gives assurance or grants the requests. In the next extract, the PR (husband of the patient) mentions his employment and hardship, which obtains the doctor's sympathy.

Extract 12

0001   DR=doctor   P=patient   PR=husband accompanying the patient

11   PR: it's not easy that we leave home to work, isn't it=
12   DR: = no, it isn't. this has cost quite a lot of money.

The instances above indicate that the pattern of convergence appears to correlate with topic types and phases of consultation. With non-medical topics (Extracts 9, 12), there is more reciprocation and development by the doctor. While treatment is being discussed, there is more reciprocal exchange of information.

This convergence has obvious effects. One patient addresses the doctor as " 老爺子 " (an intimate address form for one's father) and praises him for being amiable. Another patient addresses the doctor as "大哥" (Big Brother) which is a respectful address form in the context. What is more important, perhaps, is that patients mention that they have come to the clinic either because they have heard of the doctor himself or they acknowledge the advantages of Chinese medicine at the end of the consultation. For a Chinese medicine practitioner, nothing can be more comforting.

Patients also converge to the doctor, by trying to use medical terms. One patient uses the more technical word "記憶力減退" instead of " 記性不好 " for the idea " My memory is getting worse". She changes her dialectal " 肋插子疼 " (pain in the rib-side) for " 肋骨十二疼 ", which is the proper medical term for pain in the rib-side.

Instances of complementarity abound in the data as well. This can be seen when the doctor corrects patients when they wrongly or improperly use a medical term. The doctor is more direct in asking questions and giving explanations. When his agenda seems to conflict with the patient's, the doctor opts to pursue his own agenda by interrupting patients or ignoring their information. See the Extracts below:

Extract 13

0001 DR=doctor P=patient

5   P: just feel like vomiting just feel uncomfortable here
            when uncomfortable I vomited (.) ( ) sometimes I even
            threw up food.
6   DR: I see.
7   P: eh. most[feel like]
8   DR: [you lie   ] on the bed and I will give your stomach a
            check.

The patient gives a symptom in line 5 and seems to be trying to give her worst symptom in line 7. She is cut short (line 8) and asked to get ready for palpation.

With this same patient, the doctor tries to explain that heart disease is not hereditary after she expresses the concern that her parents have heart disease.

Extract 14

0001 DR=doctor P=patient PR=husband accompanying the patient

216   PR: heart (disease) is not hereditary?
217   DR: no. heart (disease) is not hereditary.
218   P: but my [aunt has had heart disease]
219   DR: [when people are getting older], for example father
            or mother get older, (   ) have coronary heart disease,
            and so on. that is possible. heart (disease) is not
            hereditary. (PR: (   )) right. geriatric diseases.

In line 218, the patient tries to give a counterexample (Her aunt on her father's side has heart disease). This attempt the doctor ignores and goes on with his explanation.

The doctor uses medical terms to interpret patients' narration. In Extract 15, the patient complains of breathlessness. The doctor interprets it as "depression in the chest and short of breath".

Extract 15

0004 DR=doctor   P=patient

32   P: heart ( ) short of breath (1.0) [is it]
33   DR: [depression in the chest] short of breath. ↑h.

The delivery of diagnostic information is often highly contextualized. After Inquiry or Palpation, the doctor prescribes something like "透透視", "拍片子" (have an x ray), without being explicit about which part of the body this is to be done on. The patient or the PR usually has to ask for this information.

Extract 16

0005 DR=doctor   P=patient   PR=male accompanying the patient

85   DR: ( ) you need have an x ray.
86   PR: x-ray what?
87   DR: x-ray the stomach.
88   PR: x-ray the stomach?
89   DR: right. x-ray the stomach and have an ECG.

In line 85, the doctor simply says that the patient should have an x ray without mentioning what is to be checked. The PR asks for the information in line 86 and is given the information (stomach) in line 87.

One more interesting matter is that the patients remember the name of the doctor or have even made this special trip to the clinic to see him for treatment. The doctor does not seem to remember the patients' name, even though at the beginning he has asked for it and noted it down on his case sheet. When at the end of the consultation he is prescribing biochemical tests on which he has to fill in patients' names, he asks for the names again.

Complementarity by patients can be seen in the frequent use of "en" (yeah, right), the back channelling device, in their reply to doctor's explanations and instructions.

They generally comply with the doctor, at least on the surface. When they make demands or challenges, they are made in indirect ways, and often justified in various ways. Look at Extract 17:

Extract 17

0001   DR=doctor   P=patient   PR=husband accompanying the patient

110   PR: can't have anything raw either? =
111   DR: = you'd better not. =
112   PR: = have you had any fruits?
113   DR: you can eat fruits.

The doctor has just told the patient not to eat anything raw. Apparently the patient and her companion are troubled — whether the patient can have fruit! But the PR doesn't challenge the doctor. Instead, he asks as if of his wife whether she has had fruit. The doctor amends his view in line 113.

Street (1991) does not seem to see divergence as a desirable or probable strategy in medical consultation, as this is not conducive to optimal communication in the social encounter. This may be true as far as specific communicative strategies are concerned. But when we look at the conceptual framework of the patients and the doctor, we would have to be cautious about this point. As can be seen in the extracts, the patients have come to the clinic to have their pulse examined, obviously an idea of Chinese medicine. The patients all ask about the result of pulse examination. One patient even accuses one doctor of not examining her pulsation. It seems that the patients are thinking in Chinese medicine terms. It is not clear how the doctor himself is managing the situation internally. But he does not seem to be bothered. He prescribes biomedical tests, and when this is challenged, the doctor does not explain it or change his mind. In Extract 18, the patient has gone through all the Four Examinations, and she wants to know whether the doctor is certain about her heart condition (line 233). The doctor replies that she needs to have an electrocardiogram.

Extract 18

0004   DR=doctor   P=patient

233   P: like the way you diagnose you are not sure whether I
              have[heart disease]?
234   DR: [right. (   )]. for heart, you have to have an ECG.

Discussion

Due to the small scale of this study, we are constrained from making
generalizations. Nonetheless, we hope to have illustrated some
interesting phenomena from Chinese medicine practice.

This study suggests that the overall structure of medical
consultation in Chinese medicine does not differ essentially from that
in Western medicine. This resonates with the idea that medical
consultation is a problem-solving process. The practitioner needs to
identify the problem (the condition), elicit information from the patient
for hypothesis building (diagnosis), and come up with a solution
(treatment). Whatever theory of body and illness, whatever diagnostics,
are applied, the general process is shared.

Inquiry is a very important part of medical consultation in Chinese
medicine. It allows the patient to make her complaint(s) and give the
doctor some basic information about herself and her condition. It is
organized into questioning sequences in which the doctor takes the
lead in asking questions and the patient makes replies. Drew and
Heritage (1992:49) discuss the features of institutional talk. They point
out some important asymmetries "between professional and lay
perspectives, and between professional and lay person's capacities to
direct the interaction in desired and organizationally relevant ways".
The way Inquiry is conducted in our data does in general reflect the
features. But in Chinese medicine, this process does not seem to be a
linear one. A host of factors may come into play and make the process
quite extensive. The patients are able to subvert the doctor-leading
questioning structure and pursue their own agenda. Where the patients
have clear goals and are articulate, the Inquiry can be very extensive.
Accordingly, we agree with ten Have (1991) that institutional

asymmetries are not givens but are negotiated and reproduced by the two participants in their turn-by-turn interaction.

There are more exchanges in the delivery and reception of diagnosis and treatment. This may have something to do with the method of Chinese medicine. The four Examinations are standard practice for obtaining information on the condition of the patient. There exist plenty of opportunities for patients to ask questions. Medical consultation in Chinese medicine is thus very creative, triggering off information which may be latent at the outset of the encounter. Also relevant here is the conception of the unity of body in Chinese medicine. Chinese medicine emphasizes that bodily organs are not anatomical entities, but functional systems connected to each other and the environment. Malfunction at one place may affect other parts of the body. This may be why the doctor is tolerant of the concerns over conditions other than the one directly relevant. The patients bring into the consultation their doubts, worries, and folk explanations for their condition and ask for expert opinion.

Another explanation for the lengthy diagnosis and treatment may be related to the condition patients present with at consultation. Patients try Chinese medicine for several major reasons. They are familiar with it in the first place, especially in the countryside and among older people. Secondly, herbal medicine is cheaper and is believed to have less side effect. Thirdly, patients are suffering from chronic diseases which are not cured by Western medicine. For patients suffering from chronic diseases, they are naturally concerned with the effectiveness of the new treatment. Their experience of the disease and previous treatment also equip them with a range of knowledge, like cause of the condition, possible effects, treatment. As Lupton suggests, "these well-established beliefs may underlie patients' refusal to comply with doctors' instructions and contribute to misunderstandings between doctor and patient if the former is not aware of the existence of these beliefs" (1994:101). When this occurs, the patient and the doctor are virtually in a process of negotiation and persuasion.

The doctor uses modern testing equipment quite often. Why does he use modern testing equipment in his Chinese medicine practice?

What problems are likely to arise? The data suggests that problems do arise. The doctor is an experienced Chinese medicine practitioner. He makes use of pattern identification approaches in Chinese medicine, but also prescribes biochemical or equipment tests. How does he reconcile the two different traditions internally? Perhaps more important is the question of how he handles the patients when he uses a Western medicine style of examination. It seems that the doctor is suspending his identity as a Chinese medicine practitioner, which arouses challenges from the patients.

Contemporary medical practice in China is quite complicated. Rooted in Chinese culture and having served the Chinese people for thousands of years, Chinese medicine has a profound influence in their daily life. It was not until around the end of the 19th century that Western medicine entered China. It has existed along with Chinese medicine ever since. For one period of the 20th century (early 20th century), it was the officially favoured medicine. But the government has encouraged doctors practising in Western medicine tradition to learn Chinese medicine. This is the slogan of "zhong xi yi jie he" (integration of Chinese and Western medicines). It is becoming common that Chinese medicine practitioners adopt biochemical tests to confirm their diagnosis. Stibbe (1996) discusses medical metaphors in traditional Chinese medicine and Western medicine. The idea is that there can be two sets of systems operating in medical practice in China. This study lends some support to Stibbe. For the patients with the Chinese medicine practitioner, it seems that their Chinese medicine metaphor system is activated. The two conflicting sets of medical metaphors may have created some of the tensions observed in the data, and thus divergence.

The instances of convergence deserve some comments. They may partly result from the relational work by the patients. Tracy and Coupland (1990) discuss multiple goals in social interaction. Relational goals can be pursued for transactional goals. The patients give such reasons for attending the clinic: other doctors have failed to cure them; this clinic has acquired a good reputation with experienced doctors; they have heard of the present doctor. This relational work seems to have worked well. It may also be meaningful to mention the factor that the patients pay to see the doctor. In a sense, they are buying a service, rather than enjoying something free from the doctor, as is the case with Western welfare societies. This can have a considerable effect on the relationship between the patients and the doctor.

It can be seen in the extracts that companions of the patients play a significant role in the medical consultation. They are interpreters, information providers, support to the patient, and outsiders who can be used by the patient as a sort of footing. These outsiders frequently make requests and ask questions on behalf of the patient. They even make decisions for the patient, especially when it comes to whether a medical test is to be done. As the name we give them implies, they may play a kind of public relations role. At times they appear to be the ones that are being treated rather than the real patients.

Conclusion

If we agree that medicine is a culture, then this study can claim to have thrown some light on Chinese medical culture. The way the doctor and the patients talk mirrors some of its essentials, for example, the appointment system, procedures of medical practice, appropriateness of behaviours in the setting, etc. All these are actually made explicit during the interactive processes. To use what is almost a cliché in institutional communication, they are talked into being. Furthermore, the study shows that medical consultation is also a site for struggle and negotiation. Insights into its mechanism and appreciation of its complexity can promote smooth and effective communication and the delivery and consumption of health care.

References

1.   Byrne, P. S. and B. E. L. Long. 1976. *Doctors talking to patients: A study of the verbal behaviour of general practitioners consulting in their surgeries.* London: HMSO.

2.   Cicourel, A.V. 1985. Doctor-patient discourse. In *Handbook of discourse analysis: Discourse analysis in society,* edited by van Dijk, T.A. London: Academic Press. Inc.

3.   Giles, H., J. Coupland and N. Coupland, eds. 1991. *Contexts of accommodation: Developments in applied sociolinguistics.* Cambridge: Cambridge University Press.

4.   Heath, C. 1992. The delivery and reception of diagnosis in the general-practice consultation. In *Talk at work: Interaction in institutional settings,* edited by P. Drew and J. Heritage. Cambridge: Cambridge University Press.

5.   Lupton, D. 1994. *Medicine as culture: Illness, disease and the body in Western societies.* London: Sage Publications.

6.   Sarangi, S., and C. Roberts, eds. 1999. *Talk, work and institutional order: Discourse in medical, mediation and management settings.* Berlin: Mouton de Gruyter.

7.   Stibbe, A. 1996. The metaphorical construction of illness in Chinese culture. *Journal of Asian Pacific Communication* 7:177–188.

8.   Street Jr., R. L. 1991. Accommodation in medical consultations. In *Contexts of accommodation: Developments in applied sociolinguistics,* edited by H. Giles, J. Coupland and N. Coupland. Cambridge: Cambridge University Press.

9.   ten Have, P. 1991. Talk and institution: A reconsideration of the "asymmetry" of doctor-patient interaction. In *Talk and social structure: Studies in ethnomethodology and conversation analysis,* edited by D. Boden and D. H. Zimmerman. Cambridge: Polity Press.

10.   Tracy, K. and N. Coupland, eds. 1990. *Multiple goals in discourse.* Clevedon: Multilingual Matters Ltd.

11.   Wiseman, N., tr. 1994. *Fundamentals of Chinese medicine* (revised ed.). Brookline, Mass: Paradigm Publications.

12.   Xie, Z.-F. 1995. *Best of traditional Chinese medicine.* Beijing: New World Press.

This paper was written during our visit to the Centre for Language and Communication Research at Cardiff University. We would like to express our heartfelt thanks to the staff who have helped us in various ways. Our thanks are also due to the China Scholarship Council for sponsoring our visit.

Appendix

Extract 1

0001　DR=doctor　P=patient　PR=husband accompanying the patient

191 PR:　她這人(1.0) 這麼瘦，她也不幹啥活兒啊，就在家裡呆著。

192 DR：她胃有病，她吸收得不好，消化不好，吸收得不好，她怎麼能胖呢?

193　　　(1.0)

194 P:　都説我 =

195 PR:　= 你查查她是不是還有其它的毛病? 有沒有?

196 DR:　沒有。

197 PR:　沒有?

198 DR:　嗯。別的毛病沒有。

199 PR:　嗯。

200　　　(2.0)

201 P:　你看我有沒有什麼別的毛病? 你看看。

202 DR:　沒，沒看出別的什麼毛病來，就是胃不好，你不是該查的都查了嗎?

203 P:　你拿脈拿的我心裡有沒有什麼毛病?

204 DR:　嗯?

205 P:　你[拿脈]

206 PR:　[我懷]疑她心臟有問題 =

207 DR:　=沒問題(.)。沒啥大事。

208 P:　不要緊的。

209 DR:　嗯?

210 P:　不 ↓ 要緊的。

211 DR:　嗯。

212 PR:　她心臟吧，她家吧好像有遺傳因子，她家有有不好?

213 DR:　嗯?

214 PR:　心臟呀?

215 DR:　心臟怎麼啦?

216 P:　[他説我家] (.) 父母有遺傳性，他爸有遺傳性的。

217 PR:　[(　　) 上輩]

218 DR:　沒有，心臟不遺傳。 ((笑聲))

Extract 2

0004   DR=doctor   P=patient

159 P: 半個小時就出來，多少錢吶?
160 DR: 21。
161   (1.0)
162 P: 21?
163 DR: 嗯。[對]。
164 P: [光] (.) 就是這個 (1.0) 腰腰用照嗎?
165 DR: 照 (.) 腰要照的話再加21。
166 P: 還得加21?
167 DR: 對。
168   (3.0)
169 P: 你↓咋給我診的肝呢?
170 DR: 肝?
171   (2.0)
172 P: 你好好給我看看吧，大夫。
173 DR: 脫鞋脫鞋。
174 P: 嗯。
175   (5.0)
176 DR: 你得做心電。
177   (1.0)
178 P: 還得做心電?
179 DR: 腦衝這裡 (.) 對。
180   (3.0)
181 P: 做心電就是做有沒有心臟病呀?
182 DR: 對。 心臟不好。

Extract 3

0006   DR=doctor   P=patient

10 P: 那你給我開化驗，化驗血糖吧。
11 DR: 尿不化驗?
12 P: 尿我先不化驗。
13 DR: 為啥? =
14 P: = 尿沒事。

15 DR: 你眼臉都腫了，怎麼沒事?

16　　　(3.0)

17 P: 完了再說，完了我再上別的地方化[驗]。

18 DR: [行]。

19 P: 先化驗這個。

Extract 4

0004　DR=doctor　P=patient

253 DR: 照照像帶做心電。

254 P: 帶做心電? (DR: 嗯。) (.) 心電做 ((吸氣聲)) 現在 (.) 好象有必要嗎? 做心電?

255　　　(2.0)

256 DR: 沒必要我就不提了。

257 P: 我也是問住了，俺們家情況的話，盡個量你要是能確診的話，我現在 (.) 就是那個啥少花點錢吧，(DR：嗯。) 照照像吧，(2.0) 照像得上哪去照呢？

Extract 5

0004　DR=doctor　P=patient

18 P : 那個 (2.0) 我呢你說就總覺得大脖筋疼腰疼。

19 DR : 嗯。

20 P : 就是這脖後兒這後梁骨 (.) 全都疼。

21 DR : 嗯。

22 P : 腰也疼。

23 DR : 嗯。

24 P: 心臟也跳。

25 DR : 嗯。

26 P : 腦瓜迷糊，就是腦瓜總覺得就是這後梁骨拽得兒這後梁骨拽得腦瓜子可難受了。

27 DR : 嗯嗯。

28 P : 就是挑不起精神[去]就沒精神似的．

29 DR : [口屋]

Extract 6

0005   DR=doctor   P=patient   PR=male accompanying the patient

17 DR: 還怎麼的?
18 P: 脹 (.) 硬 (.) 疼。
19 DR: 多長時間了?
20 P: 有 20 (.) 多天了。
21 DR: 20 多天了 (.) 以前沒這個情況嗎?
22 P: 也有 (.) 有吧輕。

Extract 7

0004   DR=doctor   P=patient

84 DR: ↑阿。 兩個肩酸吶。
85 P: 對。
86 DR: ↑阿。
87 P: 嗯。哪?
88 DR: 有時背痛。
89 P: 背痛。
90 DR: 嗯。
91 P: 背痛呢[就是這個部位呀] ↓ [這個部位呀]這個部位 =
92 DR: [主要是　　]　　[有時是心慌。]
93 P: =是大梁骨哇 (.) (DR：嗯。) 疼得相當嚴重。 (DR：嗯。)
　　　　　[(　　)]。
94 DR: [有　] 時候心慌。

Extract 8

0001   DR=doctor   P=patient   PR=husband accompanying the patient

51 PR: 她胃是怎樣造成的呢?
52   (2 . 0)
53 DR: 吃飯 (1 . 0) 飲食 ((拖長調))誒。
54 PR: 阿，飲食 =
55 DR: =飽一頓餓一頓(　).

Extract 9

0006   DR=doctor   P=patient

25 P: 這不離家近我就來了 (.) 要不以後我就想回單位去看。
            ↑阿。
26 DR: 什麼單位呀?
27 P: 新型啊?
28 DR: 你們有衛生所兒呀?
29 P: 呃。
30   (1. 0)
31 DR: 吃過中藥啥的沒有?

Extract 10

0003   DR=doctor   P=patient

96 PR: 照像它那 (.) 是咋回事呀?
97 DR: 我懷疑她呃過去得過心肌炎。
98 PR: 過去得過?
99 DR: 呃呃。 得過心肌炎。 (.) 小時候 (.) 或者是什麼。好感冒
            發燒。 (.) [病毒]感染的病毒性心肌炎。
100 PR: [嗯嗯。]

Extract 11

0002   DR=doctor   P=patient

34 DR: 你就治把它治徹底一點。(P: 行。) 治徹底好了 (.) 你再停
            藥。
            (P: 嗯。) 不好就別停藥。↑阿。(P: 行。)
35 DR: 這遭這病遭罪呀。 (.) 你説 (1. 0) 能吃能喝,就是遭罪,
            嘿。

Extract 12

0001   DR=doctor   P=patient   PR=husband accompanying the patient

11 PR: 俺們出門打工真不容易,是吧。=
12 DR: = 就是。 是啊。 這就花不少錢吶。

Extract 13

0001   DR=doctor   P=patient   PR=husband accompanying the patient

5 P: 就是喜歡吐就是這裡難受難過極了吐﹙.﹚﹙﹚有時連飯也
           吐出來。
6 DR: 嗯。
7 P: 嗯。 最[喜歡]
8 DR: [你倒]在床上我再摸摸胃.

Extract 14

0001   DR=doctor   P=patient   PR=husband accompanying the patient

216 PR: 心臟不遺傳?
217 DR: 誒。 心臟不遺傳。
218 P: 就我 [姑姑呀就有心臟病。]
219 DR: [年歲大了   ]，比如説父親母親年歲大了，﹙﹚有冠心病
           呀，什麼的，那都可能有心臟不遺傳 (PR:﹙ ﹚). 老年病。

Extract 15

0004   DR=doctor   P=patient

32 P: 心臟﹙ ﹚氣短 (1.0) [是不是 -]
33   [胸悶   ] 氣短。°↑阿.

Extract 16

0005   DR=doctor   P=patient   PR=male accompanying the patient

85 DR: ﹙﹚透透視吧。
86 PR: 透啥?
87 DR: 透胃。
88 PR: 透胃呀?
89 DR: 對。 透胃做心電。

Extract 17

0001   DR=doctor   P=patient   PR=husband accompanying the patient

110 PR: 生的也不能吃? =
111 DR: = 最好別吃。
112 PR: 那水果吃沒吃過?
113 DR: 那沒問題。

Extract 18

0004   DR=doctor   P=patient

233 P: 要是你這麼確診的話診不了是不是 [心臟] 病?
234 DR: [對。( )] 心臟呃，那必須得拍做心電。

Discourses of

The Academy

14

Harmony of Theory and Practice: An Engineering Lesson for Applied Linguistics?

Colin Barron

Introduction

Analysts of academic and professional discourse generally come to the disciplines they study when they are already well established. This is perhaps natural given that it is difficult to analyse a particular discourse until there is clear evidence that one has emerged. The effects, though, on applied linguistics have sometimes been pernicious in that there has been a tendency towards parasitism, that is, a dependence on the experts in the disciplines concerned. Linguistics and applied linguistics are unique in the social sciences in that they have failed to establish a critical programme similar to the social constructivist programme in sociology and related disciplines. There is, then, a lack of studies in discourse analysis on how disciplines and facts become established to complement such studies in the history and sociology of science and technology (e.g., Fleck, 1979 [1935]; Shapin and Schaffer, 1985; Latour, 1988 [1984]; Chamak, 1999). These kinds of studies are important because they are critical in a way that is different from the ideological critiques of critical discourse analysis. They raise questions such as, "Why are there disciplines?" "What are the underlying principles by which disciplines are established?" "How do the founders of a discipline ensure that it is different from other, similar disciplines?" and "How can the discourses of disciplines be identified?" In this paper I look at how mechanical engineering became established in the academy and how one of its major founders, William Rankine, ensured that it was different from the natural sciences, particularly physics.

Channell (1982) has shown how William John MacQuorn Rankine, Regius Professor of Civil Engineering and Mechanics at Glasgow University (1855–1872), played a major part in establishing mechanical engineering as an academic discipline in Britain through his "harmony of theory and practice" (Rankine, 1858) and how he successfully differentiated mechanical engineering from physics. I want to take this further in three ways:

- historically, by showing how Rankine was influenced by developments in mechanical engineering education in France;
- ontologically, by disclosing the underlying temporality of mechanical engineering that Rankine developed as distinct from the temporality of the natural sciences;
- comparatively, by suggesting how applied linguistics could learn from the example of mechanical engineering in order to move forward and take its place in the academy.

These three moves of the paper outline its underlying theme — the importance of time in the analysis of discourse. In this paper I emphasize time and temporality as key factors in the analysis of discourse. Time has not been a focus in discourse analysis up to now because "time disappears into events, processes, movements, things, as the mode of their becoming" (Grosz, 1999:1–2). As time disappears, it is represented by space and spatiality, so there is a double displacement, from becoming to being and from temporality to spatiality (Grosz, 1999:2). Consequently, time and temporality are unreflected and undertheorized in linguistics. This paper is a start in redressing the situation.

Rankine's Vision and Mission

When mechanical engineering entered the universities in Britain in the mid-nineteenth century it faced opposition from the professors of the natural sciences because it was seen as a purely practical subject, concerned with the day-to-day manipulation and change of materials. Science, on the other hand, treats substances in a fundamentally different way. Substances are "permanent, unchangeable matter" (Channell, 1982:51). If mechanical engineering were to become accepted in academia, it would have to develop a curriculum that was not purely practical while at the same time not being too theoretical and thus tread on the toes of the natural scientists. The first chair of engineering in Britain was established at Glasgow University in 1840. A chair of engineering was established soon afterwards at Edinburgh University. A number of eminent engineer-scientists had major influences on establishing engineering education in Britain, "but the brightest light of them all was W. MacQorn Rankine" (Burstall, 1963: 286). He established mechanical engineering as an acceptable academic discipline through his harmony of theory and practice (Rankine, 1858).

Rankine constructed a conciliatory discourse for mechanical engineering which enabled it to become accepted in the academy through his "harmony of theory and practice in mechanics" (Rankine, 1858). He set out his vision and mission for mechanical engineering in his inaugural lecture, which was published as the introduction to his first textbook, *A Manual of Applied Mechanics,* in 1858. This is a key text in mechanical engineering because the book went through twenty-one editions into the 1920s and the introduction appeared in all editions. Rankine summarized his vision as three kinds of knowledge.

> *"Mechanical knowledge may obviously be distinguished into three kinds: purely scientific knowledge, — purely practical knowledge — and that intermediate knowledge which relates to the application of scientific principles to practical purposes, and which arises from understanding the harmony of theory and practice."* (Rankine, 1858:8)

Rankine set out his *mission* for mechanical engineering as the harmony of two modes — the scientific and the empirical.

The framework for harmonizing the laws of science and the practice of technology was laid out in the introduction to his second textbook, *A Manual of the Steam Engine and Other Prime Movers* (1859). With his vision and framework, Rankine was able to satisfy both the natural scientists' insistence on applying the laws of science in a way that accorded with the permanent state of matter and the engineers' practices of exploiting materials to produce change.

I analyse both these texts to show how he addressed the problem through his belief in the Aristotelian method and constructed a conciliatory discourse for mechanical engineering that led to its successful establishment in the academy. I show how Rankine's texts continue in a rhetorical way the Franco-Scottish alliance by following up on earlier developments of the establishment of engineering as an academic discipline in France. I also wish to show that a constitutive perspective on the analysis of discourse and language is needed for an understanding of such rhetoric.

Influences on Rankine

Aristotle

While studying natural philosophy at Edinburgh University, Rankine read a good deal of philosophy, including the works of Aristotle and the school of Scottish Common Sense (Channell, 1982:46). To obtain inspiration for his harmony of theory and practice, Rankine looked initially at the ancient Greeks, who "are our masters" (Rankine, 1858: 1), particularly Aristotle. A fundamental concept in Aristotle's metaphysics is that of substance (ουσια). Unlike later philosophers, Aristotle defined substance as something that undergoes change during a process.

> *"Our model of change is that in all cases there is (a) a thing that undergoes change, (b) something by which it is changed and (c) something into which it changes. We further claim that the role of (b) is played by the primary mover, that of (a) by the thing's matter, and that of (c) by form"* (Aristotle, Metaphysics, Lambda 3, 1070a [1998: 359]).

Objects are created through the action of form on a substance.

> *"But then, quite generally, if to be in sphere form is itself the output of a production, then this will be a case of something being produced from something. The rule*

cannot here be suspended that all outputs of production can be split up, with this component and that component, and I am saying that the one is matter and the other form" (Aristotle, Metaphysics, Zeta 8, 1033b [1998: 194]).

Rankine incorporated Aristotle's notion of change as a central element in his engineering framework.

"The Aristotelian element, as well as the other, στοιχεια, appears, so far as we can judge, to have been understood by Aristotle himself, not as a substance, but as one of the states of which substances are susceptible " (Rankine, 1859:xxviii; emphases in original).

According to Aristotle, objects are formed when form is imposed on a substance, so that change occurs when a substance takes on a new form. This notion of change in substantial forms was central to Rankine's framework of the harmony between scientific laws of action and the properties of materials in mechanical engineering.

French Influences on Rankine

To complement his Aristotelianism, Rankine would also have looked closer to home at recent developments in engineering education. He would not have found much to help him in England where the apprenticeship system provided the corps of engineers and where there were no engineering departments in the universities (the chair of engineering at Cambridge University was established in 1875, three years after his death). Nor would he have found inspiration in the USA, where James Renwick, professor of natural experimental philosophy at Columbia University had recently published two books. The first, *The Elements of Mechanics* (1832), was a conventional exposition of the science of mechanics. The second, *Applications of the Science of Mechanics to Practical Purposes* (1842), was a survey of existing practices in the fields of civil, mechanical, marine and mine engineering (Weiss, 1982:91). Neither book provided the bridge across the gap that Rankine was seeking.

It seems reasonable to suggest that Rankine looked to France, where the École Polytechnique had been established in 1794 to train the finest mathematicians and scientists in the country (Landes, 1982: xv). There is no direct evidence to support this claim, but we can look both to history and to Rankine's engineering contemporaries in France. There have been strong links between France and Scotland since the Middle Ages when the two countries formed both political and marriage alliances to counter England. These political links have spilled over into influences on the social and economic fields.

The French Revolution established the *écoles centrales* and the École Polytechnique, which were based upon "the alliance of theory and practice" (Weiss 1982:164). We see here perhaps the beginnings of Rankine's notion of the harmony of theory and practice. A new elite was created. Before the Revolution the privileged class had power and most of the wealth, transmitting to its descendants most of its advantages. After the Revolution the middle class (*la classe moyenne*) maintained its position by education and work. The engineer (*ingenieur-industriel*) combined "[a]n aptitude for the sciences, a genius for their application, and a love of hard work" (Joseph Bélanger, cited in Weiss, 1982:220). The institution charged with creating the new technological elite was the École Centrale des Arts et Manufactures, founded in 1829.

The École Centrale was established to break completely with artisanal traditions and the apprentice system, which produced almost all British engineers. Neither did it seek to produce savants, scientists devoted to wide-ranging fundamental research and theoretical formulations in the manner of the members of the Académie des Sciences. "The realm of the engineer lay somewhere "between" these two types of activities" (Weiss, 1982:90). But what should it look like?

Auguste Comte took up the issue:

> "Between scientists properly so called (les savants
> proprement dits) and the effective directors of productive
> enterprises an intermediate class has begun to form itself
> in our day, that of the engineers, whose special mission
> is to organize the relations between theory and practice.

Not at all concerned with the progress of scientific knowledge, they consider it only in its current state of development in order to derive from it the industrial applications that it is capable of providing. Such is, at least, the natural tendency of things, although there is still much confusion on the matter" (Comte, 1949:110).

The need for harmony of theory and practice was clearly recognized by French mechanical engineers, but the method of achieving it proved to be somewhat less than straightforward. The problem centred on how to marry the theoretical with the practical, so that the engineer should not be considered inferior to the scientist while not adhering rigidly to the same scientific methods. The future of engineering could not lie in Comte's hierarchy of subjects, which progresses in an orderly fashion "from the sciences of greatest generality and independence to those of greatest complexity" (Weiss, 1982:95). The answer would have to lie in the creation of a new élite, a new Technological Man, and he was to study *la science industrielle* (industrial science), a single body of knowledge to express the unity and coherence of theory and practice, exemplified by a single *plan d'ensemble* in the curriculum of the École Centrale des Arts et Manufactures (Weiss, 1982:97).

We can start to perceive the harmony of theory and practice in the three forms of unity for the engineering curriculum at the École Centrale des Arts et Manufactures. These were:

- the poles of chemistry and mechanics
- tying together sequences of related courses along progressions from general to specialized and theory to application
- encompassing the natural and physical sciences and the arts (Weiss, 1982:152)

But there was no agreement among the founders of the École Centrale des Arts et Manufactures on how to go about achieving harmony. One of the founders, Théodore Olivier, refused to countenance the superiority of the theoretical sciences, stating "labour is a necessity of the human condition" (Olivier, 1851:iv). In the preface to his *Mémoires* (1851) he suggests that the generation and development of scientific theories is the unique province of "pure science", regardless of whether the subject is the behaviour of atoms, water flow in turbines or electromagnetic phenomena. The *application* of theories would seem to be distinct from theory, a process separate in time and space from the activities of the *savants purs* (Weiss, 1982:162). Olivier seemed to be implying that engineers' activities were derivative of scientific ones and thus seemed to be continuing "the social prominence and aristocratic pretensions of the "theoretical scientists" and their claim to the commanding heights of scientific and, hence, technological creativity" (Weiss, 1982:162). The interrelation of the subjects of *science industrielle* became evident through application. "Only in practice did one perceive the unity of theory" (Weiss, 1982:163).

Another of the founders of the École Centrale, Eugène Péclet, wrote the standard textbook, *Traité élémentaire de physique* (1847), in which "science and technology became ... open-ended enterprises" (Weiss, 1982:105). Despite the apparent marriage of science and technology — the book had extensive sections on technological innovations such as barometers — the book left many questions unanswered. In particular, it had no conceptual framework for understanding the great unifying theory of thermodynamics then unfolding.[1] For example, Peclet failed to introduce the concept of work in his discussion of the fundamentals of physics, and the equivalence of mechanical work and heat is the linchpin of thermodynamic theories (Weiss, 1982:110).

Establishing relationships and generalities between scientific theories and technological endeavours was, nevertheless, the aim of Péclet. In his discussion of electricity in his *Traité élémentaire de physique* he sought to make connections between phenomena.

Hence electricity is involved with all phenomena, and

1.   The teachers of the École Centrale were close to the tradition of scientifically oriented French engineering which was one of the centres of the development of the law of the conservation of energy (the first law of thermodynamics) (Kuhn, 1977 [1959]: 93–94).

> *we shall not discover its nature and its method of action*
> *without discovering at the same time the nature of heat*
> *and of the composition of substances* (Péclet, 1849:341).

However, this search for the relationship between theory and practice died out. In his third textbook, *Traité de la chaleur* (1860), like his other, largely an encyclopaedia of technological achievements, in this case of heating devices, Peclet presented neither the theory of thermodynamics nor a concept of energy (Weiss, 1982:112).

Rankine's Harmony of Theory and Practice

Despite their lack of agreement, the French mechanical engineering teachers had planted the seeds of Rankine's harmony. Evidence for Rankine's familiarity with developments in mechanical engineering (*la science industrielle*) in France comes from his concern with stress in mechanics. The term 'stress' was introduced by the French engineer Augustin Cauchy into mechanical engineering on 30 September 1822 (Timoshenko, 1983 [1953]:104–111; Truesdell, 1968:186), but Rankine was the first British scientist-engineer to use the term "stress" and to define it rigorously (Channell, 1982:50). His first published use of the term was in 1856, a year after his inaugural lecture (Rankine, 1856), but he also defined stress in a letter to William Thomson (later Lord Kelvin) in 1855 (Channell, 1982:50). He was also no doubt aware of French experiences in mechanical engineering education at the École Centrale des Arts et Manufactures because he was a leading figure in the emerging field of thermodynamics, which was a major concern of the engineers at the École Centrale.

Rankine outlined his vision of engineering science in his inaugural lecture at the University of Glasgow, delivered in 1855 and published in 1858 as the introduction to his first textbook, *Manual of Applied Mechanics,* with the title "Preliminary dissertation on the harmony of theory and practice in mechanics" (Rankine, 1858).

We have already seen Rankine's vision on page 370, expressed as three kinds of knowledge — purely scientific, purely practical and intermediate knowledge. It is the third part, the "intermediate kind of

instruction", in which Rankine's great insight lay. In order to rid
mechanical engineering of the charge of being a purely practical subject,
Rankine distinguished two modes, "the *empirical* and the *scientific*.
Not the *practical* and the *theoretic*, for that distinction is fallacious"
(Rankine, 1859:xix; emphases in original). The empirical is Rankine's
intermediate knowledge. For, "the empirical mode of progress is purely
and simply practical; the scientific mode of progress is at once practical
and theoretic" (Rankine, 1859:xix). Rankine set out his mission for
mechanical engineering as two modes, a combination of discovery and
practice.

Purely scientific knowledge produces the discoverer, who is:

> *"in the student that improvement of the understanding*
> *which results from the cultivation of natural knowledge,*
> *and that elevation of mind which flows from the*
> *contemplation of the order of the universe; and secondly,*
> *if possible, to qualify him to become a scientific discoverer"*
> (Rankine, 1858:8–9).

Purely practical knowledge

> *"is that which the student acquires by his own experience*
> *and observation of the transaction of business. It enables*
> *him to judge of the quality of materials and workmanship,*
> *and of questions of convenience and commercial profit,*
> *to direct the operations of workmen, to imitate existing*
> *structures and machines, to follow established practical*
> *rules, and to transact the commercial business which is*
> *connected with mechanical pursuits"* (Rankine, 1858:9).

Harmony is created by linking these two kinds of knowledge in the
empirical mode, which

> *"connects the first two, and for the promotion of which*
> *this Chair was established, relates to the application of*
> *scientific principles to practical purposes. It qualifies the*
> *student to plan a structure or a machine for a given*

purpose, without the necessity of copying some existing example, and to adapt his designs to situations to which no existing example affords a parallel. It enables him to compute the theoretical limit of the strength or stability of a structure, or the efficiency of a machine of a particular kind, — to ascertain how far an actual structure or machine fails to attain that limit, — to discover the causes of such shortcomings, — and to devise improvements for obviating such causes; and it enables him to judge how far an established practical rule is founded on reason, how far on mere custom, and how far on error" (Rankine, 1858:9).

Rankine's modes established the goals for mechanical engineering that integrated scientific theory and the laws of actions with the practical experimental data derived from the properties of materials and machines.

Although Rankine had suggested the integration of scientific laws and the properties of materials and machines in mechanical engineering, he had not established clearly the relationship between the two. He had not established a framework. The framework appears in his second book, *A Manual of the Steam Engine and Other Prime Movers* (1859). The title of the book itself is instructive since "prime mover" is an Aristotelian metaphysical construct for the fundamental cause of existence (McKeon, 1947:xviii). In this book Rankine defined heat as a "condition of bodies" which was capable of producing certain sensations (Rankine, 1859:224). This is the Aristotelian concept of "the hot element, as well as other στοιχεια, ... to have been understood by Aristotle himself, not as a *substance*, but as one of the *states* of which substances are susceptible" (Rankine, 1859:xxviii; emphases in original). Aristotle's concept of change in substance (ουσια) is central to Rankine's framework.

The Aristotelian concept of change in substantial forms explains the relationship between the laws of action and the properties of materials in Rankine's engineering science. In his *Manual of the Steam Engine and Other Prime Movers*, Rankine clarified the relationship between the scientific (laws of action) and the empirical (properties of materials) that he outlined in his vision for mechanical engineering in his inaugural lecture. His Aristotelian ideas for mechanical engineering in his inaugural lecture formed the vision, and they are explicitly stated in the title of his second book, "prime movers". The next step was to be in two stages:

- how the laws of action could apply to some substance in such a way that they created a state or condition in that matter;
- how the properties of the matter would directly influence or modify the laws of action.

The framework for connecting the laws of action and the properties of materials came in Rankine's *Manual of the Steam Engine*. He identified two modes for technological progress. I quote Rankine in full.

> "*Empirical progress is that which has been going on slowly and continually from the earliest times to the present day, by means of gradual amelioration in materials and workmanship, of small successive augmentations of the size of structures and power of machines, and of the exercise of individual ingenuity in matters of detail. This mode of progress, though essential to the perfecting of mechanical art in its details, is confined to making small alterations on existing examples, and is consequently limited in the range of its effects.*
>
> *Scientific progress in the mechanical arts takes place, not continuously, but at intervals, often distant, and by great efforts. When the results of experience and observation on the properties of the materials which are used, and on the laws of the actions which take place, in a class of machines, have been reduced to a science, then the improvement of such machines is no longer confined to amendments or enlargements in detail of previously existing examples; but from the principles of science practical rules are deduced, showing not only how to*

bring the machine to the condition of greatest efficiency consistent with the available materials and workmanship, but also how to adapt it to any combination of circumstances, how different soever from those which have previously occurred. When a great advance has thus been made by scientific progress, empirical progress again comes into play, to perfect the results in their details" (Rankine, 1859:xix–xx).

Thus Rankine established the framework for mechanical engineering: small cumulative changes, as in the empirical progress, are essential but subservient to the periodic changes of scientific progress. In mechanical engineering, scientific progress takes place when the properties of materials or machines and the laws governing action in machines are reduced to a science. This framework produces a set of rules which govern the engineer's investigations. There is one set of empirical rules, which specify what counts as being an engineer since the empirical depends on them. Rankine's genius lay in his framework of harmonizing a single set of rules with scientific laws.

The Temporality of Mechanical Engineering

In his harmony of theory and practice, Rankine made possible more than a set of rules for mechanical engineers. His twin modes of the scientific and the empirical created a Temporality for mechanical engineering that was distinct from the Temporality of the natural sciences. But it was a Temporality that remained within the dominant Western temporality, and it was these two factors — the establishment of a set of rules and the creation of a distinct mechanical engineering Temporality with its adherence to the Western Temporality — that ensured mechanical engineering a place in the academy, even though the conferring of degrees in engineering at Glasgow University did not happen until 1875, three years after Rankine's death (Parkinson, 1975: 294).

It is necessary here to define what I mean by "Temporality". Temporality is not a framework or a medium to which human beings are externally or contingently related. It is not something whose essence is entirely independent of human beings (Mulhall, 1996:145). Temporality is the human mode of constituting its general experience (Sherover, 1971:275–276). What this means is that "human beings ... exist as temporality, that human existence most fundamentally is temporality" (Mulhall, 1996:145; emphasis in original). Human beings are a complex of past, present and future.

We can now see how this applies to science and engineering. Purely scientific knowledge is based on universal laws which achieve their universality through constancy of recurrence. Because they are universal they are neither in change nor at rest. The equations based on them are reversible. Rankine's genius was to establish constancy, and therefore time, in the empirical. His distinction between the empirical and the scientific is an Aristotelian one of what is in time, i.e., the empirical because it changes, and what is not in time, i.e., the scientific because it is neither in change nor at rest (Turetzky, 1998:27). By relating the practical with the scientific to create the empirical, Rankine introduced change into scientific laws and thus located mechanical engineering in time and gave it irreversibility. In so doing he located mechanical engineering firmly within the Western Temporality by giving it two temporal planes, empirical (lay) and scientific (divine), dissymmetrical (a linear progression) (Prigogine and Stengers, 1984: 125) and symmetrical (universal laws of action).

Rankine thus gave mechanical engineering a temporal direction-forward. His intermediate knowledge enables the mechanical engineer

> "*to compute the theoretical limit of the strength or stability of a structure, or the efficiency of a machine of a particular kind, — to ascertain how far an actual structure or machine fails to attain that limit, — to discover the causes of such shortcomings, — and to devise improvements for obviating such causes; and it enables him to judge how far an established practical rule is founded on reason, how far on mere custom, and how far on error*" (Rankine, 1858:9).

By distinguishing mechanical engineering laws from the laws of the natural sciences and by clarifying the exact nature of the rules of investigation of mechanical engineering, Rankine gave mechanical engineering a distinct Temporality, consisting of the static mode (the scientific, symmetrical mode — neither at change nor at rest) and the dynamic mode (the empirical, dissymmetrical mode — that which changes). The twin modes of Temporality rid it of the charge of being a purely practical subject. But Rankine also essentialized it as a peculiarly Western Temporality which shared a unitary trait with science. Thus was it able to take its place in academia, but at the expense ultimately of denying its Aristotelianism because mechanical engineering continues the Western problematic of the domination of theory in which things have a constancy of presence.

What Rankine did was to clarify the Temporality of mechanical engineers as distinct from the Temporality of the natural sciences through specifying its rules. The Western Temporality, of which mechanical engineering became a part, evolved in its present form in the decades around the end of the thirteenth century AD.

> *"Beginning in the miraculous decades around the turn of the fourteenth century (decades unmatched in their radical changes in perception until the era of Einstein and Picasso) and continuing on for generations, sometimes swiftly, sometimes sluggishly, sometimes in one terrain of mentalité and sometimes another, Western Europeans evolved a new way, more purely visual and quantitative than the old, of perceiving time, space, and material environment"* (Crosby, 1997:227).

This Western Temporality, called the "New Model" by Crosby (1997: 227–240), is marked by several characteristics:

- it is complex
- it is quantitative
- it is both synchronic and diachronic
- it is both symmetrical and dissymmetrical
- it is visual

These are the characteristics of the Temporality of mechanical engineering.

Rankine's Achievement: The Reconciliation of Reversible Time with Irreversible Time

Rankine faced what seemed to be an intractable problem, one that was much more fundamental than the fact that engineering was considered to be purely practical. Rankine's fundamental problem was that time-irreversibility is anathema to science.

> *"We shall see that nearly everywhere the physicist has purged from his science the use of one-way time ... alien to the ideals of physics"* (G. N. Lewis, 1930; cited in Prigogine, 1997:61).

Later William Thomson made reversible processes central to the conception of mechanical engineering through his announcement that no energy could be destroyed (Thomson, 1882:118), thus negating its Aristotelianism established by Rankine. But Rankine established the temporal dissymmetry of time-reversibility in his work on the new subject of thermodynamics, specifically the thermodynamics of the steam engine. In a steam engine, the matter of study is steam and the laws of action are the creation and disappearance of heat. Rankine commented on the steam engine as follows:

> *"The combination of ... fuel with oxygen in furnaces produces the state of heat, which being communicated to some fluid, such as water, causes it to exert an augmented pressure, and to occupy an increased volume; and those changes are made available for the driving of mechanism"* (Rankine, 1859:223).

In a steam engine:

- a state of heat is created in some fuel through combustion
- this state of heat is transferred to water in a boiler, creating steam

- this heated steam creates a state of mechanical energy in the piston, which performs useful work.

Thus, in Rankine's analysis, the work of steam engine depends on:

The properties of steam + the creation and disappearance of heat in the steam

This system combines theory and practice:

- the laws of heat rely on formal theoretical concepts
- the properties of steam rely on experimental and practical data.

The system also demonstrates the harmony of time-reversibility and time-irreversibility:

- the properties of steam (time-reversibility)
- the creation and disappearance of heat in the steam (time-irreversibility).

Rankine's analysis had two effects, one practical, the other theoretical. His harmony of theory and practice led to a solution to the problem of expansion in steam engines and to the development of thermodynamics. Rankine was able to discover the reasons for lost efficiency in steam engines and to recommend procedures to reduce the negative aspects of expansion (Channell, 1982:48). In so doing he was one of the founders of the new subject of thermodynamics and a pioneer in liberating engineering science from the limitations of time-reversibility. The other effect was, of course, the establishment of mechanical engineering as a recognized discipline in the academy.

Rankine's reconciliation of time-reversibility and time-irreversibility was confirmed by the second law of thermodynamics, formulated in 1865 by Rudolf Clausius (Grattan-Guinness, 1997:625). This led to recognition of the fact that "Nature involves both *time-reversible* and *time-irreversible* processes" (Prigogine, 1997:18; emphases in original) because the second law of thermodynamics is time-irreversible (Prigogine, 1980:5–6), the only scientific law which is time-irreversible.

"The principle that the entropy of an isolated system may

only increase or remain constant under time evolution"
(Prigogine, 1997:205).

Irreversible time processes are anathema to science because they are not permanent. Irreversible processes were considered (and still are by some scientists) to be transient (Prigogine, 1997:62). This was the argument used by natural scientists to deny mechanical engineering a place in the academy in its beginnings.

Time-irreversibility: Rankine and Kuhn

The perceptive reader may be asking himself/herself that science is clearly a product of the Western Temporality, so does it have another temporal mode besides time-reversibility? Science's other temporal mode, that of time-irreversibility, lies in its historiography:

> *"every scientific revolution must be followed by a Whiggish rewriting of the discipline's history to make the victorious appear the discipline's natural heirs, thereby motivating the specialized work on which they and their students are about to embark. ... In short, the progressiveness of science lies not in the character of the work scientists do, but in the control they exercise over how they recount their collective history"* (Fuller, 2000: 28; emphasis in original).

Whig history is "the recounting of the past to vindicate the present" (Fuller, 2000:22).

Rankine's insight that science proceeds by periodic changes anticipated Thomas Kuhn's paradigms a hundred years later (Kuhn, 1970 [1962]). They were both similar and different. The projects of the two were very different in their aims. While Rankine wanted to gain acceptance of mechanical engineering into the academy, Kuhn wanted to provide a glorious account of the superiority of the Western European scientific Temporality over Communism. In his recent book, Steve Fuller (2000) advances the theory that Kuhn was promulgating a particular world-view: expression of the Cold War mentality and "inoculation ... against the siren song of Communism" (Fuller, 2000: 6). Kuhn was espousing a particular view of Temporality which emphasized the stasis of the present.

Rankine and Kuhn are similar in that both were promoting a Whig history of science, one that is historical in which the recounting of the past vindicates the present; that our present state is the result of progress through the following of scientific rules; that the future will always be better than the past. Rankine's Whig history dismisses all developments of the steam engine before those of James Watt:

> *"for ninety-one years ago a man took that model, applied to it his knowledge of natural laws, and made it into the first of those steam engines that now cover the land and the sea; and ever since, in Reason's eye, that small and uncouth mass of wood and metal shines with imperishable beauty, as the earliest embodiment of the genius of James Watt"* (Rankine, 1858:11).

A model of James Watt's first steam engine, "that small and uncouth mass of wood and metal", is exhibited at Glasgow University (Figure 14.1). It has become an icon to time-irreversibility.

Figure 14.1
Model of James Watt's Steam Engine at Glasgow University

(Rankine 1859: xxi)

Kuhn would not have considered Rankine's achievements in a positive light since he disdained the technological imperative because sciences that do not temporally progress theoretically devolve into "tools of engineering" (Kuhn, 1970 [1962]:79; see Fuller, 2000:66) and thus time-irreversibility. Nevertheless, Rankine's achievement was positive. In his reconciliation of time-reversibility and time-irreversibility both theoretically, as harmony of theory and practice, and empirically as his pioneering work on thermodynamics, Rankine not only explained what harmony should be, he actually provided an important example which changed fundamentally what mechanical engineers are and how they see the world.

Understanding for Applied Linguistics

In 1979, after trying to analyse the discourse of physicists, Larry Selinker cried out in despair, "we don't even know what we don't even know" (Selinker, 1979:201). He, like many applied linguists and discourse analysts, was following a single set of rules, those governing the investigation itself, just as Rankine suggested for mechanical engineering. But the applied linguist cannot proceed in the same way as the mechanical engineer. Mechanical engineering is an institution with meaningful social situations that usually involve language. In this sense mechanical engineering is already in the world, along with us. In studying mechanical engineering, we learn not just what mechanical engineers do, but we also learn why mechanical engineers do what they do. This entails empathy with mechanical engineering; we cannot remain detached.

> "it is quite mistaken in principle to compare the activity
> of a student of a form of social behaviour with that of,
> say, an engineer studying the workings of a machine"
> (Winch, 1958 [1990]:88).

The applied linguist must proceed by two sets of rules (Wittgenstein, 1967:80–88, 38–42); that governing the investigation of empirical method and that of human activity (see Winch, 1958 [1990]:87). The task of applied linguists is more complex than that of the engineer because they have to proceed by these two sets of rules. As an applied linguist I cannot understand the phenomena of mechanical engineering and the social actions of mechanical engineers unless I understand the interweaving of their significance and their world.

Rankine's harmony of theory and practice gave the temporal significance of mechanical engineering, but this is only fully comprehensible to somebody who already knows what mechanical engineering is and is not additionally confused by what mechanical engineers are and why they do the things they do. Applied linguists usually assume the former without the latter. Typically they analyse written texts (and sometimes spoken language) to provide us with what is there in disciplines. Their enquiry proceeds from the assumption that there is no difference between an explanation of science and an explanation of human behaviour. In this view, applied linguistics is a science in which understanding the meaning of something does not entail empathizing with it (see Lyas, 1999:61); the applied linguistic merely has to know the "facts", that is, things to be discovered.

Applied linguists cannot proceed by a single set of rules, just like the engineer, because the two sets of rules means there are two kinds of understanding. Rankine showed mechanical engineers how to be able to be mechanical engineers by combining determinacy (scientific laws) with possibility (empirical). Determinacy and possibility together make up a complex ontological whole (Blattner, 1999:42). This involves two kinds of understanding:

- understanding of mechanical engineering facts (ontic — factuality)
- understanding of mechanical engineering self (ontological — facticity)

(see Heidegger, 1996:276/254–255)

Ontic understanding is that of becoming a mechanical engineer through knowing the facts, knowing *that* something is a mechanical engineering fact. Ontological understanding means knowing *how* to be a mechanical engineer; people have not only the ability to be one, but also understand oneself and what it is to be a mechanical engineer. They understand their possibilities. This is the futural mode of temporality that applied linguistics and discourse analysis tends to ignore.

Time and temporality are the keys to uncovering the mechanical engineers' possibilities. Rather than being hidden as process, or structure, or product, time and temporality may be disclosed as the articulation of discourse, that is, differentiating their elements and interrelating them (Blattner, 1999:71) at the ontological rather than the ontic level. Language is important in this because temporal possibilities are not outwardly apparent, but language may express them. That is, linguists may be able to disclose the temporality of a discipline and by this means understand how a specialist is that particular kind of specialist by revealing the link between the ontic and ontological levels. Understanding involves sharing what is already understood. This suggests a notion of communication that does not depend on the person-to-person transmission of ideas or experiences. "Communication is never anything like a conveying of experiences, for example, opinions and wishes, from the inside of one subject to the inside of another" (Heidegger, 1996:162/152). The concerns of the applied linguist and discourse analyst, then, are not merely those features that are immediately disclosed from texts.

> *"The characteristics to be found in this being are not objectively present 'attributes' of an objectively present being which has such and such an 'outward appearance', but rather possible ways for it to be"* (Heidegger, 1996: 42/40).

As we have seen from Rankine's development of the harmony of theory and practice in mechanical engineering, possible ways to be are time and temporality. Rankine succeeded in establishing mechanical engineering as a creditable academic discipline because he placed it on a firm temporal footing in the Western tradition with both static and dynamic temporal modes for the mechanical engineer to be. The twin modes of understanding presented here show the way forward for applied linguistics and discourse analysis to locate themselves on the temporal path: a static mode of factual understanding and a dynamic mode of factical understanding. The procedures of critical theory must therefore impinge directly on the analysis of discourse, despite the reservations of some discourse analysts.

> "*Our thinking is that **critical theory**, while exerting considerable influence on discourse analysis, remains 'theory'. It is a diverse set of abstract and philosophical writing ... which does not impinge directly on the analysis of discourse, but is definitely part of the same intellectual climate*" (Jaworski and Coupland, 1999:33; emphasis in original).

Critical theory is an essential part of disclosing ontological understanding, thereby harmonizing the temporal mode with the expressed utterances to enable applied linguistics to analyse discourse.

Conclusion

This analysis of Rankine's harmony of theory and practice in mechanical engineering has disclosed a constitutive view of language (Guignon, 1983:118; Taylor, 1992) and discourse analysis by interweaving the word and the world of mechanical engineering. It shows how Rankine succeeded in gaining academic credibility for the discipline and at the same time made a substantial contribution to the establishment of the subject of thermodynamics, thus releasing time in engineering science from the clutches of reversibility. Critical theories of time and temporality are fundamental to understanding the significance of the interweaving of the word and the world. This requires more than analytical methods because adequately accounting for propositions and utterances requires understanding that they stand for much more than the sum of their parts. Then, applied linguists and discourse analysts may at least begin to know what they do not know about the disciplines they study.

Acknowledgements

Research for this paper was supported by grant no. 10201218/18740/ 43600/323/01 from the Committee on Research and Conference Grants of The University of Hong Kong.

References

1. Aristotle. 1998. *Metaphysics,* translated by H. Lawson-Tancred. London: Penguin Books.

2. Blattner, W. D. 1999. *Heidegger's temporal idealism.* Cambridge: Cambridge University Press.

3. Burstall, A. F. 1963. *A history of mechanical engineering.* London: Faber and Faber.

4. Chamak, B. 1999. The emergence of cognitive science in France: A comparison with the USA. *Social Studies of Science* 29:643–684.

5. Channell, D. F. 1974. Rankine, Aristotle and potential energy. *The Philosophical Journal* 14:111–114.

6. _____ . 1982. The harmony of theory and practice: The engineering science of W. J. M. Rankine. *Technology and Culture* 23:39–52.

7. Comte, A. 1949. *Cours de philosophie positive: Discours sur l'esprit positif,* edited by Charles Le Verrier. Paris.

8. Crosby, A. W. 1997. *The measure of reality: Quantification and western society, 1250–1600.* Cambridge: Cambridge University Press.

9. Fleck, L. [1935] 1979. *Genesis and development of a scientific fact,* translated by F. Bradley and T. J. Trenn. Chicago: University of Chicago Press.

10. Fuller, S. 2000. *Thomas Kuhn: A philosophical history for our times.* Chicago: University of Chicago Press.

11. Grattan-Guinness, I. 1997. *The fontana history of the mathematical sciences: The rainbow of mathematics.* London: Fontana Press.

12. Grosz, E. 1999. Becoming ... an introduction. In *Becomings: Explorations in time, memory, and futures,* edited by E. Grosz. Ithaca, NY: Cornell University Press, 1–11.

13. Guignon, C. B. 1983. *Heidegger and the problem of knowledge.* Indianapolis: Hackett Publishing Company.

14. Heidegger, M. [1927] 1996. *Being and time*, translated by J. Stambaugh. Albany, NY: State University of New York Press.

15. Jaworski, A. and N. Coupland. 1999. Introduction: Perspectives on discourse analysis. In *The discourse reader*, edited by A. Jaworski and N. Coupland. London: Routledge, 1–44.

16. Kuhn, T. S. [1962] 1970. *The structure of scientific revolutions,* 2nd ed. Chicago: University of Chicago Press.

17. _____ . [1959] 1977. Energy conservation as an example of simultaneous discovery. In *The essential tension: Selected studies in scientific tradition and change,* edited by T. S. Kuhn. Chicago: University of Chicago Press, 66–104.

18. Latour, B. [1984] 1988. *The pasteurization of France*, translated by A. Sheridan and J. Law. Cambridge, MA: Harvard University Press.

19. Lyas, C. 1999. *Peter Winch*. Teddington: Acumen.

20. Mayer, J. 1873. The late Professor W. J. MacQuorn Rankine. *Nature* 7:204–205.

21. McKeon, R. 1947. General introduction. In *Introduction to Aristotle*, edited by R. McKeon. New York: The Modern Library, ix–xxix.

22. Mulhall, S. 1996. *Heidegger and being and time*. London: Routledge.

23. Olivier, T. 1851. *Mémoires de géométrie descriptive, théorique et appliquée.* Paris: Carilion-Gury et Dalmont.

24. Parkinson, E. M. 1975. Rankine, William John MacQuorn. In *Dictionary of scientific biography, vol. XI*, edited by C. C. Gillispie. New York: Charles Scribner's Sons, 291–295.

25. Péclet, E. 1847. Traité élémentaire de physique. 2 volumes. 4th ed. Paris: Hachette.

26. _____ . 1860. *Traité de la chaleur*. 3 volumes. 3rd ed. Paris: Masson.

27. Prigogine, I. 1980. *From being to becoming: Time and complexity in the physical sciences*. San Francisco: W. H. Freeman and Company.

28. _____ . 1997. *The end of certainty: Time, chaos, and the new laws of nature.* New York: The Free Press.

29. _____ and I. Stengers. 1984. *Order out of chaos: Man's new dialogue with nature.* Toronto: Bantam Books.

30. Rankine, W. J. McQ. 1856. On the axes of elasticity and crystalline forms. *Philosophical Transactions of the Royal Society of London* 146:261–286.

31. _____ . 1858. Preliminary dissertation on the harmony of theory and practice in mechanics. In *Manual of applied mechanics*, W. J. McQ. Rankine. London: Charles Griffin and Company Ltd., 1–11.

32.   Rankine, W. J. McQ. 1859. *A manual of the steam engine and other prime movers*. London: Charles Griffin and Company Ltd.

33.   Renwick, J. 1832. *The elements of mechanics*. New York.

34.   _____ . 1842. *Applications of the science of mechanics to practical purposes*. New York.

35.   Selinker, L. 1979. On the use of informants in discourse analysis and "language for specialized purposes". *International Review of Applied Linguistics in Language Teaching* 17:189–215.

36.   Shapin, S. and S. Schaffer. 1985. *Leviathan and the air-pump: Hobbes, boyle and the experimental life*. Princeton: Princeton University Press.

37.   Sherover, C. M. 1971. *Heidegger, kant and time*. Bloomington: Indiana University Press.

38.   Taylor, C. 1992. Heidegger, language, and ecology. In *Heidegger: A critical reader*. Oxford: Blackwell, 247–269.

39.   Thomson, Sir W. [1849] 1882. An account of Carnot's theory of the practice of the motive power of heat; with numerical results deduced from Regnault's experiments on steam. In *Mathematical and physical papers*, vol. 1, edited by Sir W. Thomson. Cambridge: Cambridge University Press, 113–155.

40.   Timoshenko, S. P. [1953] 1983. *History of the strength of materials*. New York: Dover Publications.

41.   Truesdell, C. 1968. *Essays in the history of mechanics*. Berlin: Springer-Verlag.

42.   Turetzky, P. 1998. *Time*. London: Routledge.

43.   Weiss, J. H. 1982. Foreword to *The making of technological man: The social origins of French engineering education* by D. S. Landes. Cambridge, MA: MIT Press, xi–xvi.

44.   _____ . 1982. *The making of technological man: The social origins of French engineering education*. Cambridge, MA: MIT Press.

45.   Winch, P. [1958] 1990. *The idea of a social science and its relation to philosophy*. 2nd ed. London: Routledge.

46.   Wittgenstein, L. 1967. *Philosophical investigations*. 3rd ed., translated by G. E. M. Anscombe. Oxford: Blackwell.

15

Specifying "Purpose" in ESP: The Case of the Engineering Analytical Report

Paul Cheung

Introduction [1]

What constitutes an engineering analytical report is the focus of the present chapter, which was written against the background of the following concerns. First, published studies comparing the writings of professionals and students on the one hand and those of native-speakers of English and their non-native-speaker counterparts are extremely rare; methodologically sound ones are rarer still (see Crookes, 1986). The second concern, which follows from the first, is the lack of research-based insights concerning the teaching of the analytical report within the context of undergraduate engineering education (see Winckel and Hart, 1996). Third, there is even less available for the teaching of non-native-speaker undergraduates, despite growing demands in various countries (Marshall, 1988, 1991; Masputeriah *et al.*, 1995; Nik Suriana Nik Yusoff, 1995). The fourth, and the most fundamental concern throughout the chapter is the inadequate theorizing on the generic integrity (Bhatia, 1993) or for that matter, the generic diversity (Fairclough, 1988) of the analytical report.

In order to work towards a more thorough understanding of the engineering analytical report (henceforth AR), multiple theoretical and methodological perspectives were taken as part of a study on which the chapter is based. The chapter begins first of all with the textual-analytical-statistical perspective of the AR and a discussion of its

---

1.   The author would like to acknowledge Professor Charles Bazerman and Ms. Emily Law for their most helpful comments at different stages of the writing of this paper.

theoretical justifications. The chapter then moves on to a psychometric-statistical perspective before combining the two in a theoretical account of the AR's generic integrity-diversity. This leads to a demonstration of the complexities involved in specifying "purpose" in the teaching of AR writing within the context of undergraduate engineering education.

The Textual-analytical-statistical Perspective

While many published textual-analytical studies are pedagogically motivated, they tend to be concerned with the teaching of the research article (henceforth RA) to non-native-speaker graduate students of the natural sciences (see Holmes, 1997, for a selective review). The other major tendency is for these studies to analyse texts written by native-speakers (see Cox, 1995; Peng, 1987) or non-native-speakers (see especially Riazi, 1997), but not both. Where native-speaker (NS) and non-native-speaker writings are compared, the comparisons are across different text types (e.g., Hawes and Thomas, 1997) or across two languages (e.g., Taylor and Chen, 1991; Halliday, 1993). It is difficult to attribute any of the observed differences to first language (or whatever factor) alone. In short, there is little evidence of research on second language writing pedagogy with respect to the AR.

The only textual-analytical study of AR's written in English as part of professional engineering practice is by McKenna (1997). While his analysis of three AR's from different fields of engineering practice remains an important contribution to the study of professional discourse, there remains a limit to the applicability of his findings to second language writing pedagogy in the undergraduate setting. To model the teaching of the AR to undergraduates on McKenna's analysis is to pre-suppose too much regarding the similarities between professional and student writing. Analysis of AR's written by students is also needed for comparison. Further, in order to explore the influences of first language, AR's written by both NS and NNS are needed. The four kinds of AR's that can be compared to each other are shown in Figure 15.1.

Figure 15.1
The Ideal Design of a Pedagogically-motivated Textual-analytical Study

	AR's written in English by	
AR's written in English by	NNS	NS
Students	(Cheung, 2001)	(Cheung, 2001)
Professionals		(McKenna, 1997)

The present author took further McKenna's contribution by consistently applying his textual-analytical technique to student-written AR's (henceforth Student AR's). Student AR's were collected from NNS in the People's Republic of China and from NS in Australia. Note that due to the lack of suitable subjects, no AR was collected from NNS Professionals working in China.

The present study was designed to allow comparisons between NNS and NS AR's on the one hand and between Professional and Student AR's on the other. McKenna's textual-analytical technique led to quantitative as well as qualitative results, thereby allowing the possibility to state with a certain extent of confidence whether observed differences are due to chance. The incorporation of the inferential-statistical perspective into the textual-analytical was crucial in showing that differences found were more than random occurrences. Otherwise, only superficial and subjective judgements would have been possible as far as comparisons are concerned.

The Textual-analytical Model

McKenna's (1997) textual-analytical technique was based on a model originally developed by Gosden (1993), who used it to examine 36 scientific RA's. The Gosden-McKenna model is an elaborate classification of unmarked Themes (Fries, 1983; Halliday, 1994), which in more familiar terms are grammatical subjects in sentence initial positions in declarative clauses. That which comes after Theme in a sentence is called Rheme (Halliday, 1994). Where the grammatical subject is not found in the beginning of a sentence, the sentence initial element is called a marked Theme.

In order to concisely illustrate the theoretical bases of the Gosden-McKenna model, a sentence from a Student AR is shown below for consideration.

Extract 15.1
Sentence 260 from Report Number 964

One last coastal landform near Wollongong Harbour	is Para Reef.
Theme	Rheme

The point of departure of the sentence is "One last coastal landform near Wollongong Harbour". A different point of departure results by placing the above in the Rheme.

Extract 15.1
Version I of Sentence 260 from Report Number 964

Para Reef	is the last coastal landform near Wollongong Harbour.
Theme	Rheme

It can be said that in effect, a choice was made, consciously or otherwise, to organize the sentence by heading it up with the reference to the coastal landform as opposed to the name of the particular landform concerned. The writers of this report had been analyzing potential hazards along a proposed ferry route in preceding sentences and paragraphs as part of their AR. Notice that had their purpose been to describe the physical geography instead, then Version I of Extract 1 would have been more appropriate. It may be inferred then that the thematic choices made in all the other sentences in the AR contribute to its organization as a piece of discourse (see Fries, 1983; Halliday, 1994, Thomas and Hawes, 1994).

Gosden (1993) accepted the discourse-organizational function of Themes and attempted to make explicit the nature of this organization in RA's. According to Gosden, one dimension of this organization is the extent to which writers foreground their involvement in the text. He posited a continuum of writer visibility (recalling Martin, 1986, cited in Gosden, 1993) whereby Themes such as "We" foreground the writer's involvement most. Themes such as "This paper" likewise make the writer visible, but only to a lesser extent. Further down the continuum are Themes such as "The model", in which authorial presence is subtly displaced to the background. According to Gosden, the least writer visible Themes are references to the tangible or measurable such as "Annealing". As depicted in Figure 15.2, Gosden created four Theme domains along this continuum, viz., the Participant Domain (A), the Discourse Domain (B), the Hypothesized and Objectivized Domain (C) and the Real-World Domain (D). The above four examples belong to separate Theme categories distributed across these four domains respectively. For the ease of reference, the categories have been coded and numbered following both Gosden (1993) and McKenna (1997).

McKenna (1997) analyzed his mini-corpus of three AR's using a modified version of Gosden's model. The most important change in this theoretically and methodologically significant move was the inclusion of the Theme category C1 (see Figure 15.2). C1 Themes are "Analytical Concepts of Real-World Entities, Processes and Events" (McKenna, 1997:197). As the label suggests, McKenna believed that professionals convert the real-world (Themes in Domain "D") into the hypothesized and objectivized (Themes in Domain "C") and vice versa in the process of documenting engineering analysis. According to McKenna, the extra category was necessary to account for the lexicogrammatical realization of this two-way conversion between the concrete and the abstract. Implicit in McKenna's technique was his disagreement with the scope of Gosden's categories D3 (Real-world Event and Process) and D4 (Real-world Entity). Once again, consider the Theme in Extract 1 above. In Gosden's (1993) classification, it would have been a D4 Theme by virtue of its reference to a tangible entity. On the other hand, McKenna would have classified it as a C1 Theme because of the semi-technical nature of the term "coastal landform" and the reference to the landform as part of the ongoing analysis ("One last"). Moreover, the existence of the relatively more 'real-world' thematic option "Para Reef" (see Version I of Extract 1) suggests that the categories D3 and D4 alone may not be specific enough to reveal the discourse-organizational function of the concrete-abstract conversion. Instead, their abstract counterparts, categories C1 and C6

Figure 15.2
Categories of Unmarked Themes in McKenna's (1997)
Revised Version of Gosden's (1993) Model with Examples in Brackets

Participant Domain A	Discourse Domain B	Hypothesised and Objectivized Domain C	Real-world Domain D
A3 Interactive Participant (Smith, 1987)	B5 Interactive Discourse Entity (Previous studies)	C6 Hypothesized Entity (The model)	D4 Real-world Entity (AlFeNi alloy system)
	B4 Empty Discourse Theme (It / There)	C5 Empty Hypothesized and Objectivised theme (It / There)	
		D4 Real-world Entity (AlFeNi alloy system)	
	B3 Micro Discourse Entity (Figure 1b)	C4 Objectivised Intellectual Corpus (The data)	D5 Empty Real-world Theme (It / There)
		C3 Objectivised Viewpoint (One factor)	D3 Real-world Event or Process (Annealing)
A2 Participant Viewpoint (Our)	B2 Macro Discourse Entity (This paper)	C2 Hypothesized Viewpoint (The possibility)	D2 Non-mental Engineering Analytical Tool (Photographic record)
A1 Discourse Participant (We)	B1 Discourse Event or Process (The conclusion)	C1 Analytical Concepts of Real-world Entities, Processes and Events (The alarm sensors)	D1 Mental Pr=ocess (Deduction)

Greatest writer visibility ← - - - - - - - - - - - → Least Writer Visibility

More external community-oriented Theme ←

More internal writer-oriented Theme

(Hypothesized Entity) must be taken into account as well.

One other extract from a Student AR may help to demonstrate the necessity of McKenna's category C1. Consider the Theme in Extract 15.2 below along with Figure 15.2.

Extract 15.2
Sentence 45 from Report Number 655

Wollongong Harbour	is situated immediately west of Flagstaff Point.
Theme	Rheme

In contrast to the mention of the coastal landform in Extract 15.1, the reference here to a specific and tangible location by its proper name ("Wollongong Harbour") was not part of the technical analysis, but rather a piece of relevant background information. Unlike the case of Extract 15.1, the same classification, specifically D4, would have resulted in Extract 15.2 using either McKenna's technique or Gosden's.

The rather subtle differences in the discourse-organizational function of the Themes in Extracts 15.1 and 15.2 may be seen as a mere artefact of analysts' divergent perceptions. However, as Extract 15.3 below demonstrates, the ambiguity revealed by the textual-analytical technique discussed here is itself evidence of the concrete-abstract conversion.

Extract 15.3
Sentence 19 from McKenna's (1997:202) Civil Engineering AR

Loads on the structure from the conveyors	were estimated by our mechanical engineer based on typical values of similar conveyors.
Theme	Rheme

The word "loads" in Extract 15.3 has both the non-technical meaning of a mass and the technical meaning of force-exerting matter. McKenna regarded Extract 15.3 as a classic example of the seamless nature of the conversion from the concrete to the abstract.

The present study focussed on comparing the occurrences of Themes in the "C" and "D" domains to examine the nature and extent of the conversion between the concrete and the abstract in the NNS (Student), NS (Student) and Professional AR's. In particular, special attention was given to Themes in categories C1 and C6 and D4 and D4 as they represent the lexicogrammatical loci of the conversion (McKenna, 1997).

Results of the Textual-analytical-statistical Investigation

Figure 15.3 below shows the percentage distributions of unmarked Themes into domains across 4 NNS AR's, 4 NS AR's, 8 Student AR's, 3 Professional AR's (McKenna, 1997) and 36 Scientific RA's (Gosden, 1993).

Figure 15.3
Percentage Distributions of Unmarked Themes into Domains by Report Types

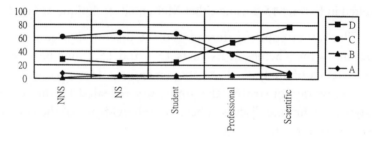

There were more "C" than "D" Themes in both NNS and NS AR's and the extent of the dominance is comparable between the two ($c^2=$ 2.865). This suggests that first language did not influence the overall balance between the concrete and the abstract in Student AR's. In this limited sense, NNS and NS AR's displayed a common discourse-organizational pattern.

While there were more "C" than "D" Themes in NS Student AR's, the pattern was reversed in Professional AR's. This "cross-over" pattern was not due to chance ($\chi^2=125.648$). This suggests that the "task" had an influence upon the overall balance between the concrete and the abstract. Precisely the same effect was found even in the confounded comparison between Student AR's and Professional AR's (χ^2=130.558), once again pointing to the lack of (mediating) influence by first language. One major difference between the Student and Professional AR's is the nature of the tasks which called for their writing in the first place. The students wrote as part of their own academic assessment while the professionals wrote as part of their employment. It appeared that Students discoursed in a more abstract fashion than their Professional counterparts. A cross-over pattern was also identified when focussing on C1 and C6, and D3 and D4 Themes (χ^2=140.672), confirming the involvement of these four Theme categories in the balancing between the concrete and the abstract. Once more, the inclusion of NNS AR's in the comparison did not lead to a different pattern (χ^2 = 142.612).

It should be noted that what distinguished Professional AR's from Scientific RA's was the significant presence and low incidence of "C" Themes respectively. Following a similar line of reasoning, Student AR's can also be distinguished from Scientific RA's.

Figures 15.4 and 15.5 show the distributions of Themes into domains across report functions of NNS AR's and NS AR's respectively. Unlike RA's, AR's are not organized structurally and sequentially into the sections "Introduction", "Method", "Results" and "Discussion". More salient perhaps are report functions, which McKenna labelled as "Introduction", "Method", "Analysis and Findings" and "Conclusions and Recommendations". The most important differences between report sections and report functions are that the latter do not imply a fixed sequential order and allow for repetition of occurrences. For instance, while it would be rare to find two introductions in a typical RA, two or more separate portions of an AR may serve the function of an introduction. McKenna's guidelines for the allocation of sentences to these functions, which were applied to NNS and NS AR's, can be found in Appendix 1 on page 417. For the ease of reference, the report functions are abbreviated to "INT", "MET", "ANA" and "CON" respectively.

Figure 15.4
Percentage Distributions of Unmarked Themes
into Domains across Report Functions in NNS AR's

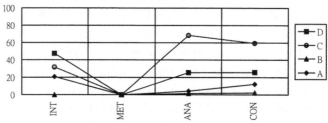

Figure 15.5
Percentage Distributions of Unmarked Themes
into Domains across Report Functions in NS AR's

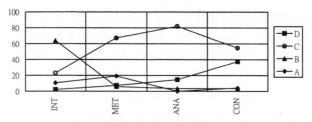

Whereas both NNS and NS AR's followed a rather abstract discourse organizational pattern overall (Figure 15.3), their differences emerge when rhetorical functions are considered. From Figures 15.4 and 15.5, it can be seen that NNS AR's did not feature the MET function, unlike their NS counterparts. In NS AR's, there was a greater decrease in the relative dominance of C1 and C6 Themes and a greater increase in the relative dominance of D3 and D4 Themes as one moves from the ANA to the CON function. This "fall-rise" pattern, which strongly suggests the conversion from the abstract back to the concrete, was less pronounced in NNS AR's.

In order to further investigate the differences between NNS and NS AR's, focus was placed on the contributions of Themes in categories C1 and C6, and D3 and D4 to the above discourse-rhetorical pattern. Based on their occurrences, it was found that the ANA and CON functions were equally abstract in NNS AR's ($\chi^2=0.002$), once again suggesting the lack of conversion of any kind. In contrast, the ANA function was more abstract than the CON function in NS AR's (χ^2= 35.813). As can be observed from the Figures 15.4 and 15.5, and as confirmed statistically, what set NS AR's apart from NNS AR's was more the increase in D3 and D4 Themes (χ^2=17.395) than the decrease in C1 and C6 Themes (χ^2=0.608) going from the ANA to the CON function. It would appear then that only the NS reconverted the abstract back to the concrete as they drew conclusions and made recommendations. The ANA function was organized differently by the NNS and NS (χ^2=8.351) lexicogrammatically while the CONfunction was not (χ^2=2.332). The latter two findings are paradoxical in the light of the ones presented immediately before.

Before discussing the effects of "task" on the conversion process, McKenna's analysis of Professional AR's is reproduced in Figure 15.6 below for comparison with Figure 15.5 in particular.

Figure 15.6
Percentage Distributions of Unmarked Themes
into Domains across Report Functions in Professional NS AR's

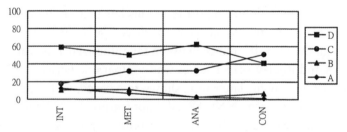

In contrast to NS Student AR's, the ANA function in their Professional counterparts was more concrete than the CON function ((2=11.143). Instead of a fall-rise pattern, a "rise-fall" pattern was evident from Figure 15.6. As a result of this finding, the foregoing construing of the abstract-concrete conversion as inter-rhetorical is cast into doubt.

It was further found that the differences between NS Student and Professional AR's stemmed more from the occurrences of D3 and D4 Themes (χ^2=41.249) than of C1 and C6 Themes (χ^2=6.109). Apparently, the differences were much more pronounced in the ANA function (χ^2=150.294) than in the CON function (χ^2=2.107). Despite the inexplicable reversal of the "rise-fall" pattern of NS AR's in their professional counterparts, the last finding presented suggests that the discourse organization of the CON function was largely shared by the two.

The results of the textual-analytical-statistical investigation strongly suggested that the concrete-abstract conversion is mediated through report functions in AR's. This is analogous to Gosden's evidence for a parallel mediating role of report sections in the case of scientific RA's. Apart from the involvement of report functions, the exact nature of the conversion across report functions remains unclear. The "rise-fall" pattern in Professional AR's is relatively inexplicable compared to the "fall-rise" pattern in NS Student AR's. Why would Professional AR's become more abstract and less concrete going from "Analysis and Findings" to "Conclusions and Recommendations" unless the conversion is not two-way as asserted by McKenna (1997)? And why were Student AR's more abstract than Professional AR's overall?

The examination of report functions has proven illuminating on the role played by first language in the discourse organization of AR's. Although the overall balance between Hypothesized and Objectivized Themes and Real-World Themes was comparable between NNS and NS Students, only the latter were shown to have converted the abstract back into the concrete. NNS AR's did not feature the "Method" report function and were equally abstract in both "Analysis and Findings" and "Conclusions and Recommendations".

Somewhat surprisingly, Themes in the categories the "Real-world Event or Process" and "Real-world Entity" appeared to be more important in the conversion in both NS and Professional AR's than their abstract counterparts. Also surprising was the apparently greater involvement of "Analysis and Findings" compared to "Conclusions and Recommendations" in the conversion.

The Psychometric-statistical Perspective

From the textual-analytical-statistical perspective, the Student AR is sufficiently distinguishable from the Professional AR that any associated writing pedagogy must take the differences into account. In order to investigate student beliefs regarding such differences, a brief questionnaire was issued to the engineering students whose AR's were analysed textually and statistically. The five items in the questionnaire of concern here are shown in Table 15.1 below (see Appendix 2 on page 418 for the questionnaire itself).

Table 15.1
The Five Items Relating to Student Beliefs of AR Writing

7.	Writing engineering reports as a student at university is different to writing engineering reportsas an engineer at work.	I agree.	I disagree.
8.	Engineers write their reports for non-engineers as well as other engineers.	I agree.	I disagree.
9.	Engineering students write reports for their markers as well as an imaginary audience (other engineers and / or non-engineers).	I agree.	I disagree.
10.	Engineers write sentences in such ways so as to attract the attention of a particular audience (e.g., the non-engineer project manager).	I agree.	I disagree.
11.	Engineering students write sentences in such ways so as to attract the attention of a particular audience (e.g., the marker).	I agree.	I disagree.

34 questionnaires were collected from a total of 36 students whose 8 AR's were analysed textually and statistically. NNS students were issued a Chinese version of the questionnaire. All questionnaires were completed following the completion and submission of the AR's.

Students tended to agree with Questions 7 ($\chi^2=12.971$), 8 ($\chi^2=13.781$) and 9 ($\chi^2=15.559$) while there was no pattern of agreement or disagreement with Questions 9 ($\chi^2=1.091$) and 10 ($\chi^2=1.091$). Responses to the questions were unrelated ($0.016<\chi^2<0.798$). The only exception was Questions 9 and 10 ($\chi^2=6.321$).

Except for Question 11, first language did not have any influence on the responses to individual questions or on the relationships between questions ($0.002 < \chi^2 < 2.047$). Specifically, more NNS students disagreed than otherwise while more NS student agreed than otherwise with Question 11 ($\chi^2 = 4.724$). Note that the relationship between first language and the responses to Question 11 was quite strong ($\chi^2 = -0.441$). Interestingly, first language and the responses to Question 10 was quite strongly related as well ($\varphi = -0.312$) even though the associated test statistic was not significant ($\chi^2 = 2.047$) at $\alpha = 0.05$.

One of the 4 NNS AR's was written by a group of Environmental Engineering students while the rest and all NS AR's were written by Civil Engineering students. Specialization in this sense was not found to have exerted any influence on the responses to any question or on the relationship between any two questions ($0.000 < \chi^2 < 0.960$). The same was found for gender ($0.015 < \chi^2 < 0.489$).

On the whole, all acknowledged that writing analytical reports as students is different to writing as professionals. Moreover, they acknowledged the fact that in either case, multiple audiences need to be addressed. However, there was an even split in deciding whether the audiences can be addressed by writing sentences in certain ways. Importantly, the opinion on Question 11, a statement concerning student writing practice, was divided along the lines of first language. Proportionally more NS Students than their NNS counterparts agreed with this question.

It is conceivable that student beliefs regarding analytical report writing reflect student writing practice. While the majority paid at least lip-service to the broad differences between professional and student writing, native-speaker students displayed greater awareness of the linguistic manifestations of these differences than non-native-speakers. Was it a mere coincidence that native-speakers also displayed clearer evidence of the concrete-abstract conversion in their writing than their non-native-speaker counterparts? Note that non-native-speakers did however display a very similar pattern of overall balance between concrete and abstract Themes in their writing. Were they not unconsciously trying to attract the attention of any audience, imaginary or real, by writing sentences in certain ways?

A Theoretical Account of the Engineering Analytical Report

The various methodological perspectives adopted in the present investigation have shed light upon the extent and to a lesser degree, the nature of the concrete-abstract conversion in engineering analytical reports. There was evidence of conversion in reports written by students as well as by professionals. There was also evidence of differences in the nature of this conversion between the three groups of reports. Among students, the differences were reflected in part by their awareness of the linguistic realizations of the conversion. All these differences point to the need for caution in specifying "purpose" in English for Specific Purposes (ESP) situations such as a written communication course for undergraduate engineering students. One of the dangers is to be simplistic in the specifying of "purpose", presuming that non-native-speaker students ought to imitate their native-speaker counterparts while they in turn ought to imitate their professional counterparts. The following condensed theoretical account of analytical reports, supplemented with references to the above findings, demonstrates why these purposes may well be invalid.

The fundamental assumption in the present account is taken from Halliday (1994), for whom text and context share a reciprocal causal relationship. Context is defined by three variables — field, or what is being described; tenor, or the relationship between all the people addressed and the writers, and mode, or the way a stretch of language is being developed and delivered (Butt, Fahey, Spinks and Yallop, 1995). Variations in field, tenor and mode are reflected in the linguistic resources used. In Hallidayan terms, the above textual-analytical investigation was a study of the modal configuration of analytical reports. Although neither field nor tenor was examined, their configuration is highly correlated with that of mode (Halliday, 1994). Thus, the modal configuration of a text broadly reflects the context in which it is used. Examining Figure 15.3 once again, it is clear that each group of reports had a different modal configuration. However, the differences in configuration between scientific research articles and professional engineering analytical reports were greater than those between the latter and their student counterparts. Among student analytical reports, those written by native-speakers and non-native-speakers were remarkably similar in modal configuration.

The modal configurations displayed in Figure 15.3 constitute evidence of the different communicative purposes of the report groups independent of the definition given to each. Figure 15.3 suggests that student analytical reports share the same generic identity (see Bhatia, 1993) with professional analytical reports. Analytical reports, as a whole, do not seem to have the same generic identity with scientific research articles. It does not necessarily follow that analytical reports are generically uniform. While all analytical reports examined in the present study fit the following definition and exhibit a degree of generic integrity (see Bhatia, 1993), they also display generic diversity:

> *"In analytical reports, engineers generally record their design of a construction or process; or present an opinion about a construction, process, or event that may be used in legal and quasi-legal situations (e.g., insurance claims)"* *(McKenna, 1997:192).*

The generic diversity and integrity of analytical reports are derived from the overlapping contexts in which they are produced and read. It is the examination of these contexts, especially where they overlap and where they do not (along with appropriate empirical studies of texts and writers) that is fundamental to the specifying of "purpose" in ESP. One of the most encompassing ways of conceptualizing "context" is provided by Tollefson (1991, cf. Fairclough, 1988). Tollefson makes a distinction between macro-sociolinguistic context and micro-sociolinguistic context. The macro pertains to the societal while the mirco pertains to the institutional. Cicourel (1992) further subdivides the latter into "broad" versus "narrow" to distinguish between the institutional from the situational respectively. Table 15.2 summarizes the elements of the macro and micro-sociolinguistic contexts with respect to the three groups of analytical reports.

Table 15.2
The Macro-sociolinguistic and Micro-sociolinguistic Contexts of the Engineering Analytical Reports Examined in the Present Study

	Professional Reports	Student Reports	
	By Native-speakers	By Native-speakers	By Non-native speakers
Macro-sociolinguistic Context	Engineering traces its roots to the Natural Sciences and established its own identity, function in society and prestige partly through its own mode of investigation and reporting.	Engineering education at the undergraduate level in Australia has been influenced somewhat by the desire to nurture students to become both scientists and practitioners with a greater emphasis on the former than on the latter.	Engineering education at the undergraduate level in the People's Republic of China has long been under the influence of the desire to produce technically-oriented personnel within the shortest possible time.
Micro-sociolinguistic Context (Institutional)	The readership was varied and included non-engineers as well as engineers.	The readership was varied and included a real audience (a postgraduate student-cum-marker) as well an imaginary one (the client).	The readership was varied and included a real audience (the present author-cum-marker) as well an imaginary one (the client).
	The reports were written in the authors' first language.	The reports were written in the authors' first language in small groups.	The reports were written in the authors' foreign language in small groups.
	The authors were very likely to have to write a similar report in English again.	The authors were very likely to have to write a similar report in English again.	The authors were unlikely to have to write a similar report in English again.
Micro-sociolinguistic Context (Situational)	Reports were collected from two engineering firms to which McKenna (1997) had provided consultancy services.	Reports were collected from the major written assessment of a compulsory semester-long subject carrying course credit in the third year of a 4-year bachelor degree programme.	Reports were collected from the major written assessment of a specially set up non-credit giving ESP course lasting three weeks in the fourth year of a 4-year bachelor degree programme.
	The reports covered the areas of Civil, Environmental and Communications	The reports covered the areas of Civil Engineering.	The reports covered the area of Civil and Environmental Engineering.
		Authors were required to evaluate designs associated with different domestic transportation options, report on their feasibility and make recommendations.	Authors were required to evaluate designs associated with different domestic transportation options and report on their feasibility and make
		Authors were explicitly instructed to document	

At the micro-sociolinguistic level, the need to address the concerns of multiple and clearly specifiable audiences, some of whom are technically oriented is the defining feature of the engineering analytical report. The implied readership (Scollon and Scollon, 1983) also includes those for whom the abstract, hypothesized and objectivized discourse may be irrelevant and / or inaccessible, and understandably so. The documentation of methodology is an important part of both professional (McKenna, 1997) and student writing, the relevant audience for which being potentially the technically-oriented readers. By omission, the non-native-speaker students were not explicitly instructed to document their methodology. The uniform absence of the "Method" report function was partly attributable to this. Despite the absence, the involvement of implied technical readers was responsible for the relatively high incidence and dominance of Hypothesized and Objectivized Themes in Professional and Student AR's respectively. In this sense, the three groups of reports can be said to share a common generic identity. It can also be said that there is some degree of generic integrity among the three groups of reports.

Simultaneously, there exists generic diversity among the three groups of reports. The diversity is also attributable to their implied readership and by extension their implied authorship. While the professionals in McKenna's study wrote in the implied role of practising engineers within their respective specializations, the students of the present study wrote in the capacity of students as well as engineers. As engineers, there was a need for them to address the non-technical as well as technical reader. As students, however, there was an additional and over-riding concern to write as scholars under academic assessment. The greater extent of the dominance of abstract Themes was attributable to this factor, which was brought to bear in turn by different influences at the macro-sociolinguistic level. The partial emphasis on training students to become professionals in the Australian context was probably related to the concrete-abstract conversion evident from the reports written by native-speakers. Conversely, the heavy emphasis on technicality in China was almost certainly related to the lack of attempts by non-native-speakers to convert the abstract back to the concrete. In other words, the training prior of the writing of the reports analysed in the present study has predisposed the native-speakers to write more like professionals and to have greater awareness of the linguistic resources available. On the other hand, the non-native-speakers were predisposed to be more technical in their writing.

Nevertheless, there remains the inexplicable reversal in the apparent direction of conversion going from "Analysis and Findings" to "Conclusions and Recommendations". Apparently, while professionals converted the concrete into the abstract in that there was a greater dominance of "C" Themes in the latter report function, native-speaker students converted the abstract back into the concrete. McKenna (1998) believed that this was partly attributable to the more hypothetical nature of the tasks that confronted the students. This would explain the greater dominance of "C" Themes overall, but not the pattern of their distributions across report functions.

The generic diversity within the over-arching generic integrity can be seen as the result of the mixing of discourse-organizational and rhetorical strategies or collectively, textualizations (Candlin, 1987). The weaving together of various textualizations in an extended stretch of discourse represents an attempt to accommodate multiple and conflicting communicative purposes brought about by the demands of the multiple implied readership. The extent to which various mixes of textualizations are produced will in turn reciprocate the influences of the macro-sociolinguistic and micro-sociolinguistic contexts (Fairclough, 1988). Hence, the reciprocal influences between text and context serve to maintain both the generic integrity and diversity among professional and student analytical reports. It is important to note that this diversity is not static but dynamic, being shaped and reshaped by factors in the relevant sociolinguistic contexts.

Evaluations and Conclusions

The comparable overall balance between abstract and concrete Themes in reports written by native-speaker students and their non-native-speaker counterparts is an interesting indication of the generic integrity of the analytical report. The limited generic integrity is made even more significant by the generic diversity demonstrated and accounted for above.

Generic integrity exists despite the considerably less time and experience the non-native speakers had in producing extended stretches of technical texts in English. They only had an average of eight months' experience in writing texts of more than 500 English words. The integrity is even more amazing in the light of the apparent and relative lack of awareness demonstrated by non-native speakers of the linguistic resources they actually drew upon and strategically deployed in their writing.

The generic diversity between professional and student reports, which can partially be accounted for with reference to relevant macro and micro-sociolinguistic contexts has a number of implications for the specifying of "purpose" in ESP. The purposes of any ESP course must take into account situational, institutional and even societal demands on the education and in particular, the written assessment of undergraduate students. This applies equally to the teaching of native as well as non-native-speakers. Thus, it may not be feasible to train students to write precisely like professionals in an academic setting. After all, students need to satisfy assessment criteria that do not apply to professionals.

Concurrently, to the extent that the training of students to become professionals is desirable or necessary in tertiary institutions, the purposes of any ESP course may include the examination and modelling of professionally written reports. As demonstrated from the textual-analytical, psychometric and theoretical perspectives, however, the premium placed on academic attainment conflicts with the emphasis on professionalization. Such a conflict is typical of language use (Fairclough, 1988) and the ability to respond by the strategic mixing of textualizations (or whatever manipulation) ought to have priority over the rote learning of any so-called "genre". This is especially important given the evidence presented above of the diversity within the genre, which makes it impossible to deal with it as a single entity.

Thirdly, given the multiplicity of purpose of analytical report writing, any associated ESP course must include the highlighting of linguistic resources available to conflicting demands of these purposes. This applies especially to the teaching of non-native speakers who need to write reports in English for identifiable reasons. While the Gosden-

McKenna model is not yet thoroughly tested by different researchers and not yet adapted for student use, students can be encouraged to conceive of the analytical report as a mix of text types (see Candlin, 1987; Fairclough, 1988), each with its unique but communicatively strategic modal configuration. Students need to be discouraged from conceiving of the mixing as the sequential arrangement of report sections. Exactly how a particular configuration can be strategic communicatively and how text types are mixed are the subjects of more detailed textual-analytical studies of report functions and ethnographic studies of the writing process, not to mention the situated analysis of reports written by non-native-speaker professionals.

Fourth, given the dynamic nature of generic diversity, ESP practitioners must pay attention over time to changes in the composition of textualizations even if the overall integrity of the genre is maintained. This implies periodic textual-analytical-statistical studies of reports produced by professional as well as students. It also implies the need to qualify prescriptive advice given to students on the structuring of sentences (see Winckel and Hart, 1992).

References

1. Bhatia, V. K. 1993. *Analyzing genre.* London: Longman.

2. Butt, D., R. Fahey, S. Spinks and C. Yallop. 1995. *Using functional grammar — An explorer's guide.* Rev. ed. Sydney: National Centre for English Language Teaching and Research.

3. Candlin, C. N. 1987. Explaining moments of conflict in discourse. In *Language topics*, edited by R. Steele and T. Treadgold. Amsterdam: John Benjamins, 413–429.

4. Cicourel, A. V. 1992. The interpenetration of communicative contexts: Examples from medical encounters. In *Rethinking context*, edited by A. Duranti and C. Goodwin. Cambridge: Cambridge University Press, 291–310.

5. Cox, J. 1995. Analyzing geotechnical engineering abstracts: Towards a pedagogical template. *ESP Malaysia* 3 (2): 136–144.

6. Crookes, G. 1986. Towards a validated analysis of scientific text-structure. *Applied Linguistics* 7v(1): 57–70.

7.   Fairclough, N. 1988. Register, power and socio-semantic change. In *Functions of style*, edited by D. Birch and M. O'Toole. London: Pinter, 111–125.

8.   Fries, P. H. 1983. On status of theme: Arguments from discourse. In *Micro and macro connectivity of texts (Papers in Textlinguistics 45)*, edited by J. Petöfi and E. Sözer. Hamburg: Helmut Buske, 116–152.

9.   Gosden, H. 1993. Discourse functions of subject in scientific research articles. *Applied Linguistics* 14 (1): 26–75.

10. Halliday, M. A. K. 1993. The analysis of scientific texts in English and Chinese. In *Writing science: Literacy and discursive power*, edited by M.A.K. Halliday and J. R. Martin. Pittsburgh, Pa: University of Pittsburgh Press, 124–132.

11. _____ . 1994. *An introduction to functional grammar.* 2nd ed. London: Edward Arnold.

12. Hawes, T. and S. Thomas. 1997. Problems of thematization in student writing. *RELC Journal* 28 (2): 35–55.

13. Holmes, R. 1997. Genre analysis, and the social sciences: An investigation of the structure of research article discussion sections in three disciplines. *English for specific purposes* 16 (4): 321–337.

14. Marshall, S. 1991. *A genre-based approach to the teaching of report-writing. English for Specific Purposes* 10 (1): 3–13.

15. Masputeriah Hamzah, Abdul Halim Abdul Roaf, Khairi Izwan Abdullah and A. F. Louis 1995. Designing learning materials for Civil Engineering students. *ESP Malaysia* 3 (2): 118–135.

16. McKenna, B. 1997. How engineers write: An empirical study of engineering report writing. *Applied Linguistics* 18 (2): 189–211.

17. _____ . 1998. *(Personal communication).*

18. Peng, J. 1987. Organizational features in chemical engineering research articles. *English Language Research Journal* 1:79–116.

19. Swales, J. 1986. English for specifiable purposes. *Occasional Papers 42.* Singapore: SEAMEO Regional Language Centre.

20. Taylor, G. and T.-G. Chen. 1991. Linguistic, cultural and subcultural issues in contrastive rhetoric discourse analysis: Anglo-American and Chinese scientific texts. *Applied Linguistics* 12 (3): 319–336.

21. Scollon, R. and S. B. K. Scollon. 1983. Face in interethnic communication. In *Language and communication*, edited by J. Richards and R. Schmidt. London: Longman: 156–188.

22. Tollefson, J. W. 1991. *Planning language, planning inequality.* Harlow: Longman Group UK Limited.

23. Thomas, S. and T. Hawes. 1994. Thematic options in reports of previous research. *Australian Review of Applied Linguistics* 17 (1): 45–72.

24. Winckel, A. and B. Hart. 1996. *Report writing style guide for engineering students.* 3rd ed. Three levels: Faculty of Engineering and Flexible Learning Centre, University of South Australia.

Appendix 1: Guidelines of Allocating Sentences to "Report Sections" in AR's (McKenna, 1997:194)

Introduction (INT)	Sentences which provide information about the circumstances of the report's commissioning, the client, the context and scope of the study.
Method (MET)	Sentences which explain the analytical method and computational devices.
Analysis and findings (ANA)	Sentences which provide objectivized empirical statements based on the engineer's data collection and applied inquiry. These statements usually reconstrue everyday phenomena into pre-existing scientific categories and taxonomies to allow analysis to take place.
Conclusions and recommendations (CON)	Conclusions are those sentences which present the implications and inferences drawn by engineers applying their professional applied-scientific judgement to the objectivized empirical statements. Recommendations are those sentences which deliver professional advice directing the clients' course of action.

Appendix 2: The Questionnaire (English)

"How do engineering students write ?" Questionnaire

This questionnaire is designed to get some information about yourself and your practices and beliefs about written communication. It is part of the research project "How do engineering students write ?" which you have agreed to participate. The information obtained will be kept confidential as explained in the information form.

1. What is your age ?

    _____

2. What is your sex ?
    Female ☐   Male ☐

3. Is English your first language ?
    Yes ☐   No ☐

    If English is not your first language, then for how many years have you been writing more than 500 words in English ?

    _____

4. What is the name of the degree course you are studying in university (e.g., Bachelor of Civil Engineering) ?

5. Have you ever contributed to an engineering report that was to be read by someone other than your university lecturer or tutor (e.g., a professional engineer) ?
    Yes ☐   No ☐

    If you have, specify the nature of your contribution and any feedback you got in the space below.

    _____

    _____

    _____

Below are a number of statements numbered 7 to 11 For each statement, circle either "agree" or "disagree", but not both. This is not a test. There is not really a 'right" or "wrong" answer for each statement.

7.	Writing engineering reports as a student at university is different to writing engineering reportsas an engineer at work.	I agree.	I disagree.
8.	Engineers write their reports for non-engineers as well as other engineers.	I agree.	I disagree.
9.	Engineering students write reports for their markers as well as an imaginary audience (other engineers and / or non-engineers).	I agree.	I disagree.
10.	Engineers write sentences in such ways so as to attract the attention of a particular audience (e.g., the non-engineer project manager).	I agree.	I disagree.
11.	Engineering students write sentences in such ways so as to attract the attention of a particular audience (e.g., the marker).	I agree.	I disagree.

12. If you have any comments about statements 7 to 11, write them in the space below.

_____

_____

_____

_____

13. If you have any other comments about this questionnaire or the research project, write them in the space below.

_____

_____

Thank you for completing the questionnaire and for participating in the research project.

16

The Linguistic Contribution to the Analysis of Professional Discourse

The purpose of this chapter is to analyze the specific role of the linguistic contribution to interdisciplinary research on the analysis of professional discourse. The opinions expressed will be drawn from relevant literature as well as from the direct experience of the writer in a research project in the field of economic discourse.[1]

The need for a linguistic analysis of a specialized text is strongly felt by specialists themselves, who often experience the need to apply appropriate linguistic analyses in order to interpret correctly passages presenting difficulties of interpretation. The reason which particularly stimulates them to seek the linguist's help is that the form of a text matters just as much as its contents. This thorough investigation of specialized discourse strengthens the specialist's interpretative skills and greatly improves his critical activity. The employment of such exegetic techniques is therefore greatly appreciated, and is subsequently felt to be a necessary part of the specialist's approach. As McCloskey states:

> *"The ignorance of rhetoric leaves economists unable to confront doubts, really confront them. Run another regression that no one else believes. Deduce another consequence that no one else is persuaded by. Adduce another institutional fact that no one else sees as relevant."*
> (McCloskey, 1988c:287)

---

1. The interdisciplinary project referred to is a research project on the analysis of the interrelations between the method and language of John Maynard Keynes, which was financed by the Italian Ministry of Scientific Research and University and which involved both economists (Prof. Francesco Silva of Turin University, Prof. Anna Carabelli of Pavia University, Prof. Riccardo Bellofiore of Bergamo University) and specialists of English language and literature (Prof. Alessandra Marzola, Prof. Maurizio Gotti and Prof. Rossana Bonadei, all of Bergamo University). The results of the project were published in Marzola and Silva (1994).

This conviction of the very important role that language plays in specialized texts has promoted two different approaches: either the setting up of interdisciplinary research in which the specialist and the linguist work together each using his own specific exegetic tools in order to reach a correct interpretation of a text (or of certain parts of it) or the adoption by the specialist himself of linguistic techniques and an attempt to apply — very frequently in a rather awkward way — his limited knowledge of the linguistic principles which he considers necessary for a more exhaustive understanding of a text. This is what has frequently occurred in recent years in a number of fields, such as the human sciences (cf. Nelson *et al.*, 1987), medicine (cf. Gusfield, 1976), biochemistry (cf. Gilbert and Mulkay, 1984), the sociology of science (cf. Mulkay *et al.*, 1983) and economics (cf. Klamer, 1984, 1987, 1988, Klamer *et al.*, 1988 and McCloskey, 1983, 1984, 1985, 1987, 1988a, 1988b, 1988c).

Such an approach, however, has proved neither very correct in the application of the linguistic models adopted nor very innovative as far as results are concerned. In fact, while claiming the superiority of linguistic models, specialists usually fail to provide a consistent, original example of discourse analysis. Moreover, very seldom is the model on which their approach is based clearly specified, and they usually fail to identify precisely the theoretical framework they are following. McCloskey, for example, when trying to specify the principles on which his criticism is based, refers vaguely to classical rhetoric and literary analysis as the models he has in mind:

> "*A good place to start might be the categories of classical rhetoric. A good place to continue would be the procedures of modern literary critics, bright people who make their living thinking about the rhetoric of texts.*"
> (McCloskey, 1985:69)

If we examine the examples of discourse analysis that specialists provide, we are led to believe that the categories applied are mainly drawn from classical rhetoric. In fact, the main rhetorical features identified in the texts are analogy, metaphor, simile, appeal to authority, symmetry, syllogism, definition and others of a similar nature.

As far as the literary paradigm followed is concerned, this is almost never explicit even though a structuralist or semiotic model could be implied.[2] Moreover, specialists usually fail to realize the great differences that exist between a literary text and a specialized one, and therefore apply specific interpretative models to texts of different natures. What particularly suggests an analogy between specialized and literary texts is the presence of metaphors and other rhetorical devices in both kinds of discourse.[3] In stressing this parallelism, however, they seem to ignore the fact that the use of metaphors and other rhetorical devices is very common not only in the specialized register, but also in everyday language, and cannot therefore be attributed exclusively to literary style. Moreover, in their analysis of metaphors specialists often fail to perceive the difference between the scientific and the literary metaphor. In fact, as has been demonstrated (cf. Hesse, 1966), the quality of striking the reader's imagination by means of unusual and unexpected analogies is a feature particularly typical of literature. In scientific argumentation, on the other hand, the creation of metaphors follows a more rational and intelligible criterion of conceptual reference, especially in the case of catachresis.

Another incorrect conclusion which seems to be drawn from many attempts of linguistic analysis carried out by specialists is that the success of a text is guaranteed merely by the fact that it contains a profusion of metaphors. Although it can be agreed that metaphors make discourse more striking and effective and therefore increase its persuasive power, it must also be admitted that if incorrectly chosen they can render a text more imprecise and at times even ambiguous. Moreover, by emphasizing the use of rhetorical devices without specifying their degree of persuasiveness, they risk giving an incorrect impression of their

---

2. For example, McCloskey refers to his literary model as follows: "The scientific paper is, of course, a literary genre with an actual author, an implied author, an implied reader, a history, and a form." (McCloskey, 1985:57). For a more detailed analysis of McCloskey's approach cf. Gotti (1993).

3. Cf., for example, McCloskey: "When an economist says, as he frequently does, 'the demand curve slopes down', he is using the English language; and if he is using it to persuade, as he very frequently is, he is a rhetor, whether he knows or likes it or not. A scientific paper, and an assertion within it such as this Law of Demand (that when the price of something goes up the demand for something goes down), does literary deeds." (McCloskey, 1985:57)

approach, suggesting a return to the traditional descriptive method of analysis of an author's style according to the teaching of rhetoric conceived as *l'art de bien dire*. This misinterpretation would reach the exact opposite effect that they had set out to reach, that is, it would emphasize the importance of figurative language and rhetorical devices as mere embellishments of specialized discourse.

The exaggerated function assigned to figurative language means they alter the nature itself of the specialized discourse they are examining, and identify it as a kind of literary form.[4] By reaching this conclusion, however, specialists do not seem to realize the great differences in the epistemological principles and expressive functions that actually exist between literature and the sciences.

Another common mistake made by specialists is the identification of language with the concept of method. The use of a new expressive system, therefore, is seen as a way to defeat an existing method (cf., for example, McCloskey, 1985). Thus they fail to realize that it is the rhetorical pattern of a text which should follow a certain methodological choice and not vice versa. Although approach to discourse analysis and choice of method are strictly related and the choice of the former has great relevance to the success of the latter, the two concepts should not be confused.

The Linguistic Contribution

The contribution that the linguist can give to the analysis of a specialized text consists first of all in the approach to the text, that is, considering the way the text is constructed to express certain meanings rather than approaching it merely to ascertain its contents. In Mulkay *et al.*'s words:

> *"The central feature distinguishing discourse analysis from previous approaches to the sociology of science is that, in the now familiar phrase, it treats participants' discourse as a topic instead of a resource."* (Mulkay *et al.*, 1983:196)

---

4.   McCloskey, for example, comes to the conclusion that economics is "a collection of literary forms" (McClockey, 1985:55) and that "a field of thought is special, after all, not because it has a certain Methodology — for these dissolve into tropes common to all persuasion — but because the conversation has a special subject, such as medieval economic arrangements or Latin poetry books." (McCloskey, 1984:115)

Thus, rather than just being interested in what is contained in the text, the linguist tries to explain the way the specialist has chosen to construct and express the contents of the text he is examining. The great difference lies in the threshold before which the discourse analyst stops: his concern is to explain the linguistic data before him, but once he has described and explained them he has no interest in going beyond them to maintain or prove a certain specialized theory.

The various features of the text are not analyzed according to the theoretical principles of the science to which such a text belongs, but rather according to the linguistic rules that govern the features of the specific register of which that text is an example. Apart from such rules concerning register, the linguist also takes into consideration the principles of discourse analysis, including those regarding the logical and pragmatic aspects of the discourse process such as Cicourel's (1973) "interpretative procedures", Gordon and Lakoff's (1971) "conversational postulates", Grice's (1975) "maxims" or Searle's (1975) "inferencing procedures".

His approach is mainly deductive as he starts from the assumption that in order to explain the true sense of each item, he presupposes that there should be specific linguistic rules to refer to. The results of his analysis do not only provide the specialist with the useful elements required for a better interpretation of the text and therefore for subsequent theoretical or applied activity, but they may also provide the linguist with deeper and newer insights as regards the features of the register and discourse that he is analyzing. On deciding to work on an interdisciplinary project these are the differing goals of the two members of the team: the specialist hopes to attain a better interpretation of the text thus enabling him to make better use of the text itself, while the linguist will see it as a chance to test the validity of the existing rules of register and discourse analysis and, possibly, integrate them with new perspectives or intuitions.

However, before starting his analytic activity, the linguist is faced by a choice. He has to decide first what features he should take into consideration. In fact, as the elements that make up a text are of various types and on different levels (morphological, syntactical, lexical, textual, pragmatic, etc.), a choice must be made as it may not be possible, feasible or convenient to take all of them into consideration. The identification of the elements to be examined will depend on the object of the analysis and on the interpretative problem that the specialist wants to solve. Once this problem has been identified, the items to be analysed are selected and relevant linguistic rules are considered. According to these rules, appropriate hypotheses are first made and then verified against the text. If existing rules allow appropriate explanations for the interpretation of the items analized, such explanations are supplied and the specialist's interpretative problem is solved. If, instead, any discrepancies are noticed, these are verified against other similar texts in order to check whether such differences are to be attributed to the author's idiosyncratic features or whether they represent additions or modifications to the general rules of register or discourse analysis.

The example of such methodology given here will be drawn from an interdisciplinary research on the language and method of John Maynard Keynes' *General Theory*[5] in which the author of this paper was involved. What particularly suggested an interdisciplinary approach was the difficulty economists encountered in understanding the true contents of that economic treatise. Such difficulties were mainly attributed to the obscurity and ambiguity of the text, which was said to have given rise to a number of misunderstandings and different interpretations.[6] In some cases the criticism by economists has been very harsh. See, for example, Yeager's words:

> *"Keynes, likewise, hardly deserves credit for what he supposedly may have meant but did not know how to say. If, more than 50 years later, scholars are still disputing the central message of the General Theory, that very fact should count against rather than in favour of Keynes's claims to scientific stature. Whatever the General*

5.   The words "General Theory" are here used to refer to Keynes' The General Theory of Employment, Interest, and Money (Macmillan, London, 1936). All quotations throughout this text have been taken from *The Collected Writings of John Maynard Keynes*. Vol. VII, Macmillan, London, 1973. The various volumes of The Collected Writings are here quoted with the initials CW.

> *Theory was, it was not great science. It was largely a dressing-up of old fallacies. Worse, for many years it crowded better science off the intellectual scene."* (Yeager, 1986:40)

These criticisms of Keynes' style are rather perplexing as in other comments Keynes has highly been praised for the elegance and clarity of the way in which he wrote.[7] When examining the accusation by economists that *The General Theory* is badly written, one should also take into consideration the hypothesis that part of the blame could also be attributed to the economists themselves as they may not have been able to decode Keynes' text correctly. Therefore, the two hypotheses to be investigated in this interdisciplinary research project were that either Keynes had not adhered to the shared rules of discourse formation and economic register or that his readers had not applied the principles of discourse interpretation correctly.

The second hypothesis was tested first by examining some of the interpretations given of Keynes' text in order to find out why the author had not reached the perlocutionary effect he had aimed to achieve. On examining these critical readings of Keynes' work, we immediately realized that such criticism has often been caused by the non-comprehension of the novelty of Keynes' methodological approach. Many economists, in fact, in spite of the clear specification given by the author of his new method, interpret his statements according to traditional views and are therefore bound to find his theory inconsistent. They generally criticize Keynes for not adopting a positivist approach,[8] although Keynes clearly states in his work that this is the method he is strongly attacking.

In this kind of interpretation of the text we can trace the attitude of several readers who approach the text incorrectly — that is, not to

---

6. The general opinion of the economists on Keynes' General Theory can be summed up in the following comment made by Samuelson: "It abounds in mares' nests or confusions" (Samuelson, 1964: 318).

7. Cf., for example, the following comment: "There are constant reminders throughout the [General Theory] that we are in the presence of a master of English style. The language is generally rich and incisive, enhanced occasionally by well-turned phrases and apt literary allusions. For Keynes' objective is to appeal not only to the intellect but also to the esthetic senses." (Patinkin, 1976: 24)

find out the actual position of the author, but to receive confirmation of their own opinions and expectations. In following their personal exegetical parameters, readers decode the various elements of the text and assign them to the categories they usually employ. For example, many economists have tried to assign Keynes' method either to static or dynamic categories without understanding that it belongs to neither, as it is a very personal method which makes use of both systems at different and very specific moments.[9] The non-comprehension of the novelty and originality of such an approach has led some economists to criticize it as "an uneasy compromise between the method of comparative statics and the concerns of process dynamics" (Chick, 1983:16).

The complexity of Keynes' method, which aims at the analysis of the interrelations and interdependencies of the various economic variables in an integrated way has important effects on the author's style, as the linearity of the linguistic instrument that he has at his disposal compels him to adapt his method of exposition so as to alternate moments of atomistic analysis of single variables to parts examining the complex result of their interrelations in a systemic way. The surface level of the text betrays this great expository effort made by the author and presents continuous references to previous parts of the text or to elements to be examined more carefully later on in the book.[10] On several occasions while dealing with a complex phenomenon, the author has to introduce new concepts or terms which might need several pages to define or deal with. He is therefore compelled to pause in his expository activity, and such pauses are often perceived as harmful digressions by the reader.

The latter, therefore, accuses the author of organizing his book badly, and on several occasions feels entitled to delete or readjust parts of the text. This attitude explains the various versions of *The General*

---

8. Cf., for example, the following critical comment: Mr Keynes neither starts from facts nor returns to them. [...] Mr Keynes starts, not from any fact, but from the definition of a concept. [...] He proceeds to a fresh series of concepts and of their definitions. [...] Mr Keynes does not return to facts for verification. There is no page throughout his work on which a generalisation is set against marshalled facts for testing. (Beveridge, 1937: 464)
9. For a detailed analysis of Keynes' method cf. Carabelli (1988).
10. For a detailed examination of this writing process cf. Gotti (1994).

Theory which exist and the consequent different interpretations attributed to this work.

Deficiencies by the Author

The second hypothesis to be tested mainly concerned the accusation of obscurity and ambiguity on the part of the text. One of the results of the analysis of *The General Theory* has been that on several occasions Keynes has failed to specify the assumptions on which his statements were based. By failing to make explicit the warrants of his claims (Toulmin, 1958), Keynes makes the reader's decoding activity much more difficult and at times impossible. The common accusation that Keynes is cryptic and obscure is mainly due to his habit of taking "short cuts" (Fouraker, 1958) to eliminate the analytical presentation of the assumptions of the various statements of his argument. In doing so, Keynes thought that the explicit mention to such presuppositions was useless and would make his theory more complicated and redundant. What induced him to neglect the treatment of such assumptions was his conviction that they were common knowledge shared by his readers.

As Keynes himself admits (CW VII: XXXI), the readers he was aiming at were mainly of his own environment, readers who were, of course, already aware of the evolution of his thought. Indeed, he did not take into consideration any "outside opinion", that is, those readers who needed a more detailed and explicit presentation of his ideas. Only with the latter reading public did Keynes not comply with Grice's (1975) maxim of quantity. Indeed, complying with the superior principle of relevance (Sperber and Wilson, 1986), he reduced his explanations to what he considered his model reader (Eco, 1979) might actually not know.

In spite of this choice of Keynes', the attitude of other readers was of co-operation, as they tried to provide their own reasons for Keynes' giving a certain solution to an intricate analytical problem. However, as the methodological and theoretical position of readers greatly differed, the interpretation of these oblique or implicit passages gave rise to very different opinions attributed to Keynes.

Yet the identification of Keynes' model readers only partially explains the obscurity of The General Theory. A more careful analysis of the macrotext shows that the excessive implicitness of Keynes' theoretical statements complies with his view of economic argument:

> *"It is, I think, of the essential nature of economic exposition that it gives, not a complete statement, which even if it were possible, would be prolix and complicated to the point of obscurity but a sample statement, so to speak, out of all the things which would be said, intended to suggest to the reader the whole bundle of associated ideas, so that, if he catches the bundle, he will not in the least be confused or impeded by the technical incompleteness of the mere words which the author has written down, taken by themselves."* (CW XIII: 470)

In thinking of economic argument as a series of "sample statements" whose function is "to suggest to the reader a whole bundle of associated ideas", Keynes attributes typically literary features to his argumentative text; rather than offering unambiguous conclusions, the author leaves it to his readers to follow the network of associated ideas that his words suggest, and takes no responsibility for any lack of success with their interpretative activity.

Another element which has caused ambiguity in Keynes' text (and which therefore has promoted its polyhedric interpretations) is the rather peculiar use made of specialized terminology. The reading of the text, in fact, shows that Keynes does not always use terms in a mono-referential way, but rather employs some of them to refer to various different concepts. One of these terms, for example, is *investment*, which in the course of the book is attributed to three different meanings. In spite of the fact that he is referring to different concepts, Keynes does not feel the need to use three separate terms or to qualify the lexeme *investment* with three different adjectives so as to avoid any danger of ambiguity.

In other cases Keynes uses two different terms to refer to the same concept. As the use of two words commonly implies two different meanings, the reader is led to believe that the concepts defined are not the same. Keynes is aware of his ambiguous use of terminology, yet he considers this an essential part of his methodological position:

> *"A definition can often be vague within fairly wide limits and capable of several interpretations differing slightly from one another, and still be perfectly serviceable and free from serious risks [...], provided that [...] it is used consistently within a given context. If an author tries to avoid all vagueness and to be perfectly precise, he will become [...] prolix and pedantic."* (CW XXIX: 36)

To a definition process of the prescriptive type (Naess, 1981) Keynes seems to prefer one of the descriptive type, which avoids the setting up of a strict relationship between *definiens* and *definiendum*. Although he feels that when writing an argumentative text of a specialized type defining a new term is often a necessity, this definition process is also perceived by Keynes as a constraint on his creativeness and is especially considered as greatly limiting the decoder's intuitive possibilities. In a letter sent to R. B. Bryce we can note a confirmation of this belief of Keynes':

> *"In my book I have deemed it necessary to go into (definitions) at disproportionate length, whilst feeling that this was in a sense a great pity and might divert the readers' minds from the real issues. It is, I think, a further illustration of the appalling state of scholasticism into which the minds of so many economists have got which allow them to take leave of their intuitions altogether. Yet in writing economics one is not writing either a mathematical proof or a legal document. One is trying to arouse and appeal to the reader's intuitions; and, if he has worked himself into a state when he has none, one is helpless."* (Quoted in Patinkin and Clark Leith, 1977: 128)

This position of Keynes' confirms the previous choices he has made in his argumentative strategies and increases the degree of literariness of his work. Confirming a position maintained a century before by Malthus (1827) and which was strongly questioned in his time,[11] Keynes endows his terms with the subjectivity of interpretation which is typical of a moral science. The extreme variability of the referents of the terms he uses, moreover, is much more appropriate — according to him — to his dynamic view of the economic system.

The fixing of the meaning of words to certain particular aspects of the reality referred to greatly limits their expressive possibilities and makes their interpretation incomplete and at times erroneous.[12] Such interpretation of the definition process reminds one to a large degree of the complexities and problems that Peirce was facing in the same period in America in trying to give a comprehensive view of the definition process. Here is, for example, one example of the problems concerning definitions as pointed out by Peirce:

> *"If you look into a textbook of chemistry for a definition of lithium you may be told that it is that element whose atomic weight is 7 very nearly. But if the author has a more logical mind he will tell you that if you search among minerals that are vitreous, translucent, grey or white, very hard, brittle, and insoluble, for one which imparts a crimson tinge to an unluminous flame, this mineral being triturated with lime or witherite rats-bane, and then fused, can be partly dissolved in muriatic acid; and if this solution be evaporated, and the residue be extracted with sulphuric acid, and duly purified, it can be converted by ordinary methods into a chloride, which being obtained in the solid state, fused, and electrolyzed with half a dozen powerful cells will yield a globule of a pinkish silvery*

---

11.   The emphasis that Keynes' contemporaries laid on the use of a more specialized lexis is pointed out by McClosky: "Since the 1930s economists of all schools have become enchanted by the new way of talking. Most journals of economics nowadays look like journals of applied mathematics or theoretical statistics." (McClosky, 1985:3)

12.   Writing about the use of specialized language Keynes states: "Too large a proportion of recent 'mathematical' economics are merely concoctions, as imprecise as the initial assumptions they rest on, which allow the author to lose sight of the complexities and interdependencies of the real world in a maze of pretentious and unhelpful symbols." (CW VII:298)

*metal that will float on gasolene; and the material of that
is a specimen of lithium.*

*The peculiarity of this definition — or rather this precept
that is more serviceable than a definition — is that it tells
you what the word lithium denotes by prescribing what
you are to do in order to gain a perceptual acquaintance
with the object of the world." (Peirce, 1931, 2:330)*

Keynes' need to exploit various meanings of the words that he
employs determines another important feature of his methodological
approach and expository style, that is, the adoption of ordinary
language. Only with the use of such language can the author provoke
the associations of ideas and interrelations between the various aspects
of the complex phenomena being dealt with and which are an essential
part of his systemic approach. As he himself states:

*"It is a great fault of symbolic pseudo-mathematical
methods of formalising a system of economic analysis
[...] that they expressly assume strict independence
between the factors involved and lose all their cogency
and authority if this hypothesis is disallowed; whereas in
ordinary discourse, where we are not blindly
manipulating but know all the time what we are doing
and what the words mean, we can keep 'at the back of
our heads' the necessary reserves and qualifications and
the adjustments which we shall have to make later on, in
a way in which we cannot keep complicated partial
differentials 'at the back' of several pages of algebra which
assume that they all vanish." (CW VII:297–8)*

Keynes, therefore, confirms his opinion that the use of a specialized
mono-referential terminology is principally valid for those exact
sciences which derive their definitions from the observation of natural
phenomena, scientific experimentation or empirical demonstration.
The use of such terminology is instead inappropriate — or even harmful —
in all sciences based on different methodological principles.

The conclusion of our analysis is therefore that the obscurity and ambiguity of *The General Theory* is not due to a fault in Keynes' stylistic power or confusion of his theoretical thought, but rather to the author's decision to leave great possibilities of personal interpretation to the reader. Keynes relies on the addressee's goodwill and intelligence to catch on to the network of associated ideas that his sample statements suggest.[13] He has meant his book to be a sort of "open-ended work" which draws up the main outline of a wholly new theory and leaves it up to the reader to decode it and complete it with his own intuition by interpreting all the implicit statements of the text and by making explicit the hidden assumptions of his argument.

Support to this interpretation comes from a comment that Keynes himself expressed in a letter written a year after the publication of his work:

> *"I am more attached to the comparatively simple fundamental ideas which underlie my theory than to the particular forms in which I have embodied them, and I have no desire that the latter should be crystallized at the present stage of the debate. If the simple basic ideas can become familiar and acceptable, time and experience and the collaboration of a number of minds will discover the best way of expressing them." (Keynes, 1937:211–212)*

In fact, by provoking a vast and long-lasting debate, the obscurity and ambiguity of the book have enabled the Keynesian theory to be better defined and completed by the exegetic efforts made by the various readers. *The General Theory* represents one of the rare examples of non-literary texts in which the author, in a clear and conscious way, assigns the addressee an important role, which does not consist in the mere decoding of the text and acceptance of its argumentative line, but rather in the much more challenging and relevant task of collaborating with him in the formulation of the final outline and in the definition of the exact meaning of his new economic theory.

---

13. As he himself states: "An economic writer requires from his reader much goodwill and intelligence and a large measure of co-operation." (CW XIII:470)

Linguistic Insights

As has been pointed out above, the linguist's main interest in taking part in an interdisciplinary research project consists in the application of specific linguistic models to the analysis of a specialized text not only to provide a more correct interpretation of such a text, but also to derive useful considerations on how such models work in reality and possibly to find new linguistic insights of a theoretical nature. This part of the paper, therefore, will be devoted to the presentation of some of the main linguistic insights which the research project on Keynes' language and method has stimulated.

An interesting linguistic insight which could be derived from the analysis of Keynes' *General Theory* concerns the use of modal verbs to express the argumentative function.[14] The persuasive goal of this function is not merely carried out by means of a clear presentation of well-formed opinions and objective evidence, but is often achieved by the author's skilful use of rhetorical devices, such as attitudinal adverbs, intensifying adverbs, parentheses, and — in particular — modality. Through modality the encoder "associates with the thesis an indication of its status and validity in his own judgement; he intrudes and takes up a position" (Halliday, 1970:336). When the author's position is not explicitly stated by performative verbs or anaphoric nouns, modality may be the sole means of assessing the illocutionary and pragmatic value of the statement.

As Coates (1983) has pointed out, the set of modal verbs is not only characterized by a continuum of meanings (cf. her "gradience model"), but also by the existence of ambiguity and merger, which may create problems in the univocal decoding of a statement. This possibility of ambiguity is clearly perceived by Keynes and often employed to make his text more persuasive. His subtlest and most effective strategy is that which gives the reader the impression of not being conditioned by him, while he is actually being led along the argumentative path which corresponds to his original compositional plan.

---

14. The argumentative function is to be interpreted here as a macrofunction consisting of various speech acts (such as explanation, generalization, assertion, inference, etc.) whose main purpose is to convince the decoder that the encoder's point of view is the correct one.

In order to compel the reader to obey his argumentative instructions and reach the same conclusions that he has come to, Keynes skilfully does not use the type of modality commonly employed to place somebody under an obligation, that is, deontic modality, as this would produce the opposite effect. His mastery, on the contrary, is shown by his adoption of a more neutral tone and the use of less subject-oriented modality such as dynamic or epistemic. In this way he gives the impression that his conclusions are not imposed on the reader, but rather that they are logically drawn from the evidence produced or the "argumentative strands" (Kopperschmidt, 1985) presented.

The two modals principally used to persuade the reader to take this "mental leap" (Brockriede, 1975) from statement to conclusion are *can* and *must*.[15] The following are some examples taken from The General Theory:

> *"Only at this point (...) can there be stable equilibrium.* (CW VII: 29)
>
> *This level cannot be greater than full employment.* (CW VII: 28)
>
> *Thus, if employment increases, then, in the short period, the reward per unit of labour in terms of wage-goods must, in general, decline and profits increase."* (CW VII: 17)

Can and *must*, rather than more subject-oriented modals such as *will*, enable the author to present his conclusions with the maximum degree of objectivity so as to gain maximum co-operation. As it is a general principle of argumentative discourse that the writer should make the strongest commitment for which he has epistemic backing (cf. Lyons, 1977), he usually employs the two forms which he perceives as being epistemically the strongest: *can't* and *must*. In using these modals, the author is not stating conclusions which might be perceived as presumable or probable, but which convey undertones of necessity or certainty.

---

15. For examples of the skilful use of modal verbs by Keynes cf. Gotti (1990).

The choice of *must* and *can't* to reproduce the persuasive effect involved in the argumentative function is not casual, as their strong epistemic value is only a gradient on their meaning continuum which also includes strong deontic modality. Although the values of *can't* and *must* in drawing conclusions is clearly not deontic, it is not at all strange to notice that in choosing the most effective modals to convince the reader of the validity of his opinions, Keynes should select such forms as may potentially imply obligation or prohibition. The gradience of the modals selected enables the writer to charge the original semantic value of his statement "It is necessarily the case that P/not P" with the illocutionary value "It is necessary for you to accept P/not P". On several occasions Keynes fulfils the perlocutionary effect of his statements by making use of those modals which enable him to charge his conclusive remarks with an ambiguous deontic tone masked by the strong epistemic value of inferential deduction, so that by accepting the validity of his argumentation the reader is forced to share the conclusions the author has reached.

Conclusion

These are only a few examples of the interesting linguistic insights that the text analyzed for an interdisciplinary research project has suggested. As has been seen, the analysis of specialized texts also has a lot to offer the linguist, provided he examines them with clear exegetic purposes and within a sound framework of linguistic theory. If carried out according to these principles, a linguist's participation in an interdisciplinary research project will not imply the ancillary position of merely helping the specialist's interpretation of a text and therefore with the sole result of serving as a mere tool for the interpretation of specialized discourse; the linguist's active involvement in such a type of research will, instead, represent another effective way of carrying out research in order to improve and better define the tenets of linguistic theory.

References

1. Beveridge, W. 1937. The place of the social sciences in human knowledge. *Politica* II 9 (September): 459–479.

2. Brockriede, W. 1975. Where is argument. *Journal of the Forensic Association* II (Spring): 179–182.

3. Carabelli, A. 1988. *On Keynes's method.* London: Macmillan.

4. Chick, V. 1983. *Macroeconomics after Keynes.* Oxford: Philip Allan.

5. Cicourel, A. 1973. *Cognitive sociology.* Harmondsworth: Penguin.

6. Coates, J. 1983. *The semantics of the modal auxiliaries.* London: Croom Helm.

7. Cole, P. and T. Morgan, eds. 1975. *Syntax and semantics.* Vol. 3. Speech Acts. New York: Academic Press.

8. Eco, U. 1979. *The role of the reader.* Bloomington: Indiana University Press.

9. Fouraker, L. E. 1958. The Cambridge didactic style. *The Journal of Political Economy* LXVI:65–73.

10. Gilbert, G. N. and M. Mulkay. 1984. *Opening Pandora's box. A sociological analysis of scientific discourse.* Cambridge: Cambridge University Press.

11. Gordon, D. and G. Lakoff. 1971. Conversational postulates. In *Papers from the seventh regional meeting*, edited by D. Adams *et al.* Chicago: Chicago Linguistic Society, 63–84. Also in Cole and Morgan (1975).

12. Gotti, M. 1990. Aspects of the use of modal verbs in the argumentative function. In *La rappresentazione verbale e iconica — Valori estetici e funzionali*, edited by C. de Stasio, M. Gotti and R. Bonadei. Milan: Guerini, 369–381.

13. _____ . 1993. Rhetoric and the language of economists: McCloskey's proposal. In *La fortuna della retorica*, edited by G. Castorina and V. Villa. Chieti: Metis, 249–258.

14. _____ . 1994. The general theory as an open-ended work. In *Language and method*, edited by A. Marzola and F. Silva. Aldershot (UK): Elgar, 154–191.

15. Grice, H. P. 1975. Logic and conversation. In *Syntax and semantics*, edited by P. Cole and T. Morgan. New York: Academic Press, 41–58.

16. Gusfield, J. 1976. The literary rhetoric of science. *American Sociological Review* XLI (February): 16–34.

17. Halliday, M. A. K. 1970. Functional diversity in language, as seen from modality and mood in English. *Foundations of Language* 6 (3): 327–351.

18. Hesse, M. 1966. *Models and analogies in science.* Notre Dame: Notre Dame University Press.

19. Keynes, J. M. 1937. The general theory of employment. *The Quarterly Journal of Economics* (February).

20. Klamer, A. 1984. *Conversations with economists*. Totowa, NJ: Rowman and Allanheld.

21. _____ . 1987. A rhetorical interpretation of a panel discussion on Keynes. In *Research in the history of economic thought and methodology*, edited by W. Samuels. JAI Press.

22. _____ . 1988. Economics as discourse. In *The Popperian legacy*, edited by N. De Marchi. Cambridge: Cambridge University Press, 259–278.

23. _____ , D. McCloskey and R. M. Slow, eds. 1988. *The consequences of economic rhetoric*. Cambridge: Cambridge University Press.

24. Kopperschmidt, J. 1985. An analysis of argumentation. In *Handbook of discourse analysis. Vol. 3, Dimensions of discourse*, edited by T. A. van Dijk. London: Academic Press.

25. Lyons, J. 1977. *Semantics*. Cambridge: Cambridge University Press.

26. McCloskey, D. 1983. The rhetoric of economics. *Journal of Economic Literature* XXI (June): 481–517.

27. _____ . 1984. The literary character of economics. *Daedalus* CXIII (3) (Summer): 97–119.

28. _____ . 1985. *The Rhetoric of economics*. Madison: University of Wisconsin Press.

29. _____ . 1987. Rhetoric. In *The new Palgrave*. Vol. 4, edited by J. Eatwell, M. Milgate and P. Newman. London: Macmillan, 173–174.

30. _____ . 1988a. Towards a rhetoric of economics. In *The boundaries of economics*, edited by G. C. Winston and R. F. Teichgraeber III. Cambridge: Cambridge University Press, 13–29.

31. _____ . 1988b. Thick and thin methodologies in the history of economic thought. In *The Popperian legacy in economics*, edited by N. De Marchi, Cambridge: Cambridge University Press, 245–257.

32. _____ . 1988c. The consequences of thetoric. In The consequences of economic rhetoric, edited by Klamer *et al.*, Cambridge: Cambridge University Press, 280–293.

33. Malthus, T. R. 1827. *Definitions in political economy*. London.

34. Marzola, A. and F. Silva, eds. 1994. *Language and method*. Aldershot (UK): Elgar.

35. Mulkay, M., J. Potter and S. Yearley. 1983. Why an analysis of scientific discourse is needed. In *Science observed*, edited by K. D. Knorr-Cetina and M. Mulkay. London: SAGE, 171–203.

36. Naess, A. 1981. *Communication and argument*. Oslo: Universitets-forlaget.

37. Nelson, J., A. Megill and D. McCloskey, eds. 1987. *The rhetoric of the human sciences*. Madison: University of Wisconsin Press.

38. Patinkin, D. 1976. *Keynes' monetary thought*. Durham, North Carolina: Duke University Press.

39. _____ . and J. Clark Leith, eds. 1977. *Keynes, Cambridge and the general theory*. London: Macmillan.

40. Peirce, C. S. 1931. *Collected papers*. Cambridge, Mass: Harvard University Press.

41. Samuelson, P. 1964. The general theory. In *Keynes' general theory: Reports of three decades*, edited by R. Lekachman. New York: St Martin's Press, 315–331.

42. Searle, J. R. 1975. Indirect speech acts. In *Syntax and Semantics*, edited by P. Cole and T. Morgan. New York: Academic Press.

43. Sperber, D. and D. Wilson. 1986. *Relevance*. Oxford: Basil Blackwell.

44. Toulmin, S. 1958. *The uses of argument*. Cambridge: Cambridge University Press.

45. Yeager, L. B. 1986. The Keynesian heritage in economics. In *Keynes's general theory: Fifty years on*, edited by J. Burton *et al*. London: The Institute of Economic Affairs, 25–44.

17

Shifting Rhetorical Focus in Student and Professional Geography Writing

Ann Hewings

Introduction

This chapter is premised on the now widely accepted view that we need to consider writing as a socially-situated activity, grounded in the context in which it is written and read (Faigley, 1986; Swales, 1990; Bazerman and Paradis, 1991; Kress, 1994; Berkenkotter and Huckin, 1995; Hasan, 1999). In academic writing this means, at a generic level for example, that academic norms and conventions influence written compositions (Berkenkotter, *et al.* 1991; Hunston, 1994; Prior, 1995, 1998; Bhatia, 1999). At a more delicate level, disciplinary differences influence the creation of texts and their reception. Adherence to disciplinary expectations has been shown to influence the ability to get work published and for researchers to be accepted as fully-fledged members of the discipline (Hyland, 1998, 2000; Myers, 1990). For students in higher education, writing constitutes their main means of receiving assessment and feedback, so success or failure is likely to be influenced by their understanding of the writing expectations in their chosen disciplines (Ballard and Clanchy, 1988; Mitchell, 1995; Ivanič, 1998). In a similar way, professional academics aiming to publish their research are influenced by the preferences of the journal to which they submit papers.

Other perspectives also address the relationships between social context and academic writing. These include, for example, work on writer identity (Ivanič, 1998; Lillis forthcoming), the influence of individual readers upon students' written output (Prior, 1995, 1998; Hewings, 1999), and hybridity and multiliteracies (Cope and Kalantzis, 2000). Like work on disciplinary differences, such research seeks to explicate writing issues in such a way that access to prestigious and powerful genres may be widened, and ultimately that the socially constructed nature of such writing may be more apparent and thus open to innovation and modification. As a contribution to this general aim, this chapter explores how the disciplinary norms of a single discipline influence the writing of academics, both professionals and students, working within it.

Its intended pedagogical outcome is a step towards overcoming what Gee (2000:68) refers to as our "unwillingness or inability to give ... the forms of instruction" necessary to increase educational access and success and to encourage critical awareness.

I take as my starting points that writing in the sciences and the humanities exhibit differences from each other, as do individual disciplines within these areas, and that these differences constitute ways of understanding and viewing different epistemological standpoints (Henderson and Hewings, 1987; Myers, 1990; MacDonald, 1994; Samraj, 1995; Hyland, 1998). This chapter looks at a method of focusing on aspects of text that reveal dimensions of the knowledge debate and its realization in a specific discipline and which could facilitate student understanding and participation. The specialist area chosen for investigation is Geography for the reason that it does not fit neatly as either a science or a humanities subject. I concentrate mainly on the writing of students rather than published academics. It is the link between epistemology in the discipline and their success or failure as judged by their academic mentors on the basis of their written essays which formed the core of this research.

The investigation of writing in geography is based primarily on a framework devised by Susan Peck MacDonald to examine writing in the social sciences and humanities. Her work was deliberately restricted to published academic research as she was testing a hypothesis concerned with "knowledge-making". She worked from the premise that academic prose had evolved

> *"...as a vehicle for constructing knowledge claims: for wielding ideas, constructing categories and concepts,*

> *weighing competing abstractions, assessing the relations between claim and evidence, developing careful distinctions and taking us out of the ephemerality of individual instances."* (1994:9)

Using evidence from studies such as those by Toulmin (1972), Bazerman (1988), and Becher (1989) she identifies criteria that are likely to differ along a continuum roughly coincidental with the move from the hard sciences to the softer humanities.

Figure 17.1
The Academic Knowledge Continuum

Science   Social Science   Arts/Humanities
◄──►
Epistemic   Phenomenal

One of the features that she looks at is language that is self-consciously directed towards the knowledge-making purposes of the disciplinary community (1994:12). Such language she labels "epistemic" and it is more generally associated with the hard end of the continuum; that is, with the sciences, which are perceived as more rigorous in their methods. This epistemic concern reflects the more focused attention of the scientific community on a group of specific problems and their working methods of building upon the research done by others. Geography as a discipline within UK educational institutions is unusual in that it straddles both the harder, more scientific side and the so-called "softer" social sciences / humanities end of the continuum. Geography students therefore read and have to write in what may be seen as competing sub-disciplinary ways. The work I report here is one part of an attempt to investigate the competing sub-disciplinary pressures and their outcomes on undergraduate students writing geography essays and also to look at the growth in disciplinary writing awareness over the course of an undergraduate degree programme. This type of analysis may prove more widely applicable in investigating students' writing throughout the course of different study programmes and in other discipline areas such as history (MacDonald, 1994; Coffin, 1997; McCabe, 1999) and economics (Hewings 1990; Henderson and Hewings, 1990) where internal disciplinary tensions may influence writing expectations.

Geography Background

The geographer's concern is with accounting for spatially distributed phenomena through the application of methodologies akin to those used in both the sciences and the social sciences/humanities. This has resulted in a discipline whose closest ties on the science side are with subjects such as geology and biology and on the humanities side with economics, sociology, history and planning. These two sub-disciplinary areas are usually referred to in the UK as physical geography and human geography respectively.

Geographers are often divided over whether or not the two wings of the discipline have an overarching similarity of purpose that unites them. The influential view below represents the integrative perspective:

> "Geography is an holistic and integrative university discipline that bridges the natural and social sciences. It is rare for a subject to make integration a priority and to do so successfully. Geography is strongly focused upon the relationships between people and the physical environment." (Conference of Heads of Geography Departments in Higher Education in the UK and the Royal Geographical Society-Institute of British Geographers, 1997)

However, historically, geography has shown a tendency to split into two broad camps and also more recently into smaller-sub-disciplines — ecology, hydrology, geomorphology, etc. This has been humorously referred to as "intellectual exfoliation" (Walford and Haggett, 1995:11). This fracturing tendency was manifest in the tension between applications of the so-called scientific method versus other forms of intellectual inquiry which dominated methodological debate in geography into the 1970s. The concern with generalizations and objectivity in science was seen as conflicting with geography's attention to the "hows" and "whys" of individual places. It has been pointed out, however (Harvey, 1969), that it was the primary influence of physics on the scientific method that led to this narrow view; other sciences are clearly also dealing with inherently unique data. The contest between uniqueness, objectivity and generalizations was resolved largely by what might be seen as a paradigm shift resulting in the so-called quantitative revolution. Based on computational and statistical analysis of data of both physical and human phenomena, this has led to methodological tools such as computerized geographical information systems which unite and underpin much of geographical inquiry today. From the point of view of the linguist, it is interesting that over 30 years ago the eminent geographer David Harvey attributed the cohesion of the discipline to a shared language.

> *"Any scientific community develops a language which is used to communicate ideas within that community. The meaning of their investigations — be it of natural or social phenomena — is partly defined by that language. Verification procedures are also developed in the context of that language and are not independent of its form. It makes sense, therefore, to speak of objectivity only within the context of some accepted language or paradigm. It follows, finally, that objectivity is a relative standard rather than an absolute measure and that this situation is ultimately true of both natural and social science."* (Harvey, 1969:58).

The quantitative revolution may be seen as a triumph for the more scientific approach but this is still being challenged, particularly by human geographers who take a different philosophical or ideological approach to the analysis of spatially distributed phenomena. Among other alternative perspectives are humanistic geography — that is, contrasting the explanation of the scientific method with the empathetic understanding of the humanistic perspective — Marxist geography, geography and feminism, and structuration (Bird, 1989). However, many of the implicit conversations between geographers with different ideological standpoints are not apparent until post-graduate level study. For the undergraduates who form the focus of this research, the underlying ferment may go unnoticed, with only the content differences being explicit. This in itself has implications for their understanding of debates within the literature, and contrasts, if they are found to exist, in the writing requirements of physical and human geography. In terms of the research reported here, this gives rise to a number of questions which are investigated below. Are student writers simultaneously learning to write both within the scientific-method paradigm and within a more humanities-social sciences framework? How different are the essays that they produce for physical and human geography and do these differences increase or decrease over the years of undergraduate study? Lastly, what does an analysis of published geography writing indicate about the epistemology of the two wings of the discipline?

The Analytical Framework

The analytical method of most significance to the work reported below is an adaptation of MacDonald's (1992, 1994) categorization of *grammatical subjects* (hereafter GS). This uses a surface, clause-level feature to shed light on the wider rhetorical underpinnings of disciplinary writing. The GS in English has a number of attributes that make it particularly useful for this purpose. The relative inflexibility of English word order means that the GS occurs at or near the beginning of most clause complexes. Traditionally the GS has been described as the agent in a sentence and it is commonly conflated with the functional roles of topic and theme. Within functional grammar, Halliday and others (Davies, 1988; Berry, 1989, 1995; Gosden, 1993; Halliday, 1994; Hasan and Fries, 1995; Ravelli, 1995) suggest that the significance of the GS is that it constitutes what is being argued about in a clause; it is the centre of the interaction and is modally responsible. Together with the finite it constitutes the Mood system — the components which carry the argument forward in a text. Thus, if the GS is the nub of what is being argued about then what a writer chooses to use as GS has consequences for the whole text. Similarly, *theme*, which, depending on definition, often or always includes the GS, may be glossed as the starting point of the message.

If the gloss of "resting point of the argument" is accepted for the GS, then it is justifiable to investigate the rhetorical significance of GS choices. The GS conveys the writer's choice of what a particular clause is saying something about. The writer can choose to say something about an infinite number of entities, both concrete and abstract. Put simply, texts which show, for example, a concern with how knowledge is built up within a discipline are likely to foreground GSs dealing with theories, opinions, experiments and work by members of the disciplinary community. On the other hand, texts in disciplines where specific people or things are studied as discrete phenomena with less emphasis on making generalizations may foreground less abstract, more concrete GSs. Gosden's work (1993) on the discourse functions of the subject is significant in classifying GS roles and tracing their uses within scientific research articles. He mapped categories of GS onto research article sections thereby demonstrating a move from more abstract to more concrete and back to more abstract GSs as the research article progresses.

The analysis of GS choices reported here is based on two broad categories containing seven classes. The broad categories are of most significance in this discussion and classes will only be discussed where particularly relevant. (See Hewings, 1999 for a full description of the analytical framework and Samraj (1995) and Masuku (1996) for alternative adaptations.) The two categories, following MacDonald, are *phenomenal* and *epistemic*. Phenomenal GSs are those concerned with the material which constitutes the research field of the discipline; in geography, that is population densities, rural-urban migration, climate change, glacial erosion, and so on. Epistemic GSs are those concerned with the methods, conceptual tools and previous research of the discipline. In terms of the human and physical geography dichotomy that I outlined earlier, we might crudely expect geographers on the human wing who reject the more quantitative objective approach of the scientific method to use a greater proportion of phenomenal GSs. We might also hypothesize that the approach of novice undergraduates is more likely to foreground phenomenal GSs in contrast to final year students and published academic writers who may be selecting more abstract epistemic GSs.

A simplified version of the classification system applied is set out below.

Figure 17.2
Grammatical Subject (GS) Categorization

	Class name	Examples
Phenomenal Category		
Class 1	Particulars	Vesuvius, the Greater Manchester Council, Typhoon Tracey
Class 2	Non-specifics	cities, people, soil, snow
Class 3	Generalized attributes	eruption of basaltic lava, the decline of manufacturing, soil erosion
Epistemic Category		
Class 4	Research constituents, theories and comment	statistics, evidence, data set, a worrying trend, the second theory, the crux of the issue
Class 5	Research studies	Roose (1975), we, they, geographers
Class 6	Audience	one
Class 7	Discoursal	Figure 2, this essay

(adapted from MacDonald 1992)

The phenomenal category is concerned with specific references to people, places or things, to more generalized, non-specific entities and to attributes, properties, actions and motivations of the specific or non-specific entities. The epistemic category contains those GSs which refer to abstractions and words used in doing and discussing the research process, references to research and researchers, inclusive audience references and discourse signposts.

The GS of each clause complex in 68 undergraduate essays was analysed — a corpus size of approximately 116,000 words. The corpus was divided into subcorpora for various analyses; e.g., human versus physical geography and first versus final (third) year student essays. No attempt has yet been made to relate type of category or class of GS to particular rhetorical sections of essays due to their length, on average just under 2000 words, and the lack of easily defined sections. A corpus of four published academic articles, two each from human and physical geography areas, was used for comparison. The published article corpus totalled just over 26,000 words.

There are obviously problems in making comparisons such as this. Although the field — academic writing in geography — is the same, there is a genre difference and the tenor relations will also be different with the unequal power relations between student writer and the more powerful assessing role of the lecturer being the most obvious. However, the status differentials are also marked for some academics trying to get papers published, and journal reviewers can represent powerful figures who assess work in a way comparable with the markers of student papers (Myers, 1990). Essays, as a pedagogic genre, do fulfil a different function from most academic articles; though in both, knowledge display of various kinds is called for. The geography students referred to here were all encouraged and often rewarded for using relevant and up-to-date journal literature. They were told to adopt the style of writing of the main geography journals — though in what ways was not made clear. This adds support to the concerns of many in the field of academic literacy that the criteria against which students' work is judged amounts almost to a hidden curriculum, a barrier which may prove a greater impediment to some than others (Mitchell, 1995; Lea and Street, 1998; Martin, 2000). Questionnaire data and an examination of reference lists showed third year students used and found most useful journal articles and collected papers on a topic. First year students still relied more on the textbook and were consequently less familiar with the journal article genre.

Findings

Figure 17.3 shows the percentages for each class and category for first and third year students. There is a noticeable difference in use of phenomenal and epistemic GSs.

Figure 17.3
The Percentage of Grammatical Subjects in Classes
and Categories for Student Essays

Year group	Class 1	Class 2	Class 3	Phenom. total	Class 4	Class 5	Class 6	Class 7	Epistemic total	Unclassified
First	11.34	27.54	36.63	75.51	15.61	5.63	0.63	1.90	23.77	0.72
Third	3.75	15.39	36.58	55.72	26.88	13.02	0.64	3.18	43.72	0.67

Phenomenal GSs in first year essays were over 75% of the total compared with 55% in third year essays. Most of this difference is accounted for by references to people, places and things either specifically or generally (i.e., classes 1 and 2, not 3). Example 1 shows GS from classes 1-3. (The coding in brackets at the end of examples refers to its designation in the sub-corpora from which they are taken.)

1. As previously mentioned, the arid lands of the Sahara and Kalahari Deserts [1] have no tsetse flies present. Similarly, the semi-arid regions [2] have a very few tsetse flies, with them only living in and nearby to the more dry subhumid pockets within the semi-arid zones (appendix 2). Clearly, the aridity of the land [3] influences where the tsetse flies live, and therefore where the trypanosomiasis which is harmful to humans is found. (First year; human 3)

In example 2 we see a shift to embedding discussion within the epistemic realm where different studies and approaches to a topic are being compared and evaluated.

2. The "Labour Process Approach" [4] investigated by Braverman (1974) re-emphasizes the classical Marxist concepts of a 'reserve army of labour'. Braverman [5] argued that the economic booms and slumps endemic to capitalism create a pool of workers who are periodically employed and made

redundant (Pinch and Story, 1992). (Third year; human 14)

This shift in attention to discussing the creation and validation of knowledge in the discipline is the most substantial difference between first and third year student essays. This is not to say that third year writers are no longer concerned with the phenomenal realm. In example 3 a specific location (Burrator catchment on Dartmoor) is referred to in the opening circumstantial adjunct, with the GS referring to researchers in the discipline.

3.   In a study of the granite-based Burrator catchment of Dartmoor, <u>Murgatroyd and Ternan (1983)</u> [5] cited the main factor increasing bank erosion as a lower net bank stability in comparison to more deeply rooted grass. (Third year; physical 18)

However, despite the specific reference, the adjunct is not focusing on the location but on the fact of the study. So, both the adjunct, a marked theme in Hallidayan terms, as well as the GS are being used to fulfil an epistemic function. The point of significance here is that both year groups are writing about real world phenomena but the occurrence of these phenomena in GS position varies significantly. First year students are more likely to foreground phenomena; their sentences are more likely to be about people, places and things rather than evidence and ideas as is the case in third year essays.

Not only is there a shift towards the epistemic in third year essays, but if all the essays are looked at in terms of the marks they received, we find that those which were awarded higher marks in both first and third year were generally those with a higher proportion of epistemic GSs. This accords with the findings of Samraj (1995) who looked at master's level writing in environmental science. She found that less successful papers have more phenomenal GSs and she attributes this to a greater concern with content rather than rhetorical construction and links explictness of content and opaqueness of rhetorical construction with novice writers. This would support the argument that what we are observing is the learning of the disciplinary writing norms of the academic discipline of geography.

At the outset I discussed the possibility that students had to learn to write in different ways for human and physical geography. This was only partially supported by the findings in this study. GS analysis which contrasts writing in human and physical geography is shown for the categories phenomenal and epistemic in Figure 17.4.

Figure 17.4
Percentage of Grammatical Subjects in Each Category by Year Group and Sub-disciplinary Speciality

	Phenomenal GSs	Epistemic GSs
First year human	75.60	23.68
First year physical	75.42	23.86
Third year human	59.30	39.76
Third year physical	52.08	47.64

The general trend towards more epistemic subjects in third year essays is evident for both physical and human geography. The first year figures are remarkably similar. In the third year a greater trend towards using epistemic GSs can be seen in physical geography essays. Closer examination of the GSs shows that the biggest increase occurs in the number of references to the literature and in a sub-classification of class 4 entitled "constituents of research". "Class 4, Research constituents, theories and comment", was sub-divided into "4a, Constituents of research" which consists of GSs concerned with what researchers do when collecting and analyzing information and their findings and "4b, Research theories and comment" which relates to mental process, particularly those used in generating ideas and theories and comparing and evaluating them. 4a is more frequent in all the essays, but the difference is more marked in physical geography essays.

In first year physical geography essays, class 4a GSs were particularly concerned with categorizing and defining, for example, "these six categories", "the term afforestation", "this type of hazard", "composite volcanoes". This is similar to the findings on geography textbooks by Peter Wignell *et al*. They noted that the

"*...discipline of geography is concerned with making*

order and meaning of the experiential world, through observing, classifying, and explaining phenomena... Geography observes the world by setting up a technical lexis; ...[and] orders the world by arranging these terms into taxonomies." (1989/1993: 165)

First year physical geography essays showed a strong classificatory tendency. Third year physical geography essays, in contrast, are more concerned with the testing of models or hypotheses through recounts of the experiments and research of others as shown in examples 4 and 5.

4. <u>Variables (internal or external) which affect the final outcome</u> [4a] could include hydraulic, glacial, periglacial factors in the short term and in the long term, climatic processes. (Third year; physical 1)

5. Using either the Penman-Monteith equation or the somewhat favoured climatic method for calculating potential evaporation, estimates [4a] have been made over differing hydrological characteristics of land according to vegetation type. (Third year; physical 18)

Both first and third year human geography essays were marginally more focused on "Class 4b Research theories and comment". GSs in this group include — "An explanation for such an occurrence...", "The reason for this...", "... a second interpretation", "This argument...", "The theoretical assumptions underlying these reforms...", and extraposed it and existential there constructions such as "It has been suggested that..." and "There are two main theories on...". Both these forms are given GS status and coded in this research and their frequency was noted as a device used to create the pseudo-objectivity associated with academic and particularly science writing. The it-clauses in particular often include markers of modality and can be analysed from the point of view of modality and interpersonal function (Halliday, 1994) or from a more pragmatics standpoint, as evidence of hedging or other metadiscoursal functions (Hyland, 1999; Hewings and Hewings, forthcoming). Hunston and Sinclair (2000) in exploring "local grammar" have also extended our knowledge of patterns conveying evaluation using it and there followed by evaluative nouns or adjectives. In these analyses the evaluative nature of most of these types of clause is apparent and they therefore come under this sub-category of "research theories and comment". Examples are:

6. It [4b] is believed that to achieve this utopia, the city must be planned. (First year; human 9)

7. It [4b] has been suggested that jokulhlaups exhibit a cyclic pattern. (Third year; physical 13)

8. It [4b] is obvious from the descriptions of the various processes that soil creep is a very slow form of movement. (First year; physical 1)

9. Clearly, there [4b] are many issues which affect the current and future role of communal housing. (Third year; human 2)

The relative frequency of these constructions in student writing compared to published academic papers is interesting. Some lecturers advise students against using constructions such as "I think" and this may influence their choice of impersonal constructions. In contrast, however, students are urged to voice opinions, to criticize, to argue. Here students face a problem. They are the novices and their markers are seen as experts. Evaluating and critiquing from this lower status position, is a probably another reason for employing impersonal structures. Martin *et al.* (1997: 69) have commented on these "explicitly objective" grammatical metaphors noting that the choice of *it*-clauses over a construction with a personal pronoun (e.g., *It is proposed* that, rather than *I propose* that) can allow the writer to depersonalize opinions. In this way, the writer presents an opinion as objective, not associated with the writer, and thus less open to negotiation. I would argue that it is this facet of "less associated with the writer", in this case the student writer, which is of significance here.

Interviews with geography academic staff were also inconclusive on the subject of human versus physical geography writing demands. Some human geographers emphasized the need for original ideas and developing arguments through writing and some saw physical geography, especially at first year level, as more concerned with factual content than ideas. In contrast, physical geography specialists perceived much less difference between the wings of the discipline and its writing norms, especially over recent years. This is taken to be a reference to the convergence between human and physical geography following the "quantitative revolution". However, one lecturer noted that physical geography essays required "harder factual content" supported by examples which show how patterns and process operated. Two other lecturers stressed the importance of debate and critical thinking and one commented that "deep down" markers of both human and physical geography essays were looking for the same "intellectual qualities".

Further detailed analysis within the different GS classes, comparisons between essays in different sub-corpora and the marks they received and the interviews with geography lecturers led me to an explanation for the generally inconclusive nature of the GS analysis as an indicator of human versus physical rhetorical differences. In the first year the phenomenal focus is high for both human and physical geography and this is, in part, a reflection of the more factual approach that students bring with them from school, what one lecturer referred to as the "A-level effect" (Bryson, 1997); that is, the influence of the type of work required to pass school examinations typically taken at the age of eighteen in England and elsewhere. In addition, physical geography essays are based on a body of scientific knowledge which lecturers are keen to teach and assess. At first year level, the lecturers were less concerned with argument, critique or evaluation in physical geography and more concerned with how much students knew. In contrast, human geography lecturers were less satisfied with the phenomenal focus of first year essays and were concerned to move students to a more analytical approach. By the third year, the analytical approach was expected in both wings of the discipline. Its greater presence in the third year physical geography essays is due to their greater preoccupation with reporting investigations and comparing models. These were often abstract and divorced from the sense of place associated with geography. Third year human geography essays in contrast showed greater evaluative language in impersonal it-constructions and a foregrounding of theories and issues. They too were more abstract and less concerned with specific locations. Thus by their final year, the students were exhibiting a convergence with the epistemic requirements of their lecturers and the discipline; a concern not with unique places and phenomena but with methods of enquiry, models and theories. Their goal was to understand and be able to evaluate competing ideas on the level of how well they helped to account for the phenomena being studied. Such an epistemic rationale united both human and physical geographers and those wedded to a scientific method paradigm and those with more humanistic research methodologies.

Comparison with Journals Corpus

The contrast between human and physical geography essays was markedly less than that found in comparing physical and human geography journal articles. Figure 17.5 shows that both journals' subcorpora used more epistemic than phenomenal GSs — a reversal of the pattern found in student writing. In addition, articles from the *International Journal of Climatology* used epistemic GSs for over 77% of clause complexes compared to 60% for *European Urban and Regional Studies*.

Figure 17.5
Percentage of Grammatical Subjects in Each Category
in Geography Journals Corpus

	Phenomenal GSs	Epistemic GSs
Human (Urban)	40.00	60.00
Physical (Climatology)	22.86	77.14

Typical epistemic examples from the human geography articles are:

10. By implication, <u>contemporary urban and regional analysis</u> [4] perhaps ought to engage in harvesting more appropriate middle-range concepts with which to rationally abstract from empirical concrete-complex forms.

11. Jessop [5] has raised similar themes when claiming that in the globalizing postnational era, new geographies of governance are emerging whereupon the state capacities are being reorganized both territorially and functionally.

12. We [5] cannot refer to a substantial record of cases at the national level.

In the climatology corpus examples are:

13. A valid climate change detection scheme [4] requires knowledge of historical as well as spatial variability.

14. Brown and Goodison (1996) [5] reconstructed historical snow cover back to 1915 for selected regions in southern Canada using a mass balance approach...Others [5] have used empirical orthogonal functions derived from satellite observations...

15. While most of the associations appear to be generally linear, a scatterplot of the association with temperature in October [4] displays a positive relationship for temperatures in the range 7.0-9.7oC...

Caution needs to be exercised in making generalizations based on only four articles and from a different genre. However, the considerable increase in frequency of epistemic GSs over the frequency found in essays is marked, as shown in Figure 17.6.

Figure 17.6
Comparison of Percentages of Grammatical Subjects
in Each Category in Human and Physical Geography Journal Articles
and Undergraduate Essays

	Phenomenal	Epistemic
Essays Human	66.57	32.63
Essays Physical	62.98	36.57
Essays Total	64.73	34.64
Journals Human	40.00	60.00
Journals Physical	22.86	77.14
Journals Total	30.93	69.07

Conclusion

Research such as this gives us only an incomplete and not necessarily generalizable fragment of the disciplinary picture. We can say that for the students at this particularly university following this particular geography course an analysis of GSs showed a change in the rhetorical sophistication of the writers from first to final year towards more epistemically-focused writing. We can also point to some variation between human and physical geography sub-disciplines at the undergraduate level. The student essays indicate that human geography is more akin to the social sciences than humanities on the continuum looked at earlier; that is, it concerns itself with both the epistemic and phenomenal realms. Physical geography, while using more epistemic GSs, is still not very far along the continuum towards the hard sciences. The journal examples used, however, showed climatology to be much more epistemic in focus and to approach problems through the experimental and modelling route. Human geography, on the other hand, had proportionately fewer epistemic subjects due to the focus on discussion of plans and strategies located in specific spatial terms, often names of places. Further research is needed in other institutions to supplement or challenge these findings and work on aspects other than the GS would complement the whole procedure. Comparative work in other disciplines would test the methodology further and contribute to our understanding of disciplinary differences and similarities. Pedagogic implications, if the findings are shown to be generalizable, would include highlighting GS choices as rhetorically motivated. This may help to illustrate to students how the more abstract disciplinary writing is constructed, that it is constructed and that the constructions vary in the choices of GS types favoured depending on discipline or sub-discipline.

References

1. Ballard, B. and J. Clanchy. 1988. Literacy in the university: An anthropological approach. In *Literacy by degrees*, edited by G. Taylor, B. Ballard, V. Beasley, H. Bock, J. Clanchy and P. Nightingale. Milton Keynes: SRHE and Open University Press, 1–6.

2. Bazerman, C. 1988. *Shaping written knowledge: The genre and activity of the experimental article in science*. Madison: University of Wisconsin Press.

3. _____ and J. Paradis. 1991. *Textual dynamics and the professions*. Madison, Wisconsin: University of Wisconsin Press.

4. Becher, T. 1989. *Academic tribes and territories: Intellectual enquiry and the cultures of disciplines*. Milton Keynes, England: Society for Research into Higher Education and the Open University.

5. Berkenkotter, C., T. N. Huckin and J. Ackerman. 1991. Social context and socially constructed texts: The initiation of a graduate student into a writing research community. In *Textual dynamics and the professions*, edited by C. Bazerman and J. Paradis. Madison, Wisconsin: University of Wisconsin Press, 191–215.

6. _____ and T. N. Huckin. 1995. *Genre knowledge in disciplinary communication: Cognition/culture/power*. Hove: Lawrence Erlbaum Associates.

7. Berry, M. 1989. Thematic options and success in writing. In *Language and literature — theory and practice: A tribute to Walter Grauberg*, edited by C. S. Butler, R. A. Cardwell and J. Channell. Nottingham: Nottingham Linguistic Circular Special Issue in association with University of Nottingham Monographs in the Humanities, 62–80.

8. _____ . 1995. Thematic options and success in writing. In *Thematic development in English texts*, edited by M. Ghadessy. London and New York: Pinter, 55–84.

9. Bhatia, V. K. 1999. Integrating products, processes, purposes and participants in professional writing. In *Writing: Texts*, processes and practices, edited by C. N. Candlin and K. Hyland. London and New York: Longman, 21–39.

10. Bird, J. 1989. *The changing worlds of Geography: A critical guide to concepts and methods*. Oxford: Clarendon Press.

11. Bryson, J. 1997. Breaking through the "A" level effect: A first year tutorial in student reflection. In *Good practice in teaching: A collection of case studies from the University of Birmingham*, edited by A. Morton and R. McCulloch. Birmingham: The Staff Development Unit, The University of Birmingham, 54–56.

12. Coffin, C. 1997. Constructing and giving value to the past. In *Genres and institutions: Social processes in the workplace and school*, edited by J. R. Martin and F. Christie. London: Pinter.

13. Conference of Heads of Geography Departments in Higher Education in the UK and the Royal Geographical Society-Institute of British Geographers (RGS-IBG). 1997. The case for Geography funding at "part laboratory" level. *The Geographical Journal* 163:286–294.

14. Cope, B. and M. Kalantzis, eds. 2000. *Multiliteracies: Literacy learning and the design of social futures*. London and New York: Routledge.

15. Davies, F. 1988. Reading between the lines: Thematic choice as a device for presenting writer viewpoint in academic discourse. *The ESPecialist* 9:173–200.

16. Faigley, L. 1986. Competing theories of process: A critique and a proposal. In *College English* 48 (6): 527–542.

17. Gee, J. P. 2000. New people in new worlds: Networks, the new capitalism and schools. In *Multiliteracies: Literacy learning and the design of social futures,* edited by B. Cope and M. Kalantzis. London and New York: Routledge, 43–68.

18. Gosden, H. 1993. Discourse functions of subject in scientific research articles. *Applied Linguistics* 14:56–75.

19. Halliday, M. A. K. 1994. *An introduction to functional grammar,* 2nd ed. London: Edward Arnold.

20. Harvey, D. 1969. *Explanation in Geography*. London: Edward Arnold.

21. Hasan, R. 1999. Speaking with reference to context. In *Text and context in functional linguistics,* edited by M. Ghadessy. Amsterdam/Philadelphia: John Benjamins, 219–328.

22. _____ and P. H. Fries, eds. 1995. *On subject and theme*. Amsterdam/ Philadelphia: John Benjamins.

23. Henderson, W. and A. Hewings. 1987. *Reading economics: How text helps or hinders*. London: British National Bibliography Research Fund Report 28, ISBN 0 7123 3115 8.

24. _____ . 1990. A language of model building? In *The language of economics: The analysis of economics discourse ELT documents:* 134, edited by A. Dudley-Evans and W. Henderson. London: Modern English Publications in association with The British Council, 43–54.

25. Hewings, A. 1990. Aspects of the language of economics textbooks. In The language of economics: *The analysis of economics discourse ELT documents:* 134, edited by A. Dudley-Evans and W. Henderson. London: Modern English Publications in association with The British Council, 29–42.

26. _____ . 1999. Disciplinary engagement in undergraduate writing: An investigation of clause-initial elements in Geography essays. PhD. diss. University of Birmingham.

27. _____ and M. Hewings. "It is interesting to note that...": A comparative study of anticipatory "it" in student and published writing. *English for specific purposes*. In Press.

28. Hunston, S. 1994. Evaluation and organization in a sample of written academic discourse. In *Advances in written text analysis*, edited by M. Coulthard. London: Routledge, 191–218.

29. _____ and J. Sinclair 2000. A local grammar of evaluation. In *Evaluation in text: Authorial stance and the construction of discourse*, edited by S. Hunston and G. Thompson. Oxford: Oxford University Press, 74–101.

30. Hyland, K. 1998. *Hedging in scientific research articles.* Amsterdam: John Benjamins.

31. _____. 1999. Disciplinary discourses: Writer stance in research articles. In *Writing: Texts, processes and practices*, edited by C. N. Candlin and K. Hyland. London and New York: Longman, 99–121.

32. _____. 2000. *Disciplinary discourses: Social interactions in academic writing.* Harlow, England: Longman.

33. Ivanič, R. 1998. *Writing and identity. The discoursal construction of identity in academic writing.* Amsterdam: Benjamins.

34. Kress, G. 1994. *Learning to write*, 2nd ed. London: Routledge.

35. Lea, M. R. and B. Street. 1998. Student writing in higher education: An academic literacies approach. *Studies in Higher Education* 23 (2): 157–172.

36. Lillis. T. *Student writing. Access, regulation, desire.* London: Routledge. In Press.

37. MacDonald, S. P. 1992. A method for analyzing sentence-level differences in disciplinary knowledge making. *Written communication* 9:533–569.

38. _____. 1994. *Professional academic writing in the humanities and social sciences.* Carbondale and Edwardsville: Southern Illinois University Press.

39. Martin, J. R. 2000. Grammar meets genre: Reflections on the "Sydney School". Inaugural lecture Sydney University Arts Association, presented at the University of Sydney.

40. _____, C. M. I. M. Matthiessen and C. Painter. 1997. *Working with functional grammar.* London: Arnold.

41. Masuku, N. 1996. A lexicogrammatical approach to the analysis of rhetorical goals in professional academic writing in the social sciences. Ph.D. diss., University of Birmingham, UK.

42. McCabe, A. M. 1999. Theme and thematic patterns in Spanish and English history texts. Ph.D. diss., University of Aston, UK.

43. Mitchell, S. 1995. Conflict and conformity: The place of argument in learning a discourse. In *Competing and consensual voices: The theory and practice of argument*, edited by P. J. M Costello and S. Mitchell. Clevedon: Multilingual Matters Ltd., 131–146.

44. Myers, G. 1990. *Writing biology: Texts in the social construction of scientific knowledge.* Wisconsin: The University of Wisconsin Press.

45. Prior, P. 1995. Redefining the task: An ethnographic examination of writing and response in graduate seminars. In *Academic writing in a second language,* edited by D. Belcher and G. Braine. Norwood, NJ: Ablex, 47–82.

46. _____. 1998. *Writing/disciplinarity: A sociohistoric account of literate activity in the academy.* New Jersey: Lawrence Erlbaum.

47. Ravelli, L. J. 1995. A dynamic perspective: Implications for metafunctional interaction and an understanding of theme. In *On subject and theme,* edited by R. Hasan and P. H. Fries. Amsterdam/Philadelphia: John Benjamins, 187–234.

48. Samraj, B. T. R. 1995. The nature of academic writing in an interdisciplinary field. Ph.D. diss. University of Michigan.

49. Swales, J. 1990. *Genre analysis.* Cambridge: Cambridge University Press.

50. Toulmin, S. 1972. *Human understanding: The collective use and evolution of concepts.* Princeton: Princeton University Press.

51. Walford, R. and P. Haggett. 1995. Geography and geographical education: Some speculations for the twenty-first century. *Geography* 80:3–13.

52. Wignell, P., J. R. Martin and S. Eggins. 1989. The discourse of Geography: Ordering and explaining the experiential world. In *Linguistics and Education* 1: 359–91. Reprinted in Halliday, M. A. K. and J. R. Martin. 1993. *Writing science: Literary and discursive power.* London: Falmer Press, pp. 136–165.

18

Legal Problem Questions: Analyzing Rhetorical Strategies Using "IRAC"

Christian Jensen

Introduction

This chapter derives from work on a 3-year Project entitled "Improving Legal English: Quality Measures for Programme Development and Evaluation" currently underway in the Department of English and Communication and the School of Law at the City University of Hong Kong. It explores a legal writing genre called the problem question. The problem question is an academic genre designed to help law students develop their legal analytical skills. This genre is absolutely central to common law legal education and is the most common type of writing encountered by law students.

The chapter focuses on rhetorical strategies in student answers to problem questions. The "IRAC method" is used as a framework for the analysis. IRAC is an analytical technique used, with some variation, in most common law-based law schools. It was hypothesized that higher grade papers would follow the IRAC approach more closely and consistently than lower grade papers. Generally speaking, this proved to be the case.

It is hoped that these insights will be used to develop more effective English for Academic Legal Purposes (EALP) pedagogy and materials.

Problem Questions and the IRAC Method

Problem Questions

A good definition of problem questions is provided by Enright (1986: 347):

> *"By a problem or problem question is meant a question or exercise where a student is asked to discuss the legal consequences of a set of facts. Normally these consequences are expressed in terms of the availability of some remedy. Further, it is a common practice to construct a problem so that the legal consequences of the facts are not immediately clear. . . The areas where the legal consequences of the facts are not clear constitute "the issues", and are the very essence of the problem question."*

Law students typically encounter problem questions in law school examinations. They are the most common type of examination. They do not, of themselves, constitute a genre from legal practice. However, although their purpose is purely academic, they have a strong practical element in that they form the basis of most legal analysis, both academic and professional. Problem questions are designed to help law students learn to "think like a lawyer". They help students develop core legal critical and analytical skills which they can later use in various professional contexts and with various professional genres. Law students at the School of Law of the City University of Hong Kong encounter the problem question in many courses.

The following is an example of a problem question taken from a City University of Hong Kong Criminal Law course. Answers to this question formed the basis of the research for this chapter.

> *"Wong, who lives in an old person's home, is a bad tempered 85 year old man who also suffers from hypoglycaemia. His condition sometimes leads to bouts of memory loss. He is also partially deaf. One morning, he was in a very bad temper and threw his medicine at a nurse. He also drank two large glasses of brandy. Later, he overheard a conversation between Betty, the nurse in charge of the home, and a doctor. Their conversation was about the need to exterminate the cockroaches in the home but Wong thought they were plotting to kill*

him. The next day, Wong secretly put some poison in Betty's tea. Suzy, another nurse drank the tea and fell into a coma. She was rushed to hospital in an ambulance accompanied by Mary, a trainee nurse. Along the way, Suzy's heart stopped but Mary, thinking that Suzy would end up in a vegetative state if she survived, did nothing to help Suzy who died. Wong says he remembers nothing after his consumption of the brandy. Discuss the liability of Wong and Mary."

The IRAC Method

"IRAC" is a mnemonic formulation which stands for "Issue, Rule, Application, Conclusion". It is a cognitive, rhetorical, analytical, organizational, and pedagogical technique taught, with some variation, in many common law-based law schools, including virtually every United States law school. Its main purpose is to provide a useful model for writing a legal analysis of individual legal issues. Yelin (1996:381) describes it as the "architectural blueprint for the legal discussion. It gives legal writing continuity and clarity and organizes the contents of the discussion. IRAC provides legal support and analysis for the issue posed by the problem and guides the writer toward a well-supported conclusion."

The idea is that, when approaching a situation from a legal perspective, one first determines what the legal issues are, states the relevant legal rules, analyzes the situation by applying the rules to the facts of this situation, and finally reaches a legal conclusion based on this analysis.

Although IRAC can be and is used in legal practice, it is first introduced and practiced in law school. It is presented to law students as an effective way of approaching problem questions.

Using IRAC to Answer Problem Questions

When using IRAC to answer problem questions, the "I", identifying the issues, is one of the most important parts of the answer. It is important because it displays the student's ability to recognize what the real problems are, the legal grey areas, the issues the court will have to decide. This is an important and difficult skill as it involves taking an everyday situation, described in everyday language, and reconceptualizing it into legal terms. Goodrich (1987:187) states:

> *"In any given instance the predominant ideological characteristic of legal argument is the highly selective manner in which it "particularizes" or translates a series of sociological relations and conflicts into a narrow set of legally relevant facts or issues. As a number of studies have argued, this particularization or decontextualization of legal discourse is its most significant ideological hallmark: concrete social relationships and real (social) people are transmogrified into the abstractly free and equal legal subjects of the legal code."*

The application portion of IRAC is also very important. This is where one uses the facts of the problem to demonstrate (i.e., not merely conclude) why and how the legal rule should apply to the issue posed. This is the legal analysis. Within the law school context, how a student goes about applying the legal rules to the facts and analyzing the various possible outcomes is much more important than the eventual conclusion reached.

Of course, having IRAC as a tool for analyzing situations from a legal perspective still does not make the task automatic or easy. Indeed, legal analysis should never be, and really cannot be, automatic. As one book cautions, "IRAC is merely a framework within which to build your analysis: It should not appear to your readers that you have merely plugged information into a rigid formula." (Charrow, 1995: 142)

Further, as Farrar and Dugdale (1984:75) point out, various analytical skills are required when performing an IRAC analysis. As stated, one must first identify the issue(s). Analogical reasoning must then be used to select the relevant legal precedents. Inductive reasoning must be used to synthesize the precedents and produce a statement of law, or rule, from these precedents. Finally, deductive reasoning must be used to answer the question posed in the issue.

Discussions of IRAC, with exercises, samples answers, and so on, can be found in a number of legal writing books and manuals, especially those written for an American audience. (See, e.g., Calleros, 1998:149; Charrow, 1995:140; Edwards, 1996:86; McVea and Cumper, 1996:16; Yelin, 1996:381.) Additional materials on IRAC can be found at a number of legal web sites.

Prior Research on Problem Questions

As Howe (1990:218) has stated, "Jurists have studied and analyzed the discourse of law for a long time, but with their own terminology and techniques and at such a sophisticated and philosophical level that works on the discourse of law were found to be only marginally helpful to the language teacher and nonlawyer." From a language perspective, prior research into problem questions, or other academic legal genres for that matter, is very limited. The most significant work on problem questions has been done by Howe (1990) and Beasley (1993 and 1994).

It is not possible to give a detailed description of Howe's and Beasley's research methodology here. It is their findings which are most important for our purposes. Howe found what she calls eight "units of discourse" in answers to problem questions, as follows:

1.	The situation	THE QUESTION
2.	The instruction	
3.	The forecast	THE ANSWER
4.	The issue	
5.	The law	
6.	Its authority (case or statute)	
7.	The application of the facts	
8.	Opinion (and advice)	

The first two units pertain to the problem question itself; the other six to the answer. Of these units, only 5, 6, and 7 were present in all the papers she analyzed.

Beasley's research more or less confirmed the presence of Howe's eight discourse units. The six units associated with the answer (3–8) can be equated with the IRAC formula as follows.

3. The forecast (relatively rare)   = Issue   [I]
4. The issue   = Issue
5. The law   = Rule   [R]
6. Its authority (case or statute)   = Rule
7. The application of the facts   = Application   [A]
8. Opinion (and advice)   = Conclusion   [C]

Methodology

To improve the validity of the analysis, three research methods were used: (1) Interviews with City University of Hong Kong and Hong Kong University teaching staff, and (2) quantitative textual analyses of various student answers to problem questions, and (3) a qualitative analysis of these same texts. This chapter focuses only on the results of (3), the qualitative textual analysis.

Papers Analyzed

The following texts were analyzed:

- Group A: Six (6) examination papers from the LLB Year 1 Law of Tort course at the City University of Hong Kong. The answer analyzed was only one out of a total of four questions the students had to answer in a three-hour examination. It was worth 25% of the total score. If students allocated equal time to each question, they would have had about 45 minutes to write this answer.

- Group B: Ten (10) take-home papers from the LLB Year 2 Criminal Law course at the City University of Hong Kong. Word limit of 1800 words.

These two courses were chosen for various reasons. First, because they included problem questions as part of their assessment. Second, because they are required courses for all law students. Third, Group A is a Year 1 course and Group B a Year 2 course. This provides a comparison between Year 1 and Year 2 students. Fourth, the papers from Group A were written under examination conditions, whereas the papers from Group B were take-home. This provides a broader view of problem questions written under varying conditions. Fifth, the fact pattern and question(s) posed for the two groups varied considerably. Finally, the overall length, and therefore the depth of analysis, was very different between the two papers, thus providing a broader perspective of different types of problem questions.

Because Group B papers were written out of class and with no time limitation, and because the assignment itself required a more complex organization, analysis, and discussion of the problem question, analysis of this group proved to be more rewarding. The length and complexity of the papers allowed for clearer rhetorical patterns to emerge, and to thus be analyzed. Consequently, more of these papers were chose for analysis (10) than those in Group A (6).

The sample papers from Groups A and B were selected according to grade received. High-, middle-, and low-grade papers were selected in order to provide a means of comparison. The main purpose of the comparison was to try to determine what makes a paper "good" or "poor" in the eyes of the marker. Special attention was paid to whether there was a correlation between the grade received and the degree to which the rhetorical structure followed IRAC.

This chapter focuses only on the results of the analysis of Group B papers. The results were substantially similar for Group A.

Type of Analysis

The analysis employed was a variant of rhetorical structural analysis. It was initially thought that Rhetorical Structure Theory (RST) would offer the best approach. (See Mann and Thompson, 1986) RST offers a tool for analyzing the organization of texts in terms of 22 "relations" which can be identified between pairs of text spans.

After struggling to apply the RST approach to the analysis of legal problem question, it was decided that it would not be the best approach after all. RST is best suited to classic student essay type writing. It breaks a paper into rhetorical units which are placed into a diagrammatic structure according to their function in the essay. Some units are classified as central arguments, called "nuclei", while others are classified as supporting arguments, called "satellites". This creates a "picture" of the essay. This picture can then be analyzed in terms of consistency and overall balance and cohesiveness of structure.

Overall balance and cohesiveness of structure, however, is anathema to problem questions. Problem questions are by nature disjointed, consisting of a number of discrete issues. Each issue is expected to be taken up and discussed one by one, and overall cohesiveness of structure is not only unimportant but actually undesirable.

RST was therefore abandoned in favour of IRAC. IRAC is more suitable for at least three reasons: (1) it is already taught to law students as part of their legal training, (2) it is specifically designed for the disjointed, issue-oriented structure of answers to problem questions, and (3) its presence in answers to problem questions has been established by prior research (see Howe, 1990 and Beasley, 1993 and 1994).

The first step in the analysis was to divide each paper into "rhetorical units" (RU). Each RU is a piece of text representing one discreet point, idea, or argument within the structure of the paper. It is not defined or delimited by grammatical structure but rather by ideational content. Most RUs consisted of one sentence. But some RUs were only a fraction of a sentence, while others were two or more sentences. Again, the determining factor for an RU was ideational content, not grammatical structure.

Once the paper had been divided into RUs, each RU was numbered according to its chronological position in the paper. It was then identified as belonging to one of the IRAC categories: Issue, Rule, Analysis, or Conclusion. The RUs were then used to create three types of diagrams. For the first diagram (D1), each RU was placed into one of four IRAC columns in a chart, moving down the page so as to create a visual image of the argument from the top of the chart moving down. (See Appendix A) This was done for each of the texts analyzed.

A second type of diagram (D2) was then created, which derived from the first. D2 is the same as D1 but with the text removed. This left a simple numerical representation of each RU. These numbers are still located within the columns of the IRAC framework, but with the text removed a clearer visual pattern of the rhetorical structure of the paper emerges. (See Appendix 2 on page 489) Again, this was done for all texts analyzed.

Finally, the D2 diagrams were taken up again and divided according to issues discussed. This was done for all Group B papers. This created a third type of diagram (D3). (See Appendix 3 on page 491)

Once the rhetorical structure of the papers had been mapped within the IRAC framework, they were analyzed according to degree to which each issue discussed followed the IRAC rhetorical pattern. This was done by analyzing the D3 charts which, as mentioned, divide the papers according to issues identified and discussed. The papers were divided into issues and analyzed from this perspective because most problem questions contain a number of issues and IRAC is meant to be used for each of them individually.

In many cases, the issue was not explicitly identified by the student. Instead, just as Howe concluded (1990:224), the issue is sometimes stated in the form of a tentative opinion, and sometimes not stated at all, but can be inferred or assumed from the context and structure of the argument.

Results of the Analysis

All of the papers were analyzed in terms of how closely their rhetorical structure conformed to IRAC for each issue identified and discussed. It was hypothesized that the rhetorical structure of the higher grade papers would follow IRAC more closely and more clearly for each issue discussed. This turned out to be quite clearly the case. As could be expected, the biggest variation in terms of rhetorical structure was between the highest and the lowest grade papers. Some of these are discussed below.

Paper B1 (Grade: A-)

This paper received the highest grade in Group B. As can be seen from Appendices 1, 2, and 3, when discussing each issue or sub-issue, the rhetorical structure of the paper follows IRAC very closely. Also, the paper identifies and discusses a large number of issues and sub-issues. The number of rhetorical units devoted to discussing each issue is remarkably similar. There is also great balance between the number of rhetorical units used to discuss "Rule" and "Analysis". Overall, the structure of the paper gives the impression of a balanced and thorough handling of the problem question generally as well as the individual issues within the problem question.

Paper B2 (Grade: B++)

This paper received the second highest grade of the papers analyzed. Again, the rhetorical structure of the paper follows IRAC when discussing each issue. It does not, however, follow IRAC as cleanly or consistently as B1, as can be seen from the Appendix 4. For example, there is a tendency to move back and forth between "Rule" and "Analysis" when discussing a single issue. But this is not necessarily "wrong" or a "violation" of the IRAC approach. Just as the name implies, the IRAC approach is meant to serve only as an "approach", a guideline, a need not (indeed, should not) be followed slavishly. Especially with the "Rule" and "Application" sections this bending of the IRAC structure is allowable. The "Rule" and "Application" sections are intimately connected and it is natural to refer back to rules while applying them to the facts.

Paper B2 devotes a relatively even number of RUs to each issue, though slightly less balanced than B1. For example, it uses a much higher number of RUs when discussing Issue 1 and Issue 7. Also, as in B1, for each Issue there is a relatively even number of rhetorical units used to discuss Rule and Analysis. When one looks at the chart, there are no "holes" in the discussion; it is balanced and thorough.

Paper B9 (Grade: D)

Along with B10, this paper received the lowest score of all the papers analyzed. In terms of rhetorical structure, it is a disaster. Appendix 5 reveals that in the B9 paper the IRAC structure is virtually absent. For most of the paper, it is impossible to even identify what issue is being discussed. Further, the number of RUs devoted to each IRAC component is grossly uneven. Instead of an interplay between the IRAC components, there are long strings of RUs devoted to discussing only "Rules". Then, toward the end of the paper, the strings of RUs switch to "Analysis". In contrast to papers B1 and B2, the discussion in B9 is unbalanced and there are gaping holes in the rhetorical structure.

A number of important conclusions can be drawn from the qualitative analysis of the ten papers.

- Higher grade papers demonstrate an ability to recognize, identify, and thoroughly analyze the relevant issues.
- Higher grade papers tend to devote a relatively even number of RUs to the discussion of each issue.
- Higher grade papers tend to employ the IRAC moves more readily and follow them more consistently when discussing each issue.
- Higher grade papers demonstrate relative balance between the number of RUs used to discuss "Rule" and "Application" for each issue.
- Higher grade papers demonstrate a more balanced interplay between "Rule" and "Application".
- Lower grade papers have a tendency to clump RUs together in strings within a single IRAC category. This creates holes in the rhetorical structure of the paper.

Conclusion — Pedagogical Implications

It is important to consider the results in terms of their pedagogic significance. These results could be used in any number of ways in the

EALP context to improve the teaching and learning of legal reading and writing. The problem question and IRAC are used in law schools to teach basic legal reasoning, which can in turn be employed in any number of legal situations and genres. In the same way, the problem question and IRAC can be used in the EALP context to teach the fundamentals of legal reasoning from a linguistic perspective, which can then be taken and applied to any number of legal situations and genres. In other words, it can be the basis for a uniform approach to teaching EALP reading and writing skills.

For example, the basic IRAC structure has been identified in legal cases. (See, e.g., Maley (1985)[1] and materials used in the English Enhancement for Law course at Hong Kong University.) This means that instruction on problem questions and IRAC in terms of language and rhetorical structure can later be applied to help law students read cases more effectively.

Similarly, legal letters often contain a legal analytical component, and thus IRAC components. Therefore, as with reading cases, that which has initially been taught and learned about problem questions and IRAC generally could later be applied to legal letters. And so the process continues. This same technique could be used for teaching other legal genres that contain an analytical component.

This is an area ripe for further research and materials development. An especially fruitful area for further research would be to analyze exactly which legal genres contain a legal analytical component (and therefore problem question/IRAC elements) and how closely the analytical component conforms to the classic problem question/IRAC model. Another potentially fruitful area would be to analyze the linguistic manifestations of the IRAC categories. This has been done to some degree by members of our Project team and by the developers of the English Enhancement for Law course at Hong Kong University.

---

1. Maley analyzed the discourse of a judgment of the High Court of Australia and identified five discourse units: the facts of the case, the issues before the court, the reasoning, the conclusion, and the finding. The only difference between this and IRAC is the "facts of the case" unit of discourse. In problem questions, the facts are provided in the problem question itself.

It is hoped that this paper can play a part in improving our understanding of the very important and difficult task faced by both teachers and students of how best to answer problem questions from the rhetorical perspective. It is also hoped that this improved understanding can lead to the development of an increasingly effective pedagogy for answering problem questions, and for legal writing generally.

References

1. Beasley, C. J. 1993. *Language and content: The case of law*. Paper presented at the 9th International Institute of Language in Education Conference "Language and Content", 15–18 December 1992, Hong Kong.

2. _____ . 1994. *Picking up the principles: An applied linguistics analysis of the legal problem genre*. Unpublished MA Paper, Edith Cowan University, Australia.

3. Calleros, C. R. 1998. 3rd ed. *Legal method and writing*. Boston: Little, Brown & Co.

4. Charrow, V. R. *et al*. 1995. 2nd ed. *Clear and effective legal writing*. Boston: Little, Brown & Co.

5. Edwards, L. H. 1996. *Legal writing: Process, analysis, and organization*. Boston: Little, Brown & Co.

6. Enright, C. 1987. 2nd ed.. *Studying the law*. Sydney: Braxton Press.

7. Farrer, J. H. and A. M. Dugdale. 1984. *Introduction to legal method*. London: Sweet & Maxwell.

8. Goodrich, P. 1987. *Legal discourse: Studies in linguistics, rhetoric and legal analysis*. London: Macmillan.

9. Howe, P. M. 1990. The problem of the problem question in English for academic legal purposes. *English for Specific Purposes* 9:215–236.

10. McVea and Cumper. 1996. *Learning Exam Skills*. London: Blackstone.

11. Mann, W. C. and S. A. Thompson. 1986. *Rhetorical structure theory: Descriptions and construction of text structures*. ISI Reprint Series, ISI/RS–86–174 October 1986, USC/Information Sciences Institute, Marina Del Rey, CA.

12. Yelin, A. B. and H. R. Samborn. 1996. *The Legal research and writing handbook: A basic approach for paralegals*. Boston: Little, Brown & Co.

Appendix 1
Criminal Law (Paper B1): Score A-)

Issue(s)	Rule	Analysis/Application	Conclusion
1. Introduction: it is possible for Wong to convict murder of Suzy and attempt murder of Betty. 2. On the other hand there are defences, such as intoxication, automatism, mistake and insanity are available to him. 3. <u>Liability to Wong – Murder – Causation – Transferred Malice</u>	4. To charge Wong murder, it is necessary to examine the actus reu and mens rea. 5. An actus reus represents the act of the accused.	6. Mr. Wong put the poison in a cup of tea is an actus rea. 7. Although it is unknown to us that what kind of the poison is, and whether the poison could cause a death instantly, it is not ridiculous	

Issue(s)	Rule	Analysis/Application	Conclusion
		to assume that a poison could cause, at least, grievous bodily harm.	8. Therefore Wong is possible to convict manslaughter. (Case cite and brief discussion of case.)
	9. However it is impossible to convict a person to murder without examining his mens rea.		
	10. In (Case Cite) the Court of Appeal held that it should be left to jury to decide whether the appellant has the mens rea while either he cut into the deceased's neck or cut her body in several pieces.		
	11. Also since it is a direct attack with a weapon, there is no need to find the appellant's intention as in (Case cite and brief discussion of case, and related cases).	12. To follow the direction in (Case Cite), a judge should direct the jury whether Wong has the intention, either kills or causes grievous bodily harm, while he put poison in a cup of tea.	

Issue(s)	Rule	Analysis/Application	Conclusion
			13. If the jury believes, beyond reasonable doubt, that Wong had the intention, then they should convict Wong for murder, which is likely to happen. [Marker: "Causation first, then transferred malice.]
14. <u>Causation</u>: The defence counsel will argue the issue of causation, since a trainee nurse did nothing and let Suzy die. 15. The question is whether Mary breaks the chain of causation.	16. In (Case cite and brief discussion of case) Bedlam LJ gave the leading judgement: (Quote re causation)		

Issue(s)	Rule	Analysis/Application	Conclusion
		17. It is no medical evidence to support that the cause of the Suzy's death was caused by the negligence treatment.	
		18. Moreover Wong is not going to escape his liability unless the jury thinks that the negligence treatment is so independent from his act.	19. Therefore the possibility of Wong to claim that Mary has broken the causation is unlikely to success.
20. Transferred malice	21. In (Case Cite) Staughton J, In the Court of Appeal, held: (Quote) 22. It is clearly show that a person is definitely convicted of manslaughter, at least, since the malice has been transferred.		
24. Attempt Murder		23. As Wong intended to kill Betty in the first place, and the malice has been transferred from Betty to Suzy.	

Issue(s)	Rule	Analysis/Application	Conclusion
	25. In (Case Cite) Lord Lane CJ held, which he appreciated (Quote)	26. The act is done, by Wong to put poison in a cup of tea, would constitute his actual commission if it were not interrupted.	27. Therefore there is an actus reu in attempt murder of Betty.
		28. According to (Case Cite), Wong has the mens rea since he realize that his action result in complete offence, no matter whether he desired this result or not.	29. Once again, there is a mens rea in attempt murder of Betty.
			30. Since the mens rea come with the actus reus, the chance of conviction on attempt murder is good.
31. Defence – Intoxication	32. In the law of England, voluntary		

Issue(s)	Rule	Analysis/Application	Conclusion
	intoxication is never a defence for any criminal case.		
	33. It simply means a person cannot escape liability because he was influenced by drugs or alcohol.		
	34. In (Case Cite) the judge held voluntary intoxication may be negated the mens rea only in the offence of specific intent.		
	35. Therefore the defence of intoxication may change a verdict of murder to manslaughter.		
	36. However it is important to realise that intoxication does not stand automatic as the accused claimed that he influenced by alcohol or drugs.		
	37. In the case of (Case Cite), McCullough J gave the direction as following: (Quote)		
	38. It means it is possible for an accused to use force to defence himself.		
	39. Moreover, the defence must be reasonable.		
		40. The accused, Wong, drank two large glasses of brandy and believed that	

Issue(s)	Rule	Analysis/Application	Conclusion
		he would be killed.	
		41. It is possible that the defence of intoxication is going to be failed by the two reasons.	
	42. Firstly, according to (Case Cite), if the cause of mistake is done by a voluntarily induced intoxication, the defence must fail.		
		43. As Mr. Wong had two glass of brandy, he might not be drunk but he could not deny that he might be influenced by alcohol.	
		44. Secondly, it is difficult to argue that by putting poison in someone's cup of tea is a denfence, which is reasonable and acceptable by the jury.	
45. Defence – Automatism	46. In the case of (Case Cite), Lord Denning gives out the definition of automatism (Quote).		
		47. It is arguable that whether the accused is able to claim automatism under the definition given by Lord Denning.	

Issue(s)	Rule	Analysis/Application	Conclusion
		48. Does a judge believe that he was unconscious when he put poison in the cup of tea.	
		49. If the judge believes that he was unconscious when he put the poison, then he is entitled to have the defence of automatism.	
		50. However, it doesn't mean that the defence of automatism changes his proposition, unless he qualifies the requirements in the common law.	
	51. In (Case Cite), Lawton LJ held that the appellant was caused by an external factor since he was affected by the medicine prescribed by the doctor. (Brief description of case.)		
		52. However, in present case, Wong did not take any medicine (he through it at a nurse), which is not similar in (Case).	
			53. So that the possibility for Mr. Wong have the defence of automatism is likely to rejected by a judge, according to the direction in (Case)

Issue(s)	Rule	Analysis/Application	Conclusion
54. Defence – Mistake of Fact	55. In (Case Cite), the appellant believed that either himself or his family was in danger being killed or grievous bodily harm by a man so he shot and killed the deceased. 56. In the Privy Council, Lord Griffiths said as the following: (Quote)	57. There is a reason that Wong may not be able to have mistake as a defence according to (Case). 58. Wong's honestly believe is not questionable (Case cite and brief discussion), 59. however it is arguable that whether Wong has used a reasonable force in the present case. 60. It is unlikely for the jury to accept the force, which used by Wong was a reasonable one, since he would have another options instead of putting poison in Betty's cup. 61. For example, he might call up the police to say that he was in a danger	and (Case).

Issue(s)	Rule	Analysis/Application	Conclusion
		and seek for help.	
		62. Moreover, he might possibly talk to the head of old person's home about the plan, from Betty, which he mistakenly believed by himself.	
63. Defence – Insanity	64. In the case of (Case Cite), Tindal CJ set the element of Insanity as the following: (Quote)		
		65. It is unlikely for a judge to believe that Wong did not know the nature or quality of that he was doing; or if he did know what he was doing that was wrong.	
		66. Therefore, the M'Naghten rule does not apply to Wong.	
	67. In (Case Cite), the House of Lords accepted that Mr. Payne was unconscious when he alleged the offence,		
	68. however his state of mind was not covered by the phase "as not to know the nature and quality of the act he was doing" (Case Cite).		
	69. It is a very strict rule.		
	70. Even Mr. Payne knew he was		

Issue(s)	Rule	Analysis/Application	Conclusion
	unconscious at the time he committed the act, he still was not covered by the rule.	71. Wong claimed that as he loss of memory, it is unlikely that the judge is going to apply the defence of insanity, since loss of memory is not covered by the phase, which was set in 1843.	
72. Liability to Mary	73. In (Case Cite) Lord Mackay of Clashdern, LC has the following judgment: (Quote)		
	74. It is unacceptable for a medical officer to do nothing simply because he or she believes that the patient is going to be a vegetative state if keeping someone's survival.	75. Therefore there is a highly possibility that the jury is going to convict Mary to involuntary manslaughter as she owed a duty to Suzy.	
		76. Also she breached this duty to save her, as a medical officer.	
		77. Besides that Suzy died as a result of	

Issue(s)	Rule	Analysis/Application	Conclusion
		her breach. [Marker: "This is not clear."]	
		78. Moreover it is no defence for Mary to claim that she is not a qualified nurse.	
	79. Lord Mackey also mentioned that (Quote and Case Cite).		
		80. As she takes up the post of a nurse, she is supposed to do what a reasonable qualified nurse could do.	
			81. Wong is likely to convict murder because Mary does not break the causation.
			82. Also the defences, that he has, are failed.
			83. Mary is likely to convict voluntary manslaughter according to the case of Adomako.

Appendix 2
(Paper B1: Score A-)

	Issues	Rule	Analysis/Application	Conclusion
	(1)			
	(2)			
	(3)			
		(4)		
		(5)		
			(6)	
			(7)	
				(8)
		(9)		
		(10)		
		(11)		
			(12)	
				(13)
	(14)			
	(15)			
		(16)		
			(17)	
			(18)	
				(19)
	(20)			
		(21)		
		(22)		
			(23)	
	(24)			
		(25)		
			(26)	
				(27)
			(28)	
				(29)
				(30)
	(31)			
		(32)		
		(33)		
		(34)		
		(35)		
		(36)		
		(37)		
		(38)		
		(39)		
			(40)	
			(41)	

	Issues	Rule	Analysis/ Application	Conclusion
	(42)			
			(43)	
			(44)	
	(45)			
		(46)		
			(47)	
			(48)	
			(49)	
			(50)	
		(51)		
			(52)	
				(53)
	(54)			
		(55)		
		(56)		
			(57)	
			(58)	
			(59)	
			(60)	
			(61)	
			(62)	
	(63)			
		(64)		
			(65)	
			(66)	
		(67)		
		(68)		
		(69)		
		(70)		
			(71)	
	(72)			
		(73)		
		(74)		
			(75)	
			(76)	
			(77)	
			(78)	
		(79)		
			(80)	
			(81)	(81)
			(82)	(82)
			(83)	(83)
Totals:	12	30	31	10

Appendix 3
(Paper B1: Score A-)

	Issues	Rule	Analysis/ Application	Conclusion
	(1) (2)			
ISSUE 1	(3)			
Sub-Issue		(4) (5)		
			(6) (7)	
				(8)
Sub-Issue		(9) (10) (11)		
			(12)	
				(13)
ISSUE 2	(14) (15)			
		(16)		
			(17) (18)	
				(19)
ISSUE 3	(20)			
		(21) (22)		
			(23)	
ISSUE 4	(24)			
		(25)		
			(26)	
				(27)
			(28)	
				(29) (30)
ISSUE 5	(31)			
		(32) (33) (34) (35) (36) (37) (38) (39)		
			(40)	

	Issues	Rule	Analysis/ Application	Conclusion
		(42)	(41) (43) (44)	
ISSUE 6	(45)	(46) (51)	(47) (48) (49) (50) (52)	(53)
ISSUE 7	(54)	(55) (56)	(57) (58) (59) (60) (61) (62)	
ISSUE 8	(63)	(64) (67) (68) (69) (70)	(65) (66) (71)	
ISSUE 9	(72)	(73) (74) (79)	(75) (76) (77) (78) (80)	(81) (82) (83)

Appendix 4
(Paper B2: Score B++)

	Issues	Rule	Analysis/ Application	Conclusion
ISSUE 1	(1) (2)		(3)	
		(4) (5) (6) (7) (8) (9)		
			(10) (11) (12) (13) (14) (15) (16)	
				(17)
		(18)	(19)	
				(20)
ISSUE 2	(21)		(22) (23) (24) (25) (26)	
ISSUE 3	(27)	(28)		
			(29) (30) (31) (32) (33)	
		(34) (35) (36) (37)		
			(38)	
				(39)

	Issues	Rule	Analysis/ Application	Conclusion
ISSUE 4	(40)			
		(41) (42)		
			(43) (44)	
		(45) (46) (47)		
			(48) (49)	
				(50) (51)
ISSUE 5	(52) (53) (54)			
			(55) (56) (57)	
		(58) (59) (60)		
				(61)
ISSUE 6	(62)			
			(63) (64) (65)	
		(66) (67) (68)		
			(69) (70) (71)	
				(72)
			(73)	
				(74)
ISSUE 7	(75)			
		(76) (77) (78) (79) (80)		

	Issues	Rule	Analysis/ Application	Conclusion
		(81)		
			(82)	
			(83)	
			(84)	
			(85)	
			(86)	
		(87)		
		(88)		
			(89)	
		(90)		
			(91)	
		(92)		
		(93)		
		(94)		
		(95)		
			(96)	
			(97)	
		(98)		
		(99)		
		(100)		
				(101)
				(102)
Totals:	10	40	42	10

Appendix 5
(Paper B9: Score D)

Issues	Rule	Analysis/ Application	Conclusion
	(1)		
	(2)		
	(3)		
	(4)		
	(5)		
	(6)		
	(7)		
	(8)		
	(9)		
	(10)		
	(11)		
		(12)	
		(13)	
	(14)		
	(15)		
	(16)		
	(17)		
	(18)		
	(19)		
	(20)		
		(21)	
	(22)		
	(23)		
	(24)		
	(25)		
	(26)		
	(27)		
	(28)		
	(29)		
	(30)		
	(31)		
	(32)		
		(33)	
		(34)	
		(35)	
		(36)	
		(37)	
	(38)		
			(39)
		(40)	
		(41)	

Issues	Rule	Analysis/ Application	Conclusion
	(42)		
	(43)		
	(44)		
		(45)	
	(46)		
	(47)		
			(48)
		(49)	
	(50)		
	(51)		
	(52)		
	(53)		
	(54)		
	(55)		
	(56)		
	(57)		
	(58)		
(59)			
		(60)	
		(61)	
		(62)	
		(63)	
		(64)	
		(65)	
			(66)
	(67)		
	(68)		
	(69)		
	(70)		
	(71)		
	(72)		
	(73)		
	(74)		
	(75)		
	(76)		
	(77)		
	(78)		
(79)			
		(80)	
		(81)	
(82)			

Issues	Rule	Analysis/Application	Conclusion
	(83)		
	(84)		
(85)			
(86)			
	(87)		
	(88)		
	(89)		
(90)			
		(91)	
		(92)	
		(93)	
			(94)
		(95)	
(96)			
(97)			
		(98)	
		(99)	
		(100)	
		(101)	
		(102)	
		(103)	

19

Academic Discourses and their Discourses of Learning: Participants, Texts and Social Practices

Robyn Woodward-Kron

Introduction

According to Bernstein, the nature of disciplinary knowledge changes according to how far a student progresses in his or her education. Disciplinary knowledge becomes "not coherence, but incoherence: not order, but disorder, not the known but the unknown" (Bernstein, 1975: 97).

Bernstein's observation appears to be the reverse of folk understandings of university learning. Students enter university with little specialist disciplinary knowledge and should leave with significantly more. Disciplinary knowledge is seen as a learnable commodity, consisting of a canon of core knowledge that is transmitted to students via authorities such as textbooks and experts in the field. A transmission model of disciplinary learning, however, does not take into account the role of participants and social practices in shaping ways of meaning in disciplinary contexts. For expert participants, learning should involve questioning and exploring transmitted knowledge, practices which are valued in the disciplinary context because they can lead to new understandings and new meanings being created.

This chapter examines how a group of undergraduate students enrolled in a teacher education course are inducted into the discursive practices of the profession. It focusses on contextual factors such as an introductory textbook, subject aims and objectives, student essays, and participant perspectives. In particular, it explores the role of these contextual factors in moving students towards a perception of disciplinary knowledge as constructed, and therefore contestable.

Discourse Communities

Bernstein's conceptualization of disciplinary knowledge as hierarchically organized from the "known to the unknown" suggests that learners and experts view disciplinary knowledge differently. To further explore these perspectives the concept of discourse community (Swales, 1990; Bizzell, 1982) is adopted as it provides the discussion with a contextual framework. It allows the relation between novices and experts and their associated discourses to be explored, and to identify contexts which to a degree determine the choices writers make (Hyland, 2000).

Figure 19.1
Elements of Academic Discourse Communities

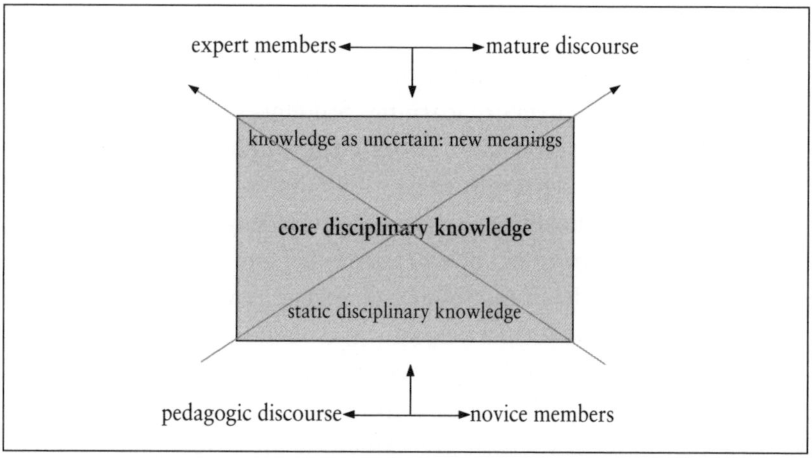

In Figure 19.1 novice and expert members of a discourse community are seen as polarized yet connected by a diagonal line intersecting the core disciplinary knowledge of the community. This knowledge consists of both static, canonical knowledge, as well as a domain where new knowledge and meanings are created. A similar relation is seen to exist between the pedagogic discourse, the discourse of learning, and the mature discourse of the discipline.

This conceptualization of a discourse community is not intended to represent an homogeneous entity, rather an abstract site in which discourses overlap, "border skirmishes" with other discourse communities occur (Bazerman, 1992:63), and where the affiliations and ideologies of its members are diverse. Member engagement with the discourse community varies considerably, as does duration of membership. Undergraduate education students studying to be teachers, for example, may only briefly experience the academic discourse of education and its associated discourses. In this respect, characterizing such members as novices is inaccurate. Such students are positioned primarily as consumers of the disciplinary discourse, and have minimal opportunities, if any, to contribute to the "conversations" of the discipline in a public forum (Plum, 1998). Despite this, the context of the discourse community determines to an extent many of the textual practices that are expected and valued in student writing. This issue will be addressed in the concluding discussion on implications for teaching and learning.

The intersecting link between novice students and expert members of a discourse community shown in Figure 19.1 is via the pedagogic discourse, the discourse of learning. While one of its functions is to make disciplinary knowledge accessible to students, the pedagogic discourse is also the main means through which novice students experience the textual practices of the discourse community.

Characteristics, Function and Status of Pedagogical Discourses

The Recontextualized Nature of Pedagogic Discourse

Bernstein's conception of pedagogic discourse (Bernstein, 1975, 1990) emphasizes its socially constructed nature. He identifies two dimensions of pedagogic discourse. The first is the regulative aspect of the discourse, which is to do with the instructor's aims for learning. The second aspect is to do with what is actually taught, the instructional dimension of the discourse. Bernstein describes the instructional discourse as embedded in the regulative one, as the regulative discourse selects and guides what is learnt. The embedding of the instructional discourse in the regulative one results in the recontextualization of the original discourse (1990). It is relocated from another context and recontextualized into a pedagogic discourse for the purpose of learning. Bernstein's characterizing of pedagogic discourse as recontextualized emphasizes the distance, not the relatedness, between the pedagogic discourse and its professional counterpart.

Similarly, the writing of novice students can be seen to have little in common with the discursive practices of the mature community, with the undergraduate culture fostering "knowledge telling" (Bereiter and Scardamalia, 1987), reproducing disciplinary knowledge. Students experience the discourse of the community via the recontextualized pedagogic discourse, and often draw on their textbooks for assignment writing, a task which functions institutionally to assess what students have learnt.

Recontextualizing in Introductory Textbooks

The focus on knowledge telling in undergraduate study mirrors the discursive purpose of the main repository of pedagogic discourse for undergraduates, the introductory textbook. The textbook, Bernstein writes, "orders knowledge according to an explicit progression, it provides explicit criteria, it removes uncertainties and announces hierarchies." (Bernstein, 1975:127). That the textbook is a site of static, canonical knowledge of the discipline is attested in part by the number of editions of a typical textbook: new editions which may only contain minor alternations. The static nature of textbook knowledge[1] is to be expected, as the function of the genre is to make disciplinary knowledge accessible to the novice, rather than convince a skeptical professional audience of potentially disputable claims, as in the research article genre (Hyland, 1999a). This means, however, that in some respects the pedagogical discourse is an unsuitable mode for apprenticing students to the specialist ways of interacting with other discourse community members via written texts.

---

1.   In some fields such as composition studies textbooks are seen as a contribution to the theory and
     pedagogy of the discipline (Alfred & Thelen, 1993; Swales, 1995).

Recontextualization in Primary Education: The Regulative and "Grand Narrative" Discourse

This section examines one instance of pedagogical discourse from the field of child development. The text is a first year introductory textbook, *Child Development* (Berk, 1997)[2], which is the core text for primary education students studying a child growth and development subject. In one regard the text is a doubly recontextualized one as it is relocated from the field of psychology to education.

The description of the lexicogrammatical resources is from Halliday (1994).

Text 1

"PHILOSOPHIES OF THE ENLIGHTENMENT
The seventeenth-century Enlightenment brought new philosophies of reason and emphasized ideals of human dignity and respect. Conceptions of childhood appeared that were more humane than those of centuries past.

JOHN LOCKE.
*The writings of John Locke (1632-1704), a leading British philosopher, served as the forerunner of an important twentieth-century perspective that we will discuss shortly: behaviourism. Locke viewed the child as **tabula rasa**. Translated from Latin, this means "blank slate" or "white piece of paper". According to this idea, children were not basically evil. They were, to begin with, nothing at all, and their characters could be shaped by all kinds of experiences while growing up. Locke (1690/1892) described parents as rational tutors who could mold the child in any way they wished through careful instruction, effective example, and rewards for good behaviour. In addition, Locke was ahead of his time in recommending to parents child-rearing practices that were eventually*

---

2.   In 1999 this text was the coursebook for EDUF111, Education 1, a core first year subject for University of Wollongong Primary Education students.

supported by twentieth-century research. For example, he suggested that parents reward children not with money or sweets, but rather with praise and approval. Locke also opposed physical punishment: "The child repeatedly beaten in school cannot look upon books and teachers without experiencing fear and anger." Locke's philosophy led to a change from harshness toward children to kindness and compassion. Look carefully at Locke's ideas, and you will see that he took a firm stand on each of the basic issues we discussed earlier in this chapter. As blank slates, children are viewed in passive, mechanistic terms. The course of growth is written on them by the environment. Locke also regarded development as continuous. Adultlike behaviours are gradually built up through the warm, consistent teachings of parents. Finally, Locke was a champion of nurture - of the power of the environment to determine whether children become good or bad, bright or dull, kind or selfish." (p. 10)

In Text 1 and the textbook as a whole, there is linguistic evidence of Bernstein's instructional discourse embedded in the regulative discourse. Use of imperatives (e.g., *Look carefully*) and the inclusive pronoun "we" are part of the regulative discourse to guide the student towards appropriate learning goals (Christie, 1998). The dominant type of process or activity in these imperative clauses are mental processes of cognition and perception, in which the functional dimension is to engage the students in the cognitive activity of the discipline (Young, 1990). For example:

"Look carefully at Locke's ideas, and you will see that he took a firm stand on each of the basic issues we discussed earlier in this chapter. (Text 1)

Consider these ideas, and you will see why Baldwin (1895) argued that heredity and environment should not be viewed as distinct, opposing forces. (Berk, 1997:13)

Recall that Piaget did not regard direct teaching by adults as important for cognitive development." (Berk, 1997:27)

Other elements of the regulative discourse are the author's intervention in how theories are to be evaluated. Competing theories and perspectives in child development are introduced to the students in the form of a synoptic history told within a narrative structure. Authorial intervention lends the narrative a grand narrative quality, with the voice of the writer evaluating the theories and perspectives with the benefit of hindsight and modern theory (Fuller, 1998).

> *"In addition, Locke was **ahead of his time** in recommending to parents child-rearing practices that were eventually **supported by twentieth-century research**. (Text 1)*
>
> *Conceptions of childhood appeared that were **more humane** than those of centuries past." (Text 1)*

Authorial evaluations are embedded within explanations of the theory as in Text 1. Evaluations also constitute distinct schematic stages in the explanations of many theories, entitled "contributions and limitations". In these evaluative sections, the author tends to present the contributions and limitations of the theories as established facts through the choice of "fact-like" reporting verbs (e.g., *indicates, shows*), (Hyland, 1999). The sources of these "facts" are generic, unspecified participants, (e.g., **Research** *indicates*, **Many researchers**), (Hyland, 1999a). It is noticeable that these 'facts' are supported with minimal or no citations.

> *"Generic unspecified participants (in bold) and verbal processes (underlined) construing propositions as "facts"*
>
> **Research** <u>indicates</u> *that Piaget underestimated the competencies of infants and preschoolers.*
>
> *This discovery has led **many researchers** <u>to conclude</u> that the maturity of children's thinking may depend on their familiarity with the task and the kind of knowledge sampled.*
>
> *Finally, **many studies** <u>show</u> that children's performance on Piagetian problems can be improved with training."*
> (examples from Berk, 1997:21)

The narrative structure is realized through temporal information organizing textual development at a macro level. That is, temporal information is foregrounded at the beginning of each paragraph, for example in Text 1 *The seventeenth century Enlightenment;* and in subsequent paragraphs: *In the eighteenth century; A century after Rousseau.* Other narrative elements are specific human participants (*Locke*), and past tense processes (e.g., *brought, viewed, described, opposed*). While the narrative structure is largely a result of the diachronic overview introducing and mapping the theories of the discipline, it is noteworthy that the explanation of theorists' ideas and theories mirrors the academic discourse community's practice of building up knowledge claims by drawing on the work of other theorists in the field. Clusters of reporting processes (e.g., *Baldwin argued, Jean Piaget theorized, Bandura has emphasized*), as well as circumstantial elements of angle (e.g., according to Vygotsky) result in a rich intertextual dimension of paraphrased and quoted texts, a dimension which is intrinsic to professional academic discourses. However, unlike the professional discourse, the supporting citations are less in evidence or even absent.

The elements of "grand narrative" structure and regulative discourse identified in the child development text function primarily to reproduce and map disciplinary knowledge in a way which is accessible to novice students. Seen from this perspective, the pedagogic discourse of child development instantiated in the textbook is an unsuitable one for apprenticing students to participate as mature members of the disciplinary discourse community. It downplays the socially and rhetorically constructed nature of academic discourse, and through the grand narrative elements presents a relatively static, uncontested map of existing disciplinary knowledge. Similar findings have been reported in the fields of geology (Love, 1991, 1993) and genetics (Myers, 1992).

The Socializing Role of Pedagogic Discourses

While the notions of recontextualization and grand narrative structures emphasize the distance between the pedagogic discourse of a discourse community and its mature counterpart, another perspective has been to emphasize the relatedness between the discourse of learning and teaching and the mature discourse. Such a perspective emphasizes the apprenticeship role that the pedagogic discourse plays in socializing novice members to the discourse and epistemologies of the discipline.

For educational linguists working within the systemic functional framework, the function of specialist pedagogic discourses has been regarded as primarily to apprentice students to the specialist ways of knowing of the discipline. Linguistic research examining textbooks from the fields of history (Coffin, 1997; Veel and Coffin, 1996; Martin, 1991; Martin *et al.*, 1991), and science (Veel, 1997; Veel, 1998; Christie, 1998) has detailed the ways in which the pedagogic discourses of these disciplines construct the experiential worlds of these fields. Of particular interest is the way in which language is used to shunt students from commonsense views of the world to uncommonsense worlds of disciplinary knowledge (Martin *et al.*, 1991; Halliday and Martin, 1993; Halliday, 1999).

Introducing the Experiential World of Child Development

This section examines the language of the textbook as a means of apprenticing students to a discipline's specialist ways of knowing. It attempts to identify in what ways the language of the textbook introduces and constructs the world of child development for novice students.

In the child development text, the logogenetic unfolding of the chapters moves the student from the commonsense world of everyday experience into the "uncommonsense" way of interpreting experience in the discipline. Many chapters begin with a story or anecdote from everyday experience, such as a sequence of events, or observations. These vignettes are written in a congruent spoken style with little grammatical metaphor and low levels of lexical density (Halliday, 1985; 1994). In some instances the anecdotes are followed by rhetorical questions which seek explanations for the observed phenomena, or explanations. In other instances, as in Text 2, the vignettes are followed by the disciplinary "naming" of the observed phenomena, which is the focus of the chapter. The lexicogrammatical choices of the rhetorical questions and explanations typically shunt the students towards the uncommonsense incongruent language of the disciplinary discourse. For example:

> *Text 2*
>
> *"(Introduction to Chapter 11: Self and Social Understanding)*
>
> *"Grandpa, look at my shirt!" exclaimed 4-year-old Ellen at her family's annual reunion. "See, it's got the three bears on it and their house and..."*
>
> *Ellen's voice trailed off as she realized all eyes were turned toward her 1-year-old cousin, who was about to take his first steps. As little David tottered forward, the grownups laughed and cheered. No one, not even Grandpa, who was usually so attentive and playful, took note of Ellen and her new shirt.*
>
> *Ellen felt a twinge of jealously and retreated to the bedroom, where she threw a blanket over her head. Arms outstretched, she peered through the blanket's loose weave and made her way back to the living room, where she saw Grandpa leading David about the room. "Here I come, the scary ghost," announced Ellen as she purposefully bumped into David, who toppled over and burst into tears.*
>
> *Pulling off the blanket, Ellen quickly caught her mother's disapproving expression. "I couldn't see him, Mom! The blanket was over my face," Ellen sheepishly explained.*
>
> *Ellen's mother insisted that she help David up and apologize at once. At the same time, she marveled at Ellen's skillful capacity for trickery.*
>
> . . . .
>
> *This chapter addresses the development of **social cognition**, or how children come to understand their multifaceted social world."*

(Berk 1994:423)

Toward the end of this narrative Ellen's combined actions are named by her mother as "Ellen's skillful capacity for trickery". There follows a disciplinary naming and classifying of this broader phenomenon as "the development of social cognition". The grammar reconstrues, or reconstructs semiotically (Halliday, 1998:185) experience construed as actions, to experience construed as a kind of entity. In the final phase of the logogenetic unfolding of this text, the disciplinary naming includes taxonomic information in the nominal group, the "kind of" cognition that is a part of a child's overall development. In this sense, the term "social" acquires a technical meaning in the disciplinary taxonomy of child development.

experience construed as process

She	purposefully	bumped into	David
Actor	Circumstance	Process	Goal

experience construed as entity

Ellen's	skillful	capacity	for trickery
Deictic	Epithet	Thing	Qualifier

taxonomizing and technicalizing

the	development	of social cognition	
Deictic	Thing	Qualifier	
		Classifier	Thing

This strategy functions not only to shift students from commonsense meanings to "uncommonsense" disciplinary ones. It also models aspects of a fundamental methodology of the discipline: the role of observation in the research process. In her introduction Berk refers to one of the philosophies of the textbook as to provide "an appreciation of basic research strategies to investigate child development" (p. xv), and the subject outline refers to the requirement to "apply the theoretical perspectives to the observation and analysis of children's behaviours"[3]. Berk lists the other aims of the textbooks as follows:

---

3.   Education 1(EDUF 111), 1999, Subject Outline, Faculty of Education, University of Wollongong.

1. an understanding of the diverse array of theories in the field and the strengths and shortcomings of each

2. knowledge of both the sequence of child development and the processes that underlie it

3. an appreciation of the impact of context and culture on child development

4. a sense of the interdependency of all domains of development: physical, cognitive, emotional and social (p. xv–xvi)

While Aims 1 and 2 are primarily knowledge transmitting aims, they are also concerned with identifying the theories of the field, the sequence of child development, and the processes. The focus of Aims 3 and 4 can be seen as transmitting understanding about methodological concerns of the discipline. In some respects, these Aims reflect the professional psychologist's task of observing and explaining the experiential world of child development. In the context of the discipline of Primary Education, an implicit goal is applying Aims 1–4 to the classroom.

The ways in which language identifies and orders the specialist world of child development in the textbook is the focus of the next section. The discussion draws primarily on the discourse descriptions by systemic functional linguists in Halliday (1994), Halliday and Martin (1993), and Martin and Veel (1998).

Defining (Naming)

The process of defining, or naming a phenomenon is a means by which technicality is built up in the discourse. Wignell *et al.* refer to technicality "as the use of terms or expressions (but mostly nominal group constituents) with a specialized field specific meaning" (Wignell, *et al.*, 1993:144). In the following examples, most of the technical terms have an everyday meaning; however, the process of naming them gives the terms a new value relevant to the field (p. 139). In the child development text the process of defining occurs mostly through relational identifying processes (Halliday, 1994). These are processes of being, in which one entity is used to identify another. Structurally, that which is to be identified is the Token, and the explanation is the Value (Halliday, 1994:122).

1. [Token:] Nature [Relational: identifying] is understood to be [Value:] the hereditary information we receive from our parents... that signals the body to grow and affects all our characteristics and skills. (p. 7)

2. Whereas [Token:] nurture [Relational: identifying] represents [Value:] the complex forces of the physical and social world that children encounter in their homes, neighbourhoods, schools and communities. (p. 7).

3. [Token:] Cognitive development [Rel: id] is [Value:] the inner process and products of the mind that lead to "knowing". (p. 211)

Technical terms are also introduced in a less direct way through clause complex sequences which include verbal and mental processes with circumstantial elements of Manner. The Senser or Sayer is typically realized as a specific human participant (e.g., *Pavlov, Vygotsky*), while the Phenomenon is realized by an anaphoric referent (e.g., *it*). The technical term is introduced in the participant role of circumstantial element of Manner (e.g., *as a zone of proximal development; as classical conditioning*). This transitivity pattern, construing how a theorist represents a particular phenomenon, results in an implicit definition of that phenomenon. The anaphoric referent typically can refer to a nominal group (e.g., 4. *make believe play*), or embedded clause in a nominal group (e.g., 5. [[*that behaviours are learnt*]]), which can be the phenomenon subsequently renamed as a technical "thing": a phenomenon which has a value in the discipline. The phenomenon is implicitly defined through how the theorist regarded or described it. In some instances, a quasi definition or explanation is provided, such as in the non-defining clause *in which children advance themselves as they try out a wide variety of challenging skills* (4). However, this implicit way of defining a newly introduced technical term, or a term that has been technicalized, can result in some ambiguity. That is, it would not be necessarily clear to a novice what relation the grammar is establishing between *make believe play* and *zone of proximal development:* whether the relation is one of defining $x = y$, whether it serves to classify in terms of x *has the characteristic of y,* or whether y *is in a part whole relationship to x.*

4.   In accord with his emphasis on social experience and language as vital forces in cognitive development, Vygotsky (1933/1978) granted make-believe play a prominent place in his theory.

[Senser:] He [Process:] regarded [Phenomenon:] it [Manner:] as a unique, broadly influential zone of proximal development, in which children advance themselves as they try out a wide variety of challenging skills. (p. 102)

5.   Ivan Pavlov had a strong belief [[that behaviours are learnt]], and [Sayer:] he [Process:] explains [Phenomenon:] it [Manner:] as "classical conditioning".

This implicit way of introducing and defining new terms, however, contributes to the constructed sense of disciplinary knowledge. The naming of a phenomenon occurs via the manner in which individual theorists regarded or interpreted that phenomenon. It also plays an important logogenetic function in developing a taxonomy of child development theories. The specific human actor is reconstrued as a deictic element in the nominal group structure, while the process of saying or perceiving becomes, through nominalization, an abstract entity in the nominal group. That is:

6.   Vygotsky's view of make believe play*

*other realizations in the text are classifying: e.g., "the Vygotskian view; the Piagetian view

Classifying (Ordering)

The process of naming phenomena and thereby introducing the technical vocabulary of the discourse enables the ordering and classification of the experiential world of child development. Once phenomena have been given a technical name, they can be systematically related to each other through taxonomies (Wignell *et al.*153). Wignell *et al.* describe a taxonomy as "an ordered, systematic classification of some phenomena based on superordination or composition (1993:

137). A preliminary investigation suggests that taxonomizing plays a major logogenetic role in the organization of the child development textbook. However, it is a linguistic one rather than a diagrammatic one. In Text 3, two perspectives on the nature of child development are introduced. These are shown in a taxonomic relationship in Figure 19.2.

Text 3

VIEWS OF THE DEVELOPING CHILD
"Recently, the mother of a 16-month-old boy named Angelo reported to me with amazement that her young son pushed a toy car across the living room floor while making a motorlike sound, "Brmmmm, brmmmm," for the first time. "We've never shown him how to do that!" exclaimed Angelo's mother. "Did he make that sound up himself," she inquired, "or did he copy it from some other child at day care?"

Angelo's mother has asked a puzzling question about the nature of children. It contrasts two basic perspectives: the organismic, or active position, with the mechanistic, or passive point of view.

Organismic theories assume that...

In contrast, mechanistic theories... (pp. 5–6)

Figure 19.2
Taxonomy of Theories of Child Development

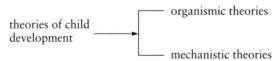

The next branch of the taxonomy involves classifying and ordering organismic and mechanistic theories of child development. In the development of the taxonomy this is a recursive process, as at one level the next branch of the taxonomy is systematically introduced mainly through composition. A typical transitivity structure is of relational possessive processes, (*a consists of x, y, z*). These relational possessive processes are typically preceded by mental processes with specific human participants as actors (*the theorists*) with whom the components of the theory are linked (e.g., *Piaget theorised*). In example 7, the relational possessive process in which the taxonomic relation of composition is established is embedded in the Phenomenon of the mental process. The taxonomic relations are shown in Figure 19.3.

7.   [Senser:] Jean Piaget [Process:] theorised
      that cognitive development may only be achieved through stages, and that each individual stage was accompanied by a period of development.
      [Senser:] He [Process:] believed [Phenomenon:] these stages to consist of the Sensorimotor Stage, the Preoperational Stage, 2–7 years, the Concrete Operational Stage, 7–11 years, as well as the Formal Operational Stage, 11 years up.

Figure 19.3
Taxonomy of Piaget's Stages of Cognitive Development

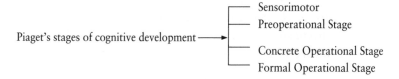

The Dual Status and Role of a Disciplinary Pedagogic Discourse: A Model

It appears that the language of the child development textbook plays a significant role in socializing students to the experiential world of child development. By moving students from commonsense views of the world towards the "uncommonsense" disciplinary ones, and by modelling the epistemological practice such as observation and the discursive ones of naming and classifying, the pedagogic discourse can be seen to apprentice students into the discursive practices of the discipline. However, as the earlier investigation from the same text showed, pedagogic discourses are in some regards unsuitable for apprenticing students as they downplay the constructed nature of disciplinary knowledge. That is, the pedagogic discourse functions primarily to transmit knowledge, a process which results in the representation of disciplinary knowledge as static and canonical.

These dual perspectives of pedagogic discourse are shown in Figure 19.4. The recontextualized aspect of pedagogic discourse is represented as characteristic of pedagogic discourse, where the instructional discourse (ID) is embedded within the regulative discourse (RD), after Bernstein (1990:183). The different perspectives on pedagogic discourse are shown in terms of their distance or relatedness to the mature discourse. The participants are shown in relation to their associated discourses.

Figure 19.4
A Model of Pedagogic Discourse in a Discourse Community

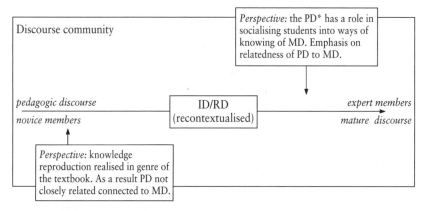

*Note: PD refers to pedagogic discourse; MD refers to mature discourse of the discourse community

Participants and Social Practices

The model of pedagogic discourse in Figure 19.4 accommodates different perspectives on the role and status of pedagogic discourse. However, it does not show the ways in which students can begin to perceive disciplinary knowledge as constructed and therefore contestable. That is, it does not explain how students can learn to understand that disciplinary knowledge can be disordered and "unknown", the point of departure for this paper. In order to do this, it is necessary to consider other contextual factors, particularly the perspective of participants and the role of social practices.

Acknowledging the socially and rhetorically constructed nature of academic knowledge is intrinsic to understanding the discursive practices of academic disciplines (Bazerman, 1992; Hyland, 2000). In academic discourse communities knowledge is perceived by its members as contestable and propositional rather than a set of "truths" or facts. Writing is therefore a process of interpreting, arguing, criticizing and persuading. Making knowledge claims involves not only reporting information but persuading the disciplinary community to accommodate new claims (Hunston, 1994). It also involves mapping out a research niche, a process which involves negotiating with prior texts and their claims (Hyland, 2000; Bazerman 1992), and engaging in politeness strategies (Myers, 1996, 1999; Hyland, 1999b).

These professional academic discursive practices are too multi-faceted to be simply labelled as "critical analysis", yet the terms *critical analysis,* a *critical approach,* and *critical thinking* are frequently used by the academy to characterize the approach required in undergraduate student writing and in student learning generally. While critical analysis is arguably not the same as the socially and epistemologically motivated discursive practices of a discipline, there are distinct commonalities which are the result of viewing disciplinary knowledge as contestable.

Analyzing and contesting received knowledge (often described as *critically analyze*) are practices which are central to undergraduate writing and learning. These values are transmitted to students in texts such as essay questions, assessment criteria, as well as in subject aims and objectives. The practice of critical analysis, however, is a source of confusion for novice students, to whom it is not necessarily clear why this discursive practice is required. That is, students are unclear whether "doing critical analysis" is an institutional requirement, or results from the disciplinary context and its practices, or is merely a reflection of tutors and lecturers' individual preferences (Plum, 1998; Lea and Street, 1998).

Data for this discussion are institutional documents from a first year Primary Education subject, Child Development (EDUF111); interviews with EDUF students; and EDUF student essays.

Participants: The Students

To successfully complete the Child Growth and Development subject, primary education students are expected to be able to:

- identify the range of theories associated with the development of children;
- apply the theoretical perspectives to the observation and analysis of children's behaviours; and
- critically evaluate the theories presented

(EDUF 111, Semester 1, 1999, Subject Outline, Faculty of Education, University of Wollongong)

Of particular interest for establishing the relation between the practices of the mature discourse community and the pedagogic discourse (here meaning the discourse in which the students learn), is the directive "critically evaluate the theories presented". Not surprisingly, the task of critically analyzing and evaluating theories was therefore a major task in both essay questions for this subject.

Six of the seven students who were interviewed from the 1999 first year cohort of *Child Growth and Development* students identified their perceptions of their lecturer's expectations of their writing in terms of critical analysis. This focus was embedded in their awareness of the intertextual nature of academic discourse. For example:

Angie

There's a big difference. ...

Well, I mean when you write at school it's ... basically you're doing a lot of copying from books, whereas now it's gotta be your own ideas, and how... they've got their own style how they want you to write. They want you to analyze it, dissect it, and that's really difficult, very difficult. Very different from what you're used to. I mean the other students all had the same problems.

Raelene

I think they like a lot of analysis, um ... I think they probably would like the kind of writing that shows that you can analyze and understand what it is you're writing about, rather than just writing to, ... to um.. just to show them that what you're writing ... you understand.

While the students recognize that lecturers want to know students' ideas, and students are expected to analyze and "dissect", it is apparent from both Angie's response, (*that's really difficult, very difficult*), as well as Raelene's hazy understanding of lecturers' expectations that the practice of critical analysis is complex and difficult to apply to received knowledge. While students may acknowledge the requirement to critically analyze and "dissect" texts, studies by composition theorists have shown that novice students see pedagogic texts as autonomous and authoritative (for example, Haas, 1994). This mismatch between students' perception of the status of knowledge in pedagogic texts, and their emerging understanding of an aspect of disciplinary discursive practice is no doubt a source of tension for students. Another likely mismatch is a lecturer's understanding of the purpose of critical analysis in assessment tasks (replicating a disciplinary discursive practice) compared to a student's perception of the same task (satisfying an institutional requirement).

Intertextuality in the Student Writing

While novice students are unlikely to be able to contribute in any real sense to making new meanings in the discipline, the institutional focus on critically analyzing received knowledge is an important step in "thinking the unthinkable". That is, the process of analyzing and critiquing established theories in some respects fosters the perception that much disciplinary knowledge is propositional, and that thinking in this way is how new knowledge is created. In this sense, critically analyzing received knowledge functions to replicate in the student writing an intrinsic academic discursive practice.

There is considerable evidence in the student essays of intertextuality to support this claim. Intertextuality is here interpreted broadly to mean reference to other texts. In the student texts the combination of paraphrased and quoted texts is the main means by which knowledge is built up and established. Evidence of intertextuality is not only established through citations, but through reporting processes (Thomas and Hawes, 1994). While this can be perceived as primarily a form of knowledge telling (e.g., *Berk reports that Piaget thought that, etc.*), the process of reporting provides the potential to question and probe received knowledge. Table 19.1 shows the ratio of quoted clauses to the overall number of clauses in the student essays (Quoted Clauses: Total Clauses = QC: TC), and the ratio of paraphrased clauses to the total number of clauses (Paraphrased Clauses: Total Clauses = PC: TC).

Table 19.1
Ratio of Citations (number of clauses) to Overall Number of Clauses in Student Essays[4]

Student	1	2	3	4	5	6	7	8
QC:TC	28:120	14:125	11:119	10:104	0:94	40:85	1:109	19:130
PC:TC	8:120	42:125	0:119	49:104	42:94	0:85	18:109	37:130
Total citations shown as % of total clauses	30 %	45 %	9 %	57 %	45 %	47 %	17 %	43 %
Number of references in reference list	2	10	11	5	0	0	3	5

The ratio of the number of clauses containing cited information to overall clauses ranged from only 9% to 57%. While a significant number of clauses containing quoted or paraphrased material is to be expected in academic texts, this data has been included to show that novice students, even those submitting their first university essays, are aware to an extent of the academic culture's practice of building disciplinary knowledge through citations.

Conclusion and Implications

An intrinsic component of disciplinary learning for novice students is learning the discursive practices of the discourse community. Yet novice students' textual experience of the disciplinary discourse is often via a

---

4. The figures given in Table 19.1 can only be viewed as an estimate, as it not always clear in the student writing how far the paraphrased citation extends. Also, it is not clear whether the number of cited clauses is indeed an accurate indication. For example, the tutor's marginal comments in student 3's essay indicated that more accurate referencing for paraphrased citations was required.

textbook, a pedagogic text which because of its generic purpose can only apprentice students to some of the discursive practices of the discipline. Moving students towards a perception of disciplinary knowledge as propositional and contestable, rather than as static and authoritative, seems to occur via regulative institutional requirements such as assessment criteria; however different participant understandings of the *function* of these requirements is a likely cause of confusion for students and frustration for teaching staff. While tutors and lecturers may intrinsically perceive the function of analysis as *replicating* an intrinsic disciplinary practice, and how new meanings are made, students are likely to view the same practice as merely satisfying an institutional requirement.

A model of discourse community which accommodates novice and mature disciplinary participants, their associated pedagogic and professional texts, and the associated social practices is one way of attempting to reconcile these different understandings, and assisting students to come to terms with the culture of a discipline and the university. Such a model may also assist students in viewing regulative institutional discursive practices as less of a prescriptive straightjacket, and more of a means to explore a populated disciplinary space in which new meanings are possible.

Reference

1. Alfred, G. and A. Thelen. 1993. Are textbooks contributions to scholarship? *College Composition and Communication* 44 (4): 466–477.

2. Bazerman, C. 1992. From cultural criticism to disciplinary participation: Living with powerful words. In *Writing, teaching and learning in the disciplines*, edited by A. Herrington and C. Moran. New York: Modern Languages Association of America, 61–68.

3. Bereiter, C. and M. Scardamalia. 1987. *The psychology of written composition.* Hillsdale, NJ: Lawrence Erlbaum.

4. Berk, L. 1997. *Child development,* 4th ed. Boston: Allyn & Bacon.

5. Bernstein, B. 1975. *Towards a theory of educational transmissions:* Class, codes and control. Vol. 3. London: Routledge & Kegan Paul.

6. _____ . 1990. *The structuring of pedagogic discourse: Class, codes, and control.* London: Routledge.

7. Bizzell, P. 1982. College composition: Initiation into the academic discourse community. *Curriculum Inquiry* 12 (2): 191–207.

8. Candlin, C., and G. Plum. 1999. Engaging with the challenges of interdiscursivity in academic writing: Researchers, students and tutors. In *Writing: Texts, processes and practices*, edited by C. Candlin and K. Hyland. London: Longman, 193–217.

9. Christie, F. 1998. Science and apprenticeship: The pedagogic discourse. In *Reading science*, edited by J. R. Martin and R. Veel. London: Routledg, 152–180..

10. Coffin, C. 1997. Constructing and giving value to the past: An investigation into secondary school history. In *Genre and institutions*, edited by F. Christie, and J. R. Martin. London: Cassell, 196–230.

11. Fuller, G. 1998. Cultivating science: Negotiating discourse in the popular texts of Stephen Jay Gould. In *Reading science: Critical and functional perspectives on discourses of science*, edited by J. R. Martin and R. Veel. London: Routledge, 35–62.

12. Haas, C. 1994. Learning to read biology: One student's rhetorical development in college. *Written Communication* 11:43–84.

13. Halliday, M. A. K. 1978. *Language as a social semiotic.* London: Edward Arnold.

14. _____ . 1985. *Spoken and written language.* Geelong, Vic: Deakin University Press.

15. _____ . 1994. *An introduction to functional grammar,* 2nd ed. London: Arnold.

16. _____ .1998. Things and relations: Regrammaticalizing experience as technical knowledge. In *Reading science: Critical and functional perspectives on discourses of science*, edited by J. R. Martin and R. Veel. London: Routledge, 185–235.

17. Halliday, M. A. K. 1999. Grammar and the construction of educational knowledge. In *Language analysis, description and pedagogy.* edited by R. Berry, B. Asker, K. Hyland and M. Lam. Hong Kong: Hong Kong University of Science and Technology and Lingan University.

18. _____ and J. R. Martin, 1993. *Writing Science: Literacy and discursive power.* London: Falmer Press.

19. Hunston, S. 1994. Evaluation and organization in a sample of written academic discourse. In *Advances in written text analysis*, edited by M. Coulthard. London: Routledge, 191–218.

20.   Hyland, K. 1999a. Talking to students: Metadiscourse in introductory coursebooks. *English for Specific Purposes* 18 (1): 3–26.

21.   _____ . 1999b. Disciplinary discourses: Writer stance in research articles. In *Writing: Texts, processes and practices*, edited by C. Candlin and K. Hyland. London: Longman, 99–121.

22.   _____ . 2000. *Disciplinary discourses: Social interactions in academic writing.* Harlow, England: Longman.

23.   Lea, M. and B. Street. 1999. Writing as academic literacies: Understanding textual practices in higher education. In *Writing: Texts, processes and practices* , edited by C. Candlin and K. Hyland. London: Longman, 62–81.

24.   Love, A. 1991. Process and product in geology: An investigation of some discourse features of two introductory textbooks. *English for Specific Purposes* 10:89–109.

25.   _____ . 1993. Lexico-grammatical features of geology textbooks: Process and product revisited. *English for Specific Purposes* 12:197–218.

26.   Martin, J. R. 1991. Nominalization in science and humanities: Distilling knowledge and scaffolding text. In *Functional and systemic linguistics*, edited by E. Ventola. Berlin: Mouton de Gruyter, 307–337.

27.   _____ and R. Veel. 1998. *Reading science: Critical and functional perspectives on discourses of science.* London: Routledge, 185–235.

28.   _____, P. Wignell, S. Eggins and J. Rothery. 1991. Secret English: Discourse technology in a junior secondary school. In *Genre approaches to literacy: Theories and practices*, edited by B. Cope, and M. KalantzisAnnandale, Sydney: Common Ground.

29.   Myers, G. 1992. Textbooks and the sociology of written knowledge. *English for Specific Purposes* 3 (11): 3–17.

30.   Plum, G. (1998). Doing psychology, doing writing: Student voices on academic writing in psychology. In *Researching academic literacies*, edited by C. Candlin and G. Plum. Macquarie University: National Centre for English Language Teaching and Research (NCELTR)/Centre for Language in Social Life, 211–288.

31.   Thomas, S. and T. Hawes. 1994. Reporting verbs in medical journal articles. *English for Specific Purposes* 13 (2): 129–148.

32.   Swales, J. 1990. *Genre analysis.* Cambridge: Cambridge University Press.

33.   _____ . 1995. The role of the textbook in EAP writing research. *English for Specific Purposes* 14 (1): 3–18.

34.   Veel, R. 1997. Learning how to mean — scientifically speaking: Apprenticeship into scientific discourse in the secondary school. In *Genre and institutions*, edited by F. Christie and J. R. Martin. London: Cassell, 161–195.

35. Veel, R. 1998. The greening of school science: Ecogenesis in secondary classrooms, In *Reading Science*, edited by J. R. Martin and R. Veel. London: Routledge, 114–151.

36. _____ and C. Coffin. 1996. Learning to think like an historian: The language of secondary school history. In *Literacy in Society*, edited by R. Hasan and G. Williams. London: Longman.

37. Wignell, P., J. R. Martin and S. Eggins. 1993. The discourse of Geography: Ordering and explaining the experiential world. In *Writing science*, edited by M. A. K. Halliday and J. R. Martin, London: The Falmer Press.

38. Young, L. 1990. *Language as behaviour, language as code: A study of academic English*. Amsterdam: John Benjamins.

Discourses of

Literature and Creativity

20

Framing Creativity: Contradictory and Complementary Discourses within the Context of Educational Reform in Hong Kong

Pauline Burton and Dino Mahoney

Introduction

In the year 2000, Hong Kong, a specially administered region of the People's Republic of China, officially embarked on a government-sanctioned series of education reforms. The proposed reforms have been embodied in a substantial text, the Education Commission's *Reform Proposals*, and in a widely distributed summary called *Excel and Grow*, both sub-titled *Education Blueprint for the 21st Century*. These documents call for a radical revision of the Hong Kong education system. They are the textual spearheads of a battle to topple the primacy of rote learning, examinations and teacher-centredness in the Hong Kong education system, and replace them with a reformed student-centred system that emphasizes the student's personal development and creativity.

This chapter examines how creativity is framed within the reform proposal documents, and investigates tensions and contradictions within the discourse of these reforms. Following Fairclough's model of discourse as text (Fairclough, 1992, 1995), which examines relationships and inherent contradictions between discourse at the level of the social situation and of the social institution, this official framing is then compared with the framing of creativity within the discourse of practising teachers. In Figure 20.1, we present a model of these contradictory discourses in the context of Hong Kong society as a whole:

Figure 20.1
Contradictory Discourses in the Context of Hong Kong Society as a Whole

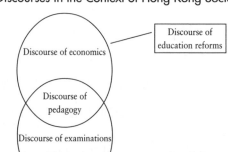

Within each of the overlapping discourses shown in this diagram, various tensions and discourse strands are apparent. We turn first to the discourse of the education reforms.

The Discourse of the Education Reforms: Tensions and Manifestations

Discourse tensions within the education reform proposals are manifest both in the text of the consultation documents and in the images chosen for the cover of *Excel and Grow*. We will examine, in turn, "shadow" discourses from the past; dominant discourses from the present; and underlying assumptions about the desired model of Hong Kong education as presented in images, as well as written text.

Shadow Discourses from the Past

Some of the underlying discourse tensions within the current proposals for education reform in Hong Kong can be identified as arising from discourses that have evolved historically. These may be present as a "shadow" or "ghost" discourse rather than being fully manifested: they serve to foreground new discourses. Occasionally they surface, but only in the context of a rebuttal. These "shadow" discourses can be identified as follows:

1. Discourse of the British colonial era, e.g., "Nevertheless, in the existing... admissions systems students are induced to

spend precious learning time on unnecessary drilling..."(*Excel and Grow*, 2000:3)

2. Discourse of Confucian Chinese culture, e.g., "...public examinations should not be used as the 'whip' or 'wand'" (*Reform Proposals*, 2000:55).

The first of these discourses arises from the British colonial education system, which was designed to produce passive, albeit numerate and literate, low-paid members of the colonial workforce. This was achieved through making the student a passive recipient of received knowledge. This approach was overlaid with colonial military notions of order in which schools were run on strict hierarchical lines, the Headmaster at the top, the student at the bottom. Students, like soldiers, were expected to give unquestioning obedience: learning was through repetition, memory drills, tests and examinations that were the educational equivalent of an assault course.

The colonial need for an obedient, functionally educated workforce was aided by the assimilation of conservative notions of Chinese educational practice, which also enshrined the transmission model of education. Traditional Chinese education involved Confucian notions of humble and respectful students, who knew nothing, being filled with knowledge from masters or teachers who knew everything. Learning was characterized as a process of copying or imitating a master or model and by rote learning of revered texts. The Confucian principle of dividing society into segregated levels was reflected in the hierarchical ordering of schools and the severity of tests needed to move up from one level of education to another.

Colonial education authorities in Hong Kong found it convenient to use perceived traditions of Confucian education to legitimize the production of a literate numerate workforce to act as economic cannon fodder for the prospering colony. If outspoken educators criticized the Hong Kong education system for being too conservative there was a convenient excuse to hand: Hong Kong schools are not conservative because that is what we wish, but because they are Chinese schools and therefore follow the conservative principles of Confucian social philosophy.

Dominant Discourses within the Reform Proposals

Two dominant and fully manifested discourses can be identified within the education reform proposals:

1. The discourse of socio-economic planning. This discourse, used to frame, justify and "sell" the education reforms to the schools and society at large, has overt features of economic discourse, e.g., "strengthen Hong Kong's competitive edge" (*Reform Proposals*:2)

2. The pedagogic discourse of liberal progressive reform, e.g., "to enable every individual to pursue all-round development through life-long learning" (*Reform Proposals*:iv).

The first of these discourses effectively frames the discourse of creativity in terms of economic justification: the economic benefits to be gained and sustained provide the rationale for the reform proposals. This discourse clearly reveals that the impetus for education reform springs from economic considerations, as did the colonial education system before it. Economic times have changed and the need for a basically educated manual workforce has given way to the need for a more cerebral and adaptable one. This has come about through a historical shift in the Hong Kong economy away from a manufacturing industrial base to a reliance on service and knowledge-based industries.

The education reform document thus assumes a convergence of objectives between the discourse of social economics, which frames educational needs in terms of economic necessity, and the discourse of progressive liberal education reform, which frames them in terms of individual self-realization, growth and development. The assumption is that an education system that is good for the economy and society must also be good for the individual, not the other way around. Giving an economic frame to the discourse of reform makes the search for "creativity" extrinsically motivated and puts it into conflict with liberal progressive notions of creativity as intrinsically motivated.

The economic framing of the reforms is highlighted in the opening paragraph:

> *Education holds the key to the all-round development of*
> *a person and prepares him/her for work and life.*
> *Education nurtures talents for the society and promotes*
> *its prosperity and progress. In an ever-changing society,*
> *it is imperative that our education system keep pace with*
> *the times and be responsive to the needs of learners. To*
> *design an education system for the future, we must*
> *envision future changes in the society in order to cater*
> *for the needs of learners in the new society and to define*
> *the new role and functions of education in the changed*
> *environment.* (Reform Proposals: 1)

The tension between the two discourses is apparent in the first sentence through the dichotomous definition of education both as all-round self-development and as preparation for work and life. The phrase "work and life" has a further, embedded dichotomy in which both are subsumed within the same defining frame, the sub-text being that they are interchangeable.

The importance of the economy as a driver of education reform is highlighted in the positioning of the following two sections, "Fundamental changes around the world" and "Developments in Hong Kong". Set at the very opening of the report, a position according weight and importance to content, the language is predominantly that of economics and commerce rather than that of education:

> *"Our staunch belief in the market economy, the level*
> *playing field, the simple tax system, the rule of law, the*
> *free flow of information and a dynamic and enterprising*
> *workforce are the key elements in sustaining Hong Kong's*
> *competitive edge."* (Reform Proposals: 2)

That economic discourse can be used to frame educational reform reflects Hong Kong's profoundly commercial culture; it also reveals the government's belief that it can best legitimize or "sell" education reform by an appeal to consumerist pragmatism.

Further evidence of this double discourse of economy and pedagogy can be found in an interview with Professor Cheng Kai-ming, one of the key policy-makers behind the reforms, in a leading Hong Kong English-language newspaper.

> *"Education is not only an economic investment but also a social investment and a leverage to create more opportunities, mobility and equity."* (South China Morning Post, 2 December 2000)

Professor Cheng is a proponent of progressive, student-centred education: but within the wider context of Hong Kong culture he is also able publicly and confidently to promote educational reform in the frame of economic discourse.

The booklet *Excel and Grow* (2000), a summary of the full edition of the reform proposals, was widely distributed in English and Chinese for public consultation. This text again foregrounds the economic necessity of the education reforms in the opening paragraph:

> *"With the political, economic and cultural changes taking place in Hong Kong and around the world, we are witnessing a trend towards globalization, a knowledge-based economy and cultural diversity"* (p. 1).

An interesting metaphor follows in which people are likened to commodities: "...there is an urgent need... for... people to... upgrade themselves" (p. 1).

This is followed by an economic clarion call: "there is an urgent need to... strengthen Hong Kong's competitive edge" (p. 1).

This foregrounded economic necessity is then backed up with several references to creativity:

> *"To achieve the above objectives, we need a huge number of talents with diverse abilities. They should possess the following qualities... adept at self-learning, articulate,*

flexible, with good organizational skills, a sense of commitment and creativity" (p. 1).

Creativity returns in a paraphrased form on the same page, "They (people)... need to... devise novel means to solve problems" (p. 1). And later, "To enable every person... (to be)... capable of critical and exploratory thinking, innovating..." (p. 2).

Creativity leaps into the limelight in the penultimate paragraph of Chapter 2:

> *"Our priority should be... enabling... our students to enjoy learning, enhance their effectiveness in communication, and develop their creativity and sense of commitment"* (p. 2).

Creativity is thus regarded as a means to an economic end — "to achieve the above objectives" — rather than an end in itself: and the areas of educational activity in which creativity is to be encouraged are implied by the images on the cover of *Excel and Grow*. It is to these images that we now turn.

Contradictory Images: The Cover of *Excel and Grow*

When asked to interpret the visual discourse of the cover of *Excel and Grow*, a group of nineteen local Hong Kong teachers were found to share a common perception of both an intentional and an unintentional message. The contradictions in the visual discourse appear to mirror the contradictions within the text.

The focus image on the booklet is an aerial view of four yellow-feathered ducks. Closer inspection reveals the ducks to be a mother and father and their two children, a boy and a girl — a duck nuclear family. The family is looking up. The children are looking at a flying laptop computer. The lid of the computer is open; there is a something colourful on the screen. The father duck looks at a flying football and the mother at a flying trumpet. Also flying around are another football, a school satchel, a violin and a tambourine. The ducks are standing in

Figure 20.2
Overlap of Discourse

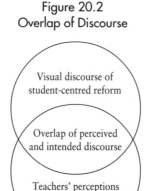

a line, the children book-ended protectively by the parents. The duck family is standing in the middle of a bright green grass field.

All responding teachers were able to read the cover image on two levels. On one level they read what they perceived to be the official intention encoded within the image. On another level they gave a parallel critical reading in which they explored what they perceived as unintentional meanings: something like visual Freudian slips, or contradictions to the officially intended meaning.

On the level of intended meaning the respondents could all see that the image was intended to project a positive image of the education reforms. The family gazing up hopefully was understood as a metaphor for a positive look into a future in which creativity and technology went hand in hand. The respondents saw the upward gaze as conveying the notion of "aspiring towards" something. The inclusion of the whole family was seen as a message that all age groups would receive the necessary education to equip them for such a future world. "The message of the picture is meant to be that education is related to the whole family and all round development."

The bright colours were understood as an intended expression of hope and life. The long shadows were seen as representing sunrise, a bright new start and hence, the education reforms. The green background was thought to mean fertility and growth and to relate to the word "*Grow*" in the title.

On a second, critical level of interpretation, all the teachers commented on the bird's-eye perspective from which the picture is constructed. "We look down on the ducks, the ducks look up. This shows a top-down approach, the reforms come from somewhere up there."

Many of the respondents commented that because the computer, school bag and musical instruments are flying above the duck family this makes these objects and the things they represent both unobtainable and threatening. Many of the responding teachers commented on the expression on the ducks' faces: "The ducks look worried and stressed"

Some respondents saw the duck family as middle class: "The father duck wears a tie and the mother duck a string of pearls, this means they are middle class and it says to me that education reforms are for the middle class only."

Many respondents commented that the notebook computer and the emphasis on music were also "very middle class images". One respondent was puzzled why there was "...too much emphasis on music. Why is there no image of painting or drawing?" Some respondents said that the two-child nuclear family with a child of either gender was "too ideal".

They all said that the choice of ducks for the cover was strange, given their significance within the context of Chinese cultural semiotics. The Chinese idiomatic expression for "spoon-feeding", literally translated into English, is "to fill a duck", in other words, force-feeding. The teachers felt that the cover signalled the message that education and the education reforms were to be "force-fed" or "spoon-fed" to students. The ducks therefore seem to be an image of the old system of "transmission of learning", rather than an image of the proposed new system of student-centred, exploratory, creative learning. One of the teachers commented that the image made her feel that "the ducks are being spoon-fed and that's what I'm doing, I'm not teaching them to think".

Ducks were also seen by the teacher respondents as being "obedient" and easily led: "Ducks like to follow each other or they follow their mother, they go wherever she wants them to go." "I am puzzled why ducks are used, ducks are stupid, they are spoon-fed and they always follow others."

The ducks were unanimously interpreted as an image of passive students following their teachers, rather than active students taking the lead in their own education.

How, then, is the discourse of creativity interpreted by teachers themselves in their professional practice? The next part of this chapter explores the discourse of creativity used by teachers in a Hong Kong secondary school and investigates to what extent this discourse complements or contradicts the discourse of reform embodied in the education reform proposals.

The Discourse of Classroom Teachers: Creativity and Constraints

The fieldwork material presented here was collected in a girls' secondary school, Band One (the upper ability range in the current Hong Kong secondary schools academic ranking system). The medium of instruction is English. The school has excellent results in public examinations and student involvement in a wide range of extra-curricular activities. It has already received Quality Education Fund support from the Government for several projects, including a school musical and developing information technology (echoing key themes from the cover of *Excel and Grow*). The school is thus an active partner in the ongoing discourse of educational reform.

Fieldwork (which started in June 1999) has so far involved interviews with five teachers in the school — two British teachers (Teachers X and Y), and three local — and informal discussions with others, including the Principal; videotaping two lessons by the two British teachers, a first-year poetry and creative writing class, and an A-level English literature class; collecting lesson plans, and extensive samples of student work; focus group interviews with first-year pupils; and participant observation of school events.

We will focus on two pieces of fieldwork data: a first-year poetry lesson, observed and videotaped, by Teacher X, and an interview on creativity with Teacher Y.

In so doing, we intend, in Fairclough's terms, "to consider how relations of power have shaped discourse practices... to situate classroom discourse historically in processes of social struggle and change" (1992:19).

Teacher X: The Lesson

The lesson, which lasted approximately 30 minutes (within a 40-minute single class period) was based on a five-stage lesson plan developed by Teacher X, a native English speaker with several years' teaching experience in Hong Kong.

The lesson—writing poetry about places—uses a poem called "Bird Street" by a Hong Kong-based writer and educator, Mike Murphy. X acknowledges a debt to his work on teaching poetry in the classroom (Murphy, 1993), and that of Maley and others (Maley and Moulding, 1985; Maley and Duff, 1989). She attended a two-day workshop on literature in language at the British Council in Hong Kong: a link to the discourse of liberal progressive educational reform, and thus (historically) to the late 20th century values of the former colonial power.

The lesson we observed is the first stage of a process in which students work in groups, pairs or individually to write their own poems, illustrate them (often with computer-generated art), and have them "published" by the teacher in a class anthology for their own and other classes to read. This, in turn, would further "inspire them to write their own poems", as X observed.

A section of the lesson transcript gives a flavour of the classroom discourse. At this point, the teacher has started to write on the blackboard vocabulary elicited from the class.

> X: Right, do we have any words that rhyme there? Perhaps I could help with a few more, because some of mine rhyme, as

I was doing it earlier on...

SS: Screaming and crying

X: Mmm... (writing on the board) OK, we've got screaming and crying

SS: Happy and lonely and dirty

X: Happy and dirty, OK, near enough... lonely... What's another word for happiness?

SS: Joy

X: Joy. Can you think of something that would rhyme with joy?

SS: Boy

X: Yes... well maybe baby boy... if you cry, what happens? (She mimes the action of wiping tears from her cheeks)

SS: Tears... fears

X: What rhymes...

SS: Fears

X: Well, obviously there's lots of words, but we're just doing this very quickly... tears and fears there... (writing on the board). Right, we're going to write a class poem called "Hospital".

Even from this brief extract, it is clear that this lesson is "traditional" in the sense of being highly structured and teacher-led. Student response is elicited within a controlled frame: responses are validated by repetition and writing on the board by the teacher, who moves freely in the front-of-class space between the seated students and the blackboard. She also controls timing, using "Right" as a discourse marker to move from one phase of activity to the next. A formal feature of poetry—rhyme—is used as a constraint on vocabulary choice, and choice is further prompted by body language.

Nevertheless, the students reply freely, without nomination. They have already gone through several similar classes, and confidently pick up the "script". At one point, where student response and teacher elicitation overlaps, they are ahead of her. They know that they need not fear rejection of their responses as incorrect: their choice of words with matching weak endings as "rhymes" draws only the mild comment "near enough". Through their subsequent writing process, they will move towards greater autonomy; they choose their own sub-topic within the overall theme, and may write in groups or individually as they wish. Their work will be published with little or no teacher intervention, and though comments are given, the work is not graded.

Can this lesson, then, be regarded as part of the pedagogical discourse of creativity? We would argue that it can, especially if seen within its wider context, as the initiating lesson in a cycle of group work and student activity. X's lesson plans are now used as a basis for teaching poetry writing to all first-year classes in the school, with additional material by Teacher Y. Thus, this professional discourse is one in which genre, in Fairclough's sense (1992:26) is privileged both in lesson plans for staff and in instructions and model poems given to students, and may be seen (paradoxically) as facilitating, not inhibiting, creativity: "framing creativity" indeed. As Fairclough comments elsewhere, "being socially constrained does not preclude being creative" (1995:28).

The most serious constraint on creativity, however, is located outside the classroom and the school, though it influences both: the discourse of examinations. Teacher X reports that poetry lessons are less popular with higher classes: Form Four students ask "why are we doing poetry? Is it in the exam?" This leads to consideration of the relationship between conflicting and complementary discourses of creativity and examinations, as shown in Figure 20.3 below. As the interview with Teacher Y indicates, the discourse of pedagogy attempts to effect a compromise between the two.

Teacher Y: The Interview

> *"Discourse is not the majestically unfolding manifestation of a thinking, knowing, speaking subject, but on the contrary, a totality, in which the dispersion of the subject and his discontinuity with himself may be determined"* (Foucault, 1969/1972:55)

Y is also a native speaker of English with several years' teaching experience in Hong Kong. He speaks Cantonese, most of his friends

Figure 20.3
Relationship between Conflicting and Complementary
Discourses of Creativity and Examinations

are local, and he regards Hong Kong as his home. He has completed a Bachelor of Education degree at The University of Hong Kong, studying part-time. Y's testimony is particularly valuable, because of his pivotal role within this particular context of practice. In his situation, different discourses overlap: recent academic and professional thinking on creativity in language and literature teaching, and the utilitarian discourse of students within a competitive examination system and a practical, achievement-oriented culture.

In his own teaching practice, and in the way he constructs that practice through professional interaction and personal reflection, Y negotiates the meaning (meanings?) of creativity through several layers of experience: his own childhood, his subsequent socialization into the discourse of teaching literature in a second language, his professional identity as a teacher, his interaction with other teachers both in the school and outside, and his sense of membership both within the school and in the wider Hong Kong community. The daily frame within which he attempts this negotiation of meaning is the senior secondary classroom, where the discourse of examination success still predominates for both teacher and taught.

Y links creativity with his own early life experience: "I became a teacher because of this word (creativity)". Y's father is an artist, and

Y's first interest was in drawing and painting. Later, he began to think that "there could be creativity involved in teaching", especially in "subjects where you could create something... where there's no exact model, there's no right or wrong". He goes on to comment "creativity in teaching should create something that's unique — each student's response is different". Creativity, he believes, can be "fostered" rather than taught: and though innate ability varies in degree, "everyone has creativity within them".

Y links the study of literature with creativity. Literature, he points out, creates new worlds for the reader. This is essentially an act of imagination on the part of the reader, as well as the writer. "When I found a book that I loved" (as a teenager) "I entered into this whole creative imaginative world... I took the characters on the bus, and I'd be thinking about them". He contrasts this explicitly with the current status of reading in English in Hong Kong: "so much of the reading is a chore in Hong Kong — they read for exams, they read for instructions". However, Y believes that if pupils study literature, "their minds will become extremely creative over time". This belief is also expressed in Cook's hypothesis (1994) that reading literary texts can bring about cognitive change in the reader, by creating new schemata: "there is a type of discourse which has a particular effect on the mind, refreshing and changing our mental representations of the world" (p. 4).

To encourage this receptive creativity, Y asks his students to keep a personal response journal for their reading. Productive creativity, on the other hand, he locates within the frame of the examination system: "that's what the exams require". He does see the product, however, as recycled into the process, as reading other students' essays can prompt further response. Thus, though Y regards creativity as stemming from and expressing the individual, group work "definitely develops it", and Y comments "if you've a good task in the first place, it can foster dialogue... a more open-ended, a more creative question — you can develop from that". Thus, in the pedagogical discourse, personal creativity is seen as a product of dialogue: between reader and text, between teacher and students, between students in group work, and (as we shall see) within the discourse community of practising teachers, both at school and university level.

This dialogic approach places the pedagogical concept of creativity within wider theories of discourse as the joint creation of meaning both by speakers and texts (see, for example, Bakhtin, 1934/1981 and Halliday, 1975). This shifts the idea of creativity away from the more conventional "sudden inspiration" view: indeed, Cropley, in a paper on creativity in the classroom, "explicitly rejects" the sudden inspiration model, because it does not fit his chosen schema: "it does not provide a basis for the systematic, purposeful broadening of students' intellectual ability"(1997:91). The phrase "systematic, purposeful broadening" encodes teacher intervention in — even teacher direction of — the students' creativity, a process which could be clearly seen in Y's A-level class, as in X's Form One class. In this respect, the frames of pedagogical discourse and examination discourse overlap, and indeed the former could be said to serve the latter.

The key question for teachers (as Y and Cropley both indicate) is how creativity can best be fostered in the classroom. The pedagogical discourse of creativity is therefore largely procedural and practical in nature: what approaches and strategies work, both in encouraging individual response and in enabling students to meet the requirements of an examination-driven curriculum — and thus, attempting to negotiate the inherent contradictions between the two.

Paradoxically, it is within the frame of the classroom — constrained by limitations of time, class size, and physical setting, as well as by the requirement to cover the A and AS-level examination curriculum — that Y sees himself most clearly as a creator. Talking about classroom activity, he uses the word "create" several times: "creating the idea to teach... creating along the way". His lexis clusters around this node: "The night before (class), I could have a dream or I could have an idea, and then it would all be changed". This is remarkably close to the popular idea of creativity as sudden inspiration. Y does not write lesson plans, because "there isn't time", but he does go into the classroom knowing what he hopes to achieve: "I do know my goal... just how to get there... creating along the way". In implementation, and sometimes even in content, he will change his mind in the classroom according to how the class seems to him, especially if they are tired or restless. This on-the-spot assessment of students' potential receptivity is in itself another mode of dialogue.

Y also sees the classroom, however, as inhibiting students' individual creative response, which needs variable time and space for development. The classroom setting is particularly valuable for examination preparation — "discipline, timing, absence of other resources" — in other words, as a training ground for a specific set of productive tasks. He prefers students to do individual written work outside the classroom, except in the immediate run-up to an examination, using "inside time" for preparation and developing response through group work and dialogue. Thus, an inherent contradiction between the discourse of examinations, and the discourse of creative pedagogy, is resolved through strategic assignment of different domains, and a conscious allocation of time to maintain a balance between them.

"I feel my school is quite a creative environment... I'm still struggling to match creativity with exam results". This word "struggling", which Y uses more than once (in an unconscious echo of Fairclough, 1992) indicates the difficulty of reconciling discourses within teaching practice. Y is ambivalent about examinations. As a teacher of A-level literature classes, he feels professional pride in getting a good record of passes at higher grades. He praises the Hong Kong A-level literature examination as a "good" examination, as it includes a coursework portfolio. He is less positive about one apparently retrograde step: the dropping of the personal journal component from this examination three years ago because teachers found it hard to assess.

Thus, Y feels that examinations and creativity "should be complementary", though he notes that some students can be highly creative in class, and still get disappointing examination results at A and AS-level. This may be (in part) because of language difficulties with some weaker students, who find it harder to express their ideas in an acceptable written form. Y believes there are cultural barriers as well, as students try to second-guess examiners' reactions, and "play safe" in suppressing their more original ideas. Students tell him local

Hong Kong markers won't understand their thinking, a notion which (from his own work as an examiner) Y does not support. Students (he believes) unjustifiably lack confidence in the system, though he keeps trying to convince them, referring to the Form 6 syllabus: "it does say you're allowed to be creative... I constantly struggle with my students to make that link — I have to spell it out".

Cultural factors also affect the discourse of local Hong Kong teachers in relation to creativity. Y relates how, at a workshop for secondary school teachers he attended, a teaching method he advocated (brainstorming ideas before reading) was gently but firmly put down by other participants: "that's the Western way, and this (comprehension questions) is the local way". He was supported by one local teacher at the workshop, who said that she approved of the "Western way", having studied overseas herself. Y was left vainly insisting "it's not the Western way, not a Chinese way, it's a creative way". The "shadow" discourse of Confucian Chinese culture is thus pitted against the discourse of liberal progressive reform, which is labeled "Western" and thus (implicitly) colonial in nature. In addition, as Y comments, local teachers may show "fear" in their contacts with native English speakers, expecting to be judged and found wanting (the "ghost discourse" of the colonial era).

Y's own views on creativity have changed since he has been a practising teacher in a Hong Kong secondary school. On the one hand, his sense of what is possible has been expanded by his professional socialization in classes for a part-time Bachelor of Education degree at the University of Hong Kong, in which he learned creative teaching strategies as described in the work of Falvey and others (Falvey and Kennedy, 1997). Y is a link in a chain of professional discourse, as some of his own former students are now doing their Bachelor of Education degree, and using his journal writing method with their own students in teaching practice — "I see myself as an agent of change".

On the other hand, Y claims to have "grown up" in taking a more realistic view of the possibilities for creativity in this society: "Sometimes, I don't think it's cool to be creative in Hong Kong". He can see that creativity has to be "more controlled, contained", and that "because it's Hong Kong, there should be a reason for doing it". At this point, the economic discourse enters his choice of arguments, especially in discussion with his students. He does his best to accommodate a local teenage view, linking creativity with mobile phone design and shopping malls: "I see this as very positive". Thus, in attempting to encourage his students to be more creative in their work, to take an individual view and make new mental connections, Y (like the authors of the education reform proposals) makes an explicit connection between creativity and the demands of the new knowledge-based economy.

Despite his personal loyalty to Hong Kong culture and the discourse of the wider society, Y still does not personally believe that creativity needs to be useful — "No, not at all". At the end of our interview, he spontaneously returned to the examination issue. As we listened to students singing outside, rehearsing for a school show, he commented that all this activity would stop as public examinations drew nearer. In the final response of the interview—his choice of "key words" he associates with creativity — Y reverts to his basic belief in creativity as enjoyment, dialogue, originality and self-expression: "expression, fun, no model answer, interaction, self, me... yes, that's it: creativity is me".

Conclusion

We would argue that contradictions and tensions are present within discourses at both ends of the educational hierarchy in Hong Kong: at the top, the policy-making level from which the education reform proposals are promulgated, and at the bottom, among teachers, by whom these proposals will ultimately be translated into professional practice. The contradictions within the reform documents between the discourses of economics and of creativity are implicit, and become apparent through the response of critical observers (such as the local teachers who commented on the cover images of *Excel and Grow*). Through the requirements of their working situation, teachers are more aware of tensions and compromises, as the discourse of creativity needs to be domesticated — framed — to fit classroom constraints, the discourse of examinations, and the expectations of the wider society (the economic discourse again).

Discourse complementarity is shown in the central overlap of Figure 20.1: the pedagogical discourse of creativity, as expressed (however framed) both in the reform documents and in the discourse of some practising teachers, especially when this is supported by the school and by in-service teacher training. This is an area of professional discourse in which dialogue between university and school-based teachers has already proved fruitful, though more remains to be done to strengthen this central discourse on which good practice can and should be based.

Does it matter, then, what discourse the education reforms are framed in if the reforms themselves lead to a better education system for Hong Kong? Perhaps there can be two co-existing but independent discourse strands: one driven by economic necessity, in which reforming education is seen as a way of keeping Hong Kong competitive in the global cyber-economy, the other driven by a liberal progressive belief in the value of student-centred self-development. Both discourses may serve common aims, and thus be complementary rather than contradictory.

The tension between these two strands, however, could affect how the education reforms continue to be framed during their implementation, and how they are realized in the classroom. It remains to be seen how the reformist discourse will be interpreted and adopted at different levels: in Fairclough's terms, "the level...of the immediate social environment in which the discourse occurs, the level of the social institution... and the level of society as a whole" (Fairclough 1989:25).

If the pressure of examinations within the Hong Kong education system is progressively reduced, as the reform documents propose, some resolution of tensions within the discourse of pedagogy may be possible. At the same time, however, more is expected of classroom teachers in Hong Kong: higher standards of professional practice are mandated in response to the demands of the new economy, new technology, and both regional and global competition. Within this context, there is a danger that creativity may become a label for everything teachers are expected to deliver in the classroom through their individual effort and collective practice.

New tensions in new discourses of educational reform and professional practice will undoubtedly continue to appear in response to rapid social and institutional change. It is a never-ending task for researchers not only to identify such discourse tensions, but to help empower teachers to reconcile them in their professional practice, and to share their insights with each other.

References

1. Bakhtin, M. M. [1934] 1981. *The dialogic imagination*, edited by M. Holquist, translated by M. Holquist and C. Emerson. Austin: University of Texas Press.

2. Cook, G. 1994. *Discourse and literature: The interplay of form and mind.* Oxford: Oxford University Press.

3. Cropley, A. J. 1997. Fostering creativity in the classroom: General principles. In *The creativity research handbook*, edited by M. A. Runco. Cresskill, NJ: Hamptonn Press, 83–114.

4. Education Commission, Hong Kong Special Administrative Region of the People's Republic of China. 2000. *Review of education system: Reform proposals consultation document* (May). Hong Kong: Government Printer.

5. _____ . 2000. *Review of education system: Reform proposals. Excel and grow. Abridged version of the consultation documents* (May). Hong Kong: Government Printer.

6. Fairclough, N. 1995. *Critical discourse analysis: The critical study of language.* London: Longman.

7. _____ . 1989. *Language and power.* London: Longman.

8. _____ . 1992. *Discourse and social change.* Cambridge: Polity Press.

9. Falvey, P. and P. Kennedy, eds. 1997. *Learning language through literature: A sourcebook for teachers of English in Hong Kong.* Hong Kong: Hong Kong University Press.

10. Foucault, M. 1972. *The archaeology of knowledge.* London: Tavistock. (Sheridan-Smith, A. M. Trans. 1969. *L'Archéologie du Savoir.* Paris: Gallimard).

11. Halliday, M. A. K. 1973. *Learning how to mean.* London: Edward Arnold.

12. Maley, A. and A. Duff. 1989. *The inward ear: Poetry in the language classroom.* Cambridge: Cambridge University Press.

13. Murphy, M, ed. 1993. *Using poems in schools.* Hong Kong: Hong Kong Institute of Language in Education.

21

Literary Discourse and Learner Autonomy

Liesel Hermes

Introduction

Autonomy has come to be a buzzword in Germany. Theories of learner autonomy, construction of knowledge, group-centred learning styles abound. Students are showered with progressive theories, but in their university courses are mostly confronted with very traditional teaching methods like lecturing, frontal teaching or a succession of student papers, in short with methods which make a mockery of the theories conveyed, i.e., student-centred learning and learner autonomy. What is sadly lacking in undergraduate programmes for future teachers and students in general is experiential learning, i.e., the actual experiencing of what is being preached such as e.g., group work and the development of learner autonomy.

One has to take into account that within the German educational context, students who train to become teachers normally come straight from high school after mostly 13 years of learning and usually have a knowledge basis which is comparable to e.g., American students after two years at college or university. Undergraduate study programs for primary and lower secondary teachers usually comprise seven semesters at university, including various phases of practice teaching and, after a state examination at university, are followed up by another 18–24 months of practical preparatory teaching before teachers can apply for temporary or permanent positions.

My research interest is to make students experience literature as a discursive event, which calls for co-operation and the negotiation of meaning. This can best be done in group work, which, if it is organized and carried out in self-determination, may lead to autonomy. I pursue this objective in all my literature courses. My theoretical foundations are first reception theory as a very fruitful literary theory, second theories of group work and last theories of learner autonomy. I will briefly look into the different theories and then turn to my own group of students and the projects I do with them in advanced literature courses at the University of Koblenz, Germany.

Reception Theory

In the history of literary theories, reception theory, which was first propounded in Germany, is commonly understood to be a branch of reader-response criticism, which also has its origin in Germany. The two concepts are sometimes even used synonymously. Reader-response criticism rejects the idea found in New Criticism that literary texts are autonomous entities with an objective meaning. Rather, according to this reader-response theory, the meaning of the literary text is created by the readers and therefore unstable and changeable. The German critic Wolfgang Iser speaks of "indeterminate elements" (Wolfgang, 1975a:228–252.) in the text, i.e., gaps which the reader has to fill in, this being a process of guesswork, creation, construction, which can be frustrating or rewarding. In the USA, the critic Stanley Fish has done research into reader response.

The German literary critic Hans Robert Jauss focuses on literary history and the changing reaction to texts by readers. Readers bring to literary texts their own cultural and literary background, their pre-knowledge and world knowledge. Their "aesthetic horizon" is a collection of assumptions, beliefs, expectations, prejudices and so on, which is constantly changing and evolving, because it is itself in the wake of traditions and interpretations that have been set up in relation to a particular text and have become part of its meaning. Therefore there is no fixed meaning within the text. The meaning is rather constructed in the dialogues between the text and different generations of readers that absorb it.

Reader-response and reception theory are in my opinion eminently fruitful for all dealings with literature at university level. Very often students come from high school with the ideas and methods of New

Criticism, i.e., they are convinced that there is a fixed meaning in the text, which the teacher knows of course and which the students are called upon to guess. If they guess the "correct" meaning of the text, it is all right, if they do not, the teacher will supply the ultimate truth and write it on the board for the students to copy. This may look like a satirical picture, but it reflects pretty adequately the truth of high school methodology.

At university level the students often have to learn that their instructor is not in point of fact the possessor of the ultimate meaning of a literary text. On the contrary: teacher and students read a text each with their own reader's background, each with their individual history as a human being. Therefore, dealing with literature in a course is an ongoing dialogue or rather multilogue, in which all participators voice their own understanding of the text, bring forward their doubts, questions, observations. Together they negotiate the meaning of the text, which holds true for this specific group. How differently texts can be understood by student groups can easily be experienced in a life of university teaching. No text that is read by different groups in the course of the years is read identically, so to speak. Each group asks their own questions, finds their own emphases or areas they want to discuss. Nothing is ever the same. Literature is an ongoing discourse.

However, this is often not clear to the students at the beginning of their studies. Therefore, they have to undergo a process of growing awareness into the potentiality of literature as a means for the development of their own discursive ability. They have to learn to tolerate ambiguities, to cope with questions to which there is no final answer, with open endings that refuse to "be closed", so to speak. The development towards literary awareness, towards becoming a mature academic reader, can therefore sometimes be painful.

At the same time it can be extremely rewarding if this process happens through group work. Interpreting literary texts in groups, acting self-determinedly as a group can open students' eyes. They learn about the diversity of meaning in literature just as they learn about themselves and the other members of the group they happen to be working with. And finally, through the process of discourse, they acquire a sense of autonomy.

Group Work

An overall consistent theory of group work does not yet exist (Gohla, 1977:21), and I will therefore restrict myself to those aspects which relate to learning groups at university. If one differentiates between formal and informal groups, a class of students is a formal group, which is characterized by a sort of membership for one semester. If within this class of students spontaneous group work is done, the students will work in informal groups, which only form for one session working on a specific task. Using the assumption that there are four kinds of group work, namely for information, training, discussion and problem solving, I will only concentrate on the discussion group.

Students often experience isolation and alienation in their university lives. They learn that one has to fend for oneself and compete with other students for grades. They are used to teacher-centred frontal teaching in which their role is reduced to taking notes. Their learning is other-determined. The initiative to let the students work in groups at all therefore rests with the teacher, and he/she has to assume responsibility not only for the overall organization, but for motivating the students through the setting of tasks that really lend themselves to group work.

Groups can be formed arbitrarily on the basis of the accidental seating arrangement. This seems to be the worst possible case, since the students are forced to work in an accidental social framework they may not actually favour, which has consequences for the quality of their work. Group formation can also be planned, e.g., on the basis of mutual knowledge of each other. Spontaneous group formation can also occur on the basis of special interests. Once the tasks are set, groups form spontaneously according to what specific task they would like to work on.

Of equal importance is group dynamics. Groups of even numbers may be of disadvantage, because they can form subgroups (Gutte, 1976: 67), whereas groups of uneven numbers cannot subdivide so easily. It is uniformly agreed in theories of group work that each member in a group assumes a certain role (Gohla, 1977:93). The larger the group, the easier it seems to be for the group members to play their specific roles such as e.g., leader. Leadership suggests a hierarchy which often evolves even in small groups. One person becomes the leader, challenged or unchallenged, usually the latter. This person normally has the longest speaking time, gets the other persons' attention including eye-contact, takes the initiative, comes up with ideas, steers the discussion, after a digression leads the others back to work and often structures the whole process. Other roles may be those of supporters, the clown or the quiet ones who just sit back and relax.

Assuming that group dynamics work satisfactorily, group work can give any group of students a kind of protection, i.e., they experience a learning arrangement where their own contributions are evaluated by just three or four. Communication is intensive and made easier especially for the introverted ones (Allwright and Bailey, (1991:148). Shy students can overcome their fear of contributing, for it is a lot easier than in a large class to make very personal comments, to utter feelings or to be emotional. Thus group work has important *psychological functions* especially for the otherwise quiet students.

Group work creates a social framework in which interaction occurs very directly. Thus group work means social learning. In groups, students have to find their own objectives, or if the tasks have been set, their own ways of reaching the objectives. They have to negotiate the tasks as well as methods to choose. This entails a high degree of *self-determination* (Meyer, 1990:245). They also experience themselves in new roles, which have to do with the functions just mentioned (Meyer, 1990:249). The objectives of group work therefore address students' communicative and social abilities as well as their intellectual and personal development. Experiential learning in groups enables the students to understand the basic principles of group work and thus helps them mature intellectually as well as socially.

Group work offers a much more communicative framework than any plenary. It is a highly dynamic process with much interaction and turn-taking. Refusing to co-operate or dropping out will be noticed at once by the others. In other words, the social framework of group work means co-operation and responsibility, negotiating one's working methods and carrying out a discussion that is based on mutual respect of each other's contributions. If the group members see their work as a self-determined joint effort, the outcome will consequently be seen as their joint achievement. This can often result in a feeling of group solidarity. At the same time, reflecting on these processes fosters students' awareness about how important social learning is.

For the sake of objectivity, some possible objections should be mentioned. The learning process in group work is more time consuming than in a lockstep class. However, who knows that students take home from a plenary and what, by the same token, they take home from a group work session? Group work is bound to fail if there is a general lack of energy or commitment or if the teacher does not supervise the students. It may fail, too, if group dynamics intimidate one member or a leader takes over and entirely controls the whole process, or if a group splits into subgroups that disengage themselves from the activities agreed upon. Lastly, group work may fail if the members of the group are incompatible or refuse to cooperate.

Learner Autonomy

David Little provides the following description of autonomy:

> *"...the basis of learner autonomy is acceptance of responsibility for one's own learning"*. He envisages the development of learner autonomy as a *"never-ending effort to understand what one is learning, why one is learning, how one is learning, and with what degree of success"* (Little:227).

The concept of autonomy presupposes an immensely optimistic vision of the human being as an ever-learning person. For autonomy to be developed, human beings have to be mature, intellectually advanced and self-assured. They have to know what they actually want to learn and therefore have to have pre-knowledge including world-knowledge in general. They have to be highly motivated. They must have a natural and sustainable drive to learn. They have to be highly critical of the whole process of learning and critical of themselves when it comes to the stage of self-evaluation. Therefore they have to be very honest and to start working again unfailingly once they have recognized that they have not yet reached the objective they have set for themselves. If autonomy is to be achieved by group work, human beings have to show good social as well as communicative competencies on top of the ones just mentioned. Ultimately, autonomy does not come by itself but has to be introduced and practically "taught" by the teacher, which means living with the paradox that autonomy can only be reached after having been denied it in the process of instruction (Benson and Voller, 1997).

Group work should take into account the individual learner's "needs, purposes, capacities" (Little, 1994:431), which he/she brings into the group and which are addressed in the process of the interaction of the group members. This strategy takes account of the individuals and at the same time of communicative processes within the group, negotiating of objectives and working methods and reflecting on the process of learning.

Even if these prerequisites are given, it takes a lot of time and indeed effort on the side of the learners. Most of our university students are so used to instruction, to being taken by the hand, to answering instructors' questions instead of asking and answering their own that they find it hard work to give up relying on the teacher's guidance. Therefore the first steps towards autonomy have to be taken by the teacher, who introduces his/her students to the concepts and objectives of autonomy. This can only be done in a process of continuous reflection together with the students about what they can decide for themselves and what effort it will cost them. Demands on the teacher are therefore high: he/she has to create a learning environment which is favourable to learner autonomy, and has to encourage constant reflection and foster self-awareness. Students have to be highly motivated for their work and have to be prepared to assume responsibility for their individual learning as well as for the activities in their groups. In this understanding learner autonomy is not isolated work, but eminently joint discourse.

Literary Discourse in Groups

Social and communicative competencies as well as the ability to work in teams have come to be highly valued in Germany since the 1990s, and these competencies are also required of school pupils in German schools. Consequently, instructors should be able to prepare the ground for the development of these competencies in their classes. That is, however, only possible if they themselves are convinced of the desirability of these objectives and if they are familiar with them. The way can be paved at university, if the students are made familiar with theoretical concepts and ideas and learn them themselves experientially. Learning in groups is just one way, but an important one to learner autonomy. But since the ability to work in teams has come to be seen as a general requirement for professional people, the arguments just put forward also hold good for other students, such as those who are enrolled in an M.A. course. For teamwork is impossible without communication, without rational negotiation of objectives to choose and methods to select. Teamwork produces its own discourse.

Previous research into student interaction has shown clearly that the overall structure of any university session has to be created by the teacher (Hermes, 1999a:199). The teacher has to pre-structure the session according to the needs, abilities and of the students and the overall level of teaching. This sounds counterproductive to the objective of autonomy, but it is a given that time is limited and that prestructuring can save time for the students' own learning process. With a view to literature, structuring can work in the following way: the students are asked to prepare a particular text at home, which will then come up for discussion in a session.

The session begins with the structuring of the text, i.e., the teacher in a plenary develops the most important structural elements of the text in hand, namely those that normally go beyond the students' immediate interest because they are more on the theoretical side (e.g., narrative perspective, point(s) of view, intricacies of setting or time scheme, style). Thus it is ensured that the students do not overlook important aspects of a text.

Then a learning environment has to be created for group work with different tasks to fulfil. This is done by brainstorming. The students brainstorm their own ideas about the text which they will later deal with. The results of the brainstorming phase are again structured in plenary discussion. Tasks for the ensuing group work stage can be chosen by the students themselves, which means negotiating the most popular topics among the groups.

The following step is group work proper with the groups forming in various possible ways. One possibility is the formation of interest groups on the basis of the results of the brainstorming phase. An alternative way is the spontaneous formation of groups, who after establishing themselves as a group negotiate which points they want to deal with. Within the groups the students negotiate their own aims and methods and at the end reflect on their achievements. At this stage the instructor only functions as a monitor.

The last stage is a plenary again, in which the results of the individual groups are presented and discussed. Each group assumes responsibility as a whole for the presentation, which means that there is no speaker but that each member of the group takes an active part in the presentation. The others are encouraged to ask questions and make comments or relate the observations to their own findings.

Group work changes the format of a seminar. In the course of a whole semester the students become used to five stages:

- structuring (teacher's guidance),
- brainstorming,
- group formation,
- group work stage,
- plenary with discussion of the results.

But one has to take into account that the ordinary time frame of 90 minutes of a usual session is too short for the students to work effectively in groups. This constraint can be overcome if the students agree to extend the time to 120 minutes. The longer time is one "sacrifice" one has to make to the goal of giving the students enough time to negotiate the aims and methods of their work and to actually agree on topics to discuss, to do the work and note it down. But it is more than compensated for by the thoroughness and depth to which these group discussions go.

Data

The aim of the project was for the students to learn to work more independently. Used to being spoon fed by the teacher, to answering questions instead of asking them, to relying on one ultimate meaning of a text, the idea was to show them through experiential learning that literary texts do not contain a prefixed meaning, but that the students themselves create meaning in a literary discourse. The whole project was discussed and negotiated with the students as an ongoing process. Metadiscussion is highly valuable for students because they normally take an instructor's methods for granted and do not ask why a particular method is chosen in a session. Therefore becoming aware of different methods and accounting for them was felt as an enrichment for the students. They continuously reflected on activities which they themselves experienced and the merits of which they were therefore able to judge in the given context.

The data collected were the following:

- two questionnaires at the beginning and end of the semester about students' learning preferences,
- four diary entries of each student about their learning experience in selected sessions,
- video-films of alternating groups,
- two structured interviews of six students in two groups in the middle of the semester about their learning experience in various groups.

The two questionnaires yielded some results as to changes in learning preferences. At the end of the semester more students preferred group discussion to other forms of learning, especially to frontal teaching, than at the beginning. The more rewarding data were the videos, the diary entries and the interviews. The videos showed how differently group dynamics work. The diaries were very candid pieces of self-analysis. What clearly emerged on the basis of the theoretical conceptualization and the experiential learning was a growing insight into the process of group work, its prerequisites and the dynamics that make it successful. Group work came to be seen as a valuable way of negotiating literary meaning, of coping with the students' own questions, doubts and observations. Interpreting a literary text in a small group instead of a large plenary made the learning environment more intimate and less threatening. At the same time the students felt that dealing with their own questions is more rewarding than answering the teacher's. Moreover, since the groups were stable throughout the second half of the semester, the students knew each other well and this created a feeling of corporate identity within the group. Students were convinced that they were able to construct meaning in a greater diversity and more independently. The way was paved for autonomy. A similarly growing awareness was reflected in the interviews.

A few remarks should be made about the videos: in each case one group was filmed, normally four or five students for about 25–30 minutes. Since the overall time of the documentation of six groups exceeds 150 minutes, I would like to concentrate briefly on some striking characteristics of each discourse. Interestingly enough, within the first five minutes roles were assumed that were "played" consistently throughout the group stage.

In one group a leader emerged right from the start, unchallenged, who directed and dominated the discussion. She made the first suggestions which topics to discuss and started: "So what are we supposed to do, who's gonna tell me that?" She suggested methods to choose, details to attend to and throughout steered the discussion, challenging anyone who was not concentrating. The film clearly shows that the others directed their comments mainly to her and kept eye contact with her. Her role as a leader was unchallenged throughout this stage, possibly all the more in view of the fact that she was among the best students in the class. Not surprisingly, it turned out that that she had the longest speaking time by far.

The fact that length of speaking time does not automatically coincide with the leader's role became apparent in another group, where a female student obviously had difficulties in expressing herself. Very early on she took the floor and sometimes monopolized it rambling along, but only because she had a hard time making herself clear to the other group members. They listened politely, asked for clarification, which provoked more rambling monologues. What the students certainly learned in this process was the negotiation of meaning. However, the results as to the discussion of the text in hand were fairly poor.

Another group, a very quiet and deliberate one, started with a period of prolonged silence, in which they reread parts of the text, made annotations and only then negotiated very amicably the points to discuss. In this group no leader emerged, and the speaking time was fairly evenly distributed among all the members. This quiet group made the best effort at clarifying and negotiating meaning at a much more abstract level than the previous one. They came up with highly original ideas which linked the text in hand with the Bible, among other texts.

A fourth group had a clown right from the start, who loved entertaining the others by sometimes silly comments, which aroused laughter. This group plunged head over heels into the text and found out after a couple of minutes that it might be advisable to restrict the number of topics to discuss. Therefore they decided on a silent period of rereading parts of the text before plunging into another discussion, which, however, moved along somewhat erratically and without any observable coherence.

In a fifth group, five somewhat older students had come together, all between 35 and 50. They did not have a leader, but an expert, since one woman was Australian and the Australian short story under discussion dealt with aboriginal topics. The other members looked to her for help, when a term needed clarifying, and she provided linguistic explanations for terms to do with aboriginal culture. On the whole they emerged as a very egalitarian group, which was also shown in the roughly equal amount of speaking time by each member.

Strikingly, in a group of four, the members sitting opposite each other talked to each other right from the start, so that at times two dialogues emerged. It appeared that the two subgroups were not actually listening to each other. Right to the end of the group stage they did not manage to develop a discussion in which all four of them were involved with each other. This may be a point in favour of groups with an uneven number of members. However, in one group of five, one student kind of dropped out. At least she had by far the shortest speaking time.

Evaluation and Conclusion

The most important result of the project is the heightened self-awareness of the students as to their own learning. This experiential learning enabled them to understand principles of group work and experience it as a fruitful method to take up a literary discourse. Constant reflection and self-reflection in the process fostered a growing awareness of the potential of this procedure on the way to learner autonomy.

Students learnt to take responsibility into their own hands. In order to be able to do this it was necessary for each of them to be well prepared. Lack of preparation immediately showed in the group discussion whereas in a larger plenary lack of preparation or motivation do not show immediately or may even go entirely unnoticed. Since the students felt responsible for their group, they showed growing motivation for thorough preparation of the texts assigned. The immediate consequence was a more lively discussion since the students in point of fact had something to say.

They experienced group work as a framework for social learning and for team orientation. Working together became a social communicative event to which each member contributed as much as possible and for which they felt responsible. Thus not only was an atmosphere of mutual confidence gradually built up, but some of the rather quieter students' self-assurance also increased. This is all the more important in the context of a foreign language, since literature seminars as well as all other courses in the department are carried out in English.

There are some literature specific results: students did not have any teacher's questions to answer, consequently guidance ended as soon as the structuring stage was over. Instead, they began asking their own questions and questioned each other about doubts or obscure points. They experienced literature as an ideal basis for dialogue, interaction and negotiation. Literature in point of fact is an ongoing dialogue between text and reader(s); it is a constructing and sharing of meaning.

A few provisos should, however, be mentioned concerning the scenario just outlined:

- A university seminar cannot do without the teacher's input. The teacher has to give information and pave the way for the activities to come.

- Structuring is necessary. Time is valuable and should not be wasted.

- However, with literary discourse in groups being at the centre of the seminar, the teacher gave a lot less input than one might usually expect. Some students complained of lack of input.

- Group work as the main methodological frame is more time-consuming than a lockstep session. Therefore more time is needed than in ordinary sessions and the usual time constraints should be loosened.

- Students need their time to get organized, to find their aims and methods of discussion, to cope with individual idiosyncrasies.

- Group work also slows down the overall pace of learning, something that is more than compensated for by the ability to reflect on the process and the depth of the individual learning experience.

Group work initiates intensive and at the same time intimate discourse which can never be realized in the same way in a plenary. Literary discourse is centred around a text, which must have been carefully prepared in advance. If then a learning environment is created by instructor and students alike, group work can produce a specific discourse which gives the four or five members the chance to negotiate aims and methodological approaches as well as topics to concentrate on and then to construct meaning in a highly autonomous way.

References

1. Allwright, D. and K. M. Bailey. 1991. *Focus on the language classroom.* Cambridge: Cambridge University Press.

2. Benson, P. and P. Voller, eds. 1997. *Autonomy and independence in language learning.* London and New York: Longman.

3. Gohla, G. 1977. *Theorie und Praxis der Gruppenarbeit. Ein Lern–und Arbeitsprogramm für gruppensoziologische Studien.* Heidelberg: Quelle & Meyer.

4. Gray, M. 1992. *A dictionary of literary terms.* London and New York: Longman.

5. Gutte, R. 1976. *Gruppenarbeit: Theorie und Praxis des sozialen Lernens.* Frankfurt a. M.: Diesterweg.

6. Hermes, L. 1999a. Learner assessment through subjective theories and action research. *Assessment and Evaluation in Higher Education* 24 (2): 197–204.

7. _____. 1999b. What do students learn in groups? Development of learner autonomy in higher education. *Fremdsprachen und Hochschule* 56/1999:34–46.

8. _____. 1999c. What do students learn in groups? Assessment of quality in higher education. *International Journal: Continuous Improvement Monitor,* Available on Web: http://llanes.panam.edu/journal/library/vol1no4/hermes.html.

9. Iser, W. 1975a. Die Appellstruktur der Texte. In *Rezeptionsästhetik,* edited by R. Warning. Munchen: Fink, 228–252.

10. _____. 1975b. Der Lesevorgang. In *Rezeptionsästhetik,* edited by R. Warning. Munich: Fink, 253–276.

11. Little, D. 1994. Learner autonomy: A theoretical construct and its practical application. *Die Neueren Sprachen* 93 (5): 430–442.

12. _____. 1997. Learner autonomy in the foreign language classroom: Theoretical foundations and some essentials of pedagogical practice. *Zeitschrift für Fremdsprachenforschung* (ZFF) 8 (2): 227–244.

13. Meyer, E. 1983. *Gruppenunterricht. Grundlegung und Beispiel.* Oberursel/Ts.: Ernst Wunderlich Verlagsbuchhandlung.

14. Meyer, H. 1990. *Unterrichtsmethoden, II. Praxisband.* Berlin: Cornelsen.

15. Pemberton, R. *et al*, eds. 1996. *Taking control. Autonomy in language learning.* Hong Kong: Hong Kong University Press.

16. Warning, R., ed. 1975. *Rezeptionsästhetik.* Munich: Fink.

Media Discourses

22

Media Interviews: An Intersection of Multiple Social Practices

Marcel Burger and Laurent Filliettaz

Introduction

Theoretical Framework

In this chapter, we will analyze the opening of a broadcast interview within the framework of what is usually called *social discourse analysis* (Van Dijk, 1997). In a very broad sense, such a perspective assumes the dialogical nature of human practices, and focuses on the role of discourse in the construction of social reality, and more precisely in producing and reproducing social structures. Thus, *social discourse analysis* takes into account the real stakes of discourse in the real world. In this view, discourse is seen as a resource for a co-operative joint construction of social reality, as it is negotiated in a public communicative act. Attending to discourse might then reveal how shared cognition shapes the ways in which interactants act and organize their talk, as well as the ways in which they anticipate how their acting and talking will be interpreted.[1] In that sense, verbal interaction becomes a relevant object of analysis in order to observe how a social reality emerges.

Considering the foregoing, a media interview is then a complex social event organized by different and closely linked professional practices, whose stakes turn out to be partly paradoxical, as we will see.

---

1. See Van Dijk (1997), Condor and Antaki (1997), Shotter (1994) for a global discussion.

Data and Problem

The data used for this analysis is that of a recent interview of the French painter Balthus by the journalist Frank Peel. This interview dates from October 2000 and was broadcast on the French-speaking Swiss public television.

Frank Peel is a 73 year old English lawyer who worked as a journalist for the American army during the Second World War, and then for various broadcast media like CNN, NBC and Channel One. He has lived in Geneva, Switzerland, for a long while and is the initiator of the only English-spoken TV talk-show with French subtitles on the French-speaking Swiss television.

Balthus is a famous French painter, one of the very few living artists whose work is exhibited at the Louvre Museum in Paris. Balthus is now 92 years old. He has been living for many years in Switzerland together with his young Japanese wife. They reside in a typically Swiss-looking house and place, near the mountains. Balthus is a rather solitary artist. For a long while he refused to appear on television. It is in fact the first time he has accepted an interview with a journalist in Switzerland. He does not have native fluency in English, and he is obviously hard of hearing.

Frank Peel describes his program as a talk-show, which implies a mix between information and entertainment, as given by the expression "infotainment" (Penz, 1996). In fact, the program's title "In Conversation in Geneva with Frank Peel" announces a playful activity more than an institutional talk. According to Peel, the show is addressed as a priority to the English-speaking community of Geneva, and aims at familiarizing the audience with the Swiss way of life. In that sense, Peel's program participates in creating a feeling of social integration. This avowed aim constitutes a constraint both on the talk (topics about Switzerland are very salient) and on the identity of the guests (all of them are somehow related to Switzerland).

Excerpt 1:   "In Conversation In Geneva With Frank Peel", Recorded on TSR2 on 6 October 2000 [2]

INITIAL CREDIT

MEDIA PREFACE

> [Camera first shows some paintings of Balthus and then his chalet in Rossinière. Schubert's music is the background for a voice-over media presentation by the journalist.]

1 Peel : tonight my program is really better called my tea with Balthus (.) now we arrived at this fantastic mythic chalet which is in Rossinière which is only two hours away from Geneva it is almost a mythic chalet we really were almost transported into another time and another place and in fact Balthus (.) what has characterized him what is what describes his life and

5 his work is that he has always gone his own way (...) my guest tonight is Count Balthazar Klossowski de Rola who is better known as Balthus the painter (.) and his wife the Countess Balthazar Klossowski de Rola are my guests on my program this evening

TRANSITION TO INTERVIEW

> [Camera now shows the guests' living room. We can hear them talk with a live sound. A servant helps Balthus to put his glasses on. Balthus, his wife and Frank Peel are having tea.]

Countess: English tea
Peel : ah English tea?!

FIRST INTERVIEW SEQUENCE

10 Peel : what I have been trying (.) to (.) to to (..) to find is who is Balthus ah humm and not but not any (.) I am trying to find who is Balthus
Balthus : nobody knows!

---

2. We use the following transcription notations: (.) (..) indicate appropriately timed pauses; underlining indicates overlapping talk; and material in square brackets indicates transcriber's commentary regarding non-verbal events.

Peel :   nobody <u>knows?</u>

Balthus :   no!

15 Peel :   not even Balthus?

Balthus :   nobody knows!

Peel :   not even Balthus?

Balthus :   even myself!

Peel :   even yourself! well (.) that is the last person to know (.)
              we are always the last person to

20   know but but in trying to in trying to (.) in trying to
              understand myself who is Balthus I (.) I I came here (.)

Balthus :   you woord uhh word (.) you used the word enigmatic!!

Peel :   enigmatic?

Balthus :   yes!

25 Peel :   enigmatic!? but you keep saying that (..) enigmatic (.)
              you keep saying that (.) enigmatic I don't say you are
              enig<u>matic at all <u>you</u></u> are not

Balthus :   <u>I don't I don't</u> think I am enigmatic
              I could not really frankly I could not answer

Peel :   you could <u>not answer?</u>

30 Balthus : <u>who I am</u> <<u>who I am</u>> There's so many different point
              of view about me that I am who is I am a bit confused

Peel :   well (.) I think I think (.) every person on this world
              <Yes!> is confused about themselves at times (..) but
              most of us (.) we somehow (.) we somehow blocked
              that out (.) we stopped <u>trying to</u>

35 Balthus : <u>do you know who</u> you are?

Peel :   I haven't got a clue! I haven't got a clue

There is no doubt that the study of media interviews can take research into very different directions. However, the question we will take up here is a rather specific one and refers to the means by which the individuals taking part in the media interview — Frank Peel the journalist and Balthus the painter — carry out the complex social practices they are engaged in. As discourse-producing agents, the participants are involved in a wide range of social actions that constrain their conduct in general and their verbal productions in particular.

From this perspective, it becomes relevant to investigate how those constraints are being fulfilled, or, to put it another way, how the participants are handling the multi-oriented processes they are being faced with.

Before proceeding to a systematic analysis of such a problem, we would like to start by expressing some intuitions regarding the sequence of the interview we are considering here. Apart from the question of the age of Balthus, which plays of course a crucial role in the way the interview is initiated and conducted, it seems quite obvious that there is something "failing" in that initial section of interaction. In a certain way, the perception we get from the excerpt above is that the participants feel rather ill at ease and come up against serious difficulties in initiating the interactional process.

But in order to present evidence for such an intuitive perception, one has to refer to theoretical categories and ground the analysis in a systematic methodological framework. From this standpoint, our main objective will be, precisely, to show that the reasons underlying the difficulties the participants are faced with cannot be determined adequately unless the organization of the social practices involved in a media interview is clearly understood. In an effort to support this hypothesis, we will try to evoke the main characteristics of media interviews as complex sites of engagementv (2) before turning the focus to the problems faced by Peel and Balthus in negotiating their joint actions (3).

Media Interviews as Complex Sites of Engagement

The Social Practices Involved in Media Interviews

As "mediated actions"[3] (Wertsch, 1998), media interviews of celebrities, such as the one under analysis here, take place in what Scollon (1998, 2001) calls a site of engagement, that is a moment in real time in which a complex range of social practices intersect.

---

3. As Scollon (1998:6) argues, media discourse is "mediated" in at least two distinct ways: on the one hand, as a practice of "the media", and on the other, as a social process accomplished through using cultural tools, that is, all kinds of mediational means.

Following researches conducted in the field of media interviews (Burger, 1999, forthcoming) as well as our own perception of Frank Peel's interaction with Balthus, it seems that an adequate way of describing the complex process carried out by an interviewer and his well known guest calls for a study of at least three distinct social practices:

a. the practice of delivering information through television media,
b. the practice of the interview itself,
c. and the practice of meeting somebody in private.

As a result, the *sites of engagement* involved in media interviews can be best described as an intersection between multi-oriented praxeological processes:

Figure 22.1
The Main Social Practices Intersecting in Media Interviews

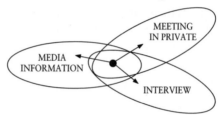

Contrary to what the above categories might seem to indicate, a clear-cut delimitation between various social practices does not come down to a reification of autonomous praxeological processes. Nevertheless, an identification of distinct purposes in the stratification of the interactional situation turns out to be very relevant, insofar as each of the social practices mentioned above involves specific *goals* and *identities*, and entails variable *discursive constraints*. From that standpoint, a clarification of what is at stake at those various levels constitutes a theoretical pre-condition for describing media interviews as complex social practices, as well as to account for the unusual way the interview is carried out by Frank Peel and Balthus. In what follows, we will try to characterize some praxeological features of the main practices entailed by media interviews, before showing how those practices intersect in the data we are discussing here.

Media Information as a Social Practice

We can briefly characterize media information as a social practice which is under paradoxical constraints. On the one hand, media information has a civic function, namely that of informing about the ongoings of the public space. It is therefore addressed to citizens and involved in the construction of public opinion. But on the other hand, the media are doing business and remain economic actors that sell information. From that standpoint, media information is addressed to customers — in a broad sense — and aims at creating customers' loyalty (Habermas, 1979; Charaudeau, 1997).

As on the diagram below, we can define what are the *goals, role identities* and *expected actions* of the participants engaged in media information:

Figure 22.2
The Properties of Media Information

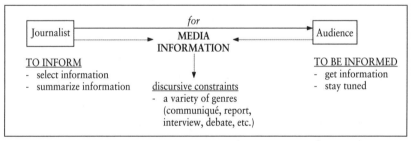

We call *journalist* the spokesperson for a complex media addressor who is in charge of informing its *audience*. The audience is a collective and anonymous addressee, which is then defined by a want to be informed. Practically, the participants engage in a unidirectional interaction: that is, the media produce a talk *for* [4] the audience.

The newsworthiness of information is an essential constraint of media information. The talk must be about current, real, out-of-the-ordinary events rather than about ordinary, fictive or past ones. In

---

4. Jucker (1995) makes the classical distinction between a "talk for" and a "talk with" relation. See also Scollon (1998) who speaks about a "watch" relation : "a watch, then, may be defined as any person or group of people who are perceived to have attention to some spectacle as the central focus of their (social) activity. The spectacle together with its watchers constitutes the watch" (Scollon 1998:92).

that sense, to inform implies at least a selection and a summary of topics in order to attract the audience and make it stay tuned.

In its regular attempts to distinguish facts from comments, media information resorts to a mix of very different genres (Jucker, 1995; Adam, 1997; Charaudeau, 1997). That is, depending on whether the media want to stress the "hard facts" or "comment" upon them, information will be achieved through genres privileging the expression of opinions (such as interviews, or debates) or through more neutral genres (such as communiqués or reports).

Each of these genres can be analyzed as being themselves complex social practices, involving specific participants, actions and goals. In the broadcast we are concerned with, media information is linked with an interview.

Interview as a Social Practice

We can briefly characterize an interview as a social practice which focuses on the discursive expression mainly of one's party, namely the "guest" party. As a consequence, the "media" party commonly refrains from comments, save when setting and delegating the floor to the guest.

The diagram below illustrates the *goals, role identities* and *expected actions* of the participants involved in an interview:

Figure 22.3
The Properties of an Interview

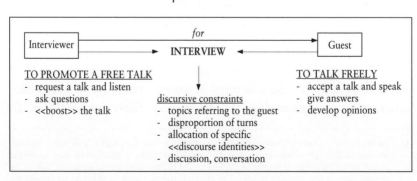

We call *interviewer* the participant who systematically questions another one, with the avowed aim of "having him speak freely". We call *guest* the respondent to these questions, who accepts to develop his opinions for the interviewer. The activity engaged in is thus an interactive communication: that is, each party talks with the other, although the floor is not equally distributed.

Considering the foregoing, an interviewer is expected to ask personal questions, then listen, and boost the talk if needed. Respectively, the guest does not initiate a talk but responds and develops his own viewpoints.

An interview is thus a sort of discussion. The interaction is led by the interviewer. That is, he is the one to propose the main topics. But it is left to the guest to express his opinion on the topic or to branch to some other topic of interest. Thus the guest is given some latitude in what he can express.

Meeting People in Private as a Social Practice

As a matter of fact, the domain of private life plays a vital role in the interview conducted with Balthus, not only because the privacy of the painter's home is explicitly and recurrently mentioned by Frank Peel ("a mythic chalet" l. 2, "we really were almost transported into another time and another place" l. 3–4), but also because the whole interview process is dramatized as a visit of the journalist to the painter at home. Consider for example the fact that Peel presents his program as "my tea with Balthus" (l. 1) and the fact that the interview sequence is preceded by a short transition during which the painter prepares himself, leaving time for brief comments about the tea offered to the guest ("English tea" — "ah English tea?!" l. 8–9).

What comes out of that set of significant details is that the action going on in our data cannot longer be reduced to a *media information process* (see page 573) nor to an *interview* (see page 574). Rather, it is carried out as a meeting in private or a visit, that is another distinct level of social practice referring to everyday life:

Figure 22.4
The Properties of Meetings in Private

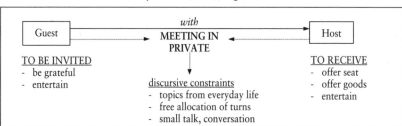

We can briefly describe meetings in private as interactive communication processes involving participants talking *with* each other. What people usually aim at in making a visit to each other lies in the sharing of a pleasant moment of time and the reinforcement of interpersonal relations (Traverso, 1996). In order to receive in an appropriate way, the host is expected to take care of the material and symbolic comfort of his *guest* by offering him a seat and various ritual goods like drinks or cigarettes, and by showing interest in the encounter. As for the commitment of the *guest*, it is usually manifested by signs of gratitude as well as by a substantial contribution to the interactional process going on.

Unlike interviews, meetings in private are usually carried out discursively in a rather unrestricted way. The topics mentioned by the interactants may be anchored in a wide range of semantic fields; the turns are allocated freely and the illocutionary forces like for instance *asking questions* or *giving answers* may be performed by each of the participants. To sum up, it seems that people mainly get involved in private meetings by producing *conversation* or *small talk* rather than restricting discursive genres.

Negotiating Multi-oriented Social Practices

From the standpoint of a *social discourse analysis*, we will not be interested so much in those practices for themselves, but in describing how they intersect in that particular moment of interaction. How are the specific goals underlying those various social practices being achieved by Peel and Balthus? How are those particular individuals dealing with the multi-oriented process they are engaged in? This is the kind of questioning we would like to address now in some details.

The first element that comes out of a close look at our data is that the multi-oriented practices we have been defining appear to be sequentially organized in Frank Peel's broadcast. Indeed, a macro-structural analysis of that initial section clearly shows that the media interview process is carried out through the opening of various and embedded frames (Goffman, 1974) referring to distinct social practices: the program starts with the initial credit, followed by a media preface (l. 1–7) focusing the interaction into a MEDIA INFORMATION process; a transition sequence then shifts into the MEETING frame by dramatizing Balthus' arrival and Peel's visit ("English tea" — "ah, English tea?!" l. 8–9). And finally, an INTERVIEW frame is initiated by Peel's first question to Balthus. Consequently, the opening section of the program can be best described as a succession of embedded frames:

Figure 22.5
The Frames Entailed in the Opening Section of the Broadcast

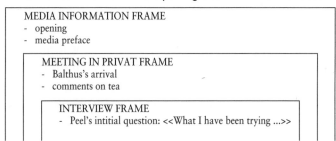

These opening frames lead to a reinforcement of the sequential organization of the process going on and present evidence that the various social practices involved in this specific site of engagement are hierarchically embedded. As shown by Figure 22.5, the INTERVIEW process turns out to be bracketed as part of a larger MEETING IN PRIVATE. And similarly, the MEETING frame is bracketed within the superordinate frame of MEDIA INFORMATION.

But taking into consideration such a sequential organization on a macro-structural level does not exhaust the problem of how interactants are negotiating multi-oriented social practices. On the contrary, important questions remain open, such as how are Frank Peel and Balthus dealing with the constant reframings required by the sequential organization of the action they are involved in? And how are they maintaining at the same time an adapted commitment to the goals linked to each of those three levels? As shown by Figure 22.5, the agents taking part to the media interview are most of the time simultaneously involved in the three social practices we have been considering. Such a layered framework has important consequences for the handling of *situated identities* [5] (Zimmerman, 1998), since interactants are expected to perform adequately in a variety of distinct social practices. More specifically, Frank Peel's position in the ongoing process can be regarded as complex in the sense that he has to behave at the same time as a journalist presenting attractive information to the audience (p. 525), as an interviewer able to promote a free talk from his guest (p. 526) and as a grateful visitor entertaining with his host (p. 527). As for Balthus, a successful outcome of his engagement requires a capacity not only to receive his guest adequately (p. 527), but also to provide the audience with relevant and attractive information (p. 525), and to develop his own viewpoints in an interview process (p. 526).

It is precisely because Frank Peel and Balthus are facing problems in negotiating such multi-voiced (Shotter, 1994) engagements that we will now turn to a more detailed analysis focused on the feeling of "failure" captured when first glancing at the data. In order to do so, we will pay attention to verbal units and consider them as a discursive expression of some framing problems.

The Discursive Expression of Some Framing Problems

The Failure of an Interview Process

When going back to the opening of the program, we can observe quite easily a typical progression from a media discourse to an interview, as

---

5.   As opposed to discourse and transportable identities, situated identities "come into play within the precincts of particular types of situation. Indeed, such situations are effectively brought into being and sustained by participants engaging in activities and respecting agendas that display an orientation to, and an alignment of, particular identity sets, for exemple, in the case of emergency telephone calls, citizen-complainant and call-taker" (Zimmerman, 1998:90).

noticed before. At first, Peel manages alone what we call a media preface introducing the interview. When turning to the interview itself, however, the transition fails because obviously Balthus *is not doing the interview*. Let us consider these two steps of the process through a diagram:

Figure 22.6
The Failure of an Interview Process

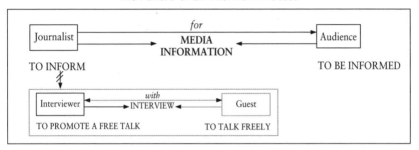

Media Process

Carrying out a media information process means to emphasize the role of a journalist engaged in a talk for the audience. Therefore, it implies a focus on the newsworthiness of information rather than on the promotion of a guest's talk, or on an ordinary conversation. Different discursive elements enable us to consider the talk as a part of a rather successful media process.

For instance, one can identify a range of **explicit markers** of "a talk for the audience" relation:

– the clear *reference* to a media interaction including the time and place of the audience:

"tonight my program is" (l. 1)
"on my program this evening" (l. 7)

– the reference to a collective speaker, namely the pronoun "we":

"now we arrived at this fantastic mythic chalet" (l. 1–2)
"we really were almost transported" (l. 3)

– and finally, the *reference to the guest as if he were absent* and more specifically the use of the third person singular instead of the pronoun "you":

> *"Balthus, what has characterized **him**, what describes*
> *his life and **his** work (l. 4–5)*

Besides these explicit markers, we also find **implicit** ones which participate in constituting the talk as a media process, that is, "a talk for the audience":

– the very emphasized *reference to the identity, the names and titles of the guests,* which are redundant information to the guests themselves, but very relevant to the audience:

> *"my guest tonight is **Count Balthazar Klossowski de Rola***
> *[...] and his wife **the Countess Balthazar Klossowski de**
> ***Rola** are my guests" (l. 6–7)*

– all the technical details regarding the *interview situation,* as well as *biographical information* about the guests, which are addressed to the audience for the same reason:

> *"we arrived [...] in **Rossinière** which is only **two hours**
> *away from **Geneva**" (l. 2)*

– and finally, the filming itself, which underlines a media process. Indeed, to show pieces of Balthus' work, the place where he lives, with a voice-over superimposed to the images is a means to clearly differentiate between two processes: the media process, which is managed by a journalist in a broadcast studio, and the interview process, managed by an interviewer and his guest in a different place and time.

Interview Process

Once the media process is satisfactorily engaged in, the journalist needs to initiate the transition to the interview. As seen before, doing an interview means to emphasize a "talk with his guest". The somewhat paradoxical stake is then to promote a free talk within a highly constrained media frame.

In fact, the interview process seems to fail due to the guest. Balthus in this case progressively refuses Peel's proposition to engage in the interview. Let us examine the proposal and its refusal in turn.

(a) Proposing the interview: Markers of the interviewer's talk

The interviewer constructs a typical interview framing by a progressive shifting from referring to "Balthus" in the third person, to speaking to him directly as the addressee:

> *"Balthus"* ➜ *"not even Balthus"* ➜ *"not even yourself"*
> *(l. 10, 15, 19)*

Of course, acting as an interviewer implies asking questions, but it leads first to expressing statements framing an ideal answer:

> *"I am trying to find who is Balthus" (l. 10–11)*

This statement anchors a complex discourse topic, that is the guest himself. The statement thus functions simultaneously as a theme and as an interactional encouragement to talk about oneself. As a matter of fact, "Balthus" can be replaced by the pronoun "you".

In the case that interests us, the questioning remains implicit, as Peel's speech is overlapped by Balthus' reaction. Acting as an interviewer is then to accept such a misfortune and to pursue the interaction by aligning with the guest's turn, as shown in his echoing of Balthus' utterances:

> *"nobody knows?" (l. 13)*
> *"not even Balthus?" (l. 15, 17)*
> *"even yourself!" (l. 19)*

Finally, acting as an interviewer presupposes recycling a request to talk when the guest has failed to provide sufficient development. Most of the time, this kind of request is formulated indirectly in order to avoid threatening addressee's face, and is expressed by unfinished statements rather than direct questions:

> *"we are always the last person to know but in trying to understand myself who is Balthus I came here" (l. 19–20)*

> *"I think every person on this world is confused about themselves at times but most of us we somehow blocked that out, we stopped trying to" (l. 32–33)*

Peel tries to reframe the interview twice using a similar strategy: he makes a concession to his guest's talk, then expresses a part of his own viewpoint. But it appears quite obviously that Balthus has no desire to do the interview. Let us consider the progressive refusal of the interview process.

(b)   Refusing the interview: Markers of the guest's talk

Balthus' first reaction on line 12 ("nobody knows") is indeed a clear marker of disagreement: it overlaps the interviewer's turn and constitutes therefore an unsolicited comment. The polemical value of the negation is consequently more acute. In general, an interviewer's guest should refrain from initiating actions (Burger, forthcoming; Heritage and Greatbatch, 1991). Instead, he should only respond, and preferably provide a long talk which is often an open invitation to story telling. Balthus' actions are systematically contradicting this procedure. On line 22, for example, he again initiates a comment on prior talk:

"you used the word enigmatic" (l. 22)

This is in fact an implicit criticism of a word not even expressed by the interviewer, as it seems. Balthus also refuses the autobiographical topic, and provides repeatedly very short reactions:

"no!" (l. 14)
"nobody knows" (l. 12, 16)
"even myself" (l. 18)

And finally, he even changes the frame of the interview in reversing its expected discourse identities:

"do you know who you are?" (l. 35)

By doing so, Balthus turns himself into an interviewer asking questions to Peel who is expected to answer. As for Peel's answer, it confirms the failure initiated at the very beginning of the interview process, and achieved here in a joint construction.

The Failure of a Media Information Process

In the preceding section, we have been considering the unsuccessful attempt by Peel to switch from a media preface to an interview process, that is the discursive expression of a particular kind of failure in the negotiation of a multi-oriented site of engagement. We will now turn to another framing problem faced by the participants in the sequence immediately following the initial section we have just been discussing:

Excerpt 2:   **"In Conversation In Geneva With Frank Peel", Recorded on TSR2 on 6 October 2000**

MEDIA PREFACE

[Camera shows Balthus' chalet, Schubert's music is played again. Camera shows photographs of Balthus in company of celebrities.]

1   Peel   we found the most incredible collection of art of decoration of the chalet itself of of the great the great the near great of this world that he has been associated with people like the Dalai Lama who who visited him at the chalet (.) and many many other people who have been to Rossinière (..)

SECOND INTERVIEW SEQUENCE

5   Balthus : did you ever go to Ro to Rome?
     Peel :   yes I have been to Rome many times
     Balthus : yes (.) many times
     Peel :   many times (.) it's a wonderful place
     Balthus : wonderful place
10   Peel :   wonderful place
     Balthus : too much traffic now
     Peel :   sorry?
     Balthus : too much traffic
     Peel :   too much traffic

15 Balthus : yes
    Peel :   yes well I'm afraid that's everywhere (.) everywhere now
              (..) and euh aa mm nobody has an answer to that nobody
              knows what to do about it
    Balthus : no
    Peel :   but we are lucky here because we
20 Balthus : because the first time (.) I went to Rome (.) it was
              marvelous (.) because you hear you could hear (..) ladies
              (.) ladies trying to play the piano
    [...]

Again, a mismatch seems to emerge between expected conduct and the rather unusual way the media interview is carried out in reality. And again, a close look at the social practices involved in that particular site of engagement can lead to an explicit description of what is at stake in that failing attempt to negotiate a multi-oriented interactional process.

The first element that can be pointed out is that this specific section of the broadcast starts once more with what we called a *media preface*, that is a discursive unit focused on the level of media information. A wide range of explicit as well as implicit markers give evidence for the idea that Peel is addressing an audience and not his guest at that point. Consider here again the filming itself, the reference to a collective speaker ("**we** found the most incredible collection of art [...]" l. 1), the reference to the guest as if he were absent ("**he** has been associated with people like the Dalai Lama [...]" l. 2–3) or the provision of redundant information from the perspective of his guest.

But the interesting point in that section of the broadcast lies in what immediately follows, that is the second attempt to open what we would call an *interview frame*. After the completion of the *media preface*, Balthus initiates a question addressed to Frank Peel ("did you ever go to Ro to Rome?" l. 5) and comments on the nuisance caused by the traffic ("too much traffic now" l. 11). In doing so, he somehow

6. Following Zimmerman (1998:90), discourse identities can be considered as "integral to the moment-by-moment organization of the interaction. Participants assume discourse identities as they engage in the various sequentially organized activities: current speaker, listener, story teller, story recipient, questioner, answerer, repair indicator, and so on".

fails to subscribe to the discursive constraints specific to interview processes (see page 574). For instance, he clearly assumes the *discourse identity* (Zimmerman, 1998:90 [6]) of a *questioner*, which is supposed to be in charge of the interviewer, and selects topics (/the city of Rome/, /Frank Peel visiting Rome/, /the traffic in Rome/) that are not clearly linked with his own experience at that point. Although Peel seems surprised and rather ill at ease, as shown by his request for clarification ("sorry?" l. 12) as well as a wide range of hesitation markers ("yes well I'm afraid that's everywhere (.) everywhere now (..) **and euh aa mm** nobody has an answer" l. 16–17), he ratifies the topics introduced by Balthus and aligns his discourse identities to those displayed by his guest. Consequently, the interviewer and his guest are not so much involved in the production of a real *discussion*, as in carrying out small talk.

Such a close attention to discursive markers is useful as it permits us to see how the routine framing of the interview is being altered once more. But we should go one step further, as the properties of that particular sequence of interaction can be linked to other levels of the multi-oriented process going on. If, on the one hand, mundane *small talk* on everyday life topics turns out to be rather unusual in interview practices, it is, on the other hand, an expected pattern in meetings in private (see page 575). As a result, the point we would like to stress here is that the failure of that second attempt to achieve an interview process stems from an excessive focus on the meeting frame in which it occurs. To put it another way, it appears that what is at stake at that point of the program refers not so much to an interview process as to the level of a meeting in private:

Figure 22.7
The Failure of a Media Information Process

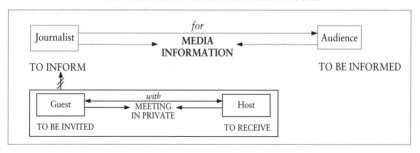

As shown by Figure 22.7, this shift into the meeting frame has also important consequences for the outcome of the media information process itself. As a matter of fact, Frank Peel's frequent visits in Rome and Balthus' consideration about traffic turn out to be rather poor information for the audience and fail to satisfy both the civic and the economic functions of media information (see page 573). Therefore, one could say that the problems encountered in the course of that second interview sequence lead in the end to a momentary failure of the media information process itself, as indicated by the broken lines and arrows in the diagram above.

Finally, it is only at the end of that sequence of small talk that Balthus starts talking freely about himself and that an effective interview frame seems to be opened. By evoking his first visit in Rome ("because the first time (.) I went to Rome [...]" l. 20–21) he provides the audience with relevant information, and displays both situated and discourse identities consistent with the role of a guest in a media interview practice.

Concluding Comments

In the above presentation, we have tried to link general considerations regarding media interviews with the description of some framing problems encountered by participants in a particular television broadcast. Starting with an intuitive perception of a "failure", we have based our analysis on the idea that agents taking part in media interviews are constrained to negotiate a complex layering of social practices associated with distinct situated identities.

What comes out of our analysis is that the study of multi-oriented sites of engagements calls preponderantly for a theory of social action as well as for a close attention to discourse units. That is why this case study illustrates emblematically that theories of discourse need to examine semiotic realities in the light of the social practices in which

7.   We want to thank the "Fondation Charles Bally" as well as the Swiss National Science Foundation (project No 12–61516.00) for their financial support. Special thanks are also due to Ingrid de Saint-Georges (Georgetown University) and Anne Vandeventer (University of Geneva) for very helpful comments on an earlier draft of this paper.

they emerge (Roulet, Filliettaz and Grobet, 2001; Filliettaz, 2000 and forthcoming; Burger, in press; Scollon, 2001).[7]

References

1. Adam, J.-M. 1997. Unités rédactionnelles et genres discursifs: Cadre général pour une approche de la presse écrite. *Pratiques* 94:3–17.

2. Burger, M. 1999. Identités de statut, identités de rôle. *Cahiers de linguistique française* 21:35–59.

3. _____ . *Les manifestes: Paroles de combat. De Marx à Breton.* Paris: Delachaux & Niestlé. In press.

4. _____ . Identités collectives et cognition: Un extrait d'entretien culturel. In *Cognition in language use*, edited by J. Verschueren. Belgium: Antwerp.

5. Charaudeau, P. 1997. *Le discours d'information médiatique.* Paris: Nathan.

6. Clark, H. H. 1996. *Using language.* Cambridge: Cambridge University Press.

7. Condor, S. and C. Antaki. 1997. Social cognition and discourse. In *Discourse as structure and process*, edited by T. A. Van Dijk. London: Sage, 320–347.

8. Van Dijk, T. A. 1997. Discourse as interaction in society. In *Discourse as social interaction,* edited by T. A. Van Dijk. London: Sage, 1–37.

9. Fairclough, N. 1992. *Discourse and social change.* Cambridge: Polity Press.

10. Filliettaz, L. 2000. *Actions, activités et discours.* Ph.D. diss., University of Geneva.

11. _____ . The expression of motives in bookshop encounters. Paper presented at the International Conference on Text and Talk at Work, Gent, 2000 August. Forthcoming.

12. Goffman, E. 1974. *Frame analysis: An essay on the organization of experience.* New York: Harper and Row.

13. Habermas, J. 1979. *Communication and the evolution of society.* Boston: Beacon Press.

14. Heritage, J. and D. Greatbatch. 1991. On the institutional character of institutional talk: The case of news interviews. In *Talk and social structure*, edited by D. Boden and D. Zimmerman. Cambridge: Polity Press, 94–137.

15. Jucker, A. H. 1995. Mass media. In *Handbook of pragmatics 1995*, edited by J. Verschuren, J.-O. Ostman and J. Blommaert. Amsterdam: John Benjamins.

16. Penz, H. 1996. *Language and control in American TV talk shows.* Tubingen: G. Narr.

17.   Roulet, E., L. Filliettaz and A. Grobet. 2001. *Un modèle et un instrument d'analyse de l'organisation du discours.* Bern: Peter Lang.

18.   Scollon, R. 1998. *Mediated discourse as social interaction. A study of news discourse.* London: Longman.

19.   _____ . 2001. Action and text. Toward an integrated understanding of the place of text in social (inter)action. In *Methods in critical discourse analysis*, edited by R. Wodak and M. Meyer. London: Sage.

20.   Shotter, J. 1994. *Conversational realities.* London: Sage.

21.   Traverso, V. 1996. *La conversation familière.* Lyon: Presses Universitaires de Lyon.

22.   Wertsch, J. 1998. *Mind as action.* New York: Oxford University Press.

23.   Zimmerman, D. H. 1998. Identity, context and interaction. In *Identities in Talk*, edited by C. Antaki and S. Widdicombe. London: Sage, 87–106.

23

Discourse and Ideology: The Taiwan Issue in the Chinese and American Media

Lu Xiaofei

Introduction

With Lee Teng-hui's statehood claim on 9 July 1999, the density of media reportage on the Taiwan issue rocketed and remained high till an earthquake struck Taiwan in late September. Notable are the many textual differences between the Chinese and American media representations of the issue. However, are these differences systematic? Are they triggered by their underlying socio-ideological contexts? How do they in turn bear upon their underlying ideologies? These are the questions that have prompted interest in the present research.

This chapter applies the framework of Critical Discourse Analysis to a comparative study of two corpora of Chinese and American Internet news discourse on the Taiwan issue during this period. The purpose of the study is to reveal how the dialectical relationship between discourse and ideology is instantiated in this particular case. The hypotheses formulated from preliminary observations of the news texts are threefold. First, we expect the textual differences between the Chinese and American news discourse to be systematic, and we aim to describe and interpret them with the aid of computer tools. Second, we expect these differences to be determined by the socio-ideological contexts underlying the production of the news discourse, and we aim to explicate how that actually works. Third, we expect the corpora of news discourse to bear different counter-impacts on their underlying socio-ideological contexts, and we aim to illustrate these functions specifically.

Framework and Methodology

Within the theoretical framework of Critical Discourse Analysis, discourse is defined as "use of language in speech and writing seen as a form of social practice" (Fairclough, 1992:63; 1995:54). This definition implies that discourse is not only a mode of representation, but also a socially situated mode of action, in a dialectical relationship with other facets of the social (*ibid.*). On the one hand, discourse is shaped by social structure: by various social relations at a societal level, by the relations specific to particular institutions, and by the situations prompting the communicative event; on the other hand, discourse is socially shaping: it may contribute to the construction of social identities, roles, and relationships as well as systems of knowledge and belief (Fairclough, 1993:134). Ideology is construed as significations or constructions of reality built into various dimensions of the forms or meanings of discursive practices, which contribute to the production, reproduction, or transformation of relations of power and domination (Fairclough, 1992:87). "The ideologies embedded in discursive practices are most effective when they become naturalized and achieve the status of 'common sense'" (*ibid.*), and critical discourse analysis has a particular stake in denaturalizing such naturalized ideologies.

To account for the nature of the ideological working of discourse, the chapter adopts a three-dimensional analytical framework, in which each discourse event is treated as a spoken or written text, an instance of discursive practice involving the production and interpretation of text, and a piece of social practice simultaneously (Fairclough, 1993, 1998). Analysis in the first dimension describes the discursive strategies in the media discourse from a multifunctional approach. Halliday's Systemic Functional Grammar (1994) is especially relevant here as it is essentially the ideological functioning of the discursive strategies that is of interest. Analysis of discourse as discursive practice focuses on the interpretation of the socio-ideological implications of the discursive strategies. In practice, these two dimensions of analysis are integrated in section three. Analysis in the dimension of discourse as social practice situates the media discourse in their underlying socio-ideological contexts, and explains the relationship between discourse structure and social structure.

The corpus-based study involves three stages. The first stage is corpus design and compilation. Taking into consideration the reputation and popularity of the source institutions and the width and depth of their coverage of the Taiwan issue, we decided to gather news texts from the four websites at http://www.peoplesdaily.com, http://www.chinadaily.com.cn, http://www.cnn.com, and http://www.abcnews.go.com. The corpus of Chinese media discourse (CMD) includes all the news texts on the Taiwan issue in the first two between 10 July and 20 September 1999, and the corpus of American media discourse (AMD), those in the rest two. The news texts collected were refined through necessary editing. The second stage is corpus processing. To maximize the extractable information, we tagged the corpora using the Constituent-likelihood Automatic Word-tagging System (CLAWS4), labelling each word with a "tag" specifying its word-class based on surface syntactic functions. The final stage is then corpus analysis, which is a combination of computer-aided and interactive work and of quantitative and qualitative approaches. WordSmith Tools 98 was used to generate relevant word frequency lists and concordances in a Keyword in Context format. In most cases the qualitative analysis of the meanings and functions of the linguistic patterns involves careful examination of the quantitative information extracted.

Discourse as Text and Discursive Practice

A General Comparison of the Corpora

Before analyzing the corpora, we need to take a brief look at some basic facts about their structures. This is relevant especially in places where statistical comparison is involved. As Table 23.1 shows, CMD comprises 293 news texts which amount to 117,264 tokens, and AMD contains 239 news texts with up to 114,292 tokens. The overall size of CMD in token is 1.026 times that of AMD. The type/token ratio indicates the degree of lexical variety of the texts. The higher ratio of AMD hints at a wider range of subject matter coverage. Besides, the longer texts and shorter sentences in AMD may bear the same implication. The hypothesis thus runs that AMD may be more heterogeneous than CMD in terms of the subject matter concerned and the ideologies encoded.

Table 23.1
Basic Statistical Facts about CMD and AMD

Item	CMD	AMD
Number of news texts	293	239
Number of tokens	117,264	114,292
Number of types	6,063	7,095
Type/Token ratio	5.17	6.21
Number of sentences	3,264	4,503
Average sentence length	34.10 tokens	25.25 tokens
Average text length	400.22 tokens	478.21 tokens

Ideational Meaning

Analysis of the ideational meaning of language is concerned with how social experiences in the real world are constructed through language. Different ways of conceptualizing social realities linguistically reveal different ideologies underlying the societies using the language. Actual analysis will focus on two aspects of language use, i.e., transitivity and lexicalization.

Transitivity

This section compares the top twenty process types of the clauses in the news texts in the two corpora by examining their top twenty non-modal verb forms. Due to the practical difficulty in differentiating the multifarious functions of the various forms of *be* and *have*, they are excluded from the analysis. Table 23.2 lists the top twenty verb forms with their tags (cf. Garside, Leech and McEnery, 1997:260) in the corpora.

Table 23.2
Top Twenty Non-modal Verb Forms in CMD and AMD

Rank	Verb Form in CMD	Number	Verb Form in AMD	Number
1	said_VVD	1043	said_VVD	1355
2	says_VVZ	291	told_VVD	171
3	split_VVI	111	saying_VVG	169
4	made_VVN	110	says_VVZ	118
5	made_VVD	90	use_VVI	85
6	separate_VVI	76	take_VVI	83
7	doomed_VVN	73	did_VDD	78
8	stressed_VVD	61	said_VVN	70
9	changed_VVN	60	do_VD0	63
10	saying_VVG	59	regards_VVZ	60
11	splitting_VVG	58	do_VDI	58
12	pointed_VVD	57	quoted_VDD	58
13	reiterated_VVD	57	warned_VVD	58
14	added_VVD	55	conducted_VVN	58
15	safeguard_VVI	55	invade_VVI	55
16	told_VVD	53	make_VVI	50
17	does_VDZ	52	reported_VVD	50
18	expressed_VVD	50	sent_VVD	50
19	stop_VVI	50	threatened_VVN	48
20	make_VVI	49	seen_VVN	47

The two corpora demonstrate considerable differences as far as their top processes are concerned. In both corpora, verb forms realizing verbal processes rank highest. However, among such neutral verbs as *say* and *tell*, we see a high density of verbs conveying a sense of verbal emphasis in CMD, such as *stress, point (out)*, and *reiterate*, and that of verbs creating a sense of verbal opposition in AMD, such as *warn* and *threaten*. This difference implies that CMD tends to foreground voices stressing mainland China's policies or reiterating supports to them through verbal processes, while AMD tends to emphasize the oppositional verbal exchanges between the parties concerned.

Ranking second are verb forms realizing material processes. Notably, CMD contains a cluster of verbs pinpointing Lee's *splitting* and *separating* the motherland, which he must *stop* and which are *doomed* to failure. The material process pertaining to the Chinese government and people, *safeguard,* bears a sense of dignified determination. Conversely, AMD characterizes the same material process as *invade,* projecting a contrastive motivation. Material processes like *split* and *separate* are not highlighted in AMD.

Lexicalization and Collocation

Lexicalization is the most obvious way in which the ideational meanings of a discourse are signalled (Halliday, 1994). Investigation of the patterns of lexical reiteration, relexicalization, and collocation of the two corpora will gain us insights into the preoccupations of the respective groups of discourse producers.

Table 23.3
Top Ten Nouns in CMD and AMD

Rank	Noun in CMD	Number	Noun in AMD	Number
1	Taiwan	2361	Taiwan	2608
2	China	1963	China	1943
3	Lee	1699	Beijing	845
4	people	879	Lee	841
5	relations	836	island	404
6	Teng-hui	709	Taipei	398
7	cross-Straits	502	U.S.	378
8	reunification	453	President	325
9	policy	410	independence	316
10	remarks	404	relations	316

A close look at Table 23.3 reveals an amount of meaningful information. In CMD, the high density of *people, reunification, policy,* and *remarks* indicates the concern of CMD over such matters as the interest of the Chinese people, reunification, China's policy, and Lee's remarks. The high frequency of *cross-Straits* implies the tendency of CMD to define relations between mainland China and Taiwan as between two sides geographically separated by the Taiwan Straits. In AMD, the high density of *Beijing* and *Taipei* shows the two governments are frequently mentioned as such. This, however, creates a strong sense of political equality between them. The presence of *U.S.* in the list hints upon an important role attached to it. The high frequency of President in AMD accompanies that of *Lee*, since Lee is consistently referred to as *President Lee*. This endorses the title unacknowledged by mainland China. Finally, in contrast to *reunification* in the list of CMD we see *independence* in that of AMD. The divergent patterns of lexical reiteration of the two corpora correspond to the different aspects of the Taiwan issue on which they place emphasis.

Whereas the key issue concerned throughout the news discourses is the same, i.e., the relations between mainland China and Taiwan, the subject matter *per se* is lexicalized rather differently in CMD and AMD.

Table 23.4
Lexical Items Defining Cross-Straits Relations in CMD and AMD

Lexical Items	CMD	AMD
cross-Straits relations, cross-Strait relations	376	16
relations across the (Taiwan) Straits	94	28
relations between the two sides of/across the Taiwan Straits, relations between both sides of the Taiwan Straits	26	9
relations between the Chinese/China's mainland and Taiwan	7	0
relations between Taiwan and the mainland/the mainland and Taiwan	5	2
relations between China and its Taiwan province	1	0
Subtotal 1	509	55
relations between China and Taiwan/Taiwan and China	6	11
Taiwan-China relations, China-Taiwan relations	0	19
Taipei-Beijing relations, relations between Beijing and Taipei	0	7
relations between the two rivals/arch-rivals	0	6
relations between Taiwan and communist China	0	2
Subtotal 2	6	45
Total	515	100

Table 23.4 differentiates two groups of lexical items used to conceptualize the "relations". Group 1 comprises wordings that avoid creating any sense of political or ideological opposition between the two sides. Rather, the idea is that they are only geographically separated by the Taiwan Straits and are both parts of a unity. Group 2 includes lexical items that tend to convey a sense of political equality or ideological opposition between the two sides.

In CMD, lexical items from Group 1 pervade, with 509 out of the 515 instances (98.8%) falling under this category. This preponderance concurs with the prevalent ideology underlying the Chinese society and serves to legitimize it. In AMD, the picture is more diversified. Although Group 1 still accounts for the majority (55%), the proportion gap between the two groups is far less notable. Relexicalization brings about a larger lexical variety in AMD, confusing the reader about the nature of the "relations" instead of clarifying the issue with a consistent definition.

One China Policy

The "one China" policy is admittedly the bottom line of mainland China's position in handling cross-Straits relations. Most countries, including the U.S., accept this policy. However, does this superficial agreement necessarily lead to convergence in treating the concept in the media?

Figure 23.1
Sample Concordance Listing of One China Policy in CMD

```
              African country will insist on a "One China"  policy, adding this
      that the UN will continue to uphold a "One China"  policy. She made the
            in October.  Myanmar Abides by "One China"  Policy: Statement
    took a clear-cut stand on the China's "one China"  policy. The support
    Bill Clinton reiterated his country's "one China"  policy on Wednesday
                    she added.   US favours 'one China'  policy WASHINGTONG
          France reaffirmed on July 21 its  one China   policy it has adopted
    "strong commitment" to adhering to its "one China"  policy on the Taiwan
        and it will continue to follow the "one China"  policy. James Foley
    reinforced the wide acceptance of the "One China"  policy and further
```

Figure 23.2
Sample Concordance Listing of One China Policy in AMD

```
     President Lee Teng-hui abandoned a "one China" policy last week, saying
 Taiwan's recent decision to scrap its "one China" policy and put relation
 Taiwan, overturning its longstanding "one China" policy. The deal was
    Beijing by dumping the longstanding "One China" policy. "It fits the
 last week by junking the longstanding "one China" policy in a bid to break
    since Taipei's decision to drop the "one China" policy that has
     basis _ a seeming departure from the "one China" policy China and Taiwan
response to Taipei's rejection of the "One China" policy, a lynchpin of
      Lee Teng-hui's repudiation of the "one China" policy. But they
  Taipei said it backed away from the "one China" policy because Beijing
```

The co-texts in which *one China policy* occurs in the two corpora differ. The concordance of it in CMD shows a preponderance of collocations with verbs and nominal groups of an affirmative nature. Typical verbs preceding it include *uphold, pursue, follow, support, advocate, affirm, reaffirm, reiterate, stress, favour, abide by, insist on, adhere to,* and *stick to.* Dominance of such collocations creates the sense that the "one China policy" is extensively "affirmed" in words and "abided by" in action. Typical nominal groups preceding it include *adherence to, commitment to, support for, acceptance of,* and *promise on.* Altogether, 167 out of the 178 instances (94%) occur in positive co-texts. Contrastively, in AMD, only 31 out of the 112 instances (28%) appear in positive environments. In the 81 negative instances, typical verbs collocating with *one China policy* include *abandon, scrap, junk, drop, dump, repudiate,* and *overturn,* and typical nominal groups include *abandonment of, rejection of, repudiation of,* and *departure from.* It is also *pushed* by China and *used by China to marginalize Taiwan.* With such patterns of collocation, the connotations *one China policy* displays in the two corpora contrast with each other. In CMD, it is consistently represented as something extensively affirmed and abided by, whereas in AMD, emphasis on the constant "scrapping" and "repudiation" of it by the Taiwan authorities lends to it a negative and pejorative nature.

Interpersonal Meaning

Analysis of the interpersonal meaning of language is concerned with how social identities of, and relations between different social subjects and groups are constructed and sustained. Actual analysis will concentrate on how the personal noun *we* as "subject" in the "mood" structure is used in this line.

Table 23.5
Who are *We* in CMD and AMD

Parties Included in We	CMD	Percentage	AMD	Percentage
The Chinese Government, people and army	103	63.1%	76	25.8%
The U.S. Government, people and army	34	20.9%	94	32.0%
The Taiwan Government and people	6	3.7%	114	38.8%
Other foreign parties	16	9.8%	8	2.7%
Irrelevant	4	2.5%	2	0.7%
Total	163	100%	294	100%

Table 23.5 indicates that in CMD, the Chinese Government, people, and army constitute the overwhelming majority of the groups of *we*, seconded by the U.S. Government, people, and army. The Taiwan Government and people are the least represented. The gap between the groups is rather obvious. In AMD, the order is almost reversed, and the gap between the three groups is considerably reduced. Compared with CMD, AMD presents a more heterogeneous picture. The more unified scene of CMD tends to identify the Chinese Government, people, and army as the dominating group whose voice carries the greatest weight in the issue. The more diversified scene of AMD, however, denies the dominance of the voice of the group, appropriating a larger portion of the stage to the Taiwan Government and people, and a more important role to the U.S. Government, people, and army.

Table 23.6
What Side Do We Take in CMD and AMD

Parties Supported	Parties Included in We	CMD		AMD	
		No.	Percentage	No.	Percentage
Mainland China	The Chinese Government and army	103	66.6%	76	25.9%
	The U.S. Government	21	12.9%	8	2.7%
	Other foreign parties	16	9.8%	1	0.3%
	Supportive Taiwan parties	4	2.5%	0	0%
	Subtotal	144	88.3%	85	28.9%
Taiwan	The Taiwan Government and army	2	1.2%	114	38.8%
	The U.S. Government and army	2	1.2%	13	4.4%
	Other foreign parties	0	0%	4	1.4%
	Subtotal	4	2.5%	131	44.6%
U.S. role	The U.S. Government	11	6.7%	73	24.8%
Comments	Other foreign parties	0	0%	3	1.0%
Irrelevant		4	2.5%	2	0.7%
Total		163	100%	294	100%

As Table 23.6 indicates, in CMD, 88.3% of the groups of *we* support the mainland China's view. These include not only the Chinese Government, people, and army, but also the majority of the groups of U.S. parties, all the groups of foreign parties other than the U.S., and two thirds of the groups of the Taiwan Government and people. Contrastively, the Taiwan authorities' view receives support from only 2.5% of the groups. The U.S. is given little space to comment on its own role in, and principles of, the issue. This overwhelming disproportion in the support of the views of the two sides serves to endorse one and marginalize the other.

In AMD, the picture is again drastically different. The view of the Taiwan authorities receives the greatest support among the groups of *we*. Furthermore, most groups of the U.S. parties support the view of Taiwan, as do most other foreign parties. Yet, the gap between the number of parties supporting mainland China and Taiwan is not so dramatic as that in CMD. Meanwhile, more space is allocated to the U.S. Government to emphasize its own role and voice its comments. In short, whereas AMD gives more support to the view of the Taiwan Government, it keeps the platform more open than CMD does.

Textual Meaning

Analysis of the textual meaning of language is concerned with how information is organized into coherent texts. Different choices in ways of organizing the same messages carry different implications. Our analysis at the macro-level of message organization seeks to differentiate meanings of different topic control strategies through comparing the news headlines in the two corpora.

Table 23.7
Topics Selected in CMD

Topics Selected	Number	Percentage
China's policy	20	6.8%
International commitments to "one China" policy	43	14.7%
Sino-U.S. relations	21	7.2%
Denouncing Taiwan's international participation	12	4.1%
Overt accusations of Lee and Taiwan's stance	86	29.3%
Negative comments on Lee and Taiwan's stance	70	23.9%
Urging Lee and Taiwan to stop separatism	8	2.7%
Military news on PLA	13	4.5%
China's determination to guard integrity and fight separatists	10	3.4%
Developments in cross-Straits exchanges	10	3.4%
Total	293	100%

As Table 23.7 indicates, the topics covered by the news texts in CMD center around two themes. Greatest prominence is allocated to overt accusations of and negative comments on Lee and the Taiwan authorities' stance. Altogether, they constitute 53.2% of all the topics. Notable prominence is also assigned to the promotion of the mainland China's policies and the commitments of international parties to the "one China" policy. Topics related to this theme take up 21.5% of the topics.

The force of the accusation is reinforced by the recurrence of two syntactic structures, i.e., NP1 (naming the accuser) + Verb (realizing the accusation) + NP2 (naming the accused), and NP (naming the accused) + VVN (past participle of the verb realizing the accusation). Typical examples of the first include "People In Eastern China Criticize

Lee's Separatist Remarks," "Taiwan Business People Slam Lee Teng-hui's Splittist Remarks," and "Bangladeshi Organization Condemns Lee Teng-hui's Separatist Remarks." Instances of the second are "Lee Teng-hui's Dangerous Step Censured," "Lee Tenghui's 'Two Nations' Theory Refuted," and "Lee Teng-hui's 'Two States' Statement Severely Condemned." Within the theme and the homogeneous syntactic structures, we see a multitude of accusers involved: apart from the official voice of the Chinese Government, various domestic groups are brought in, as are a few Taiwan parties and foreign parties. The extensity of the parties included in the pool of accusers adds up to the intensity of the accusation. The verbs selected include *refute, lash out, condemn, slam, criticize, lambast, denounce, rebut, contradict, blast,* and *disagree with.* The target of the accusation is unanimously Lee's remarks and views taking the shape of different linguistic forms. Realized in two recurrent syntactic structures, the repeated accusations from a multiplicity of parties directed towards the single target impinge upon the readers' minds forcefully.

The international community's commitments to the "one China" policy is also predominantly realized in one syntactic structure, namely, NP1 (naming the committer) + Verb (realizing the commitment) + NP2 (naming the object to which NP1 is committed to). Typical examples include "U.S. Reaffirms 'One China' Policy," "EU Supports 'One China' Principle," and "UN Chief Reiterates 'One China' Policy." Appearing in the position of NP1 is a large number of countries and international organizations. The verbs used are all associated with commitments and support: the most typical two are *reiterate* and *reaffirm;* others include *support, stress, abide by, stick to,* and *uphold.* Target of the commitments and support, i.e., the "one China" policy, remains the same all through, though unfolded in slightly different linguistic forms. The prominence given to the reiterated commitments to the "one China" policy from such a big group of parties is due not so much to their news value as to the intention of the discourse producers to sustain a consciousness of extensive support to the policy.

Table 23.8
Topics Selected in AMD

Topics Selected	Number	Percentage
Beijing against Taiwan	30	12.6%
Military reports: China	39	16.3%
China's concern over foreign intervention	10	4.2%
China's internal situation	10	4.2%
Subtotal: the voice of mainland China	89	37.3%
Taiwan against Beijing	24	10.1%
Lee and Taiwan's effort to cool the tension	11	4.6%
Internal situation of Taiwan	20	8.4%
Taiwan's international participation	8	3.3%
Military report: Taiwan	23	9.6%
Subtotal: the voice of Taiwan	86	36.0%
Other aspects of cross-Straits relations	11	4.6%
The U.S. role	36	15.1%
International concern over the issue	17	7.0%
Total	239	100%

In terms of the distribution of prominence, Table 23.8 demonstrates an extraordinary non-uniformity among the topics covered in AMD. Voices of mainland China and Taiwan take up over one third of the overall topics each, with the rest one quarter allocated to those of the U.S. and other international parties. No party dominates the stage.

Specific topics regarding mainland China in AMD differ from those in CMD, too. Primary attention is given to issues related to its military power and exercises and its claim of the force option. Typical examples include "Security Expert: China Can Take Taiwan Without Firing a Shot," "China Flaunts Military Might Amid Taiwan Row," and "War Games Reported as Taiwan Dispute Heats Up." Mainland China's accusations of and negative comments on Lee and the Taiwan authorities are reduced. Another aspect covered is mainland China's concern over foreign intervention, in which mainland China is warning foreign parties not to intervene, accusing the U.S. of its arms sales to Taiwan, and expressing worries of the U.S. involvement. As such, in AMD, mainland China is not only opposing Lee and the Taiwan authorities militarily and verbally, but also trying to warn off international parties. The policies mainland China advocates are not publicized; neither is the international support it receives.

Lee and the Taiwan authorities are granted equal opportunities to air their views in AMD. Here, the most remarkable prominence is attached to the stance they take against mainland China, particularly their statehood and democracy claims. Typical examples include "Lee Stands Firm — Taiwan's President Reaffirms His Controversial Remarks on the Island's Status," "In Volley of Harsh Words, Taiwanese Leader Fires Back at China," and "Taiwan VP Vows No Letup in Demand for Equality." Such claims are all pointedly against the mainland China's policies. Whereas in CMD, these views are explicitly discredited, in AMD they are placed in juxtaposition with the mainland China's counterattacks with an equal status as the latter. The second largest group of topics projecting Taiwan's voice focus on Taiwan's responses to the military exercises of mainland China, and Taiwan's military power and needs. Typical examples include "Taiwan's President Says Economic Problems Keep China from Military Action" "It Takes More Than War Games to Make the Taiwanese Jittery," and "Amid Tension with China, Taiwan Rolls out Upgraded Tanks." This focus constitutes a tit for tat of the large proportion of military reports on mainland China.

Summary

With the comparative analysis above, we are now in a good position to summarize the section. First, at the descriptive level, the linguistic analysis has demonstrated systematic discrepancies between the discursive strategies at various levels employed by the two corpora, as are summarized in the tables. Second, at the interpretative level, such descriptive discrepancies mean that the language in the discourses in the two corpora function in contrastive ways. Ideationally, discourses in CMD have systematically reproduced and represented those aspects of the social realities that are in favor of the policies and stances of mainland China but to the disadvantage of Lee and the Taiwan authorities. Those in AMD keep the picture more heterogeneous, emphasizing such realities as the oppositional yet equal exchanges of words or action between the two sides. Interpersonally, CMD identifies mainland China as the dominating party on the stage enjoying favorable relationships with other parties; Lee and the Taiwan authorities are isolated and marginalized; no substantial role is assigned to the U.S. or other foreign parities. In AMD, no party dominates the scene; rather, mainland China and Taiwan are positioned as oppositional equals, with the U.S. playing a significant role in the issue, too. Textually, CMD has opted for such topics that are again to the advantage of mainland China's polices and stances and disadvantage of Lee and the Taiwan authorities in terms of topic control. AMD has selected topics that convey a sense of equal opposition between the two sides of mainland China and Taiwan, or a sense of importance of the U.S. itself in the issue.

Discourse as Social Practice

This dimension of analysis situates the corpora of media discourse in their underlying socio-ideological contexts and explicates the relationship between the two. The societal contexts underlying the production of CMD and AMD differ from each other in several significant aspects: economic, political, cultural, and strategic. Economically, mainland China calls for a peaceful and stable domestic and international environment as well as reciprocal relations and exchanges with other economies, including Taiwan and the U.S. (Clough, 1999). Meanwhile, with the economic liberalization of Taiwan, the U.S. sees a new interest in fostering an economically powerful Taiwan to contribute to the management of the global economy (Lin, 1998:142). Politically, Socialism and authoritarianism in mainland China contrast Capitalism and the Westernized democracy in the U.S. and Taiwan. Culturally, mainland China places overriding priority on issues of sovereignty and territorial integrity as a result of its surging nationalism, while the U.S. and Taiwan claim emphasis on such values as freedom, equality, human rights and democracy. Strategically, Taiwan constitutes a strategic asset to mainland China, while there is an increasing mood in the U.S. to check the potential "China threat" with the "Taiwan card" (Lin, 1998:143). These considerations have resulted in substantial ideological and policy divergences between mainland China and the U.S.

In terms of the institutional contexts, Won (1989:68) observed that mass media in China serve basically as a link between the government, the Communist Party, and the people, and one expected to help push forward the Socialist cause. The dominant part of China's journalism is an organ of the Communist Party, and its political orientation and fundamental policies largely depend on those of the Party (Won, 1989:56–57). Mass media in the U.S., however, are commercialized and profit-driven; they enjoy considerable freedom and independence in news selection and are subject to minimum government control (Hiebert, 1999; Balkin, 1993).

In terms of the situational contexts, Sino-U.S. relations were rather complicated at that time as a result of a series of events, including the 1995–1996 crisis incurred by Lee's Cornell trip, NATO's bombing of the Chinese Embassy in Belgrade in May 1999, the U.S. allegation that China stole its nuclear weapons technology, the stagnating bilateral negotiations on China's accession to the WTO, the U.S. arms sales to Taiwan in between China's military exercises, and the argument over the inclusion of Taiwan in the high-tech Theatre Missile Defense (TMD). Meanwhile, mainland China has also observed a tendency of Lee and the Taiwan authorities towards independence from the 1995–1996 crisis and Lee's statehood claim on 9 July 1999.

On the one hand, we can conclude that the systematic discursive differences between CMD and AMD are determined by their different underlying socio-ideological contexts. The various considerations of mainland China lead to a policy aiming at an early "peaceful reunification" under the "one country, two systems" framework; it promotes the "one China" concept and opposes any move of Taiwan towards independence or expansion of its international space. The institutional practice of the Chinese mass media requires them to publicize and support major government policies. The societal and institutional contexts explain CMD's ideational representations of the social realities favourable to the policies and stance of mainland China and unfavuorable to Lee and the Taiwan authorities. The centralized socio-political system and thus unified policy in major political issues, the censorship policy, and the supportive attitude of the mass media towards government policies, account for the relative homogeneity in the scope of social realities reproduced. At the same time, part of mainland China's policy is that the Taiwan question is an internal matter of China, and it opposes any international interference; it insists that Taiwan is part of China and only the PRC can represent China in the international arena. However, China also needs a peaceful environment and reciprocal exchanges with other economies. The situational context shows that mainland China believes there is a strong move of Taiwan towards independence, and that Sino-U.S. relations are not on a good footing. These policies and the situational context explain CMD's interpersonal construction of the dominating position of mainland China, its favourable relationships with other parties, the isolation of Lee and the Taiwan authorities, and the marginalization of the U.S. role. Likewise, CMD's textual rendition of the messages can also be explained.

The case of AMD is of a similar nature. The intricacies of the various considerations of the U.S. have resulted in equal complexities in its policies. The U.S. maintains a policy of constructive engagement with mainland China, commits itself to the "one China" policy, and admits that the Taiwan issue should be resolved by mainland China and Taiwan; yet, it is also developing relations with Taiwan, supporting it with continuous arms sales, and warning mainland China against its force option. The institutional practice of the American mass media and the censorship policy allow minimum government control and considerable independence in news selection. Driven by commercial profits, they tend to offer what they deem as of news value to their customers. The situational context demonstrates visible complicatedness in the trilateral relations between the U.S., mainland China, and Taiwan. All the societal, institutional, and situational contexts contribute to AMD's ideational representation of the reality as an equal opposition between mainland China and Taiwan as well as its emphasis on the problematic facets of the issue. It is the opposition between the two sides and the problematic aspects of the issue that create news value. These complex contexts also explain the heterogeneity of the scope of social realities reproduced. Accordingly, in terms of interpersonal meaning, the dominating position of mainland China is denied, whereas the U.S. is attributed a substantial role in the issue. The textual rendition of the messages is determined likewise.

On the other hand, we can also conclude that the discursive strategies employed in the two corpora not only encode and embody their underlying ideologies linguistically, but also help to propagate, legitimize, and sustain them, challenging the opposing ideologies at the same time. CMD has shown an explicit function in bringing to the fore the policies and views of mainland China, giving them overruling publicity with a strong sense of legitimacy. This endowed legitimacy clearly helps to maintain the publicized ideologies among the public. Similarly, AMD reflects the complexity of the U.S. ideologies pertaining to the Taiwan issue. It challenges the dominating role of the mainland China in CMD by positioning Taiwan in an equal position, and by assigning the U.S. a legitimized role in the issue. In this sense, discourse also constitutes a site for power struggle between the different parties concerned. The dialectical relationship between discourse and ideology lies exactly in the effects and counter-effects of them on each other.

Conclusion

From the three-dimensional analysis of the two corpora of Chinese and American media discourse on the Taiwan issue, we are able to envisage a dialectical relationship between discourse and ideology in this particular case. The systematic discursive differences between the two corpora are shaped by the different socio-ideological contexts underlying the production of them, and bear upon these contexts differently. The analysis aims to help understand the naturalized ideologies embedded in the seemingly neutral news discourse, and to promote a critical awareness of political discourse in general and discourse on the Taiwan issue in particular. Further research in this line could incorporate a study of the reader's response to selected news discourse, and a re-examination of the analytical results in follow-up corpora.

References

1. Balkin, J. M. 1993. The American system of censorship and free expression. In *Patterns of censorship around the world,* edited by I. Peleg. Boulder: Westview Press, 155–172.

2. Clough, R. N. 1999. *Cooperation or conflict in the Taiwan issue.* Lanham: Rowmanh and Littlefield Publishers, Inc.

3. Fairclough, N. 1992. *Discourse and social change.* Cambridge: Polity Press.

4. _____ . 1993. Critical discourse analysis and the marketization of public discourse: The universities. *Discourse and Society* 4 (2): 133–168.

5. _____ . 1995. *Media discourse.* London: Edward Arnold.

6. _____ . 1998. Political discourse in media: An analytical framework. In *Approaches to media discourse,* edited by A. Bell and P. Garrett. Oxford: Blackwell, 142–162.

7. _____ and R. Wodak. 1997. Critical discourse analysis. In *Discourse studies: A multidisciplinary introduction,* edited by T. A. van Dijk. Vol. 2. London: Sage Publications, 257–284,

8. Garside, R., G. Leech and T. McEnery, eds. 1997. *Corpus annotation: Linguistic information from computer text corpora.* London: Longman.

9. Halliday, M. A. K. 1994. *An introduction to functional grammar,* 2nd ed. London: Edward Arnold.

10. Hiebert, R. E. 1999. The growing power of mass media. In *Impact of mass media: Current issues,* edited by R. Eldon. New York: Longman, 3–15.

11. Lin, G. 1998. The changing relations across the Taiwan Strait. In *Interpreting U.S.–China–Taiwan Relations,* edited by X. Li, X. Hu and Y. Zhong. Lanham: University Press of America, 127–150.

12. Van Dijk, T. A. 1993. Principles of critical discourse analysis. In *Discourse and Society* 4 (2): 249–283.

13. Won, H. C. 1989. *Mass media in China: The history and the future.* Ames: Iowa State University Press.

24

Hype about Hypertext

Bernard McKenna

Introduction

This chapter aims to provide a useful theoretical framework to allow tertiary educators of professional, technical, and corporate writing to make sensible decisions about the most efficacious use of hypertext technology in the classroom.

The context in which I experience life as an academic is probably very similar to that of many others: increasing workloads, reduced resources largely as a result of rapidly falling government funding, demands for a more student-focused curriculum, demands to make content more vocational, and demands that teaching strategies become more "flexible" by incorporating hypertextual and hypermediated technologies. The latter element is seen in my own university's *Faculty of Business Strategic Plan for Online Teaching.* Included in its online teaching principles are the following statements:

> 2.4 *Online teaching provides a most economical and accessible resource opportunity and support service for international students and other students with special learning needs.*
>
> 2.5 *Online teaching gives both staff and students the opportunity to balance traditional content and practice in teaching and learning with new innovative practices.*
>
> 2.6 *The quality of service offered to students and other stakeholders in the university's teaching and learning is enhanced through online teaching.*
>
> 2.8 *The development and / or modification of a unit for online teaching encourages reflection by the teacher on the content and learning experiences of the unit.*

As an academic who embraced the online teaching (OLT) system by placing all my lectures on OLT with useful web links, I was dismayed to find that lectures dwindled to less than 30% attendance[1], and that discussion tutorials were even more poorly attended. Consequently, I began my own critical appraisal of the claims made for hypertextual education. For writing pedagogy, in particular, I was forced to agree with DeWitt and Strasma, (1999) that there is "a scarcity of contextual studies on hypertext and writing ... that examine writing pedagogies and writing students" (p. 4).

Many proponents of educational hypertext claim that it is an important new technology that will unleash capabilities in students not previously possible: it

> *"has the power to reconfigure our culture's assumptions about textuality, authorship, creative property, education, and a range of other issues'; provides 'factual information and sophisticated ways of dealing with it'; encourages students 'to think in more sophisticated ways"* (Landow, 1992:195–196).

However, Gay's advice that 'the introduction of new technologies in and of itself will not solve communication problems' (In Barrett and Redmond, 1995:186) is part of a growing scepticism and outright opposition (Saul, 1997; Postman, 1986, 1993, 1995). Hypertext is, after all, only an "information presentation medium" (Dillon, 1996: 39).

This chapter firstly identifies my critical perspective that contextualizes the discourse in a political-economic framework. Then I define what is meant by the frequently synonomized terms hypertext, multimedia, and hypermedia. The bulk of the chapter then critically evaluates five prominent claims made for hypertextual / hypermedia teaching and learning. From this, I draw five conclusions that, hopefully, provide both general and practical guidance for those seeking to use this form of teaching practice.

---

1.   The fact that one subject's lecture was on Friday night at 7 p.m., it must be acknowledged, was probably also a disincentive.

Critical Perspective

By critical I mean that I specifically adopt Webster's (1997) position to take an "interrogative and sceptical view of the 'information society'", consistent with my wider critical position on the information society and the new technocracy (McKenna and Graham, 2000; see also Graham, 2000a; Postman, 1993). My critical analysis goes further than McKnight, Dillon and Richardson's (1991) injunction that we should treat any claims for the new medium "with caution" because, at a more comprehensive level, these claims are yet another manifestation of the "technoromanticism" of digital narratives which combine the romantic elements of imagination, individuality, and soul with progressivist rationalism (Coyne, 1999).

It is important to understand that the context in which this issue is practiced and discussed incorporates the non-pedagogic realm, particularly political ideology. This is perhaps best exemplified in the following extract from a paper presented by a QUT academic advocating the extension of hypermediated and hypertextual pedagogy:

> "The increasing market orientation has brought sweeping changes ... [C]hanges to government funding have forced universities to become more innovative in their resourcing. One way ... to enhance ... international competitiveness is through the flexible delivery of their programs. Flexible delivery is, by definition, a client-oriented approach because it is a commitment ... to meet the various needs of its students. Furthermore, it is tacit recognition of the "massification" of higher education" (Williams, 2000).

In this passage, the academic has combined market forces, reduced government funding, increased certification and diploma-acquisition, and individualism to form the justification for hypertextual "flexible delivery". . Another advocate, an academic vice-president at an Australian university, also justifies adopting this technology in the new pedagogy because of the "comparative advantage of the information superhighway environment" (LeGrew, 1995). In other words, its own proponents advocate technologically delivered flexible learning in highly ideologized terms

Three other discursive trajectories inflecting hypertext delivery are those of "flexibility" [2] rather than stasis; by the focus on the "client" rather than the academy or the disciplinary tradition; and the orientation towards the workplace rather than to learning *per se* (cf. Weimer, 1992). A broader context still is reduced government expenditure coupled with rising demands on the academy. Many agree to name this a "postmodern" and "postfordist" landscape (Bates, 1999, ch. 2; Dolence and Norris, 1995; Mason 1998; Katz and Associates, 1999). Notwithstanding the nomenclature, the reality for most new learners is that they

> *"will need to be able to access information ... from multiple sources in multiple formats; select, store, and reorder or recreate information; directly communicate with instructors, colleagues, and other learners; incorporate accessed or reworked material into work documents; share and manipulate information, documents or projects with others; and access, combine, create and transmit audio, video, text, and data as necessary"* (Bates, 1999:15)

Clearly this represents an interplay of significant new ideological trajectories that must be taken into account when considering the issues of hypertext/hypermedia in university pedagogy.

Definition

The terms *hypertext, multimedia,* and *hypermedia* tend to be used interchangeably. By looking at the three terms I will derive the features that are relevant to this chapter.

---

2.   For a fuller explanation of the ideological nature of "flexibility" demands see McKenna (1999).

Hypertext

The term was first coined by Ted Nelson in the 1960s to mean "non-sequential writing-text that branches and allows choices to the reader, best read at an interactive screen. As popularly conceived, this is a series of text chunks connected by links which offer the reader different pathways" (in Altun, 2000:36–37). According to DeWitt and Strasma (1999), "Hypertext as an idea is not new, but its use as a functional medium in electronic form is only a few years old" (p. 204; see also Rouet and Levonen, 1996).

Multimedia

Multimedia simply means "the use of text, graphics, animation, pictures, video, and sound to present information" (Bagui, 1998:3). The computer allows these to be integrated into one piece of technology (Najjar, 1996:129)

Hypermedia

The definition of hypermedia provided by Rasmussen and Davidson-Shivers (1998), "text, graphics, sound, animation, video, or other data" (p. 296), does not differentiate this from multimedia. However, the *Oxford Dictionary of New Words* (Tulloch, 1992), suggests that hypermedia is "the structuring [of] information in different media (text, graphics, sound etc) for presentation to an individual user in such a way that related items of information are connected and presented together" (p. 159). It is the "structuring" aspect then that separates hypermedia from other computer-based capabilities (e.g., WWW, email). This concurs with Altun's explanation that hypermedia and multimedia are "used interchangeably to refer to hypertext applications" (Altun, 2000), but the "core" of the definitions is the linking of nodes and the non-linearity (p. 37).

In this paper, by **hypertext**, I mean non-sequential text chunks that are in some way linked. By **hypermedia** I mean the assembly of written, visual, audio, and animation into a hypertext situation.

Critical Evaluation of Five Claims

Hypertext Domains Allow Students to Learn at Their Own Rate

There is much enthusiasm about hypermedia allowing reading and learning that is not constrained by the author / teacher and that reflects the knowledge representations of different learners (Welsh, 1995:275). Typical claims in this regard are

- Exploration: Active personal exploration of information for comprehension and information locating and retrieval (Guthrie, Britten, and Barker, 1991).
- Self-paced learning: "allows the learner to personally set the pace of learning" (Najjar, 1996:132).
- Meeting student needs: "Hypermedia permits the tailoring of instruction to meet individual student needs' environments" (Rasmussen and Davidson-Shivers, 1998:292).

Learner control: The notion of *Learner Control*, evident in many of these claims, is defined by Rasmussen and Davidson-Shivers (1998) as "the amount of personal responsibility or control an individual can exert in an instructional situation", (p. 296). Teachers can manipulate their teaching methods so that learning styles can be used in conjunction with learner control to facilitate and enhance student performance in hypermediated learning environments. *Learning style*[3] is defined by Dunn (1986) as "the ways in which an individual 'absorbs and retains information or skills'" (in Rasmussen and Davidson-Shivers, 1998: 292–293). Active learners will spend more time on task and have a higher frequency of selecting embedded elaborated information (in Tergan, 1997a:266; Lee and Leeman, 1993). Students who prefer interacting with others, highly organized material, and real-world activities perform better than students displaying other preferences in their first year (Matthews in Rasmussen and Davidson-Shivers, 1998: 295)

---

3.   Kolb (1985) defines four learning styles:
     (a)   diverger: can view concrete situation from multiple viewpoints
     (b)   assimilator: can understand and put into concise, logical form a wide range of information
     (c)   converger: can find practical uses for ideas and theories
     (d)   accommodator: executes plans and takes risks.

Learning styles were found to be a significant factor influencing learning in a hypertext environment (Ellis, Ford, and Wood, 1993; Rasmussen and Davidson-Shivers, 1998).

Critique

While these claims can be criticized from an empirical perspective, the concepts of epistemic beliefs and learner competence need consideration.

Empirical The empirical evidence simply does not support these claims for learning efficacy. Research has produced inconclusive findings about the claim that students in control of their instruction will achieve higher results (Stemler, 1997:348; Overbaugh, 1994[4]. Research by Jacobson, Maouri, Mishra and Kolar (1995) shows that the "free hypertext exploration group, which permitted the greatest amount of user control over navigating through the hypertext, had the lowest average attitude scores compared to students who had more structured teaching" (p. 354). This finding is reinforced by Paolucci (1998) whose research led him to conclude that "a high level of learner control, coupled with the rich learning environment provided by the hypermedia system, can lead to distraction and "hyperchaos"" (p. 144). Empirical evidence does not confirm that students 'in a self-regulated learning environment using non-linear hypertext documents will induce constructive learning activities which result in higher level cognitive processing" (Tergan, 1997b:263). Most studies showed that it does not improve comprehension and retention of subject matter. Although hypertext-based learning may improve recall performance, text based learning resulted in better comprehension and reproduction of central concepts (Tergan, 1997b:263; see Weges, Bitter-Rijpkema and Ellerman, 1993; Gordon, Gustavel, Moore and Hankey, 1988). It would appear that learning outcomes are ultimately determined by "the quality of the students' goal-oriented activity" (in Tergan, 1997a:261; see Dee-Lucas and Larkin, 1992).

---

4. However Sponder and Hilgenfield (1994) believe that this can be overcome "by providing the ability to navigate through programs at the learner's own pace and ability level" (in Stemler, 1997, p. 348).

In terms of learning style, Lee and Leeman (1993) found that "Both active and passive learners who used the hypermedia program with instructional cues outperformed their counterparts ... without instructional cues" (in Tergan, 1997a:266). Active learners are defined as those who "display tendencies towards experimentation. ... learn best when they participate in projects, homework, and small-group discussion"; whereas reflective learners' observe prior to making judgments and prefer lecture-type learning situations ... also tend to introverts, (Rasmussen and Davidson-Shivers, 1998:294).

At best, it could be claimed that increased learner control over access is differentially useful to learners according to their abilities. (Dillon and Gabbard, 1998). High-ability learners will perform better than low-ability learners, regardless of the medium of instruction. Lower ability students have the greatest difficulty with hypermedia.

Epistemic beliefs   Students' "epistemic beliefs about the nature of the learning process itself can influence learning" (Schommer, 1994; Jacobson, Maouri, Mishra and Kolar, 1995:328). Thus epistemic beliefs will affect the way that students allocate resources to different problem-solving activities, and also how they integrate prior knowledge to new knowledge, which in turn is affected by reading comprehension. Jacobson and Spiro (1995) showed that "students holding a set of simple epistemic beliefs and preferences about learning ... were less able to learn and apply their knowledge after using a hypertext system than students who possessed a more complex set of epistemic beliefs" (Jacobson, Maouri, Mishra and Kolar, 1995:328). By contrast, Altun (2000) has shown that "experienced users showed a pattern of being able to control ...[navigating through links and complex cognitive activity] based on their prior knowledge, existing schemata, ... and epistemic beliefs" (p. 52) . In fact, experienced users were bypassing the inbuilt navigational aids and developing their own strategies. Consequently, it could be argued, as Jacobson, Maouri, Mishra and Kolar (1995) do, that epistemic beliefs "constitute an independent factor from verbal and general academic ability" (p. 350). Indeed they found that students with a complex set of epistemic beliefs had more negative attitudes about the free hypertext program than those students with a simpler set of epistemic beliefs (p. 354).

Learner Competence   Although we frequently assume that younger people are computer-savvy, many learners may not have the necessary learning competence to deal with hypertext/hypermedia. This is especially so for browsing, which can often be aimless and ineffective. Despite the positive claims for hypermediated "discovery learning", critics such as Jacobs (1992) oppose the idea that browsing is an effective learning mode. In fact, there are queries about what "browsing" actually entails (Osborne, 1990).

In short, we can conclude that 'providing students with flexible access and a high degree of user control to hypertextually interconnected material is not enough' (Jacobson, Maouri, Mishra and Kolar, 1995:349). Given the complexity of learner-controlled education founded on the "individual needs" of students, it becomes clear that teachers need to customize hypermedia systems to account for individual differences such as learning styles (Yoon, 1993–1994; Yoder in Rasmussen and Davidson-Shivers, 1998:293), as well as individual differences in abilities, attributes, and motivations (Davidson, Savenye, and Orr, 1992). Whether this is feasible in contemporary cash-strapped universities with overworked academics is moot.

Multimedia Increases Interactivity and Interactivity Increases Learning Efficacy

Interaction, according to Stemler (1997) is "the major difference between traditional instruction and instruction delivered by multimedia" (see also Schwier and Misanchuk, 1993). *Interactivity* means that "the learning process is, in some degree, modified by the actions of the learners, thus changing the roles of both the learner and the teacher," Stemler (1997) claims, pointing out that interactive multimedia learning "is a process, not a technology" (p. 340). "Because computer-based multimedia instruction tends to be more interactive than the traditional classroom, interactivity is assumed to have a strong positive effect on learning" (Najjar, 1996:131).

Such claims seem to fuse two dominant educational themes of the moment: *constructivist pedagogy* and authentic learning. Whereas the former is soundly based on pedagogic theory, authentic /situated learning can often mean "vocational" learning. Situated learning, according to Ertmer and Newby (1993), grew out of a theoretical shift from "behavioral to cognitive to constructivist" learning perspectives' (p. 3 in Herrington and Oliver, 1999:402; see also Lebow, 1993; von Glaserfield, 1995). It is argued that "meaningful learning will only take place if it is embedded in the social and physical context within which it will be used" (Herrington and Oliver, 1999:402; see also Lave and Wenger, 1991; McLellan, 1996). Constructivist pedagogy sees *knowledge construction as a social activity*. The role of computer-based knowledge-building, say Scardamalia and Bereiter (1993), is to shift educational practice from knowledge reproduction processes to knowledge-building processes[5].

A key element of constructivism is that the learning process be authentic (Harper, Squires, and McDougall, 2000; cf. Hannafin and Land, 1997; Grabinger, Dunlap, and Duffield, 1997)[6]. Authenticity, constructivists say, induces higher-order thinking (Collins, Brown and Newman, 1989). This occurs when "a person takes new information and information stored in memory and interrelates and/or rearranges and extends this information to achieve a purpose or find possible answers in perplexing situations" (Lewis and Smith, 1993:136; in Herrington and Oliver, 1999:402).

Critique

The previous section showed that students with high reasoning skills and/or field independence benefit most from self-organizing of

---

5. Typical of such a pedagogy is the experiential simulation. For example, the Year 11 application activities Investigating *Lake Iluka* and *Exploring the Nardoo* (Harper, Squires, and McDougall, 2000) apply biology, physics, and chemistry to specific situations.

6. The nine characteristics of situated learning pedagogy are:
    i.   authentic context
    ii.   complex authentic activities
    iii. multiple perspectives
    iv.   expert performances
    v.   coaching and scaffolding
    vi.   opportunities for collaboration,
    vii. opportunities for reflection
    viii. opportunities for articulation
    ix.   authentic assessment

                                                    (Herrington and Oliver, 1999, p. 403)

sequences in hyperdocuments (in Tergan, 1997b:265; see Lodevijks, 1982). Thus, the claims made for learning efficacy need to be tempered by this understanding. However, the more serious criticisms of the link between interactivity and learning efficacy are based on the definition of higher-order thinking and the methodology.

Definition   The definition of *higher-order thinking* can clearly affect the results claimed. The move to a constructivist approach necessarily means a move away from canonical transmission of knowledge and processes. Such canonical approaches are clearly unfashionable especially in an individualistic ideological age: terms used to describe such as approach include *imperializing* and *top-down*. A typical constructivist's characterization of transmissionist education is that "teachers present information; through recitation and written or oral presentations, students provide teachers with evidence of learning", and that learning consists of "some kind of reproduction of the knowledge that exists out there in the objective or public world" (Scardamalia and Bereiter, 1993).

However, while the problem-solving approach with high learner control has clear benefits, there are two concerns that should be noted:

i.   It can also mask some very bad teaching practices where students are simply left to roam in an unstructured way.

ii.   Providing students with the "rules of the game", as it were, eliminates a lot of wasted time re-inventing knowledge that is already well-organized, sequenced, and workable.

Methodology   What constitutes higher-order thinking is clearly a matter of some conjecture. In an empirical study, Herrington and Oliver (1999) drew on an extensive array of cognitive theories to establish their characterization of higher-order thinking. By considering this list, one might ask whether such characteristics are agreed upon. Their hierarchy of thinking is (in order):

i.   Uncertainty

ii.   Deciding on a path of action

iii.   Judgment and interpretation

iv.   Multiple perspectives
v.   Imposing meaning, effortful thinking and multiple solutions
vi.   Self regulation of thinking.

Using this hierarchical structure to classify thinking, Herrington and Oliver (1999) concluded that "higher-order thinking was a substantial component in all the students' talk" (p. 411)[7]. This order is individualistic and anti-canonical ideologically. Such a hierarchy is also directed at functional and instrumentalist outcomes, consistent with the vocational imperative now evident in universities. There is little consideration given to the critique involving values or relations of power. By contrast, using Bloom's (1956) taxonomy would lead to the conclusion that students have reached only the two-thirds mark: Knowledge, Comprehension, Application, and Analysis. One could ask whether the fifth and sixth levels of the Herrington and Oliver (1999) hierarchy are as complex as Bloom's and whether they require dialectical engagement. Table One contrasts the fifth and sixth levels of Bloom's taxonomy with Herrington and Oliver's taxonomy.

Multimedia Presentations are More Effective than Classroom Lectures

Traditional lectures are often cast in a poor light compared to the putative advantages of "distributed learning" [North America], "networked learning" [UK], or "flexible learning" [Australia]. The new technology, Bates (1999) claims, allows students to "not so much interact with the technology as through the technology with teachers and other learners" (p. 25). Whether this idealized claim is possible with increased student:staff ratios, and whether many students prefer "a warm body" (Response by Acting Dean of Education, QUT to E-vision Working Party[8]) appears not to be tested. The least sophisticated advocacy employs the unsubstantiated claim by Treichler (1967) that people "remember 10% of what they read, 20% of what they hear,

30% of what they see, and 50% of what they hear and see".

Recognition information is better retained using visuals, according to

---

7.   Further self-acknowledged problem of their method was to use "student talk" as a manifestation of the student's thinking.

Table 24.1
Comparison of Fifth and Sixth Levels of Bloom's Taxonomy and Herrington and Oliver's Taxonomy

	Bloom (1956)	Herrington and Oliver (1999)
Fifth Level	Synthesis • use old ideas to create new ones • generalize from given facts • relate knowledge from several areas • predict, draw conclusions	Imposing meaning, effortful thinking and multiple solutions • Drawing conclusions when warranted, but with caution • Offering explanations for conclusions • Deciding what to believe • Integrating (interrelating conceptual elements) • Generating original and unconventional ideas, explanations, hypotheses or solutions to problems • Making a prediction
Sixth Level	Evaluation • compare and discriminate between ideas • assess value of theories, presentations • make choices based on reasoned argument • verify value of evidence • recognize subjectivity	Self-regulation of thinking • Applying metacognitive skills

Najjar (1996:140). More seriously, cognitive psychologists such as Glaser (1991) and Reusser (1996), and instructional designers such as Cunningham, Duffy, and Knuth (1993) claim that multiple modes of representing material in instruction will enhance learning.

There is evidence to show that multimediated instruction can improve learning, but it is not overwhelming. Liao's (1999) meta-analysis indicates that "hypermedia instruction has moderately positive effects on student achievement over the non-hypermedia instruction" (p. 269). However, he warns against the novelty effect as a factor in much of the research (cf. Liao and Bright, 1991). Left unanswered, says Liao (1999), "is the question of what factors truly affect the diverse outcomes for different types of instruction" (p. 272). Stronger evidence is provided by others. Lin and Davidson's (1996) findings show that "Hypertext instruction, structure and cognitive style have a significant effect on student performance" (Rasmussen and Davidson-Shivers, 1998:296). This is supported by Paolucci (1998) who says that

8.　(http://www.qut.edu.au/pubs/vice_chan/sub_edu.html; Accessed 14/09/00).

hypermedia systems are able to provide "an effective means for promoting and developing learner's higher cognitive skills (e.g., analysis and synthesis)". However, significantly, it was found that students using pre-structured hyperdocuments (i.e., branching and hierarchical), performed better than students using conventional hypertext (random organization) (p. 145). On the other hand, if the hypermedia environment is too structured, many students will lose interest, and learning objectives will not be achieved. Najjar's (1996) meta-analysis cites 200 studies that purport to show that "the learning is higher when the information was presented via computer-based multimedia systems than traditional classroom lectures ... [and] appeared to take less time" (p. 130).

Critique

When "higher cognitive" educational tasks are considered more closely, the claims lose strength. For example, Mayer and Anderson (1992) used an explanation of a bicycle pump as the basis of their dual channel (verbal and non-verbal) study. They claim that this shows that animation with explanatory verbal narration improves problem solving information (Najjar, 1996:13). Mayer and Gallini's (1990) study showed that students reading a text explaining the operation of automobile drum brakes accompanied by illustrations had better recall than those without illustration. Peeck (1974) found better retention for fourth grade children reading a story with illustrations (in Najjar, 1996:135). McGrath (1992) found no significant differences among groups of undergraduate pre-service teachers who used hypertext, CAI, or paper-based instruction. (Rasmussen and Davidson-Shivers, 1998: 296).

Clearly these claims, *pro tem*, need to be limited to particular types of learning. For example, auditory presentation can improve recall in short term memory[9]. Hypermedia affords the most advantage for users in specific tasks that require rapid searching through lengthy or multiple information resources and where data manipulation and comparison

---

9.   Watkins and Watkins (1980) found better short term memory for a few verbal items when presented in auditory, rather than visual, mode (in Najjar, 1996, p. 135).

are necessary. Outside of this context, existing media are better than or as effective as the new technology (Dillon and Gabbard, 1998).

Hypertext Allows Storage, Access, and Connectedness to Wide Range of Knowledge

Some claim that hypertext's capability to "store, interconnect, and provide access to a wide range of knowledge" enriches student learning (e.g., Jonassen, 1986; Kearsley, 1988). The Web now provides us with an "infinite variety of permutations" of knowledge (Anderson, in Barrett, 1993:111). Much is also made of the "liberated", "multi dimensional", and "flexible" nature of the new technology rather than the "static" and "linear" representations of old texts (cf. Redish, Wilson, and McDaniel, ch 12; Carlson, ch 3, in Barrett, 1993). Hypertextuality is considered more efficacious than the linearity of books (Jonassen, 1988) because, it is claimed, linear texts render students passive recipients of predetermined knowledge (cf. Glaser, 1991): by contrast, a non-predefined structure will enhance "active, explorative, and self-regulated learning behaviours" (Tergan, 1997b:262)

Free access to unconstrained knowledge is fundamental to constructivist learning theory. The individual takes responsibility for developing questions, constructing interpretations, appreciating and comparing alternative points of view, being aware, and manipulating the knowledge construction process (Tergan, 1997b:271). Pleasingly, the constructivist view "goes well beyond simplistic notions of learning by discovery", now deservedly in disrepute (cf. McKenna, 1995b). Scardamalia and Bereiter (1993) see knowledge construction as a process of Popperian "conjectures and refutations" leading the student "toward more complete and coherent understanding". Thus hypertextual activity becomes a form of hermeneutic activity in which students construct particularized world views. From this perspective, cognition is understood as personal interpretation based on background knowledge and beliefs (Winograd and Flores, 1986). Consistent with these philosophical arguments for the centrality of interpretation in cognition is the assumption in cognitive psychology that understanding involves making a large number of inferences.

Critique

Again, there is "limited empirical documentation of the educational efficacy of such systems" (Tergan, 1997b).

Hypertext Replicates the Cognitive Paths of the Brain

One of the most contested claims about the hypertext is that hypertextual knowledge structures and retrieval systems operate like the human brain (Dimitroff and Wolfram, 1995; Eklund and Woo, 1998). Cunningham, Duffy and Knuth (1993) claim that "users browse the hyperspace, serendipitously acquiring knowledge and the structure of the database" (in Tergan, 1997b:258): that is, that "associative browsing" corresponds to the human mind's structuring of knowledge. Bagui (1998) uses a Shannon and Weaver style model to support his information processing theory "which can be compared to an electronic computer" (p. 4). According to Reed, Ayersman and Kraus (1997), four mental models (semantic networks, concept maps, frames/scripts, schemata) may also be the organizational structure of hypermedia learning environments.

According to Tergan (1997b), the perception of hypertext as an analogue of the cognitive processes of the brain is sometimes present in constructivist principles of learning (p. 249). Social constructivists, Barrett and Redmond (1995), do not say this exactly, but do claim that 'thought and language in a virtual environment seek a higher synthesis, a re-imagining of an idea in the context of its truth' (pp. xvi; see also Thuring, Hannemann and Haake, 1995; Slatin, 1990).

Critique

Among the most popular theorists about the brain is Pinker (1994, 1997), who describes the brain as a computational mechanism. According to Graham (2000b), its "functionality is assessed in terms of its ability to calculate and represent the world; to encode and decode reality; and it its ability to effectively give 'instructions' to the rest of the body". This mechanistic analogue is best challenged elsewhere (cf. Graham 2000b; Restak, 1995). More simply, Whalley (1990) criticizes the assumptions underlying such a claim, saying that "the simple web structures of hypertext are not of the same order of complexity as human semantic knowledge structures" (in Tergan, 1997a:261).

Constructivist theorists also challenge this notion arguing that "mental representations of subject matter content are not simple representations of structures inherent in a hypertext basis ...but are actively constructed by the cognitive system" (in Tergan, 1997a:261; see Lehtinen, Balcytiene, and Gustafsson, 1993)

Empirical evidence does not support the claims that non-linearity improves learning performance. Studying with linear text often results in "higher comprehension and retention of main ideas and facts" (Tergan, 1997b:251; Rouet, 1992 reviews). Furthermore, many students feel a sense of disorientation — a form of cognitive vertigo (Schroeder and Grabowski, 1995). "Learners become easily confused and disoriented in complex interactive multimedia modules" (Stemler, 1997:345).

Conclusions

The five conclusions to be drawn from this critical review of hypermediated university pedagogy are that:

1. we should be very sceptical about the claims made for hypermediated instruction.
2. we need to adopt a coherent and defensible notion of the learner.
3. effective learning requires scaffolding.
4. educational hypertext should be properly structured.
5. doing hypertext correctly is expensive.

Scepticism about Claims

The evidence in this chapter supports Dillon and Gabbard's (1998) conclusion from their extensive meta-analysis that "the benefits gained from the use of hypermedia technology in learning scenarios appear to be very limited and not in keeping with the generally euphoric reaction to this technology in the professional arena'. This is supported by Paolucci (1998) who says that "The use of hypermedia software as learning systems does not necessarily lead to improved performance" (p. 148).

A disappointing aspect of the research is that methodologies were frequently flawed. Tergan (1997a, 1999) criticizes the fact that many approaches suffer from conceptual and methodological shortcomings in hypermedia design and research. Dillon and Gabbard (1998) are quite trenchant:

> *"... statistical analyses and research methods are frequently flawed ... Failure to control important variables for comparative purposes, lack of adequate pretesting of learners, use of multiple t tests for post hoc data, and even the tendency to claim support for hypotheses when the data fail to show statistically significant results all suggest that the basis for drawing conclusions from this literature is far from sturdy."*

These frequently excessive claims are made, according to Jacobson, Maouri, Mishra and Kolar (1995), because of a preoccupation with technological functionality; methodological problems; and a lack of attention to relevant cognitive learning theory and research (p. 322).

Research in this area can be improved in the future, say Dillon and Gabbard (1998; Dillon, 1996) by undertaking three tasks. First, research efforts should concentrate on those variables that seem most influential. This would require an understanding of the components of learning tasks so that those most likely to benefit directly from hypermedia interventions would be identified. Secondly, researchers need to more fully understand what creates individual differences among learners, rather than adopting simple binary divisions such as active or passive cognitive style. Thirdly, research needs to identify the precise combination of hypermedia design attributes, task domains, and learner characteristics that should be the focus of future research. For example, Dillon and Gabbard suggest that Jacobson's (1994) cognitive flexibility theory offers potential insights into how this technology may best be used.

Coherent Notion of the Learner

A useful guiding principle is to "put pedagogical principles first and technological whizz-bangery second" (Response by Acting Dean of Education, QUT to E-vision Working Party). The effectiveness of hypermediated learning is "the result of a complex interaction of constraining conditions on the side of the learner, ... instructional methods to support learners, ... attributes of the learning of the learning material used ..., situational constraints like authenticity of the learning situation and embeddedness in an overall instructional approach" (Tergan, 1997b:277).

Crucial to this is the need to identify what we understand the "ideal" learner to be: that is, the most typical characteristic of university learners. Are they individuals who are curious, set their own goals in a way that will maximize or optimize their learning, who select relevant content, and structure the contents in ways that will allow them to understand the discipline and deploy the appropriate disciplinary skills? Two important elements of the learner are their metacognitive processes and the learning context. Students may need to develop new metacognitive processes to deal with hypertext learning. As a result, say Reed, Ayersman and Kraus (1997) four mental models (semantic networks, concept maps, frames/scripts, schemata) may also be the organizational structure of hypermedia learning environments. The effectiveness of hypermediated learning must be tested in different learning contexts and their particular education needs (Baillie and Percoco, 2000.)

An appropriate pedagogic theory for hypermediated learning would most probably need to incorporate notions of socio-cognition, context, and "authentic" or situated action. One such pedagogic theory is Situated Action Theory (e.g.,: Clancey, 1993; Greeno and Moore, 1993). According to Jacobson *et al.* (1995), this is a "comprehensive socio-cognitivist theoretical treatment of human cognitive functioning". In other words, "it views human cognitive processing as being fundamentally situated in contexts of activity" (p. 324). It appears that hypertext-based learning "may be enhanced when it is integrated into a broader educational context" (Tergan, 1997b:265). For example Cunningham, Duffy, and Knuth (1993) implementing the INTERMEDIA program at Brown University, RI, attributed its success in university classes to the instructional arrangements of the professors and its "embeddedness in a *social context*"' (in Tergan, 1997b:265).

The three factors that affect the efficacy of varying degrees of learner-autonomy and teacher-directedness are: the structure of knowledge represented in the hypertext; the nature of the learning activity; cognitive support provided. Thus for substantive learning to occur there needs to be a situated context as well as abstract cognitive or mental models of schemas and conceptual knowledge in the learner (Jacobson, Maouri, Mishra and Kolar, 1995:355).

Scaffolding

Integral to situated learning incorporating learner schema is the technique of scaffolding support. This learning process, Paolucci (1998) claims, seems to be particularly appropriate when using hypermedia (p. 147). This means decreasing the level of hypermedia structure as the student matures [fading](see Jacobson, Maouri, Mishra and Kolar, 1995:325).

Properly Structured

Properly structured hypermedia can improve student performance and achievement (Paolucci, 1998:144). Among the practical features of proper structuring is the tailoring of navigational attributes in two ways. Firstly, different types of links [e.g., definition, other websites] are visually cued properly (Welsh, 1995; Clark and Sugrue, 1990). Secondly irrelevant or marginal information is filtered (Welsh, 1995: 276–277).

Hypertext is Expensive

Clearly, to set up a proper hypermedia learning program requires enormous effort and expense (Bates, 1999). Herrington and Oliver's (1999) program, for example, consisted of over 60 video clips and over 100 text documents (p. 403). In Australia, vastly disproportionate university asset bases and funding will probably mean an increasing division between universities that provide distance education (e.g., Deakin and University of Southern Queensland vs others) and, for intramural courses, between the well-off sandstones and the less well-off redbricks and regionals (cf. Bates, 1995).

Coda

Three pedagogic approaches might inform hypertextual teaching and learning, particularly in writing. The psycholinguistic approach might help to answer questions about whether text should effect a coherent representation in reader's mind (Sanford and Garrod, 1994; Sanford and Moxey, 1995). Barrett's (1993) social construction approach claims that, regardless of the technology, class learning situations are essentially about "people reading and talking and writing to each other in order to synthesize their thoughts" (p. 2). Systemic functional linguistic pedagogy (Callaghan, 1991; Callaghan, Knapp, and Noble, 1993; Christie, 1993; Martin, 1991a,b; McKenna, 1995a;b) asserts that meaning is context-dependent and that language is fundamentally a social practice. While the latter two are concerned with "text-in-context", psycholinguistics is concerned more with internalist accounts of scripts (Schank, 1981; Schank and Abelson, 1977), frames (Minsky, 1975) schematic frameworks (after Bartlett, 1932). It is the intersection of these three pedagogies that might well provide a coherent and practical set of principles for pedagogy in a hypertext environment.

References

1. Altun, A. 2000. Patterns in cognitive processes and strategies in hypertext reading: A case of two experienced computer users. *Journal of Educational Multimedia and Hypermedia* 9 (1): 35–55.

2. Bagui, S. 1998. Reasons for increased learning using multimedia. *Journal of Educational Multimedia and Hypermedia* 7 (1): 3–18.

3. Baillie, C. and Percoco. 2000. A study of present use and usefulness of computer-based learning at a technical university. *European Journal of Engineering Education* (March).

4. Barrett, E., ed. 1993. *Sociomedia: Multimedia, hypermedia and the social construction of knowledge.* Cambridge MA: MIT Press.

5. _____ and M. Redmond. 1995. *Contextual media: Multimedia and interpretation.* Cambridge, MA: MIT Press.

6. Bartlett, F. C. 1932. *Remembering.* Cambridge: Cambridge University Press.

7. Bates, A. W. 1995. *Technology, open learning and distance education.* New York: Routledge.

8. _____ . 1999. *Managing technological change: Strategies for colleges and university leaders.* San Francisco: Josey-Bass Publishers.

9. Bereiter, C. and M. Scardamalia. Two models of classroom learning using a communal database. In *Instructional models in computer-based Learning environments.* NATO-ASI Series F: Computer and Systems Sciences, edited by S. Dijkstra. Berlin: Springer-Verlag. In press.

10. Black, J. B. and R. O. McClintock. 1995. An interpretation construction approach to constructivist design. In *Constructivist learning environments*, edited by B. Wilson. Englewood Cliffs, NJ: Technology Publications. Also available on web at http://www.ilt.columbia.edu/ilt/papers/ICON.html.

11. Bloom, B. S., ed. 1956. *Taxonomy of educational objectives: The classification of educational goals: Handbook I, cognitive domain.* New York. Longmans.

12. Callaghan, M. 1991. Genre, register and functional grammar: Making meaning explicit for students. In *Working with genre,* LERN Conference, University of Technology, Sydney, 25–26 November 1989. Leichhardt NSW: Common Ground.

13. _____ , P. Knapp and G. Noble. 1993. Genre in practice. In *The powers of literacy: A genre approch to a teaching writing*, edited by B. Cope and M. Kalantzis.London: Falmer Press.

14. Christie, F. 1993. Curriculum genres: Planning for effective teaching. In *The powers of literacy: A genre approach to teaching writing*, edited by B. Cope and M. Kalantzis. London: Falmer Press.

15. Clancey, W. J. 1993. Situated action: A neurophysiological interpretation response to Vera and Simon. *Cognitive Science* 17:87–116.

16. Clark, R. E. and B. M. Sugrue. 1990. North American disputes about research on learning from media. *International Journal of Educational Research* 14 (6): 507–519.

17. Collins, A., J. S. Brown and S. E. Newman. 1989. Cognitive apprenticeship: Teaching the crafts of reading, writing, and mathematics. In *Knowing, learning and instruction: Essays in honour of Robert Glaser*, edited by L. B. Resnick. Hillsdale, NJ: LEA, 453–494.

18. Coyne, R. 1999. *Technoromanticism: Digital narrative, holism, and the romance of the real.* Cambridge, MA: MIT Press.

19. Cunningham, D. J., T. M. Duffy and R. A. Knuth. 1993. The textbook of the future. In *Hypertext: A psychological perspective*, edited by C. McKnight, A. Dillon and J. Richardson. Chichester, England: Ellis Horwood, 19–50.

20. Davidson, G. V., W. C. Savenye and K. B. Orr. 1992. How do learning styles relate to performance in a computer applications course? *Journal of Research on Computing in Education* 24 (3): 348–358.

21. Dee-Lucas, D. and J. H. Larkin. 1992. *Text representation with traditional text and hypertext* (Tech Rep H.P. 21). Carnegie-Mellon University, Department of Psychology.

22. DeWit, S. L. and K. Strasma. 1999. *Contexts, intertexts, and hypertexts.* Cresskill, NJ: Hampton Press.

23. Dillon, A. 1996. Myths, misconceptions and an alternative view of information usage and the electronic medium. In *Hypertext and cognition*, edited by J. Rouet *et al.* Mahwah, NJ: Erlbaum, 25–42.

24. _____ and R. Gabbard. 1998. Hypermedia as an educational technology: A review of the quantitative research literature on learner comprehension, control, and style. *Review of Educational Research* 68 (3).

25. Dimitroff, A. and D. Wolfram. 1995. Searcher response in a hypertext-based bibliogrpahic information retrieval system. *Journal of the American Society for Information Science* 46 (1): 22–29.

26. Dolence, M. and D. Norris. 1995. *Transforming higher education: A vision for learning in the 21st century.* Ann Arbor, MI. Society for College and University Planning.

27. Eklund, J. and R. Woo. 1998. A cognitive perspective for designing multimedia learning environments. Proceedings of the Fifteenth Annual Conference of the Australian Society for Computers in Learning in Tertiary Education, Wollongong, Australia, December 1998, 181–190.

28. Ellis, D., N. Ford and F. Wood. 1993. Hypertext and learning styles. *The Electronic Library* 11 (1): 13–18.

29. Ertmer, P. A. and T. J. Newby. 1993. Behaviourism, cognitivism, constructivism: Comparing critical features from an instructional design perspective. *Performance Improvement Quarterly* 6 (4): 50–72.

30. Glaser, R. 1991. The maturing of the relationship between the science of learning and cognition and educational practice. *Learning and Instruction* 1 (2): 129–144.

31. Gordon, S., J. Gustavel, J. Moore and J. Hankey. 1988. The effect of hypertext on reader knowledge representation. *Proceedings of the 32nd annual meeting of the human factors society*, Santa Monica, CA: Human Factors Society, 296–300.

32. Grabinger, R. S., J. C. Dunlap and J. A. Duffield. 1997. Rich environments for active learning in action: Problem-based learning. *Association for Learning Technology Journal* 5 (2): 5–17.

33. Graham, P. 2000a. Hypercapitalism: A political economy of informational idealism. *New Media and Society* 2 (2).

34. _____ . 2000b. Autopoiesis, language, literacy, and the brain. Available on web at http://www.uq.edu.au/~uqpgraha/publications.htm.

35. Greeno, J. G. and J. L. Moore. 1993. Situativity and symbols: Response to Vera and Simon. *Cognitive Science* 17:49–59.

36. Guthrie, J. T., T. Britten and K. G. Barker. 1991. Roles of document structure, cognitive strategy, and awareness in searching for information. *Reading Research Quarterly* 26 (3): 300–324.

37. Hannafin, M. J. and S. M. Land. 1997. The foundations and assumptions of technology-enhanced student centres learning environments. *Instructional Science* 25:167–202.

38. Harper, B., D. Squires and A. McDougall. 2000. Constructivist simulations: A new design paradigm. *Journal of Educational Multimedia and Hypermedia* 9 (2): 115–130.

39. Herrington, J. and R. Oliver. 1999. Using situated learning and multimedia to invesetigate higher-order thinking. *Journal of Educational Multimedia and Hypermedia* 8 (4): 401–421.

40. Jacobs, G. 1992. Hypermedia and discovery based learning: A historical perspective. *British Journal of Educational Technology* 23 (2): 113–121.

41. Jacobson, M. 1994. Issues in hypertext and hypermedia research: Toward a framework for linking theory-to-design. *Journal of Educational Multimedia and Hypermedia* 3 (2): 141–154.

42. Jacobson, M. J., C. Maouri, P. Mishra and C. Kolar. 1995. Learning with hypertext learning environments: Theory, design, and research. *Journal of Educational Multimedia and Hypermedia* 4 (4): 321–364.

43. Jacobson, M. J. and R. J. Spiro. 1995. Hypertext learning environments, cognitive flexibility, and the transfer of complex knowledge: An empirical investigation. *Journal of Educational Computing Research* 12 (5): 301–333.

44. Jonassen, D. H. 1986. *Hypertext/hypermedia*. Educational technology publications. Englewood Cliffs, NJ.

45. _____ . 1988. Designing structured hypertext and structuring access to hypertext. *Educational Technology* 28 (11): 13–16.

46. Katz R. and Associates. 1999. *Dancing with the devil: Information technology and the new competition in higher education*. San Francisco: Jossey-Bass.

47. Kolb, D. 1985. *The learning style inventory*, 2nd ed. Boston: McBer.

48. Landow, G. P. 1992. Bootstrapping hypertext: Student-created documents, intermedia, and the social construction of knowledge. In *Sociomedia: multimedia, hypermedia, and the social construction of knowledge*, edited by E. Barrett. Cambridge, MA: MIT Press, 195–218.

49. _____ . 1994. What's a critic to do? Critical theory in the age of hypertext. In *Hyper/text/theory*, edited by G. P. Landow. Baltimore, MD: Johns Hopkins University Press, 1–50.

50. Lave, J. and E. Wenger. 1991. *Situated learning: Legitimate peripheral participation*. Cambridge: Cambridge University Press.

51. Lebow, D. 1993. Construtivist values for instructional systems design: Five principles towards a new mindset. *Educational Technology Research and development,* 41 (3), 4–16.

52. Lee, Y. B. and J. D. Leeman. 1993. Instructional cuing in hypermedia: A study with active and passive learners. *Journal of Educational Multimedia and Hypertext.* 2 (1): 25–37.

53. LeGrew, D. 1995. Global knowledge: Superhighway or supergridlock? *Applications of media and technology in higher education.* Chilba, Japan: National Institute of Multimedia Education.

54. Lehtinen, E., A. Belcytiene and M. Gustafson. 1993. Knowledge structures, activity, and hypertext. Paper presented at the 5th European Association for Research on Learning and Instruction (EARLI) Conference, Aix-en-Provence, France, August-September 1993.

55. Lewis, A. and D. Smith. 1993. Defining higher order thinking. *Theory into Practice* 32 (3): 131–137.

56. Liao, Y.-K. 1999. Effects of hypermedia on students achievement: A meta-analysis. *Journal of Educational Multimedia and Hypermedia* 8 (3): 255–277.

57. Liao, Y. C. and G. W. Bright. 1991. Effects of computer programming on cognitive outcomes: A meta-analysis. *Journal of Educational Computing Research* 7 (3): 251–268.

58. Lin, C.-H. and G. V. Davidson. 1996. Effects of linking structure and cognitive style on students' performance and attitude in a computer-based hypertext environment. *Journal of Educational Computing Research* 15 (4): 317–329.

59. Lodevijks, H. 1982. Self-regulated versus teacher-provided sequencing of information in learning from text. In *Discourse processing*, edited by A. Flammer and W. Kintsch. Amsterdam: North Holland, 509–520.

60. Martin, J. R. 1991a. Critical literacy: The role of a functional model of language. *Australian Journal of Reading* 14 (2): 117 –132.

61. _____ . 1991b. Intrinsic functionality: Implications for textual theory. *Social Semiotics* 1 (1): 99–162.

62. Mason, R. 1998. *Globalizing education*. London: Routledge.

63. Mayer, R. E. and R. B. Anderson. 1992. The instructive animation: Helping students build connections between words and pictures in multimedia learning. *Journal of Educational Psychology* 83:444–452.

64. _____ and J. K. Gallini. 1990. When is an illustration worth ten thousand words? *Journal of Educational Psychology* 82:715–726.

65. McGrath, D. 1992. Hypertext, CAI, paper or program control: Do learners benefit from choices? *Journal of Research on Computing in Education,* 24 (4): 513–532.

66. McKenna, B. J. 1995a. Using genre-based pedagogy to teach science writing. In *Explorations in English for professional communication, edited by* P. Bruthiaux, T. Boswood and B. Du-Babcock. Hong Kong: City University of Hong Kong.

67. _____ . 1995b. *After personal growth: Principles for a critical language pedagogy in senior secondary schools.* M.Phil thesis. Griffith University, Brisbane, Australia.

68. _____ . 1999. *How Labor lost its labour: A critical discourse analysis of the Hawke-Keating years.* Ph.D. Thesis. University of Queensland. St Lucia, Australia.

69. _____ and P. Graham. 2000. Technocratic discourse: A primer. *Journal of Technical Writing and Communication* 30 (3).

70. McLellan, H., ed. 1996. *Situated learning perspectives*. Englewood Cliffs, NJ: Educational Technology Publications.

71. Minsky, M. 1975. A framework for representing knowledge. In *The psychology of computer vision,* edited by P. Winston. New York: McGraw Hill.

72. Najjar, L. J. 1996. Multimedia information and learning. *Journal of Educational Media and Hypermedia* 5 (2): 129–150.

73. Osborne, D. 1990. Browsing and navigation through hypertext documents. *Interactive Multimedia* 1 (1).

74. Overbaugh, R. C. 1994. Research-based guidelines for computer-based instruction development. *Journal of Research on Computing in Education* 27 (1): 29–47.

75. Paolucci, R. 1998. The effects of cognitive style and knowledge structure on performance using a hypermedia learning system. *Journal of Educational Multimedia and Hypermedia* 7 (2/3): 123–150.

76. Peeck, J. 1974. Retention of pictorial and verbal content of a text with illustrations. *Journal of Educational Psychology* 66:880–888.

77. Pinker, S. 1994. *The language instinct.* London: Penguin.

78. _____ . 1997. *How the mind works.* London: Penguin.

79. _____ . 1986. *Amusing ourselves to death: Public discourse in the age of show business.* New York, NY: Penguin.

80. _____ . 1993. *Technopoly: The surrender of culture to technology.* New York: Vintage Books.

81. _____ . 1995. *The end of education: Redefining the value of school.* New York: Knopf.

82. Rasmussen, K. L. and G. V. Davidson-Shivers. 1998. Hypermedia and learning styles: Can performance be influenced? *Journal of Educational Multimedia and Hypermedia* 7 (4): 291–308.

83. Reed, W. M., D. J. Ayersman and L. A. Kraus. 1997. The effects of learning style and task type on hypermedia-based mental models. *Journal of Educational Multimedia and Hypermedi* 6 (3/4): 285–304.

84. Restak, R. 1995. *Brainscapes: An introduction to what neuroscience has learned about the structure, function, and abilities of the brain.* New York, NY: Hyperion.

85. Reusser, K. 1996. From cognitive modeling to the design of pedagogical tools. In *International perspectives on the design of technology-supported learning environments,* edited by S. Vosniadou, E. DeCorte, R. Glaser and H. Mandl. Marwah, NJ: Lawrence Erlbaum, 81–103.

86. Rouet, J. F. 1992. Cognitive processing of hyperdocuments: When does non-linearity help? In *Proceedings of the 4th ACM Conference on Hypertext,* edited by D. Lucarella, J. Nanard, M. Nanard and P.Paolini. New York: Academic Press, 131–140.

87. _____ and J. L. Levonen. 1996. Studying and learning with hypertext: Empirical studies and their implications. In *Hypertext and cognition,* edited by J. F. Rouet, J. L. Levonen, A. Dillon and R. J. Spiro, Mahwah. NJ: Lawrence Erlbaum Associates.

88. Sanford, A. J. and S. C. Garrod. 1994. Selective processing in text understanding. In *Handbook of psycholinguistics,* edited by M.A. Gernsbacher. London: Academic Press.

89. _____ and L. M. Moxey. 1995. Aspects of coherence in written language: A psychological perspective. In *Coherence in spontaneous text,* edited by M. A. Gernsbacher and T. Givon. Amsterdam: John Benjamin.

90. Saul, J. R. 1997. *The Unconscious civilization.* Ringwood, Vic: Penguin.

91. Scardamalia, M. and C. Bereiter. 1993. Technologies for knowledge-building discourse. *Communications of the ACM (Association for Computing Machinery)* 36 (5).

92. Schank, R. C. 1981. Language and memory. In *Perspectives on cognitive science,* edited by D. A. Norman. Norwood, NJ: Ablex, 105–146.

93. _____ and R. P. Abelson. 1977. *Scripts, plans, goals, and understanding.* Hillsdale, NJ: Erlbaum.

94. Schommer, M. 1994. An emerging conceptualization of epistemological beliefs and their role in learning. In *Beliefs about text and instruction with text,* edited by R. Garner and P. A. Alexander. Hillsdale, NJ: Erlbaum, 25–40.

95. Schwier, R. A. and E. R. Misanchuk. 1993. *Interactive multimedia instruction.* Englewood Cliffs, NJ: Education Technology Publication.

96. Schroeder, E. E. and B. L. Grabowski. 1995. Patterns of exploration and learning with hypermedia. *Journal of Educational Computing Research* 13 (4): 313–335.

97. Slatin, J. M. 1990. Reading hypertext: Order and coherence in a new medium. *College English* 52:870–883.

98. Sponder, B. and R. Hilgenfield. 1994. Cognitive guidelines for teachers developing computer-assisted instruction. *The Computer Teacher* 22 (8): 9–15.

99. Stemler, L. K. 1997. Educational characteristics of multimedia: A literature review. *Journal of Educational Multimedia and Hypermedia* 6 (3/4): 339–359.

100. Tergan, S.-O. 1997a. Conceptual and methodological shortcomings in hypertext/ hypermedia design and research. *Journal of Educational Computing Research* 16 (3): 209–235.

101. _____ . 1997b. Misleading theoretical assumptions in hypertext/hypermedia research. *Journal of Educational Media and Hypermedia* 6 (3–4): 249–283.

102. _____ . 1999. Shortcomings in hypermedia design and research. Paper presented at the 8th European Conference for Research on Learning and Instruction (EARLI), Göteborg (Sweden), 23–28 August 1999.

103. Thuring, M., J. Hanneman and J. M. Haake. 1995. Hypermedia and cognition: Designing for comprehension. *Communications of the ACM* 38 (8): 57–66.

104. Treichler, D. G. 1967. Are you missing the boat in training aid? *Film and AV Communication* 1:14–16.

105. Tulloch. S. 1992. Dictionary of new words: *A popular guide to words in the news.* Oxford: Oxford University Press.

106. Von Glaserfield, E. 1995. *Radical constructivism: A way of knowing and learning.* London: Falmer Press.

107. Webster, F. 1997. *Theories of the information society*. London and New York: Routledge.

108. Weges, H. G., M. Bitter-Rijpkema and H. H. Ellerman. 1993. Hypertext within a distance education setting. Paper presented at the 5th European Association for Research on Learning and Instruction (EARLI) Conference, Aix-en-Provence, France, August-September 1993.

109. Weimer, B. 1992. Assumptions about university-industry relationships in continuing professional education: A reassessment. *European Journal of Education* 27 (4).

110. Welsh, T. M. 1995. Simplifying hypermedia usage for learners: The effect of visual and manual filtering capabilities on efficiency, perceptions of usability, and performance. *Journal of Educational Multimedia and Hypermedia* 4 (4): 275–304.

111. Whalley, P. 1990. Models of hypertext structure and learning. In *Designing hypermedia for learning*, edited by D. H. Jonassen and H. Mandl. Berlin. Springer, 61–67.

112. Williams, J. B., 2000. Assessment in an on-line environment: Whither the examination hall? Unpublished paper to TALSS, QUT Seminar, 17 October 2000.

113. Winograd, T. and F. Flores. 1986. *Understanding computers and cognition: A new foundation for design*. Norwood, NJ: Ablex Publishing.

114. Yoon, G.-S. 1993–94. The effects of instructional control, cognitive style, and prior knowledge on learning of computer-assisted instruction. *Journal of Educational Technology System* 22 (4): 357–370.

Discourses of

Business Communication

25

Taking an Interdisciplinary Approach in the Analysis of Multinational Business Discourse

Catherine Nickerson

Introduction [1]

This chapter investigates the use of English in the e-mail communication of Dutch and British employees working in a large multinational corporation. It refers to a number of different disciplinary traditions, including management communication (e.g., Suchan and Dulek 1998), applied linguistics (e.g., Bhatia 1993; Hyland 1998) and the theories of genre and structuration (e.g., Giddens 1984; Miller 1984; Yates and Orlikowski 1992). It focuses on the interplay between Dutch and English, and it also reports on the genres and discourse strategies that could be identified. It therefore includes details of the recurrent situations, the participants involved and the rhetorical action accomplished within the corporate context where English is invoked in e-mail communication, together with the substantive and formal characteristics of that communication (Miller 1984; Orlikowski and Yates 1994; Nickerson 1999).

The chapter begins with a brief discussion of the data collection and this is followed by the findings of the analysis of a large number of e-mail messages in English and in Dutch, including details of the genres or typified communicative practices that could be identified. The third part discusses the rhetorical moves and discourse strategies used in one of the genres most frequently invoked in English, which was used to exchange information across the corporation concerned.

---

1. A version of this paper was originally published in Nickerson (2000). The author gratefully acknowledges the permission of Rodopi Academic Publishers to reprint this work.

This final part of the analysis focuses on the similarities and differences in the strategies used by the Dutch and British writers, and discusses the possibility that the nature of these strategies is determined by both the organizational practices of the multinational concerned and the national culture of the individual writers.

Data and Data Collection

E-mail transmissions were collected from seven managers working at one of the Dutch divisions of a large multinational corporation. Two of the managers were native speakers of Dutch and five were native speakers of English. The majority of the transmissions were sent or received within one department or within the Dutch division, or they were sent to or received from other corporate divisions both inside and outside the Netherlands. A few additional messages were sent to recipients outside the corporation via an external e-mail connection. An initial analysis of the files indicated that all seven of the managers received e-mail in both languages and all but one of the English speakers also sent e-mail in both Dutch and English. There was no evidence of any other languages being used.

The messages that had been written in English by Dutch speakers within the corporation, were selected from the 939 messages that made up the notelog files provided by the two Dutch managers. This resulted in 92 messages involving 39 different writers. Several different genres could be identified within these (Dutch) English e-mail messages, on the basis of the rhetorical situations to which they were a response, the action the writer intended to accomplish and their conventional layout (see Table 25.1 on page 646 and the discussion below). A total of 60 of the 92 (Dutch) English messages were found to be textualizations of one particular genre, referred to here as Genre IE, which was used as a means to exchange information on on-going activities across the corporation. Figure 25.1 shows an example of one of the 60 e-mail messages slightly adapted from the original for reasons of confidentiality. (All the examples and extracts reproduce the original version as it occurred in the corpus. They therefore include spelling errors, typographical errors and other types of errors).

Once Genre IE had been identified, it was then possible to select an additional 40 Genre IE textualizations written by Dutch writers in English, from the notelog files provided by all seven managers, making a total of 100 messages. 100 Genre IE messages written by (British) English writers in English were also selected from the notelog files. The 100 English messages written by Dutch employees were then analyzed for a variety of discourse features, and wherever appropriate, a comparison was made with the 100 (British) English messages.

Figure 25.1
An Example of Genre IE

```
■MSG FROM: RABCM2
10:00:55
To: NLIFGAP4 J. Janssen
cc: RP889 — Secretariat

From: P. de Klein ICS-AMP/1 "Nano-tech"

Internal address: ND 32-14    tel.6161
Subject: ICS advies over Tracers Bennekom

Jan
As discussed at our meeting of last friday we have to open a
Project.
Can you please send me an official NED opdracht incl.
Account nummer for a project 'ICS advice on Tracers for Bennekom'
We wil deliver:
    - advice on tracers (stable and radioactive)
    - advice on analytical techniques to measure these tracers
    - participate in meetings/discussions

For this initial stage I think that 80 hours of our time is sufficient.
With kind regards/Met vriendelijke groeten, Paul de Klein
Nedco Centre,
Berhardlaan 5,8099 BB MOLENDORP
tel. +31 20 999 9999, fax. 8888; e-mail: KLEIN5@ics.nedco.nl
²²f  ICSNEDCO advies over Tracers Bennekom Ç
```

Findings and Discussion

Situations, Actions, Substance and Form

Situations and Actions

Table 25.1 provides details of the situations, rhetorical action and (conventional) layout that could be identified in the corpus of 92 e-mail messages written by Dutch corporate writers in English. There were four different genres in the data set, although this does not preclude the possibility that there are in fact more used within the corporation, such as for example, a travel confirmation message using an electronic template similar to the initiation of a project included in Table 25.1. Two of the genres used the conventional layout of a memo, one used a report and the fourth, the project initiation, an electronically generated form initiated by the Administrative departments at the corporation.

The most prevalent genre was used to exchange and elicit the information necessary to work towards corporate (institutional) goals on a daily basis, such as the organization of a visit to another division, the facilitation of a change in internal procedures, and the (unofficial) initiation of discussions on a possible new project. The findings discussed below relate to the substantive and formal characteristics of this genre (Genre IE), as it was textualized in the corpus, on the basis of 200 textualizations written by Dutch and British writers within the corporation.

Content or Substance

Genre IE was both Informational and Relational in terms of content (see Rogers and Hildebrandt, 1993; and Nickerson, 1999, for further details). In terms of propositional, i.e., Informational, content, information was exchanged and elicited both about language events or other texts, e.g., meetings, reports, presentations etc., and about

Table 25.1
Situations, Action and Layout

Situation & Exigence	Action	Layout	Textualizations in corpus
Effective execution of activities within existing social structures (across corporation) Need to exchange information with multiple readership and make recommendations on corporate activities and organizing process	Official means to exchange information on the activities carried out by individual corporate groupings across the corporation.	Report in Sections Headings (optional) Bullet points (optional)	22
(Internal) customer interest in product or service requiring initiation of project and/or negotiation process Need to officially initiate project and/or process of negotiation	Officially initiates and records agreement to co-operate on project	Electronically generated boilerplate (electronic template); internal quotation	6
Effective execution of activities to extend (internal) customer base Need to exchange information on activities of interest to potential customers	Means to bring about action to influence relationship with customer positively	Memo format	4
Effective execution of activities within existing social structures (across corporation) Need to exchange information on on-going activities	Means to exchange information on on-going activities across the corporation	Memo format	60

non-language events, e.g., the storage of toxic materials, job appraisal mechanisms, the allocation of space etc. The references made to non-language events within the corporation, included references to *corporate tasks or activities*, e.g., the organization of joint research projects, *corporate structure*, e.g., personnel matters or an inter-divisional employee exchange, *corporate technology*, e.g., the allocation of voice mail boxes and corporate control mechanisms, e.g., time-sheets, job appraisal, the internal accounting system and the implementation of Quality procedures. The English e-mail discourse textualizing Genre IE, therefore encompassed all four of the management sub-systems identified by Suchan and Dulek (1998) as determining factors in an organization's communicative practices. In doing so, it contributed to the maintenance of all the major systems involved in the achievement of institutional goals.

In addition to the Informational orientation in the e-mail messages, there was also a certain amount of Relational or non-propositional content, that was clearly intended to maintain the social system within the corporation, i.e., the patterns of corporate social relations between employees (Giddens, 1979;1984). Figure 25.2 shows an example of a message sent in order to create goodwill between the sender and (all) the receivers of the message and to assure the primary receiver that the sender is acting in good (corporate) faith. As such, its orientation is both Relational and Informational. An interesting aspect of this message, is that it creates goodwill not only with the primary receiver, the internal customer, but also with the manager's own staff (who must fulfil the customer's request) and his senior manager, all of whom are included on the distribution list. The writer of the message therefore takes full advantage of the characteristics of the medium and the opportunities it presents him with to achieve a multiple purpose, in this case to maximise the effectiveness of his role both as a potential supplier and as a middle manager.

Figure 25.2
An Example of Relational-informational Discourse

þMSG FROM: BBU2
To:GBTFHC6 J. Smith
cc: IMBNC9 J. Janssen   DFTX5 P. Broek

From: B. de Wit JNB-CCG/1 "Separations"
Internal address: NL 88-74 tel.9812
Subject: AB/CD analyses for GBTFC/9
John
We understand the importance and urgency of your request, but the workload at BBU
IMN/11 is very high and some people are under a lot of pressure from the Customers.
However we have shifted some priorities, and also after discussions with Piet Broek, we
will do our best to get you the required results before your meeting with IMC France.
Have a nice weekend,

With kind regards, Bart de Wit
Molendorp
WIT9@ics.nedco.nl
AB/CD analyses for GBTFC/9

Discourse: Textualizations, Organization and Strategies

Bhatia (1993) provides three levels of linguistic analysis; lexico-grammatical features, textualization and structural organization, that may be referred to in the investigation of unfamiliar genres. These form the basis of the investigation of discourse in the e-mail messages presented below. The presence of a number of Dutch lexico-grammatical features is first discussed, and this is followed by an examination of the discriminative moves that could be identified in the organization of the genre, i.e., they determined the structure of the genre. The final part of the chapter investigates how writers use a variety of *interpersonal* or *involved* strategies, realized as lexico-grammatical features in the discourse, to maintain the corporate relationship between the sender and receiver.

Figure 25.3
Dutch Lexicalizations

Krukkenoverleg
Lopendebroodje
Opdracht inclusief accountnummer
Ongeval
Knelpunt
Interneopslag
Arbo Plan/ Arbo & Milieu
Veiligheidsmeeting
Werkplaatsen
Ruimtebeheerder (RB)
Ruimte
Beoordeling formulier
OR (Ondernemings Raad)

Vatenterrein

Textualizations

A considerable amount of technical and corporate-bound lexis was present in the e-mail messages. The technical lexis referred to what the corporation did, as in for example, the technical processes involved and the goods produced, and the corporate-bound lexis referred to the way in which these activities were organized, exemplified by the acronyms and other lexical items used for procedures, corporate units and positions within the corporate hierarchy. Many of the items referring to the organizing process were Dutch lexicalizations, resulting in e-mail texts in both the Dutch-English and British-English sets of messages that were realized as English texts with single items of Dutch. Perhaps surprisingly, these also included messages sent between two British writers. Figure 25.4 shows a number of the Dutch corporate-bound lexicalizations that were used.

It was interesting to note that the items of Dutch corporate-bound lexis all occurred in messages with a readership either potentially or actually including non-Dutch speakers. In addition, although only 5 of the Dutch-English messages contained Dutch textualizations, 14 of the British-English messages contained them, all of which were used in intra-divisional communication (see Figure 25.4). This suggests that

Figure 25.4
An Example of Dutch Corporate Textualizations
in a British-English Message

þMSG FROM: NBYFR2
To: UFRSCI0 J. Janssen

From: J. Smith INBC Tel. 020 9837821
Nedco, Amsterdam
Internal address: NL 99/12
Subject: Ruimte beheerder AB
Jan, We must appoint a **RB** for the AB 02 02/JK **ruimte*** your people will soon
move into. I suggest that van Ede and Den Bosch, your trusty **RBs** from your
other **ruimtes** be nominated. OK?
Perhaps you would be so kind as to confirm this to them!
John..
With kind regards/Met vriendelijke groeten
John Smith..
Nedco HighTech B.V., Amsterdam
MOLENDORP
´y´yRuimte beheerder AB

---

* The Dutch word *ruimte* is used within the Dutch division to denote a specific physical area on site.
The *Ruimte beheerder* is an individual employee who is officially assigned to an area, and who is then
responsible for matters of safety within it.

certain items of Dutch lexis were widely referred to, at least within the
Dutch division, regardless of the language used in the text of the message
and whether or not its recipients were able to understand Dutch. The
use of Dutch reflected the communication practices internal to the
division, i.e., intra-divisional communication tolerated the use of Dutch
lexicalization. Certain Dutch items had apparently been assigned a
restricted value by the user community and were therefore examples
of what Bhatia (1993) has referred to as lexical *textualization* within a
genre. This also supports Connor's (1999) findings in fax
communication for the lexis relating to specialized terminology. For
example, the Norwegian fishing term *mandel fisk* used in a fax in
English relating to the supply of fish. As in the present study, Connor
also relates this finding and other similar findings (such as the use of
Norwegian grammatical structures in questions in English) to the
participants involved and the communication practices, exemplified
by code-switching, accepted by both sender and receiver.

Structural Organization

Four *moves* that organized the discourse structure could be identified in the e-mail messages. These are referred to here as Move I, Move IIA, Move IIB and Move III, although Move IIB sometimes occurred after Move III. Figures 25.6 to 25.7 show a series of e-mail messages sent by one manager to the same receiver, that details the communication between the Dutch and British division about a collaborative project. They are shown here in chronological order and they provide examples of the sequences of moves that could be identified in the corpus. Move I was an obligatory move that identified the subject of the message. This was often only realized by the subject line, although it could also be repeated as an additional move in the text of the message. Figures 25.5 and 25.6 show messages in which Move I, the subject of the message, is also repeated in the text. Move IIA was used to exchange information, and in several messages, such as for example Figure 25.8, it completed the Move sequence in combination with Move I, as I + IIA. In other messages, where the sender's purpose was to identify certain action that was necessary for the receiver to complete, this was realized using Move III, as in Figures 25.5 and 25.6 respectively. Move III could occur immediately after Move I, as I + III, it could also occur after the exchange of information, as I + IIA + III, or it could be used in combination with a second type of informational move, Move IIB. Move IIB was used to give an explicit reason as to why the action identified in III was necessary. Senders used this strategically to justify, and therefore moderate, the request for action implied or requested in Move III, in order to encourage the receiver to comply. Figure 25.7 provides a good example of Move III combined with Move IIB. In this message the sender needs to continue to work with the receiver in the future and he therefore justifies his request for action, despite the fact that the receiver has not responded to his original request made one week previously (see Move III of Figure 25.6). The following four sequences of moves, labelled from a to d, account for all 200 Dutch-English and British-English messages in the Genre IE corpus, in the exchange and elicitation of information:

a) I + IIA; Identify Subject/Exchange Information
b) I + III; Identify Subject/Identify Action
c) I + IIB + III; Identify Subject/Justify Action/Identify Action
d) I + IIA + IIB + III; Identify Subject/Exchange Information/
Justify Action/Identify Action

Figure 25.5
E-mail Communication between Divisions (I)

þMSG FROM: To: J. Smith

From: J. Jansen
Nedco, Amsterdam
Internal address: NL 99-83 tel.7291
Subject: AB985
MOVE I IDENTIFIES SUBJECT
John
enclosed is a brief description of the technical testing
of AB985
REPETITION MOVE I IDENTIFIES SUBJECT
Comments are welcome.
MOVE III IDENTIFIES ACTION

With kind regards, Jan Jansen
Nedco, Amsterdam

Figure 25.6
E-mail Communication between Divisions (II)

þMSG FROM: X
Internal address: NL 99-83

Subject: AB proposals
MOVE I IDENTIFIES SUBJECT

John
I hope that you survived the past festivities and are eager to
start doing research again.
I understood that Kees sent you the draft research proposals.
REPETITION MOVE I IDENTIFIES SUBJECT

Please let me know if you have any comments.
MOVE III IDENTIFIES ACTION

With kind regards, Jan Jansen
Nedco, Amsterdam

Figure 25.7
E-mail Communication between Divisions (III)

þMSG FROM: X
To: J. Smith
From: J. Jansen
Nedco, Amsterdam
Internal address: NL 99-83
Subject: comments on AB and AB985
MOVE I IDENTIFIES SUBJECT
John
Please give me asap your reaction on these documents.
MOVE III IDENTIFIES ACTION

I want to finalize them this week.
MOVE IIB JUSTIFIES ACTION

With kind regards, Jan Jansen
Nedco, Amsterdam
comments on AN and AB985

Figure 25.8
E-mail Communication between Divisions (IV)

*** Reply to note of 21/01/97 19:52
From: J. Jansen

Internal address: NL 99-83 tel.7291
Subject: AB Working Documents
MOVE 1 IDENTIFIES SUBJECT
John
We will also try to finalise our AB documents this week.
We will try to incorporate all comments and hope to have a definite version
this week. Kees en Wim will finalise our documents.
MOVE IIA EXCHANGES INFORMATION

With kind regards, Jan Jansen
Nedco, Amsterdam

AB Working Documents

  Figure 25.9 provides a final example of a message from a junior
to a senior manager within the division that combines all four moves
in the exchange of information.

Figure 25.9
An Example of All Four Moves Used within One Message

```
*** Forwarding note from OJBCT0  To: P. Jones cc: C. van Veen     B. de Wit
From: F. Huizen
Subject: Inventarisatie m2 doorbelasting van de department
MOVE I IDENTIFIES SUBJECT
Peter,
Looked at the list of buildings per department. Following adaptations are being
Suggested:
Kantoor 009/AD is a meeting room for general purposes not a NEDCO facility
Ruimte 875/DF is the robot space, which we asked to remove from our
budget by 1/12/96
Interne opslag 009/DD is the CSR opslag and thus not NEDCO
Interne opslag 007/GC is from Jansen COGS
MOVE IIA EXCHANGES INFORMATION
Further, I would like to comment that a considerable amount of staff movements
early 1997 will alter the picture quite significantly
MOVE IIB JUSTIFIES ACTION
and consequently I suggest you consider taking this as the basis for 1997.
MOVE III IDENTIFIES ACTION
Regards / Groeten,
                          Frans Huizen Nedco B.V., Amsterdam
```

Interpersonal Strategies

This final section looks at 10 linguistic features that have been identified in previous research as markers of *involved* or *interpersonal* discourse. *Involved discourse* highlights the relationship between the speaker/ writer and their audience and the interaction between them, and the use of *interpersonal* rhetorical strategies contributes to the development of the relationship between the reader and writer and also indicates the writer's attitude to the propositional information contained in the text (see Collot and Belmore, 1996; and Hyland, 1998, respectively).

The following involved/interpersonal features could be identified in both the Dutch-English and British-English data:

1.   Private verbs, such as "think" and "know", which express states or acts which are not observable (Collot and Belmore, 1996).

2. Contractions and abbreviations (Collot and Belmore, 1996; Mulholland, 1999).
3. First and second person pronouns (Collot and Belmore, 1996; Hyland, 1998).
4. Hedges (Collot and Belmore, 1996; Hyland, 1998).
5. If clauses (Collot and Belmore, 1996).
6. Emphatics (Collot and Belmore, 1996; Hyland, 1998).
7. Amplifiers (Collot and Belmore, 1996).
8. Politeness strategies, e.g., **Please** respond (Mulholland, 1999).
9. Block capitals and exclamations (Hyland, 1998; Mulholland, 1999).
10. Asides (Hyland, 1998).

Table 25.2
Interpersonal Discourse Features — Number of Messages in Corpus

Discourse Feature	Dutch-English messages No. of messages	British-English messages No. of messages
Asides	29	33
Contractions/Omissions	34	43
Block Capitals/Exclamations marks	22	30
Hedges	17	17
Emphatics	13	2
Private verbs	32	28
First or second person pronouns	85	91

Tables 25.2 and 25.3 show the quantitative findings for each of the interpersonal discourse features. The total number of running words for the Dutch-English messages was 15,201 and for the British-English messages it was 15,327. This gave an average of 152 words per message for the Dutch-English messages and 153 words per message for the British-English messages. Table 25.2 shows the total number of messages in the corpus, for each set of writers, where there was at least one occurrence of the discourse feature listed. Table 25.3 shows the total number of occurrences, for each set of writers for the discourse

features listed, including the number of occurrences per 15,000 words. The amplifiers, pronouns and if-clauses shown in Table 25.3, were isolated using the concordance programme in WordSmith Tools (Scott, 1996). Wherever necessary for comparative purposes, the number of occurrences per 15,000 words are also included in parenthesis in the text of the discussion below.

As indicated in Table 25.2, there was very little difference between the English and Dutch writers in their use of private verbs, in their use of abbreviations or contractions or in their use of block capitals or exclamation marks for emphasis. In both sets of data, writers used exclamation marks rather than capitals to emphasize propositional information in the text, for example, in the 22 messages in the Dutch-English data only two included capitals for emphasis. As Mulholland suggests, the use of capitals "remains an unsubtle and unenriching mode of presentation" (1999:79), and discussions with the managers represented in the corpus revealed an agreement not to use capitals in e-mail communication. The private verbs used, included verbs such as *hope, understand* and *feel*, and the commonly used *I/we think*. *I/we think,* was also incorporated into a number of the hedges in the data, as in "For this initial stage *I think* that 80 hours of our time is sufficient" (Dutch-English data) and *"I think* that 20 minutes followed by 10 minutes of questions would be OK, however..." (British-English data). This was used by writers in the tentative, and strategic, presentation of propositional information. For example, in the first case, the writer prefers not to commit himself in case his estimate proves incorrect, and in the second case the writer allows the receiver to disagree with his assessment of an appropriate presentation. Abbreviations and contractions were also a commonplace feature in the Dutch-English and British-English corpus, and this confirms the "preference for minimalism" that Mulholland identifies as characteristic of the medium (1999:74). Examples taken from the data, included lexical items such as *asap* and *info*, and particularly between employees in close proximity to each other within the corporate structure, radical minimalism such as "Lunch at 12:30?", "Any thoughts?", and "OK?".

Table 25.3

Interpersonal Discourse Features — Total Number of Occurrences in Corpus

Discourse Feature	Dutch-English messages (f) and (f per 15,000 words)		British-English messages (f) and (f per 15,000 words)	
Request + Politeness strategy	30	29.6	41	40.1
If clauses	17	16.8	32	31.3
Amplifiers (very + a lot)	34	33.5	9	8.8
Pronouns (we)	118	116.4	80	78.3
Pronouns (I)	153	151.0	202	197.7
Pronouns (you)	95	93.7	124	121.3

Two aspects of the discourse in which there were differences between the Dutch and British writers, were the use of emphatics and amplifiers. The most common amplifier was *very* in both sets of data, e.g., The visit of Jan was *very* beneficial..., The results are very encouraging...etc., although there were three times as many occurrences in the Dutch-English data than in the British-English data. There were a further eight occurrences of a lot in the Dutch-English data, compared to only one occurrence in the British data, such that there were four times as many amplifiers in total in the Dutch-English data than in the British-English data. Dow (1999) has suggested that German speakers have a tendency to incorporate upgraders or "strengtheners" into their presentation of propositional information, as opposed to the English tendency to use downgraders or "weakeners". The e-mail data would seem to indicate that these Dutch writers may use a similar strategy, which they then transfer into their use of English.

There were also many more emphatics in the Dutch-English data, compared to the British-English data. These were used to express a full commitment to the truth-value of a proposition and to emphasize the force or writer's certainty in the message (Hyland, 1998). The only emphatics in the British-English data were both realized as certainly, as in, "It certainly means that the skills and ABC parts of our proposal should be realizable...", as were three of the 13 emphatics in the Dutch-English data, for example, "These exchanges should *certainly* continue...". The most common emphatic in the Dutch-English data, however, was *of course*, accounting for over half of the total number of occurrences, as in for example, "This has of course quite some impact on the content of their work...". Dutch writers used emphatics to indicate that they were acting in good (corporate) faith, or to preface a request or recommendation for certain action to take place, to appeal to the reader and influence them to accept the proposal. It may be the case that the British-English writers avoided the use of emphatics, as they considered them to be high risk strategies that invite the receiver to disagree.

A further difference between the British and Dutch writers, was in the selection and use of certain pronouns and in the strategic use to which *If* clauses were put. There were just under twice as many occurrences in the British data than in the Dutch data of an *If* clause, i.e., 32 (31.3) compared with 17 (16.8). In addition, two of the Dutch occurrences were part of the electronic boilerplate that warned receivers that a message had originated outside of their division. A further three of the Dutch occurrences and eight of the British occurrences, were part of a conventional politeness strategy, as in, "Please let me know if you require further information". A total of 17 (16.6) If clauses were used strategically by British writers either to allow for disagreement on behalf of the receiver or further negotiation, or to secure the co-operation of the receiver. Examples of these included; "...we could *if* we wished bring it under point 2...", "*If* this is OK, it would be good for you, Jan and I to meet..." and "...my comments, *if* any use at all, are simply...". In comparison, although the Dutch writers used *if* clauses to accomplish the same types of purposes as the British writers, as in, "We would appreciate it very much *if* Kees could go one more time", there were only four (3.9) instances of *if* clauses used strategically in the Dutch-English messages. This suggests that this may not be a strategy with which Dutch writers feel familiar and they therefore do not incorporate it into their English discourse.

Similar numbers of messages in both sets of data included at least one first or second person pronoun as a marker of *involvement* (restricted in this analysis to *we, you* and *I*). However, the total number of occurrences for each pronoun suggested some divergence between the two groups of writers. The Dutch writers showed a preference for "we" as a first person pronoun, together with a preference for the use of "we" as a pronoun excluding the receiver, whereas the British writers showed a preference for "I" and an inclusive use of "we", including both sender and receiver. 74% of the total number of occurrences of we in the Dutch-English messages were exclusive pronouns as opposed to only 24% in the British-English messages, compared with 57% of the occurrences as inclusive in the British data and 21% in the Dutch data. One reason for the higher percentage of inclusive "we" pronouns in the British-English data, may have been the fact that a number of messages in the corpus were sent within one department. For example, three of the British managers routinely used an inclusive "we" pronoun to refer to the department or to themselves as a management team, accounting for almost half of the total number of inclusive pronouns in the British-English messages. There were eight instances of a *defocalized* "we" in the British data and five in the Dutch-English data. Defocalization occurs, for example, when "we" is used in place of "you" by a writer, *as if* it includes both writer and reader, when in fact it only refers to the writer (see Haverkate, 1992, for further discussion). These defocalizations were used in both sets of data to invoke solidarity with the receiver and therefore to bring about their agreement with the sender, as in, "we all know Jan is a good customer...", where the sender wishes to initiate an internal project with Jan, "we have a mutual interest...", and "Have we all had a go at the post-its on John's noticeboard?", where the writer knows that he is, in fact, the only one that has!

For asides, hedges and the incorporation of politeness into requests, there were also similarities between the Dutch and British writers. Asides, the interruption of the discourse, were realized in the e-mail communication by the use of parentheses, which were used in order to include extra information. As indicated in Table 25.2, these occurred in a similar number of messages in both sets of data. Much of the extra information was propositional in nature, however, a number of the asides in both the Dutch-English and the British-English data, 13 (12.3) and 20 (19.6) instances respectively, were employed strategically for interpersonal reasons. One excellent example of this occurs in one of the Dutch-English messages, where the writer, a member of the secretarial staff, requests managers to send her the names of a number of their employees who may qualify for a bonus. As part of her request, she also uses an aside to include the information as to who will ultimately be responsible for allocating the bonus:

> *"Please forward the names to me, in consultation with Jan Jansen (who is the focal point in this) we will allocate the bonuses."*

Hedges, the tentative presentation of propositional information, and the incorporation of politeness strategies in requests, were used by both Dutch and British writers alike. The realizations of hedges were similar, as in, "It *may be* useful to invite these two colleagues..." (Dutch writer) and "It *would seem* to me to be most appropriate to progress..." (British writer), as were the reasons why a writer decided to include a hedge. Hedges were used to allow for possible disagreement on the part of the receiver without either party losing (corporate) face, for example, "One option *might be* to ask support..." (Dutch writer), or to protect the sender's interests, as in, "For this initial stage *I think* that 80 hours of our time is sufficient..." (Dutch writer). Parallel texts produced in response to the same request for information, illustrate similar realizations employed in the same hedged strategy; "*As far as we know*, we have no drums at these locations..." (Dutch writer) and "ABC department has no drums in storage *to the best of our knowledge*..." (British writer).

Virtually all of the requests in both sets of data were modified in some way with the inclusion of one or more politeness markers, e.g., "*Could* this be accommodated?", "*I would appreciate* it if..." etc. One realization, "*Perhaps/maybe you could/would/should be so kind as to*...", was used only by the British writers (six instances), and the most commonly used realization in both data sets was "*Please* + send/ revert/consider..." etc. The latter provides support for Mulholland's (1999) observation that writers continue to incorporate politeness strategies despite a preference for minimalism within the electronic medium. In all 200 messages in the corpus, there was only one instance of an imperative, as in, "do this via Jansen". This occurred in a message sent from the Divisional Director to all managerial staff as the follow-up to a previous request to which there had been no response, and it suggests that unless the circumstances were exceptional, imperatives were not considered as appropriate interpersonal strategies in the formal realization of Genre IE.

Conclusion

The findings of the study indicate that the use of English in electronic communication is embedded in the organizational practices of the corporation. Electronic mail is a major source of information exchange within the corporation and there is widespread reference to electronic communication in the organizing process and in the execution of corporate activities. In both areas of activity, a considerable amount of the information exchanged and referred to is in English. Furthermore, English occurs in electronic transmissions at all levels in the corporation and across all major management systems, and the appropriate formal realization of the message, such as its lexis, is embedded within the communication practices of the corporation. Finally, although there were some differences in the discourse features and rhetorical strategies used by the British and Dutch writers in one of the organizational e-mail genres, there were also many similarities. These indicate that a typified corporate discourse may exist regardless of the national culture of the individual employee.

The interdisciplinary approach taken here is an attempt to answer the call for a "thick" description of language use, originated by Geertz and echoed twenty years later by Bhatia (Geertz 1973; Bhatia 1993). Through reference to management communication, rhetorical genre analysis and applied linguistics, it has considered both the textualization of (the corporate) context and the contextualization of text. It seems plausible that the investigation of all types of professional discourse in the future, will benefit not only from insights gained from different disciplines in the work of individual researchers, but, most especially, from the collaborative efforts of researchers active within different fields.

References

1. Bhatia, V. K. 1993. *Analyzing genre: Language use in professional settings.* London: Longman.

2. Collot, M. and N. Belmore. 1996. Electronic language: A new variety of English. In *Computer-mediated communication: Linguistic, social and cross-cultural perspectives*, edited by S. Herring. Amsterdam and Philadelphia: John Benjamins, 13–28.

3. Connor, U. 1999. "How like you our fish?" Accommodation in international business communication. In *Business English: Research into practice*, edited by M. Hewings and C. Nickerson. London and New York: Longman, 116–129.

4. Dow, E. 1999. Negotiation comes of age: Research in non-native contexts and implications for today's business English materials. In *Business English: Research into practice*, edited by M. Hewings and C. Nickerson. London and New York: Longman, 84–100.

5. Geertz, C. 1973. *The interpretation of cultures.* New York: Basic Books.

6. Giddens, A. 1979. *Central problems in social theory: Action, structure and contradiction in social analysis.* Berkeley: University of California Press.

7. _____ . 1984. *The constitution of society: Outline of the theory of structuration.* Cambridge: Polity Press.

8. Haverkate, H. 1992. Deictic categories as mitigating devices. *Pragmatics* 2 (4): 505–522.

9. Hyland, K. 1998. Exploring corporate rhetoric: Metadiscourse in the CEO's letter. *Journal of Business Communication* 35 (2): 224–245.

10. Miller, C. R. 1984. Genre as social action. *Quarterly Journal of Speech* 70:151–167.

11. Mulholland, J. 1999. E-mail: Uses, issues and problems in an institutional setting. In *Writing business: Genres, media and discourses*, edited by F. Bargiela-Chiappini and C. Nickerson. London and New York: Longman, 57–84.

12. Nickerson, C. 1999. Genre theory and intercultural communication. The usefulness of genre theory in the investigation of organizational communication across cultures. *Document Design* 1 (3): 202–215.

13. _____ . 2000. *Playing the corporate language game. An investigation of the genres and discourse strategies in English used by Dutch writers working in multinational corporations.* Amsterdam and Atlanta: Rodopi.

14. Orlikowski, W. J. and J. Yates. 1994. Genre repertoire: The structuring of communicative practices in organizations. *Administrative Science Quarterly* 39: 541–574.

15. Rogers, P. S. and H. W. Hildebrandt. 1993. Competing values instruments for analyzing written and spoken management messages. *Human Resource Management* 32 (1): 121–142.

16. Scott, M. 1996. *WordSmith Tools*. Oxford: Oxford University Press.

17. Suchan, J. and R. Dulek. 1998. From text to context: An open systems approach to research in written business communication. *The Journal of Business Communication* 35 (1): 87–110.

18. Yates, J. and W. Orlikowski. 1992. Genres of organizational communication: A structurational approach to studying communication and media. *Academy of Management Review* 17 (2): 299–326.

26

Genre Change in the Historical Development of Sales Invitations

Zhu Yunxia

Genre Change in the Historical Development of Sales Invitations [1]

This study examines genre evolution exhibited in the historical development of sales invitations used in mainland China in the economic pre-reform (1949–78) and reform (1978 to the present) periods. Here sales invitations refer to letters to invite the reader to sales exhibitions and a detailed introduction will be given later in this paper.

The study of professional genre has been an area of research interest and relevant research can be found in Swales (1990) who analyzes English academic genres and Bhatia (1993) who examines English business genres. However genre evolution is still a relative new area which is beginning to attract more interest from genre researchers. For example, Bhatia (1993) alerts our attention to the dynamic nature of professional genres, but a systematic study along this line still needs to be formulated and promoted. The reason for its under-development can be that this is a challenging area because of the process of genre change may involve a long period of time over history. An attempt to explore genre change has been made in Zhu (1996, 1999, 2000a) who further develops Swales' (1990) approach by offering a dynamic perspective to look at genre development in Chinese business communication in relation to the changing social

---

1. This chapter is based on the author's Ph.D. thesis. Thanks are given to Dr. Tony Liddicoat, Dr. Beverly Hong, Andy Kirkpatrick, and Dr. Tony Diller and for their encouragement and helpful advice. Economic reform started in 1978 in mainland China under the leadership of Deng Xiaopeng. This movement is characterised by an emphasis on gradual modernisation and privatisation of organisations and economic structures in general.

and cultural context, in particular after the economic opening-up in 1978. The advantage of using this approach lies in its strength in considering genre change as a continuous process in response to the development of business and economic contexts. This chapter further promotes the study of genre evolution by examining the historical development of another genre — sales invitations.

To be specific, this chapter accomplishes the following tasks. First, the theoretical framework is introduced and its relevance to the analysis in this study illustrated. Second, a brief introduction is given to explicate the general features of invitation letters. Third, the features of sales invitations before and after 1978 are discussed to indicate in what way they may have evolved. Finally, a corpus of 20 authentic letters collected from mainland China is examined as a specific example to illustrate the genre change at various levels of the text.

Relevant Literature

The theoretical approach utilized in examining genre change in sales invitations is a variant of what was first proposed in Zhu (1999). As a particular advantage, the approach overcomes the limitation of placing too much focus on text and discourse in genre study as pointed out by Huckin (1997). As illustrated in Figure 26.1, this approach, enables examination of genre change in relation to the changing social context, which is particularly important for the present study.

Figure 26.1
The Model of Professional Genre Study

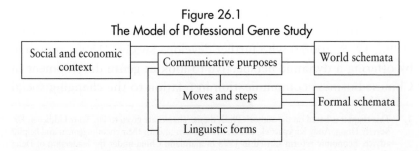

Based on Zhu's model of genre study (1999)

First, Figure 26.1 reflects Swales' top-down process of genre study which is composed of communicative purposes and moves. According to Swales, genre is characterized by a set of communicative purposes. These purposes and writing conventions shape the structure of the discourse and constrain the choice of linguistic forms, and can be realized in different layers of a text, such as moves and steps. Moves and steps are the major units of analysis. A move is defined as a communicative event by Zhu (1999), and a step is a lower unit under a move.

Swales' (1990) approach is closely related to the ethnographic communication tradition (Hymes, 1974; Miller, 1984; Saville-Troike, 1984) and offers a more holistic view than a pure linguistic-based model. Swales' model has been applied successfully in the study of English professional genres (such as Bhtia, 1993), Chinese sales genre and cross-cultural genre comparison (Zhu, 1999; 2000b).

Second, Figure 26.1 integrates knowledge structures from schema theory (Bartlett, 1932; Rumelhart, 1980), which not only makes further exploration of the cognitive aspect of genre study possible but also offers a close link between genre evolution and changes in social context. Schema theory originated from the British psychologist Bartlett (1932) within the Gestalt tradition. According to schema theory (Bartlett, 1932; Rumelhart, 1980), a text does not have meaning by itself when it is presented to the readers or learners. They have to construct the meaning based on their own previously acquired knowledge when reading or learning a text. These knowledge structures are called schemata (Bartlett, 1932; Rumelhart, 1980). The process of understanding a text is thus seen by the schematic theorists as an interactive process between the readers' background knowledge and the text. The understanding of a text does not only require linguistic knowledge but also requires world knowledge (Carrell and Eisterhold, 1983; Widdowson, 1983). Based on Carrell and Eisterhold (1983) and Cook's (1994) study of knowledge structures, Zhu (1999) further defines knowledge structures as shared by a discourse community. Although the knowledge structure of each individual may differ, the individuals share some common features of world schema that represents the general knowledge structure of this group.

In the case of sales invitations, world schemata may involve understanding the politeness behaviour of invitation and sales promotion strategies. A formal schema is seen as the background knowledge of the formal, rhetorical organizational structures of texts and linguistic forms. Formal schemata here can be seen as genre-specific. For example, Chinese sales invitations often use honorific and polite linguistic forms. The acquisition of world schemata is based on the understanding of the social context a genre involves. Social context in this paper mainly refers to the economic environment in China. Formal schemata are, in fact, closely related to the world schemata, and honorifics are considered appropriate forms to convey the meaning associated with high-level respect.

Genre can be studied from at least two perspectives. On the one hand, genre and its communicative purposes are closely related to social and economic context. Out of changing social contexts different communicative needs arise. These needs are important factors and conditions for bringing about a change in communicative purposes.

On the other hand, the top-down information process in Figure 26.1 may offer a possibility to examine how genre involves at various levels. A change in communicative purposes caused by the social change may lead to changes in lower levels of moves and linguistic forms as these levels are used to reflect the purposes. Furthermore, examining the lower levels of a text can provide specific linguistic evidence about how genre changes. Both of the above two aspects of genre need to be studied with appropriate world and formal schemata.

Politeness Behaviour

Understanding politeness behaviour in invitations may enrich the relevant schemata. Invitation is a directive; thus, politeness behaviour is examined in the light of speech act theory (Austin, 1962; Searle, 1969). Austin's (1962) major contribution lies in his conceptualization of the speech acts as comprising of locution and illocution. What is of vital importance is the illocutionary force of an utterance that is the performing of a speech act, such as invitations. According to Searle (1969), an invitation is a directive used to get the hearer or reader to do something. Politeness behaviour can thus be related to using appropriate language forms to achieve higher illocutionary force.

Research on politeness behaviour may offer some understanding to the appropriate use of language forms in sales invitations. Leech (1983) contends that polite illocutions are likely to be seen as minimizing the addressee's costs and maximizing his/her benefits, and the opposite is true for the addresser. Politeness behaviour can also be further explained in the light of Brown and Levinson's (1987) face-saving theory. Many actions we do with words are potential face-threatening acts (Brown and Levinson, 1987), such as invitations and requests. The addresser is thus often confronted with negative face and has to address it by applying Leech's (1983) principles, in which maximizing the addressee's benefits is the dominant strategy to gain politeness.

However, forms relating to politeness behaviour may vary from culture to culture. Blum-Kulka *et al.* (1989), for example, explore various forms of requests strategies across eight different cultures. Although politeness strategies may differ, they are seen as shared by the members of the culture. In a similar way, in Chinese business communication, choices of linguistic forms are often pertinent to particular politeness strategies (Gunthner, 1993; Ulijn and Li, 1995; Hu and Grove, 1991). A Chinese culture-specific politeness behavior relating to harmony and face-keeping is to show respect by using polite linguistic forms such as honorifics in sales invitations. This point is often stressed in business writing textbooks (Chen, 1991; Zhuge and Chen, 1994). The reason for this preference may be related to Chinese being a collectivistic culture in which power and status are regarded as important values. The writer may try to raise the reader's status by using appropriate linguistic device, thus achieving the purpose of indicating respect for the reader. In addition, showing respect is often discussed as a culturally shared value (Gu, 1990; Zhu, 1999).

---

2.   *Xiaxing, pingxing* and *shangxing* are used to classify Chinese official letter writing based on the reader-writer relationship. A letter is called *xiaxing* if it is directed to a subordinate, *pingxing* if it is written by person of equal status, and *shangxing* if it is to be sent to a superior. The writer has to take into consideration politeness strategies required by different kinds of reader-writer relationships when writing the letter.

Another cultural-specific feature may be related to the use of three major genres in official writing which include *xiaxing*[2] (the superior writing to the subordinate), *pingxing* (equals writing to each other) and *shangxing* (the subordinate writing to the superior). Zhu (1999) found that a *shangxing* genre may be more polite or honorific than *xiaxing*, and a *pingxing* genre may also involves a high level of politeness. All the above factors may have impact on a formal and respectful register in writing Chinese sales invitations. They will be used as important parameters to examine the development of sales invitations.

Chinese Sales Invitations

First, a general introduction to Chinese invitations is necessary. The only available literature on this is Chinese textbooks. Invitations are often described as a type of *liyi xin* (letters of etiquette), or *shejiao xin* (letters of social contact). The meaning of *shejiao* (social contact) is readily apparent; however, *liyi xin* needs some explanation. According to Zhuge and Chen (1994:361), *liyi* means etiquette and ceremonies. Accordingly, Chinese sales invitations are treated as a form of etiquette for building relationships. This can be related to the influence of Confucian concepts in which social etiquette is often emphasized. As Zhuge and Chen (1994) explain that *liyi xin* include invitations, welcome speeches, farewell speeches. and relationship building is the most important purpose in these types of letters. Since sales invitations are a sub-division of invitations they are seen as having similar characteristics as well.

Chinese textbooks tend to provide some general rules such as using respectful language for writing sales invitations, and tend not to provide a detailed list about the use appropriate forms. In spite of that, it is still possible to summarize some of the features such as polite linguistic device based on examples found in textbooks and these can be used as part of the formal schemata in understanding sales invitations. Invitations may have various forms as shown in the politeness continua of Figure 26.2.

Figure 26.2
Politeness Continua of Linguistic Forms Used In Chinese Invitations

	1	2	3	4	5
Salutations	Co. name and personal name	Personal title	Dear Customers	Your (H) Co.	Respected + personal title
Inviting Verbs	To hope and wish	To politely ask	To invite	To sincerely /specially invite	To respectfully invite
Closing	Hope that you will participate	With regards	We hereby invite (you)	To welcome your presence (H)	To respectfully invite / await your presence (H)

As shown in Figure 26.2, there are three categories in the politeness continua including salutations, inviting verbs and the closing. The numbers indicate the grades of the continuum with Grade 5 indicating the highest degree of politeness and Grade 1 the lowest. For example, *respected leading comrade, respectfully inviting* and *respectfully inviting your presence* (H) represent the highest ends of the continua; *Co. name, hoping and hoping that you will participate* indicate the lowest ends.

A detailed discussion about the writing of this genre is given to both pre-reform (1949–78) and reform (1978 to the present) periods. The year 1978 is used as a demarcation line to divide these periods as this year saw the beginning of the economic opening-up. This event is also the major factor that contributes to the changes in this genre. The features of each period are introduced as an important component of the world schemata to understand genre change.

Sales Invitations before 1978

This period is characterized by deviation from the market economy and an emphasis on a planned economy. A most prevalent strategy employed by the Chinese government was to practice market mechanisms under socialism. Under this system, the business of commodity exchange was controlled by public ownership at different levels. All the enterprises were state-owned. Products were distributed and sold through a top-down umbrella network of Ministry of Commerce, the provincial bureau, district bureau, and town bureau. The grassroots town bureaux could only get what the higher levels such as the provincial bureau, or the district bureau distributed to them.

Sales invitations in this hierarchical organizational structure played an important role to invite the subordinate organizations to the exhibition for product distribution. When there was a need to have a product exhibition, a higher-level organization such as the provincial commercial bureau would invite the subordinate town bureaux to come to the show. For example, the prices for the exhibited products were set before the show and there would be no room for negotiation. Only the heads of the organizations concerned would be invited to sign the wholesale contracts. Therefore the whole process could be seen as carrying out the government sales plan with a lot of restrictions. The participants of the exhibition did not seem to have any control of sales. Consequently there was no need to use promotion strategies in a sales invitation. Instead, the superior bureau's intention lies in distributing products at the exhibition as indicated in the following letter collected from the archives of a town commercial bureau:

X X X
      1 9 6 9   X X X

X X X

1968   11   5

Headline	Invitation to the Sugar, Cigarettes and Wine Distribution Exhibition
Salutation	The Party Secretary of the XXX City Bureau,

Exhibition	It has been decided that 1969 Sugar, Cigarettes and Wine Distribution Meeting will be held in the Conference Room in the main building of XXX Provincial Commercial Bureau at 8 am, December 1.
Inviting	We specially invite (you) to come. It is hoped that you will participate on time.
Polite closing	We hereby invite (you)
Signature and Date	Sugar, Cigarettes and Wine Office XXX Provincial Commercial Bureau November 5, 1968

The above letter is a type of *xiaxing genre* as the reader is in a subordinate position. The major purposes involve informing the subordinate organization of the exhibition and inviting the Party Secretary who was the head of the organization to come. This purpose was further realized in six moves as indicated on the left-hand column. Being informative and using the appropriate forms to invite the reader are the most important tasks of the letter. The former is conveyed by giving the specific details of the exhibition, and the latter is expressed by using invitation-related forms. The salutation addressing the reader by the personal title does not really indicate a high level of politeness (See Figure 26.2). Inviting is indicated this way:

"It is hoped that you will participate on time."

In the politeness continuum the verb *hope* is rated only as Grade 1, thus indicating a rather low level of politeness. This level fits in with the *xiaxing* register in which the writer uses typical decision-related terms such as *decided*, and *it is hoped* (Zhu, 1996; 2000a).

In spite of the fact that it is a *xiaxing* letter, the writer still tries to be polite by inviting the reader "specially" which indicates a high level of respect according to Figure 26.2. This form can be seen as required by the politeness convention of writing an invitation. However, the closing indicates a rather low respect level.

From the letter, we can see that sales elements are completely missing. The word "distribution" is used instead to reflect the nature of the planned economy. Or we may look at sales from a different perspective: the people in the subordinate organizations have to attend the exhibition in order to obtain their quota of sales. The above invitation serves this purpose very well.

Although a single letter may not give a panoramic view of sales invitations of the pre-reform period, it offers a glimpse about the preferred features of a *xiaxing* sales invitation in that period.

Sales Invitations after 1978

This period represents a link to the market economy, and sales invitations are experiencing dramatic changes in both content and language as a result of the economic opening-up.

One of the most important characteristics of this period is the change in the nature of ownership. The previous nature of public ownership was attacked and enterprises began to change from state-ownership to gradual privatization. State-owned enterprises are given more responsibility and independence in their own operation. As a result, both private and state-owned enterprises coexist. Although there still remains some public ownership by state-owned organizations, every enterprise is involved in the competitive market economy. Product promotion is becoming vital for every enterprise, and this leads to the popularity of sales invitations. Equal competition in business may contribute to the change in reader-writer relationship and sales invitations are often written in the *pingxing* (equal) genre.

As a consequence, sales promotion becomes a strong component in sales invitations and this genre involves features of both invitation and promotion. For example, relationship building and sales promotions are emphasized by Chinese textbooks. As Lu *et al.* (1993: 189) explain, the purpose of a sales invitation is to "increase friendship, and develop trade" Lu *et al.* (1993) here stress two purposes: increasing friendship and developing trade. Obviously they realize the new purpose of developing trade. In the meantime, they also pay attention to the change of the reader-writer relationship. This can be indicated by the term *friendship*. In the sales invitation context, it means more than mutual affection in its connotative meaning because the writer does not really want to be a friend to the reader but rather a business partner.

Business invitations after 1978 play a different role from those before 1978 and sales promotion becomes a strong element today. The genre also changes from *xiaxing* to *pingxing* and a higher politeness level is indicated. The specific changes of this genre will be further explored in the following analysis of the twenty sales invitations.

The Data

Twenty sales invitations were collected on a random basis from mainland China based on the following criteria: First, they had to be sales invitations; this ruled out other types of invitations for attending training classes or conferences. Second, they were selected from several cities: Beijing, Zhengzhou, Kaifeng, Shenzhen, and Zhuhai. This geographical diversity reflects the general features of the genre and also avoids a possible textural tendency to prefer a certain type of structure in a certain region.

The second source of data is composed of Chinese managers' input and their comments relating to the criteria of writing sales invitations are incorporated in the discussion where relevant.

Analysis of the Data

First and foremost, the communicative purposes are ascertained in the corpus as a starting point. The most obvious and major purpose of a sales invitation is to invite the reader to attend an exhibition and elicit a desired response. The complexity of purposes increases when the new purposes relating to sales promotion are mingled with invitation. However, if the world schemata relating to the marketing knowledge in the reform period and cultural-specific features of Chinese invitations are appropriately used, one can, on close observation, ascertain the following communicative purposes from the corpus:

1. To invite the reader to attend the exhibition and encourage

    further communication

2. To inform the reader about the exhibition
3. To build a host-guest relationship with the reader
4. To achieve a positive public image
5. To attract the reader's attention and interest
6. To give positive appraisals of the exhibition
7. To persuade the reader to attend the exhibition

The above seven purposes can be divided into two kinds: inviting the reader to the exhibition and advertising the exhibition. Generally speaking, the first three purposes in the above list are related to inviting because they focus on information about the activities and inviting the reader to come to the exhibition.

The last three purposes are related partly to the marketing model of AIDA which stands for attracting the reader's attention, making the reader interested, stimulating the reader's desire to own the product, and calling the reader to take action. All the three purposes can be seen as recent development of sales invitations in the economic opening-up. These new purposes may indicate that Chinese business practice now is influenced by the western business practice, which is characterized by privatization and competition. As competition becomes an important feature in the Chinese market, sales promotion strategies are employed as a result.

The AIDA model is activated in this manner. For example, the fifth purpose of attracting the reader's attention and interest makes up the first two stages of AIDA. The sixth and seventh are related to bringing about the desire to attend the exhibition. "Giving appraisals" is subordinate to the purpose of persuading the reader because it supports the persuasion by giving positive evaluations. "Achieving a positive public image" can be seen as a subordinate purpose to "inviting the reader" and "persuading the reader", as a good image is desirable in invitations and sales.

At the same time, sales invitations are, after all, invitations which seek to establish a guest-host relationship with the reader. Another point that is worth noting is that although the purpose of inviting the reader can be related to calling for action, this purpose does not really fit into the last stage of the AIDA model, since it is mainly related to inviting the reader.

Among these seven purposes, persuading the reader and inviting the reader are the most important because these two purposes can guarantee the success of an invitation. As can be seen from the above discussion, Chinese sales invitations have begun a transitional stage of incorporating western business practice into the purposes of inviting the reader.

The Top-Down Process of an Individual Invitation

In this section, the concept of top-down information processing is applied in the analysis of an individual letter in order to study how communicative purposes, in particular, the new purposes in the reform period, are realized in the lower levels of the text. The letter concerned was rated the best in the corpus by Chinese managers and their comments will also be incorporated in the discussion. Only the translation of the letter is provided here.

1   Banking China '93

2   China Computer Show '93

3   Invitation

4   Respected reader,

5   The Chinese economy is developing rapidly. Every industry or business has to
6   promote its technology so as to increase its competitiveness. In order to meet
7   the needs of the industries and businesses concerned, Banking China '93 and
8   China Computer Show '93 are to be held in December in Beijing. We sincerely
9   invite your (H) company to participate.

10   This show is to be held on a grand scale. (Names of the participating countries
11   omitted). Internationally well-known companies dealing with bank security,
12   computers, tele-communication and automation equipment will exhibit their
13   latest advanced equipment for financial, banking and other industrial and
14   commercial enterprises.

15   In addition, commercial councils from Australia, Singapore, and Colorado State
16   of the United States will also organize delegations to take part.

17   This show will exhibit all kinds of latest equipment and systems used in banking
18   and financial enterprises. (The detailed exhibits omitted).

19   Through participating in this exhibition, your (H) company can meet more than
20   seventy producers or suppliers from more than ten countries and districts, and
21   talk about co-operative plans with them. (You are) welcome to leave your on-
22   site exhibited products for sale.

23   In addition to this, many technology exchange discussions will also be held so
24   that visitors may have a further understanding of all the participants' advanced
25   products.

26   Our company sincerely invites managerial and technical representatives from
27   your (H) company to visit (H) this Exhibition. Enclosed is an invitation card.
28   Please bring this card with you and go to the International Exhibition Centre to
29   go through admission formalities.

30   If you need further materials, you can contact the Beijing agency of
31   Exhibition Services Ltd:

32   Miss XXX

33   Room XX, China Exhibition Services Building. No. XX, XXX Road,
34   XXX District, Beijing.

35   Telephone: XXX   Fax: XXX

36   Wish (you) good health (H)!

37   XXX Exhibition Services Ltd.

38   October, 1993.

The structure of the letter is schematized as in Figure 26.3.

Figure 26.3 indicates the various moves and steps that appear in the letter, which are also typical of the general findings in the corpus. This letter is composed of ten moves: (1) heading, (2) salutation (3) introducing the exhibition, (4) inviting the reader, (5) describing the exhibition, (6) offering incentives, (7) inviting the reader again, (8) providing registration details, (9) polite closing and (10) signature and date. The first two and last two moves can be seen as formulaic moves required by invitations. Some moves such as Move 3 are composed of more than one move, while others such as Move 4 only consist of one step. Inviting the reader is expressed twice to indicate cordiality. As pointed out by Chen (1991:106), repetitions in invitations is sometimes necessary because it emphasizes the invitation and indicates the writer's cordiality. Moves 5 and 6 reflect the new moves relating to sales promotions employed in the Reform Period. Some of the new purposes are also stressed by the managers. The following are the typical

Figure 26.3
The Structural Moves and Steps of the Sales Invitation

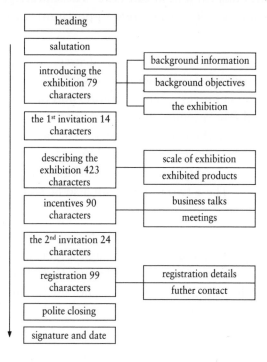

comments they made on this letter.

(1) "This letter provides a good example for writing sales invitations. The reader is sincerely invited and the exhibition is well advertised. In addition, the paragraphing of the letter is good and it is easy to follow the main ideas."

(2) "This letter represents a sincere and formal invitation to the reader which is exactly what a sales invitation should be like. The writer uses honorific forms when referring to the reader. The writer invites the reader twice, which indicates the writer's hospitable attitude."

(3) "This letter provides essential details to describe the exhibition, and there is no waste of words in order to keep the reader interested. These descriptions are also very persuasive. Unlike some

advertising materials which boast about the exhibition, the writer focuses on a detailed realistic depiction of the products and activities this exhibition can offer. These descriptions will help the reader work out possible opportunities for his/her own business."

The above comments, to a large degree, reflect the managers' knowledge structures and general expectations about genre change. The first comment gives a general impression of this letter as being well organized. The second comment is about the formal and respectful register of inviting the reader as a guest. The last comment is about what is essential for advertising the exhibition. In general, the managers stressed both the new advertising elements and the conventionalized invitation rules. These two respects can also be seen in the following analysis.

Move 1 is just a standard heading for an invitation. Move 2, the Salutation, however, indicates a very high-level respect by addressing the reader as *respected* as shown in Figure 26.1. This tendency is in alignment with the general features of sales invitations in the Reform Period discussed earlier.

Move 3, introducing the exhibition (lines: 7–10), is composed of three steps:

Step 1 Providing background information (lines 7–8)
Step 2 Indicating background objectives (lines 8–9)
Step 3 Providing information about the exhibition (lines 9–10)

The first step (lines 7–8) provides background information concerning the economic context in China, which exhibits an urgent need to raise competitive ability. This step may attract the reader's attention, and can also be related to genre change by including the market competition. In the past, the concept of competition was non-existent.

The aim of the exhibition is introduced this way:

> *In order to meet the needs of the industries and businesses concerned, Banking China '93 and China Computer Show '93 are to be held in December in Beijing (lines 8–10).*

In order to has two functions. The first is to introduce the aim of the exhibition in the subordinate clause, which is to meet the needs raised in the previous step. The second is to link this with the main clause, which provides information about the name, place and time of the exhibition. This form is also a common practice in invitation writing.

Inviting the reader (lines 10–11 and lines 25–26), is expressed in two places. Or we may say that invitation is indicated in both Move 4 and Move 7. The first is in a prominent place in the same paragraph as the introduction of the exhibition and is written in the following form:

> *We sincerely invite your (H) company to participate (lines 10–11).*

In this sentence, *sincerely inviting*, which is rated high in the politeness continuum (See Figure 26.2), and the honorific form of you is used. These forms may explicate that the writer is both sincere and respectful when inviting the reader and is also used frequently in the corpus.

The second invitation is realized in a similar way, but with more honorific lexical items:

> *"Our company sincerely invites managerial and technical representatives from your (H) company to visit (H) this exhibition" (lines 28–29).*

Besides using the same form of *sincerely inviting* as the first invitation, the writer has shown more respect by using *lilin* (H come). This term is often used in written Chinese to refer to the coming of honourable guests (Shekeyuan, 1984, p. 696). The above is related to the purpose of inviting the reader as a guest. The repetition of inviting and the use of honorific lexis all contribute to this purpose and to a higher level of respect in this *pingxing* invitation as compared to the pre-reform period. The appropriate level of respect is also indicated in the Managers' Comment No. 2.

Move 5, describing the exhibition (lines 12–21), is presented after the invitation and takes more space (423 Chinese characters in the original letter, approximately 60% of the whole text) than anything else because it is the most important section of the letter. This move deserves more attention as a major indicator of content change towards product promotion, and is composed of the following two steps:

Step 1 Providing essential details of the exhibition (lines 12–21)
Step 2 Evaluating the exhibition (line 12 and lines 13–15)

The first step is realized in three paragraphs. The second and third paragraphs of the letter describe the scale of the exhibition, supported by the name of more than ten countries as participants, while the fourth introduces various products to be exhibited. For an exhibition, the scale and variety of products can be a very appealing factor for the reader.

The major section of the second paragraph is discussed as an example to indicate the main features of this step:

> "This show is to be held on a grand scale. (Names of the participating countries omitted). Internationally well known companies dealing with bank security, computers, tele-communication and automation equipment will exhibit their latest advanced equipment for financial, banking and other industrial and commercial enterprises" (lines 12–16).

These details are introduced in a deductive manner, in which the idea develops from the general, *the grand scale*, to the specific including the names of the participating countries, and is used to support the idea of being on a grand scale. The above provides a good example of how to introduce the scale of the exhibition in a well-supported manner. The second step, evaluating the exhibition, is scattered among the first step, a typical feature of evaluating the exhibition in the corpus. For example, the first sentence in the above example can be seen as an evaluation because it gives an appraisal of the scale of the exhibition as being grand. Further evaluation can be seen in the above excerpt in the use of other forms of lexical forms. For example, the expression *internationally well-known* and the superlative degree of latest are used to give positive evaluations. This may be the reason why the managers thought this letter was *realistic* in its persuasiveness, as noted in their comment No. 3.

Move 6, offering incentives (lines 21–27), details other opportunities the writer promises the reader, including opportunities for sales and potential co-operation with foreign companies. The first incentive is achieved by promising the reader that if s/he participates in the exhibition s/he will benefit from it. Another incentive is the opportunity to leave on-site exhibited products for sale after the exhibition. This incentive is introduced by the verb *welcome* (line 23), which echoes the writer's host-like attitude in this invitation.

These incentives can be used to push the reader to a quick decision, thus helping stimulate the reader's desire to attend the exhibition. At the macro-level, it also helps realize the new promotional purposes.

Move 8, providing registration details (lines 29–37), is composed of the following two steps: giving registration details (lines 29–31) and giving further contact information (lines 32–37)

Step 1 refers to the invitation card and details the place of registration. The polite register indicated by the softener *please* (line 29) matches the high respect required by invitation letters. The second step, giving further contact information, is included to meet the reader's needs. It is written in a conditional sentence to express a polite and non-obligatory request.

Move 9, polite closing (line 39), is explicated in a very respectful tone in the form of *zhu da an* (wish great health). As a matter of fact, this form can not even be found in the relevant politeness continuum of Figure 26.2 because it is an extremely polite form. *Zhu da an* is only used in *shangxing* genre to address someone much higher in position or age and was even used by the subjects to address the emperor in the ancient times. The closing is borrowed from *shangxing* to indicate a very high level of respect. Zhu (1999) also found similar kinds of borrowing across genres to be a new tendency of lowering the writer's position in order to achieve a respectful linguistic distance.

Move 10, the signature and date (lines 41–42) is a required formulaic form to complete a letter.

In sum, this letter reflects the genre change in the following two respects. First it is a *pingxing* letter and the writer indicates a polite and respectful register throughout the letter. This is particularly true with the speech act of inviting. Second, the novel promotion elements have been incorporated successfully into this letter. Besides, the writer follows a clear organization of paragraph development as indicated in the managers' comment No. 1.

Conclusion

This chapter has explored how sales invitations involved along with social and economic changes and changes in communicative purposes were studied as a starting point for the overall examination of genre change. It has been found that the purposes of sales invitation evolved tremendously, the major purpose of earlier letters was to invite the subordinate reader to distribute wholesales, while the current invitations intend to invite the reader to sell or buy the products.

On the one hand, new advertising elements have been introduced into sales invitations and this can be shown in the adoption of AIDA marketing model. Relevant moves of "Describing the Exhibition" and "Offering incentives" are included to achieve the advertising effect. On the other hand, sales invitations have evolved from *xiaxing* to *pingxing*. This change can be shown in the preference of a more polite and respectful register in today's sales invitations as indicated in the analysis of the most successful letter.

The above findings may have implications for the study of genre change in general; changes in social context can be examined as an external factor affecting genre change. Similar research can be conducted in other business genres so that genre change in business writing can be studied extensively. Besides social change, internal changes in general cultural factors, such as in people's attitudes and beliefs may also be studied to identify further causes of genre evolution.

References

1. Austin, J. L. 1962. *How to do things with words.* New York: Oxford University Press.

2. Bartlett, F. C. 1932. Remembering: *A study in experimental and social psychology.* Cambridge: Cambridge University Press.

3. Bhatia, V. K. 1993. *Analyzing genre: Language use in professional settings.* New York: Longman Group, UK Limited.

4. Blum-Kulka, S. and J. House. 1989. Investigating cross-cultural pragmatics: An introductory ooverview. In *Cross-cultural pragmatics,* edited by S. Blum-Kulka, J. House and G. Kasper. Norwood: Ablex, 1–34.

5. Brown, P. and S. Levinson. 1987. *Politeness: Some universals in language usage.* Cambridge: Cambridge University Press.

6. Carrell, P. L. and J. C. Eisterhold. 1983. Schema theory and ESL reading pedagogy. *TESOL Quarterly* 18:553–573.

7. Chen, W., ed. 1991. *Shunxin daquan* (A comprehensive introduction to letter writing). Shanghai: Shanghai Jiaoyu Chubanshe.

8. Cook, G. 1994. *Discourse and literature.* Hong Kong: Oxford University Press.

9. Gu, yueguo 1990. Politeness phenomena in modern standard Chinese. *Journal of Pragmatics* 4 (2): 237–257.

10. Günthner, S. 1993. *Diskursstrategien in der Interkulturellen Kommunikation.* Tübingen: M. Niemeyer.

11. Hu, W. and C. L. Grove. 1991. *Encountering the Chinese: A guide for Americans.* Yarmouth, ME: Intercultural Press.

12. Huckin, T. 1997. Cultural aspect of genre knowledge. *AILA Review: Applied Linguistics across Disciplines* 12:68–78.

13. Hymes, D. 1974. *Foundations in sociolinguistics: An ethnographic approach.* Philadelphia: University of Pennsylvania Press.

14.   Leech, G. 1983. *Principles of pragmatics.* New York: Longman.

15.   Lu, P., Y. Zhang and S. He, eds. 1993. *Waimao yu shangmao yingyong wushu yuedu xiezuo 200 ti* (Two hundred issues on reading and writing skills of practical documents in business and foreign trade). Guangzhou: Zhongshan Daxue Chubanshe.

16.   Miller, C. R. 1984. Genre as social action. *Quarterly Journal of Speech* 70:151–167.

17.   Rumelhart, D. E. 1980. Schemata: The building blocks of cognition. *In Theoretical issues in reading comprehension,* edited by R. J. Spiro, B. C. Bruce and W. F. Brewerpp. Hillsdale, NJ: Erlbaum, 33–58.

18.   Saville-Troike, M. 1984. *The ethnography of communication.* Oxford: Basil Blackwell.

19.   Searle, J. R. 1969. *Speech acts: An essay in the philosophy of language.* Cambridge: Cambridge University Press.

20.   She, K. Y., eds. 1984. *Xiandai hangyu cidian.* (Modern Chinese dictionary). Beijing: Shangwu Chubanshe.

21.   Swales, J. 1990. *Genre analysis: English in academic and research settings.* Cambridge: Cambridge University Press.

22.   Ulijn, J. M. and X. Li. 1995. Is interrupting impolite? Some temporal aspects of turn-taking in Chinese-Western and other intercultural business encounter. *Text.* 15 (4): 589–627.

23.   Widdowson, H. G. 1983. *Learning purpose and language use.* London: Oxford University Press.

24.   Zhu, Y. 1996. An analysis of "Tongzhi" or "Circular Letter" genre in Chinese business communication. *Pan-Asiatic Linguistics: Proceedings of the Fourth International Symposium on Language and Linguistics,* edited by Institute of Language and Culture for Rural Development. Vol. 4. Bangkok: Mahidol University Press, 1369–1398.

25.   _____ . 1997. A rhetorical analysis of Chinese sales letters. *Text* 17 (4): 543–566.

26.   _____ . 1999. *Business communication in China.* New York: Nova Science Publishers Inc.

27.   _____ . 2000a. Rhetorical moves in Chinese sales genres, 1949 to the present. *The Journal of Business Communication* 37 (2): 156–172.

28.   _____ . 2000b. Structural moves reflected in English and Chinese sales letters. *Discourse Studies* 2 (4): 525–548.

29.   Zhuge, R. and X. Chen, eds. 1994. *Duewai maoyi wenshu xiezuo* (Practical writings in foreign trade). Beijing: Renmin Daxue Chubanshe.

Contributors

Inger Askehave is Senior Lecturer in the Department of English at the Aarhus School of Business, Denmark. Her primary research interests included expert-layman communication, business communication and communication on the Internet. She has published several articles on genre theory, business communication, translator training and expert-layman communication and is currently working on a research project concerned with language use on the Internet.

Colin Barron is Lecturer in the English Centre at The University of Hong Kong. His research interests are in the areas of the discourse of mechanical engineering and science in which he combines ethnographic methods with discourse analysis. He is one of the editors of the book *Knowledge and Discourse: Toward an Ecology of Language*, published by Pearson Education in 2001.

Charles Bazerman is Professor and Chair of Education at the University of California, Santa Barbara. His research interest include the rhetoric of science and technology, writing across the curriculum, rhetorical theory, and the history of literacy. His most recent book, *The Languages of Edison's Light*, examines the rhetorical and representational work that made Edison's incandescent light a social reality. Previous books include *Shaping Written Knowledge*; *Constructing Experience*; *Textual Dynamics of the Professions*; and *The Informed Writer*.

Vijay K. Bhatia is Professor at the City University of Hong Kong. He is well known for his work in discourse and genre analysis, English for specific purposes, professional and academic communication. His book *Analyzing Genre — Language Use in Professional Settings* is widely used by researchers in genre analysis. His major research projects include, "Teaching English in meeting the needs of business education", and "Generic integrity in legal discourse in multilingual and multicultural contexts". He is on the editorial boards of international journals, such as *English for Specific Purposes*, *World Englishes*, and *Document Design*.

Marcel Burger is Senior Lecturer at the Universities of Geneva and Lausanne. He teaches in communication and media, discourse analysis and pragmatics. His areas of specialization are the construction of identity, especially in the media. He published several articles on media interviews and debates. He is the author of *Les Manifestes: paroles de combat* (2001), Paris, Delachaux et Niestlé; and contributed to *Un modèle et un instrument d'analyse de l'organisation du discourse* (2001), Berne, Lang.

Pauline Burton is Senior Lecturer in the Division of Language Studies at the City University of Hong Kong. She is co-principal investigator for a project investigating the use of literature in English to enhance creativity and language learning in Hong Kong.

She has been a writer-presenter of educational radio programmes for Radio Television Hong Kong (RTHK) Radio 4, and a leading actor in Dino Mahoney's radio youth soap opera, "Songbirds".

Christopher N. Candlin is Senior Research Professor in the Department of Linguistics at Macquarie University, Sydney, and is a member of the Research Centre for Language in Social Life. He was the Foundation Executive Director of the Australian Government's National Centre for English Language Teaching and Research which he directed from 1987 to 1998. From 1996 to 2002 he was Chair Professor of Applied Linguistics and Director of the Centre for English Language Education and Communication Research at the City University of Hong Kong, and has previously taught at the University of Lancaster in the UK. He holds Honorary Professorships at the Universities of Lancaster, Nottingham and Cardiff in the UK.

Relevant recent research and publications include *Culture, Communication and Quality of Life of People Living with HIV and AIDS in Hong Kong* (2000); a Special Issue of the *ROLSI Journal* (co-edited with Dr. Sally Candlin) on *Discourse, Expertise and the Management of Risk* (April, 2002); The Cardiff Lecture 2000 on *New Discourses of the Clinic: Rediscovering the Patient in Healthcare* (March, 2000); *Making Sense of Viral Load: One Expert or Two?* (with A. Moore and G. Plum: *Journal of Culture, Health and Sexuality*: 3 (4) (2001); Motivational relevancies: Some methodological reflections on sociolinguistic practice (with S. Sarangi) in N. Coupland, S. Sarangi and C. N. Candlin, eds. *Sociolinguistics and Social Theory* (2001); Alterity, perspective and mutuality in LSP research and practice in M. Gotti *et al.*, *Conflict and Negotiation in Specialist Texts* (2002); Medical discourse as professional and institutional action in M. Bax and J.-W. Zwart, eds. *Papers in honour of Arthur van Essen* (2002); *Writing: Texts, Processes and Practices* (Longman, 2000), *English Language Teaching in its Social Context* (Routledge, 2000)

He is a member of the Editorial Boards of several journals, including *Applied Linguistics*, *TEXT*, *Journal of Sociolinguistics*, *Language Awareness*, and the new journal (to appear in 2004) *Communication in Medicine*, and will co-edit the new *Journal of Applied Linguistics* also to appear in 2004. He also edits or coedits seven international book series with Pearson (Longman), Continuum International, Routledge, and Palgrave (Macmillan). He is currently President of the International Association of Applied Linguistics.

Sally Candlin is a Fellow of the College of Nursing (NSW) and qualified as a nurse, midwife and health visitor in the UK. She received a B.A. (Hons) in Linguistics and Psychology from the University of Lancaster, a M.Sc. in Public Health from the University of Hawaii and a Ph.D. in Linguistics from the University of Lancaster. Her research is concentrated in the area of discourse analysis, specifically in nurse/patient communication as it concerns nurse education and the achievement of expertise. She is an Adjunct Associate Professor at the University of Western Sydney.

Paul Cheung is Senior Research Assistant in the Centre for English Language Education and Communication Research, Department of English and Communication, City University of Hong Kong. Paul Cheung has a special interest in professional–professional and professional–client discourse in law and engineering. Specifically, he is interested in the variations in such discourse that result from interactions between institutionality, intepersonality and identity. Other interests include pragmatics and research methodology.

Laurent Filliettaz in Lecturer at University of Geneva. He received his Ph.D. in linguistics in 2000 and is the author of *La parole en action* (forthcoming, Editions Nota Bene, Québec), as well as several articles dealing with situational aspects of verbal interaction. His main research areas are discourse analysis, pragmatics and theories of action. He is also one of the contributors to *Un modèle et un instrument d'analyse de l'organisation du discourse* (2001), Berne, Lang.

Arthur Firkins works for the New South Wales Department of Community Service and has had broad experience in training, social policy and clinical practice within the department's disability programme area. Currently he works with children and adolescents with challenging behaviour, applying discourse approaches to the analysis of behaviour. Arthur is also a Doctoral student in the Department of Linguistics at Macquarie University, researching discourse practices in child protection and is a research associate with the Centre for Language in Social Life at Macquarie University Sydney.

Maurizio Gotti teaches English Language and Linguistics at the Faculty of Foreign Languages of the University of Bergamo (Italy). He is the Director of CERLIS, a research centre on specialized languages.

His main field of research concerns the features and origins of specialized languages, seen both from a diachronic (*Robert Boyle and the Language of Science.* Milan: Guerini, 1996) and a synchronic perspective (*l linguaggi specialistici. Firenze: La Nuova Italia*, 1991). He has also been involved in research on English lexicology and lexicography, English syntax and foreign language teaching.

Gu, Yueguo, K. C. Wong Fellow of the British Academy, is presently a Research Professor of Linguistics at the Institute of Linguistics, the Chinese Academy of Social Sciences. His research interest includes pragmatics, discourse analysis, rhetoric and the philosophy of language. He has contributed quite extensively to several internal journals and is the editor/author of over 20 textbooks covering English, Linguistics, English Language Teaching methodology, Cross-cultural Communication and Research Methodology, published by the Foreign Language Teaching and Research Press and Longman. He is a co-chief-editor of the *Journal of Contemporary Linguistics*, and has been co-editor of a special issue of *TEXT*. He is Head of the Contemporary Linguistics Department of the Chinese Academy, Pro-Vice-Chancellor of Beijing Foreign Studies University and Dean of the School of English Language Communication.

Liesel Hermes is Dean of Faculty, Institut für Anglistik, Universitat in Koblenz. He is also the editor of the journal *Neusprachliche Mitteilungen aus Wissenschaft und Praxis* (*Journal of the Fachverband Moderne Fremdsprachen* (FMF) in Germany. He is member of IATEFL and TESOL. His research interests include 20th century English literature, Australian literature, teaching literature, intercultural education, action research and learner autonomy in university education.

Ann Hewings is Lecturer at the Centre for Language and Communications at The Open University (UK). Her research interests include academic literacy, disciplinary influences on reading and writing and EFL/ESL teacher education. She has worked as an English language teacher and trainer in Sweden, Malaysia, Australia and Brazil. Ann has recently co-edited *Innovation in English Language Teaching*, a core text on the Open University's Masters programme in applied linguistics.

Thomas N. Huckin is Professor of English and Adjunct Professor of Linguistics at the University of Utah, where he also directs the University Writing Program. His main research interests are critical discourse analysis and genre theory. Recent publications include *Genre Knowledge in Disciplinary Communication* (with Carol Berkenkotter), *Second Language Vocabulary Acquisition* (with James Coady), and *The New Century Handbook* (with Christine Hult). He is an editorial board member of *English for Specific Purposes* and *TESOL Quarterly*.

Chris Jensen is currently General Editor of *Hong Kong Lawyer*, the official journal of the Hong Kong Law Society. Prior to that he worked at the City University of Hong Kong as Senior Research Associate on the Project "Improving Legal English: Quality Measures for Programme Development and Evaluation". He also taught a course to legal translators and interpreters on understanding legal judgements.

Lu, Xiaofei is currently a Ph.D. candidate in the Department of Linguistics at the Ohio State University. He received his B.A. in English Language and Literature from Nankai University, China, and his M.A. in English Language from the National University of Singapore. He specializes in the fields of computational linguistics, corpus linguistics, and syntax.

Dino Mahoney is Associate Professor in the Department of English and Communication at the City University of Hong Kong. He is currently leading a project on using literature in English to enhance creativity and language learning. He has worked extensively in writing and presenting radio programmes for Radio Television Hong Kong (RTHK) Radio 4 aimed at a youth audience, including "Songbirds", an innovative radio youth soap opera featuring the lives of Hong Kong students. His work as a playwright includes plays that have represented Hong Kong internationally both on stage and on the air.

J. R. Martin is Professor in Linguistics at the University of Sydney. Research interests include systemic theory, functional grammar, discourse semantics, register, genre, multimodality and critical discourse analysis. Publications include *English Text*, Benjamins, 1992; *Writing Science* (with M. A. K. Halliday), Falmer, 1993; *Working with Functional Grammar* (with C. Matthiessen and C. Painter), Arnold, 1997; *Genre and Institutions* (edited with F. Christie), Cassell, 1997; and *Reading Science* (edited with R. Veel), Routledge, 1998.

Bernard McKenna lectures in the School of Communication, QUT. He has extensive research publications and consultancies in business, technical, and scientific writing, However, his most recent work includes studies of political and political-economic communication. Such areas include labourist discourses, the Pauline Hanson phenomenon, and globalized hypercaptialism. This paper arouse out of his concern for the demise of the university because of technocratic and political ideologies.

Catherine Nickerson is Lecturer in Business Communication Studies at the University of Nijmegen in the Netherlands. Her research interests include the use of English as a *lingua franca* in corporate life, the impact of corporate culture on language use, and the nature of e-mail discourse in business settings. Her study of the use of written English by Dutch writers working within multinational corporations was recently published by *Rodopi*.

Srikant Sarangi is Reader in Language and Communication and Director of the Health Communication Research Centre at Cardiff University. His recent publications include *Language, Bureaucracy and Social Control* (1996, with S. Slembrouck); *Talk, Work and Institutional Order*: Discourse in Medical, Mediation and Management Settings (1999, with C. Roberts); *Discourse and Social Life* (2000, with M. Coulthard); and *Sociolinguistics and Social Theory* (2001, with N. Coupland and C. N. Candlin). He is currently editor (with J. Wilson) of *TEXT: An Interdisciplinary Journal for the Study of Discourse*, and series editor (with C. N. Candlin) of *Advances in Applied Linguistics, and Communication in Public Life.*

Wei Shang is Associate Professor in the English Department of Guanghua College at Chuangchun University in China. She has been in the TEFL profession for 19 years offering skills training courses as well as subject courses like American Literature and History of the English Language. From May 1999 to May 2000 she was Visiting Scholar at Cardiff University under the sponsorship of China Scholarship Council. Her publications include five dictionaries, seven books, and eleven articles in professional journals. Her current research interest is history of the English language.

Sue Smith is a social worker with over 12 years experience in direct service, working with children and families in child protection and substitute care in Australia and the UK. She also has extensive experience, and post graduate qualifications, in the development, delivery and evaluation of training programs. Sue has developed a particular interest in the decision-making processes of child protection practice and the role of training and learning programs in informing such decision-making.

John M. Swales is Professor of Linguistics at the University of Michigan, Ann Arbor, and from 1985•2001 he was Director of the English Language Institute. His current interests focus on a corpus-based approach to academic speech, genre theory, and genre-based approaches to teaching academic communications. He is currently working on a successor volume to *Genre Analysis: English in Academic and Research Settings* (Cambridge University Press, 1990).

Ruth Wodak is Professor and Head of the Department of Applied Linguistics at the University of Vienna. She was recently awarded the Wittgenstein-Prize for Elite Researchers (1996). She is also Director of the Wittgenstein Center "Discourse, Politics, Identity" and, until September 2002, a Research Professor at the Austrian Academy of Sciences.

Her books include *Disorders of Discourse* (1996); *Gender and Discourse* (1997); *Die Sprache der "Miichtigen" und "Ohnmiichtigen"* (with F. Menz, B. Lutz and H. Gruber, 1985); *Language, Power and Ideology* (1989), and as co-author of *"Wir sind alle unschuldige Tiiter!". Diskurshistorische Studienzum achkriegsantisemitismus in Osterreich* (1990), *Sprachen der Vergangenheiten. Offentliches Gedenken in österreichischen und deutschen Medien* (with F. Menzl, R. Mitten/F. Stem) 1994, *Communicating Gender in Context* (with H. Kotthoff, 1997).

Robyn Woodward-Kron is a full-time Ph.D. student in the Graduate School of Education, The University of Wollongong, Australia. Her research interests include academic discourse, tertiary student writing, and the role of language in learning. Her doctoral dissertation is a longitudinal study investigating the role of writing in disciplinary learning. She is co-author of the CD-ROM, *Academic Writing: A Language-based Approach*.

Zhang, Zuocheng is Associate Professor in the School of International Studies at University of International Business and Economics in China. He has been teaching English in the school for eight years, except for one year as Visiting Academic with Centre for

Language and Communication Research, Cardiff University. His major research publications are related to writing as process and corpus-based language teaching. His current academic interest is doctor-patient interaction and analysis of intercultural discourse

Zhu, Yunxia is Principal Senior Lecturer at UNITEC. Her current research focuses on discourse analysis, genre study, and cross-cultural business communication. She has published papers in book chapters and in a number of international journals (such as *Discourse Studies, TEXT, Journal of Business Communication, Business Communication Quarterly,* and *Document Design*). Her book *Business Communication in China* was published by Nova Science Publishers, New York in 1999.

Index